UNITED STATES GOVERNMENT AND POLITICS

George Breckenridge

McMaster University

McGraw-Hill Ryerson

Toronto • New York • Burr Ridge • Bangkok • Bogotá • Caracas
Lisbon • London • Madrid • Mexico City • Milan • New Delhi
Seoul • Singapore • Sydney • Taipei

McGraw-Hill
Ryerson Limited

A Subsidiary of The McGraw·Hill Companies

United States Government and Politics

ISBN: 0–07–552771–5

1 2 3 4 5 6 7 8 9 0 BBM 7 6 5 4 3 2 1 0 9 8

Printed and bound in Canada

Sponsoring Editor:	Gord Muschett
Associate Editor:	Margaret Henderson
Developmental Editor:	Marianne Minaker
Production Editor:	Matthew Kudelka
Production Co-ordinator:	Nicla Dattolico
Designer/Typesetter:	George Kirkpatrick
Cover Design:	George Kirkpatrick
Cover Photo:	SuperStock
Typeface:	Monotype Sabon
Printer:	Best Book Manufacturers

Canadian Cataloguing in Publication Data

Breckenridge, George.
    United States government and politics

Includes bibliographical references and index.
ISBN 0–07–552771–5

1. United States–Politics and government.   I. Title.

JK421.B74 1997   351.73   C97–932265–0

CONTENTS

PREFACE

This book is about the political system of the United States, how it works, and why it works the way it does. The book's distinctive feature is that it examines the American political system by comparing and contrasting it with the Canadian one.

The book is written first of all for Canadian students. Canadians are constantly bombarded with information about American politics, yet most do not really understand how American politics works and why Americans often think and act so differently from Canadians. It is obviously important for Canadians to understand the United States. While the two nations have long boasted that their border is the longest undefended border in the world, the relationship between the two nations has always been an uneasy one. For the United States, always confident of the drawing power of its example, the very existence of Canada as a separate nation on the same continent has been a puzzle and sometimes an irritation.

Canada, for its part, has always feared being swallowed up by the United States. Throughout the nineteenth century Canadians feared American expansionism. In the twentieth century this fear has changed focus: Canadians are now worried about economic and cultural colonization. Even so, most Canadians live within a hundred miles of the border, have American relatives, and watch mostly American television. Canadians cannot ignore the American presence. As a Canadian politician once put it, "The Americans are our best friends, whether we like it or not."

Viewing the United States in a comparative context is valuable for its own sake. From the beginning, Americans have looked on their experience in the New World as unique. American "exceptionalism" has long been a bright thread running through American political studies. When we compare the American system with the Canadian one, it is easier for us to see in what respects the American system is distinctive or not.

A comparison between the United States and Canada makes sense, since the two countries have many important things in common. Both are relatively new nations, and both were built (and are still being built) by people from highly diverse backgrounds. Thus, each country has had to develop forces to hold together a disparate and geographically dispersed collection of peoples. The United States and Canada, summarizes S. Martin Lipset, "resemble one another more than either resembles any other nation."[1]

---

1   Seymour Martin Lipset, *Continental Divide: The Values and Institutions of the United States and Canada* (Routledge, 1991), 212.

The differences between the United States and Canada are equally fundamental. The historical experience of the two nations is strikingly different: the United States originated in a **revolution** that forged a strong sense of national identity; Canada was composed of two peoples that rejected the American way and evolved slowly from colonial status to independence. The two countries have been shaped by different political ideas: the Americans by liberalism, reinforced by radical Protestantism; and the Canadians by a broader mix of liberal, conservative, and democratic socialist ideas. The two nations chose radically different political systems: a system of separated institutions in the United States, and a British-style parliamentary system in Canada.

The approach to the United States used in this book emphasizes ideas and institutions. A potent combination of liberal and Protestant ideas provided the United States with both a national identity and a strong sense of national mission. The same ideas established the two poles of the national debate: individual liberty and equality. Liberty has been the dominant principle, and the comparatively unrestrained individualism of the United States has produced "the world's most dynamically evolving socioeconomic system."[2]

The main concern of the framers of the U.S. Constitution was to protect individual liberty by preventing the accumulation of political power. To that end, they fragmented power by separating the institutions of government and dividing the powers of government between them. The American institutional structure embodied a fear of government and established a system in which governmental action is difficult. "It is a political system which is prone to stasis."[3] The tension between a dynamic socioeconomic system and a rigid political structure has produced the distinctive American mode of political development. Thus, the major upheavals in American history—the **Civil War** of the 1860s, the **Progressive** reform era from 1904 to 1920, the **New Deal** of the 1930s, and the social and political turbulence of the 1960s—were all periods of rapid change that brought the political system into a new alignment with the underlying economic and social realities.

The book has three parts. The first three chapters examine the geographic and demographic environment of the United States, the development of American ideas, and the U.S. Constitution. Chapters 4 to 9 examine political institutions, the federal system, the Congress, the presidency, the executive branch, and finally the role of the Supreme Court. Finally, Chapters 10 through 15 look at the politics generated by institutions in the electoral system, with particular emphasis on electing the president, the operations of the political parties, the role of interest groups and the media, and the making of public policy.

---

2   Walter Dean Burnham, "Critical Realignment: Dead or Alive?" in Byron E. Shafer ed., *The End of Realignment? Interpreting American Electoral Eras* (University of Wisconsin Press, 1991), 113.

3   Burnham, 113.

ACKNOWLEDGMENTS

This project has been several years in the making and I have incurred many debts along the way.

I have been fortunate in having a steady stream of bright students in Political Science 2B6 and my other American courses; their interest and questions have been a continuing source of inspiration.

The staff of the McMaster Political Science Department: Mara Giannotti, Lori Ewing, and Stephanie Lisak have been unfailingly helpful in a host of practical tasks along the way. Gerald Bierling calculated some of the tables in Chapter 10 and his one-man computer help-line rescued me from many technical impasses.

I want to thank my colleagues John Seaman and Janet Ajzenstat for their encouragement and help with particular topics. Eric Monpetit generously shared his expertise in comparative federalism with me.

My research assistant, Dennis Baker, provided invaluable assistance over a range of tasks in the past year; not the least important has been his ability to cast a critical eye over my work and tell me when a draft was, well, weak.

I am very grateful to those who reviewed the manuscript at various stages, for their constructive critiques and many specific suggestions. Reviewers included: Don Abelson, University of Western Ontario; Agar Adamson, Acadia University; Daniel Austin, Edinboro University of Pennsylvania; B.H. Barlow, University of Regina; Colin Bennett, University of Victoria; Louis DeSipio, University of Illinois at Urbana-Champaign; Judith A. Garber, University of Alberta; Valerie Heitshusen, University of Missouri; Barry Kay, Wilfrid Laurier University; Geoffrey Lambert, University of Manitoba; Ron Landes, St. Mary's University; Gretchen MacMillan, University of Calgary; Daniel Madar, Brock University; Alexander Moens, Simon Fraser University; George Roseme, Carleton University; Paul Rosen, Carleton University; Thomas M. Scott, University of Minnesota; Debora VanNijnatten, Queen's University; Michael Wallack, Memorial University; and Harold Waller, McGill University.

Finally, I want to thank the staff of McGraw-Hill Ryerson who brought the project to completion: Margaret Henderson, Marianne Minaker and, particularly the sponsoring editor, Gord Muschett, whose deft blend of encouragement and pressure got a better book out of me.

George Breckenridge
McMaster University

CHAPTER 1

BUILDING THE AMERICAN NATION

ASSEMBLING THE REAL ESTATE

The "New World" of the Americas was "discovered" by Christopher Columbus in 1492. Almost certainly this was not the first European landing in America, but it was the one that led to European settlement. The conquest and settlement of the Americas by Europeans continued for four centuries, roughly from 1500 to 1900. Brazil was colonized by Portugal and the rest of Central and South America by Spain in the sixteenth and seventeenth centuries. Spanish settlement extended as far north as what is now Florida, Texas, and the American Southwest.

In North America, permanent European settlement began later.[1] France established a colony in Quebec in the early seventeenth century from which its traders and missionaries traveled to the center of the continent. The same period saw the first permanent English settlements on the Atlantic coast. The decisive period in the settlement of North America was the second half of the eighteenth century, when France and Britain engaged in a prolonged struggle for supremacy in Europe—a struggle that inevitably extended to their colonies in Asia and North America. In the course of that

---

1   A detailed examination of the process of European settlement in North America from 1492 to 1800 is in D.W. Meinig, *The Shaping of America: A Geographical Perspective on 500 Years of History*, Volume I (Yale University Press, 1986).

struggle, Britain captured Quebec in 1760, an event that brought to an end the French dream of a French, Catholic empire in North America. The same event did much to determine Canada's future as a bicultural nation.

The first British colonies in North America were Virginia (established in 1606) and Massachusetts (1629). By the mid-eighteenth century there were thirteen separate colonies along the Atlantic coast, from New Hampshire to Georgia. The British had squeezed out smaller European nations—the Swedes in Delaware and the Dutch in New York—and after capturing Quebec seemed ready to dominate the entire North American continent.

As the American colonies grew, their trading interests began to diverge from those of the mother country and the colonists began to resent being ruled from London. Britain insisted on regulating colonial trade in its own interest and on taxing the colonists to pay for their defense. Friction between the colonial power and the Americans increased steadily, until fighting broke out in 1775. The next year the colonies banded together to fight the War of Independence (also known as the American Revolution). After several years of fighting, with some help from the French, the Americans forced the British to withdraw.

In the Treaty of Paris of 1783, Britain not only recognized the independence of the colonies but also signed over to them British claims to the lands south of the Great Lakes between the Appalachians and the Mississippi. In 1803 the French emperor Napoleon, then immersed in a war with Britain, sold to the Americans the French claims to the Louisiana Territory, the vast stretch of land lying between the Mississippi and the Rockies. In less than thirty years the United States had been transformed from thirteen separate British colonies along the Atlantic coast into an independent nation of vast size.

The Separation of the United States and Canada

When the American colonies went to war with Britain, they expected the new British colony of Quebec to join them. American forces invaded Canada in 1775 and besieged the British forces in Quebec City. The French Catholic Quebecers, however, whose religious freedom the British had guaranteed, had little in common with the aggressively anti-Catholic,[2] English Americans and remained largely indifferent to the

---

2   One of the British policies that angered the Americans was the Quebec Act of 1774, whereby the British government confirmed the privileges of the Roman Catholic Church in Quebec. Nathan O. Hatch, *The Sacred Cause of Liberty: Republican Thought and the Millenium in Revolutionary New England* (Yale University Press, 1977), 75.

struggle. There was no revolt in the north, and the British were able to repulse the American attack and hold on to Canada.

The **Articles of Confederation**, the first American Constitution, drafted in 1777, provided for the speedy admission of Canada to the American union. The offer was never taken up. American attempts during the later peace negotiations to persuade the British to hand over Canada failed. The separation between the United States and Canada was reinforced in the years after the war, when thousands of Americans who had sided with the British during the War of Independence—and in some cases had their property confiscated as a result—moved north. The United Empire Loyalists moved into New Brunswick, eastern Quebec, and eastern Ontario, forming the first substantial English population in Canada. They had no desire to rejoin the country they had just left.

Even so, the Americans saw the unification of North America as inevitable. During the **Constitutional Convention** of 1787, some delegates still spoke confidently of the time when Canada would join them. The Americans' next opportunity to take over Canada arose during the War of 1812. Britain, still at war with Napoleon, was interfering with American trade; the Americans, fearful that their new independence was at stake, declared war on Britain and invaded Canada. In the early years of the century many Americans had followed the Loyalists up into western Ontario in search of good land. Indeed, by one estimate 80 percent of Upper Canadians in 1812 were American, most of them quite recent immigrants.[3] Thomas Jefferson saw the war as the occasion for "the final expulsion of England from the American continent." Upper Canada, "defended by only a few regular soldiers, and containing a predominantly American population that would presumably welcome the invaders as liberators," seemed to be "a plum ripe for the picking."[4] But again there was no revolt in the north. Americans on both sides of the border opposed the war. The British fought off the American invasion, and the war ended in stalemate. In Canada, resentment over the disruption caused by the war heightened Canadians' patriotism and strengthened their resolve to pursue a separate destiny in North America.

The British/American peace treaty of 1818 set the 49th Parallel as the boundary between the United States and Canada in the unsettled lands west of the Great Lakes. It also provided for joint occupation of the Oregon Territory on the west coast (which included what is now the states of Washington and Oregon as well as mainland British Columbia). In 1846, with American settlers effectively in control of the southern portion, Britain finally gave up its remaining claims over the Oregon Territory south of the 49th Parallel.[5]

---

3   Meinig, *The Shaping of America,* Volume II (Yale University Press, 1993), 44.
4   Meinig, Volume II, 47.
5   Meinig, Volume II, Chapter 6.

For the rest of the century Canadians feared that the Americans might still grab Canadian territory in the West. Canada's protectionist National Policy in the 1870s and its huge effort to complete the Canadian Pacific Railway in 1885 were motivated by the perceived urgency to develop an east/west flow of goods and people across Canada to counteract the strong geographic and economic pulls south toward the United States. When the Canadian prairies were finally settled between 1896 and 1914, many of the settlers were indeed Americans, but most were eastern Canadians or Europeans, and there was no serious threat from below the 49th Parallel.

The Completion of the United States

In the north, it was the British/Canadians who got in the way of American expansion; in the south, it was the Spanish/Mexicans. Between 1810 and 1821, through a series of skirmishes and land grabs, the Americans forced the Spanish out of Florida and the Gulf Coast. Inland, the boundary with Mexico, which had won its independence from Spain in 1821, still had to be settled. In the 1830s American settlers began to pour into Texas. In 1836, after a series of battles, the Americans declared Texas independent of Mexico. The United States declared war on Mexico in 1844 and annexed Texas in 1845. In 1848, as a result of the war, Mexico ceded California and the Southwest to the United States. The Americans "completed" their southwestern boundary by purchasing a parcel of land from Mexico in 1853.[6]

When the Canadian Confederation was established in 1867, the British government handed over to the new government the rights to the vast Hudson's Bay Company territories north of the 49th Parallel. In immediate response, the Americans took up a standing Russian offer, and bought Alaska. Otherwise, the Americans seemed largely indifferent to the prospect of swallowing Canada. An American magazine at the time attributed American indifference to their "belief that sooner or later—the exact time being unimportant—all the populations on the continent, whatever their present condition, must gravitate towards our political system, and ultimately be merged in it."[7]

With its continental land boundaries now fixed and the process of internal settlement of the land largely complete, at the end of the century the United States began to look abroad and to flex its muscles as a world power. At the last moment, the Americans joined in the scramble that had been going on among the European powers for the last available overseas colonies. After a short war with Spain in 1898, the Americans acquired some of the last remnants of the once-vast Spanish Empire: the Philippines and Guam in the Pacific, and Cuba and Puerto Rico in the Caribbean.

---

6   Meinig, Volume II, Chapter 7.
7   In Meinig, Volume II, 544.

During the same period, they annexed the once-independent kingdom of Hawaii. Cuba was soon given its formal independence; the Philippines only became independent in 1945; Puerto Rico and Guam remain American territories. Hawaii became a state in 1959. A last footnote: the United States purchased the U.S. Virgin Islands from Denmark in 1917.

The Settlement of North America

Between the 1780s and the early twentieth century, settlers arrived on the North American continent in waves. Most of them came from Europe, attracted mainly by the availability of cheap land. Since feudal times the land in Europe had been held by large landowners, the church, or the Crown. In America, in contrast, the land was empty (so it was perceived), and the new nations needed settlers. The flow of immigrants across the Atlantic, and the movements of settlers within North America, varied with economic and political conditions in Europe and America. Although flows were much heavier at some times than others, the process was continuous.

The movement of population within North America was from east to west though in the middle of the process there was a leap to the west coast. As one area became settled, there was always a "frontier" farther west where land was available. The first

The territorial growth of the United States.

"West" was in Tennessee and Kentucky, when Americans moved over the Appalachians in the 1780s. After that, the movement was both to the north (to Ohio, upper Pennsylvania, and New York state, and also Ontario), and to the south (the Mississippi Delta and eventually Texas).

The pattern of settlement largely disregarded political boundaries. The Loyalists had moved into Canada out of their loyalty to Britain; the later movement of Americans into Ontario and the Eastern Townships of Quebec early in the nineteenth century was simply part of the search for good land. Here, geography was affecting the flow of population. In the 1840s the movement west jumped over the inhospitable prairie lands to the fertile west coast—a population shift that was stimulated by the discovery of gold in California in 1849.

The infertile lands of the Canadian Shield lying across the top of the Great Lakes acted as a barrier to settlement. This meant that for most of the mid-nineteenth century Canada had no frontier of its own. The North American frontier lay entirely in the United States, and Canadians who sought land had to move south as well as west. With the settlement of the American prairie states after the Civil War, the United States finally ran out of new land and the movement of settlers turned north. The "last frontier" in North America was the Canadian prairies, which were settled between the 1880s and 1914 by settlers from Ontario and the United States and by immigrants from Europe.

The settlement of the North American continent in just over 100 years is a remarkable story. In the United States particularly, stories of "the frontier" and "the West" play a large part in popular history and in the national mythology. What is emphasized in these stories is the bravery, idealism, and resourcefulness of the pioneers who settled in unknown, often hostile territory, spreading civilization and Christianity. The spread of Western civilization is seen as an inevitable, benevolent, and God-directed process.

But there is another side to the story. An American historian, D.W. Meinig, has recently written: "It is important for Americans to understand more clearly than they do that their nation has been created by massive aggression against a long succession of peoples."[8] As American settlers moved relentlessly onto land claimed by others, they sparked violent clashes, a series of "Indian wars," and a war with Mexico.

A contrast has often been drawn between the settlement process in Canada, which was generally orderly and peaceful, and the one in the United States, which was often violent. In Canada the process was controlled by government: on the prairies the RCMP preceded the settlers. In the United States settlement mostly ran well ahead of government or any kind of law and order.

8   Meinig, Volume I, xviii.

Americans have generally downplayed the violence associated with their national experience. Even the War of Independence was more divisive than they usually care to remember. That war resulted in the expulsion of thousands of Americans who had remained loyal to Britain. Britain was a strong enough power during the nineteenth century to defend its remaining colonies in North America against American expansionism, but Spain and Mexico were much weaker. A great deal of American territory—Florida, Texas, California, and the Southwest—was acquired as a result of wars, most notably the Mexican-American War (1844–48). Hawaii and other territories were added when the United States became a colonial power in the wake of the Spanish-American War of 1898.

Yet the worst aggression was not against Britain or Mexico, but rather against the native peoples of North America. Right up to the end of the nineteenth century they were being forcibly swept aside to make way for European settlement. Equally horrendous was the ruthless exploitation of black slaves, on whose labor much of the early prosperity and trade of the United States was built.

The Political Growth of the United States

With the War of Independence, the thirteen British colonies became thirteen independent states. The states had banded together to fight the war, and afterwards formed a loose confederation. After this proved to be a weak form of government, between 1787 and 1789 the states hammered out the U.S. Constitution; this was ratified by the states, and the new nation was established on a firmer footing. The writing of the Constitution is examined in Chapter 3.

The U.S. Constitution provided for the admission of new states to the union on the basis of equality with the original thirteen. Once an area had sufficient settlement, it was organized as a territory of the United States and a governor was appointed. After further development and the writing of a state constitution, the territory could petition Congress for admission as a state. Between 1791 and 1912, 35 new states were added to make a total of 48; the final two "offshore" states, Alaska and Hawaii, were admitted in 1958.

The admission of new states broadly followed the spread of population across the continent. But it was also a political process. Each newly admitted state added two members to the Senate, at least one member to the House of Representatives, and at least three new votes to the **Electoral College** which elected the president. Thus, each time a new state was admitted the existing balance of power in Washington was altered; as a result, there were often partisan disputes over how quickly states should be admitted.

Table 1.1	Date	New state	Total southern states	Total states
Dates of admission of new states to the Union.	1787	Massachusetts		
		Rhode Island		
		New Hampshire		
		Connecticut		
		New York		
		Pennsylvania		
		New Jersey		
		Maryland		
		Delaware		
		Virginia		
		North Carolina		
		South Carolina		
		Georgia	5	13
	1791	Vermont		
	1792	Kentucky		
	1796	Tennessee		
	1803	Ohio		
	1812	Louisiana		
	1816	Indiana		
	1817	Mississippi		
	1818	Illinois		
	1819	Alabama	10	22

First fight in Congress over slavery in the territories: Missouri Compromise, 1820.

Date	New state	Total southern states	Total states
1820	Maine	10	23
1821	Missouri	11	24
1836	Arkansas	12	25
1837	Michigan	12	26
1845	Florida		
	Texas	14	28
1846	Iowa		
1848	Wisconsin		
1850	California		
1858	Minnesota		
1859	Oregon	14	33

Date	New state	Total southern states	Total states
Civil War 1861–1865			
1861	Kansas		
1863	West Virginia		
1864	Nevada		
1867	Nebraska		
1876	Colorado		
1889	North Dakota		
	South Dakota		
	Montana		
	Washington		
1890	Wyoming		
	Idaho		
1896	Utah		
1907	Oklahoma		
1912	Arizona		
	New Mexico	15	48
1959	Alaska		
	Hawaii	15	50

The list of southern states includes the eleven states that joined the Confederacy and the border states that at various times showed considerable southern sympathies: Maryland, Kentucky, Missouri, and Oklahoma.

The political growth of the United States also altered the balance of power between the different *regions* of the country. For this reason the process of admitting new states was a flash point between the North and the South in the first half of the nineteenth century. Across the Appalachians, settlement had moved both north and south. Thus, for the first half of the century there were new states added to both regions, and this preserved a rough balance of power between North and South in the Congress.

On two occasions, in 1820 and 1846–50, the growing tensions between the North and the South erupted into a major crisis in Congress, with some northerners insisting that new states should not permit slavery, and southerners arguing passionately that Congress could not place conditions on the admission of states. The search for new "southern" states (that is, states that would likely be sympathetic to the continuation of slavery) was one of the factors leading up to the Mexican War. One of the factors that contributed to the southern states going to war in 1861 was their realization that they had "run out of" southern states and that power in Washington was about to slip away from them once and for all.

Sources of Immigration

For the first 200 years of settlement in America, there was a small but fairly constant flow of immigrants to the various Atlantic colonies. There were small numbers of Dutch in New York, Germans in Pennsylvania, and Catholics in Maryland, but the overwhelming majority of settlers were Protestants from the British Isles. In its formative years, therefore, the United States was shaped by the language, religion, and political ideas of these British immigrants. There were also many thousands of unwilling immigrants—black slaves, who had been bought in West Africa and brought to America in chains.

The flow of immigration to America from northern Europe increased considerably in the 1830s and 1840s. Economic changes were forcing many European peasants off the land, and they were drawn to America as the interior of the continent opened up.

Table 1.2
Principal sources of immigration into the United States.

Decade	1841–50	1851–60	1861–70	1871–80	1881–90	1891–00
Total (millions)	1.7	2.6	2.3	2.8	5.3	3.7
Principal Sources (%)						
Ireland	46	35	19	16	12	11
U.K.	16	16	26	19	15	7
Germany	25	37	34	26	28	14
Italy	6	18				
Total Europe	93	94	89	81	90	96
Canada				7	14	7

Decade	1901–10	1911–20	1921–30
Total (millions)	9.0	5.7	4.1
Principal Sources (%)			
Italy	23	19	11
Austria-Hungary	24	16	
Russia	18	16	
Germany			10
Total Europe	92	75	60
Canada	2	13	23

Source: U.S. Bureau of the Census, *Statistical Abstract of the United States 1991*

It was at this time that Germany and Ireland replaced Britain as the main source of immigrants. The Irish were the first American "ethnic group" in the sense that they were significantly different from the rest of the population and retained a distinctive group identity in the new country. While some of the Irish spoke English, they were Catholic and—because of their history—strongly anti-British.

After the Civil War, immigrants were needed to settle the prairies and, increasingly, to provide labor for the growing industries of the Northeast and Midwest. Immigration increased rapidly, reaching a peak of nearly nine million people in the first decade of the twentieth century. Most of these newer immigrants were not from the traditional sources in northern Europe, but from southern and eastern Europe, as well as Russia. Most of them were Catholic, and a significant number were Jews from eastern Europe.

By the beginning of the twentieth century, Americans were beginning to realize that America was changing, and many were uneasy about the changes. The great surge of immigration from eastern and southern Europe meant that America was no longer overwhelmingly Anglo-Saxon, as it had been for most of its history. Also, America had become an industrial power. By 1880 fewer than 50 percent of Americans worked on farms. Immigrants were no longer going to the frontier; rather, they were working in the growing industrial cities of the Northeast and Midwest. In summary, the United States was no longer a nation of Anglo-Saxon, Protestant farmers; it was evolving into an urban, industrial society, and becoming more and more pluralistic in terms of ethnicity and religion.

Fears about the changes in America led to opposition to new immigrants. Immigration, which had been largely open, came under federal government regulation. Immigration from Asia was severely restricted and eventually banned. Efforts were made to screen out criminals, those with physical or mental defects, and political "radicals." A literacy test was applied to most immigrants. Finally, in the 1920s, total immigration was restricted for the first time, and quotas were set for different

Decade	1951–60	1961–70	1971–80	1981–90	
Total (millions)	2.5	3.3	4.5	7.3	*Table 1.3* *Sources of post–World War II immigration to the United States.*
Sources (%)					
Europe	53	37	18	10	
Americas	40	48	43	49	
Asia	6	13	36	38	

Source: U.S. Bureau of the Census, *Statistical Abstract of the United States 1994*

countries according to the proportion with that national origin in the existing American population. This was an attempt to freeze the population mix where it was.

Immigration was in any case reduced to a trickle by the Great Depression of the 1930s; it only increased again after World War II. In 1963, in keeping with the new domestic concern for civil rights, the law was changed to eliminate racial discrimination in immigration. The long-standing ban on Asian immigration was removed. Since the 1970s, as Table 1.3 indicates, Europe has rapidly declined as a major source of immigrants. By far the most immigrants now come from the Western Hemisphere (mainly Mexico and the Caribbean) and from Asia.

As happened at the turn of the century, when the sources of immigration switched from western Europe to eastern and southern Europe, the influx of immigrants with different characteristics from the bulk of the population is leading to some fears that the familiar America is changing. These fears are now being expressed in moves to limit the use of Spanish and to declare English the official language.

THE UNITED STATES AS A PLURALIST SOCIETY

Until the end of the nineteenth century, America saw itself as a homogeneous society embodying certain liberal democratic and Protestant religious values. Reinforcing this view was the fact that the 10 percent of the population that was black was excluded

The Statue of Liberty, a gift from France to mark the centennial of American independence.

from the mainstream (as were the smaller number of native people). The influx of immigrants who did not fit the established mold—many of them Catholics, and Jews from eastern Europe—forced a reappraisal of what American society stood for at the start of the twentieth century.

Americans were proud of their reputation as a land of freedom and opportunity to which everyone was drawn. In 1886 the Statue of Liberty, a gift from the French nation for the centennial of American independence, was erected in New York's harbor. The poem inscribed at its base has the statue, which faces Europe, declaring, "Give me your poor, your tired, your huddled masses yearning to breathe free."

America's Industrial Revolution required huge armies of new workers who could not be found internally. Many Americans were profoundly uneasy about the social changes arising from industrial growth and about the influx of strangers. They had lost confidence in America's ability to assimilate the immigrants without being changed in the process.

In the political and intellectual debate that was unleashed by these massive social changes in American society, the idea of the United States as a "melting pot" gradually became accepted as the new metaphor to describe the American experience:[9] America attracted immigrants and refugees from all over the world; on arrival, their old values would be melted down and they would emerge as new Americans eager to share traditional American values.

In order to hasten this process, much more intentional processes of education on "Americanism" were adopted, particularly in the schools. For example, it was early in the twentieth century that it became the general practice to start the school day with the raising of the flag and reciting of the Pledge of Allegiance. America slowly began to take pride in itself as an ethnically and religiously pluralist society, though—as is noted below—the process of assimilation was much slower than the melting pot metaphor suggested. The new immigrants faced real obstacles to their full integration with American society.

It has taken a lot longer for the United States to begin to think of itself as a multiracial society. The slaves were freed in 1863 as a result of the Civil War, but whites rejected social integration of the races. Legal segregation of the races had been

---

Here at our sea-washed, sunset gates shall stand
A mighty woman with a torch, whose flame
Is the imprisoned lightning, and her name
Mother of Exiles. From her beacon-hand
Glows world-wide welcome ...
"Keep, ancient lands, your storied pomp!" cries she
With silent lips. "Give me your tired, your poor,
Your huddled masses, yearning to breathe free,
The wretched refuse of your teeming shore.
Send these, the homeless, tempest-tost to me,
I lift my lamp beside the golden door!"

Box 1.1
Extract from Emma Lazarus's poem "The New Colossus" (1883), which is inscribed at the base of the Statue of Liberty in New York harbor.

---

9   On the different metaphors used to describe the American immigrant experience in this period, see Milton Gordon, "Assimilation in America: Theory and Reality," *Daedalus* XC (1961), 263–285.

Box 1.2

Extract from Act I of

srael Zangwill's play The

Melting-Pot *(1909),*

the source of the melting

pot metaphor.

America is God's Crucible, the great Melting-Pot where all the races of Europe are melting and reforming! Here you stand, good folk, think I, when I see them at Ellis Island [the entry point for immigrants in New York harbor], here you stand in your fifty groups, with your fifty languages and histories, and your fifty bloody hatreds and rivalries. But you won't be long like that, brothers, for these are the fires of God you've come to—these are the fires of God. A fig for your feuds and vendettas! Germans and Frenchmen, Irishmen and Englishmen, Jews and Russians—into the Crucible with you all! God is making the American.

introduced in the southern United States by the end of the nineteenth century, and de facto segregation was almost universally practiced in the rest of the country. It was only after racial segregation was challenged by the civil rights movement and made illegal in the 1960s that Americans began to evolve into a racially integrated society.

Also since the 1960s, racial discrimination in immigration has been removed. The influx of immigrants from Latin America and from various parts of Asia has reinforced the reality that the United States is a multiracial as well as a multiethnic and religiously pluralistic society.

Table 1.4

Racial and linguistic
composition of the
United States, 1970 to
2000: percent of total
population.

Race	1970	1980	1990	2000*
White	87.6	85.9	83.9	81.9
Black	11.1	11.8	12.3	12.8
Hispanic+	na	6.4	9.0	11.3
Asian	na	1.6	3.2	4.4
Native	na	0.6	0.8	0.9

+Hispanic is a linguistic, not a racial classification. For this reason the totals add up to more than 100%.
*Middle series projection.

Source: U.S. Bureau of the Census, *Statistical Abstract of the United States 1994.*

Composition of the Canadian Population

While both are immigrant nations, Canada's struggle with diversity has been different from that of the United States both in content and in timing. Canada originated as a French colony, Quebec. After Britain captured Quebec in 1760, British and Americans began arriving in Canada. The French, Catholic population was much too large to be assimilated into the English population; thus, from the beginning Canadians—both English and French—have had to struggle with the fact of a country divided by religion, language, and culture. Unlike the United States, Canada was founded by two homogeneous founding peoples. From the beginning, the need to accommodate both "nations" within one state has been a major factor shaping Canada as a nation and differentiating it from the United States.

For most of its history immigration was not a preoccupation in Quebec. The only significant emigration from France had taken place in the mid-seventeenth century. Because of a high sustained birth rate these original families had populated most of the province, and by the nineteenth century they were even overflowing into the New England states. It was only in the 1960s, with the fall in the French-Canadian birth rate following the social and political liberalization of Quebec during the Quiet Revolution, that population decline was seen to be a problem and immigration a necessity.

Throughout the nineteenth century most immigration into Canada continued to be from Britain, and included both Catholic and Protestant Irish. German immigration was a much smaller factor than in the United States. It was not until the rush to settle the prairies at the beginning of the twentieth century that immigrants who were neither French nor British—many of them from eastern Europe—were allowed into Canada in large numbers. This meant that the prairie provinces, and cities like Winnipeg and Edmonton, were pluralistic societies from the beginning—one of the factors that has differentiated the prairies from the rest of Canada. It was only after World War II that substantial numbers of non-British European immigrants began to settle in Ontario. As a result, Ontario only slowly came to see itself and Canada as a pluralist, multicultural society.

Since Canada comprised two distinct societies for the beginning, there was no possibility of constructing a single identity for the new nation. From early on there was a search for the right metaphor to describe Canadian society.[10] In the 1920s the concept of a "mosaic" began to be accepted as the preferred metaphor for Canadian pluralism, in deliberate contrast with the American melting pot. In Canada, it was argued, immigrants were encouraged to hold on to their own culture in order to contribute to the overall Canadian mosaic. In the 1960s an official policy of encouraging "multiculturalism" was adopted. Also in the 1960s the bias toward whites was removed from Canadian immigration policy. Since then, as a result of substantial immigration from various parts of Asia and from Latin America and the Caribbean, the larger cities in particular have been evolving into multiracial and multicultural societies.

---

10   See Alan Smith, "Metaphor and Nationality in North America," *Canadian Historical Review* 12 (1970), 247–275.

	Decade	1961–71	1981–91
	Total (millions)	1.4	1.2
	Sources %		
	Europe	69	25
	Asia	14	48
	Caribbean and South and Central America	7	16
	United States	6	4
	Africa	3	6

Table 1.5

Recent sources of immigration to Canada.

Source: Statistics Canada, *Canada Year Book, 1997*, Catalogue No. 11-402 (1996); Statistics Canada, *Historic Statistics of Canada*, Catalogue No. 11-516, Second edition (1982).

The Process of Ethnic Integration in the United States

America's conception of itself as a pluralistic society has been dominated by the metaphor of the melting pot, in which the ethnic distinctiveness of immigrants disappears relatively quickly as they are assimilated into American society. The melting pot metaphor has always been charged with ambiguity: some see it as creating a genuinely pluralist society, while others charge that it has simply disguised a policy of "Anglo-conformity" that forces immigrants to conform to dominant white Anglo-Saxon Protestant ("WASP") values.[11] Studies of ethnic behavior in the United States over several generations have indicated that while there is some truth in the notion of the melting pot, it overstates the ease and speed at which non-Anglo groups integrate themselves into the American mainstream.[12] This suggests that in spite of the contrast between the melting pot and mosaic metaphors, the actual process of "vertical" integration of immigrants into the two societies may not be very different.[13]

11 See Michael Novak, "White Ethnic," *Harper's Magazine*, September 1971, and Benjamin Schwarz, "The Diversity Myth: America's Leading Export," *The Atlantic Monthly*, May 1995.

12 The pioneering study is Nathan Glazer and Daniel Patrick Moynihan, *Beyond the Melting Pot: The Negroes, Puerto Ricans, Jews, Italians, and Irish of New York City* (MIT and Harvard University Press, 1963).

13 See John Porter, *The Vertical Mosaic: An Analysis of Social Class and Power in Canada* (University of Toronto Press, 1965).

The reality of the melting pot idea in the United States lies in the rapid acculturation of new immigrants, and in the ready adoption of an American identity by most
immigrants. From the beginning most immigrants in America have been seeking religious and political freedom and better economic opportunities than existed at home.
The basic American values of individual and economic freedom have thus had a natural appeal to immigrants. In contrast, the idea of a national melting pot has never fit
the Canadian reality. The motivation for immigration to Canada has been the same,
but in Canada the "absence of a clear and specific national faith which all Canadians
could profess, meant that there was nothing to which an immigrant could be required
to assimilate."[14]

That being said, ethnic groups in the United States have retained their cohesion and
distinctive social patterns over several generations. In part, this has been by choice—
the natural outcome of groups initially settling in homogeneous neighborhoods
("ghettos"), and of their ties to neighborhood churches and schools. There is no
doubt, however, that ethnic group cohesion has also been perpetuated by the fact that
members face discrimination from the dominant groups, as well as barriers to entry
into mainstream society. Because the United States has been an economically dynamic society and a democracy for most of its history, most of the discriminatory barriers to ethnic advancement have fallen over time. Accumulating wealth and winning
political office are the most important means of entry and upward mobility for members of minority groups.

The Political Integration of Minority Groups

As is discussed in more detail in Chapter 10, ethnic and religious group membership
has always influenced political behavior in the United States. Robert Kelley has
demonstrated how ethnicity and religion influenced party loyalties throughout the
nineteenth century.[15] Local political leaders always understood the need to reward
group loyalty by nominating candidates from the group, even at a time when America
thought of itself as a melting pot. Ethnic and religious loyalties have therefore always
been a major determinant of politics and have opened the route for new groups to
enter and move up in political office.

Minority group entry into political office has usually taken place in two stages.
The first stage is based on group cohesion at the local level: members of the group
succeed in electing one of their own to office through their strength in local electoral

---

14   Smith, "Metaphor and Nationality in North America," 254.
15   Robert Kelley, *The Cultural Pattern in American Politics: The First Century* (Knopf, 1979).

districts. Thus, minority representatives first get elected to municipal offices, to state assemblies, and eventually to the House of Representatives.

The second stage, election to statewide office—principally the offices of governor or U.S. senator—is much more difficult to achieve, since each group is a minority (often a small minority) in a much larger constituency. Elections at the first stage are won through appeals to group pride and solidarity; winning at the second stage requires an appeal to the rest of the population. Often group membership must be played down, and prejudice and stereotyping must be overcome. Typically, success at this stage marks a breakthrough in social acceptance and access to power, not just for the individual elected but for the minority group as a whole. Thus, the election in 1989 of the first black governor in modern times (Douglas Wilder in Virginia) was celebrated, as was the election in 1992 of the first Native-American U.S. senator (Ben Nighthorse Campbell in Colorado).

Public office can also be reached in the United States by appointment (as opposed to election). At the local, state, and federal levels many executive and judicial positions are filled by executive appointment; thus, they constitute another way for parties to reward group loyalty. At the federal level, all holders of Cabinet and sub-Cabinet positions and all federal judgeships are nominated by the president and confirmed by the Senate, and these appointments also have symbolic significance for ethnic groups. Thus, for example, in 1986 Italian Americans celebrated the appointment to the Supreme Court of Antonin Scalia, the first Italian-American justice.

Ben Nighthorse Campbell, first Native American elected to the U.S. Senate, with Carol Moseley Braun, first African-American woman in the Senate.

In a class by itself we find the one truly national office and the highest political prize of all—the presidency. Ascension to the highest office in the land marks the ultimate in group integration and social acceptance. To date, John F. Kennedy, of Irish Catholic descent, is still the only president to have broken the long string of presidents of northern European Protestant background. (President Reagan was of Irish extraction but was not a Catholic.)

Integration into the American Mainstream:
the Kennedys of Massachusetts[16]

The well-known Kennedy family of Massachusetts can be used to illustrate the slow process of full ethnic integration into the American mainstream through politics. The Catholic Irish were the first American ethnic group. They first came to America in large numbers in the 1840s, after the disastrous Potato Famine of 1847–48. In the United States they stood out from the established society, as Catholics in an over-whelmingly Protestant society, and as fervently anti-British in a country where the elite still had strong economic and cultural links with Britain.

The Irish immigrants encountered considerable prejudice and discrimination in America. Politics provided both a means of advancement and an outlet for their skills. By the end of the century, Irish political organizers were manning the Democratic Party organizations in many northern cities.[17] They had also moved into political office. For example, the first Irish mayor of Boston was elected in 1884. The first Irish Catholic member of the House of Representatives, John F. Fitzgerald (President Kennedy's grandfather), was elected from a Boston district in 1894.

President Kennedy's great-grandfather, Patrick, arrived in Boston from Ireland in 1848. The president's grandfather, Patrick Joseph, born in the United States, pros-pered within the large Irish community in Boston, becoming a tavern owner, a local Democratic Party leader, and a member of the Massachusetts legislature (stage one). His son, Joseph P. Kennedy, had ambitions beyond the Irish community.

Instead of being educated at Catholic high schools and universities, as was normal within the Irish community, Joseph Kennedy was sent to where the sons of the Boston elite were educated, Boston Latin School and Harvard University. Joe married Rose Fitzgerald, whose father was the first Irish Catholic elected to the House of Representatives and was later mayor of Boston. Fitzgerald's attempts to move beyond his Irish base into statewide office, as candidate for governor and senator (stage two) were unsuccessful.

When Joe Kennedy found his social ambitions and his efforts to move up in the financial community of Boston blocked by the Anglo establishment (known as the Boston Brahmins), he moved to New York, where he made a fortune in businesses out-side elite control—liquor wholesaling (including bootlegging during Prohibition in

---

16   The family stories of President Kennedy's mother and father are told in Doris Kearns Goodwin, *The Fitzgeralds and the Kennedys* (Weidenfeld and Nicholson, 1987).

17   Steven P. Erie, *Rainbow's End: Irish-Americans and the Dilemmas of Urban Machine Politics, 1840–1985* (University of California Press, 1988).

the 1920s) and the new movie industry then being developed in California, mainly by Jewish entrepreneurs.

During the New Deal, urban ethnic groups found themselves welcome in the new majority Democratic Party coalition. This was an important step in their integration into American society. The Irish, long established in the party, were well placed to take advantage of their new access to power. Joe Kennedy lavishly supported the campaigns of President Franklin Roosevelt, who rewarded him with high political appointments (though not as high as Kennedy wanted). These appointments allowed him to triumph over those who had discriminated against him in Boston. As the first chairman of the Securities and Exchange Commission (SEC), he regulated the financial community. Later, as Ambassador to Britain, he socialized with the British aristocracy.

Joseph Kennedy was in many ways a typically American success story. Although a third-generation American, he found his business and social ambitions blocked in his hometown. By moving to the melting pot of New York City and making a fortune in new kinds of businesses outside the elite's control, and by using his money to support President Roosevelt's campaigns, he was able to reach high office. Even so, Joe was not satisfied, and he transferred his ambitions to his sons, one of whom, he was determined, would become president of the United States.

When his oldest son was killed in World War II, Joe focused his ambitions on his second son, John F. Kennedy. After being educated like his father at Boston Latin School and Harvard, John started in politics in the traditional way, as congressman from an Irish district in Boston in 1946 (stage one). With the help of his father's money and contacts, he succeeded where his grandfather Fitzgerald had failed and was elected senator from Massachusetts in 1952 (stage two), defeating a leading Brahmin.

In 1960, in his drive for the presidency (final stage), Kennedy was again helped enormously by his father's money and by the active support of his family and a highly skilled group of Boston Irish political operatives (known as the Boston Mafia). Yet Kennedy still had to overcome his ethnic background. First, he had to persuade the state leaders of the Democratic Party, many of them of Irish descent themselves, that a Catholic was electable nationally. (The first Catholic to be nominated for the presidency, Governor Al Smith of New York, had been badly defeated in 1928). He did this by pouring money and supporters into West Virginia, which had a very small Catholic population, in order to win its presidential primary election and demonstrate his appeal to Protestant voters. After a series of strategic primary victories, Kennedy received the backing of the northern state party leaders and won the nomination.

In the presidential election campaign, the issue of his religion was still being raised by some Protestant leaders. Kennedy addressed the question of anti-Catholic prejudice directly by appealing for religious tolerance. In the end the issue probably helped more than it hurt him in his narrow victory. While his religion lost him a lot of votes in the Protestant rural south, it helped unite the important Catholic vote behind him in the closely contested large industrial states. It is estimated that in 1956 the Democratic candidate received only 46 percent of Catholic votes, while in 1960 Kennedy received 83 percent—a record if the estimates are accurate.

According to the **American Dream**, in the United States any child can grow up to be president. It took the Irish Americans just over 100 years to have one of their own, a fourth-generation American, reach that peak. In many ways the Irish were the pioneers for all the non–Anglo-Saxon people who came to America and had to struggle for full acceptance in American life.

Is America Still a Melting Pot?

Throughout the twentieth century the slow process of integrating the varied immigrant stock of the United States has been a central dynamic in American life and in American politics. In immigrant nations like the United States and Canada, the process never ends. Both countries received their greatest flow of immigrants in the first two decades of the twentieth century. In 1910 the proportion of the population that was foreign-born reached an all-time high of nearly 15 percent in the United States and 22 percent in Canada. After 1926, as a result of popular pressure, the U.S. government began restricting immigration, and as a consequence the proportion of immigrants fell steadily, dropping to under 5 percent by 1970. In Canada, by contrast, the proportion fell gradually to 15 percent in 1951, a level at which it has remained.

Since the 1970s immigration to the United States has been rising steadily. In 1996 the proportion of foreign-born inhabitants reached 9.3 percent, the highest proportion since 1930. Most significantly, the major source of immigrants has shifted away from Europe toward Central America and Asia. This has generated fears similar to those which rose with the great tide of immigrants from eastern and southern Europe in the early years of the twentieth century. Strengthening these fears is the fact that the new immigration from Asia, Latin America, and the Caribbean is accentuating the multiracial character of the United States at a time when Americans are becoming more unsure about how much progress they have made in racial integration since the end of segregation in the 1960s.

The fears about immigration have taken several forms: there have been calls to limit immigration and particularly to put a stop to illegal immigration, mostly across the long and porous southern border with Mexico. In 1994 voters in California passed Proposition 187 to deny all but emergency public services to illegal immigrants and their families. The welfare reforms passed by Congress in 1996 reduced public services to both legal and illegal immigrants. One reaction to the large number of Hispanic immigrants in the southwestern states has been a movement to make English the official language of government and to eliminate the provision of bilingual services to immigrants. Several states have passed such laws, and in 1996 the House of Representatives passed a bill declaring English the official language of the federal government. The bill was opposed by most Democrats, and President Clinton and has not proceeded further.

Since the 1960s there has been an increasing tendency to portray the United States as a multicultural society. The traditional metaphor of the melting pot is no longer as commonly accepted. Thus a leader of a Hispanic immigrants' rights groups has been quoted recently as preferring "the image of a 'salad bowl' or a 'mosaic,' with lots of different colors and tiles that together create a 'beautiful' and 'vibrant' picture."[18] The multicultural idea has been reinforced by calls from some black leaders (such as the Black Muslim Louis Farrakhan) and from some black intellectuals for the African-American community to focus on black separatism or autonomy rather than racial integration. On predominantly white university campuses across America there has been a significant degree of voluntary "resegregation" by black students.

These developments have produced an anguished response from American intellectuals across the political spectrum. Conservatives have supported the English-language movement on the grounds that rapid assimilation of immigrants offers them the only prospect of success in America. Nathan Glazer, who in *Beyond the Melting Pot* (1963) was among the very first to point out the persistence of ethnic identities in America, has commented with dismay on the trend toward multicultural thinking in *We Are All Multiculturalists Now*.[19] In Glazer's view, multiculturalism and the mosaic metaphor are indications of America's failure to racially integrate itself. The revulsion many Americans feel at the very notion of multiculturalism is evident in the words of liberal historian Arthur Schlesinger Jr., who wrote the following in *The Disuniting of America*:

> Instead of a transformative nation with an identity all its own, America in this new light is seen as preservative of diverse alien identities. Instead of a nation composed of individuals making their own unhampered choices, America increasingly sees itself as composed of groups more or less ineradicable in their ethnic character. The multiethnic dogma abandons historic purposes, replacing assimilation with fragmentation, integration by separatism.[20]

---

18   William Branigin, "The Great American Melting Stew," *Washington Post National Weekly Edition*, April 14, 1997.

19   Nathan Glazer, *We Are All Multiculturalists Now* (Harvard University Press, 1997).

20   Arthur M. Schlesinger Jr., *The Disuniting of America: Reflections on a Multicultural Society* (WW Norton and Company, 1992), 16–17.

Benjamin Schwarz argues that "America's anxiety over the fragmentation of foreign states and societies arises from our sense that American society is fragmenting, culturally and ethnically."[21] Arthur Schlesinger, like many American opponents of multiculturalism, holds up Canada as a negative example. "One reason why Canada, despite all its advantages, is so vulnerable to schism is that, as Canadians freely admit, their country lacks ... a unique national identity ... Inclined for generous reasons to a policy of official multiculturalism, Canadians have never developed a strong sense of what it is to be a Canadian."[22]

From a Canadian perspective, the fears expressed by Schlesinger and others seem greatly exaggerated. The proportion of immigrants in the Canadian population has been consistently higher than in the United States throughout the twentieth century. Yet the threats to Canadian unity have always been located in the relations between the two founding peoples, French and English, not in Canada's self-perception as a cultural mosaic or a multicultural society.

Historically, both the United States and Canada have successfully integrated a diverse range of ethnic and religious groups, most of them of European origin. The result has been broadly the same in the two countries, whether the integration process was given the melting pot or the mosaic label. Since the discriminatory immigration laws have been removed, the main sources of immigration into both countries have shifted considerably, so that now both the United States and Canada are faced with the challenge of creating a multiracial society. For Canada this challenge is on a smaller scale than in the United States. Thus in 1991, 6 percent of Canadians were of Asian or Arab origin and 1 percent were black. The comparable American figures are shown in Table 1.4. What adds to the challenge for the United States is that it is facing the new challenge haunted by its historic failure to treat African Americans as equal citizens.

Americans have long sensed the fragility of the American experiment and are preoccupied with preserving a unified sense of national identity. America was founded on a core set of ideas that to this day are profoundly important as a unifying force that cuts through geographic, religious, and even racial barriers. These ideas and beliefs, which are the basis for Americans' identity and patriotism, are the subject of the next chapter.

---

21   Benjamin Schwarz "The Diversity Myth," *The Atlantic Monthly*, May 1995, 58.
22   Schlesinger, *The Disuniting*, 13.

CHAPTER 2

AMERICAN IDEAS

I n order to understand how American political institutions work and how
American politics is conducted, it is essential to understand the political ideas on
which the United States was founded, for they continue to be held by most
Americans. An examination of American ideas is also the starting point for exploring
the differences between the United States and Canada. Different mixes of ideas have
produced political systems that work very differently and produce quite different
results.

Political ideas are important because to a great extent they shape political action.
Writing early in the nineteenth century, Alexis de Tocqueville argued that it was new
ideas that had brought about the French Revolution in 1789.

> It was political theory, and often that theory at its most abstract, which put
> into our fathers' hands the germs of those new ideas which have since sud-
> denly blossomed into political institutions and civil laws unknown to their
> forebears ... Political theories form a sort of intellectual atmosphere breathed
> by both governors and governed in society, and both unwittingly derive from
> it the principles of their action.[1]

---

1   As quoted in Irving Kristol and Paul Weaver, "Introduction," in Kristol and Weaver, eds.,
    Critical Choices for Americans, Volume II, The Americans: 1976 (Lexington Books, 1976),
    xviii. No citation in the original.

More recently, the British economist J.M. Keynes, who started a revolution in economic thinking in the 1930s, argued that "the ideas of economists and political philosophers, both when they are right and when they are wrong, are more powerful than is commonly understood. Indeed the world is ruled by little else."[2]

Because beliefs determine actions, the politics of any democratic country operate within boundaries set by the political beliefs of the majority of the population. Policies that are seen to violate the nation's political beliefs will not be accepted. For example, gun control laws are much weaker in the United States than in other Western countries fundamentally because Americans believe in the primacy of individual rights, and most of them have been persuaded that gun control would threaten these rights.[3] Other Western nations, including Canada, are much more willing to limit individual rights to protect the public interest.

Ideas are especially important in understanding the United States because Americans' sense of national identity has been formed around a set of political ideas and the constitutional system that embodies those ideas. The United States is unique among nations in having a sense of national identity that is essentially political.[4] Most of the early European settlers in the United States were of British ancestry, and shared a common language, culture, and religion; yet in the late eighteenth century they went to war in the name of fundamental political principles to win their separation from the mother country. It was these principles, crystallized and sanctified by the American Revolution, that forged Americans' distinct national identity.

In the past 200 years that strong sense of identity, and the political principles that compose it, have been passed on to succeeding generations of Americans and to the millions of immigrants who have come to their country from the rest of the world. As John Higham has put it: "One became an American by subscribing to the principles of republican government."[5] Americans have always taken an inordinate pride in their political system. When a sample of Americans was asked in a cross-national survey in the early 1960s what aspects of the nation they were proud of, by far the most

---

2   J.M. Keynes, *The General Theory of Employment, Interest, and Money* (Harcourt, Brace, 1936), 383.

3   On the American "gun culture," see Robert J. Spitzer, *The Politics of Gun Control* (Chatham House, 1995), 7–13.

4   Samuel P. Huntington, *American Politics: The Promise of Disharmony* (Belknap Press, 1981), Chapter 2.

5   John Higham, "Integrating America: The Problem of Assimilation in the Nineteenth Century," in George Pozzetta, ed., *Assimilation, Acculturation, and Social Mobility* (Garland Publishing, 1991).

common answer was the political system, which was mentioned by no less than 85 percent—a much higher figure than for any of the other countries polled.[6]

The American identity has been shaped by two sets of ideas: philosophical liberalism and dissenting Protestantism. Both of these are discussed below. In philosophical terms, the United States is unique among Western nations in that its commitment to liberal ideas is monolithic. So fused are liberal ideas with the national identity that American society has always strongly resisted the challenge from conservative or socialist ideas. Indeed, neither of the principal alternative philosophical traditions has been able to take root in American soil. Over the past 200 years the founding ideas have undergone development, but this development has been kept within the framework of the classic liberal ideas on which the United States was founded.

America has also been since its founding a highly religious society, one that has understood its destiny in religious terms. During the revolutionary era, the Calvinist faith of the early settlers appropriated the liberal goals of liberty and progress, and since then American religious ideas have largely reinforced American liberalism. Protestantism has injected a moral passion into the American sense of identity and mission; this is why a uniquely moralistic form of politics sometimes erupts on the American scene.

Canada and the United States are both North American immigrant nations; as a result, their sense of identity could not grow organically over the centuries (as happened in the nations of Europe or Asia), but had to be constructed. However, Canada's historical experiences and the various ideas that have influenced its development have been very different from those of the United States. It was out of these differences that the different political cultures and political institutions of the two nations grew.

The founding Americans were quite homogeneous. In contrast, Canada from the beginning was composed of two societies: a Catholic French colony that the British had captured in 1760, and British colonies originally populated by Loyalists who left America after the Revolution. This is why Canadians have never found it possible to construct a common culture or sense of identity for their country as a whole. There was never an occasion in Canada when it was necessary, or even possible, to state clearly what the ideals of the nation were. There was no Canadian Revolution. Canada's movement from British colony to fully independent nation was a gradual, evolutionary one; in contrast, the Americans declared their beliefs, seized their independence through revolution, and set up their own system of government based on their beliefs.

---

6   Gabriel Almond and Sydney Verba, *The Civic Culture: Political Attitudes in Five Nations* (Little, Brown, 1963), 64.

THE PRINCIPAL SOURCES OF AMERICAN IDEAS

The early American political culture was shaped by two interconnected sets of ideas: liberal political philosophy, and Protestantism. The colonists, who were overwhelmingly of British origin, were also heavily influenced by the historical tradition they brought from England—specifically, by the revolutionary struggles in England during the seventeenth century.

Liberal Political Philosophy

Liberal political philosophy first appeared in Europe in the sixteenth and seventeenth centuries as part of a profound shift in intellectual outlook away from the tradition of medieval Christian thought, which had been strongly influenced by classical Greek and Roman thought and had dominated European thinking for many centuries.

The key change was in the understanding of God's relationship to the world. The medieval world had seen God as the active ruler of human affairs and as the sanctifier of the existing order of things; the new thinking emphasized that God dealt with the world at one remove, through human reason. The effect of this new emphasis on human reason was to distance God from the detailed operation of the world and to open up all human affairs to the application of reason. The beginning of what is called the "modern" era was marked by the gradual emergence of new rational "scientific" thinking in all areas.

Traditional Christian political thought and most classical thought was utopian, in the sense that was concerned with discovering the best possible regime and saw political organization as existing in order to inculcate virtue in the citizens. In the modern era, a "new science of politics" began to develop that was concerned with "practicable liberty"—that is, with determining the principles on which a workable liberal regime could be built.

The two political philosophers who laid the foundations of the new liberal political science were Niccolo Machiavelli, writing in the late sixteenth century in northern Italy, and Thomas Hobbes, writing in the early seventeenth century in England. The basic liberal concepts were elaborated by many others, most notably John Locke, who wrote in late-seventeenth-century England. It was Locke who was the most important direct influence on those who founded America.

The central ideas in liberal political thought are *individual rights* and *the natural equality of all men*. All men, the liberal thinkers argued, are naturally free and equal. No man has a natural right to rule another. The individual has the natural right to life and liberty and to make his own way in the world, including the right to acquire property. What set liberal political philosophy apart from traditional thought was that it emphasized the individual rather than society as a whole as the basic political unit, and that it saw political society as a rational human creation rather than as something which had been ordained by God in its existing form and which therefore could not be changed.

Traditional (or conservative) philosophy thought of human society as an organic whole and emphasized that each person derived his significance from his part in the overall hierarchical scheme of things, which had been ordained by God. Each position in society, whether that of king, lord, or peasant, had its own duties to fulfill. Any attempt to change an individual's situation would disrupt the natural balance and order of society. The emphasis was thus on duties rather than rights.

Conservative thinkers could not imagine the individual existing outside of an organized political society. The individual found his significance by playing his ordained role in society, and the power of government was essential to maintain order and punish wrongdoing. Liberals, on the other hand, started with a free, self-sufficient individual who possessed certain basic rights. Liberals then had to explain how political society and government had come about. That is, why would a free individual agree to enter political society and submit to the power of government, which might take away his liberty?

The liberal answer to this question was that life outside of organized society, in the "state of nature," was insecure. Without law, it was not possible for individuals to fully exercise their rights. It made sense, therefore, for them to agree together on a "social contract" to establish a political society with a government that had the power to enforce the law and keep the peace. Thus, government was based not on divine authority or naked force but rather on the consent of the governed. Within society, the individual could have secure enjoyment of his rights, and indeed additional civil rights could be established.

In this way, political society was held to be a rational creation, with government existing to protect and extend the rights of individuals. By this reasoning, any government that took away the individual's basic rights was illegitimate, because it was contradicting the purpose for which it had been created; that being the case, the individual had the right to rebel against it and try to replace it.

The basic tenets of liberalism have had an enormous impact on the development of Western society. In older societies like Britain, the spread of liberal ideas, which emphasized the individual, reason, and change, was impeded by the existence of strongly entrenched feudal institutions that embodied the values of community, tradition, and continuity. The end result was a process of compromise in which ancient institutions and practices were modified rather than replaced. In America there were no such institutional obstacles to the practice of liberal ideas. America had no feudal past; indeed, as the Pilgrims had realized, here was the opportunity to establish a new form of society from scratch. To European liberals, America was the New World, where a fresh start could be made.

Protestantism

An upheaval in religious thought comparable to the emergence of liberal political ideas had already taken place in the early sixteenth century with the beginning of the Protestant Reformation in central Europe. The Protestant Reformation rejected the hierarchical structure and theology of medieval Catholicism and asserted instead the possibility and the necessity for each individual to answer to God personally, without the mediation of the church.

Protestantism shared with liberalism a number of central beliefs: the primacy of the individual; the importance of human reason and the need for a rational response to human circumstances; and a rejection of hierarchy and a belief in the equality of all persons before God. The new spirit of religious individualism was captured in the words of Martin Luther, as he nailed his list of theological objections to the door of Wittenberg Cathedral in defiance of the church authorities: "Here I stand; I can do no other."

Protestantism in several forms spread quickly across northern Europe, and split Europe into fiercely antagonistic Catholic and Protestant camps. This unleashed two centuries of religious warfare during which Catholic or Protestant minorities were persecuted in each country. The individualistic spirit of Protestantism led inevitably to the formation of many different churches and sects.

Puritanism, and similar movements in northern Europe, sharply divided Protestants. Puritans sought to build a godly society and believed that the church, the state, and the life of the individual should conform to scriptural standards. The Puritans' reforming zeal was resisted by the established churches, which allied them- selves with the state to enforce religious uniformity and persecute dissenting Protestants. Many of these dissenters sought freedom of worship in the New World, where they were able to act on their zeal for a Christian society. The antagonism between Protestants and Catholics and, within Protestantism, between Puritan "moralists" and others continued in the New World, and this would do much to shape the American religious and political experience.

◄ *The English Background*
England had "the longest and most turbulent Reformation experience in Christendom."[7] The religious and political questions that seemed to have been settled

---

7   Sydney E. Ahlstrom, *A Religious History of the American People* (Yale University Press, 1972), 124.

by the strong rule of Elizabeth I (1558–1603) were reopened under her successors, with the result that the seventeenth century was violent and uncertain. Much of the passion driving the revolutionary events of the period came from Puritanism. The struggle of their fellow Englishmen for purity in religion and against absolutist government in the seventeenth century provided the example and inspiration for the Americans in the eighteenth century. Samuel Huntington indeed argues that "the origins of American politics are to be found in the English Puritan Revolution. That revolution is, in fact, the single most important formative event of American political history."[8]

In the English struggle the political and religious dimensions were closely intertwined.[9] Politically, the opposing forces were Charles I, who claimed a divine right to exercise autocratic power, and the Parliament, which claimed the ancient right to limit the power of the king in the name of the people. In religion, the quarrel was between the supporters of the Anglican church, which had retained the hierarchical structure and some of the doctrine of the Catholic church, and those Puritans and Presbyterians who wanted a more radical reformation of the Church. The situation was complicated by the fact that Charles was also King of Scotland, where there had been a separate Calvinist reformation that had established a radical Presbyterian church.

Charles was determined to impose the Anglican Church on the Scottish Presbyterians and to raise taxes in England without the consent of Parliament in order to finance an army to fight the Scots; all of this split the English elites right down the middle along religious lines. As a result of the king's persistence, a civil war broke out in 1642 between Anglican royalists and Puritan supporters of the Parliament. The parliamentary forces eventually won, with Scottish support.

The English Revolution climaxed with the execution of Charles I in 1649 and the establishment of a republican government under largely Puritan control. English society remained badly divided, however, and the death of the charismatic leader of the Parliament, Oliver Cromwell, who had taken on a quasi-monarchical role as Lord Protector of England, effectively brought the radical experiment in republicanism and Puritan rule to an end. When the monarchy was restored in 1660 under Charles II, the underlying political and religious issues still had not been resolved.

The second stage of the struggle came in 1688, in what became known as the Glorious Revolution. James II, an autocrat and a Catholic in an overwhelmingly Protestant country, was forced to flee, and the Parliament invited his Protestant daughter and her husband to become joint monarchs in his place.[10] It was clear on this occasion that ultimate power lay with the Parliament rather than the monarch; and in fact the new monarchs were required to agree to conditions listed in a Bill of Rights, which

---

8   Huntington, *American Politics*, 154.

9   See Conrad Russell, *The Causes of the English Civil War* (Clarendon Press, 1990).

10   J.R. Jones, *The Revolution of 1688 in England* (Weidenfeld and Nicolson, 1972).

laid out some of the traditional rights of the people and limitations on executive power. The Act of Toleration brought religious persecution of the dissenting churches to an end, although the Anglican church remained established and non-Anglicans were still barred from voting or holding office in England.

Liberalism and Protestantism in America

A high proportion of those who settled in the New World in the seventeenth century were motivated by Puritan ideals. The Pilgrims who landed in the *Mayflower* at Plymouth Rock in Massachusetts in 1620 were radical **Puritans**, who were leaving what they believed was a corrupt church and society in order to be free to worship in their own way and to build a godly society in the wilderness. They were followed by many others. Sydney Ahlstrom points out that while it was the early settlers in New England who are remembered now as Puritans, Puritan ideas were in fact pervasive in England throughout the seventeenth century and influenced most of the early settlers, including the Anglicans who settled Virginia. The Puritan influence in America was so pervasive and long-lasting that Ahlstrom estimates that "Puritanism provided the moral and religious background of fully 75% of the people who declared their independence in 1776."[11]

The ideas of the liberal **Enlightenment** also found a response in America from the late seventeenth century on. The New World in America was fertile soil for liberal ideas. The central figure in liberal political thought was the independent citizen who exercised his reason and unfettered judgment. The basis for the actual exercise of unfettered judgment was economic independence, which depended at that time on the ownership of land—a realistic possibility for most people in America, which had an abundance of available land. Only in America could the liberal ideal of an independent citizenry be put into practice. The "liberal way of life" was natural in the American environment.

The closed religious world of the early Puritan settlers had to contend with the reality of an expanding commercial society and the infusion of liberal ideas. Inspired by the Great Awakening—a revival of religious enthusiasm in the colonies in the 1730s—the American Calvinist theologian Jonathan Edwards, an admirer of the liberal icons Isaac Newton and John Locke, played a key role in American religious history by reformulating the Puritan faith for the Age of Reason. The Calvinist churches' patriotic fervor was aroused by their opposition to the British government's Quebec Act of 1774, which endorsed the privileges of the Catholic church in the newly

---

11   Ahlstrom, *A Religious History*, 124.

captured colony to the north. During the revolutionary era the Calvinists embraced the ideals of liberty and popular government in their theology.[12]

By the end of the century, liberal and Protestant ideas were in substantial agreement in their vision for America. In Europe, the established churches had long opposed liberal ideas; in America, liberal and Christian ideas were working in essential harmony. As de Tocqueville observed in 1835, "In France I had almost always seen the spirit of religion and the spirit of freedom marching in opposite directions. But in America I found they were intimately united and that they reigned in common over the same country."[13] The Protestant goal was for America to become a "city upon a hill,"[14] a Christian society that would be an example to the world. This Protestant vision meshed well with the liberal goal, which was to build a free and progressive society in America. In this climate of compatibility, new forms of "democratic" Protestantism—principally Methodist and Baptist—were able to sweep across America in a second Awakening in the first quarter of the nineteenth century.[15]

The Clash Between the Old World and the New World

The system of government established in Britain after 1688 came to be widely admired as the freest in the world. Its virtues, as analyzed by political philosophers such as Locke and Montesquieu, were those of a "mixed government" that balanced the popular, aristocratic, and hereditary elements in British society as well as the legislative and executive powers in government. By the mid-eighteenth century, however, the government was in the hands of an entrenched aristocratic clique that resisted pressures for further political reforms. The opposition Whig party argued that the king was still too powerful and was able to manipulate the Parliament by handing out jobs and titles. They called for a decrease in royal power and a more representative Parliament. The American colonists, as might be expected, supported the reformist side of the argument and had close connections with the English Whigs.

The American colonies had their own argument with the king and his government in London. The colonies were allowed to elect local assemblies, but these had little

---

12   Nathan O. Hatch, *The Sacred Cause of Liberty: Republican Thought and the Millenium in Revolutionary New England* (Yale University Press, 1977).

13   Alexis de Tocqueville, *Democracy in America*, Volume I (Vintage Books Edition, 1990), 308.

14   This favorite American image is taken from a sermon preached by John Winthrop during the voyage of some of the early Puritan settlers to Massachusetts in 1630. It is a quotation from *Matthew* 5:14.

15   Nathan O. Hatch, *The Democratization of American Christianity* (Yale University Press, 1989).

influence over the royal governors and their appointed executive councils, which were controlled from London. In the 1760s serious disputes developed over British attempts to control the trade of the colonies, to tax the colonies to pay for their own defense, and to prevent their expansion into the open lands to the west. On all of these issues the economic and strategic interests of the British government prevailed over the interests of the colonies.

The colonists, with opposition support in Britain, saw themselves not simply as defending their own interests but also as defending the traditional "rights of Englishmen" against tyrannical royal government. Their key complaint, embodied in the slogan "No Taxation Without Representation," was that they were being governed without their consent in violation of liberal principles and the British Constitution. On the Fourth of July of 1776, after the political struggle had turned violent, representatives of the colonies came together and signed the Declaration of Independence.

The Declaration of Independence

The *Declaration of Independence*, drafted by Thomas Jefferson, is the American colonists' justification for going to war against Britain. The declaration was an appeal, first of all, to the colonists themselves. Their liberal principles told them that rebellion against a tyrannical government was justified, but even so, it was a momentous undertaking to challenge one of the dominant powers of Europe. It was also difficult to go to war with the mother country, whose heritage and political system they admired. The American public were divided over the wisdom of going to war and had to be won over to the cause, and the colonies had to be persuaded to act together. The Declaration was also an appeal to the British—particularly to the Whigs, who shared the colonists' political principles.

The Declaration stated the ideals on which the new nation of the United States was to be founded. The long second paragraph provides a clear statement of fundamental liberal principles:

> We hold these truths to be self-evident, that all men are created equal, that they are endowed by their Creator with certain unalienable rights, that among these are Life, Liberty and the pursuit of Happiness. That to secure these rights, Governments are instituted among Men, deriving their just powers from the consent of the governed ...

It goes on to state the right of rebellion and the right to create a new form of government to replace a tyrannical one:

That whenever any Form of Government becomes destructive of these ends, it is the Right of the People to alter or abolish it, and to institute new Government, laying its foundation on such principles and organizing its powers in such form, as to them shall seem most likely to effect their Safety and Happiness.

The rest of the document lays out the colonists' case against Britain, "a history of repeated injuries and usurpations, all having in direct object the establishment of an absolute tyranny over these States." All the blame for the situation is placed on George III: "He has refused his Assent to Laws, the most wholesome and necessary for the public good. He has forbidden his Governors to pass Laws of immediate and pressing importance ..." There follows a long catalog of the king's violations of their rights. The American colonies all owed their origins to royal charters and not acts of Parliament, and consequently they looked to the monarch and not to Parliament as the ultimate source of authority over them.

By this time in the evolution of the British Cabinet system, the king had in fact quite limited personal power. In accusing the king, however, the Americans were blaming their difficulties on abuses of the British Constitution, rather than the Constitution itself—a position with which their Whig allies in Britain agreed. It also drew a parallel between their fight for their rights and the English struggle against the king in the previous century. Many of the actions charged against George III were violations of the English Bill of Rights of 1688.

The effect of the political turmoil and the war was to crystallize American liberal ideals, most notably in the Declaration of Independence, and to ensure their triumph. It was at this point that liberal ideas were transformed into the **American Creed**. War turned the ideas of the Declaration into sacred ideals for which Americans had died and on which a new nation had been founded. In the aftermath of the revolution, the few traces of conservative institutions in America disappeared. The established churches that existed in most of the states were eventually abolished and the principle of complete religious toleration was established. In 1787 a new constitution was drawn up that attempted to embody liberal principles in a system of government, and the United States has operated within this constitution, with only a few amendments, ever since.

Because of its monolithic identification with the liberal ideas that arose during the founders' era, America has always been different from European societies, in which liberal, conservative, and socialist ideas have all shaped political developments. In American society, only liberal ideas have had any currency, and philosophically conservative ideas have never really taken root. Because the collectivist element in conservative thought has been missing, socialism has never been perceived as a viable alternative tradition in the United States.[16]

The Canadian Tradition

The monolithic liberalism found in the United States is not found in Canada, and this is the main difference between the two countries. Both in its founding and in its development, Canada has been influenced by a range of liberal, conservative, and (later) socialist ideas. Canada's distinctiveness has arisen from the fact that it originated in two founding societies with different ideological traditions. Quebec was a conservative society, originally established by the French monarchy, and was relatively unaffected by the liberal revolution in its mother country. After the British Conquest in 1760, Quebec society was on the defensive in North America, as a French Catholic island in a continent increasingly dominated by English Protestants. Quebec has responded by looking inward, identifying with its own institutions (particularly the Catholic church), stressing collective rather than individual rights, and looking to the government of Quebec to defend its distinctiveness as a society. Although it has undergone substantial change since the Quiet Revolution of the 1960s and the decline of the church, Quebec remains deeply rooted in conservative collectivist ideas.

In English Canada there has always been a viable tradition of conservative thought, and the strong tradition of liberalism has always had to contend with it. There has been considerable academic debate about the origins of Canadian conservatism. Much of the debate has centered on the United Empire Loyalists, who left the United States after the American Revolution and formed the first substantial English populations in Ontario, New Brunswick, and parts of Quebec. Were they Tories, who sided with the British against the American liberals and lost? Recent research has emphasized the extent to which the Loyalists shared basic American liberal values, but also speculates that their flight from their homeland had given them a "Tory touch."[17]

From the beginning, English Canadians were on the defensive against the much larger, expansionist, radically democratic United States. In 1775 and again in 1812,

---

16   The classic statement of this thesis is in Louis Hartz, *The Liberal Tradition in America* (Harcourt, Brace, 1955).

17   The classic article on the Tory touch is Gad Horowitz, "Conservatism, Liberalism, and Socialism in Canada: An Interpretation." Horowitz was writing in response to the ideas of Louis Hartz and Kenneth D. McRae in Hartz, *The Founding of New Societies* (Harcourt, Brace and World, 1964). Horowitz's article and the subsequent debate it triggered among Canadian scholars are in Janet Ajzenstat and Peter J. Smith, eds., *Canada's Origins: Liberal, Tory, or Republican?* (Carleton University Press, 1995).

both French and English Canadians rejected the Americans' aggressive overtures to join them. Canadians strove to differentiate themselves and clung to their British institutions. The attempted democratic uprisings of 1837, which were inspired by the American example, did not get very far either in Ontario or in Quebec. Instead, Canadians successfully pressed the British government to grant "responsible government" (domestic self-government) to the Parliaments of its remaining North American colonies. When the Dominion of Canada was being created in 1867, the U.S. Constitution was viewed as a negative model in several respects. Canada chose instead to continue with the British institutions it had inherited. Canadians have never shared the American suspicion of government. Rather, the use of governmental power has been often seen as necessary for the defense against American domination.

Religious ideas also played a role in the development of Canada, but not to the extent seen in the United States. From the beginning, Canada was an uneasy alliance between a deeply Catholic society (Quebec) and a predominantly Protestant one (English Canada). Canadian Protestants preferred a modified form of church establishment to what they saw as the anarchic religious marketplace of the United States.[18]

Canada's intellectual roots are very different from those of its southern neighbor, and its national experience has been just as different. In Canada, conservative ideas and institutions greatly moderated the impact of liberalism in a number of ways. Because it was born without a unifying national identity, and experienced no revolutionary break from its colonial past, Canada has remained open to the conservative and democratic-socialist ideas that have flowed into the country with the stream of (predominantly British) immigration. While liberal ideals are widely held in Canada, their practice has been greatly moderated by other values that are more collectivist and more deferential.

The principal student of the differences between Canadian and American society has been an American political sociologist, S. Martin Lipset. Lipset contrasts the revolutionary origins of the United States with the "counter-revolutionary" origins of Canada and argues that Canadian culture has emphasized and perpetuated the differences between the two societies. Thus, while liberal influences are strong in both, there remain distinct differences between the two political cultures. Canada, Lipset argues, is "more class-aware, elitist, law-abiding, statist, collectivity-oriented, and particularistic (group-oriented) than the United States."[19] A recent study using different value measures found some of the same differences between Canadian and

---

18   On Protestantism in English Canada, see G.A. Rawlyk, ed., *The Canadian Protestant Experience 1760 to 1990* (Welch Publishing, 1990).

19   S.M. Lipset, *North American Cultures: Values and Institutions in Canada and the United States* (Borderlands, 1990), 2.

American societies, but also suggested that the two societies may be converging inso-
far as "post-materialist" values (a concern for the quality of life) are rising in both
countries, particularly among the younger generation.[20]

THE AMERICAN LIBERAL CREED

The core liberal ideas are a belief in individual rights and the natural equality of all
men. This section examines the impact of these ideas in America as well as the closely related ideas about government, property, and democracy.

America has always been a highly individualistic culture. This bias has been
enhanced by a pervasive suspicion of authority, particularly of government. Whereas
in conservative political thought government is central, because of the primary need
for order and security, in liberal thought government is a necessary evil. The essential
purpose of government is to make possible the enjoyment of individual rights; yet at
the same time, as the experience of the early liberals and the American colonists confirmed, the power of government is also the principal threat to those rights.

This is why a deep-seated suspicion of government—what Samuel Huntington has
called an "anti-power ethic"[21]—has come to be part of the American political culture.
Americans have traditionally been very reluctant to turn to government, especially the
federal government, to solve problems. President Reagan's slogan in the 1980s—
"Government is not the solution to our problem; government *is* the problem!"—
appealed to that deep-seated American fear of government power.

In liberal thought the right to acquire property was one of the fundamental individual rights. The ownership of property was also seen as an essential guarantee of
the liberty of the individual. Without economic independence, individuals could not
be free to exercise their rights. One of the main complaints against the king in
England had been the power he claimed to confiscate property and to impose taxes
without the consent of Parliament. The American Revolution was precipitated when
the British government claimed the right to tax the colonists although they had no representation in the British Parliament. In American thinking, individual property rights
have always been fundamental. A profound reluctance to interfere with individual
property rights has been a powerful barrier against government action in many areas.

The natural equality of all men was a fundamental principle of liberal thought.
Christianity had always taught that all were equal in the sight of God. In traditional

---

20   Ronald F. Inglehart, Neil Nevitte, and Miguel Basanez, *The North American Trajectory:
      Cultural, Economic, and Political Ties among the United States, Canada, and Mexico* (Aldine
      De Gruyter, 1996).
21   Huntington, *American Politics*, 33.

Christian thought, however, spiritual equality did not translate into political or economic equality. Indeed, it was believed that God had ordained different orders in society, with some born to rule and most to be ruled over. In contrast, the practical emphasis in liberal thought was on political rights—on equality before the law.

The Declaration of Independence states that "all men are created equal." It is important to be clear about what that fundamental belief in equality did and did *not* mean to the Americans at that time. America was an egalitarian society both by conviction and, to a large extent, in practice. The Americans were opposed to the hierarchy and "privilege" that in British society took the form of ranks and titles marking the different classes. The general availability of land in the New World meant that inequalities of wealth were very much less than in Europe. America saw itself as what would later be called a "meritocracy," a land of opportunity.

The American Founders are often spoken of as "democrats" in reference to their egalitarian spirit and their belief in popular sovereignty. They were, however, eighteenth-century liberals, not modern democrats. As noted earlier, liberals argued that only someone who was economically independent—which meant a landowner—was able to freely exercise political rights. Those without land were susceptible to manipulation by those on whom they were economically dependent. This was a basic reason why women were not considered for citizenship: because they were legally and economically dependent on their husbands or fathers, they were not free to exercise independent judgment. Likewise, the poor—those without property—were not able to be active citizens.

The ownership of a certain amount of property was thus a qualification for voting in America. Since the ownership of property was much more widely spread than in Britain, the proportion of the population able to vote was much greater. It is estimated that around the time of the revolution, between 50 and 80 percent of white adult males were eligible to vote.

The more radical notion that all men should have equal political rights regardless of economic circumstance was a logical extension of liberalism. This idea was first widely propagated in France after 1789. Once the fierce controversy surrounding the French Revolution had died down, the idea of universal suffrage gained considerable support among Americans. By the 1830s almost all property qualifications for voting had been abolished; this is how the United States became the world's first modern democracy, much earlier than any other country. In Canada, some property qualifications for voting were retained until late in the nineteenth century.

While the idea of universal suffrage was an important one, it should in fact be called "universal white male suffrage." Political rights were not extended to blacks (whether slave or free), to women, or to the native people until much later. Nevertheless, the *idea* of democracy—immortalized for Americans in President Lincoln's **Gettysburg Address** of 1863: "government of the people, by the people, for the people"—became an integral part of the American Creed. The long political struggle to extend the right to vote to the excluded groups is discussed in Chapter 10.

Abraham Lincoln should also be credited with refocusing American attention on the ideal of equality. At a time when the Supreme Court, supported by his opponents both North and South, denied the fundamental equality of citizenship to black Americans, Lincoln recalled the founding promise of the Declaration of Independence that "all men are created equal." He opposed slavery as fundamentally in conflict with American values. Its extension outside the South, he argued, would undermine the moral basis of American society. After the Civil War, the 14th Amendment to the Constitution guaranteed all Americans, black and white, the "equal protection of the laws"—the first reference to equality in the Constitution.

The greatest and most persistent causes of inequality in America have been economic. In the economic sphere the idea of equality has always been subordinated to the drive of individualism and the belief in commerce as the engine of progress in America. J.R. Pole suggests that in economic terms, Americans believe not in equality but in opportunity. From the beginning, America has been revered as a land of opportunity. The belief that America is in fact such a place has justified unlimited individualism in economic affairs and the economic inequalities that have been the inevitable result. Pole argues that "the national belief in opportunity and the rhetoric of equality ... bestowed an exceptional touch of moral authority on the force of

---

Box 2.1

The Gettysburg Address, by President Abraham Lincoln, at the dedication of the Union Cemetery on the battlefield at Gettysburg, Pennsylvania, November 19, 1863.

Four score and seven years ago our fathers brought forth on this continent, a new nation, conceived in Liberty, and dedicated to the proposition that all men are created equal.

Now we are engaged in a great civil war, testing whether that nation or any nation so conceived and so dedicated, can long endure. We are met on a great battle-field of that war. We have come to dedicate a portion of that field, as a final resting place for those who here gave their lives that the nation might live. It is altogether fitting and proper that we should do this.

But, in a larger sense, we can not dedicate—we can not consecrate—we can not hallow—this ground. The brave men, living and dead, who struggled here, have consecrated it, far above our poor power to add or detract. The world will little note, nor long remember what we say here, but it can never forget what they did here. It is for us the living, rather, to be dedicated here to the unfinished work which they who fought here have thus far so nobly advanced. It is rather for us to be here dedicated to the great task remaining before us—that from these honored dead we take increased devotion to that cause for which they gave the last full measure of devotion—that we here highly resolve that these dead shall not have died in vain—that this nation, under God, shall have a new birth of freedom—and that government of the people, by the people, for the people, shall not perish from the earth.

liberated individualism."[22] It was only after the New Deal, discussed later, that the idea was accepted that government had a role to play in making "equality of opportunity" more of a reality for most Americans.

Economic Liberalism

By the end of the eighteenth century, liberal principles had begun to be applied to economic affairs. The most important philosopher of liberal economic ideas was Adam Smith, the founder of the modern discipline of economics. In *The Wealth of Nations* (1776), Smith laid out the arguments for allowing individual freedom in economic matters and for free trade between nations.

Traditionally, economic activity had been tightly controlled by government. The king granted the right to manufacture certain goods, often giving monopoly rights to individuals in return for payment. Foreign trade was controlled, since the goal was to build up the national wealth by running a surplus in the balance of payments. Smith argued that government control of economic activity led to political corruption and lowered the level of economic activity. The restriction of trade between nations had reduced prosperity and led to war. The removal of most government controls and the freeing of individuals to pursue their economic interests would, he argued, increase the general prosperity, which in turn would increase liberty and enhance political stability. Increased foreign trade would benefit all nations involved and thus encourage good relations. An important part of the argument was that important political benefits would result from economic freedom.

In response to the church's traditional moral objection to acquisitiveness (defined as the pursuit of purely individual interests), Smith pointed to how, "as though by an invisible hand," a free competitive economic system would turn the pursuit of purely private interests into a general increase in prosperity that benefited everyone.

Liberal economic ideas had a natural appeal in America, but the application of these principles in a small, developing nation like the United States was controversial. Until the Civil War, the basic question dividing the political parties was how large a role the national government should play in developing the country's economic infrastructure. On one side were the followers of Alexander Hamilton, President Washington's treasury secretary, who saw commercial development as the principal engine of national progress and who pushed for a national bank, government-supported "internal improvements," and protective tariffs. On the other side were Thomas Jefferson's followers, who envisioned America as a democratic republic of

---

22   J.R. Pole, *The Pursuit of Equality in American History* (University of California Press, 1978), 146.

small farmers and who were worried about the accumulation of power and potential for corruption inherent in government support of business.

It was not until American business grew rapidly after the Civil War and popular pressures for government regulation of business began to rise that pure economic liberalism, in the form of the doctrine of *laissez-faire*, was promoted by business as a key element of the American Creed.

Religious Liberty and the Separation of Church and State

During the revolutionary era, Protestant and liberal ideas had come together on the primacy of individual liberty and republican government; but they disagreed on the proper relationship between religion and the state. The liberal position, memorably articulated by Thomas Jefferson in the Virginia Statute of Religious Liberty of 1786, was for the separation of church and state, the argument being that state support for religion corrupted both religion and the state. Jefferson later elaborated that there should be "a wall of separation" between church and state. The Puritans and their successors countered that since the true foundation of the state was a religious one, it was incumbent on the state to support true religion.

The argument for separation and religious freedom did not originate with Thomas Jefferson and James Madison—its best-known exponents—but with religious minorities in New England, particularly Baptists such as Roger Williams and Isaac Backus, who were fighting discrimination against them by the established Congregationalist church. There was therefore a division among Protestants on the issue.[23]

At the time of the revolution, nine of the thirteen states had state-supported churches. However, the proliferation of Protestant denominations had brought a large degree of religious toleration in practice, and the privileges of the established churches were being steadily eroded. Jefferson and Madison were able to defeat a proposal that would have provided tax support for the Episcopal Church in Virginia; with the support of the Baptists and Presbyterians, they also succeeded in passing a Statute of Religious Liberty.

The First Amendment to the Constitution, drafted mainly by Madison in the first session of the new Congress, guaranteed religious freedom and forbade Congress from passing any law "respecting an establishment of religion."

The Canadian experience of church/state relations has been significantly different. In Quebec after the British Conquest, the Roman Catholic Church became the

---

23   On the early history of the separation of church and state in the United States and Canada, see E.R. Norman, *The Conscience of the State in North America* (Cambridge University Press, 1968).

principal focus of Quebec loyalties. On an English Protestant continent, the church was both the guarantor and the symbol of Quebec's uniqueness. Within Quebec the church had all the privileges and powers of an established church and wielded enormous social influence through its control of most educational institutions and hospitals. This situation lasted until the Quiet Revolution after 1960, which saw the liberalization of Quebec society, a sharp decline in the church's constituency and influence, and the rise of a modern nationalist movement.

The early years in English Canada saw a proliferation of religious denominations. The Anglican and Presbyterian churches had strong British connections. The colonial authorities were, however, concerned about the influence of the Methodists and Baptists, who had spread north from the United States, preaching republican ideals along with the Gospel. The **War of 1812** was a watershed. In its aftermath there was a widespread reaction against what were seen as the religious excesses caused by the American separation of church and state. The authorities reinforced the privileges of the Anglicans, principally through land grants for education. The status of the Anglicans as the sole established church turned out to be untenable, and the government later divided the subsidy among the principal churches (though the Baptists refused government support on principle). Canada thus rejected American separatism but also moved away from the European tradition of one established church.[24]

Whereas Almighty God hath created the mind free; that all attempts to influence it by temporal punishments or burthens, or by civil incapacitations, tend only to beget habits of hypocrisy and meanness ...; that our civil rights have no dependence on our religious opinions, any more than our opinions in physics or geometry; ... that it tends only to corrupt the principles of that religion it is meant to encourage, by bribing with a monopoly of worldly honours and emoluments, those who will externally profess and conform to it; ... and finally, that truth is great and will prevail if left to herself, that she is the proper and sufficient antagonist to error, ... errors ceasing to be dangerous when it is permitted freely to contradict them.

Be it enacted by the General Assembly, that no man shall be compelled to frequent or support any religious worship, place or ministry whatsoever, nor shall be enforced, restrained, molested, or burthened in his body or goods, nor shall otherwise suffer on account of his religious opinions or belief; but that all men shall be free to profess, and by argument to maintain, their opinion in matters of religion, and that the same shall in no wise diminish, enlarge or affect their civil capacities.

Box 2.2

Extract from the Virginia Statute of Religious Liberty (1786), drafted by Thomas Jefferson.

---

24   Nancy Christie, "In These Times of Democratic Rage and Delusion: Popular Religion and the Challenge to the Established Order, 1760–1815," in Rawlyk, *The Canadian Protestant Experience, 1760–1990* (University of Toronto Press, 1990).

Box 2.3

Extract from letter by

Thomas Jefferson to the

Danbury Baptist

Association (1802).

Believing with you that religion is a matter which lies solely between man and his God, that he owes account to none other for his faith or his worship, that the legislative powers of government reach actions only, and not opinions, I contemplate with sovereign reverence that act of the whole American people which declared that their legislature should "make no law respecting an establishment of religion, or prohibiting the free exercise thereof," thus building a wall of separation between Church and State.

The Americans pioneered the separation of church and state. Even so, they have remained a highly religious people. Starting with President Washington's proclamation of the first national day of thanksgiving in 1789, governments have sponsored various forms of religious observance. Even the new public (that is, non-church-supported) school system that the Americans pioneered starting in the 1830s was in practice a nondenominational Protestant system for most of its history.[25] In 1963 the Supreme Court rekindled the old argument over separation when it ruled that the First Amendment forbade the saying of prayers in the public schools.

There has been an ongoing argument in America over the role of religion in public life. The basic division has been between the successors to the Puritans, who believe religion to be an essential foundation for the state that should be recognized and nurtured, and those in the liberal or Baptist tradition, who cite Jefferson's belief that there should be a "wall of separation" between church and state for the benefit of both.

The irony is that the high levels of religious observance across the United States and the extraordinary variety and creativity of American religious life may well be attributable to the separation of church and state. Alexis de Tocqueville marveled at the vitality of American religious life and at the variety of forms it took. He attributed this to the separation of church and state (unheard of in Europe), which freed the churches from political divisions.[26] Others have argued that the absence of government financial and other support forced the churches in the United States to become volunteer organizations dependent on the commitment of their members.

It is certainly true that since the beginning of the nineteenth century the United States has demonstrated an extraordinary religious dynamism both in the extent of popular participation and in the variety of new denominations created. Indeed, Finke and Stark argue that it is this capacity to create new churches to meet the needs of marginal populations, free from state or church establishment controls, that has kept

---

25   On religion and education in the United States and Canada, see Norman, *The Conscience of the State in North America*.

26   Alexis de Tocqueville, *Democracy in America*, Volume I, 308–314.

the rate of religious adherence much higher in the United States than in any other Western nation.[27] A recent study found that during the 1980s, while there was a sharp decline in religious observance across Western societies (including Canada), the decline in the United States was only slight. The level of religious belief and practice in the United States remains markedly higher than in other Western societies.[28]

Until the beginning of the twentieth century, American religious life was dominated by a wide range of Protestant churches and sects. There were some Roman Catholics in the American colonies, particularly in Maryland; but it was not until the large Irish immigration in the mid-nineteenth century, and the influx of immigrants from southern and eastern Europe that followed, that the Roman Catholic Church established a strong presence in American life.[29] Most American Jews are descended from immigrants from eastern Europe, who began to arrive in the late nineteenth century.[30] In recent years, with the flow of immigration from Asia, the number of Muslims and adherents of Eastern religions has begun to increase significantly in the United States.

THE DEVELOPMENT OF LIBERALISM IN AMERICA

The United States was founded on a core of liberal ideas at the end of the eighteenth century. Because its identity was formed around these ideas and their embodiment in the Constitution, America has remained impervious to nonliberal ideas throughout its 200-year history. Political development in the United States has been driven not by an argument between liberal, conservative, and socialist ideas, as in most Western countries, but rather by arguments between different strains of thought within liberalism.

There is general agreement that the dominant intellectual influence in defining liberalism in America was Thomas Jefferson. Two distinct arguments arose in response to different aspects of Jefferson's thought: an economic and political argument, and an argument over the moral basis of American society.

The economic and political argument within American liberalism has its roots in two early, contrasting visions for the new republic: Jefferson's, and Alexander Hamilton's. Indeed, Jefferson formulated his views in opposition to the policies of

---

27   Roger Finke and Rodney Stark, *The Churching of America, 1776–1990* (Rutgers University Press, 1992).

28   Inglehart et al., *The North American Trajectory*, 77–81.

29   James Hennesey, *American Catholics: A History of the Roman Catholic Community in the United States* (Oxford University Press, 1981).

30   On the Jewish experience in the United States, see Ira Katznelson, "Jews on the Margins of American Liberalism," in Pierre Birnbaum and Ira Katznelson, eds., *Paths of Emancipation: Jews, States and Citizenship* (Princeton University Press, 1995).

Alexander Hamilton
(1789–97), treasury
secretary to President
Washington.

Hamilton, who was the first treasury secretary. Hamilton, an advocate of energetic executive leadership, believed that the powers of the national government should be defined broadly, and that the future of the republic lay in the development of commerce and manufacturing, which would lead to greater prosperity and would do the most to develop the talents of the people. To this end, he was willing to use government to support economic development.

Jefferson strongly opposed Hamilton's views on government. He believed that Hamilton was moving away from limited government back to a form of monarchical government. Jefferson saw the states as the best check on the expansion of the powers of the national government. When the Adams Administration pushed through the **Alien and Sedition Acts** in 1798 in an attempt to quash opposition press attacks, Jefferson and James Madison drew up the Kentucky and Virginia Resolutions, in which they argued that since the national government had been formed by a compact among the sovereign states, the states retained the right to disregard actions of the national government that they judged unconstitutional. This "states rights" argument was later used by John Calhoun and South Carolina to oppose tariff laws, and was taken to the extreme by the southern secessionists in 1860.

Jefferson believed that the best future for the American republic was as a nation of independent farmers, whom he saw as the model liberal citizens. He believed this was the best way to retain the greatest degree of equality among the citizens. Jefferson foresaw the inevitable growth of economic inequality that manufacturing would bring as a potent threat to America's future. In particular, he saw the support of business by government as a breeding ground for corruption and privilege.

Underlying the argument between Hamilton and Jefferson lay the tension within liberal thought between liberty and equality. Hamilton believed that unleashing the natural ambition and acquisitiveness of the individual was the key to progress, and was willing to accept the economic inequalities that would inevitably flow from that policy. Jefferson was much more concerned about balancing the liberty of the individual with the need to maintain equality among the citizens of the republic.

The second argument within **American liberalism** is over the moral basis of society. David Greenstone has described the debate as between the "humanist liberalism" of Jefferson and a tradition of "reform liberalism," which he traces from John Adams to Abraham Lincoln.[31] Jefferson's humanist views were influenced by the liberal philosophers of the late-eighteenth-century Scottish Enlightenment, whose liberal

---

31   J. David Greenstone, *The Lincoln Persuasion: Remaking American Liberalism* (Princeton University Press, 1993).

individualism was tempered by their belief in the natural benev-
olence of human beings. Jefferson was optimistic about human
nature and willing to trust the moral choices made by free individuals. Moral progress would be achieved by liberating the individual from all unnecessary constraints.

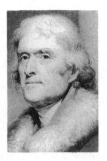

*Thomas Jefferson
(1743-1826), third
president of the
United States.*

The moralist or reform tradition within liberalism was heavily influenced by the heritage of Calvinism, a doctrine which held
that human nature is inherently sinful. According to this bleak
view of human nature, the primary task of each individual is
continuous moral improvement. A free society can only be maintained on a specifically religious foundation, and laws may be needed to encourage
moral behavior and restrain the destructive inclinations of individuals.

In the first half of the nineteenth century the Jeffersonian tradition dominated the
economic and moral debates. The Hamiltonian plans of the **Whig Party** for national
economic development were blocked, and the national bank was abolished.
Evangelical attempts to ban activity on Sunday and to legislate against alcohol were
mostly unsuccessful. The 1850s, however, saw the rise of political agitation across the
North around a number of issues that were portrayed as threats to the moral fabric of
the nation: the abuse of alcohol, the rise of Catholic immigration, and the danger of
slavery spreading outside the South. By the end of the decade the growth of opposition to slavery across the Northeast and Midwest had shattered the existing party system and precipitated the Civil War.[32]

The issue of slavery sharply divided American liberals. The humanist tradition
accepted slavery as an economic and political fact that had to be accommodated if the
Union was to continue. Divisions over slavery had to be "managed" politically
through compromise, as they had been when the Constitution was written (see
Chapter 3). The insistence that slavery was a moral issue that threatened the nation's
integrity was first injected into politics by the Abolitionist movement in the 1830s. At
first that movement's message was rejected as too radical even by reform liberals, and
the issue was overshadowed by the political battles over economic issues. But by the
mid-1850s abolitionist propaganda was tapping into a growing revulsion against "politics" within the dominant Evangelical churches in the North. In this new climate, the
desperate attempts by the leaders of both parties to find new compromises on the
slavery issue simply boomeranged. The Whig Party fell apart, and the Democrats were
left hopelessly split.

The slavery question and its aftermath dominated American politics from 1854 to
1876. This period also saw the ascendancy of the reform liberal tradition through the

---

32   See Richard J. Carwardine, *Evangelicals and Politics in Antebellum America* (Yale University
      Press, 1993).

new Republican Party. During this momentous time, the republic saw the Civil War to preserve the Union; the abolition of slavery; the federal occupation of southern states; and the congressional activism of the Reconstruction period, during which the 13th, 14th, and 15th Amendments to the Constitution were passed, along with legislation designed to improve the lot of former slaves. Republican government also meant the passage of elements of the Hamiltonian national economic program.

By the end of the 1870s, however, attention had shifted away from the great moral issue of slavery and its aftermath and toward new economic issues. The country was industrializing rapidly, and monopoly capitalism was on the rise. The reform tradition, which had little distinctive to say about economic issues, faded into the background of American politics. Meanwhile, the economic argument within liberalism took on a new form. Supporters of business dropped their call for government support and adopted a *laissez-faire* philosophy; those who were worried about the power of business began calling for government regulation. The terms of the new economic debate once again highlighted the tensions within liberalism between the fundamental principles of liberty and equality.

Laissez-faire liberalism

Adam Smith had argued in favor of liberating individual enterprise from traditional controls as a means of achieving a stable, peaceful society. In the hands of later economists, however, Smith's intricate and balanced argument was increasingly simplified into an argument for a policy of *laissez-faire* or "free enterprise." The idea was that individual economic freedom was an end in itself—that government was inherently inefficient and that any government "interference" with the "natural laws" of economics was bound to destabilize the economy and reduce overall prosperity.

The economic ideology of *laissez-faire* was reinforced by the revolution in scientific thinking following the publication of Charles Darwin's *Origin of the Species* in 1859. Darwin's argument for the evolution of animal species through natural selection seemed to legitimize the idea of competition as a law of nature; it also popularized the notion of "the survival of the fittest." The Darwinian model was quickly applied to areas beyond biology. It was used, for example, to justify the supposed superiority of the "Anglo-Saxon race," a theory that legitimized both racial segregation and discrimination against immigrants. The most popular application was by the early sociologist Herbert Spencer, who produced a Darwinian model of social development through competition. Darwin's theory was applied as a proof that social development was subject to natural and thus immutable "laws," with which government could not interfere.

Economic liberalism had a natural appeal to Americans, who generally believed in a minimal role for government and assumed that economic growth increases liberty and brings about political stability. Yet it was only toward the end of the nineteenth century, after the American economy had grown sufficiently to challenge Europe, that American business dropped its insistence on government support and became the unqualified champion of *laissez-faire*. This switch was hastened by the growing calls by labor and farmers for government regulation of business. The business community responded by using all its propaganda skills to popularize the *laissez-faire* version of liberalism.[33]

The American Dream

In the nineteenth century, as millions of immigrants poured into the United States seeking a freer and more prosperous life than they could hope for in Europe, the ideas of the American Creed were popularized in the form of the "American Dream," which combined the ideas of individual liberty, economic opportunity, and America as an open, egalitarian society. "Only in America" was it possible to rise from the humblest beginnings to the highest office in the land—"from log cabin to White House," as Abraham Lincoln had done. In America, it was said, every boy could dream of becoming president.

Toward the end of the nineteenth century, the champions of *laissez-faire* popularized another version of this dream. Only in America could a "barefoot boy" hope to become a Wall Street millionaire. The best-selling children's books of Horatio Alger told stories of boys born in poor circumstances who, through determination, courage, and clean living, achieved success in business. These popular moral tales praised not only the individual virtues of hard work and moral behavior but in particular the greatness of American society and the free enterprise system in which, it was said, these virtues were rewarded.

The American Dream presented an idealized model of American society. But while it was greatly exaggerated, there was some truth in it. Compared to the societies of Europe, the United States *was* a land of opportunity. Even in Britain, which by the end of the nineteenth century was a relatively democratic and tolerant society, the barriers to individual advancement were formidable for most of the population.

The principal barrier to economic advancement in Europe was the restricted availability of education. The United States had invented the public school, which made free basic education available to all, free of religious or economic restrictions. The creation of state universities made a university education much more widely available than in Europe. The lack of rigid class barriers, and the enormous growth of the

---

33   On the spread of *laissez-faire* liberalism in the United States, see Robert G. McCloskey, *American Conservatism in the Age of Enterprise 1865–1910* (Harvard University Press, 1951).

American economy between the Civil War and 1929, provided opportunities for economic advancement to many people that would not have been possible anywhere else.

At the same time, the myth of the American Dream distorted reality. It exaggerated the prospects for most Americans; it also glossed over the miserable conditions in which many of them lived and the barriers of discrimination and economic dependency that most of them faced. In the end, the harsh results of industrialization and *laissez-faire* produced an alternative version of American liberalism.

The Modification of Classical Liberal Ideas

The spread of liberal ideas in Europe had facilitated industrialization early in the nineteenth century. By the middle of the century, some of the effects of the transformation of traditional rural societies into urban industrial societies were being felt. The destructive effects of liberal capitalism on traditional community values was attacked by conservatives, who were the earliest supporters of legislation to improve the conditions of the urban workers. More serious was the challenge from socialist ideas. Socialism combined the conservative emphasis on the community (solidarity and brotherhood) with a radical call for governments to bring about economic as well as political equality.

In the face of these philosophical and political challenges to their ideas and policies, European liberals had to rethink the relationship between individual liberty, equality, and the role of government. What emerged at the beginning of the twentieth century was a "new liberalism" that broadened the classical idea of individual liberty beyond purely political rights and placed a new emphasis on the role of government in creating an equality of opportunity for all individuals. From this rethinking flowed various forms of government regulation of business and social welfare legislation.

In the United States the growth of monopoly capitalism after the Civil War resulted in popular protest that eventually forced a rethinking of liberalism. In the 1870s and 1880s there was a series of rural protest movements, which culminated in the **Populist Party** in the 1890s. These protests produced the first antitrust legislation; but while the Populists tried to appeal to industrial workers and the early union movement, their thinking looked back to the ideals of Jacksonian rural democracy, which had little relevance for the new urban America.

It was within the **Progressive movement** in the early twentieth century that the first rethinking of the liberal creed took place. Most Progressives were urban professionals who supported a wide range of reforms. Unifying the movement was a call for modernization of both the economy and the political system. The Progressives were also concerned about the social conditions of the urban working class, and the first social-welfare legislation was passed in some states at this time. They also recognized that the United States had become a national economy and that modernization required a larger role for the national government.

New Deal Liberalism

The Populist and Progressive critiques of *laissez-faire* liberalism never achieved broad intellectual credibility and popular acceptance in the United States. It was not until the **New Deal** of the 1930s that an intellectually and politically viable alternative model of American liberalism was produced. The Great Depression, which started in 1929 and lasted until World War II, hit North America very hard and had the effect of discrediting the *laissez-faire* philosophy for many people. The response of Franklin Roosevelt and the Democratic Party to the economic and social crisis was a mass of legislation regulating the economy, subsidizing agriculture, and laying the foundation of a national social-welfare program. This New Deal program required a massive expansion of the federal government.

While it was influenced by both Populist and Progressive ideas, the New Deal program was not dictated by a coherent set of ideas; rather, it was a pragmatic response to a crisis. Whatever its origins, however, it succeeded in challenging the traditional

The inaugural photo of President Franklin D. Roosevelt.

American view that government was a threat to individual liberty, and in producing an alternative, "new liberal" view wherein government was capable of solving economic and social problems. The publication in 1936 of the *General Theory of Employment, Interest, and Money* by English economist John Maynard Keynes revolutionized economic thinking by providing for the first time a theory that legitimated government management of the economy. The New Deal policies, underpinned by Keynesian economic analysis, thus produced a new model of activist government.[34]

Political Liberalism and Conservatism

The New Deal approach to government became the principal dividing line in American politics. Supporters of the New Deal were soon labeled political "liberals,"[35] leaving the continuing advocates of *laissez-faire* liberalism to become political "conservatives." A new majority Democratic Party coalition was built around the New Deal, drawing in many of the Progressive Republicans. Some traditional Democrats could not support the new activism and left the party. Southern Democrats retained their traditional party allegiance along with their traditional suspicion of the federal government, forming a significant conservative block within the Democratic coalition.

New Deal liberal thinking dominated American politics from the 1930s through the 1960s. After 1938, however, there was not enough political support in Washington to extend the New Deal further. The *laissez-faire* tradition had not disappeared, and most new Democratic proposals were blocked in Congress by an informal alliance between the minority Republicans and the conservative southern Democrats. It was not until the **Great Society** program was enacted between 1965 and 1968 that there was any significant further expansion of federal government authority.

The victory of the new liberalism remained limited in the United States compared to other Western societies, because of the absence of a supportive social-democratic tradition. A good example of the extent to which the United States has resisted the general movement in Western societies toward providing minimum standards of welfare, is the absence of any system of national health insurance. A program that was put in place in Scandinavia in the 1930s, in Britain in 1948, and in Canada in 1967 still does not exist in the United States. In 1968 health insurance coverage was extended to those over sixty-five by the **Medicare** program, and to those on welfare by **Medicaid.**

---

34   Walter S. Salant, "The Spread of Keynesian Doctrines and Practices in the United States," in Peter A. Hall, ed., *The Political Power of Economic Ideas: Keynesianism across Nations* (Princeton University Press, 1989).

35   Samuel H. Beer, "Liberalism and the National Idea," *The Public Interest* No. 5 (1966), 70–71.

But despite several Democratic Party attempts to create a national system, the latest by President Clinton in 1994, there are still many millions of Americans with no health insurance or with inadequate coverage.

The great expansion of the federal government's role through the new programs of the Great Society, and through strengthened business regulation in the early 1970s, created a backlash against a generation of New Deal liberal dominance. The reaction was fueled by the economic difficulties of the 1970s and the consequent loss of confidence in Keynesian techniques for managing the economy. Political conservatives turned to the alternative theories of the Austrian economist Friedrich von Hayek[36] and of University of Chicago economist Milton Friedman,[37] both strong advocates of a return to *laissez-faire*. As a new generation of conservatives took control of the Republican Party and rode to power in Washington behind Ronald Reagan in 1980, a renewed *laissez-faire* ideology, calling for reduced government and lower taxes, gained political and intellectual ascendancy in America, throwing New Deal liberals very much on the defensive for the first time since the 1930s.

Thus, in the second half of the twentieth century the contending political philosophies in the United States have been two versions of liberalism: New Deal liberalism, in which government plays a crucial role in guaranteeing and creating equality of opportunity for all Americans, and *laissez-faire* liberalism, according to which America already *is* the land of opportunity, which government interference can only diminish. What has always been missing from the American debate—and in this the United States is unique among Western societies—are philosophically conservative and socialist points of view.

Is There a Conservative Tradition in America?

The central focus in liberalism is on the free individual. Government is seen essentially as a threat to freedom, and its role therefore must be minimized. Conservatism, in contrast, places the central emphasis not on the individual but on the community as a whole. In this view, government is essential as the guardian of order and of the public good. Liberalism emphasizes political equality and individual rights. Conservatives accept inequality as natural; they have a more hierarchical vision of society, and see the rulers as responsible for the condition of the ruled. The conservative emphasis is on duties, not rights.

Most observers, following the argument of Louis Hartz, agree that conservative ideas either never took root in the United States or were rooted out in the aftermath

---

36   The best known of von Hayek's many works is *The Road to Serfdom* (University of Chicago Press, 1944).

37   Milton Friedman, *Capitalism and Freedom* (University of Chicago Press, 1962).

of the Revolution, and that there is no American conservative philosophic tradition. The best evidence of this is the pervasiveness of American individualism, the deep distrust of government, and the absence of the core conservative belief in one community, to which individual rights may be subordinated.

Nevertheless, the revival of political conservatism since the 1950s has given rise to several attempts to rediscover or construct a tradition of American conservatism. The first attempt, in the 1950s, tried to trace a tradition of conservative thought stemming from the founder of modern conservatism, Edmund Burke, the eighteenth-century Anglo-Irish philosopher and politician.[38] However, those most often cited as belonging to this tradition are literary figures, such as Nathaniel Hawthorne and Henry Adams. It is difficult to locate Burkean political thought in America since, as conservative theorist Willmoore Kendall pointed out, Burke's argument for the value of tradition and for the necessity of slow, evolutionary change had a limited audience in a society that has always been characterized by rapid social and economic change. In addition, America is a society that has produced little systematic political philosophy. "As a consequence there has not been, in the American tradition, any systematic articulation of generally recognized conservative principles that apply specifically to the American context."[39]

A different intellectual enterprise was the exploration by American historians[40] and by political philosopher J.G.A. Pocock[41] of the eighteenth-century civic humanist or classical republican tradition in the American colonies. This was an alternative strain of thought to liberalism, and one that valued civic virtue and the capacity to place the good of the commonwealth above individual self-interest. It is argued that these ideas flourished in the revolutionary era and were influential among the Federalists in the early years of the republic. The significance of civic humanism in pre-revolutionary America has been hotly debated, but even its proponents accept that it was eclipsed by the success of Jeffersonian liberalism at the beginning of the nineteenth century.

---

38   See Russell Kirk, *The Conservative Mind from Burke to Eliot*, Sixth Revised Edition (Gateway Editions, 1978), and Allen Guttman, *The Conservative Tradition in America* (Oxford University Press, 1967). There is a running controversy as to whether Burke should really be classed as a philosophical conservative. Some would categorize him as a pessimistic or "conservative" liberal.

39   Willmoore Kendall, "Towards a Definition of 'Conservatism,'" in Nellie D. Kendall, ed., *Willmoore Kendall Contra Mundum* (Arlington House, 1971), 259.

40   Bernard Bailyn, *The Ideological Origins of the American Revolution* (The Belknap Press, 1967); Gordon S. Wood, *The Creation of the American Republic, 1776–1787* (University of North Carolina Press, 1969).

41   J.G.A. Pocick, *The Machiavellian Moment: Florentine Political Thought and the Atlantic Republican Tradition* (Princeton University Press, 1973).

An important influence on the modern revival of political conservatism has been the work of University of Chicago political philosopher Leo Strauss and his many American disciples. Strauss's critical rethinking of the history of Western political thought drew its inspiration from the origins of the tradition—the thought of Plato and Aristotle—and has functioned in the American context as a comprehensive critique of the dominant philosophical liberalism.[42] Straussian thought was the main influence on many of the conservative intellectuals who served in or influenced the Reagan Administration. The best-known examples of the Straussian critique of modern American liberalism are found in the work of political philosopher Allan Bloom[43] and columnist George Will.[44]

There are two distinct components of political conservatism as it currently exists within the Republican Party: economic, anti-government conservatism and social conservatism. It seems clear that economic conservatives are, in philosophical terms, *laissez-faire* liberals who, as Ronald Reagan did, believe in individual self-reliance and minimal government.

The other major component of the conservative political revival is social conservatism, which stems mainly from the **Christian Right**. The emergence of the Christian Right as a major force in politics within the Republican Party since the late 1970s (see Chapter 12) harks back to the moralist tradition that played an important role in nineteenth-century American politics. Some have seen this recurring tradition of political moralism as the American conservative tradition. But it seems more accurate to describe this new form of moralist politics as a revival of Greenstone's "reform liberal" tradition. Certainly the contemporary form of the moralist tradition, which includes not only the Christian Right but secular Republican moralists such as Newt Gingrich and William Bennett, is thoroughly liberal in its views on economics and support for a reduced government role in all areas except certain moral ones. The fact is that **American Protestantism** had adopted the core liberal value of individual liberty by the time of the Revolution and has never presented a consistent alternative to the dominance of liberalism.

Most commentators agree that Canada, unlike the United States, has always had a conservative philosophic tradition. Usually cited as evidence is Canadians' greater respect for authority and greater willingness to use government to achieve public goals. In their analysis of political conservatism in Canada, Christian and Campbell point to two quite different strands: "business liberalism," and an authentically

---

42   See Leo Strauss, *Natural Right and History* (University of Chicago Press, 1953).

43   Allan F. Bloom, *The Closing of the American Mind* (Simon and Schuster, 1987). Bloom's book was an unexpected bestseller in the United States.

44   George F. Will, *Statecraft as Soulcraft: What Government Does* (Simon and Schuster, 1983).

conservative strain of "collectivist and hierarchical" Toryism.[45] They see business or *laissez-faire* liberalism as an element in the tradition of both the Liberal and Conservative parties in Canada, and as the dominant element in both in the 1990s. The Tory tradition of conservatism, however, has deep roots in Canada, and while it seems recently to have been submerged by the revival of *laissez-faire* thinking, it is unlikely that it has disappeared altogether from the Canadian political scene.

The Failure of Socialism in America

Socialism, which developed in the nineteenth century, draws on elements of both the other traditions. Like conservatism it is collectivist, not individualist, but the primary community is the working class, not society as a whole. Like liberalism it stresses equality, but it pushes beyond merely political equality toward the goal of economic equality. There have been two distinct socialist traditions: revolutionary socialism, which is based on the writings of Karl Marx, and democratic socialism, which stresses persuasion and democratic change rather than force as the route to achieving socialism.

As the United States rapidly industrialized at the end of the nineteenth century, socialist ideas did achieve some currency among intellectuals and trade unionists, as they did in Europe. An American Socialist Party was formed. But whereas democratic socialist parties built on trade union and working class support became significant factors in European politics from the 1920s on (and a significant minor party in Canada somewhat later), the American Socialist Party reached its peak politically in 1912, when it received 6 percent of the presidential vote. Even the prolonged crisis of the Great Depression did nothing to revive socialist fortunes. There were pockets of strength in a few cities, such as Milwaukee and New York, where German or Jewish immigrants predominated.[46] In the Dakotas and Minnesota in the 1920s there was a farmers' movement similar to the Cooperative Commonwealth Federation (CCF) in Saskatchewan in the 1930s, but it eventually was swept into the Democratic Party coalition after the New Deal. Nationally, socialism has never played a significant role in American politics.

---

45   William Christian and Colin Campbell, *Political Parties and Ideologies in Canada, Third Edition* (McGraw-Hill Ryerson, 1990), Chapter 4.

46   See Ira Katznelson, "Between Separation and Disappearance: Jews on the Margins of American Liberalism," in Pierre Birnbaum and Ira Katznelson, eds., *Paths of Emancipation: Jews, States, and Citizenship* (Princeton University Press, 1995), 200–204, on the major role of New York Jewish immigrants in American socialist politics between 1900 and 1920.

The story is quite different in Canada. While socialism has never been as strong as in Europe, democratic socialist ideas have had a significant influence, mainly through the Progressives of the 1920s, and through the CCF, formed in 1935,[47] which in 1961 became the New Democratic Party (NDP). Canadian socialism has been strongly influenced by the non-Marxist democratic socialism of the British Labour Party. It was Progressive pressure on the Liberal Party that lay behind the introduction of old age pensions in 1927, and it was the introduction of provincial health insurance by the NDP government of Saskatchewan in 1961 that brought about the national program in 1967. At different times, the CCF or the NDP have also formed the government in four of the provinces.

A number of factors have been cited as contributing to the failure of socialism in America: the failure of American socialists to adapt European Marxist socialist ideas (which called for state control) to the liberal political environment of the United States, with its strong suspicion of government; the fragmentation of the American working class along so many ethnic lines; and the hysterical opposition to communism and socialism, propagated by business, that led to the widespread political persecution of socialists and the jailing of most socialist leaders in 1920.[48]

Most explanations point to America's monolithic liberal culture as the central reason why socialism did not thrive. The clearest explanation is that of Hartz, who argued that conservatism and socialism share a belief in the importance of the community rather than the individual; and that the absence of a conservative philosophical tradition in America meant there was no collectivist sentiment on which socialists could build. Others have pointed to the strength of American liberalism in the form of the American Dream. Given the rapid growth of the American economy, the United States offered immigrants the prospect of economic advancement along with democratic rights—a prospect that undercut working-class support for major changes in the existing political and economic system.

---

47   See S.M. Lipset's first book, *Agrarian Socialism: The Cooperative Commonwealth Federation in Saskatchewan, A Study in Political Sociology* (University of California Press, 1950). Starting from the assumption that Canadian political values were the same as American values, Lipset explored why socialism had some success in Canada and none in the United States. From this study flowed Lipset's lifetime study of the differences between Canada and the United States.

48   On the failure of American socialism, see Christopher Lasch, *The Agony of the American Left* (Vintage, 1969), and James Weinstein, *Ambiguous Legacy: The Left in American Politics* (New Viewpoints, 1975). On the early Red Scares, see M.J. Heale, *American Anticommunism: Combating the Enemy Within, 1830–1970* (Johns Hopkins University Press, 1990), Part I.

The American Identity

The American Creed has always been a central part of the American identity. A strong sense of what America stands for has undoubtedly played an important role in building the sprawling American nation and assimilating millions of diverse immigrants. Indeed, at the beginning of the twentieth century, when Americans woke up to the fact that they had become a pluralistic society, the process of assimilating immigrants by inculcating patriotism and American values became a deliberate activity.[49] It was around this time that the **Pledge of Allegiance**, composed in 1892, began to be used in schools. The Pledge was formally endorsed by the U.S. Congress in 1942. Now every American child begins the school day by facing the flag and reciting the Pledge, hand on heart:

> I pledge allegiance to the flag of the United States of America and to the republic for which it stands, one nation, under God,[50] indivisible, with liberty and justice for all.

American Patriotism

Typically, Americans express their patriotism with an emotional intensity and self-confidence that surprises others, not least Canadians. A good example relates to how Americans treat their national flag. In Canada the Maple Leaf typically flies day and night, rain or shine, often until its colors have run, and it is a very faded pink and tattered at the edges. Americans are horrified at such apparently casual treatment of the flag. There is an elaborate protocol surrounding the Stars and Stripes. In schoolyards and cities across the United States the flag is ceremonially raised every morning and lowered every evening, often to the accompaniment of salutes from an honor guard and the recital of the Pledge of Allegiance. The flag is not flown in bad weather and is flown at night only if it is well illuminated. When it is raised or lowered, it must not be allowed to fall or trail on the ground. Burning is the preferred method for disposing of a worn-out flag (as opposed to, for example, stuffing it in a garbage can).

American reverence for their flag is hard to exaggerate. On some occasions when protesters have threatened to burn the flag, the police have been ordered to risk their

---

49   See Heale, *American Anticommunism*, Chapter 4, on the climate of "One Hundred Percent Americanism" in the 1920s.

50   The phrase "under God" was added during a later period of anticommunism and super-patriotism in 1954.

lives to protect the flag's honor. In 1989, when the U.S. Supreme Court ruled[51]—with obvious reluctance—that all state laws making it a crime to desecrate the flag violated the 1st Amendment guarantees of free speech and were thus unconstitutional, there was a massive outcry across the country. The outrage of many ordinary citizens that desecration of the flag (in this particular case, by burning it during a political demonstration) could go unpunished was genuine.

A fierce American patriotism is obvious not only in relation to the national symbols, such as the flag and the national anthem, "The Star-Spangled Banner," but also in relation to the American Creed and the Constitution. Americans' patriotism and sense of identity are inseparable from their political system and political values. A country like France has gone through many different constitutional systems in the past 200 years without its sense of cultural identity and superiority being in the least altered or diminished; it is impossible to imagine the United States separated from its Constitution as, say, a constitutional monarchy or a military dictatorship.

The Religious Dimension of American Life

Much of the intensity of American patriotism stems from the fact that America is and has always been a deeply religious society and from the very beginning has interpreted its national experience in that light. Many of the earliest settlers believed that God had led them out of the corruption of the Old World in order for them to establish new, godly societies in the New World. It was as if God was giving humanity a new start in a new Garden of Eden. They also drew a parallel between their experience and that of the Jews in the Bible: Had not God led the Jews (colonists) out of Egypt (Europe) across the Red Sea (the Atlantic) into the Promised Land (America)? All during the different waves of settlement in America, many settlers saw themselves as chosen people in the Promised Land.

Throughout American history, patriotism and religion have reinforced each other. The eighteenth-century Puritans saw a close parallel between their struggle to preserve the "true" (that is, Protestant) religion against Anglican or Catholic encroachment and their struggle as Americans for liberty against British tyranny. The evangelical belief that America was the Promised Land where God would bring about the millennial Kingdom[52] reinforced the faith of American liberals in progress. This fusion of religious and political ideas has imparted a theological certainty and

---

51   *Texas v. Johnson* 491 U.S. 397 (1989).
52   See Robert T. Handy, *A Christian America: Protestant Hopes and Historical Realities* (Oxford University Press, 1971).

religious fervor to the American sense of identity. Indeed, it has been argued that Americans' belief in their own ideals and reverence for national symbols function as a "civil religion"[53]—that is, as a civil faith that parallels and intertwines with the their religious faith. This is why the basic liberal beliefs are commonly referred to as the American "Creed"; and why repeated public ceremonies, such as saluting the flag and reciting the Pledge of Allegiance, have all the solemnity of religious services; and why the Declaration of Independence, the Constitution, and President Lincoln's Gettysburg Address are treated like sacred texts. "Americanism" has many similarities to a religious faith. Many Americans, it has been said, worship God and America.

ILLIBERALISM IN AMERICA

From the beginning, the United States has prided itself in being a free and open society, a refuge from religious and political persecution in other parts of the world. It gives constitutional protection to individual rights and pioneered official religious freedom. Yet there are other, illiberal, impulses built into the American psyche. Michael Zuckerman argues that the eighteenth-century towns of New England valued homogeneity of belief above all and rejected the "principled notion of legitimate differences among men," a rejection that continues in American life to the present.[54] Robert Kelley refers to "the instinctive need for unanimity" among Americans: "The role of the dissident ... has at no time been an occupation widely admired by the American people."[55] It is this fear of difference that makes the United States what a British writer (echoing many other foreign observers) recently called "the most intolerant society in the democratic world."[56]

In the same vein, Rogers Smith has recently challenged the standard argument that the United States is a monolithically liberal-democratic society. Smith points to the persistence of "illiberal undemocratic beliefs and practices" in American life. Most theorists have argued that these illiberal beliefs are marginal to the dominant liberal tradition, the product of prejudice or ignorance; but Smith argues that they are "alternative traditions" that have always coexisted with and interacted with liberalism in shaping American behavior.[57]

---

53   The classic thesis on American civil religion is Robert N. Bellah, "Civil Religion in America," *Daedalus* (1967). See also Bellah, *The Broken Covenant: American Civil Religion in Time of Trial* (Seabury Press, 1975).

54   Michael Zuckerman, *Peaceable Kingdoms: New England Towns in the Eighteenth Century* (Knopf, 1970), 258.

55   Robert Kelley, "Comparing the Incomparable: Politics and Ideas in the United States and the Soviet Union," *Comparative Studies in Society and History* 26 (1984), 707.

56   Bernard Levin, *The Times (London)*, June 4, 1990.

57   Rogers Smith, "Beyond Tocqueville, Myrdal, and Hartz: The Multiple Traditions in America," in *American Political Science Review* 87 (1993), 549–566.

Three principal forms of **American illiberalism**—religious, political, and racial intolerance—are discussed below. Clearly, these forms of intolerance are not unique to the United States. Canada has had to struggle with all of them. Each of them has, however, been an important factor shaping American society. In America these forms of illiberalism have taken on a sharper edge, and have produced more extremism and more violence than has ever been found, for example, in Canada. On the whole, Canada's reputation as a more tolerant country is justified by its history.

American forms of illiberalism are especially shocking when contrasted with the nation's noble ideals. John Higham has argued that there has always been "a deep fracture in the substance of the ideology."[58] On the one hand, America is proud of its commitment to universal liberal ideals; on the other, at its founding it was in fact a white Protestant society with a deep sense of God-given mission that excluded all those who did not share the values and goals of that society.

So while there was a commitment to religious liberty, along with monolithic Protestantism went the historic antagonism against Catholics as well as any others, such as the Mormons, who strayed too far from Protestant orthodoxy. The Declaration of Independence states that "all men are created equal," but America was a white society that took for granted the superiority of the "white race." Politically, as has been discussed earlier, the monolithic nature of the liberal creed meant that Americans rejected both conservative ideas such as monarchy and any form of collectivism.

Religious Intolerance in America

American Protestants have always seen their task as building a godly kingdom in the New World. From the founding of the earliest Puritan towns of New England, this clear sense of mission led them to want to exclude those who did not share their particular vision of a Christian America. Thus, while the Bill of Rights guaranteed religious freedom and a broad marketplace of Protestant denominations developed, non-Protestant religious groups have been treated with hostility.

The Roman Catholic Church was seen as the main threat to true religion and American values. Although there were Jewish settlers from the beginning, anti-Semitism seems not to have been a factor until the end of the nineteenth century, when the Jews became one of the targets of anti-immigrant, anti-radical agitation.[59] One religious group that was singled out for persecution throughout the nineteenth

---

58   John Higham, "Integrating America," 15.

59   On the Jewish experience in the United States, see Irving Howe, *World of Our Fathers* (Harcourt, Brace, 1989); Ira Katznelson, "Jews on the Margins of American Liberalism"; and R. Laurence Moore, "American Jews as an Ordinary Minority," in Moore, *Religious Outsiders and the Making of Americans* (Oxford University Press, 1986).

century was the Mormon Church, whose doctrine and practices, such as the toleration of polygamy, offended Christian orthodoxy.[60]

The most pervasive form of religious intolerance in America was anti-Catholicism.
The Americans did not invent anti-Catholicism. The Protestant Reformation that
swept northern Europe in the sixteenth century set off two centuries of religious warfare followed by a further two centuries of deep antagonism and suspicion between
Protestants and Catholics. The Catholic church branded all Protestants as heretics
and preached "no salvation outside the Church"; at the same time, Protestants indicted the Catholic church as the "anti-Christ" prophesied in the Book of Revelation.
Overwhelmingly, the founders of America were Protestant, and anti-Catholicism was
part of their Puritan heritage.

The Catholic church was not simply condemned in religious terms; it was also perceived as a threat to American liberties. The American colonists were angered by the
Quebec Act of 1774, through which the British recognized freedom of worship and
Catholic church privileges in Quebec, because they saw the continued presence in
North America of an authoritarian church ruled by the Pope as a threat to American
liberty. Catholics, it was argued, owed allegiance to a foreign power and as pawns in
a despotic system could not share American democratic values.[61] Like other religious
dissidents such as the Mormons, they were considered "ideological aliens" who were
unfit to participate fully in the American enterprise.

There were very few Catholics in the American colonies; only Maryland had an
early Catholic tradition. Most of the colonies prohibited Catholics from holding public office. It was the rise of Irish Catholic immigration to America in the 1840s that
stimulated an active anti-Catholicism. The Irish quickly became involved in
Democratic Party politics in the eastern cities, where they has settled in significant
numbers. For the rest of the nineteenth century, fears about growing Catholic power
did much to mobilize support for the dominant Evangelical Protestant denominations
and the Republican Party. Among the consequences of anti-Catholic sentiment was
the blocking of public financing of parochial schools; there were also various crusades
to impose prohibition and sabbatarianism on the Catholic population.

In more personal terms, Catholics faced various forms of discrimination over a
long period. Al Smith's campaign as the Democratic candidate for president in 1928
demonstrated that there was still widespread hostility to Catholics, especially in the
South. By the mid-twentieth century, however, most of the bitterness had gone out of

---

60   See "How to Become a People: The Mormon Scenario," in Moore, *Religious Outsiders*.
61   Alexis de Tocqueville argued to the contrary—that American Catholics were the citizens most
      devoted to democracy, "At the same time the most submissive believers and the most indepen-
      dent citizens." See *Democracy in America*, Volume I, 300–302.

I believe in an America where the separation of church and state is absolute—where no Catholic prelate would tell the President (should he be a Catholic) how to act, and no Protestant minister would tell his parishoners for whom to vote— ... where no man is denied public office merely because his religion differs from the President who might appoint him or the people who might elect him.

I believe in an America that is officially neither Catholic, Protestant, nor Jewish— ... where no religious body seeks to impose its will directly or indirectly upon the general populace or the public acts of its officials—and where religious liberty is so indivisible than an act against one church is treated as an act against all ... Finally, I believe in an America where religious intolerance will someday end—where all men and all churches are treated as equal— ... and where Catholics, Protestants, and Jews, ... will refrain from those attitudes of disdain and division which have so often marred their works in the past, and promote instead the American ideal of brotherhood.

This is the kind of America in which I believe.

Box 2.4

Extract from Senator John F. Kennedy's speech to the Greater Houston [Protestant] Ministerial Association, September 12, 1960.

the old religious struggles, and most Americans had come to accept religious pluralism.[62] In the 1960 presidential election, Senator John F. Kennedy tackled the issue of religious tolerance head on. His election seems to have laid to rest the long-running issue and to have completed the integration of the European Catholic immigrants into American society.

Political Intolerance in America

The monolithic nature of American liberalism, the absence of a conservative philosophic tradition, and the reasons why socialism failed to make an impact on America as it did in all other industrializing societies have all been discussed earlier. What is remarkable is not only that socialism failed in the United States but that any vestiges of socialism, real or imaginary, were opposed with so much vehemence. Anti-socialism, or more commonly anti-communism, has been a powerful and sometimes hysterical theme in American politics for the past hundred years. "Fear of socialism," says Theodore J. Lowi, "is the American disease."[63]

---

62   Robert Wuthnow, *The Restructuring of American Religion: Society and Faith since World War II* (Princeton University Press, 1988).

63   Theodore J. Lowi, "Why is there no Socialism in the United States? A Federal Analysis," *International Political Science Review* 5 (1984), 379.

M.J. Heale points out that for much of its early history the United States was a haven for radical political thinkers.[64] In his view, the climate of vehement opposition to any form of political radicalism dates back to the ascendancy of American business and *laissez-faire* liberalism after the Civil War. At the end of the nineteenth century, the most potent critiques of monopoly capitalism and its impact on working people came from the socialists and communists. Inevitably, many of those attempting to establish trade unions or calling for change in the United States were drawn to socialist ideology imported from Europe. In Canada, British trade unionism and democratic socialism were the predominant influences; in contrast, American socialism was often a more radical brand brought by recent immigrants from Germany and eastern Europe.

During the massive social upheavals that accompanied rapid industrialization and urbanization, radicals and socialist ideas were easy to stigmatize as a threat to American freedom. The early labor unions and their early strikes were met with violent resistance and official repression to a much greater degree than in Canada. The war against political radicalism intensified when the United States entered World War I in 1917. Socialists who opposed what they saw as a "capitalist war" were arraigned under the new Espionage Act or Sedition Act. The Bolshevik Revolution in Russia intensified American fears. The crackdown on radicals culminated in the "Red Scare" of 1919–20, during which hundreds of socialists and union leaders were jailed or deported.[65] While it is true that imported socialist ideas were unlikely to flourish in America's liberal climate, the severe repression of this period probably did much to prevent the growth of any significant form of democratic socialism in America. In Heale's words: "It was the misfortune of the American Left ... to be large enough to be noticed yet small enough to be crushed."[66]

The emergence of the Soviet Union triggered new American fears. Based on a collectivist ideology, dedicated to the eradication of religion, and with a tyrannical state and party apparatus, the Soviet Union was the polar opposite of everything America stood for. When after World War II the Soviet Union seized Eastern Europe and acquired nuclear weapons with the help of British and American spies, the stage was set for the Cold War stand-off between the two nuclear superpowers. For the next forty years until the collapse of the Soviet Union in 1989, the perception that the communists posed an active threat dominated and sometimes distorted Americans' understanding of the world.

In the early part of the Cold War the United States was racked by another major Red Scare. Although it is usually associated with the flamboyant crusade of Senator

---

64   M.J. Heale, *American Anticommunism: Combating the Enemy Within, 1830–1970* (Johns Hopkins University Press, 1990), Chapter 1.

65   Heale, *American Anticommunism*, Chapters 3 and 4.

66   Heale, *American Anticommunism*, xiv.

Sen. Joseph McCarthy is shown testifying on Communist Party Organization with the aid of a huge map of the United States.

Joe McCarthy from 1950 until his censure by the Senate in 1954, the anti-communist campaign actually started in the late 1930s with a hunt for disloyalty among public servants, a campaign to effectively ban the American Communist Party, and a wider-ranging "witch hunt" against intellectuals and others with real or alleged Communist contacts.[67] Heale argues that the campaign, which was strongly backed by the Republican Party, had its origins in conservative opposition to the perceived "socialism" of the New Deal.[68]

By the 1960s most Americans were recoiling against the widespread violations of civil liberties that had taken place during "the McCarthy era." The effect of those time, like that of the first Red Scare of 1920, was to demoralize the political left, leaving the United States with a spectrum of political ideas weighted much further to the right than in Canada and other Western democracies. The fear of a recurrence of **McCarthyism** would haunt the Democrats for years. Indeed, fear of unleashing another Red Scare did much to hinder the American withdrawal from the Vietnam War. President Truman had been accused of "losing" China to the Communists in 1949. Neither President Kennedy nor President Johnson wanted to be accused of losing Southeast Asia.

---

67   Richard M. Fried, *Nightmare in Red: The McCarthy Era in Perspective* (Oxford University Press, 1990).

68   Heale, *American Anticommunism*, Chapter 7.

The excesses of the McCarthy era also affected those on the right of the political spectrum. Even after President Reagan returned to a hard-line stance against the Soviet Union, branding it an "evil empire" in the 1980s, there was no attempt to revive the domestic Red Scare. With the collapse of the Soviet Union, there would appear to be no basis now for a fear of communism; but Americans' deep-seated fear of radicalism as a threat to their system is unlikely to have disappeared for good.

Racism in America

The longest-lasting and most destructive form of illiberalism in American society has been racism. There are at least three separate stories here. One relates to the treatment of Asians: their immigration was banned or restricted after 1880 in the United States and after 1885 in Canada. In the most shameful episode of racism against Asians, during World War II many thousands of Japanese, most of them born in North America, were forcibly relocated away from the continent's west coast and placed in internment camps by the Canadian and American governments.[69]

The two stories that have had the largest impact on American society are the treatment of the native peoples and the treatment of African Americans. Canada shared in the first of these stories but not the second. As a result of substantial nonwhite immigration over the past thirty years, Canada is now facing a contemporary struggle to become a multiracial society; but it has been spared the poisoned legacy of slavery that has haunted the United States from the beginning.

The Treatment of the Native Peoples

The tragic and disgraceful story of the fate of the native peoples of North America at the hands of the European settlers is at its heart one of a clash of cultures radically unequal in power. The scattered native peoples were up against an expansionist, materialistic European culture that was sure of its superiority and of its God-given mission to occupy the land. Any significant contact between two such imbalanced cultures was bound to be to the detriment of the natives. In its essence, the American story is simple enough: the natives who lived on good land were driven off it, whether by dishonest "treaties" or by force. Violent resistance was met with an even more violent

---

69   For a comparison of the Japanese experience in the United States and Canada, see Roger Daniels, "The Japanese Experience in North America: An Essay in Comparative Racism," *Canadian Ethnic Studies* 9 (1977), 91–100; see also Roger Daniels, Sandra C. Taylor, and Harry H.L. Kitano, eds., *Japanese Americans: From Relocation to Redress*, Revised Edition (University of Washington Press, 1991), and Ann Gomer Sunahara, *The Politics of Racism: The Uprooting of Japanese Canadians During the Second World War* (James Lorimer and Company, 1981).

response. Slowly, from the time of the first settlements until the end of the nineteenth century, the native peoples were driven or "removed" ever westward in front of the relentless tide of settlement. The process was punctuated by a series of "Indian wars," during which many American politicians made their reputations for valor. While the Indians won some battles, they were bound to lose the war. Those who survived were consigned to reservations, mostly on land that nobody else had wanted.

Two factors made the process of European settlement much more violent than it might otherwise have been. First, the American federal government was weak throughout the nineteenth century, which meant that the settlement process was totally beyond its control. Even when government officials desired a more humane policy toward the natives, they had no power at hand to enforce a uniform policy when faced with belligerent states and greedy settlers.

Second, the American government lacked the political will to end the violence. Commentators are agreed that the Anglo-Saxons in their dealings with the native peoples were much more racist than the French in Quebec or the Spanish in South and Central America.[70] There was nothing in either liberal or Protestant thought to make the Americans question the superiority of their civilization or the inferiority of the natives.[71] In D.W. Meinig's words:

> [The Anglo-Saxons] had neither the will nor the way to accommodate Native Americans as an integral party of an Anglo-American society. They ... could not envision a genuinely plural society that would encompass tribal, non-Christian people.[72]

It was not until late in the nineteenth century that the argument for respecting native cultures was given any credence. Native policy in the twentieth century has generally been better intentioned, but the centuries of destruction cannot be undone, and both natives and governments find it difficult to deal with the consequences.

The story of Canada's native peoples has had the same ingredients, but there have also been differences in practice.[73] The main difference was that the settlement process and native policy were firmly controlled by the British and then Canadian governments. A Royal Proclamation of 1763 prohibited land purchases from natives without government approval, and this edict was largely adhered to. Governments acquired

---

70   William T. Hagan, *American Indians*, Third Edition (University of Chicago Press, 1993), 14, 23, and Meinig, *The Shaping of America Volume 1*, 208.

71   On nineteenth-century American attitudes to the native peoples, see Thomas F. Gossett, *Race: The History of an Idea in America* (Southern Methodist University Press, 1963), Chapter 10.

72   Meinig, *The Shaping of America Volume 1*, 212.

73   Olive Patricia Dickason, *Canada's First Nations: A History of Founding Peoples from Earliest Times* (McClelland & Stewart, 1992).

land from the Indian tribes in exchange for reserves though a series of treaties that eventually covered most of Ontario and the prairies. For this reason, the advance of European settlement in Canada was essentially orderly and peaceful. After the violence that surrounded the early resistance to settlement in the Maritimes, the only major clash was the doomed attempt by Louis Riel to create a Métis homeland on the prairies in the 1880s.

If the process was more peaceful in Canada than in the United States, the result was no less tragic and shameful. The racism of the Europeans runs through the whole story. The spread of European settlement was taken for granted, and the interests of the settlers drove government policy. Policy toward the natives was entirely paternalistic. They were never consulted, and life on the reserves was controlled in minute detail. Assimilation to white society was the goal of policy, and until very recently there was no respect for native cultures and religions. The result was a people deprived not only of their way of life but of their freedom and self-respect. In recent years Canada's native people have made a concerted effort to take control of their own affairs, but the legacy of the past has left very deep scars.

❧ The Treatment of the African-American Population of the United States

White racism toward black Americans is a theme that runs through and distorts the entire history of the United States. The long history of slavery and legal segregation has no counterpart in Canada. The first blacks were brought to Canada by the Loyalists, and small numbers of former slaves moved or fled to Canada at various periods up through the Civil War. Instead of the institutionalized racism of the United States, the small and fragmented black population of Canada had to contend with "uninstitutionalized, unorganized prejudice."[74] The racial attitudes of white Canadians were no more enlightened than those south of the border.

The native peoples were on the land first, and the white immigrants came seeking freedom and opportunity; in contrast, the blacks were shipped to America in chains as slaves. Plantation agriculture dependent on slave labor was brought to the American mainland from the West Indies in the mid-seventeenth century. There was a large influx of slaves into the southern states in the first half of the eighteenth century, and by the time of the Revolution, plantation agriculture—the growing of tobacco, sugar, and, increasingly, cotton—was firmly established in the states from Maryland south. At the first census in 1790 there were 750,000 blacks, most of them slaves. This represented about 20 percent of the total American population, but over 35 percent of the population of the southern states.

It was during the revolutionary period that some Americans became convinced of the immorality of the slave trade and slavery. Many Christians, led by the Quakers,

---

74   Robin W. Winks, *The Blacks in Canada: A History* (McGill-Queen's University Press, 1971), 481.

finally realized that slavery was no longer the comparatively humane institution of the ancient world—one that the Scriptures condoned—but a thoroughly vicious and dehumanizing economic and social system based solely on race, a moral horror in their midst. Some slaveholders freed their slaves in response. Among the leading liberal figures, a great deal of attention has been given to the paradox of Thomas Jefferson, who was both an Enlightenment intellectual and a Virginia slave owner, who drafted the Declaration of Independence ("all men are created equal") yet never freed his slaves. Jefferson did persuade the **Continental Congress** to forbid slavery in the North West Territory (now Ohio and Indiana). Unlike most of his southern contemporaries, he understood the moral contradiction posed by slavery and the long-term danger it presented for the republic. As a humanistic liberal it was "his conviction that slavery, along with other social evils, would ultimately yield to the combined power of right reason and a divinely implanted moral sense."[75] He expected that progress would cause slavery as an institution to be superseded.

At the time of the Revolution, there were powerful economic and political interests supporting slavery, and this was a major roadblock to its abolition. At the Constitutional Convention in 1787 (see Chapter 3), the southern states were emphatic in their defense of slavery, for which they demanded constitutional protections. But there was also an intellectual obstacle to dealing with slavery.[76] The movement among Christians to free their slaves died out because of fears about the growing number of freedmen, for whom there was no place in white society. The general belief in the natural inferiority of blacks meant that white Americans could not envision a multiracial society. As John Higham has pointed out, in nineteenth-century America the assimilation of whites of different origins was seen as inevitable, while the assimilation of blacks (and natives) was seen as impossible.[77]

In the 1850s it was the determination of the Evangelical community in the North to prevent southern attempts to expand slavery into the West that shattered the existing two-party system and led to the formation of the Republican Party. After years of propaganda by the anti-slavery societies, a climate of moral revulsion against slavery had developed in the North, along with a fear that an expansionist South would

---

75   John Chester Miller, *The Wolf By the Ears: Thomas Jefferson and Slavery* (Free Press, 1977), xii. Miller's title is taken from Jefferson's famous description of the dilemma slavery posed for his countrymen: "We have the wolf by the ears; and we can neither hold him, nor safely let him go. Justice is in one scale, and self preservation in the other."

76   On white attitudes toward blacks in early America, see Winthrop D. Jordan, *White Over Black: American Attitudes Towards the Negro. 1550–1812* (University of North Carolina Press, 1968).

77   John Higham, "Integrating America: The Problem of Assimilation in the Nineteenth Century," in George Pozzetta, ed., *Assimilation, Acculturation, and Social Mobility* (Garland Press, 1991).

threaten American liberties. Abraham Lincoln denounced slavery as morally wrong and argued that America could not survive "half slave and half free." He believed in constitutional equality for blacks. Lincoln's victory in 1860 precipitated the secession of the southern states and the subsequent Civil War to preserve the Union. In 1863, during the war, Lincoln issued the **Emancipation Proclamation**, which freed the slaves in the Confederate states. In his second Inaugural Address in 1865, Lincoln described the war as God's punishment on Americans for slavery.

In the aftermath of the war, the Radical Republicans in Congress made great efforts to protect the position of the former slaves. They passed the 13th, 14th, and 15th Amendments abolishing slavery and guaranteeing black rights under the Constitution; they passed **Civil Rights Acts** prohibiting racial discrimination; they established black educational institutions for the first time; and they attempted for a number of years to ensure black political participation. Northern troops occupied parts of the South until 1877. In the end it was all to no avail: as is discussed in Chapter 9, the Supreme Court, by interpreting the amendments and the civil rights legislation narrowly, effectively gutted the constitutional guarantees. Black people, it was determined, were entitled to constitutional equality but not social equality. Through intimidation and administrative tricks, blacks were excluded from the political process in the South, where 90 percent of them still lived. It was in this context from the 1890s on that the apparatus of legal segregation of the races in the southern states was erected. Once in place, segregation, and also the practice of racial discrimination in the North, were allowed to survive until the 1960s.

What allowed slavery to be replaced by racial segregation was the pervasive racism of white Americans. In the middle of the nineteenth century, whites' confidence in their racial superiority was bolstered by contemporary science. The term "survival of the fittest," drawn from Charles Darwin's work on biological evolution, was taken as confirming white superiority and black inferiority.[78] The first "intelligence tests," developed around 1916, seemed to confirm the superior intelligence of whites. The superiority of the white race was treated as popular and scientific conventional wisdom and was seldom challenged until well into the twentieth century. Gossett credits the work of anthropologist Franz Boas with undermining scientific confidence in the concept of race. It was the horrors of Hitler's Germany that removed the final shreds of respectability from racist ideas.

The undermining of racist thinking helped reopen the question of racial segregation in the United States. So did the emergence of America for the first time as a world leader. At a time when the United States was proclaiming to the world its moral superiority to the Soviet Union, segregation was obviously a major international embarrassment. But the most important factor was probably the huge migration of blacks

---

78   Gossett, *Race: The History of an Idea in America*, Chapter 7.

Reverend Martin Luther King locks arms with civil rights marchers.

I say to you today, my friends, that in spite of the difficulties and frustrations of the moment I still have a dream. It is a dream deeply rooted in the American dream. I have a dream that one day this nation will rise up and live out the true meaning of its creed: "We hold these truths to be self-evident—that all men are created equal." I have a dream that one day on the red hills of Georgia the sons of former slaves and the sons of former slaveowners will be able to sit down together at the table of brotherhood ... I have a dream that my four little children will one day live in a nation where they will not be judged by the color of their skin but by the content of their character. I have a dream today.

... This will be the day when all of God's children will be able to sing with new meaning "My country 'tis of thee, sweet land of liberty, of thee I sing. Land where my fathers died, land of the pilgrim's pride, from every mountainside let freedom ring."

... When we let freedom ring, when we let it ring from every village and every hamlet, from every state and every city, we will be able to speed up that day when all of God's children, black men and white men, Jews and Gentiles, Protestants and Catholics, will be able to join hands and sing in the words of the old Negro spiritual, "Free at last! Free at last! Thank God Almighty, we are free at last!"

Box 2.5

Extract from Martin Luther King Jr.'s speech to the March on Washington from the steps of the Lincoln Memorial, August 28, 1963.

from the rural South to the industrial cities of the Northeast and Midwest. This migration started during World War I and increased considerably during World War II. The growth of a black political constituency in the North provided the incentive for liberal Democrats to actively support black civil rights for the first time in the party's history.

It was in 1954, in the midst of this intellectual and political ferment, that lawyers for the **National Association for the Advancement of Colored People (NAACP)** finally succeeded in removing constitutional support for segregation (see Chapter 9). This breakthrough led immediately to the brilliant campaign for civil rights led by Martin Luther King Jr.[79] King had the unique ability to rally the black population while also stirring the conscience of liberal whites in the North with his philosophy of nonviolent resistance. He recognized that he needed to bring into the open the white violence that maintained segregation while keeping the black response nonviolent. Between 1955 and 1968 (the year he was assassinated), King built a coalition broad enough to overwhelm southern white power in Congress. As a result, the Civil Rights Act passed in 1964, and the Voting Rights Act in 1965.[80]

It is only in the last thirty years that African Americans have had anything like political equality in the United States, and that Americans have begun to face up to becoming a multiracial society. In the immediate aftermath of the civil rights movement of 1960s there was a push to take remedial action for the centuries of denied opportunity. There was a Supreme Court–ordered effort to integrate the public schools, and a variety of government programs began requiring affirmative action for blacks (and also for women and other minorities) in the areas of employment, education, and government contracting.

From the perspective of the 1990s, there have been two major developments in African-American society since the 1960s. The first is the growth of a large black middle class, composed of those who have taken advantage of the removal of segregation in education, employment, and housing. This group has finally been able to claim the American Dream, but it also remains nervous about white society's commitment to racial equality.[81] Second, a sizable black "underclass" has been left behind in the ghettos. With their economic opportunities drastically reduced by the disappearance

---

79 On Dr. King and the civil rights movement, see David J. Garrow, *Bearing the Cross: Martin Luther King, Jr. and the Southern Christian Leadership Conference* (William Morrow and Company, 1986); Taylor Branch, *Parting the Waters: America in the King Years 1954–1963* (Simon and Schuster, 1988); and Juan Williams, *Eyes on the Prize: America's Civil Rights Years, 1954–1965* (Viking, 1987).

80 On the development of federal policies on civil rights, see Hugh Davis Graham, *The Civil Rights Era: Origins and Development of National Policy 1960–1972* (Oxford University Press, 1990).

81 See Ellis Cose, *The Rage of a Privileged Class* (HarperCollins, 1993).

of unskilled industrial jobs, and with their vulnerability to the drug culture, many inner-city dwellers have become trapped in a downward spiral of despair and family breakdown.[82]

In the 1990s there has been a reappraisal by both blacks and whites of the progress made in racial integration, and a polarized debate has developed between political conservatives and liberals of both races over racial policy. Conservatives attack the reliance on government programs, particularly welfare, in dealing with the problems of the inner city. They argue that such programs generate a "culture of dependency" and reward counterproductive behavior. Liberals counter that the problems created by generations of deprivation and racism are much too large to be solved by self-help or by the churches without government involvement.

An equally bitter political argument has developed over the policy of affirmative action for racial minorities and women. The broad consensus of the 1970s that such remedial policies were necessary has unravelled over time.[83] Conservatives charge that such policies are simply "reverse discrimination," mainly against white males, and that affirmative action is not leading toward a color-blind society. Liberals and most black leaders point to the clear evidence of continuing discrimination against minorities and argue that affirmative policies are often needed to create a level playing field for them. In recent years the U.S. Supreme Court has narrowed the permissible range for such programs.[84] In 1996 California voters passed Proposition 209, which forbids affirmative action in state hiring, contracting, and educational admission policies. President Clinton has attempted to find a middle position with the slogan "Mend It, Don't End It." He has reaffirmed the principle of affirmative action but conceded the need to reappraise the working of specific policies.

American Illiberalism: An Assessment

The universal ideals, both liberal and Christian, to which Americans committed themselves from the beginning are noble ones, but they were given meaning originally in the context of an exclusive nineteenth-century white Protestant society. Americans' identity was tied up in their unique social and political vision, and their defense of that vision as they understood it was especially vigorous. Americans were loudly

---

82   On the history of the northern black ghetto, see Nicholas Lemann, *The Promised Land: The Great Black Migration and How it Changed America* (Knopf, 1991).

83   For an assessment of the affirmative action debate, see John David Skrentny, *The Ironies of Affirmative Action: Politics, Culture, and Justice in America* (University of Chicago Press, 1996); for the perspective of a black intellectual, see Stephen L. Carter, *Reflections of an Affirmative Action Baby* (BasicBooks, 1991).

84   *Adarand Constructors Inc. v. Pena* 115 S. Ct. 2097 (1995).

confident of their nation's unique identity and mission, but they also had a sense of its vulnerability. Some commentators note that American society is especially receptive to conspiracy theories. For these reasons, American society defined as "aliens," and discriminated against, those groups they perceived either as incapable of sharing their values (such as African Americans, Asians, and the native peoples) or as posing a threat because of their beliefs (such as Roman Catholics and political radicals).[85]

At the beginning of the twentieth century, the upheavals resulting from rapid industrialization and from the inflow of non-Anglo-Saxon Catholic and Jewish immigrants on a massive scale forced an agonizing redefinition of American society. What had been a white Anglo-Saxon Protestant ("WASP") society slowly became a "melting pot," although it was not until after World War II that the multi-ethnic, multi-religious character of the United States was fully accepted. Fear of political radicals and of internal subversion was prolonged by the Cold War. However, it is white racism that has distorted America most deeply, because its roots go right back to the beginning of European settlement. For that reason it is the problem that American society has been slowest to face up to. Only since the 1960s has there been a broad societal effort to deal with African Americans on the basis of equality and with the native peoples on the basis of mutual respect. Much progress has been made, but the ideal of a multiracial society has been difficult to implement, since it has not received the full endorsement of many whites.

Rogers Smith has rightly pointed out the alternative illiberal traditions that have shaped or misshaped American society. But that does not mean that the American belief in the liberal values of freedom and equality has been a sham. Samuel Huntington argues that a recurring moralistic drive to close the gap between America's lofty ideals and its political reality has been the principal motivation for reform throughout American history.[86] As American society has changed, it has been forced, often painfully, to broaden its understanding of its ideals and to extend the opportunities they represent to more and more of its citizens. American ideals have thus provided a high standard by which to judge the existing state of society, and from the beginning they have stood as a beacon of hope for those Americans protesting their exclusion from full membership in that society.

---

85   See Samuel Huntington, *American Politics: The Promise of Disharmony* (Belknap Press, 1981), 78–81.

86   Samuel Huntington, *American Politics: The Promise of Disharmony.*

THE CONSTITUTION
OF THE UNITED STATES

The American and Canadian constitutions are so different in composition and in the functions they perform that rather than engage in a detailed comparison it may be better to summarize the different principles that underly them. In the chapter on federalism that follows, a comparison will be made of how the two constitutions have worked in certain important respects.

In the aftermath of their revolution, the Americans set out to construct a new system of government from first principles. In this endeavor, they had no blueprint to guide them. The most important model in front of them was the British constitution of the time, which they admired but which their own experience had taught them was susceptible to abuse. The fundamental principle from which they started was the liberal principle of popular government—the belief that governmental power must be based on popular consent. All political institutions were to be founded on that basis.

The Canadian authors of the British North America Act of 1867 (relabeled the Canadian Constitution Act, 1867, when the Constitution was finally patriated in 1982) were in a very different situation from that of their American counterparts eighty years earlier. They had in front of them not only the British constitution, which had evolved into a parliamentary system by that time, but also the example of the U.S. Constitution, which the Canadian founders viewed in mostly a negative light. Canada's constitutional enterprise was a reaction against the looming American presence and example. The principal motive bringing the Canadian colonies together was a shared fear of American expansionism after the Civil War.

The Constitution Act, which united the first four provinces in the Dominion of Canada, was also a more limited exercise than the U.S. Constitution. The Canadians did not invent new institutions; rather, they chose "a Constitution similar in Principle to that of the United Kingdom," a form of government that was familiar and that had the additional virtue of not being American. The only institution they invented was the Senate, and here they chose as a model not the U.S. Senate but the British House of Lords; in Canada, however, members would be appointed for life by the federal government. The Canadian Constitution was not based on the American principle of popular sovereignty; rather, it perpetuated the monarchical system, in which national power is exercised by the monarch (in practice by the Cabinet) but is checked by the popularly elected House of Commons.

The main problem to be solved by the Canadians had to do with structuring the Canadian federation. John A. Macdonald accepted the federal form of government only reluctantly, because of the realities of politics and geography. He was determined to avoid the model of the American federation, believing that its decentralized structure had been a contributing factor to the recent Civil War. In form and intent the Constitution Act describes a highly centralized federation. The listed powers of the Parliament of Canada are broadly similar to those of the U.S. Congress. But while all other powers under the U.S. Constitution belong to the states, the BNA Act lists and limits provincial powers, giving the residual power to Parliament along with the colonial powers of reservation and disallowance with respect to provincial legislation. The very different ways that the two federal systems evolved are examined in Chapter 4.

THE MAKING OF THE U.S. CONSTITUTION

To understand the United States, one must understand the U.S. Constitution. Hammered together in the summer of 1787, the Constitution is the practical embodiment of the liberal beliefs on which the new nation was founded. As such, it is an object of veneration for Americans and plays a central role in their national identity. In practical terms, the Constitution creates the three branches of the federal government, lists their powers, and carefully structures the relationship between them. In so doing, it forms the liberal framework—one critic has called it a "cage"[1]—within which national politics is conducted.

---

1   H. Mark Roelofs, *Ideology and Myth in American Politics: A Critique of a National Political Mind* (Little, Brown, 1976), 101. See also Roelofs's later *The Poverty of American Politics: A Theoretical Interpretation* (Temple University Press, 1992) for a sustained critique of the American constitutional system from the perspective of the political left.

The ideas underlying the U.S. Constitution are worth examining in some detail because they are vital to any understanding of how American politics works today. The Constitution has continued to play a central role because it has done what its framers intended it to do: it has limited power by fragmenting it.

The thirteen British colonies had quite different histories and religious backgrounds. There was considerable competition and rivalry among them. Nevertheless, they also had many common problems, and in varying degrees all felt that their interests and rights had been violated by British policy since the 1760s. It was in order to coordinate their protests against the British that the first intercolonial congresses were called.

The second \Continental Congress| met in 1775 after the first clashes with British troops. Two years later, in the middle of the American Revolution, the Congress approved a constitution called the Articles of Confederation, which came into effect once it had been ratified by all thirteen states in 1781. The Articles provided a framework for common decision-making among the states. The aim was to provide for a common defense and to minimize the obstacles to trade between states. However, each state retained its sovereignty; each, regardless of population, had equal voting power in the Congress; and each was represented on the Committee of States, which formed a sort of executive committee with a rotating presidency.

The difficulties with such a weak system of government quickly became apparent. Decision-making was difficult, and the Congress had no authority to force recalcitrant states to abide by its decisions. Money was supposed to be raised in proportion to the wealth of the different states; but the Congress could not tax directly and could only hope that the often hard-up states would pay their assessments.

Some of the more farsighted leaders began to press for a stronger form of national government, but there was a great deal of resistance. The states were not eager to surrender their sovereignty; this was particularly true of the smaller states, which feared domination by the larger ones. But none of the states was strong enough to go it alone—a truth reinforced by an economic depression that followed the Revolution. The Congress finally agreed to call a convention to consider amending the Articles of Confederation.

This convention met in Philadelphia in 1787. From the end of May until mid-September, fifty-five delegates from twelve states (Rhode Island did not send anyone) met almost every day to hammer out an agreement on a new constitution. The meetings were closed, but we know many of the details of the discussions and arguments from the notes kept by some delegates—particularly those of James Madison, secretary of the convention, which were published much later.

The prior agreement had been to consider amendments to the existing Articles; however, those who advocated a stronger national government had prepared

themselves well under the leadership of Madison and the Virginia delegation. By placing a plan for a new, stronger national government on the table at the start of the convention, they ensured that from the beginning, debate would center on a completely
new constitution.

The Task Facing the Framers of the Constitution

The delegates had "abolished" the old form of colonial government. Their task now
was, in the words of the Declaration of Independence, "to institute new Government,
laying its foundation on such principles and organizing its powers in such form, as to
them shall seem most likely to affect their safety and happiness." The rejection of
British authority by the colonies had forced the new states to consider their forms of
government, and most of the states had adopted new state constitutions. The framing
of the new national Constitution thus took place at the end of a decade of debate and
constitution-making across the states.

The principles on which the new Constitution would be based were clear enough—
they were the liberal principles laid out in the Declaration, for which the Revolution
had been fought and won. The principal function of government was to guarantee the
rights of the individual. Both in liberal theory and in the experience of the delegates,
the principal threat to those rights lay in the tyrannical use of power by an executive
that was not accountable to the people.

On the other hand, their brief experience under the Articles of Confederation had
demonstrated to the delegates that a system of government could be too weak to provide internal cohesion and protection from external threats. So the question was this:
How could a government be organized so that it was strong enough to defend the
nation's integrity without becoming tyrannical?

In drawing up such a constitution, the framers were in largely uncharted waters.
The new constitutions drawn up by the states were too new and various to provide an
authoritative blueprint. The framers had to solve both practical political problems
and theoretical problems of design. The very real practical problem was how to reach
agreement among the thirteen states, all of whom were jealous of their newly won
sovereignty, and whose circumstances and interests differed considerably. For help on
the theoretical problems, the framers turned to the available writings on government.
Several of the delegates were widely read in the Greek classics, the works of the
English and Scottish liberal philosophers, and the writers of the French
Enlightenment. Of particular importance for their task were Aristotle's *Politics*,
Locke's *Second Treatise of Government*, and Montesquieu's *The Spirit of the Laws*.

Political Divisions in the Constitutional Convention

The central political problem was how to draw up a document that had the agreement of enough delegates and the states they represented to make the new Constitution politically viable. There was early agreement that the Constitution would have to be ratified by popular conventions in the states before it could come into effect. So, while the convention worked in secret, the delegates knew that they would have to be able to defend the resulting document in front of skeptical voters back home.

There was a strong sense of urgency in the convention for an agreement to be reached. There had been considerable opposition to holding such a convention in the first place, and another opportunity might not soon arise. Yet the more farsighted delegates realized that without a much stronger national government than the Articles of Confederation provided, America's radical experiment in self-government might not survive very long in the face of the hostility of the European monarchies.

The most serious divisions within the convention were not over ideology but over political and economic interests. These lay between the smaller states and the larger, more populous ones, and between the northern and southern states.

The large/small division. There was already great variation in the size of the states. As measured by the first census in 1790, Virginia, the largest state, with 692,000 people, was more than ten times larger than the smallest, Delaware, with 59,000. Generally, the larger states could expect to play a leading role in a national government, while the smaller states felt they had the most to lose by surrendering their sovereignty.

The argument for the smaller states was led by Delaware and New Jersey, with occasional support from Maryland and New York. With Rhode Island absent and New Hampshire not present until the end of July, the smaller states were outvoted on all the key points. The bare minimum the smaller states could accept was equal representation in the Senate, and they succeeded in securing this important concession, over the strenuous objections of James Madison, by threatening to break up the convention.

The north/south division. There was a conflict between the economic interests of the northern and southern states. The northern economies were based on overseas trade and small manufacturing, while southern prosperity depended on plantation agriculture: rice, tobacco, and cotton. The profitability of the plantations depended on the availability of slave labor, and the southerners were already on the defensive on the question of slavery.

By the end of the eighteenth century, enlightened European opinion had begun to seriously question the morality of the slave trade and the existence of slavery. Such sentiment was also beginning to grow in the northern states, where slavery had never been of much economic importance. Fearing that northern interests would try to use a national government to attack their economic base, the southern states demanded and received guarantees in the Constitution to protect the interests of the slaveholders. The parts of the Constitution dealing with slavery are discussed below.

Theoretical Issues

The range of political views among the delegates to the convention was relatively small. Alexander Hamilton, who advocated giving most powers to the national government at the expense of the states, as well as an almost monarchical life-term presidency, was an isolated figure.[2] Most of the delegates were leading citizens of their states, and were well-educated men of property who held firm liberal principles. They believed in popular sovereignty and in the principle of equality, but as men of the late eighteenth century they were not democrats as we understand the word.

The most obvious problem facing the delegates was how to constitute the executive power. At that time, the universal form of the executive was some kind of monarchy. Most monarchs wielded unchecked power over their subjects. In the Declaration of Independence, the Americans blamed their own troubles with Britain on the unchecked abuse of executive power by George III. Yet one of the weaknesses of the Articles of Confederation had been that there was no real executive power at all. How should the Americans constitute and choose their executive? How could it be ensured that executive power did not become tyrannical?

The more fundamental problem to be solved was how to construct a stable system of government based on popular sovereignty. There were no contemporary examples. European governments were all traditional societies in which sovereignty belonged to the ruler. Blackstone had argued authoritatively that in Britain sovereignty lay in the Parliament (strictly, "the King in Parliament"). "Democracy" was given little respect in writings on politics. Everyone cited Aristotle, who had argued that rule by the people—democracy—was bound to degenerate into "mob rule." Recent popular uprisings in some of the states during the economic depression had reminded the delegates how easily popular passions could be stirred up.

Another problem was the size of the United States. Stretching over a thousand miles from Maine to Georgia, the territory was much larger than most nations. The

---

2   On Hamilton's views and role at the convention, see Forrest McDonald, *Alexander Hamilton: A Biography* (W.W. Norton, 1979).

ideal example of a free government was still held to be the small city-states of ancient Greece, where all the citizens could be called together. It was generally considered impossible to extend free government over a large area. Also, since the United States comprised thirteen independent states, it would have to form some kind of federation. Yet a federation was generally considered one of the weakest forms of government. Such examples as had existed had been weak and short-lived.

It was generally agreed that the country which provided the most freedom for its citizens in the eighteenth century was Britain. The explanation was held to be that Britain had evolved into a "mixed" constitution in which the three kinds of power—monarchical, aristocratic, and popular—were balanced. Montesquieu agreed with Aristotle that a government in which any one kind of power was too dominant would inevitably deteriorate: monarchy into tyranny, aristocracy into oligarchy, popular government into mob rule. In Britain, the monarch, the House of Lords (in which the land-owning aristocracy sat), and the elected House of Commons were able to check one another's powers, and this resulted in freedom for the citizen.

The problem with transferring mixed government to the United States was that there were no equivalents to the monarch and the lords, and no one wanted to invent them. Only the *popular* element existed. How could a government based on popular sovereignty be prevented from degenerating, and threatening the freedom of its citizens?

James Madison's Analysis of the Theoretical Problems

By far the best prepared of the delegates was James Madison,[3] who had spent several months reading and analyzing the fundamental problems to be solved. We know Madison's thinking in some detail, not only from his account of his speeches in the convention debates[4] but also from the essays he contributed to *The Federalist Papers*,[5] which were published shortly after the convention to explain and defend the new Constitution during the state debates over ratification. Madison was the chief architect of the Constitution. He did not get his way on every point, but the structure of the Constitution that came out of the convention largely followed his thinking.

James Madison (1751–1836), fourth president of the United States.

---

3   On Madison's role at the Constitutional Convention, see William Lee Miller, *The Business of May Next: James Madison and the Founding* (University of Virginia Press, 1992).

4   *Notes of Debates in the Federal Convention of 1787 Reported by James Madison* (W.W. Norton, 1987).

5   Alexander Hamilton, James Madison, and John Jay, *The Federalist Papers* (New American Library, 1961).

Madison presented the core of his theoretical argument in his *Federalist Paper Number Ten*. His chief concern was "to cure the diseases most incident to republican [i.e., popular] government." Popular government, he agreed, was notorious for "instability, injustice, confusion." As he saw it, the central problem was "the mischief of faction"—that is, the tendency of groups to use politics to pursue private interests rather than the public good. A particular danger was the forming of a majority faction, when the majority pushed for its own interests at the expense of the rights of minorities. The task of the convention, in Madison's words, was "to secure the public good and private rights against the dangers of a majority faction and at the same time preserve the spirit and form of popular government ..."

The main cause of faction, Madison believed, was the unequal distribution of property. The roots of this inequality lay in "different and unequal facilities for acquiring property"—in other words, in natural differences between people. For these reasons he did not believe that such inequality would disappear. Nor did he believe that one could simply rely on good legislators or on moral and religious exhortation to solve the problem of faction: it was too deeply rooted in human nature. The worst effects of the problem could, however, be contained by "a well constructed union." Within the correct structure, indeed, the ambitious and competitive aspects of human nature could be made use of to keep the constitution balanced.

According to Madison, there were a number of factors mitigating the problem in the American situation. In the first place, since direct democracy was only possible in a small area, they were dealing with "delegated" (that is, representative) government. Legislators were more likely to keep the general good in mind than the voter. Madison also argued that the size of the country was actually an advantage: a large area was likely to give rise to a larger variety of competing interests, and this made the creation of a majority faction less likely.

In this respect the federal structure would help, since the national government would deal only with "great national issues" while local issues—those most likely to stimulate factionalism—would be left to the states. The existence of separate states would act as a sort of firebreak to prevent a majority faction from forming nationally. Other federations had failed, Madison believed, because the national government had not been strong enough. Thus, a new constitution with a much stronger national government was essential.

Madison believed that a stable form of popular government could be established by careful attention to the design of the main institutions. He argued that the benefits of a mixed constitution could be achieved in the American situation by separating the branches of government, by clearly distinguishing their functions, and by splitting some of the powers of government between them so as to create a set of "checks and balances" between the three branches of government.

Madison was insistent that a balanced system of government would only work in the long run if each of the three branches was strong enough to check the other two.

Since the principal threat to individual rights in the experience of the Americans had come from the abuse of executive power, there was a strong inclination to create a weak executive. Madison, however, was equally concerned about the possible abuse of legislative power; for this reason, he argued for a strong, independent executive and for a powerful upper house of Congress. When institutions were of equal power, the competitive ambitions of each officeholder could be relied upon to check abuses by the others.

THE COMPONENTS OF THE CONSTITUTION

After a short preamble, which asserts the sovereignty of the people of the United States as the basis for the Constitution, the document provides seven articles. The first three articles set out the composition and powers of the legislative, executive, and judicial branches of government, respectively. The fourth article sets some conditions governing relations between state governments; the fifth sets up the process for amending the document; the sixth declares the supremacy of the national constitution; the seventh provides for its ratification.

For purposes of analysis the Constitution can be broken down into the following components: the theoretical design; the national/state division of powers; liberal prohibitions; and the protection of slavery.

The Theoretical Design of the Constitution

The design of the Constitution has been described by Richard Neustadt as "separated institutions sharing powers." First, the branches of government are separated from each other through different modes of election and different terms of office (Table 3.1); then the powers of government are distributed among the institutions (Table 3.2) to create a system of checks and balances on the exercise of power.

The Legislative Branch: the Congress
The Congress is composed of two houses, the House of Representatives and the Senate. Seats in the House are based on population, with each state guaranteed at least one member. Seats are redistributed among the states every ten years after the national census. Members are directly elected every two years. The short term was designed to keep the members responsive to the voters.

The House was to be the popular body; the Senate was designed as a check on sudden enthusiasms of the House. For that reason, senators were given a much longer term, six years, and were to be indirectly elected, chosen not by the voters but by the state legislators. The terms of the senators are staggered so that one-third of the

Branch	Legislative		Executive	Judicial
Body	House	Senate	President	Supreme Court
Composition	Population equality	State equality	Single executive	Unspecified
Selection	Direct election	Indirect election	Very indirect election	Nomination and confirmation
Term	2 years	6 years (staggered)	4 years	Good behavior

Senate is elected every two years. The Constitution was amended in 1913 to elect senators directly.

The most bitter fight at the convention was over the question of representation in the Senate. Madison wanted it to be on the basis of population, but he was forced, by threat of a walkout by the smaller states, to agree to equal state representation. As a result there are two senators from each state, regardless of population. Article 5 makes equal representation in the Senate the only part of the Constitution that cannot be amended.

The Executive Branch: the President[6]

The convention considered a variety of proposals on the composition of the executive power, such as a three-person executive and a council of state, but in the end Madison's argument prevailed that what was needed was not a weak executive but a strong one checked by the other branches. To this end, a single executive, the president, was agreed on. There was also much discussion on the length of term, and on whether the president should be eligible for re-election. In the end, the term was set at four years and nothing was said about re-election. An amendment passed in 1951 now limits a president to two terms.

The delegates realized that the method of election would affect how the president conducted himself in office. This proved to be the most difficult question of the convention, and it was the last matter to be agreed on. What was arrived at was an elaborate compromise that came to be known as the "Electoral College," which is discussed in detail in Chapter 11. The Electoral College method was designed to keep

---

6   On the debates at the Constitutional Convention on the executive branch, see Thomas E. Cronin, ed., *Inventing the American Presidency* (University of Kansas Press, 1989).

the president distanced from popular pressures and independent of Congress. Thus, the electors are chosen by the states, and members of Congress cannot serve as electors. The "college" never meets. By having the electors cast their votes on the same day but in the different state capitals, it was hoped that the politicking surrounding the election of the president would be kept to a minimum. This hope was to be dashed very quickly in practice.

The Judicial Branch: the Supreme Court

The independence of the judiciary from executive manipulation was agreed to be a fundamental requirement of free government. Regarding the method of selection, the choice was between appointment by the executive and election by the Congress. In the later, democratic era about half the states chose to have their judges popularly elected, but the question did not arise at the convention. In the end the power to appoint was split between presidential nomination and confirmation by the Senate. To eliminate any need for them to curry favor with either branch of government, federal judges are appointed for life ("during good behavior"); this means they can be removed only by the cumbersome process of impeachment. Note also that their salaries are protected from being cut.

Executive officials, federal judges, and the president himself can be removed by the Congress through impeachment (that is, indictment) by the House for "treason, bribery, or other high crimes and misdemeanors" followed by conviction by a two-thirds vote of the Senate, presided over in the case of a president by the chief justice. This procedure was adapted from Britain, where it provided a "last ditch" power for Parliament to remove royal appointees (but not the monarch). It was not intended to be a regular part of the government process.

The distribution of the powers of the national government was the second element in the scheme of balanced government. The institutions of government were to be separated, but the powers of government were to be shared so that each institution would act as a check on the others.

The House and the Senate are given equal power in passing legislation, except that all tax bills must originate in the House, which is the body closest to the voters. This is in recognition of the ancient parliamentary principle that the people must consent to taxation. The president also has a role in the legislative process. He may recommend legislation to Congress, but his real legislative power comes from his right of veto—that is, his right to refuse to sign a bill. Congress has the last word, but only if both houses can override the veto by a two-thirds majority.

In foreign affairs, the initiative is given to the president. In an age of very slow travel and communications, negotiations between nations were conducted by ambassadors. Agreements between nations were embodied in treaties. A measure of the importance of ambassadors at that time is that the two most prominent political

Body	House	Senate	President
Legislation	Pass	Pass	Sign/veto
Appropriations	Pass	Pass	Sign/veto
Taxes	Initiate/pass	Pass	Sign/veto
	Override veto by 2/3 vote in both houses		
Foreign policy	None	Ratify treaties by 2/3 vote Confirm ambassadors	Negotiate treaties Nominate ambassadors
War/peace	Declare war by majority in both houses		Commander in chief
Appointment of civil officers/ federal judges	None	Confirm	Nominate

figures in America, John Adams and Thomas Jefferson, who were to follow George Washington in the presidency, were not present at the Constitutional Convention because they were serving as the American ambassadors to the leading European powers: Adams in London and Jefferson in Paris. The president nominates ambassadors and makes treaties, but the Senate must confirm ambassadors and ratify treaties by a two-thirds vote.

The president is commander in chief of the armed forces, but the power to declare war is given to the Congress. The president nominates the holders of positions in the executive branch, but all top-level appointments must be confirmed by the Senate.

◄ The Design of the Constitution: Summary

In Madison's design for an American version of mixed government, each institution had a distinct function and each was separated from and independent of the others. The legislative function was divided into two parts: the House of Representatives, with its short, two-year term, would be responsive to the voters; the Senate would act as a brake on popular passions by being more insulated from short-term political currents as a result of its longer, six-year term and because it was indirectly elected by state legislators. The executive function was vested in a president with an intermediate, four-year term. The elaborate Electoral College method of election made the president independent of the Congress; it was also a means to remove the process as much as possible from popular passions and political manipulation. The independence of the judiciary was enhanced through life tenure and through the splitting of the appointment process between the president and the Senate.

In Britain, "balance" was achieved by having one elected body and two hereditary ones; in Madison's scheme, both the legislative and executive branches were "drawn from the people," as befitted a government based on popular sovereignty. Even so, balance could be achieved by applying separate methods of election with varying degrees of insulation from popular feeling. The "checks" in Madison's scheme were a result of powers being shared between the institutions. The president's power to veto legislation was made explicit, but his powers over foreign affairs and his appointive powers were checked by the Senate. It was on the Senate, not the popularly elected House, that much of the responsibility for balancing the system was placed.

The overall design, which makes the institutions of government independent of one another but then requires them to share governmental powers, is very much in line with Madison's thinking. This system is undeniably based on popular sovereignty, but at the same time immediate popular pressures are reduced by systems of indirect election and the division of powers among institutions.

Like most Americans, Madison was afraid of a tyrannical executive, but he was also afraid that legislative power would be abused by a "majority faction." He believed that he could rely on the natural ambition of the different officeholders to make the system of checks and balances work. In *Federalist Paper Number 51* he wrote that "ambition must be made to counteract ambition." He foresaw a process in which the ambition of each officeholder would be checked by equally ambitious men, all of them "striving for power which they incompletely possess."

Here, Madison was a true prophet. One of the striking characteristics of American politics continues to be the jealousy with which the different institutions guard their powers and the difficulty they have in cooperating to get things done.

The National/State Division of Powers: The Federal System

Although the states were wary about surrendering their sovereignty, there was little disagreement at the convention regarding the powers of the national government. The national legislative powers were enumerated in Section 8 of Article 1: all powers not listed there belonged to the states—a point made explicitly in the 10th Amendment, which was passed a few years later.

The listed national powers were almost all derived from what were generally agreed to be the two main purposes of forming a national government: to expand trade by creating a unified economy, and to defend the states against external aggression.

The economic power. Congress was given the power to impose taxes, borrow money, write bankruptcy laws, regulate the currency, set and police the standards for weights and measures, grant patents, establish post offices, and build roads to carry the mail. It was to regulate foreign trade and trade with the native peoples (who at that time were considered to be outside the American political system). Most importantly, Congress was also given the power to regulate commerce "among the several states." This power over interstate commerce would turn into a major source of federal power in the twentieth century, once the United States had developed an integrated national economy.

The grants of power to the national government were reinforced in Section 10 of Article 1, in which the state governments were forbidden to interfere with the national powers over the economy.

The defense power. Congress was given the power to declare war and to set up and control an army and navy, as well as jurisdiction over all military facilities. It was also given ultimate authority over the militias—part-time forces maintained by all the states. This meant that the states could not maintain military forces independent of the national government. This was specifically forbidden in Section 10, which also prohibited states from conducting an independent foreign policy.

Article 4 of the Constitution lays down some basic rules governing relations among the states. It requires each state to recognize fully the governmental and judicial actions of all the others, and provides for extradition of criminals (and runaway slaves) from one state to another. Section 3 prevents the changing of a state's boundaries without its consent. Section 4 guarantees each state federal protection against invasion, or an overthrow of its system of government; it also guarantees, if the state requests it, federal help "against domestic violence."

Article 5 sets out the procedures for amending the Constitution; these involve both the Congress and the states. An amendment may be initiated by a two-thirds vote in both houses of the Congress, or by two-thirds of the state legislatures asking Congress to call a national constitutional convention. The proposed amendment that results from either process is sent to the state legislatures or to state conventions for ratification; it comes into effect when three-quarters of the states have agreed to the amendment.

Article 6 lays down that the Constitution and all laws and treaties made under its authority are "the supreme law of the land," and that as such they take precedence over state constitutions and state laws. Along with all federal legislators and officials of the executive and judicial branches, all state legislators and officials must take an oath of office to uphold the federal Constitution.

Establishing the principle of the supremacy of the federal Constitution was extremely important, since it was common, particularly in the early years, for states that objected to federal policy to claim that the federal institutions had no right to overrule state governments or state courts. Provided that federal institutions are exercising powers given them in the Constitution, they clearly do have the right to overrule any actions by the states that are inconsistent with the Constitution.

The Liberal Prohibitions in the Constitution

As convinced liberals, the Americans believed that the purpose of government was to protect and extend the rights of individuals. In their own experience, many of these rights had been subverted by the British government. They were also well aware of the struggle by their British ancestors in the seventeenth century to protect these basic rights from monarchical abuse. Small wonder, then, that the U.S. Constitution is full of specific prohibitions against the abuse of governmental power. These prohibitions can be grouped into two categories: provisions to protect the integrity and independence of the institutions of government, and prohibitions against the violation of specific individual rights by the national government.

The independence of federal institutions. Sections 5 and 6 of Article 1 spell out the right of the House and the Senate to conduct their business free from interference from any other body. The legislative bodies need this freedom because they represent the people. The rights of the Congress are listed: the exclusive right of each House to be the judge of the qualifications and conduct of its own members; the right of each House to determine its own rules of procedure; the right of the House of Representatives to elect its own Speaker; the immunity of members of Congress from arrest and from prosecution for libel or slander while conducting legislative business. All of these rights had been interfered with by a tyrannical executive at various times in the past.

Another common executive tactic had been to influence the legislature by offering well-paid appointments to some of its key members. Section 6 provides for the payment of members of Congress out of public funds; it also prohibits members of Congress from holding any executive appointments. This was done to protect the integrity of Congress; but it is this latter provision that has prevented parliamentary-style Cabinet government from developing in the United States.

Article 2, Section 1, provides for the president also to receive compensation. Congress is forbidden either to increase or reduce his compensation during his term, and the president is forbidden from taking any other official payment or money from the states. Article 3, Section 1, provides that the compensation of the judges, who have tenure for life, shall not be reduced.

The protection of specific rights. Article 1, Section 9, prohibits Congress from suspending "the Writ of Habeas Corpus" except when there is a danger to public safety from invasion or rebellion (*habeas corpus* is the ancient right not to be held in custody for more than forty-eight hours without charge). Congress is also prohibited from passing a "bill of attainder" (a process whereby someone could be sentenced to death by the legislature without court proceedings) or an *ex post facto* law (a law that creates a crime retroactively).

Article 3, Section 2, requires trial by jury in all criminal cases, the trial to be held in the state in which the alleged offense was committed.

Article 3, Section 3, deals with the crime of treason, generally considered the most serious charge that can be laid against anyone, but also a charge that had often been abused in the past. It provides a limited definition of treason, sets strict conditions for getting a conviction, and prohibits the extension of punishment beyond the life of the guilty party, by, for example, taking away the right of that person's children to inherit property.

All of the abuses prohibited by these sections were considered absolutely fundamental, since they directly threatened the life of the person whose rights were being abused. All of these rights had long been claimed by liberals, but with the final prohibition in the body of the Constitution, the Americans were staking out another right that was not generally recognized at that time. The last clause of Article 6 prohibits the setting of a "religious test" for holding any public office, a practice that still existed in Britain, for example, well into the nineteenth century.

The Protection of Slavery

It is tragic that a document that was at the forefront in the protection of individual rights also protected the institution of slavery. The words "slave" and "slavery" do not appear in the Constitution, but at the insistence of southerners several provisions intended to prevent northern attacks on slavery were written into the document. These provisions were the price of southern participation in the Union.

Article 1, Section 2. Representation in the House of Representatives is based on population. In the southern states slaves accounted for around 35 percent of the total population. Since slaves were not considered citizens and certainly could not vote, northerners demanded that they not be counted for the purpose of determining representation, and thus voting power, in the House. The southern states wanted the slaves to be counted to maximize their population figures and thus their share of power in Washington. A compromise was reached whereby all free persons and three-fifths "of all other persons" would be counted. (Native people were excluded by general agreement.)

Article 1, Section 9. Congress was prohibited from abolishing the slave trade, "the Importation of such Persons as any of the States now existing shall think proper to admit," for twenty years.

Article 1, Section 9. Per capita taxes had to be apportioned among the states on the basis of population. This was to prevent the possibility of a heavy tax being placed on slaves so as to make slavery uneconomic.

Article 4, Section 2, paragraph 3. All states were required to send runaway slaves back to their owners.

Article 4, Section 4. The national government was obliged to protect states on their request against domestic violence, and such violence was deemed to include slave insurrections—one of the great fears that haunted southern whites.

Article 5. The provisions regarding the slave trade and taxation (see Article 1, Section 9, above) were not to be amendable for twenty years.

The Ratification of the Constitution

Once the Constitution was signed by most of the delegates on September 17, 1787, the ratification process began in the states. In order to bypass possible obstruction in the state legislatures, the delegates agreed that ratification would be by specially elected state conventions. Remembering how difficult it had been to achieve unanimity among the states under the Articles of Confederation, the delegates agreed that the Constitution would come into effect once nine of the thirteen states had ratified it.

The proposed Constitution was strongly attacked by a variety of critics, and its ratification was not a foregone conclusion. To make the case for ratification, Alexander Hamilton, James Madison, and John Jay published a series of essays, *The Federalist Papers*, which provide an authoritative contemporary justification of and commentary on the Constitution.

The main concern of the critics, collectively dubbed the Anti-Federalists, was that the new national government would come to dominate the states, and that the leaders would thus be further removed from the people and would therefore be less likely to preserve their liberties.[7] The supporters of the Constitution moved to blunt this criticism by promising to add a **Bill of Rights** once the Constitution came into effect.

---

7   Herbert J. Storing, *What the Anti-Federalists Were For* (University of Chicago Press, 1981).

Herbert Storing emphasizes that both sides in the ratification struggle shared the same liberal principles but disagreed on the best means to combine individual liberty with effective government.[8] The weakness of the Anti-Federalists' position was that they could not produce a realistic alternative to the Constitution the delegates had hammered out, although they too believed that the status quo could not continue.

Seven of the states completed the process quickly and easily, but in three states—New Hampshire, New York, and Virginia—opposition was fierce and the result was in real doubt for a time. Only after New York and Virginia, the largest states, finally agreed, in very close votes, in the summer of 1788 was the Constitution assured of going into effect. The first elections were held late in 1788, and the new president and Congress took office in April of 1789.

THE AMENDMENTS TO THE CONSTITUTION

In just over 200 years the U.S. Constitution has been amended twenty-seven times. This statement is somewhat misleading, however, in that the first ten amendments, commonly called the Bill of Rights, were passed in a batch very shortly after the Constitution was ratified. Since 1791, then, the Constitution has been amended only seventeen times. Hundreds of amendments have been put forward, but only seventeen have survived the difficult amendment process, which requires a two-thirds majority in both houses of Congress and ratification by three-quarters of the states.

The amendments can be sorted into five categories, which are shown in Table 3.3. The technical adjustments include amendments that were passed at various times to correct problems in the system's functioning. These aside, the amendments were all passed in four relatively brief flurries of activity, in the wake of periods of political turmoil and pressure for reform.

The Bill of Rights: Amendments 1–10

One of the principal complaints thrown against the Constitution during the ratification battles was that it did not include a Bill of Rights. Several states had adopted their own since independence, using as a model the English Bill of Rights of 1688. Such a list of rights had not been considered necessary at the constitutional convention, since the national government was to exercise only specified powers. In the thick of the ratification battle, however, Madison and others promised to support adding a Bill of Rights if the Constitution was ratified.

---

8   Storing, *What the Anti-Federalists Were For*, 5–6.

Category	Time	Number	Amendments	
				Table 3.3
Bill of Rights	1789–91	10	1–10	*The amendments to the*
				U.S. Constitution.[9]
Technical adjustments	scattered	6	11, 12, 20, 22, 25, 27	
Civil War	1865–70	3	13, 14, 15	
Progressive	1913–20	4+1	16, 17, 18, 19, 21	
Sixties	1961–71	3	23, 24, 26	

Almost the first business of the new House of Representatives in the fall of 1789 was the consideration of twelve constitutional amendments drafted by James Madison. Ten of these were passed by the Congress and ratified by the states in less than two years. An eleventh, as noted below, completed the process many years later.

The first eight amendments guarantee a series of rights to Americans, mainly by prohibiting Congress or the government generally from violating them.

The *First Amendment* set out more of what had come to be considered the classic rights of the citizen of a free country: freedom of speech, freedom of the press, freedom of peaceful assembly, and freedom to petition the government. But it also set out new rights to religious toleration—rights that the Americans were the pioneers in declaring: the right to freedom from a governmental establishment of religion, and the right to the free exercise of one's religion.

The meaning of the *Second Amendment* is controversial, in that it forms the principal argument made by those opposed to gun control legislation. Whether the amendment guarantees an individual the right to bear arms, as opponents of gun control claim, or such a right only in the context of the state militia (now the state national guard), is something the U.S. Supreme Court has never ruled on definitively.[10]

The *Fourth* to *Eighth Amendments* all deal with the rights of persons suspected or accused of a crime by the authorities. Having fought off British attempts to coerce them, the founding generation of Americans were well aware of the dangers of false accusations by the authorities and of the importance of strict procedural safeguards to protect the innocent. The best-known protections are the prohibition against

---

9   See Richard B. Bernstein with Jerome Agel, *Amending America: If We Love the Constitution So Much Why Do We Keep Trying to Change It?* (Times Books, 1993).

10   See Robert J. Spitzer, *The Politics of Gun Control* (Chatham House, 1995).

"unreasonable searches and seizures" in the *Fourth Amendment*, the right against self-incrimination in the *Fifth Amendment*, and the prohibition against "cruel and unusual punishment" in the *Eighth Amendment*.

The last two amendments are more general in nature. The *Ninth Amendment* states that the rights set out in the previous eight amendments and those in the body of the Constitution are not to be taken as a complete list of all the rights of the people; other rights may well exist. The *10th Amendment* makes a similar statement about the powers of government; all powers not specifically allocated to the national government or forbidden to the states in the Constitution belong to the states (that is, not to the national government) or to the people.

Obviously, the Bill of Rights is an extremely important statement in the history of human rights. While stated in abstract terms, it was written within fresh memory of some of the abuses inflicted by the British government during the struggles from the 1760s to the end of the Revolutionary War. Some of the amendments, such as the Second, Third, and Seventh, are now mainly of historical interest; but the rights of accused persons listed in the Fourth, Fifth, Sixth, and Eighth Amendments continue to be of great significance. This is just as true of the First Amendment rights (religious freedom, free speech, a free press, peaceful assembly, and the right to petition the government), and of the Fifth Amendment right not to be deprived of "life, liberty, or property, without due process of law."

The prohibitions in the Bill of Rights were held by the Supreme Court in 1833 to apply only to the federal government, and not to state governments. In the nineteenth century, few cases arose under the Bill of Rights. Sensitivity to questions of civil liberties began to grow around the time of World War I;[11] the increase in appeals to the guarantees in the Bill of Rights dates from around that time. The Supreme Court broadened the impact of the guarantees in the 1920s, when it began to incorporate them into the due process clause of the 14th Amendment and to apply the prohibitions of the Bill of Rights against actions by state governments. It was the Warren Court (1953–69) that undertook the often controversial exploration and expansion of the meaning of the rights guarantees in modern America (see Chapter 9).

An obvious question for Canadians is how the American Bill of Rights compares with the Canadian Charter of Rights and Freedoms that was adopted in 1982. Some have seen the Charter as inevitably increasing the "Americanization" of Canada through its focus on individual rights, but Alan Cairns has pointed out that in supporting the Charter, Canadians were responding to a modern global concern for rights, not just the American example.[12] In some respects the Charter is an updating

---

11   See Paul L. Murphy, *World War I and the Origin of Civil Liberties in the United States* (Norton, 1979).

12   Alan C. Cairns, *Charter Versus Federalism: The Dilemmas of Constitutional Reform* (McGill–Queen's University Press, 1992), Chapter 1.

and expansion of the Bill of Rights. In the Charter, it is Section 2 on fundamental freedoms and Sections 7 to 14 on legal rights that most closely parallel the Bill of Rights; but the Charter has additional sections on democratic rights, mobility rights, and equality rights. The equality rights section includes a prohibition against sex discrimination and allows for affirmative action.

But in other respects the Charter reflects distinctively Canadian concerns. It has sections on the two official languages, minority language educational rights, multiculturalism, the rights of aboriginal peoples, and equalization and regional disparity (a long-standing concern of Canadian federalism). The Charter also reflects a distinctively Canadian—indeed, a positively "un-American"—concern with measuring rights against the public good. Unlike American rights, which are stated in absolute terms ("Congress shall make no law regarding ..."), rights under the Charter are "subject ... to such reasonable limits prescribed by law as can be demonstrably justified in a free and democratic society." Also, in recognition of the supremacy of the political process, the Parliament or legislatures in Canada may put an act into operation "notwithstanding" the fundamental, legal, and equality rights sections of the Charter for periods of five years at a time.

Technical Adjustments: Amendments 11, 12, 20, 22, 25, and 27

These amendments were all passed to correct minor problems in the working of the Constitution that had not been foreseen by the framers. The first two adjustments were made in the early years, the other four in the twentieth century after changed circumstances exposed new flaws in the original document.

The *11th Amendment*, ratified in 1798, involved the highly sensitive questions of whether a state could be sued and whether the Supreme Court had jurisdiction in cases involving state governments. After the Court accepted jurisdiction in the case of *Chisholm v. Georgia* in 1794, widespread anger among the states led to the amendment limiting the Court's jurisdiction.

The reasons for the *12th Amendment*, ratified in 1804, which changed the operation of the Electoral College, are discussed in Chapter 11.

The *20th Amendment*, adopted in 1933, brought forward the inauguration of the president, and the swearing in of the Congress, from March to January. After the demands on the federal government increased enormously in the twentieth century, the gap between the election in early November and taking office in March was judged to be much too long. The *22nd Amendment*, adopted in 1951, limits a president to two terms. While the Constitution was silent on the question, the revered first president, George Washington, established the precedent of declining to run for a third term. This precedent was shattered by Franklin Roosevelt, who was elected to a third and then a fourth term during World War II. It was mainly the Republican Party that sponsored the amendment, in order to prevent a recurrence of such dominance by one man. Ironically, the only presidents since then who would have been eligible for a third term were Dwight Eisenhower and Ronald Reagan, both Republicans.

The Constitution provided no method of replacing the vice president when a vacancy occurred. Awareness of the problem of having no elected successor to the president was heightened after Kennedy's assassination. The *25th Amendment*, ratified in 1967, provides for nomination by the president of a new vice president, followed by confirmation by both houses of Congress. The new mechanism came into play twice in dramatic circumstances not long afterwards. When Vice President Spiro Agnew had to resign in 1973 because of a corruption scandal, President Richard Nixon nominated Rep. Gerald Ford to be the new vice president. When Nixon himself had to resign in 1974 because of the Watergate scandal, Ford became president—the first person to hold the office without having been elected to it. President Ford then used the mechanism again to have Nelson Rockefeller appointed the new vice president. The 25th Amendment also provides a mechanism for dealing with a situation in which the president is medically incapacitated, but that mechanism has not yet been tested in practice.

The *27th Amendment*, ratified in 1992, is the strangest amendment in American constitutional history, not in terms of its content but in terms of how it was ratified. The amendment provides that changes (that is, increases) in congressional pay will not come into effect until after the following congressional elections. What is strange about the ratification process is that the amendment was passed by the First Congress in 1789, along with the Bill of Rights. Whereas the ten amendments forming the Bill of Rights were all ratified by the necessary ten states (three-quarters of the thirteen states) within two years, the pay amendment was only ratified by six states and thus it did not become part of the Constitution at that time. At that time, no time limit was set for the ratification process. A seventh state, Ohio, ratified the pay amendment in 1873 to protest the latest congressional pay raise. The amendment was forgotten again until 1978, when Wyoming ratified it. Every year after 1983 the amendment was ratified by at least one more state. The process attracted almost no public attention, so that everyone was caught by surprise when it was realized that Michigan's ratification in May 1992 (state #38) completed the ratification process. The more recent impetus behind the amendment came from public anger at a number of financial scandals that had rocked the Congress in recent years.

There are four other proposed amendments that were passed by the Congress without a time limit but whose ratification by the states was never completed. Three of these—a change in the apportionment of the House, also passed in 1789; the prohibition of federal laws against slavery (1861); and the awarding to Congress of the power to regulate child labor (1924)—have all been made moot by later events. The

remaining proposal would forbid American government officials from accepting foreign honors (1810). The states could still ratify this amendment, but there is not likely to be any interest in doing so.

The Civil War Amendments: 13, 14, and 15

These three amendments were passed in the aftermath of the southern defeat as part
of attempts by the northern Republicans to safeguard the rights of former slaves.
They effectively eliminated the protection of slavery in the original document.

The *13th Amendment*, ratified quickly in 1865, abolished slavery in the United
States. On January 1, 1863, President Lincoln had issued the Emancipation
Proclamation, which freed the slaves in the rebel states. Before then, it had generally
been agreed that the federal government had no power to do this under the
Constitution. Lincoln claimed that authority as commander in chief in time of war,
but to remove any uncertainty, the amendment was passed.

The *14th Amendment* was adopted in 1868. The first sentence overruled the decision of the Supreme Court in *Dred Scott v. Sandford* in 1857 that black people were
not citizens of the United States. The rest of Section 1 is extremely important, because
for the first time it placed in the U.S. Constitution prohibitions on the *state* governments. One prohibition repeated the language of the Fifth Amendment against
depriving anyone of "life, liberty, or property, without due process of law." An
extremely important addition was the prohibition against denying anyone "the equal
protection of the laws."

The principal motivation behind this section was to protect former slaves from hostile southern state governments; but the provisions were stated in general terms and in
the twentieth century have often been interpreted more broadly. For example, the
"equal protection" clause has been used since the 1970s to strike down some forms of
sex discrimination. The "due process" clause of the 14th Amendment has been interpreted as applying many of the prohibitions of the Bill of Rights against actions of
state governments.

The *15th Amendment*, adopted in 1870, forbade the federal and state governments
from denying the right to vote on grounds of "race, color, or previous condition of
servitude." The Republicans hoped that by guaranteeing the right to vote, blacks
would be able to protect themselves against discrimination by state governments.

All three of these amendments specifically granted the Congress the power to pass
laws to enforce their provisions. Sadly, as will be discussed in Chapter 9, even such
constitutional guarantees, because of the way they were interpreted by the Supreme
Court, did not prevent segregation laws from being introduced in the southern states
by the end of the century.

The Progressive Amendments: 16, 17, 18 and 21, 19

Four amendments came out of this period of political reform, one of which later had to be repealed by another amendment. The central theme of the Progressives' various initiatives was the desire to modernize the government of the United States and to sweep away corruption by making politics more democratic.

The *16th Amendment* in 1913 declared the federal income tax to be constitutional. This overruled the 1895 decision of the Supreme Court in *Pollock v. Farmers' Loan and Trust Co.*, which struck down an income tax law on the grounds that the Constitution required direct taxes to be apportioned on the basis of population. It may seem surprising now to find such broad support for a new tax, but the Progressives had built support for new initiatives by the federal government—initiatives that needed new sources of revenue.

The *17th Amendment*, also ratified in 1913, provided for the direct popular election of the Senate. By this time the Senate was generally seen as a corrupt body dominated by state party bosses in league with big business. Since the Congress refused to approve such an amendment, its supporters went the alternative route for amending the Constitution, persuading state legislatures to ask Congress to call a constitutional convention. It was only when the number of state requests approached the two-thirds mark—which would have triggered the calling of a convention—that Congress gave in and sent the amendment out for ratification.

The *18th Amendment*, ratified in 1919, was the notorious Prohibition Amendment that prohibited the manufacture, sale, and transportation of "intoxicating liquors" within the United States. Evangelicals had long championed Prohibition, and they were joined by the Progressives, who saw alcohol abuse as a widespread social problem that also interfered with the efficiency of the work force. While many states already had prohibition laws, it was the anti-German sentiment triggered by World War I that provided the extra support to pass the amendment: the brewing industry was run by families of German descent.

Many people now interpret the prohibition movement as part of a protest at that time against immigration and changes in the nature of American society. In this light, Prohibition was a last-ditch attempt to impose traditional small-town Protestant values on the new immigrants.

The "noble experiment" of Prohibition was a complete failure. Congress never voted enough money to enforce it seriously. The laws were widely flouted, especially in the cities. The main effect was to channel the liquor trade into criminal hands. Finally, in 1933, the 18th Amendment was repealed by the *21st Amendment*, which gave regulation of the liquor business back to the states.

The *19th Amendment*, adopted in 1920, guaranteed women the right to vote. A number of western states had pioneered this reform, starting with Wyoming Territory in 1869, but by 1920 women had full voting rights in only fifteen states. The necessary expansion of women's role in the work force during World War I and the prominence of women in the prohibition movement helped to build support for the amendment.

The 1960s Amendments: 23, 24, and 26

The 1960s was a period of social change and political activism in the United States. The central issues were civil rights for black Americans and America's involvement in the **Vietnam War**. The first two amendments were a response to the civil rights issue, the third to the war. Also significant were two amendments that were proposed by the Congress but failed to be ratified.

The *23rd Amendment*, adopted in 1961, gave the citizens of the District of Columbia (Washington, D.C.) the right to vote for president by giving the District three electoral votes. As a federal territory, Washington was neither a state nor part of a state, and thus the citizens could not vote. The question was connected to civil rights, in that the bulk of Washington residents are black.

The *24th Amendment* of 1964 forbade the use of a poll tax in federal elections. Originally one form of property qualification for voting, the poll tax had been retained by some southern states, where it formed one of the many obstacles to black voting.

The *26th Amendment*, quickly ratified in 1971, lowered the voting age in all elections from 21 to 18. Congress had passed a law to this effect in 1970, but the Supreme Court ruled in *Oregon v. Mitchell* (1970) that Congress had no power to set the voting age in state elections. At a time when eighteen-year-olds were being drafted to fight in Vietnam, it was hard to deny them the right to vote. The amendment also reflected the coming of age of the large post–World War II "baby boom" generation.

American suffragette parade in New York, 1912.

Recently Proposed Amendments

Over the years, many amendments to the Constitution have been proposed that have failed to generate sufficient levels of political support. The surge of reforms in the 1960s produced three other proposals that gathered significant support but did not make it all the way through the amending process. One proposal, which arose from the chaotic presidential election in 1968, would have abolished the Electoral College and provided for the direct election of the president. It was passed by the House in 1969 but failed in the Senate. Two others, dealing with equality for women and representation in Congress for the District of Columbia, were passed by Congress but failed to be ratified by enough states.

The *Equal Rights Amendment* would have prohibited discrimination by the federal and state governments "on account of sex." This proposal had been supported in the election platforms of both major parties for thirty years, but it was the new feminist movement in the late 1960s that built new support for the cause.

The amendment passed the Congress in 1972 and looked certain of ratification. Within two years, 28 of the necessary 38 states had passed it, but at that point the momentum slowed considerably. By the mid-1970s the political climate had become much more conservative and an active campaign had begun to block the amendment. The 35th of the necessary 38 ratifications came in early 1977. Congress extended the seven-year time limit for ratification to ten years, but after 1977 no further states came close to ratifying it. In all probability, had the amendment been passed by the Congress a couple of years earlier, the reform momentum would have ensured its ratification.[13]

The more conservative climate in the mid-1970s also doomed the *D.C. Voting Rights Amendment*. This amendment, which would have given Washington one member of the House and two Senators, passed the Congress in 1978. By that time, however, sympathy for black aspirations had diminished considerably. The fact that Washington was an overwhelmingly Democratic city also limited Republican enthusiasm for the measure. Only sixteen states had ratified the amendment by the time the seven-year limit expired.

The rising tide of conservatism through the 1980s, and growing disillusionment with Washington, produced two serious proposals for constitutional change. In 1975 the conservative National Tax Limitation Committee began pushing the *Balanced Budget Amendment*. Since the Democratic majority in Congress was unsympathetic, the sponsors decided to try the alternative route to ratification, and by 1983 they had persuaded 32 (of the necessary 34) state legislatures to call for a constitutional convention to consider the proposal. Counterlobbying by liberal groups and by those worried that a convention might consider all kinds of other amendments stalled the drive at that point.

---

13   See Jane J. Mansbridge, *Why We Lost the ERA* (University of Chicago Press, 1986).

Section 1. Equality of rights under the law shall not be denied or abridged by the United States or by any state on account of sex.

Section 2. The Congress shall have the power to enforce, by appropriate legislation, the provision in this Article.

Box 3.1

Text of the proposed Equal Rights Ammendment passed by Congress in 1972 but never ratified.

Interest in the amendment was kept alive by the ballooning of the federal deficit under President Reagan and by Congress's inability throughout the 1980s to cut the deficit back. The Senate passed the amendment by the necessary two-thirds majority in 1982. In 1990 and 1992 it fell just short of passage in the House. In 1994 the triumphant capture of both houses of Congress by the Republicans for the first time in forty years seemed to make it a certainty that the amendment would pass. However, while it easily passed the House in March 1995, it failed by one vote in the Senate.

In 1994 the Republicans also promised to pass an amendment limiting the number of terms that could be served in Congress. The drive for *Term Limits* was a conservative grass-roots campaign, which by 1995 had succeeded in having twenty-two states adopt term limits for their state legislators and members of Congress. In 1994 the Supreme Court ruled that only a constitutional amendment could limit service in the Congress. In early 1995, votes on an amendment in the Republican-controlled Congress fell well short of passage.

A group of ERA demonstrators hold a rally at the Lincoln Memorial in Washington, D.C., in a final effort to obtain ratification of the Equal Rights Amendment.

The Amendments to the Constitution: Summary

Amending the Constitution is a difficult process, as it was intended to be. A successful amendment requires wide cross-party agreement in the Congress and then solid support across the nation—currently from 38 of the 50 state legislatures. Considering this, it is not surprising that most of the amendments have been adopted during those brief periods when public attention was highly aroused across the country and political activism was at its peak: during the ratification of the Constitution; in the aftermath of the Civil War; during the era of Progressive reform; and in the turbulent years of the 1960s.

The amendments vary in importance. Clearly the Bill of Rights, written in the same era as the Constitution, helped make explicit the liberal ideals on which the United States was founded. The most important of the later amendments had the effect of extending the original ideals.

The post–Civil War amendments were a noble attempt to deal with the race issue, which the framers had avoided. Sadly, there was no broad base of public sympathy, and these amendments provided no protection at all to black Americans against the racism of their fellow citizens. Nevertheless, the 14th Amendment was an extremely important addition, since it extended the liberal prohibitions of the Constitution to the state governments and placed the liberal commitment to equality explicitly in the Constitution in the form of the equal protection clause.

Likewise, the vote for women and the direct election of senators, adopted during the Progressive era, were important extensions of liberal ideals. Note that the only amendment clearly in violation of basic American principles, the Prohibition Amendment, signally failed to work and had to be repealed. It can be argued that the Equal Rights Amendment and the amendment calling for direct election of the president are two obvious extensions of liberal principles that have so far failed to be adopted.

The U.S. Constitution: An Assessment

Although the United States is a relatively new nation, its Constitution is the oldest written constitution in the world. This paradox underlines the radical nature of what the Americans undertook. Having thrown off the colonial government, they created a new form of government for themselves, shaped by their own beliefs and circumstances and based on the then-radical principle of popular sovereignty.

The U.S. Constitution has been widely admired for its political realism and theoretical sophistication. Among Americans it is an object of near-veneration, and those who framed it are held up as model statesmen who have rarely been matched by later politicians. Herbert Storing notes, however, that the Constitution was created at a unique historical moment:

> American constitutional reform occurred during a time when sharp differ-
> ences of opinion were muted and patriotic sentiments relatively great, when
> confidence in leaders was high, and when excesses of liberty had made the
> people willing to accept a sound constitution. It was the Americans' good
> fortune that the need for constitutional reform coincided with the circum-
> stances conducive to it, but these circumstances are rare and the coincidence
> unlikely.[14]

Even so, it is impossible not to admire the boldness with which the leading framers went to work within their window of opportunity to put their principles into practice.

The framers' work has lasted very well. It is remarkable that the United States, an economic and military superpower of 250 million people, is still operating with a constitution written over 200 years ago for a new nation of four million people scattered along the Atlantic coast of North America. There have been relatively few amendments to the Constitution; as will be discussed in Chapter 9, the U.S. Supreme Court through its interpretations has greatly increased the flexibility and longevity of the Constitution.

The three main elements of the Constitution have worked very much as they were intended to work. In the early period, it was the federal element that was most contentious. The federal union was nearly torn apart by the Civil War and was only held together by force and at massive cost. In the twentieth century, however, the federal system has worked well—much more smoothly, in fact, than the Canadian federation, which was designed to be much stronger. The development of the federal system is dealt with in Chapter 4.

The liberal prohibitions in the Constitution, the Bill of Rights, and the Civil War Amendments have remained an inspiration and a model for the rest of the world (for example, for the Canadian Charter of Rights and Freedoms). While the constitutional guarantees for a long time had limited impact because of public and official indifference, in the past forty years especially they have provided an important framework of protection for the rights of Americans.

It is the third element, Madison's design of the national institutions, that has had the biggest impact on American government and that current observers of the American system see as the most problematic. Again, Madison's design has worked very much the way he intended. His system of "separated institutions sharing power" has produced a highly fragmented political process in Washington in which the

---

14   Storing, *What the Anti-Federalists Were For*, 5–6

institutions and officeholders are placed in constant competition with one another for power, and cooperation is extremely difficult to achieve. Since state governments have copied the main elements of the national system, a radical fragmentation of power pervades politics at every level in the United States.

Madison shared the liberal concerns of his time about the long-term stability of popular government and the protection of individual rights both from government tyranny and from the passions of the majority. His genius was that he devised a scheme of government which solved these problems by preventing the accumulation of too much power by any one institution or person.

It is this central feature of the Constitution—this fragmentation of power flowing from a distrust of the popular will—that has often been condemned as undemocratic or conservative in the twentieth century. Some have contrasted the radicalism of the Declaration of Independence ("all men are created equal") with the more conservative cast of the Constitution and argued that the American Revolution was subverted by men of property.[15] But the American Revolution, unlike the French and Russian revolutions, was a political revolution, not a social revolution. American society was already much more open and egalitarian than European societies, due to the availability of land, but it was led by an educated economic elite.

The American founders were eighteenth-century liberals, not nineteenth-century democrats. While they proclaimed the principle of equality, they did not believe in extending political rights to those who were unqualified for citizenship. Still less did they conceive of equality in terms of a right to social and economic equality, a principle developed by nineteenth-century socialist thinkers.

In two later periods—the 1820s and 1830s, and the years from 1900 to 1920—reforms of the electoral and party systems extended political rights and made the political system more democratic, but these reforms had little impact on the basic constitutional framework. In the nineteenth century there was no problem with the organization of federal institutions. Little was demanded or expected from the government in Washington. In any case the fragmentation of power was partially offset by strong state and local parties in much of the nation.

In the twentieth century, in contrast, the demands on the federal government have grown enormously, while the party system's capacity to link officeholders and institutions has been dramatically weakened. As a result, Washington is a city full of frenetic political activity but little government action. For Canadians, who are used to a parliamentary system, in which there is clear, centralized control of the executive branch and the legislative process by the Cabinet, the fragmentation of power and the complexities of the policy-making process in Washington are startling.

---

15   This was the argument of Charles Beard and the "progressive" school of historians. Beard's *Economic Interpretation of the Constitution of the United States of America* was published in 1913.

Since the beginning of the century there have been many American commentators who have admired the efficiency of the parliamentary system and have advocated constitutional amendments that might make the American system function more like a parliamentary system.[16] However, the Constitution is so revered in the United States and is so much a part of the American identity that the prospect of any major changes to it is extremely remote. Presidents and members of Congress have no option but to continue the struggle for cooperation in a radically fragmented system.

---

16   For a review of the parliamentary critique of the American constitutional system, see Thomas O. Sargentich, "The Limits of the Parliamentary Critique of the Separation of Powers," *William and Mary Law Review* 34 (1993), 679–739. Sargentich argues that the separation of powers is superior because it increases citizen access to government and promotes a wider political dialogue.

CHAPTER 4

FEDERALISM

O f necessity, both the United States and Canada were established as federal systems, with governmental powers divided between a national government and state or provincial governments. In America the newly independent thirteen states had at first banded together under the Articles of Confederation, a very loose confederal arrangement that had no independent executive authority and under which it was up to the individual states to carry out the collective decisions. By 1787 there was a general sense that a stronger national government was necessary, but there were also widespread fears about increasing national powers. The more farsighted leaders, such as James Madison, had difficulty persuading the smaller states in particular to attend a Constitutional Convention.

At the convention, rather than tinker with the Articles, Madison and the Virginia delegation moved quickly to write a new constitution. Although the small states continued to be wary, the powers of the new national government were not much in dispute. The Congress was given powers in those areas where the main benefits from a stronger union were expected: the power to secure external defense and internal peace, and the power to allow the free flow of commerce. These powers were listed in Article 1, Section 8, and forbidden to the states in Section 10. All other powers were, in the words of the 10th Amendment, "reserved to the States respectively, or to the people."

The framers of the U.S. Constitution in effect *invented* modern federalism. The models available at the time were either a "consolidated" (that is, unitary) government, which was politically out of the question, or a confederation like the one provided for in the Articles, which by general agreement were unsatisfactory as written. The framers came up with a new form of federal government based on the central concept that each of two levels of government would have sovereignty over the same populations but different policy areas. The concept of dual or divided sovereignty was controversial; most political theorists argued that sovereignty was in principle indivisible, and that one level of government or the other was bound in practice to dominate the other. One of the fears of the Anti-Federalist opponents of the Constitution was that the new national government would become dominant over the states.[1]

The chief architect of the Constitution, James Madison, recognized that this was a new design and argued in *Federalist Paper 39* that it comprised both national and federal elements. Most scholars view it as conforming to the central federal principle of dualism, in that it gave distinct jurisdictions to both levels of government, but with a decentralist bias in favor of state powers.[2]

In the negotiations to form the Dominion of Canada between 1864 and 1867, Quebec's insistence on maintaining control of its own cultural institutions made some kind of federal system clearly inevitable. Sir John A. Macdonald and his supporters were nevertheless determined to form as strong a national government as possible. They pointed to the United States, at that time racked by civil war, as a negative example of a weak federation. The Canadian Constitution Act of 1867 established a federal union that was, on paper at least, highly centralized. Indeed, it was so centralized that it would probably not have qualified under James Madison's test of a federation.[3] The provincial governments were to deal only with local issues, and their powers were limited to those listed in Section 92. The federal government, on the other hand, was granted legislative powers in all other areas, including but not limited to those listed in Section 91. Agriculture and immigration were made concurrent powers. Provincial governments were limited to direct taxation, whereas the federal government was given general taxing powers. In addition, the federal government had the power of reservation or disallowance over provincial legislation.

In both the United States and Canada, the practice of federalism evolved in directions that their founders could not have foreseen. Alexander Hamilton, who had been

---

1   Herbert J. Storing, *What the Anti-Federalists Were **For*** (University of Chicago Press, 1981), 12–13 and Chapter 4.

2   See Robert Goldwin and William Schambra, eds., *How Federal Is the Constitution?* (American Enterprise Institute for Public Policy Research, 1987).

3   A Canadian trial of Madison's test is attempted by Jennifer Smith in "Canadian Confederation and the Influences of American Federalism," *Canadian Journal of Political Science*, XXI:3 (September 1988), 443–463.

the proponent of the strongest form of national government at the Constitutional Convention, would be delighted with the centralized American system of today, while the Anti-Federalists would consider their worst fears confirmed. The national government, which has limited powers in the Constitution, has expanded into almost all policy areas, and its supremacy over the state governments in most of these areas is now unquestioned. In contrast, Canada's highly centralized constitutional design has been replaced in practice by an institutionalized decentralization of power. The state governments of the United States are marginalized in the national policy process; the provincial governments in Canada play a leading and often determining role in many areas of domestic policy.

In light of the Canadian founders' conscious attempt to distance themselves from what they saw as the weak American model, it is ironic, as Roger Gibbins notes, that "Canadians today have a federal system not far removed in spirit from the early American model, whereas the American federal system has evolved toward the Canadian model laid out in 1867."[4] What must be explained is why the two federations developed in different directions, and why they operate so differently now.

The American and Canadian federal systems have had to deal with similar challenges. Both countries underwent enormous geographical and political expansion: the United States grew from thirteen to fifty states; Canada grew from four provinces to ten provinces and two territories. Both systems have had to accommodate severe regional conflicts. In the United States the conflict between North and South nearly tore the country apart during the Civil War. From the end of the nineteenth century there have also been significant tensions between the financially and culturally dominant Northeast and the less developed West. Canada has had to accommodate two distinct cultures, French and English. In the twentieth century relations have also been severely strained between the western provinces and the politically dominant Toronto–Ottawa–Montreal axis in central Canada.

In the twentieth century in both the United States and Canada a number of forces—industrialization, the growth of the welfare state, a larger role in the world— placed strong nationalizing and centralizing pressure on the federal structure. As governments increasingly became service providers, the lines between federal and state or provincial jurisdiction that had once been clear became increasingly blurred. In both countries, constitutional interpretation by the courts played an important role in maintaining a balance between federal and state or provincial jurisdictions up through the 1930s. Since then, both federations have tried to accommodate internal stresses by political means. Scholars differentiate between two kinds of institutional mechanisms by which federal systems regulate regional pressures: *interstate* mechanisms, in which

---

4   Roger Gibbins, *Regionalism: Territorial Politics in Canada and the United States* (Butterworths, 1982), 43.

differences are negotiated between the two levels of government, federal and state or provincial; and *intrastate* mechanisms, in which differences between the center and the regions are accommodated within national institutions.[5] The centralized American federal system relies heavily on intrastate mechanisms; in Canada, intrastate mechanisms have increasingly been replaced by interstate negotiations.

THE DEVELOPMENT OF AMERICAN FEDERALISM, 1787–1937

The framers who had united to establish a national government soon divided over the extent of its powers. James Madison and Alexander Hamilton, who had cooperated in *The Federalist Papers* to write the classic defense of the framers' handiwork, became bitter political enemies. Madison, along with Thomas Jefferson, argued for limiting national powers, Hamilton and the Federalists for broadening them. Their argument over the balance between federal and state powers came to a head in 1798 with the passage of the Alien and Sedition Acts by the Federalist administration of President John Adams. It was Madison and Jefferson's response, in the form of the Virginia and Kentucky Resolutions, that first made the case for states' rights under the Constitution. They argued that the union had been formed by a compact among sovereign states, that each government had the right to interpret the Constitution, and that states therefore had the rights of interposition and nullification against acts of the national government which they believed to be unconstitutional. This particular argument became moot with the expiry of the acts and Jefferson's election as president in 1800, but the underlying issue of the extent of national power relative to states' rights remained unresolved.

The alternative to the compact theory of the union was the national theory, espoused by the Federalists. In the national theory, the union was formed not by the states but by the people as a whole, from whom the authority of both the national government and the states derived.[6] It was another Federalist, Chief Justice John Marshall (1801–35), who laid down the constitutional foundations for a strong national government. After taking office under highly contentious circumstances (see Chapter 9), Marshall skillfully and persuasively laid down the crucial centralizing precedents, establishing the Constitution as the supreme law over both federal and state governments and the Court as its final interpreter. The Court also established

---

5   Donald V. Smiley and Ronald L. Watts, *Intrastate Federalism in Canada* (University of Toronto Press, 1985), 4.
6   Samuel H. Beer, "Introduction: The National Idea in American Politics," *To Make A Nation: The Rediscovery of American Federalism* (Belknap Press, 1993).

that the listed powers of the federal government could be interpreted expansively through a broad interpretation of the interstate commerce and the "necessary and proper" clauses of Article 1, Section 8.

Jefferson's belief in limited government lived on in the Democratic Party of Andrew Jackson, and in the first half of the nineteenth century the role of the federal government remained much more limited than Hamilton had wanted. Under John Marshall's successor, the Jacksonian Chief Justice Roger Taney (1835–64), the Supreme Court gave a broad interpretation to the inherent "police power" of the states to legislate for the public welfare. Thus, throughout the nineteenth century the United States operated a system of "dual federalism," with the state and federal governments supreme within their spheres and the scope of the federal power politically limited.

The compact theory of the Union, with its implied right of secession, remained in the background of national politics. The New England states briefly toyed with the idea of secession over the unpopular War of 1812, but it was in the South that the fear of federal government power had the most resonance. In 1832 South Carolina, following the chief exponent of the states' rights doctrine, John C. Calhoun, attempted to "nullify" the new tariff law but was unable to attract broader support in the face of President Jackson's determined opposition.

From the time the Constitution was written, however, it was the defense of slavery that fueled southerners' fears of federal power. South Carolina first threatened secession over the issue in 1851; nine years later, in 1860, it led the way as eleven southern states seceded from the Union to form the Confederacy in a panic after the election of the first Republican president, Abraham Lincoln. The southern secession enabled Lincoln to rally the North around the national idea and make the Civil War a war to save the Union. The costly northern victory settled the issues of slavery and secession; in 1869 the Supreme Court ruled that states did not have the right to secede but that the "distinct, individual existence, [and] the right of self-government by the States" was protected under the Constitution. "The Constitution," said the Court, "looks to an indestructible Union composed of indestructible States."[7]

The argument over states' rights has continued in a subdued form and indeed is a staple of American policy debate. Typically, those opposed to new federal legislation argue that there is no need for a national policy and that such matters should be left to the states. In the United States, David Nice, has argued, "debates about federalism are debates about policy in disguise."[8] Samuel Beer comments that "since the days of Hamilton and Jefferson, the opinions of American political leaders have generally

---

7   *Texas v. White* 74 U.S. 700 (1869) at 725.
8   David C. Nice, *Federalism: The Politics of Intergovernmental Relations* (St. Martin's Press, 1987), 24.

exemplified [an] instrumental view of federalism, switching back and forth with their policy aims."[9]

For most of the nineteenth century, economic and political life in the United States was based in local communities, with the federal government playing a limited role.[10] But as America developed an increasingly national economy, politics came to focus more and more on Washington and pressures for federal legislation grew. In the face of these centralizing pressures, the Supreme Court established itself as the regulator of the federal system. After 1890 the Court struck down most federal regulation of business by giving a narrow interpretation to the interstate commerce and taxing powers of Article 1, Section 8, ruling that to allow an expansion of federal powers would destroy the federal system.

Decades later, continuing along this line of constitutional interpretation, the Court struck down much of the initial New Deal legislation as beyond the power of Congress (see Chapter 9). For example, the Court struck down the Agricultural Adjustment Act of 1933, for which the federal government claimed authority under the taxing power, in the following terms:

> The expressions of the framers of the Constitution, the decisions of this court ... and the writings of the great commentators will be searched in vain for any suggestion that there exists in the clause under discussion or elsewhere in the Constitution, the authority whereby every provision and every fair implication from that instrument may be subverted, the independence of the individual states obliterated, and the United States converted into a central government exercising uncontrolled police power in every state of the Union ...[11]

It was only after Franklin Roosevelt's overwhelming re-election in 1936 that the Court quietly backed away from its restrictive interpretation of Congress's legislative authority. The result was to remove virtually all constitutional barriers to federal legislation on economic and social issues. Referring to John Marshall's original broad definition of interstate commerce in *Gibbons v. Ogden* (1824), the Court declared in 1941 that "the motive and purpose of a regulation of interstate commerce are matters for the legislative judgment [of Congress] upon the exercise of which the Constitution places no restriction and over which the courts are given no control."[12]

---

9   Samuel H. Beer, "Introduction" in Timothy Conlan, *New Federalism: Intergovernmental Reform from Nixon to Reagan* (The Brookings Institution, 1988), xii.

10 Daniel J. Elazar, *The American Partnership: Intergovernmental Cooperation in the Nineteenth-Century United States* (University of Chicago Press, 1962).

11 *United States vs. Butler* 297 U.S. 1 (1936) at 77.

12 *United States v. Darby* 312 U.S. 100 (1941) at 115.

The Development of Canadian Federalism, 1867–1937

In Canada, decentralizing pressures on the highly centralized federal structure appeared quickly. For one thing, the imbalance in fiscal resources between the provinces quickly became an issue. In 1869, Nova Scotia secured a bigger federal subsidy by threatening to secede, creating a precedent for intergovernmental negotiations over taxes and subsidies that has continued ever since. The powers of reservation and disallowance soon became politically unusable. The provinces, especially Ontario, quickly sought to increase provincial autonomy and to reduce the powers of the federal government, arguing that Confederation had been created by a compact between the provinces.[13]

The role of arbiter of the federal system fell to the Judicial Committee of the Privy Council (JCPC), the highest British court for the colonies, which until 1949 was the highest court of appeal for Canada. The effect of the JCPC's interpretations of the Constitution Act was to limit the powers of the federal government and increase those of the provinces. In the *Local Prohibition* case (1896), Lord Watson, writing for the committee, interpreted the federal government's residual powers in such a narrow manner as to render them virtually nonexistent. Thus, Canada moved toward a system of dual federalism. As Stevenson notes, "the practical effect of the 1896 decision was to place the federal and provincial levels of government on a basis of equality."[14]

After World War I, Canada experienced some of the same pressures to increase the role of the federal government that were experienced in the United States, and the JCPC played a constraining role similar to that of the pre–1937 American Court. Viscount Haldane, a leader on the JCPC from 1912 to 1928, reduced the powers of the federal government through a series of rulings[15] that narrowly interpreted the federal power to regulate trade and commerce.

While the committee was restricting federal power, it was expanding the jurisdiction of provincial governments by broadly interpreting their power to legislate in the area of "Property and Civil Rights in the Province." This line of reasoning was used to strike down parts of Prime Minister R.B. Bennett's "New Deal" program in the 1930s. In the Unemployment Insurance Act reference of 1937,[16] for example, Lord Atkin ruled

---

13   On the early provincial rights movement in Ontario, see Robert C. Vipond, *Liberty and Community: Canadian Federalism and the Failure of the Constitution* (State University of New York Press, 1991).

14   Garth Stevenson, *Unfulfilled Union: Canadian Federalism and National Unity*, Third Edition (Gage, 1989), 50.

15   See *In Re The Board of Commerce Act, 1919,* and *The Combines and Fair Prices Act, 1919,* [1922] 1 A.C. 191, extracted in Peter H. Russell, Rainer Knopff, and Ted Morton, *Federalism and the Charter: Leading Constitutional Decisions* (Carleton University Press, 1989), 61–67.

16   *Attorney General of Canada v. Attorney General of Ontario* [1937] A.C. 355, in Russell et al., *Federalism and the Charter*, 97–100.

that the federal government could not legislate a national unemployment insurance program because it would clearly affect property and was thus a provincial matter.

While the U.S. Supreme Court retreated from its narrow interpretation of federal powers after 1937, the JCPC did not, and even after its Canadian jurisdiction was removed in 1949 its precedents continued to be followed by the Canadian Supreme Court. The legacy of the JCPC was therefore a form of dual federalism, with much less extensive federal powers and much more extensive provincial powers than Macdonald and the Fathers of Confederation intended. Some scholars have argued that the JCPC, because of its distance from the Canadian situation, distorted the founders' centralized constitution into the decentralized federation it is today. Others reject the contention that the committee's rulings created regional cleavages instead of merely reflecting them.[17] The error, they argue, was committed by the founders, who misread the entrenched nature of provincialism in the nation. If the JCPC had not decentralized the Constitution, the results could have been disastrous. As Pierre Trudeau argued in 1964, without the JCPC's interpretation of the 1867 Act, "Quebec separatism might not be a threat today; it might be an accomplished fact."[18]

Federalism in the United States Since the New Deal

The Great Depression strongly increased the centralizing pressures in the United States and Canada. In both countries, the federal government was being called upon to provide an increasing range of services. Many of the new areas lay within the traditional jurisdiction of the states and provinces, but the federal governments had greater fiscal and bureaucratic resources. Also, the increasing national integration of the economy and the equalizing philosophy that lay behind the welfare state required national regulation and national standards for services.

Under these nationalizing pressures, both countries moved away from dual federalism, in which the separate jurisdictions of the two levels of government had been respected, toward "cooperative federalism," in which the federal government took the lead in policy areas that traditionally had been under state or provincial jurisdiction. In the United States a typical product of the new federalism was the Social Security Act of 1935, a set of programs largely funded from Washington but administered by the states according to national standards. It was "a new pattern of authority, shared but sharply more centralized."[19]

After the New Deal an informal coalition of Republicans and southern Democrats controlled the Congress and there was no majority for extending federal programs. A

---

17   See Alan C. Cairns, "The Judicial Committee and its Critics," *Canadian Journal of Political Science* IV (1971), 301–345.

18   Pierre Elliot Trudeau, *Federalism and the French Canadians* (Macmillan, 1968), 198.

19   Beer, "Introduction," xxi.

notable exception was the massive interstate highway program of the Eisenhower Administration, which was sold as essential for national economic development and the national defense. But it was not until the 1960s that the political climate supported a significant expansion of the federal role. Daniel Elazar argues that although federalism had become increasingly cooperative after the turn of the century, most politicians still paid lip service to the principle of dual federalism and there was reluctance to invade state jurisdiction.[20]

This reluctance was swept away in the 1960s. The way was paved by the crisis over civil rights in the early 1960s. The traditional southern states' rights argument had been discredited through its association with last-ditch racist opposition to civil rights. Under intense pressure from the civil rights movement, Congress invaded what had been the most sacrosanct areas of state jurisdiction, with only the southern Democrats and a handful of the most conservative Republicans in opposition. The Civil Rights Act of 1964, which forbids race and sex discrimination in most public activities, was based on the interstate commerce clause. The Voting Rights Act 1965, which mandates federal supervision of voting in the southern states and some parts of the North, was based on congressional authority to implement the 15th Amendment. Both acts were upheld unanimously by the Supreme Court.[21]

President Johnson's Great Society program of 1965–68, which followed closely behind the civil rights revolution, saw an explosion of new federal legislation in many more areas of state jurisdiction, such as education, welfare, urban development, and transportation. In a massive process of national equalization dubbed "creative federalism," a whole series of new programs poured federal grants tied to national standards into state governments as grants-in-aid; still more funds were poured directly into local governments and local organizations. By the end of the 1960s the dominant northern Democrats, through their support for Great Society programs and civil rights, were unequivocally in favor of the expansion of federal authority and national standards, in doing so abandoning their party's traditional sensitivity to states' rights.

Republican attitudes toward federalism were more complex. After the New Deal, the central Republican principle was opposition to the expansion of government—the federal government in particular—but the strength of that party's opposition to government varied. Until the late 1970s the party was dominated by moderates who accepted the need for some new government programs. Their hesitancy about expanding the role of government often took the form of arguing that issues should be left to

---

20   Daniel J. Elazar, "Cooperative Federalism in the United States," in Daniel J. Elazar, *Federalism and the Way To Peace* (Institute for Intergovernmental Relations, Queen's University, 1994).

21   *Heart of Atlanta Motel, Inc. v. United States* 379 U.S. 241 (1964); *South Carolina v. Katzenbach* 383 U.S. 301 (1966).

the states. Thus, President Eisenhower called for a return to dual federalism but sponsored the massive interstate highway program. President Nixon proposed a New Federalism in which the states would be given greater discretion in the use of federal money through the use of block grants—a proposal largely blocked by the Democratic Congress. Nixon nevertheless presided over the massive expansion of federal regulation of the environment and the workplace in the early 1970s.

Although Republicans were more sensitive to state concerns than Democrats, John Kincaid argues that by the end of the 1960s attitudes in Washington had shifted so much across the board that cooperative federalism had become "coercive federalism."[22] Neither party had any qualms about imposing its own priorities on the states. In 1972, Michael D. Reagan assessed the working of modern American federalism as follows:

> There is a sharing of power ... between the national and state governments but ... the state's share rests upon the permission ... of the national government ... The legal authority to impose whatever degree of restrictiveness it wishes exists unquestionably in the national government.[23]

The new breed of conservatives who took over the Republican Party in the late 1970s posed a much more determined threat to the expansion of the federal government than their moderate predecessors. The rise of the conservatives was in part fueled by a growing backlash against the earlier massive expansion of federal programs and regulation. Even some Democrats had second thoughts about some of the new government programs.[24]

The principal goal of the new conservatives was to dismantle the New Deal–Great Society approach to governing. This involved depriving the federal government of the means to expand by cutting taxes as much as possible and by eliminating as many federal programs as possible. President Reagan accomplished the first objective; his massive income tax cuts increased the budget deficit so much that any expansion of federal programs (except for defense) has been almost unthinkable since then. Eliminating programs turned out to be much more difficult, since most were well entrenched, with vocal constituencies and often widespread popular support. In the face of this opposition, Reagan tried an alternative strategy. In 1982 he proposed a radical form of New Federalism: the transfer of over forty federal grant programs

---

22   John Kincaid, "The New Coercive Federalism: Places versus Persons," in Franz Gress et al., eds., *The American Federal System: Federal Balance in Comparative Perspective* (Peter Lang, 1994).

23   Michael D. Reagan, *The New Federalism* (Oxford University Press, 1972), 163–164.

24   For the views of a disillusioned Democrat on what went wrong with the Great Society program, see Daniel Patrick Moynihan, *Maximum Feasible Misunderstanding: Community Action in the War on Poverty* (Free Press, 1969).

from Washington to the states, along with a share of federal excise taxes.[25] The proposal went nowhere in Congress.

The conservatives' goal was to reduce government at all levels, not to reform the federal system, and their posture toward the states remained coercive. Thus, Washington continued to enforce its own policies on the states by attaching a multitude of conditions to federal grants, by imposing mandates on state and local government, and by continuing to preempt state regulatory authority in new areas. Kincaid notes that President Reagan "signed more preemption laws than any president in U.S. history."[26] The Republicans were also pursuing a national social agenda. Typical of how the Congress imposed its policy in areas of state jurisdiction was the 1985 law reducing highway funds to the states by 5 percent unless they raised their minimum drinking age to twenty-one.

The Supreme Court continued to sanction broad federal powers. Thus, the law to induce the states to raise the minimum drinking age was upheld in *South Dakota v. Dole* (1987) as a valid exercise of the congressional spending power. The Court agreed that Congress could achieve a national minimum age for drinking indirectly through coercive state action, although it did not have the jurisdiction to legislate on the matter directly. The Court's most important statement on the working of the federal system came in *Garcia v. San Antonio Metropolitan Transit Authority* (1985). One of the pillars of dual federalism had been that neither level of government had the power to tax or regulate the other. One of the manifestations of coercive federalism has been the unilateral erosion of state tax immunity and the progressive extension of federal regulation of state employees. In *Garcia* the Court narrowly upheld federal regulation of the hours and wages of municipal transport workers, arguing that there was no way in principle to limit federal authority. The only protection the states have against federal intrusion, the majority decided, lies in the political process in Washington, in which the states have a great deal of influence through their elected representatives.

Only in the 1990s did signs of a lessening of federal dominance began to appear. One reason was that the initiative in policy innovation had shifted to the states. Conservative presidents and the constraints imposed by the budget deficit had produced few new federal programs. State governments were being forced to find innovative ways to manage with sharply reduced federal funds. In addition, President Clinton, who had previously been governor of Arkansas for ten years and a leader among the governors, was more sensitive to the states' perspective than any of his predecessors. While the Democrats remained committed to maintaining federal standards, Clinton moved toward a more "permissive" federalism that allowed the states more room to experiment in how they used federal funds.

---

25   The Nixon and Reagan proposals for a "New Federalism" are both examined in Conlan, *New Federalism.*

26   Kincaid, "The New Coercive Federalism," 46.

The trend toward decentralization was reinforced by the Republican capture of Congress in 1994. The conservatives were intent on scrapping as much federal regulation as possible. While their assault on regulation failed in most areas, a compromise overhaul of welfare legislation left much more responsibility with the states and retained only a few of the federal standards. The Congress also passed a bill restricting its power to impose "unfunded mandates" on the states—that is, to impose new obligations without providing the funds to carry them out. One example of a recent unfunded mandate is the "motor-voter" law (1994), which requires the states to register voters at state licensing and welfare offices.

In 1995 the Supreme Court for the first time in many years placed a limit on the extension of federal authority. In *U.S. v. Lopez* a bare majority struck down as beyond federal jurisdiction a 1990 federal law prohibiting the carrying of guns in school zones. The carrying of guns, the Court argued, was unrelated to the congressional power to regulate interstate commerce.

Federalism in Canada since the 1930s

The Canadian federation faced the same centralizing pressures as the United States, and a similar pattern of cooperative federalism developed under federal leadership. Although the federal government did not have the unrestricted powers to legislate of the U.S. government after 1937, questions of jurisdiction were largely bypassed. There were federal-provincial agreements to amend the Constitution in 1940 to give the federal government jurisdiction over unemployment insurance and in 1951 to allow the federal government to legislate in the area of pensions. Most programs, however, consisted of conditional federal grants to the provinces to administer national policies.

Garth Stevenson argues that the era of cooperative federalism came to an end in 1967 when the federal government used its fiscal muscle to force the (mostly) reluctant provinces into the national Medicare program.[27] It was at this point that Canadian federalism developed in a quite different direction from the American kind. In Canada in the 1970s there was strong provincial resistance to federal attempts at coercion. Policy discussions and fiscal negotiations between the two levels of government became much more contentious, requiring extended negotiations between federal and provincial ministers and first ministers. A key factor in this shift toward a pattern of "executive federalism" was the radical change in the constitutional climate. The period of cooperative federalism had been one of "constitutional conservatism." The constitutional calm was shattered by the massive changes taking place within Quebec society.

---

27   Stevenson, *Unfulfilled Union*, 165.

Quebec emerged from the Quiet Revolution of the 1960s a very different place
from the traditionalist Catholic province whose place in Canada had always been
secured by the processes of elite accommodation between Ottawa and Quebec City.
The new, secular Quebec society looked to the provincial government as the guarantor of the survival of the French language and culture. As a result, Quebec governments demanded both increased powers in some areas and greater constitutional protection for Quebec as a "distinct society" within Canada. The new assertiveness in
Quebec clashed with trends in the rest of Canada, which increasingly viewed itself as
a multicultural rather than a bicultural nation. While Quebec's push for increased
provincial powers was echoed in the wealthier provinces, its demands for what was
seen as special status within Confederation were greeted with hostility, especially in
the West, where the equality of the provinces had become an article of faith.

Behind Quebec's demands lay the ultimate federal issue—the right of secession, a
threat made explicit after the sovereigntist Parti Québécois first took power in 1976.
Quebec's demands set off an almost continuous process of federal-provincial negotiations in the vain search for a new constitutional settlement that would both stave off
Quebec separation and satisfy the demands of the western provinces for equality.

The Diefenbaker government, with its 1960 Bill of Rights, and the Trudeau government of the 1970s, with its policy of national bilingualism and the constitutionally
entrenched Charter of Rights and Freedoms in 1982, both attempted to downplay the
regional divisions by emphasizing individual over group rights. The Mulroney government in the 1980s undertook two arduous rounds of federal-provincial negotiations to
reach a new constitutional accommodation, but both the Meech Lake Accord of 1987
and the Charlottetown Agreement of 1992 collapsed at the last minute for lack of broad
popular support. So far, all attempts to reach a new national settlement have failed.

Part of the explanation for the strikingly different development of the American
and Canadian federal systems in the past thirty years has to do with the strength of
the intrastate mechanisms—the ways that policy-making at the federal level accom-
modates regional interests.

INTRASTATE FEDERALISM IN THE UNITED STATES

In the American political system there are strong intrastate mechanisms that enable
regional interests to be negotiated and accommodated as federal policy is shaped in
Washington. The effectiveness of the intrastate process has minimized the need for
interstate negotiations between the two levels of government.

In the twentieth century the American federation has become progressively more
centralized and the federal government has come to dominate many policy areas that
were previously under state jurisdiction. This shift in power to Washington has produced a very different design from that envisaged by the framers of the Constitution.

It is not difficult to explain the shifting of power to the national level. Samuel Beer argues that this centralization was driven not by theory but by policy concerns, "from the perception widely shared ... that certain problems were both urgent and national and for that reason required the exercise of new forms of power."[28] What is more difficult to explain is why such a high degree of policy centralization was politically acceptable in a country with such a long history of resistance to control from Washington. A major factor was the strength of the intrastate mechanisms in the American federal system.

The strength of the intrastate mechanisms flows from the fragmentation of power in the American system of government. The U.S. Constitution established a fragmentation of power at the center by separating the executive branch and the two houses of the legislative branch and then requiring them to share power. There are in addition strong decentralizing forces within the executive branch (see Chapter 8) and in Congress (see Chapter 5). For most of the twentieth century, power in Congress was effectively decentralized to committees and committee chairs. Since the 1970s a great deal of legislative power has flowed further down to the subcommittees and to individual members. For a variety of reasons, the principal unifying force in the Congress, party loyalty, has remained limited.

In such a decentralized form of government with a relatively weak party system, there is plenty of room for various interests—prominent among them regional and local interests—to wield considerable influence. Members of Congress have always seen their primary task as representing constituency interests. The House of Representatives was from the beginning viewed as a body dominated by purely local concerns. While the Senate has always been a more nationally oriented body, its relaxed rules allow maximum scope for senators to pursue their home-state interests. In Congress it is generally accepted that constituency interests come first for the members, and party loyalty second.

The decentralization of power within both houses of Congress, together with the reliance on seniority for distributing powerful positions, has generally meant that power is widely distributed geographically and that members from small states are often in a position to wield considerable power. Probably the most powerful Democrat in the Senate for the past twenty years has been Robert Byrd from the small, poor state of West Virginia. Even the party leadership positions that are filled by election by the party caucus usually result in a dispersal of power geographically. For example, the last three Democratic leaders in the Senate have come from West Virginia, Maine, and South Dakota, and the last three Republican leaders from Tennessee, Kansas, and Mississippi.

Because power is so decentralized in Washington, the basic mode of operation is bargaining. Majorities must be built at every stage of the legislative process. Party

---

28   Beer, "Introduction," xxi.

loyalty is rarely sufficient to ensure a majority. In the course of building majority support, legislation must be modified and adjusted to bring more members on board, and
it is in the course of building these majorities that regional and state interests are usually accommodated. Sometimes this is done by adjusting distribution formulas, sometimes by allowing individual members to write specific local projects into the bill.

Support for local interests is not the same as sensitivity to the federal structure and
support for state governments. Up until the 1960s, support for state government was
strong in Congress. Many members had previously served as governors or state legislators, and strong local party organizations had their representatives in Congress. It
was against this political background that dual federalism evolved into cooperative
federalism. The federal balance shifted sharply in the 1960s as the remaining
party organizations weakened and state and local government fell into disrepute:
"Federalism became associated with states' rights, and states' rights became associated with racism."[29] In addition, as the party organizations declined there were fewer
members of Congress who had served a political apprenticeship in state or local government. It was against this changed political background that cooperative federalism
became coercive federalism. Only in the 1990s have state governments recaptured a
reputation for effective government and policy innovation.

The operation of effective intrastate mechanisms in Washington has meant that
national goals can be pursued while genuine regional differences are accommodated
and benefits are spread across the country in a broadly equitable manner. These
intrastate mechanisms have also kept the amount of formal interstate bargaining
between governments to a minimum. Representatives of state and local governments
meet regularly in organizations such as the National Governors Conference and the
United States Conference of Mayors, but these organizations operate essentially as
pressure groups attempting to wield influence within the intrastate system in
Washington. The American intrastate model has managed to reconcile regional differences with national goals without bringing about the kind of radical institutional
decentralization that now exists in Canada.

Intrastate Federalism in Canada

Most students of Canadian federalism agree that the decentralization of Canadian
federalism since the 1960s has been exacerbated by the erosion of intrastate mechanisms at the federal level. From the beginning the Canadian federal system regulated
itself through a combination of interstate (fiscal negotiations between governments)
and intrastate processes. In Canada the main intrastate mechanism was not the legislature, as in the United States, but the political party. The kind of intrastate

---

29   Kincaid, "The New Coercive Federalism in Perspective," 37.

bargaining that operates in Washington is precluded in Canada by the requirements of the parliamentary system, in which governments are created and sustained in office through strict party discipline. For Canadian MPs, provincial and local interests have always been overridden by the requirements of party loyalty.

The one intrastate mechanism built into the Canadian Constitution was the principle of equal representation of the regions in the Senate. But the Senate's ability to represent regional interests in Ottawa is weakened by two things: all senators are appointed by the prime minister, and those appointed are almost always party loyalists.

At the time of Confederation there was also an understanding that the regions would be equitably represented in the federal Cabinet, and this convention has been followed. The representation of each province (if possible) has remained a fundamental principle of Canadian Cabinet-making. For Cabinet ministers, however, there remains a conflict between representing regional interests and the overriding requirement of Cabinet and party solidarity. The possibility of regional differences being accommodated by intrastate mechanisms therefore depends on how the party system functions.

For much of Canadian history, regional pressures were managed within the dominant party, which operated as the principal intrastate regulator of the federal system. In the first party system from 1967 to 1917,[30] the dominant party—first the Conservatives under Sir John A. Macdonald, then the Liberals under Sir Wilfrid Laurier—played the leading role in nation building by building a national party organization. "For Macdonald, and then Laurier, party-building was simply the necessary political dimension of state-building."[31] The local party sent its representative to Ottawa, and local interests were satisfied by the distribution of federal patronage—jobs and grants—which was usually managed by the prime minister himself. The second party system, from 1921 to 1957, was dominated by the Liberal prime minister William Lyon Mackenzie King. King perfected the art of brokering interests and regional demands through party management. King relied on having strong regional ministers in his Cabinet, though overall party strategy remained in his own hands.

The brokerage style of party management began to break down in the 1950s as styles of politics changed. Conservative prime minister John Diefenbaker and his Liberal successors, Lester Pearson and Pierre Trudeau, all spoke in terms of national citizenship and directed their appeal to the individual voters. The shift toward political individualism was symbolized by Diefenbaker's 1960 Bill of Rights and even more

---

30   The discussion of the Canadian party system is based on David E. Smith, "Party Government in Canada," and R.K. Carty, "Three Canadian Party Systems," in R.K. Carty, ed., *Canadian Political Party Systems: A Reader* (Broadview Press, 1992).

31   Carty, "Three Canadian Party Systems," 564.

by Trudeau's entrenchment of the Charter of Rights and Freedoms in the Constitution in 1982. As regional tensions increased, the integrative capacity of the national parties was further weakened as the provincial wings of the Liberal and Progressive Conservative parties established separate organizations.

Concern about the decentralization of the federal system since the 1960s, and about the possibility that Quebec may secede, has led to a search for improved intrastate mechanisms. Alan Cairns has pointed out how the first-past-the-post electoral system has tended to polarize Canadians by consistently underrepresenting each province's political minority in the House of Commons.[32] Many people have called for a loosening of party discipline in the House of Commons to allow for the representation of local interests. At present, because of the demands of party discipline, the regional advocacy that does take place within the Cabinet and party caucuses in Ottawa is done behind closed doors.[33] This has left the provincial governments as the most vocal and seemingly most effective representatives of regional interests.

The most attention, however, has been devoted to various proposals for reviving the Senate as the body where regional interests are represented in Ottawa. The western provinces, for example, have supported an American-style "Triple E" Senate—a Senate that would be *elected* and *effective* and in which the provinces would have *equal representation*. Whatever the utility of the different proposals, the defeat of the Meech Lake and Charlottetown intergovernmental agreements has made the prospect of any significant change in the federal structure through constitutional amendment remote at present. It seems clear that the decentralizing forces in Canadian federalism are now too strong to be reversed by revamped intrastate processes in federal politics, even if it were possible to create them.[34]

THE NATIONAL IDEA IN THE UNITED STATES AND CANADA

The United States has survived and become increasingly centralized politically mainly because of the strength of "the national idea" in that country, something which Canada lacks. Since its inception the United States has been held together by the belief that it was founded as one nation united by a common set of values and a common national vision. The alternative, state compact theory nearly tore the nation apart when the southern states pushed it to its logical conclusion and seceded over the issue of slavery. National disintegration was prevented when the rest of the country rallied

---

32   Alan C. Cairns, "The Electoral System and the Party System in Canada, 1921–1965" *Canadian Journal of Political Science* 1 (1968), 55–80.
33   Smiley and Watts, *Intrastate Federalism in Canada*, 30.
34   Smiley and Watts, *Intrastate Federalism in Canada*, 26.

reluctantly behind the weak federal government and fought to save the Union. In this regard, Samuel Beer cites "the immense formative influence of the Civil War on the American political mind" in strengthening the emotional commitment to the idea of one nation.[35]

In the twentieth century the federal government gradually became the main exponent of the national idea, and the struggle to define the national vision increasingly took place in Washington. In this context the centralization of the federal system makes sense. In 1972, federalism scholar Michael D. Reagan saw the new centralized federalism as fulfilling the national idea: "It should be clear at once that this is not federalism at all in the classic conception. Federalism in that sense is dead. We have at last become one nation, indivisible ..."[36]

In this respect, the history of Canada is strikingly different from that of the United States. It is marked by "the absence of a clear and specific national faith which all Canadians could profess."[37] Canada has always lacked a national idea uniting French and English Canada. The different attempts to override or obscure that fact— Macdonald's centralized constitution, the growth of the welfare state, and Trudeau's attempts to create a bilingual nation focused on individual rights—have all in the end failed to contain the profound division at the heart of Canada. In recent years the original problem has been complicated by the growth of multiculturalism and the growing strength and assertiveness of the western provinces, particularly British Columbia and Alberta.

Canada finds itself in the 1990s caught between competing visions: the traditional French-Canadian conception, largely shared by Ontario, of Canada as a compact between two nations, French and English; the alternative conception, an elaboration of the original provincial rights position, of Canada as a decentralized federation of equal provinces; and the newer vision held by Quebec sovereigntists of an association between two sovereign nations, Quebec and the rest of Canada. The lack of a clear national identity and American-style national idea does not mean that the Canadian federation is doomed to fall apart. The linkages of habit and emotion that have held the country together are much stronger than they often appear. What is beyond Canada's reach is the kind of centralized federation that Sir John A. Macdonald established and which can now be found south of the border.

---

35   Beer, *To Make A Nation*, viii–ix.
36   Reagan, *The New Federalism*, 164.
37   Allan Smith, "Metaphor and Nationality in North America," *Canadian Historical Review* LI (1970), 254.

CHAPTER 5

CONGRESSIONAL ORGANIZATION

The Congress sits at the heart of the complicated, even chaotic, policy-making process that is the sole industry in Washington, D.C. It occupies a sprawling, domed building on Capitol Hill that overlooks both the White House and the office buildings that house the offices of interest groups and government departments. In a more metaphysical sense, the Congress is completely surrounded by a multitude of people, interests, and institutions, all of them competing to influence its decisions.

As a legislative body, the Congress operates quite differently from the Canadian House of Commons: individual members are much more powerful; party discipline is much weaker; and the decision-making processes are much more complex and more open to outside influences. And these are only some of the more important differences. To understand how the Congress works, one must know how it is organized and how power is distributed within it. The next chapter looks at the behavior of the members and at how their goals influence the legislation that Congress passes.

CONGRESS IN THE CONSTITUTIONAL SYSTEM

The first Article of the Constitution establishes as the legislative branch of government a Congress composed of two houses: the House of Representatives and the Senate. The Congress was placed first in the Constitution because it was composed of the people's representatives. Throughout the struggle against the British, the popular-ly elected legislatures had been the focal point of the colonists' fight with the British governors and their appointed executive councils. This is why the Congress was seen as the cornerstone of republican government.

In setting up two legislative houses, the framers were following the generally accepted wisdom that legislation should be written in a popular "lower" house and reviewed in a second chamber somewhat removed from popular passions. In Britain, the landed aristocracy filled the upper house of Parliament, the House of Lords. In America, a new and more egalitarian society, representation explicitly based on class was unthinkable for most of the framers. Instead, senators were to be indirectly elect-ed by the state legislatures. Members of the House of Representatives were elected to two-year terms to emphasize their accountability to the people, while senators were elected to six-year terms that ensured more distance from popular pressures. One-third of the Senate is elected every two years.

Representation in Congress

At the Constitutional Convention of 1787, the question of how representation in Congress was to be distributed among the states was one of the main points of con-tention between the larger and smaller states. Representation by population in the lower house inevitably gave the larger states more power. To balance this, the smaller states held out for equal representation in the Senate. This demand led to some of the bitterest arguments at the convention; in the end, the larger states were unwilling to risk the breakup of the convention, and agreed grudgingly to equal representation for the states, regardless of population. The agreement was for two senators per state; this was for fear that a single senator would too easily become a mere delegate of the state legislature.[1]

Equal representation of the states in the Senate meant that an undemocratic princi-ple was built into the constitutional system. The small states even insisted on a clause (at the end of Article 5) forbidding the amendment of this part of the Constitution (which means that it would take two amendments to change the basis of Senate repre-sentation). At the time the largest state, Virginia, had nearly twelve times the popula-tion of the smallest state, Delaware. The growth of the United States has magnified the democratic discrepancy. The effect of equal representation today is that the smallest state in population, Wyoming, has two senators for less than half a million people, while California, the largest state, has two senators for over thirty million people.

---

1   On the debates on congressional representation in the Constitutional Convention, see William
     Lee Miller, *The Business of May Next: James Madison and the Founding* (University of
     Virginia Press, 1992), 67–77.

State	Number of House Seats After 1990 Census	Gains/Losses 1950–1990	Gains/Losses 2000 Census*	
California	52	+22	+3	
Florida	23	+15	+1	
Texas	30	+8	+2	
Arizona	6	+4	+1	
New York	31	-12	-2	
Pennsylvania	21	-9	-2	
Illinois	20	-5	-1	
Ohio	19	-4	-1	
Massachussets	10	-4	-1	
Iowa	5	-3	—	
West Virginia	3	-3	—	

Table 5.1

States with biggest gains (+) and losses (-) in House seats, 1950–1990.

*Congressional Research Service projections based on the Bureau of the Census 1994 population projection.
Source: U.S. Bureau of the Census, *Statistical Abstract of the United States 1993.*

The first Senate had twenty-six members representing the original thirteen states. It grew gradually with the admission of new states, and reached its present size of 100 senators in 1958 when Alaska and Hawaii were admitted to the Union. The original House of Representatives had sixty-five members apportioned between the states according to their population, with every state guaranteed at least one member. The Constitution provides for an official census at the start of every decade, after which House seats are redistributed between the states. The size of the House grew until it reached 435 members after the 1910 census; at that point it was agreed not to let it expand any further.

The freezing of the size of the house has meant that now after each census those states whose populations have grown more slowly than the national average lose seats in the House to those states which have grown faster than the average. In the last forty years this has meant a gradual shift of seats, and therefore power, from the industrial states of the Northeast and Midwest (particularly New York and Pennsylvania) toward the fast-growing states of the Sunbelt in the South and Southwest (especially California, Florida, and Texas).

The Powers of the House and the Senate

The House and the Senate have equal legislative power in that legislation must pass both houses. Each house has some unique powers. The House of Representatives has the power to impeach (indict) executive or judicial officers and send them for trial to the Senate. In line with the ancient parliamentary principle that all government expenditures and taxes must be approved by the representatives of the people, the House must also initiate all financial legislation.

A number of important checking powers over the executive were given to the Senate. All treaties negotiated by the president must be approved by a two-thirds majority of the Senate. The Senate must confirm all of the president's high-level executive and judicial nominations, and it is responsible for trying cases of impeachment. For all its extra constitutional powers, during the first twenty years of its existence the Senate did not assert itself, in deference to public fears that it might become an "aristocratic" body like the House of Lords. It played a subordinate role to the House, with a high membership turnover and low public visibility. Gradually, however, the innate advantages of the Senate—its additional powers, its smaller size, its longer terms, and especially its superior ability to speak to national issues (while the House was becoming more local in its concerns)—led to its emergence as the more important and powerful of the two houses.[2] Since then the Senate has generally been considered a more powerful and prestigious body than the House of Representatives. In every election, several representatives give up their seats in the House to run for the Senate. No senator would dream of giving up his or her seat to run for the House.

The United States is in fact unique among democratic systems in having an upper legislative house that is more powerful than the lower house. It seems unlikely, however, that the Senate could have remained so powerful in the twentieth century if the original indirect method of election by state legislatures had not been changed to popular election by the 17th Amendment of 1913. In this century, popular election has been considered the only acceptable basis for exercising political power in a democracy. In Britain, for example, the once powerful but hereditary House of Lords was made subordinate to the House of Commons by the Parliament Act of 1911. In Canada, the Senate has always lacked popular legitimacy because senators are appointed by the federal government on the basis of party patronage. By reluctantly responding to overwhelming public demand and passing the 17th Amendment, the U.S. Senate in fact retained its status as the more powerful house by renewing its popular legitimacy.

The Separation of Institutions

The Congress may look familiar to Canadians, but it operates very differently from the legislative branch in a parliamentary system, mainly because of the constitutional

---

2   Elaine K. Swift, "Reconstitutive Change in the U.S. Congress: The Early Senate, 1789–1841," in John R. Hibbings and John G. Peters eds., *The Changing World of the U.S. Senate* (IGS Press, 1990).

separation of institutions in the United States. The president, who is the chief executive, is elected separately from the Congress. In addition, Article I, Section 6, of the
Constitution forbids members of Congress from holding any executive office. In sev-
enteenth-century England one way that the king attempted to control Parliament was
by bribing members with salaried executive appointments. So to preserve the independence of Parliament, the principle of the complete separation of legislative and
executive bodies was adopted by reformers. Later, as the Cabinet system evolved in
Britain, government ministers were made the only exceptions to this general rule. In
adopting the British-style parliamentary system, Canada followed this practice.

For the framers of the U.S. Constitution, the principle of separation was the key to
establishing a free government. This is why they prohibited any joint membership
between the legislative and executive branches, and had the branches elected for different terms by different methods, and guaranteed the president's salary against congressional interference. The framers went further: in order to ensure an active opposition between the branches, they gave each branch active checking powers over the
others. Thus, the Senate can check the president's foreign policy and appointive powers, while the president's veto over legislation gives him some influence in the legislative process.

Because of this separation of institutions, the Congress operates in a very different
manner than Canada's parliamentary system in two fundamental respects: Congress
does not determine the composition and length of term of the executive; and the
executive does not control the legislative process in Congress.

In the Canadian system the leader of the party (or coalition of parties) that has a
majority of seats in the House of Commons becomes the prime minister. He or she
appoints the other government ministers from the House and Senate and remains in
office as long as he remains leader of his party, and as long as his party (or coalition)
continues to have a majority in the House for its major policies. In the United States,
the president is elected separately from the Congress. He appoints the rest of the government (subject to Senate confirmation, which is almost always given) and will remain
in office for his four-year term regardless of whether his party has a majority in Congress, and regardless of whether Congress passes or defeats his legislative proposals.

The fact that the president and the Congress are elected independently makes it
possible for the executive branch to be in the hands of one party and for the Congress
to be controlled by the other—a situation that cannot arise in Canada. Indeed, for
most of the last twenty-five years the United States has had "divided government,"
with the Republicans generally in control of the White House and the executive
branch, and the Democrats usually controlling the Congress. (Since 1995 the reverse
has been true.)

In Canada the Cabinet is composed of the leaders of the majority party. Because
party discipline is almost complete, the government is able to control the legislative
process and get its legislation passed. Government bills dominate the legislative

agenda. The government largely controls the timetable of the House of Commons, and its bills are passed in the form in which the government presents them. Thus, in Canada the House does not legislate; rather, it provides a forum for debating legislation shaped within the executive branch.

In the United States the president and his Cabinet are not members of the Congress and are not in a position to control its operations, even when the president and the congressional majority are from the same party. The Congress remains genuinely independent of the executive and must control its own legislative process. Legislation is shaped within the congressional process. The president must try to persuade Congress to pass the legislation he wants in something close to the form in which he wants it—always a difficult task.

THE ORGANIZING STRUCTURES OF CONGRESS

Since the executive cannot control the legislative process, the Congress must organize itself in order to manage its principal tasks, which are these: to approve the federal budget, which must be passed every year if the government is to continue to operate; to consider and pass legislation; and to oversee the operations of the executive branch in executing the laws that Congress has passed.

Two distinct structures have evolved over time in the Congress to enable it to accomplish its tasks: the *standing committee system* and the *party leadership structure*. The interaction between these two structures defines the legislative process. The House of Representatives and the Senate operate in basically the same way. The main differences between them are a function of size. The House, being a large body of 435 members, is more institutionalized and more controlled by rules. The Senate, with only 100 members, prides itself on being more informal and on operating more by "gentlemen's agreements." Specific differences between their procedures will be pointed out in the course of the following discussion.

The Committee System

In the Canadian House of Commons, a bill is first approved in principle by the whole House before being sent to a standing committee for detailed consideration. Since the government has a majority on the committee, it remains in control of the process. The only changes made in committee are those acceptable to the government. The legislation is then returned to the whole House for final passage.

In the Congress the committees are at the center of the legislative process. Early in their history both houses found it useful to refer bills and legislative proposals first of

House Committees	Senate Committees	
Agriculture	Agriculture, Nutrition, Forestry	*Table 5.2*
Appropriations	Appropriations	
Banking, Financial Services	Banking, Housing, Urban Affairs	*House and Senate*
Budget	Budget	*Committees in the*
Commerce	Commerce, Science, Transportation	*104th Congress*
Economic and Educational Opportunities	Labor and Human Resources	*(1995–97).*
Government Reform, Oversight	Governmental Affairs	
House Oversight	Rules and Administration	
International Relations	Foreign Relations	
Judiciary	Judiciary	
National Security	Armed Services	
Resources	Energy and Natural Resources	
Rules		
Science		
Select Intelligence	Select Intelligence	
Small Business	Small Business	
Standards of Official Conduct	Select Ethics	
Transportation, Infrastructure		
Veterans' Affairs	Veterans' Affairs	
Ways and Means	Finance	
	Environment and Public Works	
	Indian Affairs	

Source: *Congressional Quarterly, Weekly Report*, Supplement March 25, 1995.

all to a specialized standing committee for examination and recommendation to the whole house. Standing committees continue in existence from one Congress to the next and have the power to recommend legislation. For the most part, committees operate independently of the party leadership. The number of committees has a tendency to expand, and periodically there have been reorganizations of the committee structure. When the Republicans took control of the House in 1995, they reduced the number of standing committees by three and cut the number of subcommittees more heavily. The House now has 20 standing committees with a total of 86 subcommittees. The Senate currently has 19 standing committees with 78 subcommittees.

Table 5.2 attempts to list opposite each other the committees in each house with equivalent jurisdictions. In some cases, such as the two Budget or Select Intelligence Committees, and the House Ways and Means Committee and the Senate Finance Committee, jurisdictions match exactly. In other cases the two houses divide up their business differently. Thus, environmental questions that are handled in the Senate by the Environment and Public Works Committee are split in the House between the

Resources and Transportation and Infrastructure Committees. In the Senate, aboriginal questions go to a separate standing committee (Indian Affairs); in the House, the same questions are dealt with by a subcommittee of the Resources Committee.

The party that has a majority of seats controls the House in the sense that it has a majority on, and provides the chairs of, each committee and subcommittee. Members are allocated to committees by their party. In the House each member is on average a member of two committees and four subcommittees. In the Senate, which is much smaller than the House but has even more business to cover, each senator is likely to have three committee and six subcommittee positions.

The Party Leadership Structure

Every two years at the beginning of the new Congress, the party leaders are elected by the party caucus (or Republican conference) in each house. In the House of Representatives, the leader of the majority party is elected Speaker of the House. In Canada's House of Commons, the Speaker is a neutral presiding officer and carefully avoids partisan connections after being elected to the chair. In the House of Representatives, the Speaker combines the presiding function with leadership of the majority party.[3] His second in command is the majority leader, who is followed in the party hierarchy by the whip. The leader of the other party is the minority leader, who is followed in the party hierarchy by the minority whip.

Under the authority of each whip are a large number of deputy and assistant whips, whose job it is to channel information back and forth between the members and the party leadership. Each assistant whip is responsible for a small group of members, and collects information on the attitudes and voting intentions of those members regarding legislation coming to the floor. He relays to those same members information from the party leadership (including requests for support for various bills).

In both parties, the leadership group includes the chairman and secretary of the caucus and the chairman of the Congressional Campaign Committee, whose job it is to channel assistance to members of the party at election time. The House Democrats coordinate party decisions through a Steering and Policy Committee, which includes the leadership, the chairmen of several key committees, several members elected by the caucus, and other members nominated by the leadership. The House Republicans have no equivalent committee but include the chairs of their caucus Policy and Research Committees in the leadership.

In the Senate there is no equivalent to the Speaker, since the Constitution gives the presiding role to the Vice President of the United States. Because senators want no executive branch interference in their affairs, the vice president has always been

---

3   See Ronald M. Peters, *The American Speakership: the Office in Historical Perspective* (Johns Hopkins University Press, 1990).

House of Representatives

Republicans

Speaker	Newt Gingrich, Georgia
Majority leader	Dick Armey, Texas
Majority whip	Tom DeLay, Texas
Conference chair	John Boehner, Ohio
Conference vice chair	Susan Molinari, New York
Policy committee chair	Christopher Cox, California

Democrats

Minority leader	Dick Gephardt, Missouri
Minority whip	David Bonior, Michigan
Caucus chair	Vic Fazio, California
Caucus vice chair	Barbara Kennelly, Connecticut
Steering committee co-chair	Steny Hoyer, Maryland

Senate

Republicans

Majority leader	Trent Lott, Mississippi
Majority whip	Don Nickles, Oklahoma
Conference chair	Thad Cochran, Mississippi
Policy committee chair	Larry Craig, Idaho
Conference secretary	Connie Mack, Florida

Democrats

Minority leader/ conference chair	Tom Daschle, South Dakota
Minority whip	Wendell Ford, Kentucky
Conference secretary	Barbara Mikulski, Maryland
Policy committee co-chair	Harry Reid, Nevada

Table 5.3

Republican and Democratic party leaders of the House and Senate, 1995–96 (104th Congress).

Source: Congressional Quarterly, *Weekly Report Supplement,* March 25, 1995; *Weekly Report* June 15, 1996.

restricted to a purely ceremonial role. His only power is that of breaking a tied vote, a situation that arises a few times every year at most. Apart from that difference, the Senate leadership structure is similar to that in the House.

The Legislative Process

In Canada, a bill must receive approval in principle from the whole House before it can be sent to committee for detailed consideration. In Congress a bill is first referred to a standing committee. Each bill that is introduced by a member is automatically sent to the committee that deals with its subject matter. The committee in turn will usually send the bill on to the relevant subcommittee. Thousands of bills are introduced every year, but only a few hundred will be passed. A bill that is not approved by the subcommittee and full committee will go no further. The initial consideration of a bill in committee and subcommittee is therefore the crucial stage of the legislative process.

The legislative process by which a bill becomes a law consists of the following stages, which are the same in the House and the Senate except for stage two (see below). The two houses operate independently of each other. A bill may very well pass in one house but be blocked or defeated in the other. Each Congress is divided into two year-long sessions. Bills carry over from one session to the next but not from one Congress to the next.

1. Committee stage. After it decides to consider a bill, the subcommittee will normally hold public hearings at which interested parties may testify for or against the bill, or for the inclusion of certain provisions in the bill. After the hearings, the subcommittee members meet in closed session to "mark up" the bill—that is, to decide on the details of the bill. Once approved, the bill goes to the full committee, where it may be amended.

Congressional committees are specialized not only in their subject matter but also in their membership, in that members typically serve on the same committees for many years. Committee expertise enhances their authority and their autonomy from the rest of the House. Since the committee stage is the first stage in the legislative process, committees have great power to shape bills and determine their fate.

2. Floor scheduling. In the House, once a bill comes out of committee it goes to the Rules Committee, which schedules bills for consideration by the full House and decides the "rule" under which the bill will be debated on the floor. The rule specifies how long debate on the bill will last (with the time normally divided between supporters and opponents), and whether the bill will be open to amendment or not, and how many—sometimes even *which*—amendments will be debated. Floor debate in the House is always restricted, usually to a few hours. The kind of rule a bill receives—that is, open or closed—may help or hurt its chances of passage.

There is no comparable committee in the Senate, and bills are scheduled for debate on the floor by the majority leadership. Since debate in the Senate is unrestricted, it is not usually possible to place any advance restrictions on amendments, or on the length of debate, except as part of a general agreement between the parties.

3. Floor debate. This is the stage at which the whole house votes the bill up or down. The bill is usually managed on the floor by the chair of the committee from which it came, assisted by the party leadership. Managing a bill involves leading the

debate on the bill and on proposed amendments, if these are allowed by the rule, as well as trying to muster a majority of votes for the bill, with the assistance of the party whips.

In the House the floor debate always has a strict time limit, but in the Senate there is a long tradition of allowing unlimited debate. This gives opponents of a bill an additional weapon, the **filibuster**. If they are not certain they can defeat a bill when it comes to a vote, the bill's opponents can filibuster by holding the floor to keep the debate going, thus preventing a vote from being taken. Under Senate rules the only way to end a filibuster is for sixty senators to vote to close debate, something many senators are reluctant to do, preferring to preserve the tradition of open debate. The smaller states, who are in a stronger position in the Senate than in the House, particularly value the ability to filibuster. In a recent example, the two Nevada senators used the filibuster and other procedural delaying devices to stop passage of a bill creating in their state a temporary depository for nuclear waste from across the United States. Although there were strong majorities in both houses for the bill, the senators were able to publicize the issue through their filibuster and get the president to promise (in an election year) that he would veto the bill.[4]

Since floor time is often scarce at the end of a session, when many bills may be waiting for approval, the filibuster, or even the threat of a filibuster, is a powerful weapon. The objective of those filibustering is usually to force the leadership to compromise with them and agree to changes in the bill or to drop it altogether in order to let other bills come to the floor for a vote. The filibuster used to be a rarely used, last-ditch legislative weapon. The most famous filibusters were the attempts by southern Democrats to block civil rights bills in the 1950s and 1960s. In recent years, however, the filibuster has become a standard method of obstruction, particularly for the minority party. The constant threat of a filibuster means that the effective majority to pass legislation in the Senate is now 60 votes rather than 51.

4. Conference. When bills on the same subject have been passed by both the House and the Senate, the two will almost always contain different provisions. Before a bill can be sent on to the president for his signature, both houses must agree on a common form of the bill. To negotiate the differences between the House and Senate bills, a group of members from each house meet in a Conference Committee. For a new bill to emerge from this committee, a majority of the members from each house on the committee must agree on a compromise. Once a conference bill has been agreed on, it is taken directly to the floor in each house for passage in the new form. Possibly, one house or the other will reject the conference bill because of the changes made in the conference committee. Only after an identical bill has been passed by both houses can it be sent to the president for signature.

---

4 *Congressional Quarterly, Weekly Report*, September 28, 1996, 2751.

5. Presidential signature. Usually, for a bill passed by the Congress to become law it must be signed by the president. Once the Congress sends him a bill, the president has ten days to decide what to do. He has four options:

- He can sign the bill, in which case it becomes law.
- He can do nothing, in which case it becomes law without his signature.
- He can veto it by sending it back with a message stating why he is not willing to sign it. When the president vetoes a bill, Congress can override the veto and make the bill law without his signature, but only if the bill is passed again in both houses by a two-thirds majority instead of the usual simple majority. On average, less than 10 percent of presidential vetoes are overridden.
- If both houses of the Congress adjourn before the ten-day period is up, the president can "pocket veto" the bill by simply doing nothing. This is normally only an option right at the end of a Congress, when a large number of bills are passed in the last few days before adjournment.

The Budget Process

The annual budget process starts when the president's proposed budget, drawn up by the **Office of Management and Budget** (OMB), is sent to Congress at the end of January. Whereas in Canada the budget announced by the Minister of Finance each spring is sure to be passed intact by the House of Commons, in the United States, the president's budget is simply a proposal, to which the Congress reacts in the course of drawing up its own version.

In Congress the expenditure side of the budget is dealt with by the **Appropriations** Committees of each house, and the revenue side by the House Ways and Means Committee and the Senate Finance Committee; while the Budget Committees are concerned with the overall size and shape of the budget. The Congress is advised by the Congressional Budget Office (CBO) on the economic and program implications of alternative budget proposals.

Under procedures adopted in 1974, both houses first need to adopt Budget Resolutions (proposed by their Budget Committees), which set the overall size and the main expenditure and revenue components of the budget. The Appropriations and Revenue Committees then must work within the parameters of the Budget Resolution to adjust spending and revenues to meet the targets. The goal is the adoption of the thirteen appropriations bills to authorize government spending before the start of the next fiscal year on October 1.

Federal expenditures are grouped into thirteen categories, each of which is the responsibility of an appropiations subcommittee. Each subcommittee recommends an appropriations bill, first to the full Appropriations Committee and then to the House for approval. Differences between the bills passed by each house are dealt with in a conference committee in the usual way. Like other bills, the appropriations bills must be signed by the president to become law, or they may be vetoed.

Traditionally, the appropriations subcommittees operate with the autonomy of full committees. They are powerful within each house because they approve expenditures, and most members of Congress are preoccupied with maximizing federal expenditures within their own constituencies. The freedom of operation of the appropriations committees has, however, become more and more limited since the Budget Committees were set up, and especially since cutting expenditures has become a major preoccupation in Washington (as is discussed below).

On the revenue side of the budget there is not the same urgency for action, since most taxes are permanent, until altered, or are authorized for several years, and since there is no constitutional requirement for the budget to be balanced. Efforts in recent years to pass a constitutional amendment that would require Congress to balance the federal budget have been narrowly defeated in Congress. The budget deficit is covered annually by new government borrowing that increases the national debt. Congress sets a "ceiling" on the national debt, and periodically the debt ceiling has to be raised—another piece of legislation that must be passed so that government does not grind to a halt.

Most pieces of legislation take several years to work their way to final passage. The appropriations bills, however, must be passed by Congress every year. If any of the appropriations bills are not passed by the beginning of the next financial year, October 1, Congress must pass a short-term Continuing Resolution that continues expenditures in that category at the previous year's levels. Otherwise the money to pay for the activities will run out and departments will shut down. This is exactly what happened twice in the winter of 1995–96 when President Clinton and the Republican Congress deadlocked over several of the appropriations bills.

❧ The Struggle for Control over the Budget

Until early in the twentieth century, there was no federal budget that brought together federal government expenditures and revenues. Federal expenditures were limited, and were more than covered by revenues, which came mainly from tariffs. Government expenditures were handled on an individual basis by the Appropriations Committees in Congress. With the development of a national economy and increasing pressure for action by the federal government, federal expenditures rose rapidly (this was also partly a result of World War I), and a federal income tax was made permanent. One of the goals of the modernization drive by the Progressives was to create a coherent budget process for the federal government. Finally, in 1921 Congress established the Bureau of the Budget in the executive branch; this office was to be responsible each year for drawing up and presenting an executive budget to Congress.

After the Bureau of the Budget was created, the main influence over government expenditures shifted away from Congress toward the executive branch. The president sent his budget, prepared by the bureau, to the Congress for approval every year. The appropriations subcommittees then examined the particular budget requests from the executive departments. They increased some requests, cut others, and made sure that items of particular interest to themselves were included. The effect was to vary the president's proposals only at the margins.

The authority of the executive branch over budget policy was further increased in the 1940s, when it came to be recognized (thanks partly to Keynesian economic theorists) that federal expenditures and budget deficits or surpluses had a strong impact on the level of economic activity. Congress, with its appropriations process divided among almost autonomous appropriations subcommittees that focused politically on particular expenditures, had no mechanism for focusing on the budget as a whole or for preparing an overall budgetary and economic strategy to challenge that of the executive branch.

Finally, in 1974, as part of a more general reform of congressional processes, Congress established the Congressional Budget Office (CBO), as well as a Budget Committee in each house. The job of the CBO is to provide the Congress with analyses of the economic implications of budgetary proposals that are independent of the Office of Management and Budget (OMB), which is the successor to the Bureau of the Budget. The creation of the Budget Committees, which had a mandate to shape the overall budget, set up an ongoing power struggle in both houses with the traditionally powerful Appropriations Committees, which jealously controlled the details of expenditures. This is why the House Budget Committee was composed differently from other committees, with representation from the appropriations and tax committees and a time limit on membership. All of this was intended to prevent the Budget Committee from developing the expertise to challenge the other committees.

But the main political struggles over the budget are still between the Congress as a whole and the president. The changes in the congressional process brought about a greater balance of expertise in the ongoing political struggles between the branches over the budget. However, the president's budgetary priorities and his political agenda are almost always different from those of members of Congress, who are always concerned about the political impact of budget decisions in their districts.

The election of President Reagan in 1980 began a new era in which the annual fight over the federal budget became the centerpiece of an ideological struggle between conservative Republicans, who wished to eliminate many federal programs, and liberal Democrats, who wished to maintain those programs. In 1981 Reagan persuaded Congress, including the Democrat-controlled House of Representatives, to cut income taxes substantially, on the "supply side" theory that cutting taxes would stimulate economic activity so much that government revenues would actually increase.[5] Reagan also increased defense spending considerably, but his efforts to cut domestic expenditures were resisted by most Democrats as well as by many Republicans in Congress. When the increased revenues failed to materialize, the net result was a ballooning of the annual federal deficit and a massive annual increase in the national debt.

By the mid–1980s many in Washington shared the conviction that the deficit had to be brought under control. This overriding concern had the effect in Congress of increasing the power of the Budget Committees at the expense of the Appropriations and Revenue Committees. The Budget Resolutions were used to instruct the other committees as to how much to increase revenue, and how much and even where to cut expenditures. Even so, it was difficult to make much impact on the deficit, since cutting expenditures was politically unpopular and raising taxes even more so. As a result, there was a search for long-term package deals to "force" Congress to reduce the deficit.

The first of these was the Gramm-Rudman Act of 1985, which attempted to bring about automatic reductions in expenditures if reduced deficit targets were not met. So many exceptions had to be included in the bill to secure its passage that its effect on the deficit was limited. In 1990, with the Budget Enforcement Act, President Bush and the Democratic Congress reached an agreement to both reduce expenditures and raise taxes over five years. Most importantly, the agreement included the pay-as-you-go principle that any new expenditure proposals had to be accompanied by a matching proposal to pay for them, either by reducing other expenditures or by raising revenues. But the budget battles of the 1980s, which had led to several very brief government shut-downs, were nothing compared to the monumental struggle over budget-balancing strategies between President Clinton and the newly Republican Congress in 1995–96.

THE DISTRIBUTION OF POWER IN CONGRESS

A description of how Congress organizes itself does not tell us where the power lies in the legislative process. For example, it does not tell us how much control, if any, the party leaders have over the committees, or how much influence the president, as the national leader of his party, has over Congress in spite of the constitutional separation of institutions. In historical terms, there has been no fixed answer to the question of where the power lies. Congress has operated very differently at different times.

5   On Reagan's outmaneuvering of the majority Democrats in the House of Representatives over the 1981 budget, see Daniel J. Palazzolo, *The Speaker and the Budget: Leadership in the Post–Reform House of Representatives* (University of Pittsburgh Press, 1992), 90–127.

There have been periods when power was highly centralized, and others when it was radically dispersed. There have been periods when a president was the legislative leader, and many more when his influence on Congress was minimal. To discover where the power lies, we must examine three further aspects of Congress:

- How decisions about the composition of committees are made.
- How the party leaders in Congress perform their roles.
- The extent of party discipline in Congress.

Power in Committees

The congressional committees and subcommittees play the key role in shaping legislation. For individual members of Congress, committee positions are the main opportunity to exercise legislative power—to have some impact on what happens in Washington. Some committees are more powerful than others. Some committees are of particular interest to members from certain types of districts or certain regions of the country. Who goes on which committee, how long a member stays on a committee, and who becomes chair of a subcommittee or of the full committee are all extremely important questions for the members of Congress. Whoever makes or influences these decisions is bound to wield a great deal of power in the Congress. Locating where these key decisions are made is one way of locating the real power center in Congress. What follows is a brief survey of the three different kinds of power structure that have existed in Congress in this century: centralized party leadership, automatic seniority, and modified seniority.

Centralized Party Leadership

By the beginning of the twentieth century a great deal of power in the House of Representatives had accumulated in the hands of the Speaker. The rules gave him considerable power over floor proceedings. He chaired the Rules Committee, but most significantly, he allocated members to committees and appointed the chairs. With the Speaker's power behind them, chairmen dominated their committees. Clearly, these procedural powers gave the Speaker the power to dominate the process of crafting legislation. He could appoint chairmen who agreed with him and remove those who defied his wishes. In the Senate, similar power was exercised by a small clique of Republican senators.

The advantage of centralized power within Congress is that it makes for an efficient legislative process. David Brady and colleagues suggest that such a high degree of centralized power was tolerated by the members of the majority Republican Party as long as they agreed with the kind of legislation that was being passed.[6] But increasingly, the Republicans were split between progressive and conservative factions. When Speaker Joseph Cannon used his powers to exclude Progressives from power, unrest grew within the party. Finally, in 1910 the Progressive Republicans joined with the minority Democrats to radically change the House rules, stripping the Speaker of most of his powers.

The Automatic Seniority System

The system that was established after the revolt of 1910 lasted for over sixty years with only minor changes.[7] The power to allocate new members to committees was taken from the Speaker and given to a committee of each party. More importantly, a binding seniority rule was adopted to govern the allocation of members and the selection of committee chairs.

Seniority in each house was determined by length of continuous service. In competition for vacant committee positions the member with more seniority was chosen. Seniority was also used to determine committee chairs. Seniority in this case meant seniority on the committee. The longest-serving member on the majority side automatically became chair of the committee, with subcommittee chairs normally going to the next most senior members of the majority. The advantage of the seniority system was that it was a completely automatic way of making the key decisions about power on committees. It meant that power could not be concentrated in a few hands; at the same time, it avoided the constant scramble for power that would have ensued had committees been allowed to elect their own chairs.

The long-term effect of using the seniority system to distribute power in Congress was twofold:

First, the seniority system established the autonomy of the committees by reinforcing the specialization and expertise of committee members. Once on a committee that suited him, a member had every incentive to stay put and accumulate seniority and therefore power on the committee. Since the party leaders could not influence how power was allocated within committees, the committees became largely independent of the leadership. The committee chairmen, who could not be removed, became extremely powerful as a result. Committee members had no incentive to "rock the boat," and most waited quietly as their seniority rose with each re-election.

The power of the majority party's leadership to control what happened in Congress had been considerable before 1910, but declined greatly after that. This

---

6   David Brady, Richard Brody, and David Epstein, "Heterogeneous Parties and Political Organization: The U.S. Senate, 1880–1920," in John R. Hibbing and John G. Peters, eds., *The Changing World of the U.S. Senate* (IGS Press, 1990).

7   On the use of seniority in the House of Representatives, see Michael Abram and Joseph Cooper, "The Rise of Seniority in the House of Representatives" *Polity* 1 (1968), 53–85.

meant that there was no central control over the legislative process. Power in Congress became fragmented among the powerful committee chairmen, the congressional "barons," each of whom dominated his area of jurisdiction.

Second, the seniority system concentrated power in Congress in the hands of elderly members from one-party states. In order to reach a committee chair, a member usually had to serve at least twenty years, and this was much easier in noncompetitive states where re-election was guaranteed. A member who finally reached a committee chair found it difficult to give up power, and was protected from the challenges of younger men back home by his ability to use his power to benefit his district or state. As a result, many important chairs were held on to by very old men, some of whom stayed on into their nineties.

In the 1940s the drawbacks of the seniority system—that it rewarded longevity, and gave one-party areas of the country disproportionate power in Congress—became a problem for the majority Democratic Party. With Democratic majorities in Congress after the New Deal, a disproportionate share of committee chairs went to conservative southern Democrats, most of whom fell increasingly out of sympathy with the party as it tried to extend New Deal programs and particularly as it began to support black civil rights. Southern politicians had long used the strategy of sending young men to Congress and re-electing them while they accumulated seniority and power. Their principal mandate was to defend racial segregation.

The problem with the seniority system came to a head in 1961 when President Kennedy, whose party controlled both houses of Congress, found most of his legislative program blocked by a handful of elderly conservative southern chairmen, such as Rep. Howard Smith of Virginia, who chaired the Rules Committee. When the president wanted to get a tax cut passed to stimulate the economy, he had to do a deal with Wilbur Mills, who was chair of the House Ways and Means Committee and one of the most powerful and skillful of the congressional barons. Attempts to change the seniority system failed. Many members were reluctant to defy the existing power structure, and there was no agreement on an alternative method of distributing power. Pressure for change continued to build until finally, in 1973, a majority in the Democratic caucus favored a major reform of the system.

The Modified Seniority System

The changes made in 1973 are still in operation today. The most important changes were made by the Democratic Party in the House. The power to allocate new members to committees was given to a more broadly representative Steering Committee composed of the leadership and members elected by the caucus. It no longer had to follow seniority rigidly, and had more discretion in making its allocations. In the most important change, the Steering Committee was given the power to nominate committee chairs at the beginning of each Congress, but its nominations were made subject to a vote of the whole party caucus.

The effect of these changes was to make committee chairmen much more sensitive to majority sentiment in the party. Seniority has generally been respected; but in the first few years of the new system several recalcitrant chairmen were defeated by the caucus, while others indicated that they had "got the message" and moderated their behavior. In 1985 the long-time chairman of the Armed Services Committee was removed by the caucus because of his age, and a much less senior member with considerable expertise was elected in his place. In recent years, several less senior committee members have challenged long-standing committee chairs in the caucus—some of them successfully.

A second reform was to open up and democratize the operations of the committees. In general, chairs were made more responsible to committee members for how they conducted business. For example, it is no longer possible for a chair to avoid dealing with an issue simply by refusing to call a meeting of the committee. Some of the powers that chairs had exercised alone, such as the power to select subcommittee chairs, were given to the committee caucus. The effect has been to increase the number and importance of the subcommittees.

In the Senate the effect of seniority on committee assignments was always less restrictive than in the House, since with a smaller number of members there were more good positions to go around. But seniority was and still is a binding rule in the selection of committee chairs. No exceptions have been agreed to. This is why Senator Jesse Helms, whose views are out of line with those of virtually all of his colleagues, was allowed to chair the important Foreign Relations Committee from 1981 to 1987, and why he has chaired it again since 1995, and why Senator Strom Thurmond took the chair of the Armed Services Committee in 1995 at the age of 92.

Political scientists have noted that major change is most likely to occur in an organization like the Congress after the influx of an unusually large number of new members. One such influx was of reform-minded Democrats after the Watergate scandal in 1974; another was of "revolutionary" Republicans after their party captured both houses in 1994. In the 1970s the new rules and the influx of new members led to radical changes in how both houses operated. The behavioral norms of deference and apprenticeship, and the belief that new members should keep their heads down until they had learned the ropes and "paid their dues," practices which the seniority system had fostered, gave way to a much more individualistic, entrepreneurial spirit among members.

Under the seniority system power had been concentrated in the hands of long-serving committee "barons" at the expense of the party leadership and of individual members. The changes of the 1970s radically decentralized power. In the House, a great deal of power flowed downwards to the subcommittees, which grew in number and became more active. In the Senate, power fell more and more into the hands of individual senators, who developed much greater scope for both initiating and blocking legislation.[8]

All of this decentralization in Congress made the legislative process even harder to control or predict. One notable effect in the Senate was the greatly increased use of the filibuster by individuals or small groups of senators. The filibustering of bills is becoming increasingly routine, and this means that in practice the majority required to pass legislation is sixty votes—the number needed to end a filibuster. The increased unpredictability of the legislative process encouraged the party leaders to try to assert more control.

The Recentralization of the Legislative Process in the 1990s

The rule changes of 1973 added to the Speaker's powers. Through his influence on the Steering Committee, he increased his role in allocating members to committees. Also, he was given the power to nominate new members of the Rules Committee, and this gave him effective control over the scheduling of legislation for floor debate. In addition, the Speaker gained more control over how bills were referred to committees, and over the nomination of members to conference committees, in which much of the final shaping of legislation is carried out.[9]

The first Speaker to use the new powers to the full, and to play a much more directive role in the House, was Jim Wright, who became Speaker in 1987. Wright intervened actively in the committee process in order to push a Democratic legislative agenda largely developed by himself. Wright's experiment as an assertive Speaker did not last long, however; he was forced to resign in 1989 after an ethics investigation that had been aggressively pushed by Republican Representative Newt Gingrich.[10]

Newt Gingrich became Speaker in 1995 in unprecedented circumstances. Almost single-handedly he had plotted the Republican capture of the House after forty years of Democratic control—a feat that few had thought possible. Part of his unique election strategy was to commit Republican candidates to a ten-point program, the Contract with America. When the Republicans won a majority, Gingrich enjoyed an unusually high standing with his caucus as the architect of their victory; he also had a ready-made agenda in hand.[11]

From the start, Gingrich used the powers of his office in a way not seen since the days of Joe Cannon in 1910. He played a large role in allocating the new members to committees, disregarding the normal practice by assigning some freshmen to the most

---

8   Barbara Sinclair, *The Transformation of the U.S. Senate* (Johns Hopkins University Press, 1989).

9   Roger H. Davidson, "The New Centralization on Capitol Hill," *Review of Politics* 50 (1988), 345–363.

10   On Wright's tenure as Speaker, see Peters, *The American Speakership*, 264–280.

11   On Gingrich's role in building a Republican majority in the House, see Connie Bruck, "The Politics of Perception," *The New Yorker*, October 9, 1995.

powerful committees. He personally chose each committee chair, in several cases pass-ing over the most senior member for someone likely to be more effective. He openly disparaged the committee structure and set up independent task forces to deal with some issues. And he threatened to bypass the committee stage of the legislative process if a committee did not produce the required bill.[12]

Gingrich's extraordinary power as Speaker proved to be short-lived. His grand strategy—to force the president to sign the radical Republican budget by allowing much of the government to shut down for three weeks—collapsed in the spring of 1996 as his own popularity sank, along with that of his party. After that, House lead-ers had a struggle to contain the divisions within their ranks and many of the stan-dard institutional pressures began to reassert themselves: pressure from committee chairs to control their own jurisdictions, and pressures from individual members to protect spending in their districts.[13]

In the 1996 elections Republicans were on the defensive and many members of the House made an effort to separate themselves from the unpopular Gingrich. The Republicans retained control, but with only a narrow majority. Gingrich's position was further weakened when at the start of the new Congress he was found guilty by the bipartisan House Ethics Committee of financial irregularities associated with GOPAC, his principal fund-raising organization. By a vote of the entire House, he was formally reprimanded and fined $300,000. He entered his second term as Speaker in 1997 weakened politically, without a clear agenda or strategy, and with several com-mittee chairs openly proclaiming their control over different policy areas. All the signs were that the House was reverting to its former decentralized mode of operation.

The Role of the Congressional Party Leaders

The leaders of the Congress are elected by the members of the party caucuses. Attempts by presidents to influence the selection of congressional leaders have always been fiercely resisted, as have been all attempts by the executive branch to play a direct role in the Congress. Lyndon Johnson had been an unusually powerful Democratic majority leader of the Senate from 1955 to 1961; yet when he became vice president in 1961 and tried to continue to influence the Senate, he was quickly rebuffed by the new Democratic leaders.

The responsibilities of the congressional leaders are roughly four: to manage the party in Congress, to manage the legislative process, to act as intermediaries between the president and the Congress, and to act as national advocates for their party.

---

12   *Congressional Quarterly, Weekly Report*, October 7, 1995, 3049–3053
13   For a summary of the House Republican leadership problems in 1996, see Jackie Koszczuk, "For Embattled GOP Leadership, A Season of Discontent," in *Congressional Quarterly, Weekly Report*, July 20, 1996.

Party Management

The leader's goal is to maximize the unity of his party caucus. This is a difficult task for three main reasons: both parties are of necessity fairly broad coalitions; members of Congress are preoccupied with the needs of their individual districts; and the leaders have very few means to reward or discipline members. There have been periodic attempts to use caucus meetings to develop party positions on issues and to bind members to vote accordingly. These attempts have sometimes succeeded for brief periods, when there was substantial unity on particular policies; but they have all failed eventually, because there is no effective way to enforce caucus decisions.

In most cases, it would be counterproductive for the party to discipline its members. Stripping members of their seniority or throwing them out of the caucus might drive them into the other party. Preventing representatives from putting the interests of their district before those of their party would only result in their defeat in the next election; this would simply reduce the party's control, or prospect of control, of the house. This is why such discipline has been used only in extreme cases of disloyalty to the party. Party discipline is discussed in more detail in the next section.

Creating party unity in Congress involves developing positions around which as many party members as possible can rally; it also involves persuading members it is in their own best interest to go along. Skillful party leadership brings an important degree of cohesion to what always tends to be a highly fragmented legislative process.

Management of the Legislative Process

There are so many points at which legislation can be blocked in the Congress that it is very difficult to get any laws passed. Yet at least one piece of legislation, the budget, absolutely must be passed every year if the government is to continue to operate, and there is always public pressure for legislation to deal with current problems. Committees and subcommittees have considerable autonomy in their own spheres, but it is the responsibility of the congressional leaders to keep the legislative process moving. Too much disorganization would lower even further the already shaky public reputation of the Congress.

The management task is particularly difficult when the presidency and the Congress are controlled by different parties. In this situation, the leaders of the two branches inevitably clash over what should be done, and the interests of the two parties conflict. Neither branch and neither party wants to be dominated by the other. Yet neither can afford to use its power over the legislative process simply to block the other. The task of finding some strategy for cooperation in spite of institutional and partisan rivalries falls mainly on the congressional leaders. Most of them are very conscious of the central role they play in making the separation of powers work, and have a sense of national responsibility that goes beyond partisan interests.

An excellent example of a new leader coming to terms with the difficulties of managing the legislative process under divided government is the case of Gingrich and the

Republican House in 1995–96. The Republicans took control with a "revolutionary" program. Speaker Gingrich had little difficulty in getting most of the agenda passed by the House, with only a few modifications to satisfy the moderate Republicans. The centerpiece of the Republican revolution was a seven-year plan to balance the federal budget, which would have sharply cut many of the Democrats' treasured programs. Once it passed the House, the plan bogged down in negotiations with the less conservative Republican Senate, and this led to some compromises. The next obstacle was the president's veto.

Initially, Gingrich was very confident that he could force the president to agree to most of what the Republicans had passed. After much of the federal government was forced to shut down for three weeks because several of the appropriations bills were deadlocked between Congress and the president, Gingrich had to concede that he had overplayed his hand and that he would not be able to accomplish several of his major legislative goals in the 1995–96 Congress. After months of stalemate both the House Republicans and the president realized that they needed some record of accomplishment for the election, and in the summer all sides reached compromise agreements to pass the appropriations bills and several other important pieces of legislation.

Intermediary Role

Besides managing the congressional process, congressional leaders are the intermediaries between the president and the Congress. The party leaders of both houses meet with the president regularly to learn his legislative plans and to inform him of the state of opinion in the Congress. The party leaders are always involved in the frequent negotiations between the executive and legislative branches over particular pieces of legislation. The president works most closely with the leaders of his own party, who usually feel bound to adopt his legislative priorities as their own, and who meet with him to plan party strategy.

National Party Advocates

The president is leader of his party and cannot but overshadow the congressional leaders of his party. There is, however, no Leader of the Opposition in the American system. Except for the three-month period between the national convention and the presidential election every four years, the party that does not occupy the White House has no designated leader. In this situation, the congressional leaders of the party out of power become of necessity advocates for their party on national issues.

Until recent years, congressional leaders were chosen for their political skills in the complex world of the Congress—skills that did not require them to be good at public communication. Indeed most were not very effective on television. The ability to act as an effective public advocate for the party has now become a major consideration in choosing congressional leaders.

Party Discipline in Congress

In the Canadian House of Commons, party discipline in voting approaches 100 percent. The parties take positions on almost all questions that come to a vote, and the members of the party are instructed to vote accordingly. It is news when a member defies the instructions of the party whip. MPs who do are liable to be disciplined, perhaps by being tossed from a committee position. Any MPs who repeatedly defy their party are likely to be dismissed from the party caucus, which means they will be ineligible to run for the party in the next election. In the Congress, party discipline is very much weaker. The parties take positions on fewer issues, and on "party votes," where the majority of one party is opposed by the majority of the other, members on average vote with their own party only about 75 percent of the time.

The Reasons for Weak Party Discipline

Reason #1. In the Canadian system, if the government party does not maintain the voting loyalty of its own members, its continuance in office is threatened. Party leaders use this argument to require almost complete loyalty in voting. Opposition parties feel obliged to show similar degrees of discipline to demonstrate their ability to form an alternative government. In the American system this argument does not apply, since what happens in the Congress has no effect on the president's tenure.

Reason #2. In Canada, party leaders control each member's promotion both within the party and within government. A rebel cannot expect to become a minister. In Congress the party leaders can do little to reward or punish members. Once the member has the committee assignments he wants, his tenure is protected by the seniority system. In any case, party leaders are generally unwilling to try to punish members, since they recognize that party loyalty can only be maximized through persuasion.

In cases of extreme disloyalty, the party caucus can strip members of their seniority, thereby damaging their future prospects for exercising power within the Congress. A few southern Democrats were punished in this way after they actively supported the presidential candidates of other parties—Barry Goldwater in 1964 and George Wallace in 1968. In 1983, Rep. Phil Gramm of Texas, a Democrat, was removed from the House Budget Committee by his party after he used his position to betray party strategy to the Republicans. Gramm's response was to resign his seat and win re-election in his conservative district as a Republican. In 1984 he was elected as a Republican senator from Texas.

Reason #3. In Canada, a rebellious MP would be worried about being renominated in his riding, since every candidate's nomination papers must be signed by the party leader. In the United States, nominations are by the primary system, and party machinery is usually nonexistent, so a member's prospects for renomination and re-election depend entirely on his or her own personal ability to retain popular support in the district. Voters traditionally resent any electoral interference from Washington. In sum, party leaders have no control over a member's re-election prospects.

Reason #4. It is generally accepted in Canada that political parties are necessary if government is to work. In the United States this is not the case: political parties have always been viewed as, at best, a necessary evil. The general expectation is that members of Congress will represent the interests of their districts. A Canadian MP will try to further the interests of her constituents within the government and within the party caucus, but her vote in the House will be dictated by the interests of her party. Members of Congress always place the interests of their district (and their personal re-election) before the interests of their party, and Congressional leaders accept this reality.

✒ Reasons for Party Loyalty

Canadians ask why party discipline in the Congress is as low as 75 percent, but considering the disincentives to party loyalty listed above, one might ask why it is as *high* as 75 percent. Although it is at a much lower level than Canadians are used to, party voting remains an important factor in the functioning of the Congress. There are a number of reasons why.

Reason #1. Most members of the Democratic and Republican parties in Congress are likely to be in broad agreement with one another on the major policy questions. Most Democrats can be classed as political liberals, and most Republicans as conservatives. The parties remain coalitions, however, and there are minorities (often regionally based) in each party that are somewhat out of step with the majority. The average 75 percent score for party loyalty conceals a range of behavior on the part of individual members, running from over 90 percent to around 50 percent. In the Democratic Party, some of the conservative southern Democrats are on the lower end of the loyalty scale; among Republicans, the low scorers are almost all from the generally liberal northeastern states.

In recent years the party caucuses have become more homogeneous: the Democrats have continued to lose their traditionalist support in the South, and the Republicans have become increasingly conservative. Yet even at the height of the highly partisan battles in the 1995–96 Congress, there were distinct groups of more conservative Democrats and more moderate Republicans, and their leaders had to accommodate them on some issues.

Reason #2. Belonging to a party caucus is like belonging to a team. Members are expected to work together whenever possible. Also, most of the contacts members of Congress have at work are likely to be with other members of their own party. Members are called upon to vote on all sorts of issues about which they have little personal knowledge, and they often need to be "cued" on how to vote. Most representatives finder it safer to take their cues from party colleagues, unless there is a clear conflict with the interests of their district.

Reason #3. The job of the party leaders is to maximize the unity of the party in the House. They must judge when there is sufficient potential unity among their members to make an issue a party matter. Then they must try to persuade wavering members to support the party line. While there is little the leaders can do to punish or reward members, small favors from party leaders—like making sure an expenditure for the congressman's district is included in a bill, or arranging an invitation to a White House dinner—may help "persuade" a member to vote as requested.

The Consequences of Weak Party Discipline
The gap between the 100 percent party discipline, which is standard in Canada's House of Commons, and the 70 to 80 percent average in Congress means that there is "room" in Congress for factors other than party to influence how a member of Congress votes. The principal other influences are district, ideology, and special interests.

District influence. Each member is expected to represent the interests and views of his or her constituents. This general expectation is reinforced by the reality that members are responsible for their own re-election, which neither the party leaders in Washington nor the party organization at home can ensure. It follows that members are not likely to vote against the clear interests of any large number of their constituents. This is particularly so when it comes to the House of Representatives. House districts, with about half a million inhabitants each, are often fairly homogeneous in their interests. Senators are generally freer from direct constituency pressures, because the populations they represent tend to be more diverse and less monolithic.

Ideological influence. Ideology, as is noted above, is related to party affiliation in that most liberals are Democrats and most conservatives are Republicans. It is also related to demographics. Members from inner-city and working-class districts are likely to be liberal Democrats who vote for government action to help people. Members from the suburbs or prosperous rural areas are likely to be conservative Republicans who want to cut taxes. There are, of course, exceptions to these generalizations. Ideology may also be an independent factor that leads conservatives to oppose abortion and foreign aid (which are not integral to the stands of their party or the interests of their district), and liberals to support civil rights and international peacekeeping.

The influence of special interests. Members of Congress are free to choose how they will vote on most issues. In particular, committee and subcommittee votes by individual members of Congress may have a major impact on what laws are passed, because it is these votes that actually shape legislation. It follows that for all those who have a stake in which laws are passed in Washington—and that is just about everyone in the United States at one time or another—members of Congress are well worth influencing. All of this explains why Washington lawmakers are the target of lobbying by special interests to a very much greater extent than is true in Ottawa. Individual legislators are the key point at which the legislative process becomes open to special interests. This topic will be discussed further in Chapters 6 and 14.

THE ROLE OF THE PRESIDENT IN THE LEGISLATIVE PROCESS

The sharing of powers in the design of the Constitution makes the president part of the legislative process in two principal ways. First, under Article II, Section 3, the president is to "give to the Congress Information of the **State of the Union**, and recommend to their Consideration such Measures as he shall judge necessary and expedient." Second, under Article I, Section 7, the president has the power to veto legislation when the Congress presents it to him, though his veto may be overridden by a subsequent two-thirds vote in both houses.

In addition, since the presidency is a party office (though the framers of the Constitution did not intend it to be), the president's role as leader of his party gives him influence with the members of his party in the Congress.

The President as a Legislative Leader

George Washington delivered the first State of the Union message to the Congress. While Presidents Washington and Adams had read their message to the Congress, the third president, Thomas Jefferson, was worried about the growing monarchical trappings of the office and simply sent Congress a written message. This practice was followed over the next hundred years. In 1913 Woodrow Wilson reverted to the original practice and delivered his message in person in the House chamber, and his precedent has been followed ever since. Nowadays the president delivers his message to the members of Congress assembled in the House chamber on television in prime time around the middle of January every year.

The State of the Union message performs the same function as the Canadian Throne Speech, which opens every new session of Parliament. The message, in the course of a survey of domestic and world affairs, recommends to Congress what amounts to a presidential legislative program. The speech is couched in general terms; more specific proposals are sent to the Congress later. The Throne Speech, while it is read by the governor general, is written by the government and lays out its legislative program for the coming year.

There is a crucial difference between the two situations. In the parliamentary system the government is announcing what it is going to do, since with its majority in the House of Commons it is sure of being able to pass the bills it is proposing. For the president, however, the proposals contained in the State of the Union message are just that, proposals. The chances of a president's proposals becoming law are often quite slim. In the United States, the president makes proposals but it is Congress that decides which of those proposals, if any, will become law.

The model of the president as an active legislative leader who makes proposals and works actively to persuade Congress to pass them is a twentieth-century one. The first president to act this way was Theodore Roosevelt, who campaigned publicly to get Congress to pass the Hepburn Act in 1906.[14] Woodrow Wilson, between 1913 and 1916, was the first president to demonstrate how a president working actively with the Congress could push through a whole program of legislation. The most famous example of a legislative program being enacted swiftly through cooperation between the president and Congress was the New Deal legislation of 1933–36. It was not until President Truman, however, that presidents started to draw up an annual legislative agenda for submission to Congress. This has been the general practice ever since, though the president's success rate in persuading the Congress to pass his proposals varies considerably from year to year.

The Veto Power[15]

For most of American history, the veto was used by presidents as a last-ditch weapon to curb congressional extravagance or encroachment on executive powers. The first president to use the threat of a veto as a regular bargaining tool in negotiating with the Congress over the content of legislation was Franklin Roosevelt in the 1930s, and this has become standard executive practice. The veto power allows the president to play a major role in shaping legislation, particularly in the later stages of floor passage

---

14   David R. Mayhew, *Divided We Govern: Party Control, Lawmaking, and Investigations, 1946–1990* (Yale University Press, 1991), 149.

15   See Richard A. Watson, *Presidential Vetoes and Public Policy* (University of Kansas Press, 1993).

and conference committee negotiations. Congressional leaders in turn expect the president to indicate his intentions well before the bill is in its final shape: that is, whether he intends to veto it, and if so, what his specific objections are.

There are two ways the president can veto a bill. In a "regular" veto (close to 60 percent of vetoes are of this type), the president sends the bill back to Congress with a message giving his reasons. There is also the "pocket" veto, which arises when the Congress adjourns at the end of a session before the ten days allowed for presidential action are up. Once Congress has adjourned, the president simply does nothing and the bill dies.

In the case of a pocket veto there is no opportunity to override since the Congress is no longer in session. With a regular veto, the Congress's first option is to try to override it. Usually, the level of support for the bill at final floor passage gives a good indication whether there is any chance at all of an override. Often an override is not even attempted. If it is, one house will hold an override vote. If it fails there is obviously no need for the other house to vote, since a two-thirds majority in both houses is required. If an override is not possible, one option is to pass the bill again without the features to which the president objected. Alternatively, the bill's supporters may prefer to let it die, with the objective of trying again in the next Congress or with the next president.

The requirement of a two-thirds majority in both houses indicates that the framers intended a veto override to be difficult to achieve. It has indeed proved difficult, but not impossible. In the period between presidents Kennedy and Bush (1961–92), 18 percent of regular vetoes were overridden (11 percent of all vetoes).[16] Since the president's party is usually reluctant to override his veto, an override is only possible when a bill commands broad partisan and popular support. For example, the only one of President Bush's forty-five vetoes to be overridden, shortly before the 1992 elections, related to a bill to control the rise of cable subscription rates.

◂ The President and His Party in Congress

As the acknowledged leader of his party, the president can expect party loyalty to play an important role when it comes to commanding the support of fellow Democrats or Republicans in Congress. The question is, how much of a role? The reasons for party discipline discussed earlier also apply to relations between the president and fellow party members in Congress.

In the first place, there is usually considerable ideological agreement between president and party. The president's proposals are usually consistent with the party's general positions on issues. In the second place, there is a strong motivation to help the president, since he, as the leader and most visible member of the party, largely defines

---

16   *Statistical Abstract of the United States 1995* (U.S. Bureau of the Census, 1996), Table 446.

in the public mind the party's image at the time. The main concern for a member of the president's party is how popular the president himself is in the member's district. Will cooperation with the president help or hinder the member's re-election? It is a standard political tactic for an opponent to "tie" an incumbent to an unpopular president of the same party. A large number of Republican members were defeated in 1974 because of the **Watergate** scandal, although the Republican Party had nothing to do with it. On the other hand, an effective and popular president helps all members of his party at election time. During the 1984 election, even some Democratic members boasted about their support for President Reagan.

The mobilization of party support for the president also depends on leadership. Usually, the congressional leaders of the president's own party mobilize support in the Congress for his proposals, but the president is also expected to provide leadership, and does so in two ways.

First, he is expected to provide backup for congressional support by making the case for his proposals to the general public. Thus, the president plays up the issue while making speeches around the country. He sets up "photo opportunities" to dramatize the issue for television—for example, by going to a national park to talk about the environment. He also brings to the White House groups of opinion leaders, business leaders, editorial writers, and leaders of relevant interest groups, and attempts to persuade them to support his position.

Second, the president is expected to actively lobby members of Congress in the final stages of the legislative process. The Congressional Liaison Office, located in the White House, handles the continuous routine contacts with members of Congress, but the president himself is considered essential when it comes to lobbying wavering members. This he does by telephoning them or by inviting them to the White House. Presidents vary greatly in their willingness to get involved in congressional lobbying. The most skillful was Lyndon Johnson, who both as majority leader of the Senate and as president was a legendary cajoler and arm-twister. Other presidents, including Kennedy, Nixon, and Carter, found the business distasteful and got involved only reluctantly. By most accounts their legislative programs suffered accordingly.[17]

For all the pressures on the president's party in Congress to offer support, the reality of the constitutional separation of institutions places limits on party loyalty. Unlike the Canadian prime minister, the president can never expect 100 percent support from his party. All senators and representatives have their own constituencies, which are different from the president's national constituency. The first concern for any member is how popular the president's policy is likely to be back home. In a conflict between the president's policy and the clear interests of the district or state, the president is likely to lose.

---

17   See the case studies in Barbara Kellerman, *The Political Presidency: Practice of Leadership* (Oxford University Press, 1984).

An example of how presidential leadership can make a difference in the legislative process was the passage of the **North American Free Trade Agreement** (NAFTA). On this issue, President Clinton was at odds with a majority of Democrats in Congress. Most trade unions were worried about how NAFTA would affect their members' jobs, and pressured many northern Democrats to oppose the agreement, which the president had decided to sign. In a highly unusual move, two of the leaders of his own party, the majority leader, Dick Gephardt, and the majority whip, David Bonior, campaigned openly against the president and tried to defeat the agreement.

November 17, 1993: Final House Passage
of the North American Free Trade Agreement

	234	:	200
Democrats	102	:	156
Republicans	132	:	43
Independent	0	:	1

Most Republicans supported the agreement, which had originally been negotiated by President Bush. But because of widespread concerns about how the agreement would affect employment, the Republican leaders were wary of making the issue of free trade versus protectionism a partisan one. They told the president they would only work to pass the agreement if he could deliver at least 100 Democratic votes. The president had to lobby his own party hard to find enough votes for passage.

Patterns of Voting in Congress

Voting in the House of Commons is almost entirely along party lines. In Congress, voting is much more fluid and unpredictable. In Canada the leaders of each party indicate the position to be taken, or the party caucus reaches a consensus, and then MPs vote accordingly. In Congress, members are fundamentally independent, and party loyalty is only one of many factors in a voting decision. Usually the only vote in which there is 100 percent party discipline is the vote at the beginning of each Congress to elect the Speaker of the House. This vote is like a vote of confidence in the House of Commons: it is the fundamental test of which side a member is on and which party controls the House.

After the initial organizational votes, there are always some members who defect from their party's position for one reason or another. Even at the height of his power in 1995, Newt Gingrich as Speaker could not command all Republican votes:

October 26, 1995: 1995 budget reconciliation package

	227	:	203
Republicans	223	:	10
Democrats	4	:	192
Independent	0	:	1

The budget package was central to Gingrich's legislative agenda. Yet even on a partisan vote of such importance, both parties had a small number of defectors: northeastern and midwestern moderate Republicans worried that the proposed cuts in some programs would be extremely unpopular in their districts; and four fiscally conservative southern Democrats supporting the Republican proposal.

On most issues the number of defections is higher:

June 17, 1995: Amendment to strip a ban on government-funded abortions at overseas military bases from the defense authorization bill

	196	:	230
Republicans	41	:	187
Democrats	154	:	43
Independent	1	:	0

This vote was fairly typical of the many votes involving the abortion issue over the last twenty years. Most Democrats are supportive of abortion rights, and most

Newt Gingrich holds a copy of the allegations of possible misconduct by then–House Speaker Jim Wright of Texas during a 1988 press conference in Washington, D.C.

Republicans are opposed; but in each party can be found a significant minority that votes "against the grain" of the majority position.

Because party defections are common, there is cross-party voting on virtually every vote, and every majority is bipartisan to some degree. The proportion of roll call votes that are party votes, in which a majority of one party opposes a majority of the other, varies greatly from session to session but is usually around 60 percent of the votes called on the floor of either house. In the other votes, either the majority of both parties are in agreement, or both parties are badly split. While the party leaders schedule all votes, the party usually commits its full weight only to issues regarding which a public stand is considered important (often because an election is coming).

In the 1990s the Congress has become much more partisan, and the parties are more polarized. One reason is that each party has become more homogeneous. The conservative, particularly southern, wing of the Democratic Party has shrunk, as has the number of moderate to liberal Republicans from the northeastern states. Another reason is the much more aggressively partisan stance taken by Republicans in the House since Newt Gingrich became minority whip in 1989. This culminated in the Republican-controlled 1995–96 Congress, which according to *Congressional Quarterly* was the most fiercely partisan since early in the twentieth century.[18]

In the 1995 session the number of partisan roll call votes reached an all-time high of 73 percent in the House and 69 percent in the Senate. Likewise, as can be seen in Table 5.4, the average party unity score for Republicans in both houses reached an unprecedented 91 percent, compared to an average in the low 70s throughout the 1980s. The Democrats remained at 80 percent—a level that has been fairly stable for several years.

The Legislative Process in Canada and the United States

The congressional legislative process is characterized by a decentralized committee structure and by relatively weak party discipline. In Canada the legislative process is highly centralized; most bills are government bills and are steered through the parliamentary process, each stage of which is controlled by the government majority. Most bills are passed during the session of Parliament in which they are introduced, and are passed by a partisan government majority, with the opposition parties usually voting in the minority against the bill.

There are a number of significant differences in the way the congressional process works. In the first place, neither the president nor the party leaders take a position on

---

18   *Congressional Quarterly, Weekly Report,* January 27, 1996.

Table 5.4 *Party Unity*		Republicans	Democrats
Average Scores in	1981-90	73	77
Congress	1991	78	81
	1992	79	79
	1993	84	85
	1994	83	83
	1995	91	80

A party unity roll call vote is one in which the majority of one party opposes the majority of the other. The party unity score measures how often on average the members of the House and Senate voted with the majority of their party in party unity votes.

Source: Congressional Quarterly, *Weekly Report*, January 27, 1996. Reprinted with permission.

every issue before the Congress. The president usually concentrates on a few proposals that are important for his agenda. Usually, the party leaders will not let a bill come to the floor unless it has accumulated enough support that it has a chance of passage.

Even when a bill is made a party issue by the president or the leaders, the weak party discipline means that there will always be defectors from the party line. It also means that most votes will be bipartisan to some extent. It is standard practice for supporters of a bill to seek support across party lines. Few bills are passed on a purely partisan vote. In his study of the impact of divided party government on the legislative process, David Mayhew found that most major pieces of legislation in the past forty years were in the end passed by large bipartisan majorities. Only 8 percent of such legislation had been carried into law by a one-party majority in both houses, and only 26 percent by a one-party majority in one of the houses.[19]

It is unusual for a bill, unless it is an appropriations bill, to be passed through all its stages within one Congress. More typically, proposals linger at the committee stage from one Congress to the next until the political climate is supportive and the right compromises have been found to build the broad coalition of support that is necessary for floor passage—a process described more fully in Chapter 15.

---

19   David R. Mayhew, *Divided We Govern: Party Control, Lawmaking, and Investigations, 1946–1990* (Yale University Press, 1991), 126

CHAPTER 6

CONGRESSIONAL BEHAVIOR

The main organizational features of the Congress—the committee system and the party leadership structure—have developed over time to enable the Congress to get its job of legislating done. These structures are quite flexible in how they operate and relate to each other. An important influence on the working of the congressional process is the needs and goals of the individual members. To understand how the congressional process actually works, one must understand first what motivates members of Congress and the pressures they feel. The main pressure facing members is the need to ensure their own re-election, so they spend a great deal of time and energy trying to make their districts electorally secure. This inevitably shapes the way the Congress legislates.

The life of members of Congress is dominated by two realities: the pressure to act, which comes from many different sources; and a constant sense that their political future is at risk. Members of Congress are the focus of pressure because their votes matter, both on the floor and in committee, and because members are not bound by strict party discipline. Members of Congress are the focus of lobbying from a variety of sources: party leaders, the president, other executive officers, voters and particular interests in their district, and special interests generally. All of these try to persuade them to act or vote a certain way.

At the same time, members are (or believe themselves to be) in constant political danger. A member's political career—the process of getting re-elected and gaining seniority, or moving to a higher office—is almost entirely in the member's own hands. Neither party leaders nor the party organization can provide much help. These twin realities—the exercise of power and political insecurity—constitute the parameters for congressional behavior. Each of the many decisions a representative is called upon to make has consequences both for public policy and for his or her own political career.

Each member of Congress has to find a strategy for doing the job that takes these realities into account. Richard Fenno has argued that the behavior of members of Congress is governed by three basic goals, usually ranked in this order: to get re-elected; to increase their influence in the House; and to make good public policy.[1] These goals are examined in the following sections; later on, we discuss how the survival strategies of members of Congress shape the legislative process.

MEMBERS OF CONGRESS AND RE-ELECTION

It may seem unduly cynical to insist that the first goal of every member of Congress is to secure re-election. The reality is, however, that no member of Congress can achieve the more admirable goals, such as making good policy or helping constituents, without first being re-elected. This is especially true in the House of Representatives, where terms last only two years. It is generally agreed that it takes at least a year to prepare for a serious election campaign, so members of the House are running for re-election almost continuously. Senators, who enjoy six-year terms, face less direct electoral pressure, at least for the first four years of their term.

Members of Congress are almost always conscious of their vulnerability and of the need to work to prevent electoral defeat. The two potential threats are to their renomination and to their re-election.

Renomination. There is no strong party organization at home to guarantee renomination. This means that early in election year, any member may find himself challenged for the party nomination (which is decided in a primary election). There are always ambitious state legislators and others who are eager to move to Washington— more of them than there are House seats available. A member who appears politically "vulnerable" is likely to be challenged for the nomination.

Re-election. Many members do not face a serious challenge from the other party. Since the New Deal, American voters have tended to divide between the parties on the basis of class. Working-class and poor rural areas usually elect Democrats, while the

---

1   Richard F. Fenno Jr., *Congressmen in Committees* (Little, Brown, 1973), 1.

suburbs and prosperous rural areas return mostly Republicans to Washington. The class division has been considerably blurred by social issues in recent years, but there are still many members who are safe from a challenge by the other party because of the nature of their district.

But security against challenge from the other party may be weaker than it seems. For one thing, each party has periodic bad years in which voter sentiment across the country moves more heavily than usual against its candidates. For example, in 1974, the first election after the Watergate scandal, many long-established Republican representatives were defeated. And in 1994 voters moved strongly to the Republican Party and defeated the House Speaker, Tom Foley, a thirty-six year veteran. For another, congressional districts may change their character over time through population growth or contraction. Since 1963 the courts have required that congressional districts be equal in population. As a result, all district boundaries are redrawn to some extent every ten years after the national census. Every member's nightmare is that the state legislature will abolish or radically alter the district that he or she has worked so hard to secure.

A good example of what redistricting can do to a previously entrenched member is the case of Stephen Solarz, who represented a safe Democratic district in Brooklyn, New York, from 1975 to 1993. Solarz chaired the Asian and Pacific Affairs Subcommittee of the House Foreign Affairs Committee and became well known for his skill at raising large amounts of campaign money from Asian-American groups across the country.[2] He made no secret of the fact that he had accumulated a campaign fund of over $1 million to ward off possible Democratic challengers. After the 1990 census, however, New York state faced a reduction of two seats in its House representation and also the legal requirement to create a second majority-Hispanic district in New York City. Solarz's district was abolished. Rather than challenge a neighboring Democratic incumbent (who had also collected a large campaign fund), he chose to contest the Democratic nomination in the new Hispanic seat. He lost. For all his precautions, his promising congressional career had come to an end.

Not even the most powerful members are safe from unexpected challenges. In 1982, a year of economic recession, the Republican minority leader in the House, Robert Michel, came within an inch of defeat in Peoria, Illinois, after twenty-five years without a serious challenge by a Democrat. In 1990 the House Republican whip, Newt Gingrich, a nationally known conservative, won by fewer than 1,000 votes in what everyone had assumed was a safe seat in the Atlanta suburbs. As noted earlier, House Speaker Tom Foley was defeated in 1994.

The electoral vulnerability of members of the House would seem to be contradicted by the fact that usually well over 90 percent of incumbent members who run again

---

2   *Congressional Quarterly, Weekly Report*, March 11, 1989.

are re-elected. A record for incumbent security was reached in 1988, when only six of the 412 members who were running for re-election were defeated, and only one lost a re-nomination contest. Even in the Republican sweep of 1994, 90 percent of Democratic incumbents who ran were re-elected.

The Senate is a different matter. Most states are sufficiently heterogeneous that either party can win. Since the solid Democratic hold on the South ended in the 1960s, there has been no state that can be considered safe for either party. In the past thirty years only Louisiana[3] and West Virginia have not elected a Republican senator, and only Kansas has not elected a Democrat. Potentially at least, any incumbent senator is beatable. Between 1980 and the present, an average of twenty-eight incumbent senators have sought re-election at each election; of these, only four have been defeated.

Despite the impressive re-election record of incumbents, most members of Congress, then, believe that they are electorally vulnerable and that they must use the means that incumbency provides to protect their position in their district. For this reason, they devote much of their activity in Congress to securing re-election. In his 1974 analysis of the Congress, David Mayhew argued that because of the preoccupation with re-election, much of congressional activity can be slotted into three categories: "advertising," "credit claiming," and "position taking."[4] To elaborate on this analysis, the election-oriented activities of incumbents can be divided up as follows: image building, servicing the district, searching for benefits, establishing a secure voting record, cultivating important interests, and building a campaign fund.

Image building. Because House elections attract little publicity compared to Senate and especially presidential elections, name recognition and a positive image are invaluable aids to re-election. Members have the advantage of free mailing to communicate with their constituents, though some limits have been put in place to prevent abuse. Through videotape and satellite technology, they are able to appear frequently in the local media. Most return to their districts often to attend local events. Some even leave their families in the district and return home from Washington every weekend. (This is why congressional leaders can schedule important votes only from Tuesday to Thursday.) Most surveys show that only about 40 percent of Americans can name their member of Congress, but even that level of recognition is likely to be much higher than for any challenger.

Servicing the district. Unlike Canadian MPs, members of Congress are provided with a large staff—fifteen in the House and more in the Senate, depending on the size of

---

3   In 1996 the Republican candidate was beaten by 0.4% by Democrat Mary Landrieu, a result that was investigated by a Senate committee after Republican allegations of voting irregularities.

4   David R. Mayhew, *Congress: The Electoral Connection* (Yale University Press, 1974).

the state. Members typically locate up to half of their staff back in the district, so that they can more easily respond to the problems of constituents. In particular, members are expected to act as intermediaries between their constituents and the federal government. To build gratitude and therefore support back home, members of Congress consider it essential to answer district mail, phone calls, and e-mail, and to make themselves available to greet visiting constituents.

Searching for benefits. Most members of Congress believe that the best way to impress their constituents with their concern for the district and with their power in Washington is to arrange federal expenditures for the district. Earlier in the century, such expenditures mainly involved infrastructure projects such as the building of roads, canals, and post offices. Nowadays there is a much wider range of possibilities: government contracts and tax breaks for local industries, grants for small businesses, research grants for colleges, subsidies for farmers, and so on. Any area of government expenditure can be used to provide a local benefit.

Since legislation and expenditures can best be influenced in committee, an important factor in a member's choice of committee is how much scope it will afford for acquiring "goodies" for constituents. This is why members from farm districts fill the agriculture committees, why those from inner-city districts flock to the committees dealing with housing and urban renewal, and why everyone wants to get on the appropriations and tax committees, which approve expenditures and tax loopholes, respectively. The effect on policy of the relentless search for constituency benefits is discussed later in this chapter.

Voting record. The first thing that someone does when considering whether to challenge an incumbent member, is scrutinize his or her votes in Congress to find an issue to use as a weapon. "Did you know that your congressman voted against the tax cut?" is the kind of charge an incumbent dreads. A major objective, therefore, is to build a voting record that is immune from political attack. The first rule is not to miss too many votes. The unexpected defeat of Senator Huddleston of Kentucky in 1984 was blamed on a television commercial sponsored by his opponent in which a pack of bloodhounds set off across the countryside to search for the "absent" senator.

On some issues, the interests of the district or the views of a majority of the voters are clear, and members vote accordingly. Thus, members from rural or southern districts where hunting is popular vote against gun control regardless of their personal views. But there are few votes in which the interest of a member's district is clear. With most votes, the member's constituents are likely to be uninformed, indifferent, or divided. On issues where opinion in the district is uncertain, a member will often "look for cover" by voting the same way as the other members from her state, or by following a prominent or expert member whose opinion can be cited as a defense.

Cultivate special interests. It has been said that the thing an incumbent fears most is "determined opposition" in his district—some group or interest that is so offended by his voting record that it is willing to back his opponent. To prevent this, most members are strongly inclined to appease, through voting or doing favors, any interest that they perceive to be influential in the district. The relationship between members of Congress and special interests will be examined more fully in a later section.

Campaign funds. Running for election to Congress is very expensive, and becoming more so every year. Proposed changes to the campaign finance laws in 1995 assumed that the cost of a contested race for the House is $600,000. The bulk of this money goes for television time and commercials. Most members therefore feel the need to have a large campaign fund on hand in case they are challenged. Challengers, who do not have the name recognition or mailing privileges of incumbents, usually have to spend even more money than incumbents and can often be scared off by the existence of a large campaign fund. Key sources of campaign funds nowadays are the political action committees (PACs) run by special interests; these PACs are especially interested in helping members of Congress who sit on committees that are relevant to their interests. The problem of campaign funds will be discussed more fully later on.

Senators face essentially the same pressures as House members, but there are some differences. Because they enjoy longer terms, senators do not face the same constant electoral pressures, but nowadays this advantage is offset by re-election rates that are lower than those for representatives. Most senators have constituencies so large that they cannot rely on personal service to build support. On the other hand, senators find it much easier than House members to get media coverage for their actions and views. For this reason, and because they are viewed as having more individual power in Washington, senators find it easier to raise campaign contributions from individuals; in fact, they rely less on PAC contributions than do House members.

The Conflict Between Re-election and Law-making

The struggle for electoral security is a fundamental reality that no member of Congress can escape, but most members want more than simply to be re-elected. In Fenno's words, they also want to increase their influence in the House and make good public policy. Increased influence both helps re-election and translates into the power to shape policy. The trouble is that the activities which aid re-election, discussed in the previous section, are different from those which increase a member's influence with his or her colleagues, and which shape legislation—indeed, the two sets of activities are often in direct conflict. Most valued inside Congress are the development of expertise, the ability to negotiate and compromise, and, above all, hard legislative work.

Members specialize through their committees, but the development of real expertise goes well beyond that. A member who is recognized as speaking knowledgeably on a subject can achieve considerable influence in that area of policy. Recent examples of members who were widely respected in both parties for their expertise were Senator Sam Nunn of Georgia (on defense policy) and Senator Bill Bradley of New Jersey (on financial matters). Other legislators, such as Senator Nancy Kassebaum of Kansas, gained respect from their hard-working, practical approach to issues. Because it is so easy to block legislation in Congress, members who take an active role in negotiating differences and creating compromises that can command majority support play an essential role in the congressional system. The work is time-consuming, and mostly invisible to the public, and requires flexibility and creativity.

The conflict between election-oriented activities and law-making activities is, first of all, one of time. Activities like visiting the district, attending to constituents' requests, and fund-raising are time-consuming and severely limit the time available for legislative work. In addition, to the degree that a member is afraid to offend constituents or special interests, her freedom to speak from her expertise and to be flexible in negotiations is diminished. What most members want, therefore, is a strategy for handling their relations with their districts that secures their re-election but also provides them with some freedom of action in Washington. They are looking for some leeway—for some room to maneuver in the midst of the electoral pressures that they feel.

Richard Fenno has studied what he calls the "home styles" of members of the House—that is, the strategies they use in dealing with their districts.[5] He describes two principal styles: one relies on building personal trust, the other on the development of a strong issue profile.

A home style based on personal trust plays down issues and emphasizes the personal qualities of the representative, who makes himself highly visible in the district, turns up at many local events, and stresses his accessibility to his constituents. Fenno suggests that this style works best in rural and small-town districts.

A striking example of how well this style can work and how much leeway on issues it can give a member is provided by the career of Lane Evans, a Democrat from central Illinois. Evans's district is comprises small towns and a prosperous farming area that had been solidly Republican since the party was founded. Only in a very bad year for the Republican Party does a Democrat have a chance. In 1974, after Watergate, a Democrat was elected, only to be replaced by a Republican at the next election. Evans similarly won in 1982, in the middle of a recession; but far from being defeated in 1984

---

5   Richard F. Fenno Jr., *Home Style: House Members in Their Districts* (Little, Brown, 1978).

(which was a very good year for the Republicans), he was re-elected and has been ever since, to the frustration of the Republican Party.

What is unusual about Evans is that instead of behaving cautiously, as most Democrats would in a Republican-leaning district, he has compiled a strikingly liberal voting record in the House, even by Democratic standards. Americans for Democratic Action, a liberal group that monitors congressional voting, has consistently given him a 100 percent liberal rating for his voting on key issues, while the corresponding conservative group, the American Conservative Union, scores him at close to 0 percent.

Evans is able to get away with such a liberal record in a rather conservative district because of his high visibility and great personal popularity in the district. *Congressional Quarterly* explains: "Evans wins in part because he works tirelessly at home—conducting meetings to study the district's economic problems, popping up at every county fair and small-town celebration, making himself available to the local media, and putting in countless hours helping constituents."[6]

Not long after his first election, a frustrated local Republican official was quoted as follows by *Congressional Quarterly*: "He's a very personable guy. He holds the door for old ladies. If he steps on your shoe he apologizes ... But it's obvious to me that the man is a socialist with a mission."[7]

It has proved hard, however, for the Republicans to persuade the voters of the 17th District in Illinois that their "friendly, good-looking, modest, sometimes inarticulate young congressman is someone to worry about."

There are two kinds of home styles based on issue profiles. In one, the member advertises himself as either a liberal or a conservative, depending on the district. Fenno argues that this style works best in middle-class districts where voters and especially party activists are ideologically aware. The drawback to this style is that it commits the member to a whole set of positions in advance and restricts his flexibility in law-making.

With the other issue style, the member develops a very high profile on a few issues or on the major interests that are important to the district; this gives the member leeway on other issues. An unusual example of this style is provided by Charlie Wilson, a Democrat who until 1997 represented a small-town, Baptist district in east Texas. Wilson's voting record was a mix: conservative on defense and foreign policy issues, but much more liberal on social issues, such as civil rights and abortion, than would be expected of a member from such a district.[8] Nor did his lifestyle seem to fit his socially conservative district. In 1983 he was ticketed in a hit-and-run accident in Washington and was investigated for cocaine use, though no charges were laid. In

---

6   *Congressional Quarterly, Politics in America 1992*, 466.
7   *Congressional Quarterly, Weekly Report*, May 31, 1986.
8   *Congressional Quarterly, Politics in America 1992*, 1421–1423.

1987 he made headlines when the press discovered that from his position on the Appropriations Committee he had had six planes removed from the budget of the Defense Intelligence Agency, apparently because the agency had refused to transport his girlfriend when she was in Pakistan. In spite of such bad publicity, Wilson had little difficulty getting re-elected. The main reason was that Wilson used his position to help independent oil producers—the principal employers in the district—and supported the oil workers' unions. This gave him a solid base of support in the district; it also provided him with enough campaign funds to outspend any rivals.[9]

Evans has been untypical in the use he has made of the leeway his home style provides. So was Wilson. Most members are much more cautious, both in their policy stands and in their personal style. However, they use the same basic methods for handling their districts—personal trust and access, or a high profile on key issues—with the goal of trying to secure re-election while attending to their legislative tasks.

THE EFFECT OF ELECTION-ORIENTED ACTIVITY ON THE LEGISLATIVE PROCESS

The search for electoral security has a major impact on how Congress legislates: it leads to the stacking of committees with members whose districts have an interest in the relevant subject matter; it reinforces a basic "logrolling" style of decision-making; it encourages the wide distribution of benefits; and it facilitates "pork barrel" spending habits. A further consequence of the preoccupation with re-election is that members come to depend on campaign contributions from interest groups.

Committee Composition

Members want to deliver benefits to their districts, and try to get on the committees and subcommittees that will best enable them to do that. Not all committees are equally important. Using the scheme devised by Richard Fenno, we can divide congressional committees into three main categories: power committees, policy committees, and constituency committees.

Power committees. These deal with the central questions of expenditure, taxation, and trade. They include the appropriations committees, which approve all spending, and the House Ways and Means Committee and the Senate Finance Committee, which deal with most taxation and trade matters. Also included are the House Rules

9   *Congressional Quarterly, Weekly Report*, November 14, 1981.

Committee, through which all committee bills must pass for floor scheduling, and the Senate Foreign Relations Committee, because of its importance for the many senators with presidential ambitions. The power committees of the House are designated as "exclusive" committees, meaning that members of these committees cannot serve on any other committees. Any member would gladly serve on a power committee because of the wide impact of their jurisdiction, and because of the opportunities they provide for arranging benefits for their districts and for doing favors for other members.

Policy committees. These deal with areas such as education, labor, banking, energy, transportation, and science, in which major policy issues that divide the parties are fought out. These committees tend to change in popularity from one decade to the next as the current debate shifts. While these committees deal with broad issues of national policy, they also provide opportunities for members to steer projects to their districts, particularly in areas like transportation and science. In recent years they have also provided opportunities for raising campaign funds. When legislation affecting the health care, banking, insurance, or telecommunications industries has been before Congress, interest groups with a stake in the legislation have showered the members of the relevant committees with PAC money.

Constituency committees. These deal with issues that have distinct geographical constituencies. For example, the agriculture committees and the resources committees have jurisdiction over federal land use, water distribution, and mining—all issues that are important to the western states. Some other committees have constituency subcommittees; for example, the House Transport and Infrastructure Committee has a Coast Guard and Marine Transportation Subcommittee. These committees are stacked with members from those areas which have a stake in the subject matter. A member with a position on such a committee is able to legislate for her district, and enjoys all the campaign funding and presumed electoral benefits that flow from having such power.

Policy-making in the power committees affects the whole country, and all regions want a say in their decisions. Maintaining a broad geographical representation is an important consideration when new members are added, especially to the appropriations and tax committees. Otherwise, there is a very strong tendency for committee and subcommittee memberships—and therefore policy-making power—to be given to members representing those districts most interested in the policy outcomes. This pattern of policy-making by interested parties is very marked in the House, whose members can serve on only one or two committees. This is less true in the Senate, where all states have a wider range of interests and senators serve on more committees.

One example of such "clustering" is the Space and Aeronautics Subcommittee of the House Science Committee. Virtually all the members of this subcommittee hale from districts in which the aerospace industry is prominent. Thus, the Kennedy Space Center in Florida and the Johnson Space Center in Texas are both represented on the Republican side, as is the Marshall Space Flight Center in Huntsville, Alabama, on the Democratic side. This means that the subcommittee members are writing legislation that affects the major economic interests and sources of employment in their districts. We can be certain that no committee member is going to vote against these interests. Indeed, the members choose this subcommittee precisely so that they will be able to demonstrate their importance to the district by favoring these interests.

Logrolling

Through their committee positions, members representing the districts most affected by legislation are able to shape that legislation in its early stages. But a subcommittee cannot pass legislation by itself; it must first get the support of the full committee, and then of the Congress as a whole. This is made easier by the eagerness of members of Congress to defer to one another's interests in return for support for their own.

Often, a piece of legislation is important to only a few members—the ones whose districts are clearly affected by it. To get a particular measure passed, the interested members will need the help of those who are not interested in the measure and who are free to vote either way on it, but who have other measures in which they do have a strong interest and for which they need support. This diversity of interests leads to the universal practice of logrolling. In effect, each member says, "If you will support this measure that is important to me, in return I will support a measure that is important to you if I am free to do so." Members of Congress have a strong tendency to defer to one another's interests, provided they have leeway on the issues at hand and are not under pressure to oppose them.

The Distribution of Benefits

In addition to logrolling, there are two other techniques widely used to build support for legislation that affect the way legislation is designed. These are the disaggregation of benefits, and pork barrel politics.

The disaggregation of benefits. To disaggregate benefits is to distribute them widely—to design a bill in such a way that a large number of members, not simply the members of the committee, will get benefits for their district and will therefore support it.

A good example of how this technique works is the Clean Water Act, which became law over President Reagan's veto in February 1987.

The bill was vetoed by the president on the grounds that it cost too much and would increase the budget deficit. Reagan appealed to members who were concerned about the size of the deficit, and particularly to the Republicans, not to vote to override his veto. The Democratic majority leaders in both houses were anxious to override the veto to demonstrate their strength and the president's lame duck status after the 1986 elections. The Republicans held more than one-third of the seats in each house, and so they had the votes to block the override if party loyalty was their main concern.

In the event, the House voted 401 to 26 and the Senate 86 to 14 to override the veto, with a large majority of Republican members and even some Republican leaders voting against the president's position. The reason for this massive desertion of the president was not simply that providing cleaner water was likely to be a popular idea across the country, but that the bill distributed billions of dollars among the fifty states (and therefore to every House district) in federal grants for sewer construction projects. Since all states and districts benefited, most Republican members felt unable to vote against it in the name of the more abstract principles of reducing the budget deficit or supporting the president.

The principle of spreading benefits to build congressional support affects another category of decisions—the awarding of contracts for large-scale projects such as new weapons systems and major science projects. When large-scale government contracts are awarded, the crucial element is the willingness of Congress to fund the project, especially in its early stages. Once a project has been securely launched it is usually impossible to cut off funding, because so much money has already been spent and a broad coalition both inside and outside Congress has been built up in its support.

Here is one example of how important the support of highly placed members of Congress can be for landing a contract. In 1991 a consortium of Lockheed, Boeing, and General Dynamics was chosen to build a new, advanced tactical fighter plane for the Air Force. Reportedly, there was nothing to choose technically between the winning bid and the losing one (from Northrop/McDonnell Douglas). What most likely tipped the balance in the Defense Department's decision was the winners' influential congressional support, which consisted of the following: chair of the Senate Armed Services Committee, Sam Nunn, in whose state (Georgia) Lockheed had announced the plane would be built; chair of the Senate Finance Committee, Lloyd Bentsen, in whose state (Texas) General Dynamics' plane works are located; and the Speaker of the House, Tom Foley, whose state (Washington) is home of the Boeing Corporation. The losers could not match this level of support.[10]

---

10   *Newsweek*, May 6, 1991.

When corporations go after government contracts, they must take into account the location of their plants. For example, after it lost a competition in 1988 to supply a new fighter for the Navy, the Grumman Corporation decided to decentralize its production facilities, which had been concentrated in Long Island, New York. This was specifically in order to broaden the company's potential support in Congress.[11]

Winning contractors spread subcontracts widely across the country. The advantages of this mode of operation can be seen in the difficulties encountered by the budget-cutting 1995–96 Congress when it tried to discontinue production of the B–2 bomber. For all the declarations of President Clinton and the Defense Department that more B–2 bombers were not needed, and for all the long-standing skepticism of most liberal Democrats about military spending, and for all the budget-cutting zeal of the Republican chair of the House Budget Committee, John Kasich, the House repeatedly voted to continue funding production of the plane. The margin of victory came from liberal Democrats worried about the loss of jobs among B–2 subcontractors in their districts or states. A frustrated Kasich later said, "I don't think facts had anything to do with the outcome. We could have announced that the B–2 couldn't fly ... and it wouldn't have made any difference."[12]

A classic case of how Congress makes decisions on major projects was the decision to build the superconducting supercollider (SSC), the world's largest particle accelerator, at an estimated cost of $5 billion. The first decision was where to build it. The decision by the Department of Energy in 1988 to choose Texas over six other equally suitable sites was generally attributed to the influence of President Bush and House Speaker Jim Wright, both from Texas. The decision to build was dependent on Congress subsequently voting funds for the necessary research and development and, later, for construction contracts. The initial research contracts were widely distributed in the classic fashion. Additional support for the crucial early construction appropriations was built in the usual way, by cutting influential members in on the deal (a major contractor announced that it would build a new plant in Louisiana, the home state of Senator J. Bennet Johnson, chair of the Senate Energy Committee), and by voting money for other projects in the districts of other key members. By 1990 it was estimated that 815 universities, research labs, and companies in thirty-nine states had received SSC-related funding. The contract to build the SCC's research lab was divided between companies in New York, Idaho, and Texas. This led the local Texas congressman to boast that the building contract would "give collider supporters a leg up in lobbying the members of New York's huge congressional delegation."[13]

With over $1 billion already appropriated and construction of the massive project well underway, the SSC seemed secure. The fact that the conventional wisdom did not

---

11   *Washington Post, National Weekly Edition,* May 2–8, 1988.
12   *Congressional Quarterly, Weekly Report,* September 9, 1995.
13   *Newsweek,* July 2, 1990.

hold in this case is an indication of how serious the pressure to balance the budget had become by the 1990s. In 1993 the large, mainly Democratic freshman class in the House provided the majority to kill the SSC project, despite the continuing support of the major committees and of the party leaders in both houses. The fact that the B–2 bomber and the other major science project, the space station, narrowly survived similar elimination attempts has been attributed to the fact that they generated more jobs in local districts than the SSC.[14]

Pork barrel politics. An expenditure that is designated for a specific project is commonly described as "pork." Distributing pork has long been a traditional method of building majorities; the process involves trading favors and generally "greasing the wheels" of the legislative machinery in Congress. In earlier times, pork took the form of money for roads, bridges, canals, and dams—money that was authorized by the public works committees in each house. A commonly told joke is about the traveler who was driving down a narrow country dirt road when all of a sudden the road turned into a four-lane highway. On inquiring at the next gas station, he discovered that he had just crossed into the district of a member of the House Public Works Committee.

Pork is no longer confined to roads and dams. Other committees have long since found ways to benefit their own districts and increase their influence in the House by approving expenditures requested by other members. Special tax loopholes are another common form of pork. The House Ways and Means Committee and especially the Senate Finance Committee have long been notorious for writing specific tax breaks for industries (and even for individual businesses) into the Tax Code at the request of powerful members. The adjustment to the Tax Code, which is passed hurriedly at the end of each session, is commonly referred to as the "Christmas tree bill," so festooned is it with "gifts" for particular businesses. The members of Congress responsible will of course argue that each "gift" is economically justified on its merits.

So deeply engrained is this practice that even the Tax Reform Act of 1986, which simplified the Tax Code by eliminating many of the tax loopholes that had been written into it in the past, contained a large number of specific exemptions, labeled "transition rules," which had quietly been inserted by members of the committees. For example, an exemption was provided from the general limit on foreign tax credits for any corporation that was incorporated on June 13, 1917, and that had its principal place of business in Bartlesville, Oklahoma. This clause, inserted by Senator Boren of Oklahoma, a member of the Finance Committee, fit only the Phillips Petroleum Corporation.[15]

Nowadays almost no part of the federal budget can escape having special expenditures carved out of it to benefit a member's district—usually over the protests of the

---

14   *Congressional Quarterly, Weekly Report*, October 23, 1993.
15   *Newsweek*, June 16, 1986.

government agency whose budget is being plundered. One form of pork that has grown rapidly is "academic pork," which includes research and other grants steered to specific colleges without competition. *Congressional Quarterly* reported that between 1980 and 1992 the number of such grants had grown from seven worth $10.7 million to 499 worth $708 million.[16]

There are endless other examples of how the distribution of political power in the Congress influences the distribution of government expenditures. Both inside and outside the Congress, there are plenty of critics who assail the system as corrupt and wasteful. Others argue that most of the expenditures are justified on their merits and that the system ensures a wide distribution of resources across the country. In any case, they point out, given the lack of executive or party control of the legislative process, and given the individualistic nature of electoral competition, the scramble by legislators to acquire benefits for their home districts is difficult to prevent.

Some members openly boast of their ability to bring home the bacon for their districts. The current "king of pork" is Democratic senator Robert Byrd of West Virginia. In 1989, Byrd gave up the powerful position of Senate majority leader to take over the chair of the Appropriations Committee. On doing so, he vowed that he would capture $1 billion in federal expenditures for his state in the next five years. In fact, he succeeded in less than two years and kept on going. As chair of the full committee, Byrd was able to insert a host of relatively small items in most of the thirteen appropriations bills each year. These items were projects for West Virginia. One of his biggest coups was getting the CIA fingerprint lab and its 2,600 jobs transferred from Washington, D.C., to West Virginia. Senator Byrd does not apologize for his efforts to spend federal money in his state. West Virginia, he says, is a poor and otherwise powerless state that needs federal government help. All of the projects are justified in his eyes and in the eyes of most West Virginia voters, who have been re-electing the senator since 1959.

The case of Robert Michel of Illinois illustrates just how difficult it is for members to resist using their influence to steer expenditures to their districts. Michel served in the House from 1957 to 1995. He became a senior member of the Appropriations Committee, and from 1981 to 1995 he was Republican minority leader. Michel represented the 18th District of Illinois, a traditionally Republican district that centers on the city of Peoria and includes prosperous farming country. A conservative from a conservative district, Michel believed that government expenditure should be minimized; accordingly, he voted against many new government programs. Michel refused to use his increasing influence in the Congress to shower his district with benefits, yet he had no difficulty winning re-election.

By 1982, however, the farm economy in the Midwest was suffering, and Caterpillar Tractor, the largest employer in the district, was laying off thousands of workers.

---

16   *Congressional Quarterly, Weekly Report*, December 4, 1993.

Michel suddenly found himself in a fight for his political life against a well-financed Democrat. In the end, he squeaked back in by less than 6,000 votes out of nearly 200,000 cast.

An article in the *Congressional Quarterly* describes what happened next:

> Since the first of the year, it has been raining federal funds in the 18th district—public housing money, rural electrification loans, community development block grants, mass transit assistance.
>
> The public works jobs bill that cleared Congress in March contained $1.4 million to spruce up the runway at Greater Peoria Airport. Next year the city will become the training site for Mobile Army Surgical Hospitals. A long-debated bridge is to be built over the Illinois River ...
>
> In 1983 alone, Michel's list of "grants, loans, and projects secured for the district ..." comes to well over $60 million—a striking demonstration of what a powerful member of Congress can do for his district if he puts his mind to it.[17]

Like many members before and since, Michel found himself faced with a conflict between his principles and his career. Like most of the others, he chose his career. Another perspective is this: As long as the district remained prosperous it could afford to do without government money. Once it ran into hard times, however, like every other district it turned to the government and its member of Congress for the help it needed.

⍦ Closing Military Bases

It is next to impossible for members to resist securing new expenditures for their districts; it is equally difficult for them to eliminate existing spending. The most acute example of this one-way pressure on the federal budget relates to redundant military bases. There are thousands of military installations of varying size and importance scattered across all fifty states. Every time the United States was at war or defense expenditures were rising, members of the armed services committees and the defense appropriations subcommittees of both houses delighted in creating new military installations, mainly for their own districts. The result was that new bases were added but few if any were closed. By the mid-1980s it became generally recognized that declining defense budgets would have to be concentrated on personnel and equipment, and that many surplus bases would have to close.

While everyone recognized the need to close bases, given the deeply engrained deference that members accord each other's interests, it proved all too easy for them

---

17   *Congressional Quarterly, Weekly Report*, July 15, 1995. Reprinted with permission.

to get the bases in their own districts excluded from any list of base closures. In the end Congress had to adopt a special procedure to limit its own ability to protect bases from closure. The procedure adopted in 1988 established a Defense Base Closure and Realignment Commission, composed of nonmembers, to examine a list of base closings proposed by the Defense Department and to make final recommendations to the president. The president must decide whether to transmit the commission's list, as it stands, with no amendments, to the Congress. The Congress then has forty-five working days to pass a joint resolution disapproving the list; otherwise the closings will proceed. Under the procedure there is no power to amend the commission's list.

The procedure has been used four times since 1989. Each time, the president has transmitted the commission's list to Congress and attempts by members with district bases on the list to reject the list have been overwhelmingly defeated. Members campaign strenuously, first in hearings before the commission and later in the Congress, to save their bases. But as was intended, their hands are tied by the procedure. The vast majority of members, relieved that their own bases have been spared this time round, vote down attempts to override the commission's recommendations. In 1995 President Clinton strongly disagreed with some of the decisions of the latest commission, particularly about the closing of bases in California, a state that was vital to his re-election. Nevertheless, the prospect of refusing to transmit the list to Congress was even less appealing politically, given the pressures to cut expenditures, and he reluctantly went through with the process.[18]

The kind of bread-and-butter politics that emphasizes the delivery of concrete benefits to voters has a long history in the United States. It was the kind of politics practiced by the urban political machines well into the twentieth century. In the past, however, it was the party organization that delivered the goods. Now, with the disappearance of most strong party organizations, the onus to deliver falls on the individual member of Congress. Because of the lack of executive control of the legislative process and the decentralization of congressional operations since the 1970s, it is possible for many individual members to influence such decisions.

In Canada, decisions on the withdrawal of funding for major projects, such as the 1989 decision to close fourteen military bases across the country, and the 1994 decision to withdraw funding for the KAON particle accelerator project in British Columbia, are subject to the same political pressures as in the United States. The strongest pressures are usually regional ones. In Canada, however, it is the Cabinet that weighs the conflicting technical, financial, and political considerations and makes the decisions. Individual MPs lobby ministers privately, and some may even protest publicly, but they have very little influence on the final decisions.

---

18   *Congressional Quarterly, Weekly Report*, July 15, 1995.

The Problem of Money

In recent years increasing concern has been expressed, both outside and inside Congress, about how the legislative process is apparently being influenced by money from interest groups.[19] The problem has two facets: interest groups want to gain access to and curry favor with members of Congress, and members need to raise large sums of money on their own for their election campaigns.

In the House of Commons this problem does not arise to any serious extent. There are strict limits on how much money candidates can spend during elections, so MPs need much less in the way of campaign funds. In any case, the ordinary MP has little impact on legislation and has no freedom when it comes to voting in the House, and so is scarcely worth lobbying on most issues. In Canada, most political money is raised by the federal and provincial party organizations. Corporate donations are an important source of funds for the Liberal and Progressive Conservative parties. At the same time, small individual donations to parties are encouraged through tax breaks. As a result, the smaller parties have been able to remain at least somewhat competitive when it comes to campaign spending.

Money flows from interest groups to members of Congress in two legal ways: direct payments to members for their personal use, in the form of honoraria or gifts in kind (such as travel expenses); and campaign funds. The latter constitute the more pervasive and serious problem.

Before we look at the problems with legal fund-raising, it should be noted that bribery is also a persistent, though minor, problem in Congress. Bribery, defined as the accepting of money in exchange for legislative services, has long been illegal. In recent years several members of Congress have been accused of or convicted of accepting bribes, or of violating the laws governing personal or campaign financing. For example, in 1988 one long-serving member of the House from New York City, Mario Biaggi, was convicted of accepting illegal gratuities as well as extortion. During the 1988 elections, two senior committee chairmen, Fernand St. Germain of Rhode Island, chairman of the House Banking Committee, and Bill Chappell of Florida, chairman of the House Defense Appropriations Subcommittee, were defeated after repeated allegations were made that they had engaged in corrupt relations with interests doing business with their committees.

The biggest scandal in recent times over congressional corruption was the Abscam scandal in 1980, which involved an FBI sting operation. Congressmen and senators were invited to meet "Arab businessmen," who offered them money for help in circumventing the immigration laws. The congressmen's responses were secretly taped.

---

19   See, for example, Elizabeth Drew, *Politics and Money: The New Road to Corruption* (Collier, 1984).

One was filmed stuffing 100-dollar bills into his pockets! As a result, six members of the House and one senator were convicted of accepting bribes. In a perceptive comment on the Abscam case, columnist Meg Greenfield pointed out that the line between outright bribery and the other kinds of financial dealings common in Washington was a fine one. "The people who lobby for a tax break for your trade group, for a mortgage benefit for me, for all the rest, are—in some sense—with their contingent offers of money and support doing what the FBI bribers did."[20]

Honoraria and Gifts

Most people would consider it perfectly appropriate for the chair of the Banking Committee in the House or the Senate to address the annual convention of the American Bankers Association, and to be modestly reimbursed for that effort. Such acceptable practices began to be abused more and more as interest groups looked for ways to curry favor with influential members of Congress. Members were accepting honoraria and expenses to attend "conferences" put on by interest groups at expensive resorts, where their main task seemed to be to socialize with interest-group members on the golf course and at cocktail parties. Congressional staff members were being wooed in the same way.

In the 1980s, in the face of adverse publicity, both houses placed limits in on how much members could add to their congressional salaries through honoraria. House members could supplement their income by only 30 percent, and senators by 40 percent. Money collected above that had to be donated to charity. The charity aspect also turned out to be open to abuse. Interests began to donate to charities in the member's district in his name. Some of the resort trips were made into charity fund-raisers. While some members argued that this was a good way to raise money for charity, critics saw simply another example of interest groups doing favors for certain members.

In 1989, after an extended, agonized debate, the House voted to forbid members from keeping honoraria; in return, their pay was increased substantially. The Senate, whose members have a higher profile and attract more than most House members in honoraria, declined to follow the House's lead on this issue. Public criticism of Washington's ways continued. The common practice whereby lobbyists paid for expensive meals for members or gave gifts such as sports tickets attracted criticism. Finally, in 1995, under pressure from the 1994 freshman Republicans, who had promised to clean up Washington politics, both the House and the Senate voted to ban all gifts to members of Congress except those from family members, and to place strict limits on the kinds of expenses-paid trips that members could accept.

---

20   *Newsweek,* February 25, 1980.

Campaign Funding

The Watergate scandal of 1972–74 pushed the Congress to write new laws governing campaign financing. One of the factors feeding the scandal had been the enormous amount of money raised by the Nixon re-election campaign in 1972, much of it in illegal corporate contributions.

The important changes in the law were these: a limit of $1,000 was placed on individual contributions to a candidate's campaign, with primary and general election campaigns considered separately; interest groups would have to establish separate political funds, called political action committees (PACs), to which their members could contribute if they wished to donate to political campaigns; PAC donations were limited to $5,000 per candidate; and partial public funding, with an accompanying limit on total campaign spending, was to be provided for presidential campaigns, which was where the biggest problems seemed to lie. There was not sufficient support to extend public funding to congressional campaigns.

In the past twenty years the cost of campaigning has escalated. In the discussions in 1995 about campaign finance reform, the generally accepted figure for the cost of a House campaign was $600,000. This means that a House member must raise at least $300,000 per year, leaving aside the question of a primary election challenge. An additional complication is that sometimes very much more may have to be spent. Members fear the emergence of a wealthy or well-financed challenger and feel that they must be prepared for such a contingency. Collecting a large and well-publicized "war chest" is a good way of warning off potential challengers.

In the Senate, the fact that elections are every six years only partially offsets the fact that much larger sums are required. A House district has around half a million people; almost all states are much larger both in population and in size. Senate races routinely cost millions of dollars. In 1994 a new record for Senate campaign spending was set in California: the challenger, Republican representative Michael Huffington, spent close to $30 million, most of it his own money. As a result, the incumbent, Diane Feinstein, was forced to raise $15 million to eke out a narrow victory.

Election results have demonstrated repeatedly that the candidate who spends the most money does not always win. It is generally agreed, however, that to have a fair chance of winning a candidate must have enough money to run a serious television campaign and to be able to reply to attacks by an opponent. Nowadays candidates who are seriously underfunded compared to their opponent rarely win congressional elections.

There are only a few possible ways for a member of Congress, or a potential challenger, to raise the money necessary for a campaign: from personal funds, from party funds, from donations from individuals of up to $1,000, and from PAC funds in amounts of up to $5,000.

	Senate	House
	Percent of total	
Candidate contributions	2	3
Candidate loans	11	11
Individual contributions	62	49
PACs	19	32

Table 6.1

Sources of receipts of congressional candidates, 1991–92.

Remaining receipts include contributions from party committees, transfers from other funds, and interest payments.

Source: Federal Election Commission as reported in U.S. Bureau of the Census, *Statistical Abstract of the United States 1995*, Table 469.

Personal funds. The 1974 law placed a limit on the amount of personal funds a candidate could spend on her own campaign. In 1976, however, the Supreme Court declared such a limit to be a violation of the First Amendment.[21] This gave an enormous advantage to wealthy candidates. While personal funds do not usually loom large, in some campaigns they have been crucial. In the 1988 Senate race in Wisconsin, for example, Herbert Kohl, a wealthy businessman who had never run for public office before, scared several prominent local politicians out of the Democratic primary by spending an estimated $3 million of his own money. In November Kohl spent a further $2 million in the process of outspending and defeating his Republican opponent. Similar examples of huge personal spending could be drawn from other years.

For the 1996 Senate elections, the Democratic Senatorial Campaign Committee concentrated on recruiting wealthy candidates to challenge conservative Republican incumbents.[22] Wealthy candidates are able to contribute large amounts to their own campaigns; paradoxically, they also find it easier to raise money from others, who are more willing to give to what appears to be a viable campaign. Wealthy candidates can claim with more credibility that they are not dependent on special interests.

Party funds. The campaign financing laws have increased the importance of the political parties as a source of funds. Funds are provided through the national committees and through the House and Senate campaign committees of both parties, The limits on donations that can be made to the parties are higher than for candidates: $20,000 for individual donors and $15,000 for PACs. The parties, in turn, can give up to $10,000 to House candidates, plus nearly double that amount in the form of services, such as polling. For Senate campaigns the amounts are higher.

---

21   *Buckley v. Valeo* 424 U.S. 1 (1976).
22   *Congressional Quarterly, Weekly Report*, February 24, 1996.

Individual donations up to $1,000. For most members of Congress this is the preferred source of contributions and still the major one. That being said, finding enough donors and persuading them to contribute (for example, by direct mail techniques) is time-consuming and expensive. It follows that the temptation to raise money in larger amounts from PACs is very strong. Some (read *very few*) members of Congress refuse to accept PAC money. Senators rely less on PAC money; this can be attributed to their greater visibility, which makes it easier to attract individual contributions.

Money from political action committees. The 1974 law triggered a large increase in the number of PACs, and twenty-five years later, their numbers are still growing. While PACs have been set up by a wide variety of groups and individuals, the greatest increase has been in the number of those established by corporate and trade organizations. Campaign contributions from PACs are entirely legal, but a great deal of concern is now being expressed over their steadily increasing importance as a source of campaign funds.

Two features of PAC funding stand out:

First, most PAC money—as much as 90 percent in some election years—is given to incumbents. This means that even though business groups would normally be more sympathetic to Republican policies, most of their money went to incumbent Democrats before 1995. There are two reasons for this: PACs prefer to back winners; and PACs give most of their money to those holding positions of power in the Congress.

Second, PAC money is heavily targeted to members of those committees dealing with legislation of interest to the PAC. The American Medical Association's PAC, for example, gives most of its money to members of the committees concerned with health policy. The amount of campaign money handed out by the AMA and by other groups related to the health industry ballooned in the 1993–94 Congress when health care reform was President Clinton's top priority.

Members of Congress deny that their decisions are influenced by the sources of their campaign funds. Some people indeed have argued that the initiative in dealing with PACs usually lies with the member of Congress. Some members in fact virtually require groups with legislation before their committee to contribute to their campaigns. When Senator Lloyd Bentsen became chair of the Senate Finance Committee in 1987, he announced that he would hold regular breakfast meetings with lobbyists for which the annual charge would be $10,000 (the maximum PAC contribution for a primary and an election campaign). This arrangement attracted so much public criticism that the senator canceled it, but similar arrangements have been set up by other powerful members.

Some members argue that there is now so much campaign money available from PACs that it can free members from dependency on specific interests. Democratic representative Al Swift of Washington put it this way: "There is so damn much money out there that anybody who gives anybody anything for it is an idiot. If you can't get it from the oil guys, you can get it from the natural gas guys. If you can't get it from the communications guys, you can get it from the rail guys."[23]

It is probably true that a campaign contribution does not buy a member's vote; still, everyone agrees that a contribution does buy access to the member. Members agree that it is very difficult to refuse to listen to someone who has contributed to your campaign. In 1996 the *Wall Street Journal* reported that Senator Robert Dole of Kansas did a number of political favors over the years, in the form of sponsoring tax breaks or interventions with federal departments (some successful, some not), for companies that had contributed regularly to his senatorial and presidential campaigns. It is clear that Senator Dole is not unique in this respect.[24] Interest groups argue that all they want is the right to make their case to the member. The danger in this situation is that because members of Congress are so desperate for campaign funds, they will end up listening mainly to the people who provide those funds.

Most members of Congress are very unhappy with the pressures of fund-raising. Some senators have stated that in an election year they must spend as much as half their time not making laws or meeting their constituents, but attending fund-raising events and talking potential contributors into providing the millions of dollars needed for a campaign. The ethical conflicts involved in the current system have been well publicized by the media and by public interest groups such as Common Cause. More and more loudly, both the public and the members themselves are calling for reform of the campaign funding laws.

Campaign Finance Reform

The campaign spending reforms of 1974 had the unintended consequence of encouraging the growth of PACs, and by the 1990s sufficient loopholes had been discovered that the law's impact was weakened. There is now general agreement that further reform is needed. Some political conservatives argue that since campaign funds are spent by candidates to communicate with voters, what is needed is more money, not less. They advocate removing all restrictions on raising and spending campaign money with the sole proviso that the amount and source of all campaign funds be made public. This way, they argue, the voters will be able to make up their own minds about the

---

23   *Congressional Quarterly, Weekly Report*, March 17, 1990
24   *Wall Street Journal*, February 12, 1996.

connection between funding and the member's behavior in Congress. However, most politicians and commentators worry about the enormous advantage that such a free-for-all would give to monied interests, and argue that more restrictions on campaign funding are needed.

Attempts to rewrite the campaign financing laws in recent years have run into two major roadblocks. In the first place, both parties are wary about changes that would handicap them and benefit their opponents. Since the late nineteenth century the Republican Party has had the advantage in fund-raising due to its greater support in the business community. Thus, Republicans typically oppose spending limits, as well as federal subsidies in any form, while the Democrats take the opposite positions. Various attempts from 1990 through 1996 to change the law were blocked by partisan differences.

The second obstacle is the Supreme Court's extension of the First Amendment guarantee of free speech to cover campaign spending. In 1976 the Court argued that limits on campaign spending were only constitutional if they were voluntarily accepted in exchange for a benefit.[25] This means that most presidential candidates are legally restricted in their spending because they accept federal matching funds. Recent proposals for benefits that could be offered to candidates in exchange for limiting spending have included the following: discounts on television time and postal rates, and exemption from a proposed tax on campaign contributions. It has also been suggested that additional benefits could be provided for candidates opposed by candidates who do not accept spending limits. Recent decisions of the Supreme Court have broadened the definition of free speech in campaigning[26] and restricted the application of the campaign spending law.[27] Some commentators are now arguing that the only way to be sure that laws limiting campaign spending are constitutional would be to pass a constitutional amendment—an unlikely prospect.

The objectives of campaign finance reform are relatively easy to agree on: to maintain free speech and encourage communication with the voters; to lessen the burden of fund-raising on political candidates; to create a level playing field between the political parties and between rich candidates and the others; and to loosen the connection between political fund-raising and the legislative activities of members of Congress. It is genuinely difficult, however, to write a law that meets these diverse, even contradictory objectives, especially in a society like the United States, which finds it so difficult to place any restrictions on free speech or on the right of interest groups to lobby the government.

---

25   *Buckley v. Valeo* 424 U.S. 1 (1976).

26   *McIntyre v. Ohio Elections Commission* 115 S.Ct. 1511 (1995)

27   *Colorado Republican Campaign Committee v. Federal Elections Commission* 116 S.Ct. 2309 (1996)

CHAPTER 7

THE PRESIDENCY

The office of President of the United States is unique. The definition of this novel position was the key element in the carefully balanced constitutional structure that the framers invented for the United States. Their model was the British "balanced constitution," in which the power of the monarch was balanced by the two houses of the legislature. There was no blueprint for what was really an elected monarch. The example of dignity and modesty was set by George Washington, the first president, who insisted on behaving in a constitutional fashion and decided to retire after two terms. Washington helped define the new office, but it was some time before fears that it would inevitably develop into a monarchy finally died away.

The office of prime minister evolved quite differently out of British constitutional practice. During the eighteenth century, effective executive power gradually passed from the monarch to his or her ministers, led by the prime minister. By the nineteenth century the ministers were only able to govern with the support of a majority in the House of Commons. As a consequence, the monarch lost the power even to choose the members of his Cabinet and was relegated to the ceremonial and symbolic role of "constitutional monarch." These developments separated the roles of head of state (monarch) and political chief executive (prime minister), roles that are combined in the office of president. This chapter looks at how the office of president was established and at how this eighteenth-century creation has developed as American society has changed over the past two centuries.

The President in the Constitution

The major problem confronting the framers of the Constitution was how to set up the executive power.[1] Their knowledge of history and of political theory told them that executive tyranny was the principal threat to individual liberties. Their own experience in dealing with the British had confirmed this (the Declaration of Independence had charged George III with a long list of rights abuses). The Articles of Confederation, under which they had operated since the War of Independence, had a rotating executive, and that made for a very weak form of government. As the most astute of them realized, they would need a stronger national government if their bold political experiment was to survive, and this would require an executive that was strong enough to provide leadership but not so unchecked that a tyranny might possibly develop.

At the convention, most of the argument on this question related to how the executive would be chosen. There was no precedent in modern times for an elected executive, and the framers realized that the method of election would have an important bearing on the kind of person elected. Agreement on an elaborate electoral "college" was the final piece of the constitutional puzzle to fall into place (see Chapter 11). The framers also established a system of checks and balances between the executive and legislative branches of government. This design was based on their interpretation of the eighteenth-century struggle in Britain to find the right balance in the constitutional system between order and liberty. A system in which the legislature was totally dominant might lead to tyranny of the majority. The framers gave the executive independence from the legislature; but at the same time, made the exercise of some key executive powers dependent on the cooperation of the legislature.

THE POWERS OF THE PRESIDENT

One question about which there was little disagreement at the convention was what the necessary executive powers were. These must have seemed fairly obvious. Article II, Section 1, of the Constitution vests "the executive power" in a President of the United States and then goes on to spell out the method of election.

In Section 2, the president is made commander in chief of the army and navy and required to supervise the executive departments. The president is given the power to

---

1   For a thorough discussion of the various aspects of the presidency as they were debated at the Constitutional Convention of 1787 and at the precedents established by the first four presidents, see Thomas E. Cronin ed., *Inventing the American Presidency* (University Press of Kansas, 1987).

pardon criminals—a power traditionally exercised by the king. While the power of clemency was considered a normal executive function at the time, its use has become highly controversial in recent times. When President Ford pardoned former President Nixon in 1974 for crimes surrounding the Watergate scandal (to which he had not admitted), there was a storm of protest.

Section 2 also gives the president key powers in foreign policy, to make treaties and appoint ambassadors as well as to appoint the other members of the executive branch and the Supreme Court justices. The exercise of these powers is, however, to be checked by the Senate. Treaties must be ratified by a two-thirds vote, and appointments must be made "with the Advice and Consent of the Senate."

Section 3 requires the president to provide the Congress with "information of the State of the Union"; this is the basis for the State of the Union message, which is nowadays delivered to a joint session of Congress each year in late January. The president is to recommend legislation to Congress and may convene it in an emergency. His most important check on the legislative branch, the veto power, is set out earlier, in Article I, Section 7. At the end of Section 3 there is another general statement of executive responsibility: "he shall take care that the laws be faithfully executed."

As the ultimate check on presidential abuse of power, Section 4 makes it clear that the president, like all appointed officials, may be removed from office if he is impeached by the House of Representatives and convicted by the Senate.

Of the later amendments to the Constitution, only four directly affect the presidency. None of them deal with the powers of the office.

- The 12th (ratified in 1804) adjusted the working of the Electoral College to provide for the separate election of the president and vice president.

- The 20th (1933) brought forward the inauguration of the new president and Congress elected in November from March and the following December, respectively, to January. This reflected the need for a quicker transition of power in modern conditions.

- The 22nd (1951) limited a president to two terms. This was intended as an additional safeguard against executive tyranny. It was enacted after Franklin Roosevelt had broken the tradition, established by George Washington, that a president should serve only two terms.

- The 25th (1967) reflected growing concerns about how to maintain the continuity of executive leadership at times of crisis. (President Kennedy had been assassinated four years earlier.) It provided methods for filling a vacancy in the vice presidency and for handling the serious illness of a president.

For the most part, the powers of the president are stated in general terms in the Constitution. Throughout American history there has been a running debate as to whether the president also has prerogative powers that are inherent in the office although they are not spelled out in the Constitution.[2]

THE DEVELOPMENT OF THE PRESIDENCY

While the constitutional powers of the president have remained unchanged for 200 years, the role of the presidency has been transformed by changes in American society. Some important changes affecting the office came about quickly. The most significant changes, however, have been those which have shaped the modern office of the president in the twentieth century. The early changes can be summarized under two headings: the intrusion of party, and the growth of democracy.

The intrusion of party. The framers of the Constitution distrusted political parties and saw no need for them in their new political system. They believed that their ingenious indirect method of election would insulate the president from partisanship. In this they were mistaken. George Washington was a national hero, a figure above politics, but before he retired at the end of his second term, his Cabinet was bitterly divided into two opposing parties, both of them organizing to capture the presidency and control the government. By the time of the second battle between Adams and Jefferson in 1800, voting in the Electoral College was entirely along party lines. Ever since the development of the two-party system in the 1830s, no one has been able to win the presidency without first being nominated by a major party.

The growth of democracy. The Constitution allows each state legislature to decide how to select its presidential electors. Originally, in most states the legislature itself chose the electors, although right from the start a few states allowed a popular vote. With the spread of democratic ideas in the 1820s, popular election of the presidential electors became an irresistible idea (only South Carolina held out until the Civil War). This meant that the president was in effect elected by the people.

The Presidency in the Nineteenth Century

Although the presidency was the center of political attention and the focus of ambition for every politician right from the beginning, in the nineteenth century the office

---

2   For a recent argument that certain perogative or discretionary powers are inherent in the executive offices, see David K. Nichols, *The Myth of the Modern Presidency* (Pennsylvania State University Press, 1994)

conferred more prestige than power. Power in Washington lay in the Congress, especially in the hands of those who rose to the top through their political skills or oratorical powers. In the second half of the century power increasingly lay in the hands of the leaders of the powerful state party organizations in the large states of the Northeast and Midwest. The parties controlled many House districts and, through their influence on the state legislatures, controlled elections to the Senate.

The state party bosses also played a major role in nominating presidential candidates. However, agreement on a candidate at the national convention required compromise between the bosses. Most nominees came from a small handful of large, pivotal states: New York, Illinois, Ohio, Pennsylvania, and Indiana. Governors were much more likely to be nominated than members of Congress. Another popular category in the nineteenth century was army generals: Jackson, Harrison, Taylor, and Grant all ascended to the presidency after transferring their prestige from the battlefield to the political arena.

The situation of the presidency in the nineteenth century was summed up by Lord Bryce, a British observer of American politics, in *The American Commonwealth* (1888) in a famous chapter, "Why Great Men Are Not Chosen Presidents." Generally speaking, presidents tended to be secondary political figures, like Abraham Lincoln, or generals with untested political skills, who were surrounded in Washington by the powerful state bosses, either in their Cabinet or in the Senate. As a result, most presidents were politically weak. Although the president was the only politician who could have claimed a truly national and popular mandate, there was a strong taboo against the president taking his case directly to the public. The one nineteenth-century president who tried to do so was Andrew Johnson, and he was impeached by the House of Representatives.[3]

The two most important nineteenth-century presidents were the exceptions who proved the rule. Andrew Jackson (1829–37) provided the model of the president as "tribune of the people" and leader of his party. In his policy battles with the Congress, Jackson used every constitutional and political weapon available to him as president and party leader. For example, he was the first president to use the veto power as a political weapon. Jackson was the transitional figure between the elite, Washington-based politics of the first thirty years and the democratic, party-based politics of the rest of the century, and none of his successors could equal his popularity and control over his party.

Abraham Lincoln (1861–65), generally reckoned now to be the greatest of all the presidents, did not have an impressive record before his election. A former one-term Congressman and defeated Senate candidate from the swing state of Illinois, who had taken a more moderate position on slavery than the leading Republicans, he was the classic compromise candidate. In office he was surrounded by a Cabinet of powerful

---

3   Jeffrey K. Tulis, *The Rhetorical Presidency* (Princeton University Press, 1987), 87–93.

and experienced state bosses. Lincoln, however, was president during the greatest crisis in American history, the Civil War, and turned out to have the qualities of courage, wisdom, and political astuteness needed at that time. The bold, even unconstitutional, use of executive powers, such as the suspension of the right of *habeas corpus* and the freeing of the slaves in the rebel states, for which he is rightly famous, was possible only because the nation was at war. Such a crisis required strong executive leadership, which Lincoln provided.

The Transformation of the Presidency in the Twentieth Century

By the start of the twentieth century, America was no longer an ethnically and religiously homogeneous society of farms and small towns. After the Civil War, America had developed into a major industrial power with enormous concentrations of financial and industrial capital. To staff the mills and factories, immigrants had poured into the cities of the Northeast and Midwest from southern and eastern Europe. The transcontinental railroads and new developments in agriculture had opened up the prairies to farming, thus completing the settlement of the continent and closing the era of the western frontier.

The increased economic and social complexity of American society brought a shift in political culture—changes in voters' attitudes toward, and expectations of, both politics and politicians. These changes can be summarized under three headings: the nationalization of politics, the weakening of the parties, and the personalization of the presidency.

The nationalization of politics. As the American economy expanded, it became increasingly integrated and national in scope. Pressures for changes in financial policy and for government regulation were increasingly directed toward the federal government. The main focus of political life began to shift away from the locality and the state toward Washington, D.C.

The weakening of political parties. Pressures for the government to modernize in response to the changes in the business world came to a head in a series of reforms sponsored by the Progressive movement. These reforms were carefully designed to weaken the influence of the political parties on politics and on government. Parties were depicted as generally inefficient, unprofessional, and corrupt—as a throwback to an earlier age.

The Progressive reforms largely succeeded in weakening the parties, especially at the state level. The widespread adoption of direct primary methods of nomination reduced party control over nominations except at the local level, thus undermining a central function of the party. The direct election of U.S. senators weakened the state bosses and removed most of them from the Senate.

The personalization of the presidency. As politics became more "national," more attention came to be paid to the chief executive's role in policy-making. The decline of the influence of the party bosses in Washington removed some of the party constraints on the president and strengthened his role as national leader of his party. Other, related developments also increased the importance of the president.

The style of presidential campaigns changed. The "military" style, based on the mobilization of the party faithful through appeals to party loyalty, gave way to an "advertising" style, in which the focus was on the candidate rather than his party. William Jennings Bryan, the Democratic Populist candidate of 1896, was the first to undertake an exhausting national campaign on a grand scale. (He lost.)

Another important development was the growth of cheap, mass-circulation newspapers in the cities, and of national magazines with a large, middle-class readership. It was now possible for a publicity-conscious president to dominate the headlines and communicate directly with his national constituency over the heads of the party and the Congress. Later, radio (in the 1930s) and television (beginning in the 1960s) would make it much easier for a president to speak directly to the voters. This would give the advantage to politicians with strong media skills.

The first president to demonstrate the new potential for personalized leadership was Theodore Roosevelt, undoubtedly the most flamboyant character ever to become president. Roosevelt rose to national fame through a military operation, as many of his predecessors in the nineteenth century had done. He achieved this not as a general, like the others, but as an enthusiastic amateur leading a volunteer cavalry regiment in Cuba during the Spanish-American War of 1898. The press publicity from this exploit helped to him achieve the governorship of New York in the same year. The Republican state party boss found him too difficult to control and in 1900 got rid of him by "promoting" him to the prestigious obscurity of the vice presidency. Shortly afterwards, President McKinley was assassinated and the energetic Roosevelt took over.

Teddy Roosevelt believed that the president could take any necessary action unless it was forbidden by the Constitution. He was the first president to actively set out to influence public opinion to support his policies. He initiated an energetic role in foreign policy, actively encouraging Panama to break away from Colombia so that he could secure American rights to build the Panama Canal. His visit to Panama was the first time a sitting president had traveled outside the United States. In 1904, Roosevelt became the first vice president who had succeeded to the presidency to be elected president in his own right.

Roosevelt's presidency provided a new, activist model for the office that would eventually become the standard. Of his immediate successors, only Democrat

Woodrow Wilson (1913–21) followed his example, but there were long-term factors at work that were increasing the importance of the president at the expense of the Congress and making activist presidencies inevitable. The new factors were the expanding role of the federal government and the rising importance of the United States in the world.

◢ The Expanding Role of the Federal Government

The American tradition has always been to minimize the role of government, especially the federal government. This is one important point on which the American and Canadian traditions differ. This traditional resistance to government action was intensified with the development of strong intellectual arguments for *laissez-faire* and social Darwinism toward the end the nineteenth century. The increasingly powerful business community, which in the early years argued for government support, discovered the merits of unqualified *laissez-faire*.

Even in the face of this powerful resistance, as American society grew more complex and the economy more integrated, popular demands for government action to solve problems grew. The politicians responded with legislation and new executive agencies to administer the new laws. One of the key reforms the Progressives sponsored led to the professionalization of the federal public service, which increased the stability, experience, and expertise of the executive branch. As the executive branch grew in size and expertise, so did the potential power of the chief executive.

The Great Depression of the 1930s and President Franklin Roosevelt's New Deal policies brought about a major shift in American attitudes toward the federal government. For the first time, most Americans saw the government in a positive light, as the solver of economic and social problems. This new attitude was powerfully reinforced by the widespread acceptance of Keynesian economics (after John Maynard Keynes, a British economist), which after the late 1930s largely replaced *laissez-faire* as orthodox economic thought.

The classical economic theory was that the economy was governed by natural laws, which in the long run brought about the full employment of resources. Consequently, government interference in the market—for example, trying to reduce unemployment—could only be counterproductive. In contrast, Keynes argued that market forces could not always produce full employment and government could and therefore should intervene to influence the level of economic activity. As a result of the spread of his new theory, voters began to hold governments responsible for managing the economy.

Along with the steady expansion of the federal government in the twentieth century, there has been a corresponding rise in the importance of the president as manager of the executive branch. These developments have also increased the need for the president to provide leadership in the legislative process.

◀ The Rising Importance of the United States in the World

From the beginning, the president has asserted the leading role in shaping American foreign policy, and Congress has largely conceded it to him. This is mainly because any state needs to speak with one voice when dealing with the rest of the world.

Between the War of Independence (1776–81) and the War of 1812 (1812–14), the United States was struggling to retain its independence, and was heavily preoccupied with its relations with Britain and France, the superpowers of that day. For the rest of the nineteenth century, however, the United States was preoccupied with its internal affairs and had neither the desire nor the economic and military weight to play a role in world affairs.

The Spanish-American War of 1898, as a result of which the United States acquired the last remnants of the old Spanish Empire, marked the end of the long period of American isolation and the emergence of the United States as a major economic and military power. The renewed importance of foreign policy increased the importance of the president, and enhanced his constitutional role as commander in chief of the U.S. military.

America's involvement in World War I and President Wilson's ambitious efforts to restructure Europe and establish a new world order through the League of Nations after that war led to disillusionment at home. As a result, the United States drew back again from overseas involvement, except in the Western Hemisphere, which it had declared to be its "sphere of influence" as early as the Monroe Doctrine of 1823.

The reluctance of the United States to get involved in the affairs of Europe in the 1930s ended abruptly when the Japanese attacked the American Pacific Fleet at Pearl Harbor, Hawaii, on December 7, 1941 and the United States declared war on Japan. Germany then declared war on the United States, which reciprocated. The Americans emerged from World War II with the satisfaction of having saved the world from the evils of fascism. The ruin of Germany and Japan and the profound weakening of the British Empire left the United States and the Soviet Union as the new superpowers, their unique status reinforced by the fact that at the time, they alone possessed nuclear weapons.

Since 1945, every American president has been "the man with his finger on the nuclear trigger"—a statement that underlines the central role the United States has played in the world since then and the correspondingly enhanced role that the president has played in Washington because of the overwhelming importance of foreign and defense policy. The expansion of government has forced the president to play an activist role in shaping domestic policy; in the same manner, the greatly increased role of the United States in the world has required active leadership from the president in foreign policy. Some analysts have suggested that the ending of the Cold War may eventually lead to a diminution of the president's power.

THE INSTITUTIONALIZATION OF THE PRESIDENCY SINCE WORLD WAR II

New public expectations and new government tasks led to an expanded role for the president in the twentieth century; obviously, presidents required more staff to cope with the increased role. Traditionally, presidents had functioned with the help of a handful of personal secretaries, and worked with some of their Cabinet secretaries or others in government on particular problems. In his first years, Franklin Roosevelt gathered around him a "brains trust" of young members of his administration, who shaped the early New Deal legislation under his authority. Many presidents relied on a "kitchen cabinet"—that is, on friends outside government who gave the president support and advice. The staff assistance that was developed for the president has two main elements: the Executive Office of the President; and the White House staff.

The Executive Office of the President

In 1937 the Brownlow Commission, which had been set up to study government administration, opened its report with the words: "The President needs help." As a result, the Executive Office of the President was established. Since then, a number of government functions, for which the president has been given direct responsibility, have been located in the Executive Office, making it in effect the president's "department." The principal components of the Executive Office at present are the Office of Management and Budget, the Council of Economic Advisers, and the National Security Council.

The Office of Management and Budget (OMB) is the successor to the Bureau of the Budget, which was established in the Treasury Department in 1921 to coordinate and present to Congress an executive budget. All departmental budgets had to be approved by the bureau before being transmitted to Congress. President Roosevelt expanded the bureau's functions to include approval of all departmental legislative proposals. In 1939 the Bureau of the Budget was transferred to the Executive Office of the President. In 1970 President Nixon renamed the bureau the Office of Management and Budget and expanded its functions further to include the reviewing of all departmental regulations.

The OMB has thus emerged as the central office for managing the vast executive branch of government. Its director, responsible directly to the president and given Cabinet rank, is always potentially a powerful figure in Washington. The best recent example of how much power this person can wield is that of David Stockman,

President Reagan's first OMB director (1981–85), who was the principal architect of the "Reagan Revolution" in economic policy.

The Council of Economic Advisers was established in 1946 to provide the president with economic advice. Its creation signified that government had accepted responsibility for managing the economy. The three members of the council, including the chair, have usually been academic or business economists.

The National Security Council (NSC) was established in 1947 as part of the reorganization of the foreign and defense policy machinery of government after World War II. The new structure reflected America's new role in world affairs and the centrality of the president in directing that role. The NSC is a coordinating committee, chaired by the president, that brings together key government officials in the areas of foreign and defense policy: the state and defense secretaries, the CIA director, the military chiefs of staff, the vice president, and others at the president's discretion. The NSC staff, located in the Executive Office, provide the president with his own source of foreign policy advice independent of the other agencies of government. The head of the council, the national security adviser, has often played a major role in shaping foreign policy. The most powerful of the advisers was Henry Kissinger, who with President Nixon ran America's foreign policy from the White House between 1969 and 1973.

Other offices have been attached to the Executive Office at different times. Some of these have later been transferred to other parts of the executive branch. The offices that have survived over time are the Office of Science and Technology Policy, which has advised the president on science policy since 1962; the Office of the President's Special Representative on Trade, who exercises the authority that the Congress gave to the president in 1963 to negotiate foreign trade agreements, such as the North America Free Trade Agreement (NAFTA) with Canada and Mexico in 1993; and the Council on Environmental Quality, which was established by President Nixon in 1969. President Clinton established a National Economic Council to coordinate economic policy in 1993.

The White House Staff

While the principal officials in the Executive Office, like other executive appointees, are nominated by the president and confirmed by the Senate, the members of the White House staff are exempted from confirmation, since they are considered to be the president's personal staff helping him carry out the core functions of his office. Traditionally, the president was allocated one official secretary, though many of them made use of unofficial advisers and assistants. With the expanding role of the president in the twentieth century, the need for more assistance grew. President Hoover was the first to employ additional professional staff to deal with Congress and the press. By one count, Franklin Roosevelt had eleven staffers by the end of his presidency. Under Eisenhower the count rose to thirty-four. Kennedy, reacting to his predecessor's military-style staff structure, cut his team of aides to twenty-two, but the number soon crept upward again.[4] President Nixon inaugurated something like the current staff structure with fifty-two assistants. Although most presidents have vowed to cut back when they take office, the number has continued to trend upward.

In mid-1995, for example, the *U.S. Government Manual* listed 123 members of President Clinton's White House Office, not counting support staff. This included the three top officials (chief of staff Leon Panetta, adviser George Stephanopoulos, and counselor Mack McLarty), twenty-two officials with the rank of assistant to the president, twenty-nine deputy assistants, forty-seven special assistants, eleven staff in the counsel's office, and one additional adviser. Five of the staff were assigned to the First Lady.

Walcott and Hult divide the functions performed by the White House staff into three categories: outreach, policy processing, and coordination and supervision.

Outreach. This involves relations with Congress (through the Office of Congressional Relations), with the rest of the executive branch, with states and local governments, with the president's party, and with a variety of special interest groups—business, unions, religious groups, and so on—whose support the president particularly wants to cultivate. Hoover was the first to appoint a press secretary, and briefing the now-large White House press corps remains a key task. The aspect that has expanded most in the last twenty years, in this new era of "continuous campaigning," is the Office of Communications, whose function is public relations, continuous opinion-polling, and advising the president on how to present himself and his message.

Policy processing. The NSC machinery facilitates the president's leadership in foreign and defense policy. Since FDR, presidents have worked systematically to develop domestic policies and get them passed. Since Truman, presidents have presented an annual legislative agenda to Congress. Presidents have experimented with different forms of organization within the White House to handle domestic policy. Nixon established a Domestic Council and Clinton a National Economic Council (by analogy with the NSC), but neither format has so far become a permanent part of the White House structure.

Coordination and supervision. As the president's public role has expanded, the staff who manage his schedule, his travel, and the flow of paper have grown in number.

---

4   Charles E. Walcott and Karen M. Hult, *Governing the White House: From Hoover through LBJ* (University Press of Kansas, 1995), 8.

Included in this category are the speechwriters who draft speeches and remarks for the president's many public appearances. As the White House staff has swelled, the task of managing it has become more complex. Since Nixon, every president has needed a chief of staff, but presidents vary greatly in how large a role the chief of staff plays.

The Vice Presidency

The office of Vice President of the United States is the most paradoxical in the whole of the American system. The vice president is surrounded by the trappings of power: he has an official residence in Washington; he has round-the-clock protection from the Secret Service; and wherever he travels, in the United States or around the world, he goes in Air Force Two and in limousines with flags flying and a police escort. Yet the Constitution lists no real duties for the vice president except to be on stand-by in case anything happens to the president.

The vice presidency was "an incidental by-product" created during the invention of the Electoral College system (see Chapter 11), added to ensure that the presidential electors did not waste their second vote.[5] The Constitution makes the vice president the presiding officer of the Senate. But from the beginning, the Senate has refused to allow vice presidents to exercise any real authority. As a result, the vice president only presides on ceremonial occasions or when needed to break a tie vote. Even then, he votes as directed by the president.

The vice president is the subordinate member of the party ticket, chosen by the president, who alone has the political authority that arises from being elected by the people at large. The first two vice presidents were major figures who became president since, originally, the runner-up in the Electoral College became vice president. However, the awkwardness of having a president and vice president from different parties soon became apparent, and the 12th Amendment in 1803 provided for the presidential electors to vote for the two offices separately. The result of the reform was that the vice presidency sank into obscurity.

The parties used the vice presidential nomination to balance the presidential ticket, the intention being to unite the party and extend the appeal of the presidential nominee. Typically, the vice presidential nominee was chosen from a different region of the country and sometimes from a different faction of the party than the presidential candidate. The choice of the vice presidential candidate used to be part of the bargaining by the state party leaders over the presidential nomination at the convention; but since Franklin Roosevelt in 1940, the presidential nominee has been allowed to choose his own running mate.

---

5   Shlomo Slonim, "Designing the Electoral College," in Thomas E. Cronin, ed., *Inventing the American Presidency* (University Press of Kansas, 1987), 53.

President Bill Clinton gives his 1997 State of the Union Address to the 105th Congress. Vice-President Al Gore (left) and House Speaker Newt Gingrich look on.

In the 1950s, attitudes toward the vice presidency began to change, making it once again a desirable office for an ambitious politician. Television gave the young and ambitious Vice President Richard Nixon a new public visibility. Surveys in recent years show the vice president second only to the president in public recognition. John Kennedy tried to get the Democratic vice presidential nomination in 1956 as a stepping-stone to the presidential nomination. Nixon succeeded in being nominated for president in 1960, and since then most vice presidents have received the presidential nomination of their party for the next election. The exceptions are Nixon's first vice president, Spiro Agnew, who resigned in a corruption scandal, Gerald Ford's appointed vice president, Nelson Rockefeller, and Dan Quayle, George Bush's vice president, who was never able to establish himself as a major political figure. Vice presidents can capitalize on their high visibility and have learned that they can use their office to work on behalf of their party across the country—a good way to build up grass roots support for a future presidential bid.

Kennedy's assassination in 1963 underscored the need for the vice president to be ready to be president. It also emphasized the political opportunity inherent in the position. In the twentieth century, five of the sixteen presidents have failed to complete their term: McKinley and Kennedy were assassinated; Harding and Franklin Roosevelt died in office; and Nixon resigned in disgrace. In addition, Reagan was shot and wounded, and Roosevelt, Truman, and Ford were shot at but not hit. Both Wilson and Eisenhower were seriously ill while in office. In sum, the odds of a vice president succeeding to the presidency are quite high.

Because every vice president is a potential president, presidents have begun to make better use of them. President Carter set a new standard by using Vice President Walter Mondale as a key adviser and involving him in a wide range of decisions. The same was broadly true of President Reagan's use of Vice President Bush. President Clinton set a precedent by ignoring the traditional advice to balance the ticket when choosing a running mate. In selecting Senator Al Gore, Clinton chose someone from the same part of the country, the same part of the Democratic Party, and the same age cohort. The Clinton-Gore ticket was presented as much more of a "team" than was usual, and by all accounts President Clinton has stuck with the concept while in office. Besides being allocated the usual special projects, Gore has functioned as a close adviser to the president.[6]

The office remains a paradoxical one. The vice president arrives in Washington with no job description. As vice president, says Norman Sherman, "you are what the president allows you to be, but you have no real authority, no real responsibility, and no independent clout."[7] How the vice president is used in the administration is the president's decision. A good vice president keeps a low profile and stays loyal to the president. His or her political future is largely tied to that of the president. Although most modern vice presidents have gone on to win the presidential nomination, only George Bush became president directly by the vice presidential route (Nixon was elected later, on his second try), and his victory was largely attributable to the continued popularity of his predecessor. Nevertheless, an invitation to join the president's ticket is one that few ambitious politicians turn down.

ANALYSES OF THE MODERN PRESIDENCY

The American presidency is a much-studied office, particularly in its modern form, which by general agreement started with Franklin Roosevelt. FDR was a dominant and charismatic figure who in many ways has overshadowed his successors in the office.[8] In the last thirty years an almost unbroken string of presidential failures has resulted in an ongoing re-examination of the problematic character of the office in the current American political system. One way of examining the problems of presidential power is through a brief summary of some of the leading scholarly analyses of the modern presidency.

---

6   On Gore's role, see Anne Devroy and Stephen Barr, "Reinventing the Vice-Presidency," *The Washington Post National Weekly Edition*, February 27–March 1, 1995.

7   Norman Sherman, "Pity Anyone with the 'Soul of a Vice-President,'" *Washington Post National Weekly Edition*, January 25–31, 1988. Sherman was press secretary to Hubert Humphrey, President Johnson's vice president, 1965–69.

8   See William E. Leuchtenburg, *In the Shadow of FDR: From Harry Truman to Bill Clinton*, 2nd Revised Edition (Cornell University Press, 1993).

The first major analysis of the post-FDR presidency was Richard Neustadt's *Presidential Power* (1960).[9] Neustadt's analysis drew on the example of Roosevelt, his own experience of working in the White House with Truman, and his observation of Eisenhower, whom most Democrats considered a passive, do-nothing president compared to his Democratic predecessors. Neustadt reiterated the traditional Democratic belief, which had been greatly reinforced by FDR's powerful example, that strong presidential leadership was necessary to make the American system work. Against the now-conventional belief that the presidency is a powerful office, Neustadt pointed to the constitutional limitations. The president is not automatically powerful—in fact, unless he devotes his energies to *making* himself powerful, he may find himself simply a clerk, signing documents and cutting ribbons.

In contrast to the popular notion that the president sits in the White House giving orders, Neustadt argued that in the American constitutional system, the president's power is "the power to persuade." To get others to do what he wants, he must persuade them that it is in their interest to do so. The sources of a president's persuasive power are what Neustadt called his "prestige," meaning his popularity with the voters, and his "professional reputation" in Washington among those who make policy. Since presidential leadership is essential if the American system is to work, the president must devote his energies to cultivating these sources of power.

Neustadt's analysis has been highly influential, but by the early 1970s the context of the argument had changed. President Johnson had been widely denounced for misusing his power and deceiving the Congress in pursuing the undeclared war in Vietnam. When it was confirmed that President Nixon had used the powers of his office to punish his "enemies," to interfere with the Democratic presidential campaign in 1972, and to permit and then cover up illegal activities by his associates, the ancient American fear of executive tyranny was rekindled.

The changed context is reflected in Arthur Schlesinger Jr.'s *The Imperial Presidency*,[10] published in 1973 during the Watergate scandal. Schlesinger charted the increasing assertion of prerogative powers by modern presidents in foreign affairs and its spillover into domestic politics. The increased power of the executive branch in general and of the president in particular at the expense of Congress had dangerously unbalanced the constitutional system. "Nixon's Presidency," he argued, "was not an aberration but a culmination." Schlesinger argued for a restoration of the constitutional balance between the legislative and executive branches.

The argument in Richard Pious's *The American Presidency* (1979)[11] also reflected the Watergate experience but drew a different conclusion. Pious argued that the

---

9   Richard E. Neustadt, *Presidential Power: The Politics of Leadership* (John Wiley, 1960).
10   Arthur Schesinger Jr., *The Imperial Presidency* (Basic Books, 1973).
11   Richard M. Pious, *The American Presidency* (Basic Books, 1979).

president is seriously hemmed in, politically as well as constitutionally. The president's resources are much weaker than Neustadt believed. In this situation, presidents fall back on the undefined prerogative powers of the office to get things done. Since the use of prerogative power is easiest to justify in a crisis situation, presidents are driven to create an atmosphere of crisis to justify unilateral action. Any assertions of power that win popular support establish new precedents and permanently expand the powers of the office. But some actions are not successful. Truman seized control of the steel mills to end a national strike, but his action was overruled by the Supreme Court. Nixon constantly tried to expand the powers of the office, but in the end he so overreached in his efforts to control both the government machinery and his opponents that he was forced out of office in disgrace.

The analyses of the presidency published in the 1980s were reacting to the political changes that had taken place in the previous decade—especially the complete collapse of party organization, the decentralization of power in Congress, and the increasing individualization of politics, all of which made the president's leadership task more difficult. All saw the development of a "plebiscitary" presidency. In *Going Public* (1986),[12] Samuel Kernell argued that the radical individualization of politics and the absence of party ties had forced the president to depend on cultivating his own popularity, which further undercut his ability to bargain with members of Congress.

In *The Personal President* (1985),[13] Theodore Lowi argued that the demands for presidential leadership had grown, but without any expansion in his actual power. Indeed, the weakening of the political parties has left the president increasingly on his own. He has to appeal to the public for personal support, but the reality is that almost every action he takes in domestic policy offends some group and reduces his support. Action in foreign policy may increase his general popularity, but not for long. The modern president is thus doomed to fail in a no-win situation. The gap between the pressures for leadership and the obstacles facing them in reality means that "presidents operate on the brink of failure."

In *The Postmodern President* (1988),[14] Richard Rose emphasized how the domestic weakness of the presidency weakened America's leadership in the world. Rose, a British academic of American origins, compared the weakness of the president with the much stronger position of the prime minister in parliamentary systems. Unlike most prime ministers, who spend years in Parliament learning to govern, a president often arrives in Washington as "an absolute beginner" with an inexperienced

---

12   Samuel Kernell, *Going Public: New Strategies of Presidential Leadership* (Congressional Quarterly Press, 1986).

13   Theodore Lowi, *The Personal President: Power Invested, Promises Unfulfilled* (Cornell University Press, 1985).

14   Richard Rose, *The Postmodern President: The White House Meets the World* (Chatham House, 1988).

administration that lacks cohesion. Like the other analysts, Rose pointed to the problems caused by the president's heavy dependence on personal popularity. Not only
must the president spend much time and energy cultivating his public support, but
when he loses support he loses his leverage with Congress as well as control over the
executive branch. An unpopular president is much more crippled politically than an
unpopular prime minister, who can usually still rely on party support and can continue to control government until his or her popularity revives.

The most recent scholarship on the presidency has tried to get away from the
overemphasis on the president that has characterized American political analysis over
the past fifty years. In his analysis of legislative productivity since the 1940s, David
Mayhew in *Divided We Govern* (1991)[15] discovered that unified party control of the
presidency and Congress had nothing to do with the rate at which important legislation was passed. Further, presidential leadership was only one of a number of factors
involved in passing legislation. There is, he noted, "a problem-solving mentality" in
Washington that works on legislation until enough support is in place to pass it.

In *The Presidency in a Separated System* (1994),[16] Charles O. Jones emphasized the
American constitutional design: "The plain fact is that the United States does not have
a presidential system. It has a *separated* system."[17] The role of the president and the
opportunities he has for leadership vary considerably according to a variety of factors
outside his control. The American system is not as dependent on presidential leadership to make it work as the traditional view has believed. Instead of the traditional
"presidency-centered party government perspective," Jones argues for a "separa-
tionist, diffused-responsibility perspective" on the American system.

In his innovative historical analysis of the presidency, *The Politics Presidents Make*
(1995),[18] Stephen Skowronek emphasized that because of the centrality of the office,
all presidents have an important impact on the politics of their time. He argued, however, that different presidents face very different opportunities for leadership, depending on their relationship to the dominant party and policy regime at the time. Thus,
while the time was ripe for change in the New Deal/Great Society policy regime by the
1970s, President Carter found it difficult to effect change because he was tied to the
Democratic Party, which had created and remained invested in the New Deal regime.
It was much easier for President Reagan to bring about change. A president's success
should be measured, Skowronek argued, against the opportunities for leadership he
was faced with.

---

15   David Mayhew, *Divided We Govern: Party Control, Lawmaking and Investigations,
      1946–1990* (Yale University Press, 1991).

16   Charles O. Jones, *The Presidency in a Separated System* (Brookings Institution, 1994).

17   Jones, *The Presidency*, 2.

18   Stephen Skowronek, *The Politics Presidents Make: Leadership from John Adams to George
      Bush* (Belknap Press, 1993).

The President and the American People

The scholarly analyses of the presidency over the last twenty years demonstrate a consensus that public expectations surrounding the presidency are too high and that the pressures these unrealistic expectations place on the president are destructive. Faced with a string of "failed" presidencies from Johnson through Bush, with Reagan the sole exception, commentators are agreed that the presidency is a much less powerful office, both constitutionally and politically, than Americans have believed since the time of Franklin Roosevelt. A more realistic assessment of the president's position should lead to a lowering of expectations as to what he can be expected to accomplish. Yet lowering expectations surrounding the president is difficult, for several important reasons:

First, the decline of party organization and party identification since the 1960s has forced presidential candidates to campaign separately from their party and to rely heavily on their own personal appeal. To get elected, a president must raise expectations. Those who cannot communicate a "vision" are criticized. In her analysis of presidential speeches, Barbara Hinckley found that in office presidents typically isolate themselves in history, rarely referring to their party or their predecessors.[19] There is no doubt that the office of president has become more highly personalized than ever before—something that the blanket media coverage of his every movement and utterance cannot help but reinforce.

Brace and Hinckley[20] note that successful presidential campaigns raise great expectations about the new president, and that his popularity is highest when he takes office, after which it inevitably declines. In their detailed analysis of presidential popularity as measured by the monthly opinion polls taken since President Truman, they found a "decay curve"[21] in the president's popularity. Independently of the state of the economy or overseas incidents that may affect his rating, every president's popularity declines steadily over his first three years, rising somewhat only in the fourth. The high initial expectations always lead to disappointment, and for all his efforts there is little the president can do about it.

Second, besides being the chief executive, the president is also head of state and thus combines two roles that are separated in the British parliamentary tradition. By the early nineteenth century, the British monarchy had surrendered its executive powers to the Cabinet and was left to play the ceremonial role of head of state. Later in the century, Prime Minister Benjamin Disraeli realized the potential in the monarch's

---

19   Barbara Hinckley, *The Symbolic President: How Presidents Portray Themselves* (Routledge, 1990).

20   Paul Brace and Barbara Hinckley, *Follow the Leader: Opinion Polls and the Modern Presidents* (Basic Books, 1992).

21   Brace and Hinckley, *Follow the Leader*, Chapter 2.

role above politics as a symbol of unity and stability for the nation and persuaded the reclusive Queen Victoria to appear more in public. Ideally, the role of the head of state is to unify the nation and speak for the nation as a whole in times of celebration and crisis, above the divisions of politics and partisanship. The prime minister, on the other hand, always remains a political figure, admired by some, reviled by others.

In Canada the distinction between the roles is rather blurred: the Queen is constitutionally the head of state, but in practice she is not able to exercise that function. Most of her formal functions have been transferred to the governor general, a prime ministerial appointment who is usually a secondary political figure and so lacks the high public profile needed for an effective head of state.

In the United States the president takes on an extraordinary degree of popular significance, well beyond that normally accorded a politician. Surveys show that virtually 100 percent of Americans, including even elementary schoolchildren, can identify the president correctly. Few other politicians reach even a 50 percent level of identification, even among their own constituents.

The evidence suggests that the figure of the president plays an important psychological role in the public's attachment to the political system. Studies of people's reactions to the assassination of President Kennedy in 1963 found that many people reacted as if a close relative had died.[22] Similar stories are told about public reaction to the death in office of President Roosevelt in 1945, and of President Harding in 1923. Brace and Hinckley found that a president's popularity rises when he acts and speaks in such a way as to "rally" the nation; when he draws attention to the nation's problems or divisions, his ratings go down.[23]

The main problem with combining roles is that it leads to contradictory public expectations about the president. The qualities required to perform these different roles successfully are not only not the same; they are in conflict. To be a successful chief executive requires considerable political skill. This is particularly true in a system as complex and as fragmented as the American one. The qualities necessary for a successful head of state, however, seem to be essentially personal and nonpolitical. The president must therefore be highly political without seeming to be so to the public.

While the president automatically becomes head of state, in reality not every president is successful in the role. Of the last nine presidents, going back to Franklin Roosevelt, only three—FDR, Eisenhower, and Reagan—clearly achieved the degree of widespread respect, admiration, and affection to which a successful head of state inspires. President Kennedy should probably be added to the list. While in the White House, Kennedy generated the kind of public excitement that was more often associated with Hollywood than with Washington. Brace and Hinckley found that while the

---

22   Fred I. Greenstein, "What the President Means to Americans," in James David Barber, ed., *Choosing the President* (Prentice Hall, 1974).

23   Brace and Hinckley, 94–5 and 111–13.

popularity of every president is subject to the "decay function," levels of basic popularity have been higher for some presidents—notably Reagan, Eisenhower, and Kennedy (there was no regular polling in FDR's time)—than for others.[24]

It is a mystery to political commentators why some presidents maintain their popularity no matter what. It is also frustrating to the president's opponents. One Democrat labeled Reagan "the Teflon President" because failed policies did not stick to him as they normally do to ordinary politicians, including most presidents. The explanation seems to be that voters responded to President Reagan as the head of state rather than as a politician and did not blame him personally for what happened. By comparison, the other presidents in the same period—Truman, Johnson, Nixon, Ford, Carter, and Bush—were never able to connect with the American people at the level of head of state. They were judged simply as politicians, and their popularity fluctuated widely according to whether their policies were successful and popular. They had no cushion of respect and affection on which to draw when their policies became unpopular.

The question of why some presidents are successful heads of state, while most are not, is not easy to answer. It is difficult to generalize from the four successful examples, but the ability to communicate with the public seems to be important. FDR was a skillful public speaker and was the first president to master the art of radio communication, through his "fireside chats." Both Kennedy and Reagan used television brilliantly, Kennedy in live press conferences, which displayed his wit and quick mind to advantage, and Reagan in scripted speeches, in which his experience as a movie actor was used to powerful effect. Eisenhower, on the other hand, was quite inarticulate in public but nevertheless conveyed a sense of "fatherly" reassurance. By contrast, none of the other presidents was an effective communicator in public.

Brace and Hinckley suggest that the most popular presidents—Reagan, Eisenhower, and Kennedy—while very different from one another, were the most "public-regarding"—that is, they cared the most about being liked by the public.[25] By this standard, President Clinton would seem to have the potential to be a successful head of state. While at first sight this might seem unlikely, by the spring of 1996 commentators were noting how well President Clinton was playing some parts of the head of state role—in opening the Olympic Games, for example, and particularly in playing the role of "mourner in chief" during the funeral of his commerce secretary and others killed in a plane crash and during the anniversary of the bombing of the federal building in Oklahoma City.[26]

The ability to connect with the American people at the level of head of state does not necessarily make the president an effective chief executive. Franklin Roosevelt

---

24   Brace and Hinckley, 32–8.
25   Brace and Hinckley, 35.
26   Richard Cohen in *The Washington Post National Weekly Edition* April 15–21, 1996.

certainly had a major impact on his country, but a strong case can be made that
President Truman, in foreign policy, and President Johnson, in domestic policy,
achieved much more in office than Eisenhower, Kennedy, or Reagan. Because high levels of personal popularity do not spring from agreement on policy, they are difficult
to translate into public support for a particular policy. For example, although
President Reagan repeatedly proclaimed his support for the anti-communist Contra
insurgents in Nicaragua throughout his presidency, he was never able to generate
majority public support for his policy.

On the other hand, popular support as head of state does give a president a great
deal of leeway in Washington that other presidents do not enjoy. Members of
Congress and the others in Washington whom the president must persuade are always
extremely wary of opposing a popular president. It does not pay politically to attack
the head of state. Whether a president has the will and the political skill to make effective political use of this leeway is another question.

The Problem of Presidential Power

The problem of the presidency can be stated simply: The public expectation of strong
leadership and the need of modern government for central direction bear little relation to the constitutional powers and political influence of the office. The American
system of government was founded on eighteenth-century liberal principles that
feared the power of government. The framers of the Constitution therefore established a system based on separated powers with checks and balances between the
branches of government. The presidency was intended to be an energetic and not a
purely ceremonial office, but it was set—as Charles Jones points out—in a separated
system in which responsibility is diffused.

But even in America the public demands results from its government, and the burden of trying to make such a fragmented set of institutions work in the late twentieth
century falls inevitably on the president. The pressure on the modern president to produce results is great, yet his resources are extremely limited. As a result, some presidents resort to asserting extra-constitutional prerogative powers, as Nixon did with
disastrous results. Some presidents find domestic politics too frustrating and spend
most of their energies on foreign policy, as both Nixon and Bush did.

The analysts agree that the president is dependent on his popularity, his ability to
"go public." This means that a great deal of time and effort goes into public relations—into the creation of "pseudo-events"—and into finding ways to package and
"spin" what the president does, for the media to transmit to the public.[27] The kinds of

---

27   John Anthony Maltese, *Spin Control: The White House Office of Communications and the
Management of Presidential News* (University of North Carolina Press,1992).

skills that used to be confined to election campaigns are now indispensible for governing. Modern presidents are obsessed with the opinion polls. Yet, as Brace and Hinckley's analysis demonstrates, there is in fact little a president can do to influence his bedrock level of popularity or to keep his poll ratings from inevitably declining.

The key suggestion analysts make for easing the problems surrounding the presidency is to lower expectations; but given the central role the president plays in the constitutional system, as both chief executive and head of state, and the way the media personalize politics, it is difficult to see how the attention and the expectations focused on the president can be made to revert to premodern levels.

Others have proposed various constitutional amendments—for example, to change the term of the House of Representatives from two to four years to align it with that of the president and thus increase the president's influence over Congress. It is not clear that such an amendment would have the desired effect, and in any event the chance of any amendments being passed that would seriously alter the relationship between the branches of government is close to zero. American presidents will have to continue to try to provide executive leadership without many of the powers possessed by parliamentary leaders.

CHAPTER 8

THE EXECUTIVE BRANCH
OF GOVERNMENT

The Constitution vests "the executive power" in the President of the United States and requires him to "take care that the laws be faithfully executed." The Constitution also refers to "executive departments" headed by executive officers who are to be nominated by the president and confirmed by the Senate. The president is thus commonly called the "chief executive"; and under him there has grown a vast network of government departments and agencies whose basic job is to execute the laws that have been passed by Congress. Laws are necessarily written in general terms; it follows that in the administration or execution of the law, considerable discretion is left in the hands of the executive officers.

The executive branch of government, because of both the discretion it exercises and the professional expertise it has accumulated, has become a major force in Washington policy-making. One of the principal jobs of the president is to manage the vast executive branch of government. This chapter looks first at the growth, organization, and personnel of the executive branch and then at the president's task of managing the executive branch.

THE GROWTH OF THE EXECUTIVE BRANCH

The First Congress established three executive departments: the State Department (which dealt at that time with both domestic and foreign affairs), the Treasury

Department, and the War Department. Each was headed by a secretary. President Washington used the secretaries as his principal advisers and formed them into a Cabinet council, along with the vice president and the attorney general (who did not have a department—the Justice Department—until 1870). The Department of the Navy was created in 1798 at a time when the Americans feared being caught up in the war between Britain and France. In 1829 the postmaster general was added to the Cabinet.

The Department of the Interior was created in 1849. The idea of a department for domestic affairs had been discussed from the beginning and often proposed. It was the increased volume of work generated by the expansion westward—particularly the acquisition of vast new territories in the Southwest from Mexico in 1848—that led to one finally being created. The new department brought under one administrative roof various domestic functions that had been the province of other departments and left the State Department concerned exclusively with foreign affairs. Since its main responsibilities, such as federal lands and Indian affairs, are of greatest concern to the western states, Interior has always been the "western" department.

For the first century the federal Cabinet's modest expansion was the result of growth in the core functions of government, such as defense, law and order, and management of the western territories. All subsequent expansion was the result of the federal government expanding into new areas of jurisdiction in response to pressure by interest groups. After Congress passed legislation in a new area, a new office or bureau in the executive branch had to be established to administer the law. Typically, these offices were attached to one of the existing departments as subordinate units. Once such an office was established, the interests involved began a campaign to have the office elevated into an independent department with a secretary in the president's Cabinet. Since there was always great reluctance to expand the role of government and increase spending, the battle for Cabinet status was always a prolonged one.

The first entirely new department was for agriculture. The settlement of the prairies and the extension of the railroads westward transformed American agriculture into a major export business and a nationally important sector of the economy. This led to the establishment of the first national organization of farm interests, as well as demands for government help in promoting agriculture and agricultural trade. The struggle over the original proposals for the creation of a Department of Agriculture ended in a compromise in 1862: agriculture was given an office independent of the Interior Department but was headed by a commissioner rather than by a Cabinet secretary. It was not until 1889, after many years of pressure by western agricultural interests, that the Department of Agriculture was established.

Rapid industrial development in the last quarter of the nineteenth century made the United States a major exporter of manufactured goods; as a result, business began pressuring the federal government for help in trade promotion. At the same time, industrialization was causing a rise in confrontational and often violent labor relations, with both sides demanding government intervention. A Bureau of Labor was created in the Interior Department in 1884. Union pressure for an independent Cabinet department was only partly successful. In 1888 Congress made the bureau an independent department but refused to grant it Cabinet standing. The Labor Department became caught up in renewed demands for a Department of Trade and Commerce. In 1903, Congress created a new Cabinet Department of Commerce and Labor; this pleased business but not the unions. Finally, in 1913, the Democrats created two separate Departments of Commerce and Labor.

Independent Regulatory Agencies

Although the scope of the federal government expanded greatly in the twentieth century, no more Cabinet departments were created until 1953. A major reason for this was that many new government functions, instead of being added to the departmental structure, were established under a different form of organization: the independent regulatory agency. The intention was to shield these governmental functions from day-to-day political pressures and give maximum scope for professional expertise. Regulatory agencies are organized in many ways, but generally such an agency is run by a board. The board members are nominated by the president and confirmed by the Senate, in the usual way, but they serve for set terms. Unlike those appointed to the departments, who can be removed at any time by the president, a member of a regulatory board cannot be removed until his or her term ends. A new president cannot immediately replace the agency boards, but must wait until the members' terms expire.

The first regulatory agencies established by Congress in this way were the Civil Service Commission in 1886 and the Interstate Commerce Commission, which in 1887 was given some powers to regulate railroad rates. A number of other agencies were created during the Progressive years, including the Federal Reserve System, which functions as the central bank, and the Federal Trade Commission. The New Deal saw another set of agencies established as the federal government expanded its regulatory powers into new areas. Thus, the Federal Communications Commission (FCC) now regulated the new broadcasting industry; and the Securities and Exchange Commission (SEC) now regulated the stock market; while the National Labor Relations Board recognized the rights of trade unions for the first time.

The *United States Government Manual* for 1995–96[1] lists a total of sixty-five independent establishments and government corporations. Some of the best-known ones

---

1   U.S. National Archives and Records Administration, Office of the Federal Register, *United States Government Manual 1995–96*.

Table 8.1	Department	Date of Creation or Elevation
Executive	State	1789
departments.	Treasury	1789
	Attorney General	1789
	War	1789–1947
	Navy	1798–1947
	Post Office	1829–1971
	Interior	1849
	Justice (Attorney General)	1870
	Agriculture	1889
	Commerce and Labor	1903–1913
	Commerce	1913
	Labor	1913
	Defense	1947
	Health, Education and Welfare	1953–1979
	Housing and Urban Development	1965
	Transportation	1966
	Energy	1977
	Health and Human Services	1979
	Education	1979
	Veterans Affairs	1988

are the National Aeronautics and Space Administration (NASA), 1958; the Peace Corps, 1961; and the Federal Election Commission (FEC), 1971. Also in 1971, the post office—long a government department—was removed from direct political control and re-formed as the U.S. Postal Service. The newest regulatory agency, the Corporation for National and Community Service, was established in 1993.

The Growth of the Cabinet Since 1945

One result of American involvement in World War II was a reorganization of the military departments. The old departments of War and Navy were merged to create a new Department of Defense. In 1953 the Department of Health, Education and Welfare (now the Department of Health and Human Services) was created; this reorganized the administration of social programs created during the New Deal. The new government programs of the Great Society period resulted in two new departments: the Department of Housing and Urban Development (HUD) in 1965, and the Department of Transportation in 1966.

Two new departments were established during the Carter presidency. One of Carter's highest domestic priorities was to solve the "energy crisis" of the mid-1970s;

to this end, he established the Department of Energy in 1977. Lastly, in 1979 the old Commission on Education, established in 1867 during the Reconstruction period, was removed from HEW (which then became HHS) and reborn as a separate Department of Education. This change had long been advocated by the teachers' unions.

President Reagan campaigned in 1980 on reducing the size of the federal government, and promised to abolish the departments of Energy and Education; but Congress did not agree to disband them. In political terms, it was difficult to resist interest group pressures and cut the bureaucracy—a fact that was underlined when President Reagan agreed in 1988 to create a new Department of Veterans Affairs out of the Veterans Administration, an independent agency set up in 1930. The latest candidate for promotion to full departmental status is the Environmental Protection Agency (1970). There is general support for the change; however, since 1990 disputes over secondary issues have stalled the legislation that would create the new department. When the Republicans took control of Congress in 1995, they promised to abolish the Departments of Energy, Education, and Commerce. But again, they could not overcome the entrenched support that executive agencies build up in Congress.

In addition to the fourteen heads of the executive departments, the Cabinet roster also includes the vice president, as well as other executive officials who may be granted "Cabinet rank" by the president. Under President Clinton these have been the White House chief of staff, the director of the Office of Management and Budget, the U.N. ambassador, the U.S. trade representative, the chair of the Council of Economic Advisers, the administrator of the Environmental Protection Agency, and, since 1995, the CIA director.

THE PERSONNEL OF THE EXECUTIVE BRANCH

The executive branch is staffed by two distinct groups: civil servants and political appointees. These two groups differ in how they are recruited and in the conditions under which they serve.

The Civil Service

Civil servants are career officials employed under civil service rules of the type that are common to most of the Western democracies: they are recruited on the basis of merit, often by competitive examination, and can only be fired for cause and according to established rules and procedures. They are in effect guaranteed career service; in return, they must avoid active involvement in party politics, since they may have to work for administrations of both parties during the course of their careers.

In the nineteenth century, government departments were staffed by political patronage. The party in power appointed its supporters to federal government positions across the country, with the post office and the customs service being particularly rich sources of jobs. Government workers paid dues to the party and provided much of the manpower for the party at election time; a change in the party controlling government meant the turnover of most government jobs. The patronage system was a major target of the various movements for government and political reform. Reformers pressed both to increase the professionalism of the government service and to weaken the party machines. The first step toward reform was the creation of the Civil Service Commission in 1886 to establish a merit system for recruitment, and slowly over the next forty years more and more government positions were brought under civil service rules.[2]

Nowadays most federal government jobs are covered by civil service rules. This means that the vast majority of federal government employees, from the drivers, janitors, and filing clerks up to the higher executive grades—which include many professionals, lawyers, economists, engineers, diplomats, and so on—are nonpartisan career civil servants. The exceptions are the roughly 3,000 top officials who are appointed by the president at his pleasure or for a set term.

Political Appointees

The top officials in the executive branch are appointed to their positions by the president. This includes the Cabinet secretaries who head the fourteen departments, but also the two or three layers of officials who serve immediately under them—the deputy secretaries, undersecretaries, assistant secretaries, and so on. There are roughly 300 such positions in all. In addition, the president makes another 300 appointments to the boards of the independent regulatory agencies, when the terms of the existing members expire. It is these approximately 600 people who collectively form the "Clinton Administration."

This layer of noncareer political appointees who head up the executive departments and agencies is the distinctive element in the American executive branch. In Canada this layer does not exist. Each government department in Canada is headed by a Cabinet minister, who is an MP. Directly under the minister is a deputy minister, who is a career public servant. Canadian departments are thus staffed entirely by politically neutral civil servants who serve whatever party is in power. The prime minister has some influence on the choice of deputy ministers, and people from outside government have sometimes been brought in at that level, but there is nothing like the

---

2   Stephen Skowroneck, *Building A New American State: The Expansion of National Administrative Capacities, 1877–1920* (Cambridge University Press, 1982).

American practice, which relies on large numbers of political appointments to staff the highest levels of the departments. Government patronage, which is used extensively in Canada to reward ex-politicians and party workers, rarely affects the core departments.[3]

The president's appointing authority covers about 4,000 positions in all. Another important group is the ambassadors, of whom there are about 150. Most of these come from the career diplomatic service but some are always political appointments, often from the ranks of large contributors to the president's campaign. There are also about 1,000 legal appointments: U.S. attorneys and U.S. marshals for every federal judicial district, and several hundred federal judges. Since federal judges serve for life, appointments can only be made when vacancies arise or when new judgeships are created by Congress.

In the United States the civil service system has never been extended to cover the top positions in the executive branch. Heclo argues that it would be more difficult for the Canadian system to work in the United States, where because of the separation of powers there is not the same unified control of the executive branch. In the United States, departments are responsible both to the chief executive and to Congress, and the agency heads need good political skills to negotiate such an environment.[4]

An additional argument for the American system is that it helps the president take control of executive branch policy-making. It is generally agreed that in order to perform his function as chief executive, a president must be able to choose his own top officials. This is why the necessary Senate confirmation of the president's executive appointments is very rarely withheld, even when the opposition party controls the Senate. Most of President Clinton's Cabinet nominations in early 1993 were confirmed without serious opposition from the Republicans in Congress.

Only ten presidential nominations to the Cabinet have ever been rejected in a Senate vote, and only two in this century, the last under President Eisenhower. It is more common for a nomination to be withdrawn to avoid certain defeat or a prolonged confirmation fight. Either is more likely to happen when the president's party does not control the Senate. In 1981, President Carter withdrew his original nomination for CIA director, Theodore Sorensen, because of his earlier opposition to the Vietnam War. In 1989, President Bush withdrew his nomination of former senator John Tower as Secretary of Defense after several weeks of controversy over his personal life and his financial connections with defense contractors. In 1993, President

---

3   See Patrick Weller, *First Among Equals: Prime Ministers in Western Systems* (George Allen and Unwin, 1988), 93–102.

4   Hugh Heclo, "The In-and-Outer System: A Critical Assessment," in G. Calvin Mackenzie, ed., *The In-and-Outers: Presidential Appointees and Transient Government in Washington* (The Johns Hopkins University Press, 1987), 203–204; Heclo also discusses why the American system of appointment evolved the way it did and its advantages and disadvantages.

Clinton's first two nominees for attorney general had to withdraw when the press discovered their minor tax problems. Clinton's first nominee to head the Civil Rights Division in the Justice Department, Lani Guinier, was forced to withdraw after controversy over some of her writings on racial districting.

The In-and-Outers

Political appointees to executive positions are referred to as "in-and-outers," since they necessarily lose their positions with a change in government. The changeover is most dramatic when party control of the presidency changes. In early 1993, for example, President Bush's Republican appointees made way for Clinton's Democrats. Even when there is a "friendly takeover" within the same party, as between Presidents Reagan and Bush in 1989, most of the appointments change. Within each administration there tends to be a high turnover, particularly in the middle-level positions. Appointees average just under two years in any one position, and just under four years all told in the administration.[5] Turnover is lower in the top Cabinet posts; ten of President Clinton's original fourteen Cabinet secretaries served out his first term.

Some people hold appointive office only once; others make a career of these appointments, working their way up from junior to senior positions, interspersed with periods in nongovernment employment. These people find it necessary to alternate government and nongovernment work, since the political parties tend to alternate in power in Washington and both parties overwhelmingly appoint their own supporters. Until the Reagan-Bush regimes of 1981–93, neither party had occupied the White House for more than eight years straight since 1953.

Another reason for alternating government and outside employment is financial. In relative terms, government service is modestly paid, but often years of government service can be balanced with years of much more lucrative employment in business or a law firm. High-level experience in government tends to enhance a person's career prospects. This sometimes results in a "revolving door" between government and business, whereby those who negotiated with or regulated an industry in government leave to work for that industry, which values their government experience and contacts. The lobbying industry in Washington is always eager to employ those with useful experience in government or Congress.

Heclo suggests that in-and-outers "are most easily characterized by what they are not: they are not politicians and they are not usually bureaucrats ..."[6] They are

---

5   Linda L. Fisher, "Fifty Years of Presidential Appointments" in Mackenzie, ed., *The In-and-Outers*, 21–26.
6   Heclo, "The In-and-Outer System," 195.

Elizabeth Dole first served in the Johnson Administration and was already well launched in her *In and Out Profile:* appointive career when she married Senator Robert Dole in 1975. Because she was appointed *Elizabeth Hanford* by President Nixon to a six-year term on an independent regulatory agency, she served into the *Dole.* Carter Administration. Appointed to the Cabinet by both Reagan and Bush, she is now the woman with the most high-level government experience.

OUT OF GOVERNMENT	IN GOVERNMENT
Lawyer	
	Staff assistant to assistant secretary, HEW, 1966–67
Private law practice, 1967–68	
	Executive director, Presidential Commission on Consumer Affairs, 1968–71
	Deputy director, White House Office of Consumer Affairs, 1971–73
	Board of Federal Trade Commission, 1973–79
Presidential campaign of Senator Dole, 1979–80	
Presidential campaign of Ronald Reagan, 1980	
	Presidential assistant for public liaison, White House, 1981–83
	Secretary of Transportation, 1983–87
Presidential campaign of Senator Dole, 1987–88	
	Secretary of Labor, 1989–90
President of American Red Cross, 1991– ; on leave for presidential campaign of Bob Dole, 1996–97	

In and Out Profile: Christopher, President Clinton's former secretary of state, is a classic in-and-outer. He has

Warren Christopher. served in every Democratic administration since President Johnson, while spending the

Republican years in private law practice in Los Angeles.

OUT OF GOVERNMENT	IN GOVERNMENT
International trade lawyer, Los Angeles, 1950–67	
	Adviser to governor of California Deputy attorney general, 1967–69
Private law practice, 1969–76	
	Public service volunteer Deputy secretary of state, 1977–81
Private law practice, 1981–93	
	Public service volunteer Secretary of state, 1993–97

"politically-connected technocrats."[7] Both parties have a pool of in-and-outers composed of lawyers, businesspeople (particularly the Republican Party), academics, and other policy specialists who either have served in previous administrations or are eager to get a start in government service. Many interest groups are eager to place their people in the administration, both to influence government policy and to gain experience in Washington.

During the two-month transition period between election and taking office, the major task of any new president is to appoint his government—to find the 600 people to fill the policy-making positions in the departments and regulatory agencies. As part of his transition team, which negotiates the transfer of power with the outgoing administration, the president forms a committee to undertake the talent hunt, to screen applications, and to advise him on appointments.

A number of the appointments will be rewards for political support during the campaign. The names of potential appointees are also canvassed from a variety of party sources, members of Congress, governors, and senior party figures. People close to the new president are deluged with requests from office seekers or their patrons. Lee Atwater, who had been George Bush's campaign manager and who was known to be fond of hot sauce, reported that in 1988 he received fifty bottles of sauce from people hoping he would use his influence to get them a government appointment.

7   Heclo, "The In-and-Outer System," 202.

The Selection of the President's Cabinet

In both the United States and Canada, the executive branch is managed through the Cabinet, the political heads of the executive departments. The two Cabinets function in different ways that serve to illustrate the fundamentally different principles on which the presidential and parliamentary systems operate. This section looks first at how the Cabinets are selected in both countries and then at how they function.

Under the conventions of the parliamentary system, the prime minister must draw the Cabinet from the ranks of the House of Commons, with not more than one or two from the Senate. A Canadian government is a party government, so the prime minister must find places for the leading members of the party, and include political rivals if they are MPs. Prime ministers attempt to recruit potential ministers from outside politics, but they must be willing to run for office; if willing, they must then be nominated and elected to the House of Commons before they can serve. When Prime Minister Chrétien, in order to strengthen the Cabinet representation from Quebec, recruited Stephane Dion and Pierre Pettigrew in mid-term, by-elections had to be called for them to run in.

On the face of it, the president has a freedom that any prime minister would envy, which is the freedom to call on anyone in the United States to serve in his Cabinet. The only constitutional restriction is that sitting members of Congress may not accept an executive appointment; however, some members are willing to resign for a high-level position, as Rep. Dick Cheney did in order to become defense secretary in 1989, and as Senator Lloyd Bentsen did to become treasury secretary in 1993. Also, a president normally picks only people associated with his party. A president will sometimes appoint a member of the other party for a particular reason, as President Roosevelt did during World War II (to enhance national unity), and as President Kennedy did in appointing Douglas Dillon treasury secretary (to reassure the financial community).

For the top positions, presidents usually look to people with experience in Washington. Not everyone is able to function successfully in such a complex and high-pressure bureaucratic and political environment. This is where the in-and-outers are particularly valuable, especially when the president has no previous experience in Washington (as in the case of Carter, Reagan, and Clinton). About half of President Clinton's initial Cabinet-level appointments had prior Washington experience, either in Congress or as appointees in the Carter Administration. Since as a former governor, Clinton had no foreign policy experience, the appointment of an experienced in-and-outer like Warren Christopher as secretary of state was particularly important.

There are in addition particular political pressures that surround each Cabinet position. Each government department and agency has its own "attentive public," that segment of the public and set of organized interests directly affected by government policy. It follows that these people pay particular attention to appointments in that area of policy-making. Thus, the financial community is particularly concerned about who the treasury secretary is, the business community about the treasury and commerce secretaries, teachers' unions about the education secretary, the western states about the interior secretary, and so on.

The Representative Nature of the Cabinet

In both Canada and the United States, the overall composition of the Cabinet is dictated partly by symbolism. In Canada, given the permanent concern for national unity, geography—that is, the need for the Cabinet to represent every province, and for the largest provinces to be represented in sufficient strength—has always been a principal factor. This greatly explains why Canadian Cabinets have often been substantially larger than American ones—sometimes as large as forty members as opposed to twenty (including those granted Cabinet rank). The central concern in Canada is always the representation of Quebec, and it is here that governments have most often resorted to recruiting people from outside Parliament. In the United States the interior secretary is almost always from the West, since most of that department's clients are there, and the agriculture secretary usually comes from the Midwest, the largest agricultural area. Beyond that, however, state or regional representation in the Cabinet has not generally been an issue.

Since the 1960s, attention has also been paid in both countries to the representation in Cabinet of certain social groups previously underrepresented in the political process. In the United States this has meant a focus on black, female, and now Hispanic representation. In Canada, besides the representation of Quebeckers, only women's representation has become an issue.

In the United States, the first black Cabinet secretary was Robert Weaver, who in 1966 was made the first head of the new Department of Housing and Urban Development by President Johnson. President Kennedy had promised to appoint Weaver but had difficulty persuading Congress to establish the new department, partly because of that promise. Since then, every president except Nixon has included one or two African Americans in his Cabinet. In 1989 President Bush broke new ground by appointing two Hispanic Americans to his Cabinet, in recognition of the growing size and political importance of that group in several key states.

Only in the 1970s did the representation of women come to be seen as necessary in both the United States and Canada. The first American woman to head a Cabinet department was Frances Perkins, who was labor secretary throughout Franklin Roosevelt's three full terms, 1933–45. Ovetta Culp Hobby was appointed the first HEW secretary (1953–55) by President Eisenhower. But then, for the next twenty

years, including the terms of Presidents
Kennedy, Johnson, and Nixon, no woman
served in the Cabinet. Since then the
"required" number of women has slowly
inched up. President Ford's Cabinet contained one woman and President Carter's
two. Four women held Cabinet rank under
President Reagan, although never more than
two at one time. President Bush had one
female Cabinet member during his four
years in office and another in a position of
Cabinet rank.

*Frances Perkins, first
American woman to
be a Cabinet secretary.*

In Canada the first woman Cabinet minister was Ellen Fairclough, who held several
such positions from 1957 to 1962. Since then
every Cabinet has included at least one
woman. In the mid-1960s, when Pauline
Jewett suggested to Prime Minister Pearson
that it was time for her to be promoted to the Cabinet, he famously replied, "But we
already have a woman in the Cabinet." The number of women Cabinet ministers was
long constrained by the small number of women elected to the House of Commons;
it was only in the late 1980s that the representation of women rose above purely token
levels. In 1984 the Conservative Cabinet had six female members out of thirty-nine. In
1993 Prime Minister Chrétien appointed four women to his streamlined Cabinet of
twenty-three, plus two women out of eight in the new "junior" category of secretary
of state.

By far the most deliberate in picking minority representation for his Cabinet has
been President Clinton, who promised during his campaign to appoint "a government
that looks like America." He set up an elaborate selection process in which gender and
minority status were advertised factors. For example, he decided in advance to appoint
the first female attorney general. His first Cabinet contained three women: Donna
Shalala at HHS, Hazel O'Leary at Energy, and Janet Reno as attorney general. Three
other women were given positions of Cabinet rank: Madeline Albright, U.N. ambassador, Laura Tyson, the CEA chair, and Carol Browner, the EPA administrator. The
Cabinet had three black members, another record: Ron Brown at Commerce, Hazel
O'Leary, and Jesse Brown at Veterans Affairs. Clinton also matched Bush's record of
two Hispanic representatives: Henry Cisneros at HUD and Frederico Pena at
Transportation.

THE WORKING OF THE U.S. CABINET SYSTEM

The president's Cabinet is composed of the political heads of the executive departments and a handful of other executive officers with Cabinet rank. The American
Cabinet thus looks like the Canadian Cabinet but it operates very differently because
the underlying constitutional and political realities are very different.

In Canada the Cabinet operates on the principle of collective responsibility. The
members are all MPs or senators drawn from the majority party. The prime minister
has the power to select and fire the other ministers, but he or she is always bound by
the fact that the government's tenure depends on maintaining a majority in the House,
and that this requires a united party. The fundamental rationale for collective Cabinet
responsibility remains as it was stated by Sir Robert Walpole, the first British prime
minister, in the mid-eighteenth century. Faced with a political crisis, Walpole advised
his colleagues: "Gentlemen, if we don't hang together, we will assuredly hang separately."

Ministers accept collective responsibility for the actions of the government. The
major decisions are made collectively by the Cabinet, which nowadays operates
through a system of Cabinet committees. While the prime minister is almost always
the most influential single voice in the Cabinet (traditionally, "the first among
equals"), he or she will rarely try to proceed with a policy to which a substantial number of Cabinet members are opposed.[8]

On the other hand, "the United States is the one major democracy without some
kind of system of collective responsibility."[9] The president (with the vice president) is
the only elected member of the executive, and ultimate constitutional authority for
the executive branch rests with him alone. Politically, the president is elected separately from his party in Congress, and the congressional leaders are prohibited by the
Constitution from serving in the Cabinet. The president can thus claim the moral
authority of election, as well as a popular mandate for his policies that cannot be
challenged by any other member of the executive branch. In this respect, the president's personal authority is stronger than that of the prime minister. While the prime
minister campaigns nationally, he does so as the head of his party, as the leader of a
team of ministers, and he is directly elected only in his own constituency. The president, by comparison, is elected by a national constituency. Thus, the president combines the constitutional authority of the chief executive with the political authority of
a national popular mandate.

---

8   On the different models of prime ministerial leadership of the Cabinet in Canada, see Peter
     Aucoin, "Prime Ministerial Leadership: Position, Power, and Politics," in Maureen Mancuso,
     Richard G. Price, and Ronald Wagenberg, eds., *Leaders and Leadership in Canada* (Oxford
     University Press, 1994).
9   Theodore J. Lowi, *The Personal President* (Cornell University Press, 1985), 98.

In the era of strong parties (roughly from the 1830s to the end of the century), the president's Cabinet resembled the Canadian Cabinet more closely in that the president normally felt it necessary to place the leaders of his party—the state party leaders, who were also influential in Congress—in his Cabinet. But even in that situation it was clear that both constitutionally and politically the president could not be bound by his Cabinet. The story is often told of President Lincoln summing up a Cabinet discussion in which the members had all disagreed with him: "Seven noes, one aye—the ayes have it."[10] In the last analysis, the only vote that counts in the Cabinet is that of the president, because he is the one who has been elected chief executive.

Each Cabinet secretary is responsible for the duties of the office to which he or she was confirmed but not for any other decisions. There is no collective responsibility for government decisions as there is in Canada. Another way of making the same point is this: although twenty people sit around the Cabinet table, each secretary "has an audience of one," the president. While the president relies on the secretary to manage the department and the issues involved, the secretary will not launch major initiatives without presidential support. If the secretary has the support of the president for the policy he or she is proposing, the views of the others at the table are not important.

This is why the American Cabinet cannot really function as a decision-making body or even as a forum for real discussion. At best it may act as a clearinghouse for information. Both the secretary and the president prefer to discuss policy bilaterally rather than open it up for general discussion. While presidents often start out intending to govern through the Cabinet, the underlying political and constitutional realities sooner or later reduce Cabinet meetings in every administration to largely ceremonial occasions.

Presidential Management of the Executive Branch

Having emphasized the president's constitutional and political authority as the elected chief executive, we must also stress the other side of the equation—the difficulties built into his management of the executive branch. In *Presidential Power*, Richard Neustadt tells the story of President Truman commenting on the management problems his successor Dwight Eisenhower would face: "'He'll sit here,' Truman would remark (tapping his desk for emphasis), 'and he'll say, "Do this! Do that!" *And nothing will happen.* Poor Ike—it won't be a bit like the army. He'll find it very frustrating.'"[11]

Every president finds managing the executive branch frustrating. John Kenneth Galbraith, who was an adviser to President Kennedy and then his ambassador to

---

10   Richard J. Fenno Jr., *The President's Cabinet: An Analysis in the Period From Wilson to Eisenhower* (Harvard University Press, 1959), 29.

11   Richard E. Neustadt, *Presidential Power: The Politics of Leadership* (John Wiley, 1960), 9.

India, tells of visiting the president in the Oval Office and suggesting a change of policy to him. "That's a good idea," replied the president, "but I don't think the government would buy it." The question is this: Why should the chief executive have so much difficulty getting "the government" to do what he wants?

The core reason why the president has difficulty controlling the executive branch relates to the constitutional separation of powers. The separation of powers, by denying the president control over the legislative branch, also denies him complete control over the executive branch. With its powers of legislation, appropriation, and oversight, Congress has considerable influence over the operations of the executive branch. The executive agencies are established by Congress, which sets their jurisdiction and delegates regulatory powers to them. Agency budgets are approved by Congress annually. And through its oversight authority—an extension of its legislative and budgeting powers—Congress has the right to investigate the operations of executive agencies.

Departments and agencies need to maintain close links with the committees in Congress that process their legislation and approve their budgets. They are also in communication with the major interest groups in their field. Both Congress and the interest groups can put unwanted pressure on a department for their own purposes; but they can also provide them with support in their struggles within the executive branch.

As a result of the separation of powers, executive agencies and departments are effectively responsible both to the president, through the Cabinet structure, and to the Congress. The responsibility that in Canada is concentrated in the Cabinet is diffused in Washington between the president and the Congress. The departments and agencies are caught between them and can often play one end of Pennsylvania Avenue against the other. The chief executive must therefore contend with the Congress for control of the executive branch.

This situation does not arise in Canada. The Canadian Cabinet system provides for a *unity* of control, not a *separation* of powers. The legislative branch cannot compete with the Cabinet for control of or influence over the executive branch because the Cabinet controls the House of Commons through its partisan majority. This means that the internal struggles that are a normal part of executive branch functioning— the struggles for control between a minister and his or her department, and the competition between departments for resources or control over a particular policy area— all take place *within* the executive branch and are sorted out largely away from public scrutiny.

In the United States, because of the independent role of the Congress these executive branch struggles often get caught up in the competition *between* the branches and are commonly fought out in a much larger and much more public arena. For example, there is a built-in tension in the executive branch between a department staffed by career civil servants that has its own view of policy (or a stake in continuing existing policy), and a minister or political appointee who often has little experience in the area and will only serve for a short time but who may want to make a mark by changing policy. The "departmental" view of policy may often differ from the view of its political boss or from the political priorities of the Cabinet or president. In Canada these struggles are fought out by the bureaucrats and politicians within the executive branch, with the final decision in the hands of the Cabinet. In the United States the bureaucrats have the additional option of quietly enlisting congressional and interest group support against the secretary or the president.

The extreme case of an agency that had built so much congressional, interest group, and public support that it became virtually immune from executive control was the Federal Bureau of Investigation (FBI) under its notorious long-time director, J. Edgar Hoover. Administratively, the FBI is part of the Justice Department and reports to the attorney general, but Hoover, who was director from 1924 to 1972, was so skillful in his use of publicity to build public and therefore congressional support for the FBI that he was able to ignore the various attorneys general and pursue his own policies. Although every president from FDR to Nixon wanted to fire Hoover, none was willing to risk the inevitable congressional and public outcry, and Hoover stayed in command until he died at the age of 77.

In the United States, government does not have a military-style command structure where orders from superior officers are unquestioningly obeyed. In Washington there are many ways that agencies can obstruct, and delay carrying out, decisions with which they disagree. Also, as noted above, the agency may well have congressional and interest group support for its position. Civil service rules forbid agency staff from campaigning openly against their political bosses, but those staff can use their close contacts with congressional subcommittees and their agency's attentive publics to make their case.

Another technique used by virtually everybody in Washington is to leak information to the press with the objective of pushing one particular side of a policy argument. Journalists cultivate confidential relations with people at every level of government (the Supreme Court is the exception) and are given "inside information" to publish provided they preserve the confidentiality of the source. The president or a Cabinet secretary may read his proposals on the front page of the *Washington Post* one morning before he is ready to announce them. At some point every administration becomes so frustrated by leaked information that it tries to crack down on leakers. (The Nixon Administration actually resorted to phone taps.) In fact, everyone in Washington, including the White House staff, regularly leaks information for their own purposes. In Ottawa policy is usually shaped by a small number of bureaucrats and ministers who maintain a strong tradition of secrecy, so leaks are much less common. In Washington, by contrast, press leaks are a standard part of the ongoing bureaucratic and political warfare.

The president may even have difficulty getting his political appointees to carry out his policies. An American administration, staffed by several hundred appointments made hurriedly after the presidential election, is what Heclo calls "a government of strangers." In Ottawa, *both* groups of key policy-makers—the party leaders who become Cabinet ministers, and the deputy ministers and other top civil servants—will probably have worked together for some time. In Washington, especially when there is a change of party, a large group of appointees will be assembled to work closely with others whom they have never met. President Kennedy had never met his secretary of state, Dean Rusk, until shortly before he took office. Among recent presidents, only President Bush, who had held a series of executive appointments in the Nixon and Ford Administrations, was able to staff many of the key positions in his administration with experienced former colleagues.

In Ottawa policy-makers are also bound together by party loyalty and discipline, or by the strongly disciplined culture of the civil service. In Washington, while most appointees are loosely affiliated with the same party, party discipline is weak. There is no common working culture—only a mix of personal ambition and a willingness to enter public service.

Once a Cabinet secretary is nominated by the president and confirmed by the Senate, he or she is sworn in to take responsibility for the department. The secretary performs two roles: political head of the department, and adviser to the president as a member of Cabinet. If there is a difference between the policy favored by the department and that favored by the president, the secretary stands between the two. He or she will either accept the advice coming from the department and oppose the president, or side with the president and be at odds with the department.

Presidents have developed different strategies to extend their control over the executive branch. One method utilizes the appointment process. While it is impossible to vet every appointee for loyalty to the president or ideological agreement, some administrations have attempted to have at least one prominently placed loyalist in each agency. President Kennedy relied on loyalists in the departments to keep him informed outside of the formal channels of communication. During the Reagan Administration, conservatives saw to it that there was a network of true believers throughout the executive branch who were willing to push conservative policies in the ongoing struggle across the administration between conservatives and pragmatists. Other presidents, as will be discussed below, have bypassed the departmental structure and directed policy through their advisers in the White House.

Policy Coordination

In managing the executive branch, one of the president's principal tasks is to coordinate policy between the different agencies. In some policy areas there is one principal department or agency to deal with; in others, there are a number of agencies with a stake in the policy. Especially in the areas of the economy, trade, and foreign policy, the president has no choice but to be continuously involved with several agencies advising him. In Canada, policy also has to be coordinated, but there are far fewer agencies and matters can usually be handled through the Cabinet committee structure. The Canadian Cabinet is also assisted by coordinating agencies such as the Privy Council Office (PCO) and the Prime Minister's Office (PMO).[12]

On economic policy, the president's official advisers are the Secretary of the Treasury, the chair of the Council of Economic Advisers, the OMB director, and the chair of the Federal Reserve Board. In addition, the commerce and labor secretaries are likely to have an interest in economic policies. Each of these agencies was established for a different purpose, and has a different type of expertise and a different attentive public, and so is likely to have a different perspective on policy. Note here that the Federal Reserve Board, which plays a central banking role similar to that of the Bank of Canada, was set up as an independent agency and has a different relationship to the president than the other agencies. The board's chair advises the president but is not subject to presidential direction. "The Fed" is generally reckoned to be the most influential economic institution because it controls monetary policy.

Each of these offices gives the holder a potential voice in shaping the administration's policies. For example, in President Reagan's first term the OMB director, David Stockman, played the leading role in pushing through the "Reagan Revolution"; he succeeded through sheer energy, command of figures, and good connections with the Congress. Unless the president, directly or through a delegate, gives clear direction, there is a built-in tendency for administration policy to dissolve into a set of contradictory positions. President Clinton established the National Economic Council (NEC) in the White House to coordinate economic policy; this council is analogous to the long-established National Security Council.

On trade issues a different set of agencies is involved. For dealing with the massive imbalance in American trade with Japan—an issue he chose to highlight—President Clinton established a team that included high-level representatives from the Departments of the Treasury, Commerce, and State and the Office of the Trade Representative, chaired by the NEC director. Also included were the chair of the CEA, Laura Tyson, a foreign trade economist, and another Japan specialist then serving on the CIA National Intelligence Council. It was reported that this arrangement for coordinating policy tended to downplay the role of the State Department, which has traditionally been concerned with maintaining good diplomatic relations. This made a tougher policy against Japan likely.[13]

---

12   The degree to which the PCO and/or PMO manage the Cabinet is left to the discretion of the prime minister. See Herman Bakvis and David MacDonald, "The Canadian Cabinet: Organization, Decision-Rules and Policy Impact," in Michael M. Atkinson, ed., *Governing Canada: Institutions and Public Policy* (Harcourt Brace Janovich Canada, 1993), 47–80.

13   Clay Chandler, "A Degree from the School of Hard Knocks," *Washington Post National Weekly Edition*, February 28–March 6, 1994.

The most crucial area of policy in which coordination is needed is foreign and defense policy. Here the heavyweight advisers are the state and defense secretaries, with the CIA director and U.N. ambassador also involved. The official coordinating body is the National Security Council (NSC), of which the principal advisers are members. Its director, who doubles as the national security adviser to the president, has been a major player in most administrations.

Even with the NSC structure, it is up to each president to determine how best to determine policy. The modes of operating have varied considerably. At one extreme, President Nixon conducted his high-risk foreign policy with his national security adviser, Henry Kissinger—bringing the Vietnam War to a belated end, establishing relations with China, and creating a detente with the Soviet Union—while largely bypassing the secretary of state. Under President Carter there was a continuing struggle between the secretary of state, Cyrus Vance, and the national security adviser, Zbigniew Brzezinski, to control policy. To avoid this problem, President Reagan downplayed the national security adviser's role but left his strong-minded state and defense secretaries, George Schultz and Caspar Weinberger, to contend with each other. To complicate matters, the CIA director, Bill Casey, was given a free hand by the president, and there were a number of second-echelon conservatives pressing for hard-line policies. It was in this rather chaotic environment, which lacked presidential direction, that the Iran/Contra scandal developed.[14]

By far the smoothest foreign policy operation was run by President Bush, who placed his closest adviser, James Baker, at the State Department and Dick Cheney and Brent Scowcroft, both of whom he had worked with in the Ford Administration, at Defense and the NSC, respectively. The U.N. and CIA positions were placed in the hands of career professionals. After a rather shaky start, President Clinton put together a noticeably low-key but quite effective team of Warren Christopher at State, William Perry at Defense, Anthony Lake at the NSC, Madeline Albright at the U.N., and John Deutch at the CIA.

Presidential Management of the White House Staff

Faced with the difficulties of coordinating the executive branch and with the obstacles that executive agencies can place in the way of their policies, presidents have come to rely increasingly on their personal staffs in the White House both for policy advice and for help in managing the government. The resulting situation generates tensions between the White House and the other political executives. The White House staff

---

14   See Theodore Draper, *A Very Thin Line: The Iran-Contra Affairs* (Hill and Wang, 1991). A documentary history is in Peter Kornbluh and Malcolm Byrne, eds., *The Iran-Contra Scandal: The Declassified History* (New York: The New Press, 1993).

are the president's personal staff. They are not executive officers who are appointed to a position established by the Congress, and thus they do not require Senate confirmation and cannot be required to testify before Congress. The president has total freedom in choosing his staff and assigning tasks to them.

The growth of the president's staff has led to management problems within the White House itself. Several recent presidents have been damaged politically by the activities of members of their staff. The most spectacular case was the Watergate scandal, which led to the resignation of President Nixon and sent his attorney general and several of his staff to jail.[15] Three of President Reagan's staff were convicted in the Iran/Contra affair, and all recent presidents have been plagued by controversies or scandals involving current or past staff members.

The problems presidents have had with their staff can slotted into two broad categories: personnel, and management style.

◂ White House Personnel

When a president chooses his Cabinet and other executive appointees he searches widely for experienced talent and appoints people he has never met to key positions. When it comes to choosing his personal staff, however, every president feels the need to have people around him whom he knows and feels comfortable with. Most draw their staff from those who have worked for them in their previous office or in their presidential campaign.

Thus, President Kennedy entered the White House with his "Boston Mafia"—a group of aides, most of them Irish Americans from Boston, who had worked with him for years. When Lyndon Johnson succeeded to the presidency after Kennedy's assassination, most of Kennedy's Cabinet and other appointees stayed on to serve the new president, but Kennedy's White House aides left and were replaced by Johnson's own people, most of them from Texas. A similar story can be told of the other presidents. Nixon's notorious "palace guard," led by Bob Haldeman and John Ehrlichman, had worked on his unsuccessful campaign for governor of California in 1962 and then on his national campaign. Clinton appointed a lot of FOBs (Friends of Bill), many of them from Arkansas.

Presidential staffers typically lack experience in handling the enormously complex Washington political scene and the sudden glare of publicity that is focused at all times on the White House and its occupants. They are working under an entirely new

---

15   There are a host of books about Watergate. Of those by the participants, John W. Dean, *Blind Ambition* (Simon and Schuster, 1976), best conveys the atmosphere in the Nixon White House. Elizabeth Drew, *Washington Journal: The Events of 1973–74* (Random House, 1975) is a good account of the slow unfolding of the drama. More recent re-assessments are Stanley Kutler, *The Wars of Watergate: The Last Crisis of Richard Nixon* (Knopf, 1990), and Fred Emery, *Watergate: The Corruption of American Politics and the Fall of Richard Nixon* (Times Books, 1994).

level of pressure, and the stakes are higher than ever before. Some of those who come to Washington with the new president quickly lose their enthusiasm. Several of President Clinton's FOBs had to be replaced; some were caught up in "Whitewater" (the generic term for Congress's investigations of the president's financial dealings in Arkansas); one, Vince Foster, committed suicide after lamenting how the merciless Washington environment destroyed people's lives.

Proximity to the president generates great intensity within the White House as aides compete for access to the Oval Office and therefore power in Washington. The peculiar pressures generated in and around the modern White House have been best described by George Reedy.[16] Reedy, who was an aide to Lyndon Johnson in both the Senate and the White House, started by wondering why his boss, who had been a legend in the Senate for his sophisticated understanding of the Washington political process, started to make elementary political mistakes in the White House. Reedy concluded that in the Senate Johnson had had to deal with his colleagues face to face every day; but in the White House, surrounded by deferential aides, he grew removed from political reality. Reedy compared the White House to the court of a medieval monarch where the courtiers compete for the monarch's favor. This tendency for a "court" to develop in the White House may be encouraged or constrained by the president's management style.

The President's Management Style

Whether the White House staff facilitate the president's achievements and enhance his reputation or involve him in distracting problems and scandals depends in large part on how the White House is managed. Each president has his own characteristic style of making decisions, which the organization of the White House staff must accommodate. Every decision-making style has strengths and weaknesses. The most successful White House operations are those which complement the president's style, reflecting its strengths and compensating for its weaknesses. The worst operations have magnified those weaknesses and damaged the president's reputation.

The central question regarding the president's management style is this: How actively involved does he want to be in decision-making? At one extreme was President Reagan, who operated as "chairman of the board." He set broad policy directions and had to sign off on the major decisions, but otherwise—according to the unanimous testimony of his admirers and critics alike—he did not involve himself at all in the details of policy-making. At the other extreme are the hands-on presidents like Carter, who immersed himself in detailed briefing books, and Clinton, universally described as a "policy wonk" who loves nothing better than to talk for hours about abstruse aspects of policy.

---

16   George E. Reedy, *The Twilight of the Presidency* (New American Library, 1970).

The "chairman" model requires a strong chief of staff to coordinate the flow of information and access to the president. Eisenhower, who was used to the military command system, operated this way; so did Nixon, except on foreign policy, where he worked closely with his national security adviser. The most successful application of this model was actually a modified version. The first-term Reagan White House was run by a troika of top managers: James Baker, a skilled, pragmatic manager, was chief of staff but worked closely with two of Reagan's old associates, Ed Meese, who acted to make sure the president's conservative views were followed, and Mike Deaver, who knew the president and his wife well personally and concentrated on managing the president's image. This unusual team worked brilliantly to compensate for the president's extreme disengagement from most issues and to present him in the most positive light. It also helped to control the infighting between pragmatists and conservatives in the administration.

Exhausted by their efforts, the Reagan management team left at the end of the first term. Deaver set up his own lobbying firm to cash in on his connections with the president; Meese became attorney general; and Baker simply swapped jobs with Don Regan, the treasury secretary. Regan was not a successful chief of staff. Lacking good political skills, he failed to recognize the weaknesses in the president's style. Specifically, he failed to prevent the NSC staff from operating out of control and was forced out when the Iran/Contra scandal broke.

The most disastrous application of this model was that of President Nixon. His chief of staff, Bob Haldeman, ran an extremely efficient White House operation, but one that magnified the president's weaknesses—especially his paranoia and vindictiveness. Instead of deflecting or ignoring the president's more extreme wishes, the loyal staff unquestioningly carried them out, thus setting in train a series of illegal activities now known collectively as the Watergate scandal.

The chairman model with a strong chief of staff has two major disadvantages: First, it places a great deal of pressure on the chief of staff. The problems with Haldeman and Regan have already been noted. Eisenhower's chief of staff, Sherman Adams, eventually had to resign after he accepted gifts from a businessman. John Sununu, President Bush's abrasive chief of staff, was eventually forced out over a minor matter after alienating everyone in Washington except the president. Second, by prescreening so much of the information the president receives, this model runs the risk of isolating the president and depriving him of a full range of decisional options.

The "hands-on" president aspires to run the executive branch himself and wants access to a wide range of information and people. The organizational model that fits the activist style is sometimes referred to as the "spokes of the wheel" model, in the sense that the president is at the center dealing independently with a number of different aides, including the chief of staff. For Democrats this has been the preferred model, especially since both Franklin Roosevelt and John Kennedy operated this way, though with a much smaller staff than current presidents.[17]

The "wheel" model spreads responsibility among several top aides and keeps the president involved in the shaping of decisions. The danger is that the president will be swamped with information. President Kennedy is generally reckoned to have worked successfully by knowing when to involve himself in an issue and when to leave it to others. President Carter, on the other hand, is generally thought to have handled his staff poorly. By trying to micro-manage too much himself he expended too much energy on unnecessary details.

The most studied White House operation to date is President Clinton's. Accounts of the president's first two years by experienced journalists, Bob Woodward[18] and Elizabeth Drew,[19] described a chaotic atmosphere in a White House that operated like a continuous "graduate seminar." There seemed to be few clear lines of authority. While this highly unstructured mode of operation clearly reflected the president's love of policy debate, decision-making was slow and confusing. Finally, in mid-1994, Leon Panetta, an experienced Washington operator, was brought in as chief of staff to bring greater order to White House operations. Under Panetta the Clinton White House moved closer to the wheel model. Such a system reflected the president's need to be engaged in the policy debate. Unlike some presidents, Clinton ran little risk of becoming isolated or unaware of the policy options, but his White House reflected his own lack of discipline and always seemed to be on the brink of collapsing into the chaos with which it started out.

How the president manages the White House staff is extremely important. Greenstein makes the point that "leadership in the modern presidency is not carried out by the president alone, but rather by presidents with their associates."[20] As the record of the last twenty years indicates, a president can be greatly helped or badly hurt by his staff. The record also shows the variety of presidents' working methods, from the extreme efficiency of Nixon to the barely controlled chaos of Clinton. There is no one method of organizing the White House that is guaranteed to work. The White House organization must accommodate the president's decision-making style, but it must also find ways to compensate for the weaknesses of that style.

---

17   See Charles E. Walcott and Karen M. Hult, *Governing the White House: From Hoover Through LBJ* (University of Kansas Press, 1995), Chapter 11.

18   Bob Woodward, *The Agenda: Inside the Clinton White House* (Pocket Books, 1995).

19   Elizabeth Drew, *On the Edge: The Clinton Presidency* (Simon and Schuster, 1994).

20   Fred I. Greenstein, ed., *Leadership in the Modern Presidency* (Harvard University Press, 1988), 352.

THE PROBLEM OF EXECUTIVE BRANCH MISCONDUCT

From their colonial experience and their knowledge of British history, the framers were fully aware of the danger of executive misconduct and the need to provide mechanisms to deal with it. This section looks at three of the ways that executive misconduct has been handled: the constitutional mechanism of impeachment; congressional investigation; and the use of special prosecutors.

The Impeachment Process

In the Constitution the framers constructed an intricate balance between the executive and legislative branches, but they gave the ultimate power to Congress when they decided to include the British mechanism of impeachment, whereby ministers of the Crown (but not the monarch) could be removed by Parliament. Raoul Berger argues that in the minds of the framers the "fear of presidential abuses prevailed over frequent objections that impeachment threatened his independence."[21] Under Article II, Section 4, of the Constitution, "the President, Vice President and all civil Officers of the United States, shall be removed from Office on Impeachment for, and Conviction of, Treason, Bribery, or other high Crimes and Misdemeanors." Article I gives the House of Representatives "the sole Power of Impeachment [in the sense of indictment]" and the Senate "the sole power to try all Impeachments." A two-thirds majority is necessary for conviction. If the president is on trial, the president of the Senate (that is, the vice president of the United States) has a conflict of interest and is replaced by the Chief Justice as the presiding officer.

The process of impeachment and conviction of executive officials by the legislature was always thought of as the last resort when normal political pressures had failed to remove corrupt or oppressive ministers. In the British parliamentary tradition impeachment became essentially obsolete once the government was required to maintain a parliamentary majority. A minister who is credibly accused of wrongdoing will almost always be removed by the prime minister. A prime minister can be removed by a simple vote of nonconfidence. In the United States the president has the power to remove political appointees, which means that the impeachment procedure is relevant only for the president and for federal judges who have life tenure.

The first use of the procedure was the attempt to remove Supreme Court Justice Samuel Chase in 1805 on charges of judicial misconduct. Chase, a highly partisan

---

21   Raoul Berger, *Impeachment: The Constitutional Problems* (Harvard University Press, 1973), 5. Berger explores the British background and the thinking of the framers on the impeachment power.

Federalist, was impeached by the Jeffersonian majority in the House, but the Senate failed to convict him, although the Jeffersonians held a two-thirds majority.[22] Most commentators believe that if Chase had been convicted, the Jeffersonians would have gone after other Federalist justices, probably including Chief Justice John Marshall. In the highly charged partisan atmosphere of the time there was a danger that impeachment might become established as a regular weapon in the partisan struggle, threatening the independence of the executive and judicial branches. As it was, the next use of the procedure was the impeachment of President Andrew Johnson in 1868.

Johnson was a Union Democrat from Tennessee who had been chosen as President Lincoln's running mate in 1864 to broaden the electoral appeal of the Republican ticket. As vice president he succeeded to the presidency on the assassination of Lincoln in April 1865. Johnson and the Republican majorities in Congress carried on a vicious battle over Reconstruction policy in the South, and in the end the president was charged with violating the law by removing the Secretary for War without the Senate's approval. Johnson was overwhelmingly impeached by the House, but fell one vote short of conviction in the lopsidedly Republican Senate.[23]

After being a dead issue for over one hundred years, impeachment re-entered the American political vocabulary with the Watergate scandal. The investigation of executive branch misconduct was triggered in June 1972 by the arrest of six burglars in the offices of the Democratic National Committee in the Watergate office building in Washington, D.C.. By the spring of 1973, allegations in the *Washington Post* connecting the burglars to White House operatives had led to a congressional investigation by a special committee of the Senate and to a criminal investigation by a special prosecutor appointed by the attorney general.

There were allegations of extensive wrongdoing by presidential aides and officials of the Committee to Re-elect the President, and of President Nixon's active involvement in covering up their activities and obstructing justice. Conclusive proof depended on the tapes of White House conversations in the possession of the president. When the special prosecutor persisted in going to court to obtain relevant tapes, he was fired on the president's orders. An unprecedented public outcry led to the immediate appointment of a second special prosecutor and the start of impeachment proceedings in the House. At the end of July 1974, the House Judiciary Committee, after weeks of televised hearings, voted for three articles of impeachment. A few days earlier, the Supreme Court had unanimously ordered the president to hand over the relevant tapes. Examination of the tapes revealed the "smoking gun" of the president's

---

22   Berger, *Impeachment*, Chapter 8. Berger believes Chase should have been impeached for
     allowing his partisan biases to affect his judicial decisions.

23   Berger, *Impeachment*, Chapter 9. Berger believes that Johnson's trial was a misuse of the
     impeachment process by partisan Republicans in Congress.

earlier involvement in the cover-up. Nixon's remaining Republican support in the Congress evaporated. It was then certain that the entire House would vote overwhelmingly to impeach him and that the Senate would convict him. Faced with this prospect, President Nixon resigned on August 8, 1974.

While the unsuccessful trials of Justice Chase and President Andrew Johnson were immersed in partisanship, few would argue that the launching of impeachment proceedings against President Nixon was unjustified. Yet few regret that the spectacle of an impeachment trial of the president was avoided by Nixon's resignation. Impeachment is likely to remain an awesome weapon of last resort.

Congressional Investigations

Two congressional committees played a major role in investigating and resolving the Watergate scandal: the special Senate Watergate Committee in the summer of 1973; and the House Judiciary Committee, which a year later investigated whether the president should be impeached. Both committees held extended televised hearings that did much to educate the public on issues involved in the scandal.

The Congress has often used its power of oversight to investigate the executive branch. Because oversight is an extension of the legislative power, the Congress can investigate policy matters as well as allegations of executive misconduct. What the Congress cannot do is undertake a criminal investigation—a job that usually falls to

Members of the media and spectators watch the House Judiciary Committee open debate on the possible impeachment of President Nixon.

the Justice Department. In recent years allegations of misconduct in the executive branch have usually triggered separate but parallel investigations: a congressional investigation by a standing committee or special committee, and a criminal investigation by the Justice Department or a special prosecutor. While the two types of investigation have different functions, they tend to have competing priorities. Members of Congress inevitably want to capitalize on the issue for partisan or personal reasons and seek quick and highly publicized hearings. Criminal investigations are necessarily slower and private. If due care is not taken, the congressional investigation can impede the criminal investigation.

Under the Fifth Amendment, a witness cannot be compelled to testify. Congress, however, has the power to extend "use immunity," under which a witness is required to testify (or be cited for contempt of Congress, with possible criminal penalty) in exchange for immunity from prosecution on the basis of evidence given to Congress. The convictions of John Poindexter and Oliver North for their role in the Iran-Contra affair were thrown out on appeal because the evidence at their trial was judged to be tainted by the evidence they had been compelled to give under immunity before the joint congressional committee investigating the affair.

Congressional investigations of the executive branch are obviously open to partisan manipulation. For example, Democrats charged that the investigation of President Clinton's involvement in the Whitewater land deal by the Banking Committee in 1995–96 was highly partisan. But when Mayhew examined major congressional investigations from 1946 to 1990, he found that they were no more likely to occur in periods of divided government, with one party investigating the other, that in periods of one-party control of both the executive and legislative branches.[24]

Special Prosecutors

The Watergate scandal revived the use of special prosecutors to investigate allegations of executive-branch misconduct. Presidents had appointed a special prosecutor on three previous occasions to investigate charges against Cabinet officers. But in all other such cases the investigation had been carried out by the Justice Department.[25] It was, for example, the Justice Department that investigated the allegations, unconnected to Watergate, against President Nixon's vice president, Spiro Agnew, at the same time the Watergate investigations were going on. Agnew was charged with conspiracy, extortion, and bribery while governor of Maryland. In a plea bargain, he pled no contest to one charge and resigned from office in October 1973.

---

24   David R. Mayhew, *Divided We Govern: Party Control, Lawmaking, and Investigations,*
      1946–1990 (Yale University Press, 1991), Chapter 2.

25   Terry Eastland, *Ethics, Politics and the Independent Counsel: Executive Power, Executive Vice*
      1789–1989 (National Legal Center for the Public Interest, 1989), Chapter 2.

Special prosecutors were appointed to investigate the Watergate scandal out of political necessity. Since Nixon's first two attorneys general and FBI director were among those suspected of wrongdoing, there was no question of leaving the investigation in the hands of the Justice Department (which includes the FBI). The first special prosecutor, Archibald Cox, was appointed by the new attorney general, Elliot Richardson, who gave assurances to Congress about Cox's complete independence. When President Nixon ordered Cox fired, Richardson and his deputy resigned. The political pressure was so great that a second special prosecutor, Leon Jaworski, was immediately appointed. Jaworski won access to the White House tapes in the Supreme Court, and the convictions of several of the president's top associates, including his first two attorneys general.

In the aftermath of Watergate there was pressure from Democrats and public interest groups for Congress to mandate the appointment of special prosecutors whenever there were allegations of misconduct by high executive officials. After much debate, such a law was passed in 1977 as part of an Ethics in Government Act. The special prosecutor law was reauthorized as the Independent Counsel Act in 1982 and again in 1987,[26] in spite of Republican opposition. The law was allowed to lapse at the end of 1992, but was reauthorized in 1994 when the Republicans discovered an interest in investigating President Clinton.

The law requires the attorney general, either on her own initiative or at the request of Congress, to investigate allegations of wrongdoing by high-level government officials. If the initial investigation indicates that the charges are credible, she must ask a special panel of three federal judges to appoint an independent counsel and set the terms of the investigation. The independent counsel then operates outside the supervision of the Justice Department.

The attorney general also has the discretion of calling for an independent counsel in any other investigations where a conflict of interest might arise for the Justice Department. This could include the criminal investigation of members of Congress, though the law has not yet been used in this way. The House Ethics Committee has appointed independent counsel to investigate allegations of violations of House rules—for example, to investigate House Speaker Jim Wright in 1988 and Speaker Newt Gingrich in 1996—but these appointments were not made under the special counsel law.

Since the law was first passed, fifteen special prosecutors/independent counsel have been appointed: two under President Carter, seven under President Reagan, two under President Bush, and four in President Clinton's first term. In only six of the fifteen cases has the investigation led to any convictions. By far the most high-profile and controversial independent counsel investigations since Watergate have been those by

---

26   The origins of the law and the changes made in the 1982 and 1989 reauthorizations are in
      Eastland, *Ethics, Politics and the Independent Counsel.*

Lawrence Walsh in the Iran/Contra affair and by Kenneth Starr into the Whitewater land deal. Both of these investigations were embroiled in partisan political charges from the beginning.

Republicans maintained that Iran/Contra was about the struggle between a Republican administration and a Democratic Congress for control of foreign policy, and that a criminal investigation was not called for; Democrats argued that there had been serious violations of law, and perjury by several administration officials. Walsh obtained convictions against John Poindexter, President Reagan's national security adviser, and Oliver North, a member of the NSC staff, but both convictions were overturned on appeal for technical reasons. Walsh also obtained indictments against six officials, including Reagan's defense secretary, Casper Weinberger, but the case against Weinberger was thrown out and President Bush pardoned all six shortly before he left office. In all, Walsh's investigation lasted six years.

The Whitewater investigation, started in 1994, was into President Clinton's financial dealings while governor of Arkansas in the 1980s, including his involvement in the Whitewater land development scheme. This was the first use of an independent counsel to investigate the conduct of the president and his wife. It was also unusual in that it involved alleged misconduct before the president took office, though it expanded into whether the White House had tried to obstruct the investigation of the case. Democrats charged that the investigation was simply a Republican "fishing expedition" intended to undermine the president; Republicans argued that there were serious questions about the conduct of the president and the first lady.

The increasing resort to the use of independent counsel has generated considerable argument. The argument for appointing an independent counsel is quite clear: that there is at least the perception of a conflict of interest if the criminal investigation of executive officials is left to the Justice Department, which is part of the executive itself and whose head, the attorney general, is often a close associate of the president. Certainly in Watergate the case for a special prosecutor was compelling, given that the charges included White House attempts to use executive agencies such as the FBI and the Internal Revenue Service for partisan purposes.

The case against the use of independent counsel has been laid out by a former Justice Department official, Terry Eastland. He argues that the independence of the special prosecutor removes him or her from the checks and balances of the normal prosecutorial decision process. "Each counsel ... has only one subject matter to investigate and unlimited resources to do so."[27] As a result, he argues, executive officials are made much more vulnerable to criminal prosecution that ordinary citizens. This is not only wrong in principle but is a deterrent to public service. Eastland also disagrees with the Supreme Court decision upholding the constitutionality of the independent

---

27   Eastland, *Ethics, Politics and the Independent Counsel*, 129.

counsel law,[28] believing that the law tips the system of constitutional checks and balances against the executive branch.

It certainly seems that the independent counsel law is being overused. In only a minority of the investigations were charges actually laid, and these were most often against secondary figures. Some of the high-level investigations have been of relatively minor matters, such as whether President Carter's aide, Hamilton Jordan, used cocaine in a New York nightclub (there was no indictment) and whether an assistant attorney general in the Reagan Administration had lied to Congress (he was cleared).

Americans have always been distrustful of executive power. Watergate fulfilled their worst fears and created a climate of deep suspicion about executive branch manipulation. Public suspicion has been fanned in recent years by other developments: the political climate in Washington has become increasingly partisan and adversarial; and the style of investigative journalism that Watergate stimulated has often deteriorated into "attack" journalism (see Chapter 15). Both the press and the partisans are looking for another "-gate" scandal, and in such an environment it is difficult for allegations of executive misconduct to be weighed dispassionately. Yielding to the clamor to appoint an independent counsel is often the easiest way for the administration to deal with such charges. There is, however, a danger of discrediting the mechanism through overuse.

---

28   *Morrison v. Olson* 487 U.S. 654 (1988).

THE ROLE OF THE SUPREME COURT

The U.S. Supreme Court has played a major role in shaping American policy and politics almost since its founding. A look at some of the most important decisions of the last fifty years gives some idea of the impact its decisions have had on American society:

- *Brown v. Board of Education of Topeka, Kansas* (1954). By declaring the segregation of pupils by race to be unconstitutional, the Court set in motion the civil rights movement, which ten years later brought an end to the legal segregation of the races in the United States.

- *Baker v. Carr* (1962). In this case and in a series of subsequent related cases, the Court ordered that seats in all legislative bodies, at the federal, state, and municipal levels, be apportioned on the basis of equal population (one person, one vote). The effect was to dramatically shift legislative power away from the rural areas to the cities and suburbs, and a corresponding shift in policy priorities right across the country.

- *Roe v. Wade* (1973). In this case the laws in most states that made almost all abortions a criminal offense were declared unconstitutional. This decision outraged many Americans and set off a bitter political and legal conflict between pro-life and pro-choice forces that is still raging across America.

- *U.S. v. Nixon* (1974). In this case the Court denied President Nixon's claim of executive privilege and ordered him to hand over to the special prosecutor investigating the Watergate scandal the tapes of conversations recorded in the Oval Office. In doing so the Court precipitated the president's resignation from office.

The U.S. Supreme Court has always been immersed in political controversy. It was established as a national institution by the U.S. Constitution in an era when the power of national institutions was being hotly contested. The Court has wielded great influence as the final interpreter of the Constitution—particularly of the Bill of Rights and the 14th Amendment, which guarantees rights against actions by state governments. The high profile and often highly controversial role played by the Court through most of its history contrasts sharply with the much lower profile that Canadian courts displayed until recently.

The Supreme Court of Canada was not established by the British North America Act; rather, it was set up by the federal government in 1875. Until 1949 the Judicial Committee of the Privy Council in Britain, the appeal court for British colonies, was the final court of appeal for Canada, and the Supreme Court had an inferior role in every respect.[1] As Patrick Monahan notes, "for most of its ... history, the Supreme Court of Canada was the forgotten institution of Canadian politics."[2]

Only after 1949, and then very gradually, did the Supreme Court of Canada begin to take on the role of the "third branch of government." Its role was transformed, and its traditional low profile raised considerably, by the adoption of the Canadian Charter of Rights and Freedoms in 1982. "The single greatest factor altering ... public attitudes towards the Court has been the enactment of the Charter [which] has meant that a broad range of controversial issues that had previously been decided in the political arena are now being channeled into the courts."[3] The role of Canada's Supreme Court has thus become much more similar to that of the U.S. Court, though its decisions have yet to attract the political and public attention that surrounds the Supreme Court in Washington.

Concern has been expressed that the Charter will increase the influence of liberal ideas in Canada at the expense of other philosophical traditions. However, Alan

---

1   Peter H. Russell, *The Judiciary in Canada: The Third Branch of Government* (McGraw-Hill Ryerson, 1987).

2   Patrick Monahan, *Politics and the Constitution: The Charter, Federalism, and the Supreme Court of Canada* (Carswell, 1987), 245.

3   Monahan, *Politics and the Constitution*, 246.

Cairns argues that the Charter is in fact a "generous, eclectic document."[4] The emphasis on individual rights is clearly liberal, but other elements of the Charter, such as the recognition of multiculturalism and the protection of linguistic and religious minorities, are not. Moreover, in contrast to the absolutist language of the American Bill of Rights ("Congress shall make no law ..."), all the rights guaranteed in the Charter are explicitly "subject ... to such reasonable limits prescribed by law as can be demonstrably justified in a free and democratic society" (Section 1). Further, in recognition of the Canadian doctrine of parliamentary sovereignty, Parliament or a provincial legislature may actually override some provisions of the Charter (Section 33, the "notwithstanding" clause)—a provision that astounds Americans. One of the questions for the Canadian Court is how much weight it should give to American precedents in the light of their much longer experience with a Bill of Rights. Some have urged that rather than follow the American example too closely, the Court should carve out a distinctly Canadian judicial path that recognizes Canada's different philosophical mix and experience.[5]

The Charter of Rights and Freedoms has raised the profile of Canada's Supreme Court and begun to increase public "ownership" of judicial decisions. This has inevitably also raised interest in the parallel American judicial questions. As happens with so many things American, Canadians are bombarded with information about the American courts and their decisions on individual rights; but as Roger Gibbins has pointed out, there is also a great deal of ignorance and misunderstanding about the role the Supreme Court has actually played in American life.[6] For that reason alone, it is worth looking at the role of the U.S. Supreme Court in some detail.

The Court Systems in the United States and Canada

The American and Canadian court systems were set up on a different basis. Canada has an integrated court system in which both the federal and provincial governments play a role. With the exception of the Supreme Court and a handful of specialized federal courts, the courts are established and maintained by the provinces; however, the judges of the higher-level provincial courts and the three federal courts are appointed by the federal government. Criminal law is federal; civil law is provincial; and the

---

4   Alan C. Cairns, *Charter Vs. Federalism: The Dilemmas of Constitutional Reform* (McGill-Queen's University Press, 1992), 79.

5   Monahan, *Politics and the Constitution*, Chapter 11.

6   Roger Gibbins, "The Impact of the American Constitution on Contemporary Canadian Constitutional Politics," in Marian C. McKenna, ed., *The Canadian and American Constitutions in Comparative Perspective* (University of Calgary Press, 1993).

Supreme Court is the final court of appeal in both areas, as well as the final interpreter of the Constitution.

The United States has a dual system of federal and state courts. In each state, therefore, there are two separate sets of courts. Since the District of Columbia is federal territory, it is governed by federal law and federal courts. The federal courts deal with all cases that arise under the Constitution, with federal laws, and with treaties ratified by the United States. Congress can pass laws only on the subjects listed in Article I, Section 8, of the Constitution; however, as is discussed below, federal authority has come to be defined broadly, and the amount of federal legislation has expanded enormously in the last fifty years.

The fact is, however, that most of the laws that govern Americans are state laws. Most private law—dealing for example with commercial or domestic relations—and most criminal law is state law. Cases that arise under state laws are handled by each state's system of state courts. Cases in which a state law is claimed to conflict with federal law or to violate the U.S. Constitution may be heard in federal court.

The U.S. Supreme Court was established by Article III of the Constitution to head the judicial branch of the federal government. Congress was given the power to establish lower federal courts. The First Congress in 1789 established local federal trial courts, known as district courts. There are now eighty-nine district courts in the fifty states, plus one for the District of Columbia. Each state has at least one federal court district; the more populous states are divided into two, three, or four court districts. There is also a district court in Puerto Rico.

For a long time, Supreme Court justices and district court judges doubled as members of appeal court circuits, and traveled around the country to hear appeals from District Court decisions. In 1891, Congress set up an intermediate level of courts, the Courts of Appeal, with their own judges to deal with the growing volume of appeals cases. The United States is now divided into eleven appeals court districts. There is also an appeal court for the District of Columbia, and another that deals with appeals from the decisions of various administrative bodies.

Under the Constitution, federal judges are nominated by the president and confirmed by the Senate. To protect their independence, they are appointed for life

	No. of Courts	No. of Judges
Supreme Court	1	9
Court of Appeals	13	179
District Court	90	625

Table 9.1
Federal courts and judges in the United States, 1996.

Source: *The United States Government Manual 1996–97* (Office of the Federal Registrar, 1996).

("during good behavior") and their salary may not be cut by Congress. The only way to remove a federal judge is through the impeachment process. This step has only been taken a few times, to remove a District Court judge who has been convicted of an offense but has refused to resign. No Supreme Court justice has ever been removed by impeachment.

The number of justices on the Supreme Court varied in the early years between four and ten but has been stable at nine since 1869. The Court is composed of eight associate justices and the chief justice. The chief justice is the presiding officer and has certain leadership prerogatives, but he votes as an ordinary member.

The Working of the Supreme Court

The U.S. Supreme Court, as the "third branch of government," has played an important political role in the development of the United States. As the final interpreter of the Constitution, the Court deals inevitably with political issues, but it deals with them differently than the other branches of government. It is a court and operates as a court, not as a legislative or executive body. Charles L. Black explains: "The term 'constitutional law' symbolizes an intersection of law and politics, wherein issues of political power are acted on by persons trained in the legal tradition, working in judicial institutions, following the procedures of law, thinking as lawyers think."[7]

Because decisions of the U.S. Supreme Court can have a profound impact on American society and may arouse strong political opposition, the Court is often at the center of political controversy and the target of efforts to influence its decisions. For most of its history, the Court has been well aware of its vulnerability in dealing with the other branches of government. While it is difficult to attack the justices directly, since they can only be removed by impeachment and their salaries may not be cut, the Court is ultimately dependent on both the legislative and executive branches in certain important respects:

- Congress controls the appellate jurisdiction of the Court. On one occasion in the aftermath of the Civil War, Congress removed a category of cases from the Court, and such action has often been threatened even in recent times. Congress could overwhelm the Court with cases by making certain kinds of appeals mandatory. In fact, Congress has given the Court a great deal of freedom to choose the cases it hears.

---

7   Charles L. Black, *Perspectives in Constitutional Law* (Prentice-Hall, 1963), 1.

•   The Court has no capacity to enforce its own judgments; it depends on the executive branch to enforce them. While this is taken for granted nowadays, it was not always so. Faced with the Court's decision in *Worcester v. Georgia* (1832), which contradicted his Indian policy, President Jackson is reputed to have stated: "John Marshall [the Chief Justice] has made his decision. Now let him enforce it." Jackson then ignored the decision.

The Court has usually been aware of the dangers inherent in getting involved in too many contentious issues, and has developed a number of decisional rules that it can use to limit its involvement in constitutional questions until it is ready to deal with them. The Court will only hear a genuine case in which the parties to the case can claim some substantial wrong has been done to them. Also, it will hear a case only after all legal proceedings in the lower courts are finished. The Supreme Court does not sit in review of the actions of government; indeed, unlike the Supreme Court of Canada, it has always refused to give advisory opinions—that is, to judge the constitutionality of a law referred to it by government without an actual case being brought. Usually, the Court will not give a constitutional ruling if there are other grounds for deciding the case. Finally, the Court has at its disposal a number of technical rules through which it can avoid or postpone dealing with an issue.

Each case is heard by all nine justices, though there may be fewer in cases of illness, an unfilled vacancy, or recusal (where a justice removes himself or herself from the case because of some previous involvement with the parties to the case). It takes a majority of the Court to overrule the decision of a lower court. The vast majority of the cases that reach the Supreme Court are on appeal, either from a federal appeals court, involving the interpretation of federal law or the Constitution, or from the highest level of a state court, involving a question of constitutional interpretation.

The first decision the Court has to make is whether to hear a case. Around 4,000 cases are sent to the Court each year; of these, the Court can hear a maximum of about 200. There are very few types of cases that the Court is *obligated* to hear. Thus, the Court has almost complete freedom to choose its cases. Each of the justices, who has a staff of law clerks, looks over the cases and votes on which ones to hear. The rule on the Court is that a case will be heard if four justices vote to hear it. The Court does not provide its reasons for not hearing a case. When the Court chooses not to hear a case, the decision of the lower court stands.

When a case is scheduled for hearing by the Court, the lawyers for both sides submit their written arguments. The solicitor general, who represents the administration's positions before the Court, often also submits a brief on a case. In addition, the Court allows *amicus curiae* (friend of the court) briefs to be filed by any other groups or organizations with an interest in the case. Some particularly important cases attract a great number of *amicus* briefs. The largest number of *amicus* briefs ever filed was in 1989 for *Webster v. Reproductive Health Services*, which dealt with abortion. In that instance seventy-six different groups, including the American Medical Association, the American Civil Liberties Union, members of Congress, several state attorneys general, and various groups on both sides of the abortion issue, submitted briefs, since it was widely believed that the Court was about to use that case to change its policy on abortion.

The next stage is that of oral argument. The lawyers for each side are given just half an hour to argue their case and to respond to questions from the justices. Having read the briefs and listened to the oral arguments, the justices then go into conference to come to an initial decision in the case. If with the majority, the chief justice decides who will write the Court's majority opinion. If the chief justice is with the minority, then the most senior justice in the majority makes that decision. When the majority opinion of the Court is circulated, the other justices must decide whether to sign it, or write a concurring opinion (that is, one that agrees with the result but for different reasons), or write or sign a dissenting opinion.

The decision facing the justices is whether to affirm or overrule the decision of a lower court; that being said, the reasons the Court gives for its decisions are even more important. It is through the Court's decisions, and even more through its reasoning, that the meaning of the law and the Constitution is clarified and develops. Lower courts are bound by the decisions of the Supreme Court. This is why lawyers across the country scrutinize the Court's decisions when assessing their chances of winning particular cases. The opinions are also analyzed and debated within the legal community for their coherence and persuasiveness, for their consistency with precedent, and for what they reveal about the method of constitutional interpretation being used. The decisions of the Court are also followed closely by politicians and interest groups for their impact on public policy and for their potential to set off political protests.

Dissenting opinions are also carefully scrutinized, since several times in the Court's history a minority line of argument has later become the opinion of the Court. The opinions of the justices are thus the basis for an ongoing and often fierce debate among lawyers, academics, politicians, and sometimes the general public about what the clauses of the Constitution mean or ought to mean at the present time. The issues are important, since the operative meaning of the Constitution defines the powers of government and the rights of citizens.

THE CHANGING ROLE OF THE SUPREME COURT

Most legal scholars divide the history of the Supreme Court into three major periods:[8]

---

8   The classic short history of the Court to 1960 is Robert McCloskey, *The American Supreme Court* (University of Chicago Press, 1960).

From 1789 until the Civil War.   In this period, the Court started to build its authority, particularly between 1801 and 1835 under the leadership of Chief Justice John Marshall. The chief issues were national unity, the division of powers between the federal and state governments, the establishment of the Constitution as the supreme law of the land with the Court as its final interpreter, and the independence of the justices from partisan pressures.

From the Civil War to 1937.   The questions about national unity were ended by the war, and America turned to making money. This was a period of rapid economic growth that brought major transformations to American society. As economic change transformed their lives, first farmers and then industrial workers called on governments for protection. Political and constitutional debate during this period centered on the role that governments should play in regulating economic activity.

From the New Deal to the present.   The Great Depression ended the argument over economic regulation and started the period of activist government. The Court began to turn its attention to the civil rights of citizens. In the 1950s and 1960s, under the leadership of Chief Justice Earl Warren, the Court redefined and enforced the Bill of Rights, which places restrictions on the federal government, and the 14th Amendment, which restricts the actions of state governments. The changes brought about by the Court's activist role eventually brought a political reaction, and the 1970s and 1980s were marked by bitter controversies over the role of the Court.

The Role of the Supreme Court from 1789 to the Civil War

The reputation of the United States as a litigious society dominated by lawyers, and one where the courts are resorted to to solve political problems, goes back almost to its founding. The French writer Alexis de Tocqueville wrote in 1835 that "scarcely any political question arises in the United States that is not resolved, sooner or later, into a judicial question."[9] In its first decade, however, there was no sign that the Court was likely to play a major role in American life. There was considerable turnover in its membership. The Court was soon entangled in the dispute over the extent of national power that had begun during the ratification process. One of its first decisions, *Chisholm v. Georgia* (1795), was quickly overridden by a constitutional amendment (the 11th).

Not for the last time in its history, the Court found itself caught in the bitter political struggles of the time. One issue was the perennial one of how large a role the

---

9   Alexis de Tocqueville, *Democracy in America*, Volume I (Vintage, 1990), 280.

courts should play. The Constitution itself does not give the Supreme Court the role of final interpreter. An activist role for the Court to uphold the Constitution as the supreme law over congressional, executive, and state action was championed by the Federalists, who saw the courts as a bulwark against the excesses of democratic populism. The Jeffersonians took exactly the opposite view: they looked on judges with deep suspicion, and argued that each branch of government was free to interpret the Constitution in the light of its own responsibilities.

The fierce partisan battle spilled right into the Court in its most famous case, *Marbury v. Madison* (1803). It was Chief Justice John Marshall's skillful handling of this case that laid the foundation for the Court's later role.

◄ *Marbury v. Madison* (1803)

The background to the case was the bitter struggle for power between the Federalists and the Republicans. Federalist John Adams had succeeded George Washington in 1796, having defeated Republican Thomas Jefferson. Relations between the parties were greatly embittered over the Federalist Alien and Sedition Acts of 1798, which attempted to silence opposition newspapers. The Federalists accused the Republicans of supporting the French Revolution; the Republicans accused the Federalists of repeating the worst excesses of the British government against the colonies. Each side believed that the other would wreck the new and fragile American experiment in republican government. In the rematch election of 1800, Jefferson defeated Adams and the Federalists were faced with the prospect of handing over power to their political enemies.

Having lost the presidency and the Congress, the Federalists turned to the appointed judiciary as the last defense against the "revolutionaries." The new president and Congress did not take office until March 1801, and the lame duck Federalists set about creating new judgeships and appointing solid Federalists to the positions. In other words, they packed the judiciary with their own supporters. The Federalist secretary of state, John Marshall, was appointed the new chief justice, but continued to act as secretary of state up to the last minute.

In the scramble to complete the appointment process, a few of the documents certifying the new judicial appointments were not delivered to the appointees. One of these documents had been intended for Marbury, who had been made a justice of the peace in Washington, D.C. When Marbury asked the new Republican secretary of state, James Madison, to hand over his commission, Madison refused. Marbury then went to court to try to force the new government to honor his appointment.

When the case reached the Supreme Court two years later, Chief Justice Marshall was faced with a dilemma. On the one hand, he clearly wanted Marbury to take up his appointment. Marbury had been legally appointed, and the government was obligated to recognize the actions of its predecessor. On the other hand, Marshall knew that if the Court ordered Madison to hand over the commission, he would certainly refuse and there would be nothing the Court could do about it. Such open defiance would simply weaken the Court's authority.

Marshall recognized that the most important issue in the case was not Marbury but the role of the courts. His solution was ingenious. First, he came down on the side of Marbury, who clearly was entitled to the commission. The next question was this: Did the Court have the power to order the secretary of state to hand it over? Such power was not granted in the Constitution; however, in the 1789 Judiciary Act Congress had given the Court the power to issue writs of *mandamus* ("we order"). In doing so, however, Congress had added to the original jurisdiction of the Supreme Court as stated in Article III of the Constitution—and this, Marshall declared, had been an unconstitutional action.

While weak in legal terms, Marshall's argument was strategically brilliant. He declared Marbury to be in the right, but avoided an open clash with the Republicans by declaring that the Court did not have the power to order the government to act. Most importantly of all, by declaring an action of Congress unconstitutional, he had asserted the Court's right to overrule the Congress by interpreting the Constitution— a right that the Federalists supported and that the Republicans strongly opposed. In this way, Marshall neatly made his point and established a crucial precedent while avoiding a direct clash with the president. Marbury did not receive his commission.

It took a while for the fierce political passions surrounding the Court to die down. In 1804 the Republican House of Representatives impeached a Federalist justice, Samuel Chase, for his partisan activities, but enough Republican senators balked at such drastic action that the Senate failed to convict him. Had the attempt succeeded, other justices would have been removed for partisan reasons, possibly including Marshall himself, and the Court's authority would have been dealt a very serious set-back. It was Marshall's skill in getting out of tight corners that enabled the Court to survive and slowly build up its authority.

◄ The Legacy of John Marshall

Marshall remained chief justice until he died in 1835 and dominated the Court during that whole period. In the Court's earliest years the practice had been that each of the justices wrote an opinion on every case. Under Marshall the Court announced each decision in a single opinion of the Court, and this greatly increased the impact of its arguments. There were very few dissents, and most of the important decisions were written by Marshall himself.

Marshall's lasting importance was that he set in place the early precedents that established the supremacy of the Constitution as the supreme law of the land; that established a strong role for the Supreme Court as a national institution; and that gave a broad interpretation to the powers of the federal government. His actions were consistent with his Federalist political philosophy and were controversial at the time, but his skill enabled the Court's precedents to survive and its prestige to grow in spite of the controversy. From the perspective of the twentieth century, the early precedents were crucial to the building of a strong and unified nation, and they enabled the Court to play a significant role in the nation's development.

Following are some key precedents relating to the role of the Court:

Marbury v. Madison (1803). The first time an act of Congress was declared unconstitutional.

Fletcher v. Peck (1810). The first time the act of a state legislature was declared unconstitutional.

Martin v. Hunter's Lesee (1816). The first time the decision of a state court was overruled. The Court asserted its right to hear appeals from state courts involving the U.S. Constitution.

Cohens v. Virginia (1821). The Court took jurisdiction in a case involving a state and its citizens.

The key precedent giving an expansive reading of the powers of Congress was *McCulloch v. Maryland* (1819), which dealt with the constitutionality of the Bank of the United States, which had been established by Congress. The bank had been bitterly attacked by the Jeffersonians (and later the Jacksonians) as a symbol of growing federal power being used to support financial interests. Chartering a bank is not listed under the powers of Congress in Article I, Section 8, and the opponents claimed that Congress therefore had no such power. Marshall, however, argued that Congress had an implied power under the last clause of the section "to make all laws which shall be necessary and proper for carrying into execution the foregoing powers." Thus, he rejected a narrow, literalist reading of the Constitution.

Marshall played a key role in the history of the United States in several respects. By gradually establishing the authority of the Supreme Court as the final interpreter of the Constitution, he provided a uniform interpretation of the Constitution that made it in fact the supreme law of the land, and one to which Congress, the states, and the state courts had to conform. This was an important unifying factor in an age when struggles between state and regional interests dominated politics.

At the time, it was more important for the Court to establish its ultimate authority to overrule state laws and state court decisions than to establish its authority to overrule Congress. Indeed, the precedent of *Marbury v. Madison* was not used again until the Dred Scott decision of 1857, discussed below.

Marshall saw the revival of Jeffersonian ideas under President Jackson and was succeeded in 1836 by Roger Taney, who had been Jackson's treasury secretary and who served as chief justice until 1863. The Court was gradually filled with Democratic appointments, but some of these justices were supporters of national powers. While Marshall's key precedents relating to the role of the Court were not overturned, the Taney Court generally favored a broad interpretation of state police powers. However, the Taney Court is remembered chiefly for its disastrous foray into the issue of slavery in the Dred Scott case of 1857.

Dred Scott v. Sandford (1857)

The background to the case was the first major fight in Congress over slavery in 1819, which raised the question whether Congress had the power to attach conditions to the admission of new states—specifically, to forbid slavery in Missouri. In 1820 an agreement, the Missouri Compromise, was reached whereby the new states of Maine and Missouri were both admitted without conditions but slavery was prohibited in the northern parts of the Louisiana Territory (roughly the vast territory lying between the Mississippi River and the Rocky Mountains).

In 1854 the Democrats had pushed through the Congress the Kansas-Nebraska Act, which repealed the Missouri Compromise and allowed the people of the vast territory to decide the issue of slavery for themselves. This action did much to fan anti-slavery activity in the North, and the Scott case arose in this inflamed political atmosphere. Dred Scott was a slave who was claiming his freedom because he had lived with a previous owner for some time in the 1830s in a part of the Louisiana Territory in which slavery had been forbidden by the Missouri Compromise of 1820. The Court had dealt with very few cases involving slavery and could have dismissed this case on narrow technical grounds. Instead, privately encouraged by the incoming Democratic administration of President Buchanan, the Court decided to try to cut through the political controversy and "settle" the question of slavery.

The Court held that black people were not intended to be citizens of the United States and thus were not protected by the Constitution; and that prohibiting slavery deprived individuals of their property (slaves) "without due process of law," in violation of the Fifth Amendment. The Missouri Compromise was thus unconstitutional, and Scott must remain a slave.

The Scott decision, seen in the North as blatantly pro-southern, was greeted by the biggest outcry in the Court's history and badly damaged the Court's reputation for political impartiality. It galvanized the supporters of the new Republican Party, who swept the North in the 1858 elections and in the presidential election of 1860. In turn, this precipitated the outbreak of the Civil War.

The Role of the Supreme Court from the Civil War to 1936

The issue that dominated this period was the struggle between those who advocated the philosophy of *laissez-faire*, which prohibited any government interference in economic affairs, and those who supported various forms of government regulation of the economy. Also, the Court had a profound impact on the development of American society in the aftermath of the Civil War through its interpretation of the constitutional rights now guaranteed to black citizens.

◆ Civil Rights After the Civil War

After the North emerged victorious in the Civil War, the Republicans dominated Washington for a decade, during which considerable efforts were made to guarantee the rights of ex-slaves. The most important milestones in this regard were the passage of the 13th Amendment to the Constitution, which prohibited slavery; the 14th Amendment, which placed restrictions for the first time on the actions of state governments; and the 15th Amendment, which prohibited discrimination in voting rights on the grounds of race. Also, a number of laws were passed forbidding various forms of discrimination based on race and providing educational and other assistance to the ex-slaves.

It was the 14th Amendment that was to have the broadest impact on constitutional law. Its purpose was to protect individual rights against violation by state governments. Its most important clauses forbade the state to do any of these:

- Abridge the privileges or immunities of citizens of the United States.

- Deprive any person of life, liberty, or property without due process of law (the same wording as the Fifth Amendment prohibition on Congress).

- Deny to any person the equal protection of the laws.

These efforts to help black people were greeted with hostility by the white majority in the South and, once the immediate passions of the war had passed, with indifference in most of the North. Eventually cases under these laws came before the Supreme Court, which gave them a very narrow interpretation.

- *The Civil Rights Cases* (1883). These cases involved the Civil Rights Act of 1872, which prohibited discrimination on the basis of race in public accommodations. The Court ruled that the law applied only to the official actions of a state government, and could not apply to discrimination by individuals.

Box 9.1

Extract from Justice

rown's majority opinion

in Plessy v. Ferguson.

The object of the [14th] Amendment was undoubtedly to enforce the absolute equality of the two races before the law, but in the nature of things it could not have been intended to abolish distinctions based upon color, or to enforce social, as distinguished from political equality, or a commingling of the two races upon terms unsatisfactory to either ...

We consider the underlying fallacy of the plaintiff's argument to consist in the assumption that the enforced separation of the two races stamps the colored race with a badge of inferiority. If this be so, it is not by reason of anything found in the act, but solely because the colored race chooses to put that construction on it ...

The argument also assumes that social prejudices may be overcome by legislation, and that equal rights cannot be secured to the negro except by enforced commingling of the two races. We cannot accept that proposition.

- *Plessy v. Ferguson* (1896). Louisiana had passed a law requiring black and white people to travel in separate railroad cars. Plessy, defined as a black person, was fined for insisting on traveling in a "white" car. He claimed that the state law denied him the equal protection of the laws. The Court ruled that the 14th Amendment only guaranteed political equality, not social equality. The Louisiana law was held to be a reasonable reflection of social differences between the races, and one that did not imply that blacks were inferior. Only Justice John Marshall Harlan dissented, in an opinion in which he passionately laid out a broad interpretation of the amendment as intended to guarantee the fundamental rights of all citizens. The Constitution, he argued, must be "color blind."

The effect of the Court's very narrow interpretation of these laws was to deny black people any constitutional protection against discrimination. Only the most blatant forms of official discrimination were declared unconstitutional—for example, a West Virginia law which declared that only white people could serve on juries: *Strauder v. West Virginia* (1880). However, the total exclusion of blacks from juries in practice was ruled not a violation of due process of law in *Virginia v. Rives* (1880).

Since they were a minority in every state, blacks also had no political protection against whites' general demands that the races be kept separate. In fact, by the turn of the century black people were excluded from the political system altogether through many forms of discrimination and intimidation. The Court struck down the official exclusion of blacks (in *Guinn v. U.S.*, 1915), but turned a blind eye to their actual exclusion by other means.

In *Plessy v. Ferguson* the Court had in effect proclaimed the constitutional doctrine of "separate but equal." Because of their total lack of any political power, however, facilities for blacks were never equal to those provided for whites. The ex-slaves were gradually returned to a condition close to slavery under segregation laws and the gen-

The white race deems itself to be the dominant race in this country. And so it is, in pres- *Box 9.2*
tige, in achievements, in education, in wealth and in power ... But in the view of the *Extract from the dissent-*
Constitution, in the eye of the law, there is in this country no superior, dominant ruling class *ing opinion of Justice*
of citizens. There is no caste here. Our Constitution is color-blind, and neither knows nor tol- *Harlan in* Plessy v.
erates classes among citizens. In respect of civil rights, all citizens are equal before the law. The *Ferguson.*
humblest is the peer of the most powerful. The law regards man as man, and takes no account
of his surroundings or of his color when his civil rights as guaranteed by the supreme law of
the land are involved. It is, therefore, to be regretted that this high tribunal ... has reached the
conclusion that it is competent for a State to regulate the enjoyment by citizens of their civil
rights solely on the basis of race.

In my opinion, the judgment this day rendered will, in time, prove to be quite as pernicious
as the decision made by this tribunal in the *Dred Scott* case ...

eral practice of discrimination, while the Supreme Court, reflecting the public's indifference, looked the other way.

Government Regulation of Economic Activity

After the Civil War the pace and scale of economic activity in the United States began
to increase rapidly. The new transcontinental railroads opened up the prairie states to
commercial grain-growing and cattle-rearing and provided access to the mineral
deposits in the Rocky Mountains. Vast new industries, such as oil and steel, were
developed; and new forms of business and financial organizations enabled large
monopolies and huge accumulations of wealth to be built up by entrepreneurs like
Andrew Carnegie (steel) and John D. Rockefeller (oil).

The new economic conditions generated protest movements calling for government
regulation. First, American farmers began protesting the power of the railroads, grain
companies, and banks; soon after, industrial workers began protesting their conditions under unregulated capitalism. However, the new business interests became
increasingly influential in the political parties, particularly in the dominant
Republican Party. To ward off the threat of regulation, businessmen preached the doctrine of *laissez-faire*. One sign that business was increasing its influence in politics was
the appointment of corporate lawyers to the Supreme Court by both Republican and
Democratic presidents. In the words of Louis Fisher, "lawyers from the corporate sector helped translate the philosophy of laissez faire into legal terms and constitutional doctrine."[10] Whenever they lost the battle against regulation in the state legislatures

---

10   Louis Fisher, *Constitutional Dialogues: Interpretation as a Political Process* (Princeton
University Press, 1988), 17.

or the Congress, corporations appealed to the courts, arguing that laws which, for example, regulated railroad rates violated the property rights that were guaranteed by the Fifth and 14th Amendments.

For most of this period, business found a staunch ally in the Supreme Court, which extended to corporations the guarantees of the Bill of Rights. The Court saw itself as defending the traditional rights of property and contract against invasion by state governments and Congress. In the protesters' view, the Court was defending the interests of the rich and powerful against the interests of the people and distorting the intent of the Constitution.

It was in this period that the Court moved to much more active use of the precedents that John Marshall had laid down, giving the Court the power to overrule legislative actions. Through its interpretation of the "due process of law" clause of the 14th Amendment, the Court declared most state efforts at economic regulation to be unconstitutional. Also, it struck down most federal regulation through its narrow interpretation of the interstate commerce and tax clauses of Article I, Section 8.

Due Process of Law

The 14th Amendment prohibits the states from depriving anyone of their property "without due process of law." Traditionally, this wording had been interpreted as requiring governments to follow the correct procedures, such as giving the property owner the chance to object and make his case. After the Civil War, however, the supporters of *laissez-faire* began to argue that the clause should be interpreted more broadly and that the intention of the clause was to prevent the violation of fundamental rights, most importantly property rights. Gradually, the justices began to adopt this interpretation, known as "substantive due process." Under this interpretation, the Court argued that property rights were fundamental and that no violation of these rights should be allowed unless the Court judged the law to be "reasonable." The most famous case was *Lochner v. New York* (1905), in which a New York state law limiting the hours of work in bakeries to 60 hours per week was held to be an unreasonable violation of the right of contract of both the employers and the workers. In this way, most of the efforts by the state and federal governments to regulate wages, hours, and working conditions were declared unconstitutional.

Interstate Commerce

The Constitution gives Congress the power "to regulate commerce ... among the several states." In the first case under this clause, *Gibbons v. Ogden* (1824), John Marshall had given "commerce" a broad interpretation. At that time most commercial activity took place within states. By the end of the century, however, with an enormous increase in production and improved transportation, the economy had become a national one and most goods were shipped between states. The question for the

Court was how broadly "commerce" was to be interpreted in this new situation. The Court consistently defined the clause narrowly to cover "commerce" but not "production," arguing that if the power of Congress was allowed to expand, the powers of the states would be overwhelmed and the federal system unbalanced. Thus, in *Hammer v. Dagenhart* (1918) the Court struck down the federal law that attempted to eliminate child labor by banning the products of companies employing children under fourteen from interstate commerce. The Court's narrow interpretation of the commerce clause also prevented federal attempts to protect union rights to organize. In *Adair v. U.S.* (1908) the Court declared that union membership had nothing to do with interstate commerce and thus Congress could not legislate in that area.

◄ *Federal Taxing Power*

In its attempts to find constitutional ways to regulate some economic activity, Congress used its power to tax. After the Court had struck down its ban on the interstate shipment of the products of child labor in *Hammer v. Dagenhart* (1918), Congress tried again in 1919 by placing a tax of 10 percent on the net profits of companies that employed child labor. In *Bailey v. Drexel Furniture Co.* (1922), however, the Court ruled that this was not a legitimate use of the power to tax since it was really an attempt to regulate employment and thus an invasion of the powers of the states.

While not every government regulation of economic activity was struck down in this period, the Court placed effective constitutional barriers in the way of most forms of regulation. Many state laws were struck down as unreasonable violations of freedom or property rights, based on the Court's interpretation of the due process clauses. And most federal regulation was disallowed as being beyond the scope of the interstate commerce or taxing powers of Congress and as intrusions into the powers of the states.

While the positions taken by the Court were controversial, in fact there were powerful political forces on both sides of the argument over economic regulation. For most of the period from 1900 to 1929 the American economy was booming, which made it harder to argue for changes in the dominant political and constitutional philosophy of *laissez-faire*. The political climate changed dramatically, however, with the onset of the Great Depression in 1929. During the economically depressed 1930s, those arguing for government regulation of the economy were finally able to win a decisive victory, first in the Congress and eventually in the Court.

The Impact of the New Deal on the Supreme Court

Led by President Franklin Roosevelt, the Congress started in 1933 to pass a whole set of new economic regulations that went far beyond anything that had been done before. Inevitably, cases under some of these laws came before the Supreme Court; and the Court, sticking with the line of constitutional interpretation it had been developing for forty years, declared several of the key New Deal laws unconstitutional. Eight of the ten pieces of New Deal legislation that came before the Court in 1935 and 1936 were declared unconstitutional.

In *Schechter Poultry Corp. v. U.S.* (1935), the Court struck down the National Industrial Recovery Act (NIRA) of 1933, which allowed the federal government to set regulations governing hours and conditions of work in different industries, as an unconstitutional regulation of production. In *U.S. v. Butler* (1936), the Agricultural Adjustment Act provision that taxed the processors of agricultural products in order to pay growers to reduce their acreage was declared to be an unconstitutional use of the federal taxing power to regulate agricultural production.

The striking down of legislation central to the New Deal caused the biggest storm around the Court since the *Dred Scott* decision of 1857. The justices were widely denounced as "nine old men" who were out of touch with the needs of a society in economic crisis. After his overwhelming re-election in 1936, President Roosevelt asked Congress to give him the power to add a new justice to the Court for every sitting justice who was over seventy (of whom there were six). In spite of their anger against the Court, many Democrats felt that Roosevelt's "court packing" plan went too far.

The crisis was defused by the Court itself. In its next term, the Court narrowly approved (5 to 4) the next New Deal case to come before it, *National Labor Relations Board v. Jones and Laughlin Steel Co.* (1937). The National Labor Relations Act of 1935 established the rights of labor unions to organize and forbade employers to discriminate against union members or to interfere with lawful union activities. The Court held that the prevention of labor strife was a legitimate concern of Congress under its power to regulate interstate commerce. The Court thus overruled its decision in *Adair v. U.S.* (1908).

The turnaround in the Court's attitude toward economic regulation was most visible in two decisions in consecutive years relating to state minimum-wage laws. In 1936, in *Morehead v. New York ex rel. Tipaldo*, the Court in a 5 to 4 vote had struck down New York's minimum wage for women as a violation of the 14th Amendment. But a year later, in *West Coast Hotel Co. v. Parrish*, the Court upheld by 5 votes to 4 the minimum wage law in Washington state.

The Court was composed of four staunch defenders of the Court's traditional position, two more moderate conservatives, and three liberal justices who argued for a broader interpretation of government regulatory powers. One or both of the moderates had provided the majorities to strike down the New Deal legislation in 1935 and 1936. In the 1937 cases, however, both moderates voted with the liberals to uphold the legislation. The timing of the switch by the moderates was interesting. Roosevelt introduced his proposal to pack the Court in February 1937. The newly favorable decisions were announced in May 1937, though the decisions had actually been taken before February. Whatever the precise motivation, the moderates had pulled the Court back from a major political confrontation; Roosevelt's proposal to add members to the Court, which could have created a dangerous precedent for congressional interference with the Court, went nowhere. The Court's switch on economic regulation soon became permanent, as serving justices retired and were replaced by Roosevelt's nominees.

An example of how broad a definition later Courts have given to federal regulatory powers arose in 1964. The sweeping Civil Rights Act of that year, which prohibited racial discrimination in all public facilities, was based on the congressional power to regulate interstate commerce. The act was challenged by the proprietor of Ollie's Barbeque Restaurant in Birmingham, Alabama, on the grounds that he was not engaged in interstate commerce since almost all of his customers were local. The Court, however, ruled unanimously in *Katzenbach v. McClung* (1966) that since much of the food served by the proprietor came from out of state, the Civil Rights Act applied to his restaurant.

The Role of the Supreme Court Since 1937

The period since 1937, when the Court removed its objection to government economic regulation, can be divided into four segments: a transition period from 1937 to 1953 in which the Court was searching for a new direction; the Warren Court, from 1953 to 1969, during which the Court embarked on a new period of activism, concerned this time with civil liberties and their protection against government action or neglect; the Burger Court, from 1969 to 1986, during which the Court was under pressure to reverse the activism of the Warren Court; and the Rehnquist Court, since 1986, the first Court since 1937 with a conservative majority.

◄ Transition: 1937 to 1953

Between 1937 and 1945, President Roosevelt was able to appoint all nine members of the Court. With the question of economic regulation now settled in favor of government, the Court turned to new constitutional issues. The most significant cases in this period were those dealing with First Amendment rights and with race. A series of cases were brought before the Court by Jehovah's Witnesses, a small religious sect, who claimed that various state and local restrictions on their proselytizing activities violated their right to free speech and free exercise of religion under the First Amendment. The Court generally supported their position. In the most famous case, *West Virginia State Board of Education v. Barnette* (1943), the Court struck down a state law that made the ceremony of saluting the flag compulsory in all public schools on the ground that it violated the religious freedom of the Witnesses. In the Witness cases the Court began to develop the doctrine that the rights guaranteed in the Bill of

Rights were "fundamental rights"—a doctrine that would later flourish during the Warren Court.

The ruling precedent on racial segregation was *Plessy v. Ferguson* (1896), in which the Court had declared that public services must be provided for both whites and blacks but could be provided separately; this was the doctrine of "separate but equal." In practice, because black people were generally excluded from the political system, most of the public facilities provided for them were flagrantly unequal. During this period, lawyers for the NAACP argued in a series of cases that the Court should reconsider the situation and look more closely at the actual practice of racial discrimination. In *Missouri ex rel. Gaines v. Canada, Registrar of the University of Missouri et al.*, (1938) the Court rejected the southern practice of segregating universities and offering scholarships to study out of state to the few blacks who sought professional education; it also ruled that the state was obligated to provide equal opportunity for higher education within the state to both races. In *Sweatt v. Painter* (1950) the Court ordered a black student admitted to the University of Texas Law School on the grounds that the "black" law school that the state had hurriedly created was not equal in facilities and reputation to the long-established "white" law school. Clearly, the Court had begun to enforce the equality side of the "separate but equal" standard; but it was still unwilling to face the question of whether *Plessy* itself should be overruled. It would take new leadership on the Court for this to happen.

◄ The Warren Court: 1953 to 1969

The appointment of Earl Warren, Republican governor of California, to be chief justice in 1953 marked the beginning of a new period of activism on the Court, this time in defense of the rights of the individual against the actions or neglect of governments. In this period the Court created many new precedents, most of them controversial in both legal and political terms.

The Warren Court expanded three areas of constitutional interpretation:

* It applied most of the provisions of the Bill of Rights to the states by arguing that the due process clause of the 14th Amendment should be understood to include most of the specific rights listed in the first eight amendments. This line of interpretation had originated in the 1920s but the Warren Court greatly expanded its use.

* It adopted the doctrine, developed by a minority of justices in the early 1940s, that the rights guaranteed by the Bill of Rights should be treated as "fundamental rights." Laws that violated these rights were given "strict scrutiny" by the Court and were presumed to be unconstitutional unless government could demonstrate a "compelling governmental purpose" for such a law.

We come then to the question presented: Does segregation of children in public schools *Box 9.3*
solely on the basis of their race, even though the physical facilities and other "tangible" *Extract from Chief*
factors may be equal, deprive the children of the minority group of equal educational oppor- *Justice Warren's opinion*
tunities? We believe that it does. *in* Brown v. Board of

In *Sweatt v. Painter* [1950], in finding that a segregated law school for Negroes could not Education *(1954).*
provide them equal educational opportunities, this Court relied in large part on "those qualities which are incapable of objective measurement but which make for greatness in a law
school." ... Such considerations apply with added force to children in grade and high schools.
To separate them from others of similar age and qualifications solely because of their race generates a feeling of inferiority as to their status in the community that may affect their hearts and
minds in a way unlikely ever to be undone ...

We conclude that in the field of public education the doctrine of "separate but equal" has
no place. Therefore, we hold that the plaintiffs and others similarly situated ... are, by reason
of the segregation complained of, deprived of the equal protection of the laws guaranteed by
the Fourteenth Amendment.

- It broadened the interpretation of the equal protection clause of the 14th
  Amendment. Constitutional amendments are prohibitions against state (that is,
  governmental) action, and the Court substantially broadened the meaning of
  "state action" to include the actions of any body supported or financed by the federal or state governments. Freedom from discrimination on racial or religious
  grounds was declared to be a "fundamental right."

This section will look briefly at the Court's new precedents in five areas: racial discrimination, legislative apportionment, the separation of church and state, the rights
of the accused, and the right of privacy.

Racial discrimination. In 1954 the Court finally agreed to reconsider the interpretation
of the equal protection clause in relation to racial segregation. In *Brown v. Board of
Education of Topeka, Kansas*, led by Chief Justice Warren, it unanimously overturned the narrow interpretation in *Plessy v. Ferguson* and ruled that "segregated education is inherently unequal" and thus a violation of the Constitution.[11] The decision
in *Brown* was extremely important: not only did it remove the constitutional approval
of racial segregation, but in follow-up decisions the Court ordered that public school

---

11   On the background to *Brown*, see Richard Kluger, *Simple Justice: The History of Brown v
      Board of Education and Black America's Struggle for Equality* (Knopf, 1976).

Guardsmen in Sturgis,
Kentucky, escort a
group of black students
out of the school on
September 10, 1956.

authorities take steps to integrate their school systems racially. Since public education was segregated by law in the South and in some other states, and by traditional practice in many northern states, the Court was ordering a major social revolution across the United States.

The Court's decisions were met with wild opposition from southern whites. In 1957, President Eisenhower had to send troops to Little Rock, Arkansas, to enforce a Federal District Court order integrating the Central High School. Generally, school boards dragged their feet and had to be ordered by the lower courts to implement integration plans. Since racial integration in schools was hindered in most places by segregated patterns of housing, the Court eventually approved integration plans in some cities that involved substantial busing of students across the city; an example: *Swann v. Charlotte-Mecklenberg* (1971). While busing children to school was a very common practice, busing to achieve racial integration aroused a great deal of hostility, particularly in many northern cities. In Boston in 1975, in the face of mob violence and school board intransigence, a federal judge temporarily took over control of the schools from the school board to implement an integration plan.

Legislative apportionment. Drawing the boundaries for legislative districts, whether for the state legislatures or the House of Representatives, is the responsibility of each state's legislature. From the beginning of the twentieth century there had been a general movement of population from rural areas, first into the cities and eventually into the suburbs. In many states the rural-dominated legislatures had not redistricted seats to fully reflect the population shifts; as a result, rural areas became overrepresented and the cities and suburbs grossly underrepresented in the state legislatures and in the House of Representatives.

In 1943 in *Colegrove v. Green*, the Court had ruled that the question of representation was a "political question"—that is, an issue that was not appropriate for the courts to deal with and that had to be left to the political process. The trouble with this was that rural legislators held disproportionate power, and that the only way to achieve redistricting was to persuade them to give up some of it. There was no other way of changing the situation.

In *Baker v. Carr* (1962) a majority of the Court finally decided to tackle the situation. It ruled that the fact that the state legislature of Tennessee had not been redistricted since 1901, in violation of the state constitution, denied suburban voters the equal protection of the laws. This decision forced the Court to come up with a constitutionally acceptable standard for distributing legislative seats.

In follow-up cases the Court ruled that every vote had to be given equal weight in any form of legislative districting; this became known as the "one person, one vote" standard. It even ruled that state upper houses also had to have districts of equal population—something that had never been true before. These decisions were very unpopular, particularly in rural areas; there was much criticism of the rigid standard of equality that was being set, which made no allowance for geography or tradition. In some cases, when a state legislature refused to redistrict as thoroughly as a District Court demanded, the court hired its own experts to draw the boundaries.

The separation of church and state. The most controversial issue in this area was (and still is) how to interpret the First Amendment prohibition on laws "respecting an establishment of religion." The Court applied the prohibition to the states through the 14th Amendment. In *Engle v. Vitale* (1962) the Court ruled that a school board could not require the saying of a nondenominational prayer at the beginning of the school day. In *Abington v. Schempp* (1963) it struck down a state law requiring bible reading in public schools. These decisions abolished a long-standing tradition in most public schools and outraged conservative Christians.

As a result of the Warren Court's broad definition of "establishment of religion," many of the other ways in which government and religion had traditionally been "intermingled" were eventually challenged. The Court ruled that government action that had a religious purpose was unconstitutional. Action that supported religion was only allowable if it was incidental to a secular purpose. For example, is it constitutional for a city council to put up a Christmas creche on public property? Only if it also includes secular symbols of the season, like Santa Claus; see *Lynch v. Donnelly*

(1984). Can a state legislature pay a Christian chaplain to open its daily sessions with prayer? Yes; see *Marsh v. Chambers* (1983). Can a state require a "moment of silence" for prayer or meditation at the beginning of the school day? No; see *Wallace v. Jaffree* (1985).

The rights of accused persons. The Bill of Rights guarantees a number of specific rights to persons accused of a crime:

- The Fourth Amendment guarantees security against "unreasonable searches and seizures" of their person and property.

- The Fifth Amendment provides guarantees against double-jeopardy and self-incrimination.

- The Sixth Amendment guarantees a fair trial.

- The Eighth Amendment provides guarantees against excessive bail or fines, and against "cruel and unusual punishment."

The Warren Court applied these guarantees to the states through the 14th Amendment and broadened their meaning. In *Mapp v. Ohio* (1961) it forbade the use in a state court of evidence obtained from a police search without a warrant, thus tightening the rules under which police searches were conducted. In *Gideon v. Wainwright* (1963) it ruled that to ensure fair trials, states must provide poor defendants with a lawyer. By far the most controversial precedent in this area was *Miranda v. Arizona* (1966). Here, a kidnapper and rapist was freed because the police interrogation was ruled to have violated his constitutional right against self-incrimination. The Court ruled that police had to inform suspects of their constitutional rights before questioning them—that is, to inform them that they had a constitutional right to remain silent and to have a lawyer present during questioning. This has become regular police practice. Thus, American police dramas show suspects being read their "Miranda rights" or being "Mirandized" on arrest. The right against self-incrimination had always been applied in court proceedings. The *Miranda* decision extended that right to cover the whole period of police custody. Many people argued that the new "Miranda rules" went too far and made the work of the police too difficult.

The right of privacy. In *Griswold v. Connecticut* (1965)[12] the Court declared that individuals have a constitutional right of privacy against government intrusion into their

---

12   On the background to *Griswold*, see David J. Garrow, *Liberty and Sexuality: The Right to Privacy and the Making of Roe v. Wade* (Macmillan, 1994).

lives. The Court struck down a Connecticut law that made it a crime to use a birth control device or to counsel anyone to do so. A right of privacy is not listed in the Bill of Rights; even so, the Court declared that it could be deduced from the right to liberty in the Fifth Amendment or, alternatively, could be understood as being one of the additional, unlisted rights referred to in the Ninth Amendment. The full impact of the new doctrine of privacy became clear in 1973, when the Burger Court declared in *Roe v. Wade* that it included a woman's right to have an abortion. This struck down the laws in most states prohibiting abortion.

The Warren Court marked a return to the tradition of activism of the pre–New Deal court, this time on behalf of basic civil rights rather than economic rights. Some of the Court's decisions had an enormous impact; for example, they ended long-established social traditions such as racial segregation, and religious exercises in the public schools. The Court's decisions in the areas discussed above all generated a great deal of public opposition, and by the late 1960s conservative politicians had begun to make the liberal activism of the Court a political issue. In 1968, Richard Nixon promised to appoint "strict constructionists" (that is, justices who would interpret the Constitution narrowly rather than broadly) to the courts if elected president.

❧ The Burger Court (1969–86)

Starting with the appointment of Chief Justice Burger by President Nixon in 1969, all the new appointments to the Court in this period were made by Republican presidents: Nixon made a total of four; Ford one; Carter none (which made him the first president since 1850 not to have a vacancy on the Supreme Court during his time in office); and Reagan three, including one during Burger's tenure as chief justice. But there was no sharp turnabout in the Court's decisions—in fact, the Burger Court was as active in striking down legislation as the Warren Court had been. In spite of considerable political pressure, particularly during the Reagan years, the Court upheld the precedents established under Warren. It did not have the reformist zeal of the 1960s, but it did move into some new areas.

Typical of the more cautious approach of the 1970s were the decisions on the death penalty, starting with *Furman v. Georgia* (1972). Only two justices considered the death penalty to be a violation of the Eighth Amendment's prohibition of "cruel and unusual punishment," but a majority agreed that the lack of procedural safeguards in the application of the death penalty made it unconstitutional under existing state laws. Later, the Court upheld new state laws that imposed the death penalty with better procedural safeguards: see *Gregg v. Georgia* (1976); but the same Court disallowed some related state laws—for example, those that imposed the death penalty for rape: see *Coker v. Georgia* (1977).

Similarly, the Court was cautiously reformist in dealing with the politically contentious issue of affirmative action. In an attempt to provide some remedy for the long history of racial segregation, starting in the late 1960s Congress passed several laws

requiring positive integration. This principle was originally applied to racial integration, but subsequent laws extended the principle to women, to other minorities, and
to the disabled. Affirmative action to give preference to racial minorities in admissions
policies or in hiring was opposed by many people as "reverse discrimination." It was
argued that the practice violated the 1964 Civil Rights Act, which forbade most forms
of discrimination, and denied equal protection to non-minorities.

The first affirmative action case to reach the Supreme Court was *Bakke v. Regents
of the University of California* (1978). In order to increase the number of minority
students in its medical school, the university reserved 16 of its 100 places annually for
students who could demonstrate some educational disadvantage. Although his test
scores were higher than those of some of the students admitted to the minority places,
Bakke was twice denied admission, so he took the university to court. The Court was
almost evenly divided, and split its decision into two parts. By 5 to 4 it declared that
the university's use of a fixed quota of 16 places for minorities violated the Civil
Rights Act; but by 5 to 4 it also stated that it was not unconstitutional for universities
to take the race of candidates into account in their admission policies.

The effect of *Bakke* was to give general approval to affirmative action plans, provided they did not use fixed quotas and had some flexibility. The Burger Court held
to this position and later approved a number of affirmative action programs involving
minorities and women.

It was the Burger Court that pioneered the application of the equal protection
clause of the 14th Amendment to sex discrimination. This argument was pressed by
lawyers for the American Civil Liberties Union (ACLU), with many of the early cases
being argued by Ruth Bader Ginsburg (later Justice Ginsburg). Starting with *Reed v.
Reed* (1971), the Court struck down a series of laws and practices that discriminated
against women. But it refused to go so far as to make sex discrimination a "suspect
category" like racial or religious discrimination, where the discrimination is subject to
"strict scrutiny" by the Court and is almost impossible to justify in constitutional
terms.

The most important and controversial women's issue in which the Burger Court
broke new ground related to abortion; see *Roe v. Wade* (1973).[13] Most states had laws,
dating from the nineteenth century, that made it a criminal offense to perform an
abortion. A handful of states had liberalized their abortion laws in the 1960s. The
Burger Court's decision to hear an abortion case surprised many people; the judgment, written by Justice Harry Blackmun (who had been recently appointed by
President Nixon) and supported by seven justices, was even more surprising.

Using the precedent of *Griswold v. Connecticut* (1965), the Court in *Roe* declared
that a woman's decision about abortion was protected by the right of privacy from

---

13   On the background to *Roe*, see Garrow, *Liberty and Sexuality.*

government regulation. Since abortion was a safe medical procedure in the early stages of pregnancy, the state could not claim the right to regulate it on grounds of public health. The state had more claim to be able to regulate in the later stages, at which time it might also protect the life of the child. The Court divided the normal pregnancy of nine months into three trimesters. In the first three months, the woman's right to decide was absolute and the state could not regulate. The state might make a case for some regulation in the second trimester, and a stronger case in the final trimester.

The effect of *Roe* was to eliminate most state laws on abortion. Opinion was very sharply polarized. Those opposed to abortion were outraged, and several states passed new laws placing a variety of restrictions on the performance of abortions, almost all of which the Court struck down in subsequent cases.

⊛ The Rehnquist Court (1986 to the present)

Presidents Reagan and Bush, responding to strong conservative pressures from within their party, determined to appoint only conservative justices to the Court. Between 1981 and 1991 they appointed five justices, and Reagan promoted Justice Rehnquist to be chief justice. The subsequent behavior of these five Republican appointees on the Court illustrates the dilemma facing judicial conservatives opposed to the liberal activism of the Warren years: Should they overturn the Warren precedents, many of them in place for thirty years, in a campaign of conservative activism? Or should judicial conservatives, above all people, respect the hallowed rule of *stare decisis*, which calls for precedents to be accepted for the sake of the stability and integrity of the law? Only Justices Scalia (appointed by Reagan) and Thomas (Bush), mostly joined by Chief Justice Rehnquist, have chosen the activist course; the others, Justices O'Connor (Reagan), Kennedy (Reagan), and Souter (Bush), have generally left the precedents intact.

The fate of *Roe v. Wade* provides the best example of the conservative Court at work in the early 1990s. From the time of the battle over the nomination of Robert Bork in 1987 (discussed later), anti-abortion campaigners hoped and abortion rights supporters feared that a majority was developing on the Court that disagreed with the decision in *Roe* and might vote to overturn it and allow the states to regulate abortion again. The expected clash was slow in coming. In *Webster v. Reproductive Health Services* (1989) and *Hodgson v. Minnesota* (1990), a majority voted to allow states to impose additional restrictions on abortions but declined to discuss the underlying question of the right of privacy. The constitutional issue was finally joined in 1992.

The case of *Planned Parenthood v. Casey* (1992) involved a Pennsylvania law that placed a number of restrictions on abortion procedures, such as requiring a twenty-four-hour waiting period. In its judgment the Court split into three groups: Justice Blackmun, the author of *Roe*, and Justice Stevens still supported the original decision.

An anti-abortion protestor waves a doll and an American flag outside the U.S. Supreme Court during the hearing of Planned Parenthood vs. Casey.

Chief Justice Rehnquist and Justice White (who had dissented in *Roe*), along with Justices Scalia and Thomas, wanted the Court to overrule the *Roe* precedent. The decisive votes lay with Justices O'Connor, Kennedy, and Souter, who signed a joint opinion. While they upheld most of the state restrictions (except the requirement that the woman have her spouse's consent for the procedure), they affirmed the central point in *Roe*, that being "the right of the woman to choose to have an abortion before viability and to obtain it without undue interference from the State."

The argument of the moderate conservatives was a procedural one: "After considering the fundamental constitutional questions resolved by *Roe*, principles of institutional integrity, and the rule of *stare decisis*, we are led to conclude this: the essential holding of *Roe v. Wade* should be retained and once again reaffirmed." The three justices rejected the reasoning in *Roe* and allowed the state to regulate abortion procedures from the earliest stages of pregnancy, provided only that the woman's exercise of her fundamental right to choose an abortion was not "unduly burdened."

Casey seems to have brought the constitutional argument over abortion to at least a temporary halt with what amounts to a compromise: the precedent and the basic constitutional right of privacy have been affirmed, but are now subject to regulation that may modify the practice of abortion to some extent. This is typical of the approach the Rehnquist Court has taken in the past ten years. In some areas, such as affirmative action and the rights of the accused, the Court has moved in a restrictive direction. The era of school integration under court order has been brought to an end. As *Casey* demonstrates, however, there is no stable conservative majority, and the Court can still produce surprises, such as the flag-burning cases. In *Texas v. Johnson* (1989) a Court majority composed of the three remaining liberals and two conservative justices (Kennedy and Scalia), ruled that the act of burning the American flag as a protest was protected by the free speech guarantee of the First and 14th Amendments. This decision, which struck down laws against flag desecration in forty-nine states, was greeted with howls of patriotic outrage. Congress passed a federal law to the same effect, which the Court struck down in *U.S. v. Eichman* (1990). Attempts to pass a constitutional amendment to protect the flag have failed in Congress.

One area in which the Rehnquist Court has continued to break new ground is women's rights. For example, the Court has made it easier for women to sue for sexual harassment in the workplace; see *Meritor Savings Bank, FBD v. Vinson* (1986) and *Harris v. Forklift Systems* (1993). More surprising was the Court's ruling in *Romer v. Evans* (1996) on gay rights, an issue that is increasingly coming before the courts. In *Romer* the Court ignored the precedent in *Bowers v. Hardwick* (1986) that upheld a Georgia law against sodomy, and for the first time extended the equal protection clause of the 14th Amendment to cover discrimination on the basis of sexual orientation.

THE ARGUMENT OVER THE ROLE OF THE SUPREME COURT

For the past thirty years the U.S. Supreme Court has been surrounded by raging political controversy. Pickets have regularly marched outside the Supreme Court building on Capitol Hill; there have been mass marches supporting and opposing its decisions; and the appointment of justices to the Court has become highly politicized and has become a factor influencing presidential elections. The political battle is being fought over the legacy of the Warren Court. At the center of the controversy has been the case of *Roe v. Wade*, a decision made by the Burger Court in 1973 but set up by the Warren Court's earlier proclamation of the constitutional right of privacy in *Griswold v. Connecticut*.

Contained within the political struggle over issues such as abortion and prayer in schools is a genuine argument over the role of the courts in a democratic society—an argument over where the line between the judicial process and the democratic political process should be drawn. Given that judges are appointed for life (or until retirement, as in Canada), they cannot be held accountable for their decisions. Their very independence and separation from political life, it is argued, can also leave them out of touch with ordinary concerns. On the other hand, in a democratic country majority rule takes place within the constraints of the Constitution when it comes to questions of governmental jurisdiction and particularly of individual and minority rights. It follows that judges are necessarily in a position to overrule political actions on occasion through their interpretation of the Constitution.

Although the Canadian Supreme Court has been active in interpreting the Charter of Rights and Freedoms since 1982 and deals with many of the same issues as the U.S. Supreme Court, a public debate over the judicial role has been slow to develop in Canada. While specialists debate the use of "interpretivist" (restrained) and "non-interpretivist" (activist) modes of interpretation by different justices, the Court's decisions have stimulated almost no public debate. This is in part because the Canadian

Court has proceeded fairly cautiously. It has been most activist in the area of accused rights, but there has been no major controversy like that which surrounded the *Miranda* decision in the United States. The Court was cautious on the explosive issue of abortion. The law restricting abortion was struck down in *R. v. Morgentaler* (1988) because the process for securing an abortion violated the Charter. Only one justice declared that there was a right to an abortion under the Charter. As a result of the lack of burning controversy, the Court has not become a political issue and little attention is paid to its composition. The nomination of a new justice is always front-page news in the United States; a new appointment by the prime minister to the Canadian Supreme Court is buried on the inside pages.[14]

Both Thomas Jefferson and Andrew Jackson were strongly opposed to "elitist" judges overruling political decisions and argued that each branch of government had the right to interpret the Constitution for itself. The Constitution itself does not locate the interpretive function, but it was probably inevitable that John Marshall's argument for the Supreme Court's role in *Marbury v. Madison* would in the long run be generally accepted. But even if the role of judges as the final interpreters of the Constitution is accepted, it is still worth debating how expansive a role they should play.

In the United States there have been two schools of thought regarding the scope of the Court's interpretive role. Advocates of "judicial restraint" have argued that the courts should usually defer to the decisions of the political process, overruling them only when there has been a clear violation of established constitutional interpretation. The most principled and consistent advocate of this position was Justice Felix Frankfurter (1939–62), who on many occasions refused to vote to overrule laws he clearly disapproved of because he believed that the Court should play a limited role in a democracy.[15] On the other side of the argument is "judicial activism," a position that sees the Court as the guardian of the Constitution's values, which often must be defended against violation by careless political majorities. The strongest advocates of judicial activism, such as Justice William Brennan, who was the principal architect of many of the Warren Court's decisions, go even further and argue that the Court must creatively adapt the eighteenth-century Constitution to contemporary values.[16]

In response to the judicial activism argument, conservative critics of the Warren Court have attempted to develop the position of judicial restraint into a coherent philosophy of constitutional interpretation. The best-known variant of the restraintist

---

14   See Rainer Knopf and F.L. Morton, *Charter Politics* (Nelson, 1992).

15   For examples of Frankfurter's restraintist position at the beginning and the end of his career on the Court, see his dissents in *West Virginia Board of Education v. Barnette* (1943) and *Baker v. Carr* (1962).

16   Justice William J. Brennan, "The Constitution of the United States: Contemporary Ratification," in Jack N. Rakove, ed., *Interpreting the Constitution: The Debate over Original Intent* (Northeastern University Press, 1990).

philosophy is "originalism" or "original intent." Originalists argue that any kind of activist position simply results in judges writing their own values into the Constitution. But the nine justices of the Court are no wiser, writes Justice Scalia, than "nine people picked at random from the Kansas City telephone directory."[17] The proposed alternative is to interpret the Constitution in accordance with the meaning intended by its framers or by the sponsors of the amendments. Thus, judges are not entitled to discover "new" rights, such as the right of privacy, in the Bill of Rights. The way to update the Constitution is through the democratic amending process, not through judicial interpretation. The principal exponent of originalism has been Robert Bork; Justices Scalia and Thomas have attempted to apply the originalist position from their seats on the Court.[18]

As noted above, the debate surrounding judicial activism is really an argument over the activism of the Warren Court in the 1950s and 1960s. Before looking at the argument, it is worth recapitulating the relevant aspects of the Court's history. It was Chief Justice John Marshall who established an activist role for the Court. Marshall held firm Federalist convictions about the importance of the judiciary as a "check" in the republican system. His political skill, exemplified in *Marbury v. Madison*, enabled him to lay down the basis of the Court's active, centralizing role in interpreting the Constitution, and to steer the Court around direct partisan entanglements toward a position of authority and independence. Later, *Dred Scott v. Sandford* showed that the Court, by mistaking the temper of the times and overestimating its own powers, could seriously damage the reputation Marshall had built for it. In the clash over the New Deal between the Court and FDR, the Court's established line of constitutional interpretation, which favored economic rights and a limited role for government, ran into a president backed by a party and public opinion that demanded government regulation of the economy. Public sentiment had shifted dramatically in only a few years, and in that situation the Court had to give way. The obstacles the Court had placed for many years against an expansion of federal government powers were removed.

It is worth noting that judicial activism can produce either conservative or liberal political results. Thus, John Marshall's activism in establishing the role of the Court, and the activism of the pre–New Deal Court in limiting the government's power to regulate the economy, were generally applauded by the political conservatives of the

---

17   *Cruzan v. Director, Missouri Department of Health* 497 U.S. 261 (1990) at 293.

18   Robert Bork lays out his philosophy in *The Tempting of America: The Political Seduction of the Law* (The Free Press, 1990). See also Justice Antonin Scalia, "Originalism: The Lesser Evil," *Cincinnati Law Review* 57 (1989), 849–865. For a legal conservative who is critical both of judicial activism and the philosophy of originalism, see Charles Fried, *Order and Law: Arguing the Reagan Revolution – A First Hand Account* (Simon and Schuster, 1990). For articles on both sides of the originalist debate, see Rakove, ed., *Interpreting the Constitution*.

Justice Thurgood Marshall, former NAACP chief counsel, is shown outside the Supreme Court in 1958 after having made an appeal for desegregated education.

time, and deplored by the liberals. More recently, the activism of the Warren Court (1953–69) on individual rights drew strong liberal political support and passionate conservative condemnation.

The Warren Court inaugurated the new era of activism on rights with its pioneering decision in *Brown v. Board*. *Brown* was the culmination of a twenty-year "campaign" by NAACP lawyers, led by Thurgood Marshall (later Justice Marshall), to persuade the Court to overrule its precedent in *Plessy v. Ferguson*. The *Brown* decision not only removed the constitutional sanction from racial segregation but gave a green light to the civil rights movement. Few people now doubt the wisdom of the Court's decision, or question Chief Justice Warren's careful management of it, though some conservatives argue that the constitutional reasoning should have been more sophisticated.[19] There is also general approval now of *Baker v. Carr*, where the Court cut through a long-standing political impasse over legislative districting.

The most vociferous and lasting objections to the Warren Court's activism have been in other areas: to the series of cases starting with *Engle v. Vitale* in which the Court adopted Jefferson's strict "wall of separation" interpretation of the establishment clause of the First Amendment, thus outraging the sensibilities of conservative Christians; to the Court's broadening the interpretation of the rights of the accused, in *Miranda v. Arizona* and other cases, which many felt tipped the scales too far against law enforcement; and to the Court's "discovery" of a "right of privacy" in the Bill of Rights in *Griswold v. Connecticut*, which provided the constitutional basis for the reasoning in *Roe v. Wade*, the most politically explosive case of all.

These decisions generated a considerable conservative political reaction that was encouraged by Republican politicians, starting with Richard Nixon, who during the 1968 presidential election campaign promised to appoint "strict constructionists" and conservative southern justices to the Court. Anger at the Supreme Court was instrumental in mobilizing the New Christian Right behind the Republican Party in the

---

19   Because he knew the importance of the decision and the political turmoil it was bound to create, Chief Justice Warren went to great lengths to persuade all of his colleagues to support a unanimous decision. He wanted a short opinion that newspapers could print in full. For a conservative critique of the Court's reasoning, see Robert H. Bork, *The Tempting of America*, 74–84.

1970s, and in disillusioning many socially conservative working-class voters with the Democratic Party leadership, which generally supported the Court's decisions.

The anger at the Warren Court was stoked partly by the fact that constitutional rulings by the Court are so difficult to change. If the Congress disagrees with the Court's interpretation of a federal law, it can change the law, and quite often does. For example, in 1982 the Congress passed an amendment to the 1965 Voting Rights Act in order to overturn *City of Mobile v. Bolden*, a 1980 decision of the Court that gave a narrow interpretation to a section of the act. A constitutional interpretation by the Court, however, can only be overruled by a constitutional amendment. This has happened historically—the 11th, 13th, 14th (overruling *Scott v. Sandford*), 16th, and 26th Amendments all overruled Court decisions or were passed in response to them—but it is extremely difficult to accomplish. Repeated attempts to pass amendments to overrule the Court on school prayer and abortion fell well short of the required two-thirds majorities in Congress.

The only other methods of changing a constitutional ruling are to persuade the Court to change its mind or to change the composition of the Court. Unlike the other institutions in Washington, the Supreme Court cannot be lobbied directly. It has no constituents it must listen to and no need of campaign funds. The way to influence the Court is through legal argument—in briefs before the Court, in the legal journals, and in the media. The best example of this kind of campaign to change the Court's interpretation of the Constitution was the one by the NAACP against racial segregation, but it took nearly twenty years of work to finally overturn a fifty-year-old precedent.[20] A similar campaign to have the death penalty declared unconstitutional has been waged for over twenty years, with only limited results. Since the vote in *Roe v. Wade* was 7 to 2, the prospect of changing the mind of the Court on abortion was obviously remote.

The conservative campaign to change the Court's mind, particularly on abortion, has focused on changing the composition of the Court. This is also a slow process. On average a justice leaves the Court every two years, but this is not a regular process. For example, while there were four vacancies on the Court between 1969 and 1972, there was only one vacancy between 1972 and 1981. It is also an unpredictable process, in that many justices, once established on the Court, do not make the rulings that were expected of them by the president who appointed them. The best examples are Chief

---

20   On the NAACP campaign, see Mark V. Tushnet, *The NAACP's Legal Strategy Against Segregated Education, 1925–1950* (University of North Carolina Press, 1987). The legendary NAACP legal campaign provided the model for many others, including, it is worth noting, the Women's Legal Education and Action Fund (LEAF), founded in 1985 to press for women's rights under the Charter. See Sherene Razack, "The Women's Legal Education and Action Fund," in F.L. Morton, ed., *Law, Politics and the Judicial Process in Canada,* 2nd Edition (University of Calgary Press, 1992).

Justice Warren and Justice Brennan; both were appointed by President Eisenhower, yet they became the principal liberal activists on the Court, which was not at all what the president expected or wanted.

President Nixon was the first Republican to promise to appoint conservative justices to end the Court's liberal activism. Making the Court a campaign issue in 1968 had the effect of politicizing the appointment process, and in 1969 two of Nixon's nominations were defeated by the Democratic majority in the Senate. Between 1969 and 1972, Nixon had the unusual opportunity to make four appointments to the Court. Yet in 1973, three of the Nixon appointees voted with the majority in *Roe v. Wade*. Indeed, one of them, Justice Blackmun, wrote the landmark liberal opinion! Only one, Justice Rehnquist, turned out to be the kind of solidly conservative justice that President Nixon had in mind.

In the 1980s Presidents Reagan and Bush, under pressure from Republican conservatives, were much more deliberate in selecting conservative judges for all the federal courts, using opposition to *Roe v. Wade* as a "litmus test" of true judicial conservatism.[21] This politicized the nomination and confirmation process even more, particularly for nominees for the Supreme Court.

Appointments to the Supreme Court have often been politically contentious.[22] Between 1789 and 1898, 20 of the 78 nominations by the president were defeated in the Senate, usually for partisan reasons. In the twentieth century, there has generally been a concern to "keep the Court out of politics," and only 5 of 59 nominations have been defeated. Three of the defeats have come since 1969, that is, during the latest period of polarization around the Court.

The most spectacular and important confirmation clash in the modern history of the Court began when President Reagan nominated Judge Robert Bork in 1987.[23] In his earlier academic career, Bork had carved out a reputation as a conservative judicial theorist and caustic critic of the activism of the Warren Court. Bork's reputation as an aggressive conservative who was totally opposed to *Roe* had earned him the nomination for the Supreme Court, but also made him a lot of enemies among liberal interest groups. In 1987 the stakes seemed particularly high for abortion rights supporters, because Bork would have been replacing Justice Powell, a supporter of *Roe*, and would probably have created a majority on the Court for overturning that

---

21   On President Reagan's judicial appointments, see Herman Schwartz, *Packing the Courts: The Conservative Campaign to Rewrite the Constitution* (Scribner, 1988).

22   On the judicial appointment process, see David M. O'Brien, *Judicial Roulette* (Priority Publishers, 1988).

23   For opposing views of the Bork nomination fight, see Patrick B. McGuigan and Dawn M. Weyrich, *Ninth Justice: The Fight for Bork* (University Press of America, 1990); and Michael Pertschuk and Wendy Schaetzel, *The People Rising: The Campaign Against the Bork Nomination* (New York: Thunder's Month Press, 1989).

decision. A coalition of women's, civil rights, and union groups waged an unprecedented grass roots and media campaign to persuade the Democratic majority in the Senate to defeat the nomination, which it did. In hindsight, the defeat of the Bork nomination did prove to be the key to saving at least the core of the *Roe* decision; in 1992, Justice Anthony Kennedy, who was appointed instead of Bork, was part of the moderate conservative block that upheld the *Roe* precedent in *Planned Parenthood v. Casey*.

President Bush avoided controversy when he nominated a low-profile judge, David Souter, to replace Justice Brennan in 1990. But his second nomination, of Judge Clarence Thomas to succeed Justice Thurgood Marshall, was highly provocative and set off another storm of political controversy.[24] Marshall was a legend for his role as an NAACP lawyer in battling segregation, and had been a leading liberal voice on the Court; Thomas was an outspoken black conservative who had much less impressive credentials.

The controversy surrounding the Thomas nomination escalated sharply when public pressure forced the Senate Judiciary Committee to hold hearings based on the allegation by Professor Anita Hill, a former subordinate of Thomas's in government, that he had sexually harassed her. The Hill/Thomas hearings were one of the most bizarre spectacles in all of modern American politics, as the committee of male senators questioned Hill, Thomas, and others about the intimate details of the charges before a transfixed TV audience. While the black community had been united against Bork, it was split on the Thomas nomination. A handful of southern Democratic senators, responding to evidence of southern black support for Thomas, broke with their party and provided the votes to confirm Thomas by 52 votes to 48, the narrowest margin for confirmation in the Court's history.

Anxious to avoid a political fight, President Clinton nominated two "safe" moderate liberals to the Court, Ruth Bader Ginsburg in 1993 and Steven Breyer in 1994. Both were confirmed easily. Faced with a Republican Senate, it seems likely the president will pursue a similar noncontentious appointment policy in his second term, should there be further vacancies on the Court.

The Political Role of the Court: Overview

In the past thirty years the work of the U.S. Supreme Court has become highly politicized. Questions about the role of the courts have become hopelessly entangled with political positions. On the Court itself, the individual justices have not always been

---

24   For opposing views of the Thomas confirmation process, see Jane Mayer and Jill Abramson, *Strange Justice: The Selling of Clarence Thomas* (Houghton Mifflin, 1994); and David Brock, *The Real Anita Hill: The Untold Story* (The Free Press, 1993).

able to keep their judicial philosophies separate from their personal political views, as Justice Frankfurter was able to do throughout his career. The appointment process has become highly partisan, culminating in the public campaigns against Bork and Thomas. The controversy surrounding the Court, while not unprecedented, is setting a dangerous trend. To the degree that the Court is perceived as simply another partisan body, and its rulings as no more than expressions of the political views of a majority of the Court, the Court loses its distinctive moral authority to be the final interpreter of the Constitution, and the problem of its lack of accountability becomes more pressing.

Blame for politicizing the Court tends to be allocated politically. Conservatives blame the Warren Court for pushing much too far on too many issues and thus generating an inevitable political backlash. Liberals blame Republican politicians who, from Richard Nixon in 1968 to Bob Dole in 1996, have made the courts an election issue.

Did the Warren Court go too far? Politics aside, to answer this question we must consider the relationship between the interpretive process and public opinion. In liberal democracies the courts are deliberately insulated from the direct popular pressures of the political process.[25] So is the Constitution, which cannot be amended by the normal legislative process. But in the long run the Court's interpretation of the Constitution must be politically viable. Thus, when John Marshall established the Court as an important nationalizing institution, he aroused political controversy at the time, but he was also moving the nation in the direction it had to move. In the same way, when the Judicial Committee of the Privy Council altered the legal balance of Canadian federalism, its actions broadly corresponded to the changing federal/provincial political relationship (see Chapter 4).

The Supreme Court's relationship to public opinion can be studied through its three major decisions on race. The Court's attempt to solve the slavery issue in *Dred Scott v. Sandford* was a disaster because it flew directly in the face of the changes in northern opinion on the issue. It was dismissed as a purely political decision and was overridden by the 14th Amendment after the Civil War. *Plessy v. Ferguson*, while in retrospect a tragically narrow reading of the equal protection clause, was very much in tune with popular opinion, in the North as well as the South. Justice Harlan's famous lone dissent ("Our Constitution is color-blind") was more prophetic than politically viable at the time. In *Brown v. Board of Education* the Court initiated a social revolution well in advance of the nation's political capacity to end segregation. In spite of the instant controversy, this decision—the boldest in the Court's history—

---

25   In roughly half the American states, state judges are elected rather than appointed. In most cases the direct election of judges was adopted during the Progressive era as a way of reforming a judicial appointment system than had been corrupted by partisan abuses. In most cases efforts are made to keep judicial elections out of the main partisan battles.

was soon accepted as wise and inevitable and as pointing out the direction in which the American nation had to move.

Archibald Cox has stated the relationship between the Court and public opinion as follows:

> The aspirations voiced by the Court must be those that the community is willing ... in the end to live by. The legitimacy of the great creative decisions of the past flowed in large measure from the accuracy of the Court's perception of this kind of common will and from the Court's ability ... to strike a responsive chord equivalent to the consent of the governed. To go further—to impose the Court's own wiser choice—is illegitimate.[26]

Most of the key decisions of the Warren Court were controversial. The most controversial decision of the era, however, was the Burger Court's decision in *Roe v. Wade*. On his retirement in 1984, Justice Blackmun, who wrote the opinion on *Roe*, justified the decision on broad political grounds as "a step that had to be taken as we go down the road toward the full emancipation of women." Critics argue that the political process was at work to change the restrictive abortion laws and that a number of states had already liberalized their laws. It was unnecessary and unwise, the argument goes, for the Court to impose a sweeping national standard, particularly since it had to engage in a controversial form of constitutional interpretation (the right of privacy) to do so.

Certainly, *Roe* exposed the Court to an enormous political backlash. It did more than anything else to motivate the sustained effort by conservatives to change the composition of the Court. It also made opposition to abortion the single greatest mobilizing issue behind the rise of political conservatism. Since being injected into the political arena, the abortion issue has generated heated rhetoric and even some violence on the anti-abortion side. It is notorious for being an issue on which compromise seems impossible.[27] It is the Court itself that may in the end have found a way to put the issue to rest. Until 1986 the Court majority had repulsed a series of state efforts to get round the blanket protection of early-term abortions. The conservative appointments by Presidents Reagan and Bush did change the Court's position, but as was discussed earlier, three of the five new justices balked at overruling *Roe* after more than twenty years. Instead they affirmed the right to an abortion but scrapped Justice Blackmun's reasoning and allowed states to legislate some restrictions. This left the issue in a position largely in tune with the majority of the American public.

---

26 Archibald Cox, *The Court and the Constitution* (Houghton Mifflin, 1987), 377.
27 See Barbara Hinkson Craig and David M. O'Brien, *Abortion and American Politics* (Chatham House, 1993) and the discussions in Laurence H. Tribe, *Abortion: The Clash of Absolutes* (Norton, 1990) and Elizabeth Mensch and Alan Freeman, *The Politics of Virtue: Is Abortion Debatable?* (Duke University Press, 1993).

The aim of judicial and political conservatives has been to end the activism of the Court, reduce its role, and lower its profile. They are discovering that this is not easy to do as new rights are claimed and the cases make their way up through the various court systems. Thus, the Rehnquist Court has broadened the definition of sex discrimination to include sexual harassment. More surprisingly, in *Romer v. Evans* (1996) the Court has reopened the issue of gay rights that it had effectively dismissed in 1986. In 1997 the Court found itself in the middle of another intensely controversial issue: whether there is a constitutional "right to die."

The twentieth century has seen a slowly growing "rights revolution" in the United States. As a result of efforts by organizations such as the NAACP and the American Civil Liberties Union (ACLU), a heightened concern for individual rights has been slowly spreading through American society. While the preoccupation with rights is seen by many conservatives as excessive,[28] the rights campaigners are, after all, simply appealing to the foundational American tradition of "unalienable rights" proclaimed in the Declaration of Independence. Conservatives also argue that such issues should be dealt with by the political process and not by the courts; but here again they are working against the grain of American society. As Alexis de Tocqueville testified in the 1830s, "scarcely any question arises in the United States that is not resolved, sooner or later, into a judicial question."[29]

---

28   For a conservative critique of the American focus on rights, see Mary Ann Glendon, *Rights Talk: The Impoverishment of Political Discourse* (The Free Press, 1991).

29   Alexis de Tocqueville, *Democracy in America*, Volume I (Vintage, 1990), 280.

CHAPTER 10

THE AMERICAN ELECTORATE

The founding generation of Americans were not democrats in the modern sense. While they believed in the sovereignty of the people, they also believed in qualifications for voting, which usually meant ownership of a certain amount of property or payment of a certain amount in taxes. Since land was quite readily available in the New World, the proportion of the adult male population qualified to vote was much higher in America at that time (as high as 80 percent in some states) than in Europe.

The Constitution allows states to set their own qualifications for voting, although Congress has the power to regulate federal elections. After 1800 the states began lowering property qualifications for voting; by the 1840s these qualifications had been abolished, and the United States could claim to be a democracy with universal suffrage—the first modern democracy.

Throughout the nineteenth century, Canada, in contrast to the United States, retained the concept that voting should be restricted to those with a property stake in the community. The provinces had property qualifications that allowed most male heads of households to vote—an estimated 15 percent of the total population (perhaps 50 to 60 percent of adult males). After Confederation, Canada alternated between using provincial qualifications and setting a uniform standard for federal elections. In the last decade of the century most provinces adopted adult male suffrage with the result that the return to provincial standards for federal elections in 1898 came close to achieving universal male suffrage across the country. The process was completed in 1920, when a uniform federal franchise was established.[1]

COMPLETING THE DEMOCRATIC ELECTORATE

The achievement of universal suffrage was an important political landmark; but by contemporary standards the United States was not democratic at all, since most adults were explicitly excluded from voting. The four main excluded groups—African Americans, women, Asians, and native people—were not granted the right to vote, and full citizenship, until well into the twentieth century.

African Americans. As slaves, most blacks were considered the property of their owners. Even after slavery was abolished by the northern states in the early nineteenth century, free blacks were not seen as part of the political community and were generally prohibited from voting. Before the Civil War, they were permitted to vote only in the New England states. In the aftermath of the war, as part of efforts by Republicans to guarantee the rights of the former slaves in the South, the 15th Amendment was passed forbidding states to deny the right to vote "on account of race, color, or previous condition of servitude."

The legal position of blacks was clear after 1870; even so, by the end of the century the southern states had taken steps to effectively exclude the black population from politics. One method was the use of poll taxes and literacy tests as qualifications for voting. Poll taxes were a major deterrent to the poorer segments of the population, both black and white. Literacy tests were easy to manipulate so that even well-educated black people were generally prevented from voting. Another method was to forbid blacks from voting in Democratic primary elections on the ground that the Democratic Party was a "private" organization and thus not covered by the 15th Amendment. It was only in the 1940s that the Supreme Court ruled the use of "white primaries" unconstitutional.[2]

In the North, while blacks could not be prohibited from voting, it was only after the New Deal that much effort was made to mobilize the black vote. In the South, obstacles to black voting were formidable. The civil rights movement increased its efforts to register black voters and was met with intimidation and violence. The 24th Amendment abolished the poll tax in federal elections in 1964, but it was not until the

---

1   See Norman Ward, *The Canadian House of Commons: Representation*, 2nd Edition (University of Toronto Press, 1963), Chapter 12.

2   *Smith v. Allwright* 321 U.S. 649 (1944).

Voting Rights Act of 1965 that the final legal and administrative obstacles to black voting were removed. This act permitted federal officials to supervise registration and voting in any area where voting participation was unusually low. As a result of federal intervention, black voting rose steadily, although by the late 1980s the black participation rate was still lower than that of whites.

Women.   Women were denied the vote because their social role was seen as essentially domestic; in contrast, a man was the "head" of his household and its representative in the public sphere. The movement to gain equal rights for women, including the right to vote, began in the 1840s but was at first overshadowed by the campaign against slavery. Some expected that women, who were the strongest supporters of black rights, would achieve their rights at the same time as the freed slaves, but women bitterly discovered how little independent support woman suffrage had, and their campaign had to begin again.[3]

The traditional and religious opposition to women voting weakened gradually in the nineteenth century as women took on increasingly active roles in the churches and charitable organizations. The most popular argument was that women, who were usually the strongest supporters of reform movements, would be a good influence on politics. The first place to give women the vote was the Wyoming Territory, in 1869. There it was argued that women's "civilizing influence" would change the territory's wild image and attract more settlers.[4] Early in the twentieth century a number of western states extended the vote to women. The most important breakthrough occurred when the women's movement won a referendum on the issue in New York state in 1917. By that time the movement to give women the vote nationwide had become unstoppable, especially after women had replaced men in a wide range of jobs during World War I. The 18th Amendment to the Constitution was ratified in 1920.

In Canada the debate over female suffrage followed essentially the same course as in the United States. The western provinces gave women the right to vote in 1916, Ontario in 1917, the federal government in 1918, and the Maritime provinces between 1918 and 1925. In Quebec, however, where the opposition was led by the Catholic church, women were not enfranchised in provincial elections until 1940.[5]

Initially, the voting participation of women lagged well behind that of men. For example, a study of voting in Chicago in the 1920 presidential election, the first in which all women were eligible to vote, showed that 70 percent of men but only 46 percent of women voted. The participation gap between men and women narrowed

---

3   On the history of the struggle for female suffrage in the United States, see Paul Buhle, *The Concise History of Woman Suffrage* (University of Illinois Press, 1978).

4   Alan P. Grimes, *The Puritan Ethic and Woman Suffrage* (Oxford University Press, 1967).

5   Catherine L. Cleverdon, *The Woman Suffrage Movement in Canada* (University of Toronto Press, 1950, 1974).

slowly. By the early 1950s there was a 10 percent difference; by the 1970s the gap was under 5 percent; it was not until the 1980s that women voted at the same rate as men.[6]

Asians. Asian immigrants were barred from citizenship in the United States by a federal statute of 1870 that limited the right of naturalization to "white persons" and "persons of African descent." Without citizenship, they could not vote. The rights of their American-born children, including the right to vote, were upheld by the courts in the 1920s.[7] The racist restrictions on immigration and naturalization were finally lifted in 1952.

In Canada, Asians were not barred from citizenship. However, they were denied the vote in British Columbia, where most lived; also, the first federal franchise law of 1885 defined "person" to exclude Chinese and Mongolians. The federal Franchise Act of 1898 removed the ban on Asians voting in federal elections, but the ban was in effect reimposed in 1920 when those who were disenfranchised by provincial law were also excluded from voting federally (except for war veterans). As late as 1944 there was a federal law extending the voting ban to include those who had moved to other provinces after 1938 (mostly the Japanese who had been forcibly relocated from the west coast by the federal government in 1941!). The ban on Asian voting was removed in 1948.[8]

Native people. In the United States, native people were not allowed to vote before the twentieth century because they were not considered citizens. Article I, Section 2, of the Constitution specifically excluded Indians from the population census, as did the 14th Amendment of 1868. Some were granted citizenship on the condition that they abandon tribal life and enter "civilized society." Others who volunteered for the U.S. Army during World War I were given citizenship, but it was not until 1924 that the native peoples as a whole were defined as citizens. Even after that, several states prohibited some categories of native people from voting. In 1948, lawsuits under the 14th and 15th Amendments removed the last vestiges of discrimination in New Mexico and Arizona.

In Canada, the native peoples were considered wards of the Crown and thus not qualified to vote, especially since they paid no taxes. As part of the government's policy of assimilation, Indians living east of the Great Lakes were given the federal franchise in 1885, but this was withdrawn in 1898. The Inuit were first explicitly excluded from the federal franchise in 1934—a provision that was removed in 1950. In general, it was not until 1960 that the last obstacles to native people voting were removed.

---

6   Keith T. Poole and L. Harmon Ziegler, *Women, Public Opinion and Politics* (Longman, 1985).
7   Roger Daniels, "The Japanese Experience in North America: An Essay in Comparative Racism," *Canadian Ethnic Studies* 9 (1977), 95.
8   See Norman Ward, *The Canadian House of Commons*, Chapter 13.

Voter Participation

The United States was the first modern democracy. Since the nineteenth century, democracy has been considered a fundamental characteristic of the American system. Americans commonly use "free democratic elections" as the touchstone for judging the legitimacy of any political regime. Americans are called upon to vote often, and to elect federal, state, and local officials, including judges in many states. In many of the western states, proposed laws or amendments to the state constitution (propositions) regularly appear on state ballots through voter initiatives (see Chapter 13). Many states and localities require referendums to approve government bond issues. There are congressional and state elections every two years and often local elections in the intervening years.

One of the paradoxes in a country that places so much importance on elections is that the proportion of the voting age population that actually exercises its right to vote is startlingly low, very much lower than in any other Western country. Since the 1970s the voting turnout in presidential elections has been just over 50 percent. In 1996 it fell to 49 percent—the lowest level since the early nineteenth century. In congressional elections in off-years (nonpresidential years), turnout has averaged around 35 percent.[9]

By comparison, the turnout in national elections in other Western countries is almost always in the 70 to 80 percent range, and over 90 percent in those, such as Australia, where voting is compulsory. In Canada the turnout in both federal and provincial elections fluctuates around 75 percent and rarely falls below 70 percent.[10]

There is considerable variation in turnout among the American states, though even those with the highest participation fall below what is considered normal in Canada and other Western countries. In 1992, when the national turnout was 55 percent, the range was from a high of 73 percent in Maine to a low of 43 percent in Hawaii.[11] The southern states in particular have a long tradition of low voter turnout, since the techniques that were used to exclude blacks from voting in the South also excluded many poor white voters.

It is thus reasonable to argue that in American voter participation there is a "hole" comprising some 20 to 30 percent of Americans. Studies of voting behavior show that voter turnout is highly correlated with education and income. The millions of "missing" voters come overwhelmingly from the poorer, less educated segments of American society, which are thus badly underrepresented in the political process.[12]

---

9   U.S. Bureau of the Census, *Statistical Abstract of the United States 1995*, Table 146.
10   Ruy A. Teixeira, *The Disappearing American Voter* (The Brookings Institution, 1992), 8.
11   *Statistical Abstract of the United States 1995*, Table 462.
12   Teixeira, Chapter 3.

Why is voting turnout in the United States so much lower than in Canada and other Western democracies? Studies of the problem suggest that there are two main factors involved: registration barriers, and a failure to mobilize potential voters.

Registration

At the beginning of the twentieth century, when southern states were finding ways to prevent black voting, barriers to voting were also being raised in the North. Many states introduced poll taxes or literacy tests for voting. Also, most states started to require the advance registration of voters, particularly in the cities. Targeted by these reforms were not black voters but new immigrant voters. It was argued that these changes were necessary to reduce electoral corruption by urban political machines, which depended heavily on immigrant voters for their support; but the changes were clearly also motivated by middle-class fears about the changing composition of American society.

Over the years poll taxes and literacy tests fell out of use; they were finally abolished in the 1960s. In most states, however, voter registration is still a substantial obstacle to voting. The problem lies in the method of registration used in the United States, which places the onus for registration on the voter.

In other Western countries the government takes responsibility for compiling an accurate register of eligible voters, usually through politically neutral officials, such as the chief electoral officers in Canada. In most countries, including Canada since 1997, there is a permanent voting register that is updated annually. In the United States, the system is characteristically *laissez-faire*: it is up to each individual voter to make sure that he or she is registered to vote in advance of the election.

So in the United States, voting is a two-stage process—registering to vote, then voting—and less well-educated, less informed people are much less likely to take both steps. The proportion of registered voters who actually cast a ballot is fairly high—comparable to the turnout figures in those other countries where voters have their registration done for them. The "missing" American voters, then, are largely those who have failed to register. In 1994 the Democrats passed the "Motor-Voter" Act, which requires states to make voter registration available when people go to renew their driving, hunting, and other licenses or pick up a welfare check, but it is too soon to tell whether the new opportunities will have the desired effect on registration levels.

Various analysts have estimated that an easier voter registration system would raise the turnout rate by about 10 percent; this suggests that registration difficulties are only part of the problem and account for less than half of missing voters.[13]

---

13   Walter Dean Burnham, "The Turnout Problem," in A. James Reichley, ed., *Elections American Style* (The Brookings Institution, 1987), 139.

The Failure to Mobilize Voters

Walter Dean Burnham has pointed out that the low level of voter turnout in the United States is entirely a twentieth-century problem. Voter turnout in federal elections, which was low at the beginning of the nineteenth century, doubled in the Jacksonian period and often reached 80 percent during the second half of the century.[14]

In the twentieth century there was a general fall in voting participation. In the South, as already discussed, there was a deliberate and successful effort to prevent blacks from voting. The methods used for this also depressed voting among poorer whites. Southern voting in national elections fell sharply: between 1904 and 1952 it rarely even reached 30 percent. Since the removal of obstacles to black voting in the late 1960s, southern turnout has risen, though it remains under 50 percent.

Outside the South, voter turnout in presidential elections also declined steadily from the start of the twentieth century, falling to under 60 percent in the 1920s. During the New Deal it rose somewhat and stabilized at close to 70 percent until 1964. Since then it has declined steadily again.[15]

The main reason for the decline in voter turnout outside the South relates to how the party system operates. The end of the nineteenth century was a period of intense national competition between the Republican and Democratic parties; it was also the time when state party organizations were at their strongest. The parties had both the incentive and the organizations to get as many voters as possible to the polls.

This situation changed rapidly beginning in the late 1890s. Competition between the parties dropped off as the Democrats lost ground outside the South. As the Republicans became the dominant party in most of the North and West, Democratic Party organizations became weaker. The Republicans had less incentive and the Democrats had less ability to maximize their voting strength. Public attitudes were more hostile to parties during the Progressive era; and party organizations, especially at the state level, were weakened by the Progressive reforms. Between 1896 and 1924, turnout in presidential elections outside the South fell from 86.2 percent to 57.5 percent. There is much evidence that most of the "missing" voters belonged to the urban working class.

The working class was strongly attracted to President Roosevelt's New Deal, and this revived Democratic Party organizations in the North and raised voter turnout during the 1930s by over 10 percent. This new level was maintained until the late 1960s, when voter turnout started to drop steeply again. This latest fall-off is believed to be the result of the collapse of the parties as organizations capable of mobilizing marginal voters.

---

14   Walter Dean Burnham, *Critical Elections: the Mainspring of American Politics* (Norton, 1970).

15   Historical data for voting in presidential elections by state from U.S. Bureau of the Census, *Historical Statistics of the United States: Colonial Times to 1970* (1975), Series Y, 27–28.

As is discussed in Chapter 13, the role that party organizations once played in political campaigns has been undermined by candidate-centered organizations that use impersonal techniques, such as television and direct mailing, to influence voters. Party workers no longer knock on doors reminding people to vote. The capacity of the traditional party organizations to mobilize indifferent voters has thus been lost. Other organizations sometimes try to mobilize particular voting groups. Thus, Jesse Jackson has often run registration and voting drives in black communities, and in recent years groups such as the **Christian Coalition** have done the same in conservative churches. These efforts, however, remain partial.

It is clear that voter participation rises as public awareness of an election increases. This is why turnout is always higher in presidential years than in off-years. When a particular contest attracts unusual publicity, voter turnout can rise dramatically. An example was the run-off election for the Louisiana governorship in November 1991, which involved David Duke, a former official of the Ku Klux Klan and a neo-Nazi sympathizer. Local and national opposition to Duke attracted unprecedented publicity to the election, and voter turnout was reported around 80 percent. However, it appears that only in exceptional circumstances can American voters be persuaded to vote at a rate seen as normal in Canada and other Western democracies.

THE VOTING BEHAVIOR OF THE AMERICAN ELECTORATE

The base for studying American voting behavior has been provided by the American National Election Studies undertaken since 1948 by the Survey Research Center at the University of Michigan. The explanations that emerged from the early studies centered on two concepts: party identification as the main determinant of voting behavior, and the importance of social group membership as an influence on party identification.[16] Party identification has clearly weakened in recent years among voters, and this has opened the search for other explanatory factors and reopened the debate over how "rational" voting behavior is.[17] Even so, party identification remains a useful starting point for examining voting behavior. Social group membership is still a significant factor in voting behavior, although the groups having the greatest political significance have changed over the years.

The explanation of Canadian voting behavior is based mainly on the National Election Surveys conducted in conjunction with every federal election since 1965

---

16 The first major study was Angus Campbell et al., *The American Voter* (John Wiley, 1960).
17 A survey of the literature on voting behavior and the state of current theoretical discussion is in Richard G. Niemi and Herbert F. Weisberg, *Classics in Voting Behavior* (*Congressional Quarterly*, 1993).

(except for 1972). Analyses of the survey results have made it clear that the determinants of voting behavior in Canada are quite different from those in the United States. The key explanatory factors in America—long-term party identification and social group identification with a party—are very much weaker in Canada. Only about one-third of the Canadian electorate are "strong, stable, and consistent identifiers" with a political party—a much lower figure than in the United States (see Table 10.1). The bulk of Canadian voters can be classified as "flexible partisans."[18] Some religio-linguistic group alignments played a role in the earlier party systems; but in the current system, social group alignments are only marginally significant in explaining Canadian voting behavior.

Explanations as to why voting behavior is determined so differently in the two countries tend to be circular. Because "Canadian political parties cannot call upon legions of loyal followers whose attitudes are reinforced by strong group or ideological commitments ... they attempt to harness a variety of less predictable short term forces

Identification	1952	1956	1960	1964	1968	1972
Strong Democrat	22	21	20	27	20	15
Weak Democrat	25	23	25	25	25	26
Independent Democrat	10	6	6	9	10	11
Independent	6	9	10	8	11	13
Independent Republican	7	8	7	6	9	11
Weak Republican	14	14	14	14	15	13
Strong Republican	14	15	16	11	10	10

	1976	1980	1984	1988	1992
Strong Democrat	15	18	17	18	18
Weak Democrat	25	23	20	18	18
Independent Democrat	12	11	11	12	14
Independent	15	13	11	11	12
Independent Republican	10	10	12	13	12
Weak Republican	14	14	15	14	14
Strong Republican	9	9	12	14	11

Table 10.1
Party identification in presidential election years, 1952–92.

Source: From Miller and Traugott, *American National Election Studies Data Source Book*. Copyright 1989 by the President and Fellows of Harvard College. Reprinted by permission of Harvard University Press. Figures for 1988 and 1992 from the U.S. Bureau of the Census, *Statistical Abstract of the United States 1994*.

18   Harold D. Clarke, Lawrence LeDuc, Jane Jenson, and Jon H. Pammett, *Absent Mandate: Interpreting Change in Canadian Elections* (Gage, 1991), 48.

to achieve their goals."[19] Presumably, this process undercuts the basis of stable party identification. One factor that has worked against stable party identification is the separation that has developed between the federal and provincial parties since the 1960s. Clarke and colleagues hypothesize that it is the length of the American ballot, on which voters must vote for a long series of offices and propositions at the same time, and the greater frequency of American elections, that have made party identification such a strong factor in American voting behavior.[20]

Party Identification

The concept of party identification was developed by researchers at the University of Michigan, who undertook the first in-depth studies of voting behavior in the 1950s. They discovered that most voters did not approach elections with an open mind but had a prior "psychological identification" with a political party that heavily influenced their view of politics and that was the central factor in explaining how they voted. As Table 10.1 indicates, in some voters party identification is strong, in others weaker. Some voters can only be said to lean toward a party; others, classed as independent, have no party identification.

The sources of party identification lie in the political events that create new alignments of the political parties. But party **realignments**, discussed below, have only occurred at intervals of about thirty years. Most people acquire their party identification through the processes of political socialization. As children become aware of the political world, they often pick up feelings and attitudes toward the parties from the family and other surroundings; thus, they enter the political world with a built-in identification with one of the parties. Such an identification is deep-seated and resistant to change.

Party Identification and Voting

Since party identification is not easily changed, it is an important long-term factor influencing how people vote. The stronger the party identification, the more likely it is that people will vote and that they will vote for the party with which they identify. In each election, however, there are also short-term factors specific to that election: namely, the candidates in that election, the issues that have come to the fore at that time, and the images of the parties at that time. An individual's actual voting decision

---

19   Clarke et al., *Absent Mandate*, 51.
20   Clarke et al., *Absent Mandate*, 47.

in each election thus involves an interaction between long-term factors (party identification) and short-term factors (candidates, issues, and party images).

The strength of the short-term factors varies considerably in different elections, as does the direction in which the short-term factors point. The long-term and short-term forces may reinforce each other. In fact, they have a strong tendency to do so, since voters view candidates and issues through the "filter" of their party identification. Thus, the committed party voter is likely to view a new candidate for her own party and her party's position on a new issue favorably—at least initially—because of her identification with the party.

It is also possible that the long-term and short-term forces will be in conflict. A voter may be attracted to the candidate of the other party or repelled by that of his own. Likewise, he may agree with the other party on an issue rather than with his own. In such situations his voting decision will be more difficult to make. A voter who feels cross-pressured may solve his problem by not voting. How a person votes is likely to depend on the relative strengths of his party identification and of the short-term forces.

It is important to emphasize that party identification is not determined by voting behavior. A voter who identifies with one party yet votes for the other party's candidate in a specific election is said to have "defected." Defection does not change party identification, and the voter is likely to return to voting in accordance with party identification in subsequent elections. However, repeated defections are likely to erode party identification.

The strength of the short-term forces in an election normally depends on how much information the voter has; in turn, this depends on the amount of publicity generated by the particular election. Typically, the level of information/publicity is highest for a presidential election and declines rapidly for elections to lower political offices. This means that the impact of short-term forces is potentially highest in a presidential election (or any other election that attracts a lot of publicity). It also means that in most elections, where the level of information/publicity is low, shortterm forces are weak and the long-term force of party identification is by far the biggest influence on the outcome.

The fact that most voters identify with a party and are predisposed to vote accordingly has a stabilizing effect on American politics. Most elections between the major parties are reasonably predictable, especially at the local level. The most difficult elections to predict are primary elections—that is, the elections parties hold to nominate their candidates. Since a primary election takes place within one party, party identification is not a factor in voting. This means that the only factors at work in a primary election are short-term ones: the candidates, and the issues specific to that election. The absence of the stabilizing effect of party identification makes voting behavior in primary elections highly volatile and difficult to predict. Voting on ballot propositions is usually volatile. Since candidates usually do not take sides on propositions, voters are deprived of the usual cues on how to vote and are highly dependent on advertising during the campaign.[21]

Canadian voting behavior is much more volatile than American because stable party identification plays a much smaller role. Two-thirds of the Canadian electorate are "flexible partisans [whose] party ties undergo substantial changes over relatively short periods of time."[22] Without the stabilizing factor of long-term party identification, most voters decide on the basis of the short-term factors—their attitudes toward the parties, the party leaders, and the local candidates, all of these specific to each election. As well, since the major Canadian parties do not present consistent choices to the voters, voting behavior is highly volatile from one election to the next. In such a context, the concept of realignment (a major explanatory factor for political change in the United States) has little relevance. Historically in Canada, regional realignment was an important factor in the transition between party systems;[23] but the low levels of party identification would seem to rule out realignment as a change mechanism in the future. In American terms, Canadian voting behavior is in a permanent state of **dealignment**.

Party Identification and Realignment

The concept of party identification helps us understand the process of political realignment (see Chapter 13). The distribution of party identification in the population created by a realignment underlies the majority/minority party pattern. The stability of party identification, once established, helps to explain why party systems have lasted up to thirty years.

Studies of the creation of the New Deal party system indicate that the main factor in the realignment was that a large portion of the urban working class (whose identification with the Republicans was weak) was strongly attracted to the policies and personality of Franklin Roosevelt. The critical election that created the realignment was that of 1936, in which the Republicans opposed the New Deal, while the Democrats defended it and promised further government programs.

Once a new alignment of parties has been established, elections tend to fall into one of two patterns: maintaining or deviating. An election in which the result corresponds to the underlying distribution of party identification in the electorate—that is, in which the short-term forces are either weak or cancel each other out and defections are low—is a *maintaining election*. An election in which the result is substantially different

---

21   David B. Magleby, "Direct Legislation in the American States," in David Butler and Austin Ranney, eds., *Referendums Around the World: The Growing Use of Direct Democracy* (Macmillan, 1994), 249.

22   Clarke et al., *Absent Mandate*, 47.

23   R.K. Carty, "Three Canadian Party Systems," in R.K. Carty, ed., *Canadian Political Party Systems: A Reader* (Broadview Press, 1992), 563–586.

from what would be expected from the underlying pattern of identification—that is, in which the short-term forces work strongly in favor of one party and defections are high—is a *deviating election*. The presidential victories of President Eisenhower in 1952 and 1956 and President Reagan in 1980 and 1984 are examples of deviating elections. In each case, the Republican won in spite of the continuing Democratic lead in party identification (see Table 10.1). Many Democrats defected temporarily to Eisenhower or Reagan but continued to vote Democratic at other levels.

An example of a deviating election won by the Democrats is President Johnson's colossal victory in 1964. In that election the short-term factors—the emotions generated by President Kennedy's assassination in 1963 and the unpopularity of the issues supported by the Republican candidate, Senator Barry Goldwater—heavily favored the majority Democrats, and Republican defections were high.

Party Identification and Dealignment

Surveys of party identification have been taken since 1952 (see Table 10.1). The figures indicate the long-term stability of party identification and the dominance of the Democratic Party through 1968. The figures from 1968 through 1992 show a clear trend toward partisan dealignment—that is, a general weakening of identification with either party: a decline in those identifying strongly with the parties (particularly the Democrats), an increase in those simply leaning toward both parties, and an increase in those without any party identification.

The overall trend since the 1960s toward partisan dealignment rather than realignment is most visible when we compare the strength of party identification in 1960 and 1992:

Identification	1960	1992
Strong party identifiers	36	29
Weak party identifiers	39	32
Independent party identifiers	13	26
Independent identifiers	10	12

Table 10.2
Summary of party identification, 1960 and 1992.

In spite of Republican dominance in presidential elections, it is clear that there has been no partisan realignment since 1968. The decline in Democratic identification in the 1980s did not lead to an increase in Republican identification. Rather, the increase was in those with very weak or no partisan identification, at the expense of the strong identifiers with both parties. Even in 1992 the Democrats still retained a significant advantage over the Republicans in the number of identifiers, though the combined independents were by then the largest single group.

Table 10.3		1960	1964	1968	1972	1976	1980	1984	1988	1992
Democratic percentage										
of party identification	Party ID	51	61	55	52	52	52	48	48	50
and the presidential	President	49	68	46	36	51	44	42	46	43
and congressional	Congress	56	65	52	56	57	55	55	53	54
two-party vote in										

presidential election Party identification is the sum of Strong Democrat, Weak Democrat, and Independent
years, 1960–92. Democrat.

Source: Adapted from Warren E. Miller and Santa A. Traugott, *American National Election Studies Source Book 1952–1986* (Harvard University Press, 1989). Reprinted by permission. Figures for 1988 and 1992 from *Congressional Quarterly, Weekly Reports*.

Dealignment—a decline in the strength of party identification—should increase the potential impact of short-term forces on voting behavior. Modern campaigning styles should have the same effect: television is used in political campaigns mainly to enhance the impact of short-term factors—the candidates and selected issues—at the expense of party loyalty.

However, the actual effect of the dealignment trend seems to have been less than would be expected from the theory. Gant and Luttbeg examined the rates of defection from party identification in presidential elections, and note that the independents who identify very weakly with a party nevertheless have been loyal to party candidates at about the same rate as strong identifiers.[24] There has been no trend to increasing defection from party identification; rather, the defection rate varies with the circumstances of each election, being higher when there is a third-party candidate—as in 1968, 1980, and 1992—or a candidate with a particularly strong personal appeal, such as Ronald Reagan.

One noticeable effect of the trend to partisan dealignment has been an increase in split-ticket voting.[25] Those who identify strongly with a party are likely to vote a "straight ticket"—that is, to vote for the party's candidates for all the offices on the ballot. As identification weakens and the impact of short-term factors increases, the potential grows for split-ticket voting—that is, voting for candidates of both parties for different offices on the ballot. Indeed, since the 1960s there has been a substantial increase in split-ticket voting across the country. For example, in 1988 there was a record number of districts in the House of Representatives (148 out of 435; or 34 percent) in which there was a majority for the presidential candidate of one party and a representative of the other party.[26]

---

24   Michael M. Gant and Norman R. Luttbeg, *American Electoral Behaviour: 1952-1988* (F.E. Peacock, 1991), 41.
25   Gant and Luttbeg, 37.
26   *Congressional Quarterly, Weekly Report*, July 8, 1989.

It is also possible to explain the divided party system since 1968 in terms of party identification. The greatest Republican successes since that year have been in the presidential elections, where information/publicity and the use of television are highest and the potential impact of short-term forces on party identification is greatest. The Republicans have also had some success in Senate and gubernatorial elections, which are statewide elections that nowadays are also high-publicity, television-intensive elections. In local elections, including elections to the House of Representatives and the state legislatures, the level of information and publicity is usually much lower and there is much less use of television in campaigning. It is at these local levels that the continued underlying dominance of the Democratic Party has been expressed in voting behavior. The Republicans did extraordinarily well in the 1994 elections for the House of Representatives and for the state legislatures generally, but it is not clear yet whether these victories indicated a more permanent shift in voters' loyalties or a fluctuation influenced mainly by circumstances.

The trend toward partisan dealignment since 1968 helps explain how the two parties can dominate different levels of politics and how the Republican Party—the minority party in terms of party identification—can win more easily at the national level than at the local level. It is important to note here that dealignment does not explain why the Republicans have been so successful in presidential elections. The explanation for this since 1968 lies in how the two parties have handled the issues and chosen their candidates. As Gant and Luttweg point out, the relatively weak state of party identification certainly means that neither party can win the presidency by relying on party loyalty alone.[27]

Group Voting Behavior

In the United States group membership has always been an important influence on party identification and voting behavior. Voters have responded to parties, candidates, and issues not simply as individuals but as individuals whose place in American society is defined by the groups to which they belong. Robert Kelley and others have traced the patterns of attachment of different religious and ethnic groups to the political parties throughout the nineteenth century.[28] Analyses of voting patterns in that period bear out that different groups were disproportionately attached to one party or the other.

The significance of group membership was well understood by the party organizations, which made sure they appealed to as many different groups as possible. It was standard practice, especially in the pluralistic cities, for each party to nominate a

---

27   Gant and Luttbeg, 74.
28   Robert Kelley, *The Cultural Patterns in American Politics: The First Century* (Knopf, 1979).

"balanced ticket" composed of candidates for the different offices drawn from all the groups whose support it needed.

Every voter belongs to groups defined by different characteristics. Of these, race or ethnicity, religion, social class, and region have been the most important in shaping political attitudes. For many of these groups, patterns of close interaction through residence, education, and social relations have persisted over many generations. Many groups have also experienced varying degrees of discrimination in their attempts to move up in American society. Thus, it is not surprising that various groups have formed distinct attitudes toward politics and transmitted those attitudes to others over a long time.

Whether membership in a particular group influences a person's voting behavior depends on three things: the relative importance of that group membership to the individual voter; the salience of issues affecting that group in the election; and whether the voter perceives any difference between the parties on the issues salient to the group.

There have been many examples of solid group loyalty to one party. The most obvious example of regional loyalty was the almost unanimous support of white southerners for the Democratic Party for a century after the Civil War—a solidarity that arose out of the experience of defeat and occupation at the hands of the Republicans. This party loyalty was passed on to succeeding generations through political socialization until the 1960s, when the national Democratic Party shifted its civil rights policy. Even after the reasons for this party solidarity no longer held, strong elements of the old pattern persisted. Until the early 1990s, Democrats still held a majority of southern congressional seats and continued to dominate all the state legislatures in the South. It was not until 1994 that the Republicans, as part of their national sweep, won a majority of congressional seats in the South.

Another example of a group that often closely identified with one party is Catholic voters. Here, religion and ethnicity were both factors. The number of Catholics in the United States was originally very small. The Catholic population increased with the influx of Irish immigrants in the mid-nineteenth century, who were followed by immigrants from southern and eastern Europe at the beginning of the twentieth century. The Democratic Party was traditionally more pluralistic and open to new immigrants, and the Irish in particular were strongly Democratic. This loyalty to the Democrats was reinforced by periodic outbreaks of anti-Catholicism among Protestant groups associated with the Republican Party. By the early twentieth century, however, the attractiveness of the Democratic Party to urban Catholic voters was diminished by the increased rural and southern influences in the party.

Catholic support for the Democratic Party rose in 1928, when the Democrats nominated the first Catholic candidate for President—Al Smith, governor of New York. But it was during the New Deal that the strongest Catholic loyalty to the Democrats developed. The basis of this new loyalty was class: most Catholics at that time were the working-class children of recent immigrants and strongly attracted to the New Deal programs. However, religion was also important, since integration into the new majority Democratic Party coalition provided opportunities for many Catholic politicians.

Over time this strong identification with the Democratic Party eroded as later generations of Catholics became increasingly prosperous and integrated into the general population. Many Catholics defected to vote for Eisenhower, but Catholic support for the Democrats took a massive jump in 1960 (see Table 10.4). In that election not only did the Democrats nominate a Catholic for president again, but John Kennedy's religion was made an issue by some Protestant leaders. In that situation, the political saliency of their religion rose sharply and Catholics voted overwhelmingly for Kennedy. In the 1970s the erosion of Democratic support among Catholics resumed; by the 1980s Catholic voters had become almost indistinguishable from the population as a whole in their voting behavior, though they remained more Democratic than white Protestants.[29]

	1952	1956	1960	1964	1968	1972	1976	1980	1984	1988	1992
Catholic	52	46	83	79	60	40	58	46	46	53	50
Total population	42	40	49	68	46	36	51	44	42	47	47
% above national average	+10	+6	+34	+11	+14	+4	+7	+2	+4	+6	+3

Table 10.4
The percentage of Catholic voters who voted for Democratic presidential candidates, 1952–92.

Source: American National Election Studies, 1948–1992 Cumulative File (CD-ROM) (Center for Political Studies/Institute for Social Research, University of Michigan, 1995).

The impact of Catholicism on political behavior has declined, but another form of religious identification—namely, white evangelical Protestantism—has become significant, as Table 10.5 indicates.

This rise in white evangelical support for the Republican Party can be explained by the ending of the traditional Democratic allegiance of white southerners—a high proportion of whom can be classed as evangelicals—and also by the very deliberate attempts by the Republicans since the late 1970s to appeal to and mobilize evangelicals around moral issues such as abortion and prayer in the public schools.

---

29   Lyman A. Kellstedt and Mark A. Noll, "Religion, Voting for President, and Party Identification, 1948–1984," in Mark A. Noll, ed., *Religion and American Politics* (Oxford University Press, 1990), 360–364.

Table 10.5		1960	1964	1968	1972	1976	1980	1984	1988	1992
The percentage of white evangelical voters who voted for Republican presidential candidates, 1960–96.	White evangelical	62	37	51	82	54	63	73	69	51
	Total population	50	33	45	64	49	56	58	53	34
	% above national average		+12	+4	+6	+18	+5	+7	+15	+16	+17

Source: American National Election Studies, 1948–92 Cumulative File (CD-ROM) (Center for Political Studies/Institute for Social Research, University of Michigan, 1995).

It is important to note that black evangelicals have not joined the white evangelical move toward Republican politics. At present, African Americans are the group with the most distinctive voting behavior. For the last twenty years, black voters have consistently supported Democratic candidates for office to an overwhelming degree. The reasons for this high group consciousness among black people are obvious: black people have always been treated as a separate group by the white majority and have always been oppressed in all areas of life. Policies affecting black people therefore have always had a very high saliency for them as a group.

For seventy years after the Civil War, the relatively small number of black voters in the North were strongly supportive of the Republican Party, which had freed them from slavery. This pattern shifted in two distinct stages during the New Deal party system.

First, black voters, along with other poor and working-class voters, were attracted by New Deal policies. This attraction was reinforced by the fact that by the 1920s the Republican Party had ceased to have a distinctive policy on civil rights, while for the first time a few prominent Democrats, led by Eleanor Roosevelt, the president's wife, were making sympathetic overtures to black people.[30]

The Democratic Party first committed itself to supporting black civil rights in 1948, but it was not until President Kennedy and the Democratic Party demonstrated their full commitment to civil rights by their actions in the 1960s that black voters moved overwhelmingly into the Democratic column (see Table 10.6). As a result of the Voting Rights Act of 1965, the number of black voters, particularly in the South, expanded considerably; and by the 1980s the participation rate of blacks was close to that of whites.

Since the 1960s the African-American community has remained overwhelmingly loyal to the Democrats, not simply out of gratitude but because the Democrats—as

---

30   See Nancy J. Weiss, *Farewell to the Party of Lincoln: Black Politics in the Age of FDR* (Princeton University Press, 1983).

	1952	1956	1960	1964	1968	1972	1976	1980	1984	1988	1992
White	40	39	48	65	41	30	47	37	37	40	39
Black	80	64	71	100	97	87	95	93	91	86	82

Table 10.6

Percentage of white and black voters who voted for Democratic presidential candidates, 1952–92.

Source: Miller and Traugott, *American National Election Studies Data Source Book 1952-1986* (Harvard University Press, 1989). Reprinted by permission. Figures for 1988 and 1992 from the New York Times/CBS exit poll.

the party committed to using the federal government to tackle social and economic problems—have remained much closer to the black outlook. It took action by the federal government and federal legislation to bring segregation in the states to an end and to create programs helpful to many blacks. Since 1964, when Senator Goldwater voted against the Civil Rights Act, the Republican Party has consistently refused to identify itself with black interests.

African-American loyalty to the Democratic Party since the 1960s presents an example of how one group loyalty can overwhelm the potential impact of another group identification. As Kellstedt and Noll point out, a larger proportion of blacks than whites identify themselves as evangelical Christians and have similarly conservative views on social questions. Yet black evangelicals have entirely resisted the movement that white evangelicals have made toward the Republican Party since 1980. It is clearly race, not religion, that presently determines the black community's political behavior.[31]

The fundamental basis of partisan choice in the electorate remains the class division of the New Deal. Generally, poorer and less well-educated voters are likely to be Democrats, while the upper ends of the income and education scales produce mainly Republicans. However, there are some group loyalties that cut across the class division. As noted, black voters are strongly Democratic regardless of income and education, while white evangelicals have become increasingly Republican over the past twenty years. These overwhelming group loyalties are likely to persist so long as one party is sympathetic and the other unsympathetic to the group's main concerns.

A small number of Republicans, such as former congressman Jack Kemp, have argued for years that the party should make a greater effort to appeal to black voters. The potential Republican candidacy of Colin Powell in 1996 offered one way to split the black Democratic vote, since it seems certain that as candidate for president or even vice president, Powell would have attracted a large black vote for reasons of racial pride and group solidarity. The prospect of Democrats appealing to white evangelicals

---

31 Kellstedt and Noll, 365–366.

seems very limited in the short run, though that group is much less monolithic than are black voters.

The main "swing" voters in the past twenty years have been socially conservative working-class voters, often called "Reagan Democrats." Many of these voters still lean toward the Democrats on issues of economic security but are drawn to the Republicans on social and foreign-policy issues. They have left behind their former New Deal Democratic loyalties, but they have not been permanently captured by the Republicans. This is the group that provides the votes by which most presidential elections are now decided.

CHAPTER 11

ELECTING THE PRESIDENT

The presidency has always been the focal point of American politics, the summit of every politician's ambition. The national political parties have always organized themselves around the goal of electing a president. The four-year term of the president thus sets up a four-year cycle in national politics.

Since the members of the House of Representatives and one-third of the Senate are elected every two years, the four-year cycle is split in two by the **off-year elections**. Since the presidential election so dominates politics in the fourth year of the cycle, a majority of states choose to elect their governors in the off-year in order to insulate state elections from national politics. Five states go even further and elect their governors and state legislatures in odd-numbered years, which is also when most municipal elections are held.

In the second half of the cycle, the next presidential election increasingly dominates politics in Washington. In the fourth year, politics across the country is dominated by the nomination of the presidential candidates and then by the election itself.

There are two separate processes involved in electing the president: the nomination process *within* each party to select the presidential candidates; and the election campaign *between* the candidates of the two major parties.

The nomination process. For the Democratic and Republican parties, this process culminates in a national convention in July or August of the presidential election year. To win the nomination, a candidate must acquire the most convention delegates from the

Table 11.1 *The four-year election* *cycle*	**Year I**	**1997**	
		Early January	Start of 105th Congress
		Mid-January	Inauguration of the president
		November	Odd-year elections in two states
		December	End of first session of 105th Congress
	Year II	**1998**	
		January	Start of second session of 105th Congress. Through the year, politics is increasingly dominated by the approaching off-year elections.
		October	Adjournment of 105th Congress.

		November	Off-year elections:
			    All of the House of Representatives
			    One-third of the Senate
			    36 governors
			    Most state legislatures

	Year III	**1999**	
		January	Start of 106th Congress. Through the year speculation increases about possible presidential candidates; activity increases among those considering running for president.
		Summer/Fall	Announcements of candidacy or noncandidacy.
		November	Odd-year elections in three states.
		December	End of first session of 106th Congress.
	Year IV	**2000**	
		January	Start of second session of 106th Congress.
		February-June	Selection of delegates in all states for both parties' national nominating conventions.
		Mid-July	National convention of the out-party; formal nomination of presidential candidate.
		Mid-August	National convention of the incumbent party; formal nomination of presidential candidate.
		October	Adjournment of 106th Congress.

		November	Elections:
			    President
			    All of the House of Representatives
			    One-third of the Senate
			    12 governors
			    Most state legislatures

different states. This competition runs from February through early June. Before the first state party begins to select its convention delegates there is usually a period of overt competition between the declared candidates for the nomination, usually from October or November of the previous year until February. Before the start of overt competition, most candidates will have engaged in months—even years—of planning and fund raising.

Summer/Fall of previous year:	Declarations of candidacy for the presidential nomination. Early competition between the candidates for each party's nomination.	**Table 11.2** *Timetable of the nomination process.*
February to early June:	Selection of delegates to the national conventions of both parties. Campaigning by candidates in each party for delegates who will pledge to vote for them at the convention.	
Mid-July:	National convention of the out-party.	
Mid-August:	National convention of the party holding the presidency.	

The election campaign. The race between the nominees of the two major parties is shorter than the nomination process. Traditionally, the campaign started after both conventions had been held, running from Labor Day until election day in early November. In recent years, however, the party nominee often has the nomination wrapped up long before the national convention, sometimes as early as March. So there is pressure to start the campaign against the other party as early as possible.

But until the national convention, the focus of the prospective nominee is still on his own party. He must unite the party behind him; heal rifts with defeated opponents and their supporters; negotiate positions on disputed issues for the party's election platform; and select a running mate. After this starts the most intense part of the election campaign: the two months before election day in early November.

The president is elected on the first Tuesday after the first Monday in November. For both major-party candidates, election day is the culmination of the long nomination and election processes. Late on election night the loser gives a concession speech before his downcast staff and supporters; soon after, the winner appears before a rapturous crowd. According to the Constitution, however, the president is not elected until the presidential electors meet in December, and the result is not official until the electoral votes are counted in the newly elected Congress early the following January.

The president is not elected by direct popular vote but must receive a majority of votes in the Electoral College. Because the result in the Electoral College has been the

Table 11.3	March/June to the national convention in July or August:	Consolidation of party support behind the nominee. Some early campaigning against the other party.
Timetable of the presidential election campaign.	Late August to election day in early November:	National campaign against the candidate of the other party.

same as the popular vote at every election in the twentieth century, the Electoral College machinery usually seems little more than a historical curiosity. In certain circumstances, however, the Electoral College could cause major complications in the presidential elections.

THE ELECTORAL COLLEGE

The framers of the Constitution spent a great deal of time debating how the chief executive should be chosen. They understood that the method of election would be an important influence on what kind of person was chosen and how he would behave in office. After rejecting direct popular election on the one hand and election by Congress on the other, the framers arrived at what seemed like a brilliant compromise: indirect election, through what was later called the Electoral College.[1]

The original version of the Electoral College in Article II, Section 1, of the Constitution can be summarized as follows: Each state appointed a number of electors, the number matching the number of the state's representatives in Congress (House plus Senate). The electors, who were not to include any members of Congress, met on the same day in each of the state capitals and voted for two persons, one of whom had to be from another state. The votes were tallied in Congress, and the person having a majority of the electoral votes became the next president and the runner-up became vice president. If no one had a majority of the votes, the House of Representatives chose among the top five candidates, but with each state delegation casting only one vote.

Several things should be noted about this carefully devised scheme: the distribution of electoral votes between the states reflected the compromise reached earlier at the convention over the distribution of representation in the Congress; members of Congress were forbidden to be electors; and all the electors never met in one place in order to to minimize the opportunities for politicking over the presidential election.

It seems that the framers hoped that their very indirect method of election would produce a widely respected elder statesman who was above party, like General George

---

1   Shlomo Slonim, "Designing the Electoral College," in Thomas Cronin, ed., *Inventing the American Presidency* (University Press of Kansas, 1989).

Washington, whom everyone recognized was going to be the first president. Some scholars argue to the contrary: that the framers must have expected it would be difficult for anyone to get a majority of the electoral votes and that therefore the election would often be decided by the House of Representatives.

Once party politics began to intrude, the character of the Electoral College changed quickly. President Washington's administration was increasingly split over policy, and when he declined to accept a third term, the battle for the presidency was on between the leaders of the two factions: **Federalist** John Adams and Republican Thomas Jefferson. The two parties scrambled to line up electors behind their candidates. Adams won, and Jefferson, as the runner-up, became vice president—an awkward situation for both men.

In the rematch election of 1800 the result was awkward in a different way. Party discipline was so tight this time that the two members of the winning Republican ticket, Jefferson and Aaron Burr, received the same number of electoral votes. This meant that the out-going House of Representatives, controlled by the Federalists, had to choose between them. Since Burr was even more objectionable to the Federalists than Jefferson, the latter was eventually chosen. The complications caused by the injection of party politics into the process led to the 12th Amendment to the Constitution, ratified in 1803, which separated the election of the president and vice president.

In the revised Electoral College, which has never been altered since, the vice president is elected separately instead of being the runner-up for the presidency. Electors cast one vote for president and one for vice president. If there is no majority of electoral votes for president, the House, voting by state delegation, chooses between the top three candidates. If there is no majority for vice president, the Senate chooses between the top two candidates. The parties, of course, pick nominees for both president and vice president and run them as one ticket.

The injection of party competition into the Electoral College forced party leaders to pay attention to two aspects of the process for electing the president: the method for choosing the electors in each state, and the method for nominating the party's presidential candidate.

Choosing the Presidential Electors

The Constitution allows the state legislatures to decide how to choose the electors, and at first the legislatures did the selecting themselves. With the introduction of party competition, however, alternative methods began to be used in the states as the parties looked for ways to increase their chances of winning. Some states changed their methods frequently as the parties struggled for advantage. There was also increasing pressure for popular election of the electors. At first, two different methods of popular election were used:

- The district method, whereby the state was divided into electoral districts and each elector was separately elected.

- The general ticket method, whereby a statewide election was held between two party lists of electors. The winning list became the state's electors, who cast all of the state's electoral votes for their party's candidate.

Of these, the district method was agreed to be the more democratic, since it reflected the preferences of the voters most closely; but it had the disadvantage of splitting each state's electoral votes in most instances and thus diluting the state's impact on the outcome of the election. Some democrats wanted a constitutional amendment to require the use of the district method by all states, but that did not transpire, and by 1832 the general ticket method, which maximized each state's impact on the result, had become almost universal.[2]

The shift to popular election of the electors transformed the presidential electorate: instead of being composed of small groups of political insiders, it was now a national constituency. However, the use of the general ticket method by the states preserved the structure of the Electoral College, in that the objective was not to win the most votes nationwide but rather to win states. The continued existence of the Electoral College is thus not merely of historical interest: it continues to affect the outcome in presidential elections.

The Effect of the Electoral College on Presidential Elections

The size of the Electoral College is currently determined as follows:

Number of members of the House	435
Number of members of the Senate	100
Electoral votes given the federal district (Washington, D.C.) by the 23rd Amendment	3
Total	538
Required majority	270

Each state has the same number of electoral votes as it does members of the House and Senate. When the 435 seats in the House of Representatives are redistributed

---

2   For the operation of the Electoral College in the early years, see M.J. Heale, *The Presidential Quest: Candidates and Images in American Political Culture, 1787–1852* (Longman, 1982).

between the states after each census, the votes in the Electoral College are also redistributed. A national census has been held every ten years since 1790. The composition of the House (and thus the Electoral College) was adjusted for the 1992 congressional and presidential elections as a result of the census of 1990.

Currently, California (54), New York (33), Texas (32), and Pennsylvania (23) hold the most electoral votes. At the other end of the scale, Alaska, Delaware, North Dakota, South Dakota, Montana, Vermont, and the District of Columbia all have the minimum number—three votes (equal to one House seat and two Senate seats).

The continuing use of the Electoral College can complicate presidential elections in two types of situations: when the candidate with the most popular votes does not win, and when no candidate gets a majority in the Electoral College.

Regarding the first situation: Since winning the presidency depends on winning states, it is possible for a candidate with more popular votes across the country to end up with fewer electoral votes. This can happen in a close election when one candidate wins several big states narrowly, while the other piles up votes in most of the other states. This has happened only twice, in 1876 and 1888.

The situation in 1876 was obscured by disputed results in Florida and Louisiana, both of which were still partially controlled by federal troops in the aftermath of the Civil War. The Republican-controlled House awarded both states to the Republican candidate, Rutherford Hayes, which gave him a one-vote margin in the Electoral College. Yet both parties agreed that nationwide, the Democrat, Samuel Tilden, had garnered around 250,000 more votes than Hayes.

In 1888 the situation was more clear cut.

1888	Popular Vote	Electoral Vote
Grover Cleveland, Democrat	5,540,329	168
Benjamin Harrison, Republican	5,439,853	233

President Cleveland did not win his votes in the right places: 13,000 more votes in his home state of New York, with its thirty-six electoral votes, would have secured his re-election.

The closest election in modern times was the election of 1960. In that year the Electoral College magnified John F. Kennedy's very narrow margin in popular votes:

1960	Popular Vote	Electoral Vote
John F. Kennedy, Democrat	34,227,096	303
Richard M. Nixon, Republican	34,107,646	219

It is not clear how worried Americans would be nowadays if the Electoral College winner came second in the popular vote. This situation arises from time to time in parliamentary systems when the party winning the most votes does not win the most seats, but this has not undermined public confidence in the electoral system.

Regarding the second situation: This is the scenario that most observers dread. Only once has the presidential election had to be decided in the House of Representatives: in 1824, when the House chose John Quincy Adams over the front-running Andrew Jackson amid great controversy. In most presidential elections there are the two major-party candidates and the usual host of fringe-party candidates, and this situation cannot arise. It is a different matter when there is a third-party or independent candidate with broader support.

The last time there was serious concern that no candidate would get a majority in the Electoral College was in 1968, when George Wallace ran as the American Independent candidate.

1968	Popular Vote	Electoral Vote
Hubert Humphrey, Democrat	31,274,503	191
Richard Nixon, Republican	31,785,148	302
George Wallace, American Independent	9,901,151	45

There was considerable apprehension in the run-up to the 1968 election that in a close contest between the main candidates (which was likely), Wallace might win enough southern states to deprive either of a majority of electoral votes. There were then two possibilities: the president might have to be elected by the House of Representatives; or before the electors met in December Wallace might try to bargain with the other candidates, possibly offering his electoral votes in exchange for promises on policy or appointments.

As can be seen above, these fears were not realized. Wallace took 13.5 percent of the total vote and won five southern states. The race between the principal candidates was indeed very close in votes, but Nixon won so many states (thirty-two to Humphrey's thirteen), including several large states, that he won a comfortable victory in the Electoral College.

Wallace's candidacy was a threat because his vote was geographically concentrated in the Deep South, which meant he could win states and get on the Electoral College scoreboard. The only other example of that in this century involved another dissident southern Democrat protesting his party's support for civil rights: Governor Strom Thurmond, running as the States' Rights ("Dixiecrat") candidate in 1948, got only 2.4 percent of the vote nationally but won four southern states with thirty-nine electoral votes—not enough, however, to interfere with President Truman's victory.

Support for most third-party candidates is more evenly spread, which makes it more difficult for them to win electoral votes. Thus, while Ross Perot won an impressive 19 percent of the popular vote in 1992—the highest share for a third-party candidate since former President Theodore Roosevelt in 1912—because his vote was fairly evenly spread across the country he did not win any electoral votes. A third-party candidate with evenly spread support would need to win closer to 30 percent of the popular vote to have a chance of winning many states. Third-party candidates may, however, affect the result indirectly by taking more votes from one major-party candidate than the other.

The most famous three-way race in American history was in 1912, when the dominant Republican Party was badly split between the incumbent president, William Howard Taft, and the former president, Teddy Roosevelt, who had decided he wanted to be president again. When Taft won the party nomination, Roosevelt ran as a Progressive. The charismatic Roosevelt outpolled Taft and won six states to Taft's two, but the main effect of the Republican split was to allow the Democratic candidate, Woodrow Wilson, to win easily in the Electoral College with 42 percent of the vote.

The 1968 election and the speculation that Wallace might try to use his electors to bargain with the other candidates raised the question of the role of the electors. While the founders clearly intended for the electors to exercise their independent judgment, the realities of party politics have meant that the electors are bound by party loyalty to vote for their party's candidate. Once chosen, however, the electors are not legally bound to obey party dictates. At times a few electors have not voted as expected. In 1960, fifteen Democrats from three southern states cast their electoral votes for Senator Harry Byrd of Virginia rather than John F. Kennedy, who had won their states. The only time defections from party loyalty affected a result was in 1836, when the Virginia electors refused to vote for the Democratic vice presidential candidate; this resulted in a tie for the vice presidency that had to be broken by the Senate.

Why Not Abolish the Electoral College?

The most serious effort in recent years to change the method of electing the president was made after the 1968 election. One proposal was to abolish the fall-back arrangement whereby the House of Representatives would elect the president. Instead, it was suggested, there should be a run-off election between the top two candidates if no one had a majority in the Electoral College. The most common proposal, however, was simply to abolish the Electoral College and elect the president by a straight popular vote. There has been no movement on either proposal.

Changing the way the president is elected requires a constitutional amendment; this in turn requires a broad consensus for change, both in Congress and across the country. No such consensus has developed. The smaller states tend to oppose any change, since the Electoral College formula (House seats plus two) gives them slight-ly more weight in the process than a straight popular vote would. At the same time, there is no group that sees a strong interest in changing the process.

Since in every election but two the electoral vote winner has also won the popular vote, and since no election has been determined in the House of Representatives since 1824, few people see the Electoral College as a threat to democracy. Even so, the elec-tions of 1968 and 1992 demonstrated its potential to complicate the election process. It will probably take another scare like that of 1968 before changes to the method of electing the president are considered seriously again.[3]

THE NOMINATION PROCESS FOR PRESIDENTIAL CANDIDATES

The introduction of party politics into the framers' carefully constructed scheme made it essential for each party to agree on a single candidate who would maximize its support across the states. The first partisan candidates, in 1796 and 1800, were obvious choices: George Washington's vice president, John Adams, for the Federalists and Thomas Jefferson for the Republicans. After that, the choices were not so obvi-ous and some form of consultation within each party became necessary.

The first nominating forum used was the party caucus in Congress; that is, all the House and Senate members who supported the party met to reach agreement on the nominee for president. Since members of Congress usually had good connections with their home state legislatures, this method worked well for the Republicans, who used it to nominate James Madison in 1808 and 1812 and James Monroe in 1816 and 1820. The Federalist Party began to fade after its defeat in 1800, and it had much more difficulty agreeing on its presidential candidates. Its congressional caucus was smaller and less widely representative. Federalist candidates were nominated by their home state legislatures, but this method did not help to build nationwide support for them.

This method of nomination by the congressional caucus finally broke down for the Republicans in 1824 over the question of who should succeed President Monroe. By this time the Federalist Party had disappeared. The Republican caucus was unable to choose between three leading contenders. In addition, there was for the first time a popular challenger from outside the Washington establishment: General Andrew Jackson of Tennessee.

Jackson had become a national hero for his exploits during the War of 1812 and in driving the Spanish out of Florida. He was a political outsider in several respects: he

---

3   The most recent discussion of the Electoral College is Michael J. Glennon, *When No Majority Rules: The Electoral College and Presidential Succession* (*Congressional Quarterly*, 1992).

had served in Congress only briefly; he was a "westerner" from the frontier state of Tennessee; he was of Scotch-Irish background (historian Robert Kelley calls him the first ethnic president); and he did not have the polished manners of the Virginia or Massachusetts gentry, who had provided all the presidents to that point.

In the election of 1824 Jackson ran first but did not get a majority of the electoral votes, which were split between four candidates. Rather than Jackson, the House of Representatives elected the runner-up, John Quincy Adams (the son of former President Adams). When Henry Clay, who had run fourth, was appointed secretary of state by Adams, the Jacksonians charged that there had been a corrupt deal for Clay's support. Angered that he had been robbed of victory by the political establishment, Jackson and his followers set out to organize for victory the next time.

Jackson thus began a process that eventually polarized the old Republican Party into two groups: Jackson's Democratic Republicans, later called the Democrats; and the National Republicans, later called the Whigs, whose leading figure was Henry Clay. Jackson's political crusade for the presidency helped democratize American politics by expanding the electorate. Since the number of voters was increasing, new political techniques had to be developed, so it was during this time that the characteristic American forms of political organization, such as the urban political machine and the national nominating convention, were invented.

The National Party Convention

In 1828, Jackson and President John Q. Adams were the obvious candidates for president. Jackson was elected on his second attempt. By 1832, however, the parties were again faced with the problem of how to nominate a candidate who would be supported by all the state parties and have a wide appeal to the voters.

The first national nominating convention was actually held by a short-lived third party, the Anti-Masonic Party, in 1831. Later that year Jackson's opponents held a convention to nominate Henry Clay. In 1832 the Jacksonians also held a national convention to rally behind Jackson's choice for vice president, Martin Van Buren. The Democrats were the only party to hold a convention in 1836, to nominate Van Buren for president. Since 1840, both major parties have held national conventions every four years to nominate candidates for president and vice president.

In the earliest conventions the nominee had already been designated by the party leaders, and the convention was called mainly to rally the delegates from the different states behind him prior to the election. The Whig convention of 1840 was the first one to actually decide on a nominee; the Democrats followed suit at their convention of 1844. For roughly the next hundred years the national party conventions, held in the summer of each election year, were the battlegrounds on which the state party leaders fought and bargained among themselves to choose a candidate with the potential to unite the party and win the presidency. Nowadays, nominations are again decided before the convention opens; conventions are once again mainly party rallies, as they were when first invented.

National Party Conventions: Format and Functions

At a national convention, delegates from every state and the various U.S. territories gather in one of the larger American cities for a week in the summer of the presidential election year. The number of delegates has tended to swell, with the Democrats traditionally favoring larger conventions than the Republicans. Thus, in 1996 there were 4,295 delegates at the Democratic Convention compared to 1,984 for the Republicans. The delegates are apportioned among the states and territories, mainly according to population, but with additional delegates awarded to those states where the party has done well in recent presidential and state elections.

The two party conventions are held a few weeks apart in July or August. Traditionally, the party that does not hold the White House goes first. Both parties run their conventions in very similar ways. In recent years the organization of the conventions has been largely dictated by the needs of the television networks for lively prime-time coverage and by the desire of the parties to present a positive image to the television audience. The first convention to be televised was the Republican convention of 1940, and every convention since 1952 has been televised. From the 1950s through the 1970s the major networks covered most of the convention proceedings live. Such blanket coverage proved to be a mixed blessing for the parties when they had divisive conventions, as the Republicans did in 1964 and 1976 and the Democrats in 1968 and 1972. Since 1980 the networks have cut back their coverage, and the parties have attempted to "package" the conventions for television to present the desired image of unity to the voters.

The conventions of both parties follow the same general course. On the first day the credentials of the delegates are accepted and the rules of the convention are adopted. The rules for delegate selection have become much more standardized since the 1970s, so disputes over delegate credentials, which used to be common, are now rare. Similarly, the last major fight over the convention rules was at the Democratic convention in 1980. The supporters of Senator Edward Kennedy, who were in a minority, tried to change the rule requiring delegates to vote for the presidential candidate to whom they had pledged support during the selection process. The Kennedy supporters hoped that once freed of that obligation, some Carter delegates might change allegiance. The Carter delegates voted down the rule change and went on to renominate the sitting president.

The business of the second day is to adopt the party platform for the election. The platform is a fairly comprehensive statement of the party's position on the major issues of the day. A Platform Committee holds hearings for weeks before the convention and prepares a draft to present to the convention. The prospective nominee usually tries to control the platform-writing process, but cannot always do so without a fight. Factions within the party press the Platform Committee on particular issues and threaten to appeal to the convention if they do not get their way. In order to present the image of a unified party to the press and the public, the party managers go to great lengths to avoid divisive floor votes at the convention.

The most famous floor fight over a party platform in modern times was in 1968, at the raucous and bitterly divided Democratic convention in Chicago. The convention was controlled by supporters of the nominee, Vice President Humphrey, and by President Johnson, but protesters against the Vietnam War were out in force both in the convention hall and on the streets of Chicago. All efforts to have the platform condemn the war were voted down amid the wildest scenes at a convention in anyone's memory. The fact that all of this chaos was being televised nationally clearly did nothing to help Humphrey's election prospects. In the run-up to their convention in 1996, Republican leaders spent a great deal of time negotiating the platform's statement on abortion, trying to broaden the party's appeal to pro-choice women without provoking a convention floor fight from the strongly entrenched pro-life forces within the party.

The third day is given over to the central purpose of the convention, which is to nominate the presidential candidate. During the roll call, the state leaders announce for whom their delegation's votes are being cast. In the days when multiple ballots were necessary before one candidate received the required majority of delegate votes, this procedure was full of suspense. In recent years the process has been a complete anticlimax because the nominee has been known for months, since quite early in the delegate selection process. The last convention to require more than one ballot to nominate the candidate was the Democratic convention of 1952.

The vice presidential candidate is nominated on the last day of the convention. Here again, there is no longer any suspense. The presidential candidate used to select his running mate only in the twenty-four hours after his own nomination amid wild speculation and lobbying. This practice changed in 1972, after the hurriedly chosen Democratic vice presidential candidate had to withdraw and be replaced after the convention. Jimmy Carter in 1976 was the first nominee to announce his running mate before the convention, and this is now standard practice in both parties. The only suspense relates to the slight possibility that the vice presidential choice might be challenged on the floor by a disgruntled faction of the party. The climax of the convention is the acceptance speeches. The vice presidential nominee goes first; the candidate for president follows.

The national conventions have traditionally performed several functions for the parties. For most of American history each party actually chose its nominee for president at its convention. Since the 1950s, however, the delegate selection process has settled the nomination in advance of the convention and the second function of the convention—that of rallying the party behind the nominee—has become the most important one.

The convention is the only large national gathering of the party, and with the presidential election in the immediate offing, there is great incentive for party unity. Badly divided conventions, like the Democratic conventions of 1980 and especially 1968, hurt the nominee's electoral prospects. So do conventions that send out too extreme a message, as did the Democratic convention of 1972 and the Republican convention of 1992. At the convention the party displays itself to the voters, and much effort goes into managing the convention so as to present the party as united and with its most appealing face.

Party Conventions in Canada

The Americans invented the national party convention. Canadian parties later picked up the concept and adapted it to a different system of government. The first national party convention in Canada was called by the opposition Liberal Party in 1893 to rally its members behind a series of policy resolutions and was directly inspired by the Democratic Party convention of 1892. In 1919 the Liberals were the first federal party to use a national convention to choose the party leader. This was a break with the British parliamentary tradition, in which the party leader was chosen by the parliamentary caucus or after consultation among party notables. After 1919, leadership conventions gradually became standard practice for all parties in Canada, both federal and provincial.

Canadian leadership conventions are held only when a party needs to select a new leader. Usually leadership candidates have only a few months before the convention to travel the country seeking support from the local constituency party members, who elect the convention delegates. The competition to line up delegates has been growing increasingly sophisticated, and the amount that must be spent for this purpose has been rising. Since a candidate is almost never able to lock up the nomination in advance, the leader is still chosen at the convention itself. The uncertainty is increased by the use of secret ballots at the convention (as opposed to public roll-call votes, which is what the Americans use). Typically, suspense builds over several ballots as the candidates garnering the fewest votes are eliminated, until one candidate wins by receiving an absolute majority of delegate votes. Canadian leadership conventions have retained much of the suspense and drama that American conventions have lost in recent years.

The drama of Canadian leadership conventions, while exciting for TV viewers and journalists, is often divisive for the party. Like the Americans, Canadian party strategists have become increasingly concerned about presenting a unified and moderate face to the TV cameras. Another factor is also leading to major changes in the leadership convention, increasing pressure in the 1990s for more active partticipation by the party membership in selecting the leader. Several provincial parties have moved to some form of one-person, one-vote system whereby all party members have the right to vote, by mail or telephone, for the leader. Others have attempted to combine a direct membership vote with a convention, in order not to lose the publicity and excitement a convention usually generates. The national parties are now all committed to some form of combined system when their next leaders are chosen.[4]

The Delegate Selection Process

At a national convention in the United States, the delegates come from the state parties. How these delegates are selected determines the politics of the nomination process and what happens at the convention. In that light, the history of the presidential nominating process can be divided into three periods: 1840 to 1952, when the nomination process was dominated by state party leaders; 1956 to 1968, when various forces began to undermine the control of the state leaders; and 1972 to the present, during which delegates have been selected by party activists in primaries or caucuses.

The Presidential Nominating Process, 1840 to 1952

Throughout this period it was the state party leaders who selected the delegates to the convention and controlled how they voted. The delegates, usually party or elected officials, were dependent on the party leaders and voted as they were instructed. This meant that state leaders controlled blocks of convention votes. In order to exercise maximum influence on the presidential candidate, the leaders invariably cast all the state's delegate votes in a block for one candidate, rather than splitting them among different candidates. This meant that control of the convention and thus the presidential nomination lay in the hands of the party leaders in a handful of the largest states—New York, Pennsylvania, Illinois, Ohio, and Indiana—provided that these leaders could reach agreement on a candidate.

In deciding which candidate to support, the state leaders took two factors into account: how well the candidate would run in their own state, and the likelihood of the candidate winning the presidency. The impact of the party's presidential candidate at home was important, since on the ballot he was placed "at the top of the ticket." A popular candidate for the top spot was likely to have strong coattails and

---

4   An exhaustive study of Canadian national leadership conventions, including recent reforms, is in John C. Courtney, *Do Conventions Matter?* (McGill-Queen's University Press, 1995).

increase the vote for the party candidates for state office further down the ticket. The leaders' main concern was winning the state offices, since doing so would give them control of state patronage. Also, if their candidate became president the state leaders could expect a say when it came to filling the many federal jobs the president controlled—for example, in the local post offices and customs houses. For themselves, the party leaders could aspire to a place in Cabinet, where they would control still more jobs. As is discussed in Chapter 13, the party organizations maintained their grip mainly through their ability to distribute patronage to party workers in the form of government jobs.

Thus, until 1952 the political dynamics of the nominating convention involved bargaining among a small group of party leaders. For the state party leaders the best candidate was sometimes obvious but often not. A common strategy for postponing a difficult choice was to support a "favorite son"—that is, a candidate from the state, often the governor or a senator, who was not a serious contender for the presidency but whom the state could vote for on the early ballots while the leaders assessed the strengths of the serious candidates.

The bargaining between the state leaders took place at the convention. Only when there was an incumbent president was the voting likely to be over in a few ballots. The situation was particularly complex in the Democratic Party, which required the winning candidate to get two-thirds of the convention votes. If the nomination was not decided after a series of ballots, the leaders of the large states would enter a "smoke-filled room" (cartoonists always portrayed party bosses as smoking big cigars) in order to bargain. It was in such circumstances that a "dark horse" might emerge as the nominee. A dark horse was a compromise candidate, sometimes someone who had not had much support in the early ballots. Sometimes a compromise could not be reached easily among the bosses. The most extreme case of convention deadlock occurred in 1924, when it took the Democrats 103 ballots to nominate a candidate. Franklin Roosevelt had the two-thirds rule abolished in 1936.

Thus, in the nineteenth century the nomination of presidential candidates in both parties was dominated by the party bosses of the large states in the Northeast and Midwest, who controlled the largest blocks of convention delegates. Almost all the presidential and vice presidential nominees came from the same large states—particularly fiercely competitive states like Ohio, Illinois, and New York—since a strong presidential candidate was expected to win his home state in November.

The Progressive period from 1900 to 1916 saw major reforms of the American party system. These reforms are discussed in more detail in Chapter 13. The most important reform was the introduction of the primary-election method for nominating candidates. While the reforms reduced the power of the old-style state party bosses, they had little effect on the presidential nomination process.

The first state to use a primary election to choose its national convention delegates was Florida in 1904, followed by Wisconsin. By 1912 the Democratic and Republican parties were using the primary election method in twelve and thirteen states respectively, and bypassing the state party leaders. However, that year's race for the Republican nomination showed how little the introduction of primaries had changed the nomination process. Former president Teddy Roosevelt wanted to take the nomination away from his successor, President Taft. While he was campaigning in the primaries he ran up against two realities: nearly 60 percent of the delegates were still chosen by the state party leaders, who were staying loyal to President Taft; and delegates from primary states were not always legally bound to vote at the convention for the candidate who had won the primary. Taft kept the nomination.

Between 1912 and 1968 the number of states using presidential primaries to select delegates to the national convention fluctuated between twelve and twenty. On average around 40 percent of the delegates were chosen in primaries, but state leaders continued to dominate the nomination process. The decisions of a single state boss of the earlier period were replaced by negotiations among strong local leaders and officeholders as to which candidate the state should support. There remained a strong incentive for the state to put all its delegates behind one candidate. Candidates who wished to impress the party leaders with their vote-getting ability would campaign in selected presidential primaries as a strategy (John F. Kennedy did this is 1960), but they still needed the support of the party leaders at the convention.

The impossibility of winning a nomination through a primary campaign alone was demonstrated again in 1952. In that year Senator Estes Kefauver of Tennessee won fourteen of the fifteen Democratic primaries but was blocked by the leaders of the big states, who delivered the nomination to Governor Adlai Stevenson of Illinois, who was not a declared candidate and had entered none of the primaries.

The Presidential Nominating Process in Transition, 1956 to 1968

The Democratic convention of 1952 was the last national convention where more than one ballot was required to nominate the party's presidential candidate. The old style of nomination whereby party bosses negotiated for a candidate was being undermined by new political forces.

In John F. Kennedy's successful campaign for the nomination in 1960 there were elements of the traditional process, in that he needed to win the support of the large-state party leaders, but there were also elements of a new style, in his aggressive and high-spending primary campaigns. Senator Kennedy was a relatively junior figure in the party and was backed mainly by his father's money and his own ambition. The two main obstacles to his getting the nomination were, first, the party's dominant New Deal liberal wing, who favored either Senator Hubert Humphrey or Adlai Stevenson and, second, the fact that Kennedy was a Roman Catholic. The only previous Catholic candidate, Al Smith in 1928, had lost heavily.

The majority of convention votes were controlled by state party leaders. These included Richard Daley of Illinois and David Lawrence of Pennsylvania, who though Catholic themselves were skeptical about whether a Catholic could be elected. The only way for Kennedy to convince them of his popularity was by entering presidential primaries in some of the states. Kennedy entered about half the primaries held in 1960, but the ones crucial to his winning the nomination were those in Wisconsin and West Virginia.

By defeating Humphrey in the Wisconsin primary, Kennedy demonstrated to liberal Democrats, who doubted his liberal credentials, that he could beat their champion on his home territory (Wisconsin being next door to Humphrey's home state of Minnesota).

To demonstrate his electability among Protestants, Kennedy entered the West Virginia primary against Humphrey. West Virginia, a small state with few convention delegates, was chosen because it was 95 percent Protestant. After his earlier defeat by Kennedy, Humphrey badly needed a victory. Kennedy put on a massive campaign in the small state, spending much more money than Humphrey could afford. After Kennedy's decisive victory in the primary, Humphrey dropped out of the race and Kennedy more or less clinched the nomination by getting the support of the key state-party leaders.[5]

In 1964 Senator Barry Goldwater stunned the Republican Party establishment by winning the nomination in spite of their strong objections to his right-wing views. The Goldwater victory came not so much by winning primaries as by organizing local conservative activists in the many states where party organization was weak.[6]

The 1968 Democratic National Convention

In 1968 the two forces, the traditional style of presidential politics and the new activist politics, met in a violent clash at the Democratic convention in Chicago. The old politics won that year, but it was a pyrrhic victory. The fallout from the convention was such that the rules governing the delegate selection process were radically rewritten to remove the last traces of boss control. By 1972 the presidential nomination process had been transformed.

What precipitated the clash was the Vietnam War. The Democrats fought out this issue within their own party while the Republicans, who were critical of President

---

5   On Kennedy's nomination strategy, see Theodore H. White, *The Making of the President 1960* (Atheneum, 1961). White pioneered a new style of journalism that chronicled presidential selection through both the nomination process and the presidential election. White himself covered the presidential elections from 1960 through 1972. Since then his general model has been followed by other journalists. For every presidential election now there are several volumes by teams of journalists covering the campaigns.

6   An account of Goldwater's insurgent campaign for the nomination is in Robert D. Novak, *The Agony of the G.O.P. 1964* (Macmillan, 1965).

Johnson but not of the war, looked on. President Johnson defended his conduct of the war and the need to pursue it. In this, he was strongly supported by most state party leaders and most working-class Democrats. Opposition to the war was strongest on university campuses, with the students receiving growing support from the liberal wing of the party.

The challenge to President Johnson's renomination came first from Senator Eugene McCarthy, who with the support of an army of student volunteers very nearly defeated Johnson in the first Democratic presidential primary in New Hampshire. Soon after, Senator Robert Kennedy, the late president's brother, also entered the race for the nomination in opposition to the war. President Johnson then decided not to run for re-election, leaving it to his vice president, Hubert Humphrey, to defend his position. Kennedy and McCarthy won most of the primaries, with Humphrey entering only a few of the late ones. The emotional climate surrounding the campaign became supercharged when Bobby Kennedy was assassinated on the night he beat Humphrey in the last of the primaries, in California.

At the convention, while anti-war protesters were being clubbed and tear-gassed by the Chicago police outside the hall, Humphrey received the Democratic nomination for president. In spite of the rebels' primary victories, 60 percent of the delegates had been named by the state party leaders, who remained loyal to the vice president.[7]

The Presidential Nominating Process After 1968

After the chaos of the 1968 convention and Humphrey's defeat the following November, the Democrats found it hard to ignore calls for reform of the delegate selection process. The party set up a commission dominated by reformers to rewrite the rules for the 1972 convention. These rules, with some modifications and additions for later conventions, are the basis of the present nomination process. The Democratic Party led the way in transforming the nomination process; the Republican Party has moved in roughly the same direction, while generally leaving more choice to the state parties.

The goal of the party reformers was to make the presidential nomination process more democratic and to eliminate the power of party leaders to control the delegates. To this end, they laid down new rules governing several key aspects of the delegate selection process:

- Delegates now must be chosen by one of two methods: a presidential primary or a grass-roots caucus system. (Both methods are discussed below.)

---

7   One account of the turbulent Democratic convention is David R. Farber, *Chicago '68* (University of Chicago Press, 1988).

- Delegates must now be chosen in the year the convention is held. A schedule has been established that starts with the first caucus meetings in early February (in Iowa); these are followed by the first primary election (in New Hampshire). All other states must select their delegates between the end of February and the first week of June. (The Republicans have allowed some states to start their caucus meetings earlier than February.)

- The Democrats have tried to restrict participation in primaries and caucuses to registered Democratic voters. It has been impossible to enforce this, however, since voter registration practices vary considerably between states. In thirty of the states, when voters register themselves to vote they are required to "declare" themselves (that is, as Democrat, or Republican, or independent). Many of these states hold *closed* nomination processes—that is, only registered party voters may participate in the party's primaries or caucuses. In other states nominating events are *partially open*, meaning that those registered as independent may choose to participate in either party's nomination procedures. Still other states, including the twenty states that do not register voters by party, hold *open* nomination events—that is, voters indicate at the polling place which party's nomination procedure they wish to participate in.

- It had long been standard practice for each state party to vote solidly for one candidate; the point of this was to maximize the impact of its delegates. Under the new Democratic Party rules, each state's delegate slots must be divided between the candidates getting at least 15 percent of the primary or caucus vote in proportion to the share of votes won. The Republicans have no set rules for delegate allocation. In 1996 eight states used a proportional system, and eight gave all the delegates to the winner statewide; most of the others allocated delegates through some combination of proportional and district "winner take all" systems.

- Originally, the new rules required each delegation to reflect its state's population. This was an outcome of the battle in the 1960s to force the southern Democratic parties to select some black delegates. In 1972 the McGovern anti-war forces who controlled the convention took great delight in excluding Mayor Richard Daley of Chicago, their nemesis from 1968, on the grounds that his Illinois delegation was not representative enough. In 1980 this rule was changed again, so that each state delegation was simply required to have an equal number of men and women.

Many Democratic officeholders had found themselves excluded from conventions under the new selection processes. In 1980, in response to this awkwardness, each state delegation was expanded by 10 percent, with the additional places to be filled by elected officeholders from the state. In order not to undermine the rules, the additional delegates are required to cast their votes in the same proportions as the state delegation as a whole. In 1984 a second category of "superdelegates" was added for prominent officeholders, who are free to cast their own votes.

Presidential Primaries

A presidential primary is an adaptation of the primary-election method of nominating party candidates for office that has been used almost everywhere in the United States since the early twentieth century. In *direct* primaries, the voter votes directly for a candidate. A presidential primary is an *indirect* primary in that the voter is asked to choose a slate of delegates who will, in turn, vote for a presidential candidate at the national convention. To simplify matters for the voter, the ballot in most states lists the names of the candidates for the nomination rather than the names of the delegates.

Since the party reforms of the 1970s, the presidential primary has become the most popular method for choosing delegates to the national convention. The number of states holding presidential primaries has increased greatly in recent decades. In 1996 there were forty-one Republican and thirty-five Democratic primary states. The other states use some form of the caucus method.

Presidential Caucuses

A **caucus** is a gathering of members of the same party. The presidential caucus system was invented in the 1970s as an alternative to the primary election method. The best way to explain how the caucus system works is to follow what happened one nominating year in Iowa, which has become the most famous of the caucus states because it is the first to start its delegate selection process.

Level One: Precinct Caucuses. On the evening of Tuesday, February 7, 1988, starting at 7 p.m., an estimated 126,000 Democrats and 108,000 Republicans met separately in approximately 2,500 precinct caucuses all across the state. The purpose of the meetings was to elect delegates to the county conventions. Those who attended the precinct meetings were grouped according to which presidential candidate they supported. Each group that amounted to more than 15 percent of the attendance at its meeting was entitled to select a share of the delegates to be elected to the next level.

Level Two: County Conventions. The Iowa county conventions met on March 5 for the Republicans and on March 26 for the Democrats. The county conventions elected delegates to the six congressional district conventions, using the same proportional system to divide the delegates among the candidates still in the race.

Level Three: Congressional District Conventions. These were held on May 14 for the Democrats and on June 24 for the Republicans. The six district conventions elected some of the delegates to the national party conventions (between five to seven per district for the Democrats, three per district for the Republicans), as well as delegates to the Iowa state party conventions.

Level Four: State Conventions. The remaining delegates to the national conventions were elected by the state Democratic and Republican conventions, both of which met on June 25.

The precinct caucus meetings thus began a four-tiered process of electing the state party's national convention delegates. (Other states use a three-tiered process.) Because the process starts at the grass roots and because the sets of delegates are selected in proportion to each candidate's support, the state's delegation to the national convention will reflect the support each candidate has at the local level. Delegates pledged to a candidate who later drops out of the race are free to support another candidate.

Public Financing of Presidential Campaigns[8]

Starting with the 1976 election, the presidential nomination process was radically altered by the introduction of public financing for presidential campaigns. Public financing was part of a wholesale reform of the laws governing political contributions and expenditures, and was a reaction to the financial abuses perpetrated by the Nixon re-election campaign of 1972. The new rules limited campaign contributions for all elections.

- Individual contributions to political campaigns are now limited to $1,000 per candidate per campaign. Campaigns for nomination and election are treated as separate campaigns.

- Corporations, unions, and interest groups can only contribute to political campaigns by setting up special political action committees (PACs), which can donate up to $5,000 per candidate per campaign.

- The new rules also restricted how much of their own money candidates could spend on their own campaigns. However, in *Buckley v. Valeo* (1976) the Supreme

---

8   A summary of the history and current state of presidential campaign finance is in Charles C. Euchner and John Anthony Maltese, *Selecting the President: From Washington to Bush* (*Congressional Quarterly*, 1992), Chapter 2.

Court struck down that restriction as a violation of the First Amendment guarantees of free speech.

Public financing in the form of matching funds is provided only for presidential campaigns and is available for each stage: nomination, convention, and general election. To qualify for matching funds during the nomination process a candidate must first raise $5,000 in each of twenty states in amounts of $250. For every candidate who qualifies, the government matches the first $250 of each individual campaign contribution received. A candidate loses the right to matching funds if he or she fails to receive at least 10 percent of the votes in two consecutive primaries. In return for the public funds, candidates must disclose all donations and expenditures of $100 or more and accept limits on how much they can spend in each state and in total on their nomination campaigns.

The Supreme Court accepted the campaign spending limits since they are voluntary, and apply only if the candidate accepts public matching funds. Otherwise, there is no restriction on spending. Since 1976 only two candidates, both Republicans, have opted not to take public funding: John Connally (1980) and Steve Forbes (1996). Neither was successful. In addition, Ross Perot, who ran as an independent in the 1992 presidential election, spent an estimated $60 million of his own money.

Under public funding the major parties receive a subsidy for their national conventions ($12 million in 1996). For the general election, the two major-party candidates receive a public subsidy and are limited to spending that amount ($74 million in 1996). Other parties can also qualify for a subsidy if they received at least 5 percent of the national vote in the previous presidential election. In 1996 Ross Perot qualified for a total of $30 million on the basis of his showing in the 1992 election. He accepted the subsidy for his Reform Party candidacy and was therefore limited to spending that amount.

The system of public funding for presidential elections is generally thought to have worked well through the 1980s. The prospect of matching funds enabled more candidates to contest the nominations. In the general election the federal subsidies provided a more level playing field between the parties; previously, the Republicans almost invariably had an advantage in fund-raising because of their greater support from business.

There have always been loopholes in the system of public financing. Independent committees can raise and spend money to support or oppose a candidate provided that the expenditures are not coordinated with the official campaign. In 1979 an amendment was passed allowing political parties to raise money outside the normal restrictions for "party building" activities, such as voter registration drives. "Soft money" raised this way cannot be used to support particular candidates.

It is this loophole that has in the end torn the party financing system wide open. The line between party activities and support for the party's candidates was always a fine one and in the 1990s it was increasingly disregarded. The attraction of soft money is that large donations—hundreds of thousands of dollars in some cases—can be raised from individuals and corporations outside the campaign finance limits. The raising of soft money by both parties to support their presidential candidates had become increasingly flagrant by 1992. In 1996 the fund-raising activities by both parties made a mockery of the entire campaign finance system. Each party, claiming it was only trying to match the other's expenditures, set out to raise and spend $120 million *in addition to* the supposed limit of the $74 million public subsidy.[9] The raising and spending of such enormous amounts in this unrestrained fashion made the discovery of various fund-raising "scandals" inevitable.

In 1996 the Clinton campaign was accused of violating the law by directly controlling the expenditure of soft money for the president's campaign.[10] The size of some soft money contributions (some as high as $250,000) raised questions about the expectations of the donors. Many donors had obvious policy interests, and this left both parties, and especially the incumbent president, wide open to accusations of influence peddling. There were also questions about the methods the parties used to attract large donations. For example, the Clinton campaign was accused of "selling" overnight stays at the White House for large donations. The system of controlling the financing of presidential campaigns that had worked well for nearly twenty years had obviously collapsed; by 1996 the whole system of campaign financing for presidential elections seemed to be back where it was in 1972—awash in corporate money and in drastic need of reform.

The Impact of the New Rules on the Presidential Nominating Process

The new rules governing the selection of delegates transformed the nomination process by removing it altogether from the control of state party leaders. Delegates could no longer be delivered to a candidate in blocks; they had to be won over almost one by one in each state. Starting in 1972 the candidates were faced with more than fifty (when one includes the U.S. territories and Washington, D.C.) separate delegate selection processes spaced over a period of less than four months, most of which they needed to contest in their search for a majority of convention delegates.

Now that seven sets of presidential nominations have been made under the current rules (from 1972 through 1996), it is possible to summarize how the current presidential nominating system works. Clearly, the preparatory stage of fund raising and putting together a campaign organization is extremely important. The early stages of

---

9   *New York Times*, October 18, 1996, A1.
10   Bob Woodward, *The Choice* (Simon and Schuster, 1996).

the delegate selection process move so fast and are so unpredictable that candidates absolutely must have enough money and organizational support in place to survive any early defeats and stay in the process. In the 1970s the process allowed lesser-known candidates, such as McGovern in 1972 and Carter in 1976, to build support on the basis of early victories and go on to win the nomination; since then, the process has increasingly benefited the well-financed front-runners. In fact, in the Republican nomination contests, the front-running candidate has always won.

Before the delegate selection process starts, the competition between candidates is largely shadow boxing—there is much maneuvering to create publicity, demonstrate popularity, and raise funds. The uncertainty mounts as the starting date for the selections comes closer: Will the front-runner hold up or start to falter? Who will emerge in second or third place, in the best position to replace the front-runner?

This uncertainty, and the importance that voters and financial contributors attach to backing a winner, makes it absolutely vital for candidates to do well in the first few states, especially Iowa, which holds the first caucuses, and New Hampshire, which holds the first primary. Neither of these states has a large number of convention delegates, and neither is typical of the country as a whole. They are crucially important simply because they provide the first indications of a candidate's grass roots appeal.

The delegate selection process has developed its own dynamic that weeds out the weaker candidates very quickly; this is why most nominations have been effectively decided before the end of the second month of the process. Two concepts that are important in understanding how the modern nominating process works are *momentum* and *expectations*.

Momentum.   Some primary voters will be strongly attached to a particular candidate, perhaps for reasons of geography, ideology, or ethnic or racial identification, but most have little basis for preferring one candidate over another. In this circumstance primary voters are strongly attracted to a candidate who looks like a winner. A candidate who wins or does well in one primary usually attracts votes in the next one. This is how momentum builds.

The media is an important factor in developing momentum. The print and broadcast media cover candidates who are doing well and largely ignore the others. A good early performance greatly increases media coverage, which in turn helps a candidate attract more voters. Also, most financial contributors would rather contribute to a successful campaign than throw away their money on a losing one. Most candidates have difficulty raising enough campaign money. Good early results attract more money; with poor results, the money dries up quickly. This need for early success is reinforced by the rules governing federal funding: a candidate who gets less than 10 percent of the vote in two consecutive primaries loses his or her claim to future federal matching funds.

Expectations. In the early stages of the race, voters, contributors, and the media are all trying to spot the winner. One of the measures of a candidate's prospects is whether he or she is doing better or worse than expected. Front-runners are expected to do well, and so are candidates running at home (that is, in their home state or region). By the same token, little is expected of little-known candidates. A candidate who does worse than expected loses momentum, while one who does better gains momentum.

The first example of the power of expectations was in the New Hampshire Democratic primary in 1972, in which Senator Ed Muskie defeated Senator George McGovern 46 percent to 37 percent. Muskie was the front-runner for the nomination and came from next-door Maine. Although he won the primary, his margin of victory was so much lower than expected that his candidacy went into a tailspin from which it never recovered. McGovern, whose chances had been generally discounted, started to gather momentum from his close second-place showing and went on to win the nomination.

The Presidential Nominating Process in 1996

The current delegate selection process squeezes out trailing candidates quickly, leaving one candidate in a dominant position. As a result, the nomination has effectively been decided by mid-April at the latest, and those states which choose their delegates later than that find themselves without influence. For this reason, several states decided for 1996 to move their primaries or caucuses forward into March. Most significant was California's move from its traditional position at the end of the process (early June) to the end of March. New York moved from early April to early March, while Ohio, Wisconsin, and Oregon all moved forward from April or May into mid-March.

There was also maneuvering by rival regions. Starting in 1988 most of the southern states agreed to hold their delegate selections on the same day in mid-March, creating what became known as "Super Tuesday." This was done explicitly to increase southern conservative influence, especially on the choice of Democratic candidates. For 1996 all the New England states except New Hampshire coordinated their events to create another regional primary a week earlier than Super Tuesday.

These moves front-loaded the nominating process even more than before. The Iowa caucuses and New Hampshire primary were allowed to keep their traditional first places in mid-February (although Louisiana provocatively moved its Republican caucus just ahead of Iowa's). After a few other scattered state events, the real crush started on March 5 with ten states, including the rest of New England, holding Republican primaries or caucuses. The New York primary followed on March 7; the Missouri caucuses on March 9. Then on March 12, Super Tuesday, seven more, mostly southern, states selected their delegates. Thus, in the space of one week—March 5 through

March 12—no fewer than nineteen states, including such large states as Texas, New York, and Florida, selected 38 percent of the total Republican convention delegates, with a further 23 percent to be selected before the end of March.

It seemed clear that only candidates with massive advance organizations and huge amounts of campaign money could hope to survive the month of March. The opportunity that had existed for an unknown candidate like Jimmy Carter in 1976 to gradually build up support and money after early successes was no longer open. In 1996 too much money and too much organization was needed too quickly for lesser known, underfinanced candidates to stay in the nomination race.

The Democratic Party in 1996

No incumbent president has been denied renomination by his party in the twentieth century. This is not to say that an incumbent's nomination always goes unchallenged. In 1912 former president Teddy Roosevelt mounted a massive challenge to the renomination of his successor, President Taft. In more recent times, President Johnson was challenged by Senators Eugene McCarthy and Robert Kennedy in 1968 and withdrew from the contest; and President Ford had to fight off a serious challenge from Ronald Reagan in 1976, as did President Carter from Senator Ted Kennedy in 1980. In 1992, in the early stages of the nomination process, President Bush had to deal with a noisy and damaging challenge from Pat Buchanan.

In early 1994 it seemed quite possible that President Clinton might be challenged for renomination. His performance in office had pleased neither the liberals nor the centrists in the party. There was speculation that Jesse Jackson, who had run creditably in 1984 and 1988, or former New York governor Mario Cuomo might challenge him from the left; and that Senator Bob Kerrey, who had run against him in 1992, or Senator Bill Bradley might challenge from the right. Governor Casey of Pennsylvania, an abortion opponent, also talked about a possible challenge to the president.

Well aware of these possibilities and of how Presidents Carter and Bush had been weakened politically by divisive renomination contests, Clinton and his advisers acted to ward off any challenge, mainly by starting high-profile fund-raising as early as the spring of 1995. Clinton was letting potential challengers know that he was prepared and would be in position to overwhelm any opponents.

The president also benefited in the fall of 1995 from his budget battles with the self-styled "revolutionary" Republicans who had won control of the House of Representatives in the 1994 mid-term elections. By consistently outmaneuvering the congressional Republicans, Clinton increased his approval ratings and rallied his party against Republican attempts to dismantle many of the Democrats' past legislative accomplishments.

By the end of 1995 it was clear that there would be no challengers and that President Clinton's renomination would not be contested. This was an enormous advantage for Clinton: throughout the spring of 1996, at a time when his prospective Republican opponent was locked in an especially nasty and expensive struggle for that party's nomination, he was able to continue to act "presidentially" rather than as a partisan candidate for office. Because he had had to spend comparatively little to campaign for the nomination, Clinton was able to afford a television campaign against the Republicans through the spring.

The Republican Party in 1996

After his defeat in November 1992, President Bush quickly retired from public life. There would be an open contest for the Republican nomination in 1996. Potential candidates started their groundwork soon after. By late 1994 the potential candidates had all assessed their chances and decided whether they had the stomach for a nomination campaign. The announcements of candidacy (and of noncandidacy) started appearing in early 1995, a year before delegate selections actually started.

In recent years the nomination process has been shaped as much by those who decided not to enter as by those who chose to run. For example, after Senator Al Gore, Representative Richard Gephardt, and Governor Mario Cuomo decided not to be candidates for 1992, there is no question that Bill Clinton found it much easier to win the Democratic nomination. The noncandidacy decisions were equally important for the Republicans in 1996.

Promising candidates stay out of the races for various reasons. Sometimes the reasons are largely personal (as in the case of Cuomo). Other decisions to stay out turn out to be political miscalculations (such as Senator Gore's decision, and Richard Gephardt's, not to run for 1992, on the assumption, reasonable at the time, that President Bush was unbeatable). There is no doubt that the long, nightmarish nature of the delegate selection process, the need to raise massive amounts of money in advance, and the increasingly intrusive nature of press coverage have turned away some promising candidates. Few have put it as succinctly as Senator Walter Mondale, who in 1974 explained that he would not run because he did not want to spend the next two years in Holiday Inns.

Republican Noncandidates: the First Round

August 1994	Bill Bennett, former Cabinet secretary
January 1995	Dick Cheney, former defense secretary
	Jack Kemp, former congressman and candidate in 1988
February 1995	Dan Quayle, Bush's vice president
	Bill Weld, governor of Massachusetts

Cheney and Kemp particularly would have been highly credible candidates. Both had seriously considered running, as had Quayle. In modern times many former vice presidents have been front-runners for the next presidential nomination, but Quayle had never been able to shake his image as a political lightweight. Other possible candidates, including Jim Baker, the former secretary of state, and prominent governors Thompson of Wisconsin and Engler of Michigan, made no moves to become candidates. Ten Republicans did declare their candidacy for the 1996 presidential nomination.

Republican Candidates

February 1995	Phil Gramm, conservative senator from Texas
	Lamar Alexander, ex-governor of Tennessee; Cabinet secretary
March	Pat Buchanan, conservative commentator
	Alan Keyes, conservative radio talk-show host
	Arlen Specter, senator from Pennsylvania
April	Bob Dole, Senate majority leader from Kansas
	Bob Dornan, ultraconservative congressman from California
	Dick Lugar, senator from Indiana
	Steve Forbes, millionaire businessman
June	Pete Wilson, governor of California

Among the declared candidates, Dole stood out as the obvious front-runner. Dole had been President Ford's running mate in 1976 and had sought the nomination in 1980 and 1988. He had been Senate republican leader since 1985. Gramm and Wilson also seemed serious contenders; Alexander was rated a long shot; Buchanan had challenged Bush in 1992 but was not thought likely to do as well in 1996; the remaining candidates, including the well-respected Lugar and Specter, were thought to have virtually no chance.

Republican Noncandidates: the Second Round

September 1995	Pete Wilson
November 1995	Colin Powell, former chairman of the Joint Chiefs of Staff
	Arlen Specter
	Newt Gingrich, Speaker of the House of Representatives

Specter, a social liberal, had never stood much chance. Wilson's failure was a surprise, but he had badly miscalculated his strategy and found it impossible to raise sufficient funds in California. Gingrich had rocketed to prominence as leader of the

Republican take-over of the House of Representatives and then as Speaker. It always seemed unlikely that he would leave that key position to run for president, but he refused to rule himself out until the end of the year.

Colin Powell's decision not to run was by far the most important of any potential candidate in shaping the nomination race. Powell had retired in 1994 as chairman of the Joint Chiefs of Staff, the top military position in the United States. Before that he had been national security adviser to President Reagan. During his military career Powell had had no party affiliation, though most of his associations had been with Republican officials and presidents. Speculation about a possible Powell candidacy, as either an independent or a Republican, grew steadily during 1995 and reached a frenzy when he went on a national book tour in September to promote his autobiography. Pre-nomination maneuverings were suspended until Powell announced in early November that, while he was a Republican, he would not run. As a reason he cited his lack of sufficient "fire in the belly" for such a contest.

For several weeks, until he took himself out of the race, the prospect of a Powell candidacy had thrown the calculations of the other Republican candidates and of President Clinton himself out the window. Powell was seen by his supporters as "a second Eisenhower"—as a man untainted by politics, who nevertheless had experience in high-level military and White House decision-making (during the Gulf War, for example), and who radiated strength and integrity. Although a social moderate in an increasingly conservative party, polls showed him leading the Republican field in many states. The fact that Powell is black, the son of Jamaican immigrants, opened up the prospect of heavy Republican inroads into the black vote, which had usually gone overwhelmingly to the Democrats; yet at the same time, the polls showed no sign that his race would be held against him by Republicans, even in the South. After Powell removed himself from the running, the Republican contest resumed, and Democratic calculations returned to their previous assumptions.

◄ The Republican Delegate Selection Process, 1996

The question at the beginning of the process was whether the front-runner, Senate majority leader Bob Dole, would establish his dominance and lock up the contest from the start, or whether he would begin to falter and open up the race to the other candidates. Since the 1970s the first major contest has been the Iowa caucuses, but in 1996 the Louisiana Republicans, with the encouragement of Senator Gramm, decided to hold caucuses six days ahead of Iowa. The furious Iowa Republicans persuaded most of the other candidates to stay away from the Louisiana contest, but Pat Buchanan decided to take on Gramm. Gramm had boasted that a win in Louisiana would give him momentum going into Iowa, but his entire game plan fell apart when Buchanan beat him in Louisiana.

Iowa Republican Precinct Caucuses, February 12, 1996

Dole	26%
Buchanan	23
Alexander	18
Forbes	10
Gramm	9
Others trailing	

Dole, the best organized and financed candidate, had been expected to do well in Iowa, which is next to his home state of Kansas. He eked out a win but came in below expectations. Louisiana had indeed provided momentum into Iowa, but for Buchanan not Gramm. In both states Buchanan, with his uncompromising anti-abortion stance, had received strong support from conservative Christians and Catholics. Alexander performed respectably and would now be taken more seriously. Gramm, by raising high expectations for himself in Louisiana and failing to meet them, had started a tailspin; he would be the first to leave the race, on February 15.

The traditional second event is the first primary, in New Hampshire. Forbes had concentrated his efforts here and had spent unprecedented amounts of his own money on a TV campaign attacking Dole. The questions going into New Hampshire were therefore these: Would Forbes's massive outlay enable him to do well? Would Buchanan retain or increase his momentum? And how well would Dole hold up to the attacks by Forbes and Buchanan, who were already seen as his main challengers?

New Hampshire Republican Primary, February 20, 1996

Buchanan	28%
Dole	26
Alexander	23
Forbes	16
Others trailing	

Buchanan was clearly on a roll, with an unconventional Republican message combining economic populism with extreme social conservatism—a message that alarmed the Republican establishment. Dole was clearly wounded after a second disappointing result; Alexander had again done better than expected and was positioning himself as the mainstream alternative to Dole. Forbes was judged to have done adequately and was clearly willing to spend money to stay in the race.

Forbes kept himself in the race on February 24 by winning the Delaware primary, one in which only he had campaigned actively. There were three primaries on February 27: North and South Dakota, generally conceded to Dole, and Arizona, where both

Buchanan and Forbes were making a major effort. In Arizona, Forbes won, running slightly ahead of Dole and Buchanan, with Alexander trailing. The next primary would be in South Carolina on March 3. This was not only the first contest in the South but also the prelude to the crucial week of March 5 through 12, which contained no fewer than nineteen contests for 38 percent of the delegates. Dole's challengers needed strong momentum from a win in South Carolina if they were to have any hope of competing with Dole's broad organizational support the following week.

South Carolina Republican Primary, March 3, 1996

Dole	45%
Buchanan	29
Forbes	13
Alexander	10

In South Carolina, a solidly conservative Republican state, the party organization led by the governor, in alliance with the leadership of the Christian Coalition, threw all its support behind Dole in an effort to bring a quick end to the contest. Dole won handily.

The contest for the Republican presidential nomination in 1996 effectively ended in South Carolina, less than a month after it started. Dole went on to win all nineteen contests in the ensuing week. Alexander left the race after March 5, Forbes after March 12. Both endorsed Dole. Only Buchanan refused to surrender: he continued to compete in some states but was unable to get more than around 30 percent of the vote anywhere and ended up with only 8 percent of the convention delegates. Dole was duly nominated at the national convention in August.

The Current Presidential Nominating Process: Pro and Con[11]

To many people the current process is a bizarre roller-coaster, especially in the early stages. This can be illustrated by what happened to Bob Dole in February 1996. A good case can be made that if Dole had run second in Iowa instead of first, and third in New Hampshire instead of second—a difference in both cases of three percentage points—his candidacy would have been so damaged that the party establishment would not have been able to rally around him in March. As it was, Dole's candidacy nearly collapsed in spite of the money he had raised and the large number of endorsements he had collected from Republican governors and other party notables.

---

11   An assessment of the nominating process, with proposals for changes, is Alexander Heard et al., eds., *Made in America: Improving the Nomination and Election of Presidents* (HarperCollins, 1991).

Dole's weak performance in the early delegate selection events was a harbinger of his weak performance during the presidential election, in which he was defeated. Yet by the time the delegate selections started in February the party establishment had no good alternative to Dole. Mainstream candidates such as Lugar and Gramm were gaining little support. Forbes, lacking any political experience, was not a plausible candidate. Buchanan also lacked experience of office, and furthermore would have split the party. Only Alexander would have been at all feasible. Under the pre-1972 nominating system, faced with Dole's weak performance, party leaders might well have rallied behind a Cheney, a Kemp, or a Powell before the convention; but nowadays candidates cannot be nominated if they do not enter the process. The Republican Party was stuck with Dole once the delegate selections began in February.

There has been much criticism of the speed with which the nomination decision is made and of the disproportionate influence of a handful of unrepresentative early states. Yet the states that moved their delegate selections forward into March in 1996 still had no impact on the result. The Republicans were so unhappy with the trend toward front-loading that at the 1996 convention they adopted tighter rules for the year 2000. To avoid competitive date-setting among the states, all will have to stipulate their delegate selection process by July 1, 1999. No selection process will be allowed to start before February 1, 2000. In the most significant rule change, a bonus increase in delegates is being offered to states selecting their delegates later rather than sooner: +5 percent for between mid-March and mid-April; +7.5 percent for between mid-April and mid-May; and +10 percent after May 15.[12]

One of the most incisive critics of the presidential nomination process is Thomas Patterson. He argues that the removal of the political parties from the process has forced the press to become the intermediary institution informing the voters and structuring their options. But this is a role that the press is not suited to play: "The press is in the news business, not the business of politics, and because of this its norms and imperatives are not those required for the effective organization of electoral coalitions and debate. Journalistic values and political values are at odds with each other."[13]

Patterson argues that the news media are not oriented to provide the kind of information the voters require and that their relentless search for new stories increases the volatility of the nomination process. He proposes that the delegation selection process be shortened and moved back to May and June and that the over-concentration of the results in Iowa and New Hampshire be eliminated.

One suggestion for reform that has attracted attention is to encourage regional primaries, such as those already in place in the South and New England, but to also space

---

12   *Congressional Quarterly, Weekly Report*, August 17, 1996.
13   Thomas E. Patterson, *Out of Order* (Alfred A. Knopf, 1993), 36.

these events much more evenly—say, one month apart. Better spacing, it is argued, would give the candidates time to regroup, and party members time to reflect, and might allow the late entry of new candidates. Whether the national parties have the will to push the states into such an arrangement remains to be seen.

Another criticism of the current nomination process is that it is so grueling and requires so much money to be raised that good candidates are discouraged from running. It is certainly true that the out-party nominations in 1992 and 1996 were greatly affected by candidates who did not run. Supporters of the current system argue that the mettle of potential presidents must be tested. A president must be able to handle stress, think quickly, make decisions under pressure, and win the public over to his policies, and the primaries are an appropriate test of these abilities.

Another deterrent is the intense media scrutiny that all candidates for the presidency or vice presidency must now face. Investigators working for other candidates, the other party, and the media (both serious and tabloid) spend enormous resources trying to unearth any aspects of the candidate's record, finances, schooling, health, family, and private life that can be used as ammunition. Candidates have been forced to drop out because of allegations of marital infidelity (Gary Hart in 1988) or plagiarism (Joe Biden in 1988). Others have been damaged by questions about their spouse's finances (Geraldine Ferraro in 1984) or about how they avoided the military draft during the Vietnam War (Dan Quayle in 1988; Bill Clinton in 1992).

There must be many potential candidates who hesitate to expose themselves and their families to such relentless scrutiny. Yet it can legitimately be asked what relevance this kind of information has. It seems highly doubtful, for example, that President Kennedy, whose risky sexual exploits only became public knowledge some time after his death, could have survived a modern campaign for the nomination. The same is probably true of Franklin Roosevelt, who might not have been elected if the full extent of his physical disability (his legs were substantially paralyzed as a result of polio in 1921) had been widely known, as it would have been today.[14]

THE PRESIDENTIAL ELECTION CAMPAIGN

Until the twentieth century the tradition was that a presidential candidate did not campaign personally for the office. Presidential campaigns were vigorous but were conducted by the state parties. The only candidates to break with this tradition and undertake a personal campaign of speeches were Stephen Douglas, the northern Democratic candidate in 1860, and William Jennings Bryan, a fiery orator and Democratic Populist

---

14   See Hugh Gregory Gallagher, *FDR's Splendid Deception* (Dodd, Mead, 1985) on how Roosevelt and the press dealt with his disability.

candidate in 1896. Both were defeated. It was not until the successful campaign of Woodrow Wilson in 1912 that it became standard and necessary practice for candidates to appear widely across the country and speak on their own behalf.

In each party, the task of coordinating the presidential candidate's campaign fell to the National Committee, which was chaired by the candidate's own nominee. Once elected, the president commonly appointed his National Committee chair to a Cabinet position—often postmaster general—and placed him in charge of distributing federal patronage to the state parties.

By the 1950s some candidates were choosing to run their national campaigns with their own staff, separate from the National Committee. This trend was reinforced by the changes in the nominating process after 1968. Once the delegate selection process opened up, a candidate had to first run a national campaign with his own organization to win the nomination. Successful candidates were then unwilling to entrust the general election campaign to the National Committee staff, who of necessity had been neutral during the nominating process. The use of a personal campaign team during elections was also encouraged by the federal financing of presidential election campaigns, which started in 1976.

A modern presidential election campaign is a highly specialized operation run by a team of pollsters, media consultants, and "spin doctors." The political strategists attached to the campaign develop a Svengali-like mystique if their candidate wins. In the 1980s a group of Republican strategists, including Roger Ailes and Lee Atwater, seemed to have a monopoly on the necessary campaign skills. President Reagan's re-election campaign of 1984, which had as its slogan "Morning in America," was regarded as a model (one that President Clinton tried to copy in 1996). In 1988 the Bush campaign, with its emphasis on Bush's patriotism and its attacks on Democratic candidate Michael Dukakis's "liberalism," was also admired by political professionals for carrying Bush to victory after Dukakis had built a large early lead in the polls. After 1992 the new masters of the presidential game were considered to be Clinton's strategists, James Carville and Paul Begala.

The unique atmosphere of frenzied activity and wild mood swings in the later stages of a modern presidential campaign is well captured by the documentary film *The War Room*, which is about the 1992 Clinton campaign. Because modern communications are instant and media coverage is unceasing, the rival campaign strategists are forced to engage in a round-the-clock tactical competition: How do you capitalize on an opponent's gaffe? How do you recover from your own candidate's gaffe? Should you respond to the latest opposition attack? How? Should you open up a new line of attack on the opposition? When? And what "spin" should you put on each new development? An interesting and amusing account of the battle of wits between two skilled campaign staffs running two very different campaigns is provided in *All's Fair*, an insider's account of the 1992 campaign written by James Carville, Clinton's campaign manager, and his wife Mary Matalin, political director of the Bush campaign.[15]

Since the 1960s presidential candidates have relied more and more on television to get their message out. Television is used in two key ways: as advertising, and as free exposure. All campaigns make heavy use of 30 or 60 second "spots" on the national networks and in local television markets. But candidates also travel relentlessly across the country in a modern campaign in order to attract local news coverage and to provide the network newscasts with varied events to cover. Candidates commonly fly in to several different locations and television markets each day. Another form of free exposure that was used heavily for the first time during the 1992 campaign was appearances by the candidates on national TV talk shows and national and local call-in shows.

The strategic decisions to be made during a campaign fall into two broad categories: presentation, and resource allocation.

Presentation

The candidate with his advisers has to decide how to present himself and his party to the electorate—that is, which issues and themes to emphasize and which ones to play down. The decision is often made to appeal to particular segments of the electorate, often called "target groups"; usually these groups are of somewhat fluid party loyalty. Groups whose loyalty to one or other party is considered secure are usually taken for granted. Large sums of money are spent on opinion polling to guide the strategy decisions.

The successful Bush campaign of 1988 targeted socially conservative Democrats who had supported President Reagan. It did so by emphasizing patriotic themes and attacking the liberal social values of the Democratic candidate. The successful Clinton campaign in 1992 won back many of these wavering Democrats by blaming President Bush for the weak state of the economy and by accusing him of ignoring social problems. Not all attempts at presentation succeed. The efforts of the Republicans to steer public attention away from economic issues in 1992 did not work because of the widespread public concern about unemployment. In 1996 the Dole campaign was severely criticized for never settling on a clear theme for the campaign.

Resource Allocation

The two principal campaign resources are money and the candidate's time. The campaign team has to decide how and where to use these resources. The bulk of the money is spent on the television campaign and on polling. The candidate's time has

---

15   Mary Matalin and James Carville, *All's Fair: Love, War, and Running for President* (Simon and Schuster, 1995).

President Bill Clinton listens to Republican presidential candidate Bob Dole during their presidential debate in 1996.

to be allocated between campaign travel, preparation for debates and interviews, and—for an incumbent—presidential duties. For a while, public funding eliminated the need for fund raising during the campaign. With the increasing reliance on "soft money" in the 1990s, however, fund raising by the candidates continued right through the general election campaigns. In 1996 President Clinton built so large a lead in the polls that he was able to devote some of his time to raising money for Democratic congressional candidates.

The main influence on how resources are allocated during a campaign is the Electoral College. Since presidents are elected by state electoral votes, not a national popular vote, campaigns naturally focus on the large states with their clumps of electoral votes. Thus, it is rare for a presidential candidate to appear in, say, North or South Dakota during the last two months of the campaign.

By custom almost all the states cast all of their electoral votes for the candidate with the most popular votes in the state. Because money and time are limited, a campaign will neglect even a large state if the polls say the candidate is either far ahead or far behind, and will concentrate its advertising and appearances heavily on those large states where the polls say the election is close. In sum, most campaigns focus sharply on a limited number of large target states.

The first televised debate between presidential candidates was the Kennedy/Nixon debate of 1960. It is generally believed that the less well-known Kennedy benefited most from that debate. Since then, challengers have usually been more eager than incumbents to arrange a debate. The first incumbent to agree to debate his opponent was President Ford in 1976, at a time when he was behind in the polls. Debates have since become a regular feature of campaigns, as have debates between the vice presidential candidates.

It would be difficult nowadays for a candidate to refuse to take part in a debate; even so, at each election the candidates and their managers argue and negotiate over the number of debates, their timing (early or late in the campaign), and the specifics of the format. The many fringe candidates for president are excluded from the debates, but independent candidates with wider support are sometimes allowed to participate. In 1980 President Carter refused to debate with John Anderson, but in 1992 neither Bush nor Clinton was willing to exclude Perot from the debates for fear of alienating his supporters. In 1996, however, Perot was excluded on the grounds that he was too low in the polls to be considered a serious contender.

All candidates are nervous before the debates—afraid of making a gaffe or of giving the wrong impression in front of millions of voters—and they spend a great deal of time preparing for them. Still, there is no evidence that the debates have affected the outcome in any presidential election.

Politicians, political professionals, and even some of the public get caught up in the day-to-day unfolding of the presidential campaign as it comes to dominate the news through September and October. There is a school of thought, however, which argues that all the effort, ingenuity, and money spent on presidential campaigns has no bearing at all on the result. According to this view, the result reflects underlying economic, international, and political factors, most of which are in place long before the fall of election year. Most attempts to explain presidential election outcomes (and thus to predict future outcomes) link the result to the state of the economy. The most elaborate explanatory model is that of Allan J. Lichtman and Ken DeCell.[16]

The model's basic premise is that each presidential election is a referendum on the performance of the outgoing administration. In an era of dealignment when neither party can win solely on the basis of party identification, this premise is persuasive. Besides the state of the economy and America's international performance, this model takes into account two other factors. The first is how united the rival parties are: experience suggests that the public shies away from an obviously disunited party. The remaining factor is the candidates; however, a candidate makes a difference to the outcome only if he has a high degree of charisma, like John Kennedy or Ronald Reagan, or is a national hero, like Eisenhower. The Lichtman–DeCell model is essentially a body of past experience dressed in deterministic robes. Many other analysts would

---

16   Allan J. Lichtman and Ken DeCell, *Thirteen Keys to the Presidency* (Madison Books, 1990). Their introduction includes a list of other predictive models that have been proposed.

argue that a good or bad campaign does make a difference, though a much smaller one than all the effort that goes into them would suggest.

The Presidential Campaign of 1996

The 1996 presidential campaign was the classic case of a campaign that seemed to make no difference at all to the final outcome. President Clinton's lead in the polls of ten points or more remained fixed from well before Labor Day. The Republicans' various efforts to cut into his lead or shake up the campaign had no effect.

The campaign was dominated by the strongly entrenched position of the incumbent president. There were two main reasons why his lead was impregnable: the state of the economy, and his positioning as a political moderate. A strong economy usually creates optimism among the electorate, and this is good for any incumbent. However, optimism about the economy is not in itself enough to guarantee victory for an incumbent. In the 1994 elections the economic outlook was strong, yet the Republicans were able to harness widespread anger against Washington to sweep into control of Congress. At the beginning of 1995 Clinton's chances for re-election looked exceedingly dim.

Ironically, it was the Republican control of Congress that secured Clinton's victory in 1996. The Republican "revolutionary" agenda did two things for Clinton: it enabled him to position himself as the moderate defender of popular programs, such as Medicare and environmental regulation, and it unified the Democratic Party behind him, which precluded any challenge to his renomination.

From the beginning of the delegate selection process, Senator Dole had shown himself to be a poor campaigner. Dole was a highly respected legislative leader, a consummate Washington insider skilled at constructing compromise deals to push legislation through its final stages. To campaign for president, however, a candidate must be able to "connect" with the public. Dole had never needed this skill and did not have it, but Clinton had it in abundance.

Given Clinton's large early lead, the Dole campaign staff had difficulty deciding how to present their candidate. They tried to attack the president on issue after issue, but had to abandon each when it had no effect. The allocation of resources presented a similar problem for Dole: Clinton was so sure of his base in the Northeast and Midwest and on the west coast that he could afford to spend time and money campaigning in states the Republicans had won in 1992 (he succeeded in stealing Florida and Arizona). Dole had to spend most of his resources on efforts simply to hold his shrinking base.

Could Clinton have been beaten? Given the state of the economy and Clinton's political skills, it would have been very difficult for *any* Republican to win in 1996. It would have taken a candidate like Colin Powell to change the dynamics of the race. With his nonpolitical appeal, strong character, and potential to swing the overwhelmingly Democratic black vote, Powell as the Republican candidate would probably have run strongly against Clinton. It was Clinton's good fortune that Powell decided not to run.

The Presidential Campaigns of Ross Perot in 1992 and 1996

The highly unconventional campaigns for president by H. Ross Perot, the Dallas billionaire, illustrate a number of characteristics of contemporary presidential campaigning. The two campaigns were structured differently: in 1992 Perot ran as an independent candidate in the general election, spending his own money; in 1996 he ran as the candidate of the Reform Party, which he had created with his own money.

◄ Perot's 1992 Campaign

Perot's first campaign fell into two distinct parts: the pre-campaign from April to mid-July 1992, and the actual campaign in October.

The spring campaign. Perot had never run for political office before, although he had sometimes involved himself nationally or locally on specific issues. The issue that concerned him in 1992, which he felt was being ignored by the two main parties, was the size of the federal budget deficit.

Perot launched his campaign in April by going on the national television talk shows, and immediately generated a huge wave of popular support—some polls showed him leading both Bush and Clinton. He had unlimited amounts of his own money to spend. Since he had no party to support him, his first task was to get volunteers across the country to collect the signatures on the petitions that were required to get his name on the general election ballot in each state.

In June, Perot hired two experienced political operatives to run his campaign: Ed Rollins, who had run President Reagan's re-election campaign in 1984, and Hamilton Jordan, who had run President Carter's campaigns in 1976 and 1980. The managers advised him to formally declare his candidacy and launch a television campaign in the summer to consolidate his support and counteract the increasingly negative press he was receiving. Perot responded by firing them. In mid-July he abruptly folded his campaign, complaining about harassment by the other parties and the media.

The October campaign. Even though Perot had decided at the last minute not to run, his volunteers continued the process of getting his name on the ballot in all states and eventually completed the task. By September he began hinting that he might yet enter the race, and in early October he declared his candidacy. There was no precedent for such a late entry, and his October campaign broke all the rules of modern campaigning: he did almost no campaigning in person; he fought with reporters, who where almost uniformly critical of him; and he spent heavily on television, though not for the sophisticated 30 or 60 second "spots" that most candidates used, but rather for earnest "infomercials" about the deficit.

Perot's independent candidacy for president in 1992 was the most unusual and also the most successful since that of Theodore Roosevelt in 1912. He was "successful" in that he received 19 percent of the total vote, yet in the end he had little impact on the election result. Since his support was spread evenly across the country, he did not come close to winning any electoral votes. Survey evidence suggests that he drew his support quite evenly from the other candidates; if so, he did not influence the outcome of the election even indirectly. Perot is generally credited, however, with putting the problem of the budget deficit firmly on the political agenda for the next four years, as President Clinton and the Republicans in Congress maneuvered to appeal to Perot's sizable block of discontented voters.

⚶ Perot's 1996 Campaign

After his impressive showing in 1992, Perot formed a national organization, United We Stand, which he was careful to emphasize was not a political party. At least in public, he was steadfastly equivocal about the prospect of running again in 1996. In September 1995, Perot moved to create the Reform Party and to collect the large number of signatures that most states required to get a new party on the presidential ballot. He created an innovative two-stage nominating convention but refused to declare his own intentions. His equivocation tempted Richard Lamm to declare his candidacy for the Reform Party nomination. Lamm, a former Democratic governor of Colorado, had long criticized both major parties for avoiding difficult issues. No sooner had Lamm entered the race than Perot declared his own candidacy. Reform Party members (that is, registered voters who had signed a petition to put the Reform Party on the ballot) voted for their nominee by mail or e-mail, and in a very low turnout Perot (to no one's surprise) defeated Lamm for the new party's nomination.[17]

Running as his party's nominee, Perot decided to accept the $30 million public subsidy that was due to him as a result of his performance in 1992. In doing so, he was accepting the spending limits that went with it (for example, he could spend no more than $50,000 of his own money). Perot was counting on the presidential debates to raise his national profile, as they had in 1992, but since he was running under 10 percent in the polls in October, the bipartisan Presidential Debates Commission recommended that he not be included in the presidential debates. Perot ran a much more

---

17   Laura Lippman, "How Ross Perot led Lamm to the Slaughter," *George*, November 1996.

conventional campaign, making more personal appearances and running some short television spots. In the end he won 9 percent of the popular vote, with his support quite evenly spread across the country, as it had been in 1992.

The Significance of the Perot Candidacies

Historically, the appearance of significant third parties has signaled a change in the alignment of political forces. The fact that Perot could win 19 percent of the vote in 1992, and even 9 percent when the economic outlook was good in 1996, suggests that a potential opening exists for a third party. David Broder of the *Washington Post* has argued that the failure of the major parties to face up to the impending crisis in the funding of main entitlement programs is creating space for a third party. To break through, however, a third party needs not only a cutting issue that distinguishes it from the major parties but also (probably) a compelling candidate. Clearly, Perot is too eccentric a figure to attract more support than he already has. In the fall of 1995 there was serious talk of Colin Powell running as an independent, but in the end he declared himself a Republican. Because of the substantial dealignment of party identification, the electorate is now fluid enough that a serious third-party challenge for the presidency is distinctly possible in the right circumstances.

Another conclusion that can be drawn from Perot's independent candidacy in 1992 is that someone who is rich enough and determined enough could probably "buy" the presidency. Perot's unusual candidacy illustrates vividly the power of money in modern campaigning. He was able to get on the presidential ballot in all fifty states and enter the campaign late only because he was able and willing to spend vast amounts (estimated at $60 million) of his own money. And because he did not seek federal matching funds, there was no limit on how much he could spend legally.

In the past, wealthy men and women often spent large amounts of money supporting their favorite candidates. Since the reform of the campaign finance laws, however, they can only spend unlimited money on their own behalf. On several occasions wealthy candidates have won Senate seats by spending millions of their own dollars, but Perot was the first to try for the presidency this way—a much more expensive proposition. In 1996 Steve Forbes, another wealthy man with no political experience, spent an estimated $30 million of his own money in a credible attempt to win the Republican nomination.

While Perot did not win, receiving 19 percent of the national vote without any party support was a remarkable achievement for him. One can only wonder how well a candidate with Perot's resources but with greater political skills might perform. It is possible that Perot has pioneered a new route to the presidency, one that bypasses the established party machinery altogether.

CHAPTER 12

PARTY SYSTEMS IN
AMERICAN POLITICS

American politics has always been dominated and shaped by the competition between two political parties. Since 1856 the competition has been between the Democratic and Republican parties. The major parties thus have a long and continuous history, but inevitably they have also had to change over time as evolving economic and social conditions raise new concerns among the electorate. For examples, the Republican Party originally favored an active federal government but is now strongly opposed to big government; the Democratic Party, which for most of its history opposed black rights, is now overwhelmingly supported by black voters.

American parties have always been broad coalitions of different groups and interests. In order to assemble and maintain a national coalition that can win the presidency, a political party must develop national policy themes that broaden and unite its own coalition and differentiate it from the other party. It must respond to the prevailing national concerns. As the issues that concern the voters change, each party must adapt to keep its coalition together and possibly add to it. Sometimes the parties have succeeded at this, sometimes not.

As Table 12.1 shows, in the competition between the parties one party has usually dominated for several decades at a time. Each of these periods can be viewed as a distinct party system during which the pattern of competition between the two party

Table 12.1	Period terms/party	Presidential terms/party	Years	House control	Years
Party systems: Tenure of majority and minority parties.	2. Democratic system,				
	1828–60	6D	24	11D	22
		2Wh	8	3Wh	6
				2R	4
	3. Civil War system,				
	1860–96	7R	28	10R	20
		2D	8	8D	16
	4. Industrial system,				
	1896–1932	7R	28	15R	30
		2D	8	3D	6
	5. New Deal system,				
	1932–68	7D	28	16D	32
		2R	8	2R	4
	6. Divided government,				
	1968–96	5R	20	1R	2
		2D	8	13D	26

Parties: Democratic = D; Republican = R; Whig = Wh.

coalitions was basically stable. In each system one party was the majority party, meaning that it won the presidency and controlled the Congress and usually a majority of state governments most of the time. For the purposes of analysis, the 200-plus years of American history can be divided into six distinct two-party systems, each lasting around thirty years.

Canadian Party Systems

Recent scholarship has divided Canadian political history into three distinct party systems: 1867–1917, 1921–57, and 1963 to the present.[1] Because the Canadian and American political systems work differently, and because the political parties within them play different roles, a detailed comparison of the two sets of party systems is difficult. Several obvious differences are worth noting, however. In the United States, both major parties have enjoyed long periods of dominance; in Canada, the Liberal

---

1   See the three complementary articles that deal with different aspects of the party systems and the transition periods between them: David E. Smith, "Party Government in Canada," R.K. Carty, "Three Canadian Party Systems," and Richard Johnston, "The Electoral Basis of the Canadian Party Systems, 1878–1984," in R.K. Carty, ed., *Canadian Political Party Systems: A Reader* (Broadview Press, 1992).

Party has dominated politics since the middle of the first party system in 1896. Although this dominance has been in steady decline throughout the second and third party systems, the Liberal Party is still the "party of government."

A second difference is seen in the role third parties have played in the two countries. In the United States, third parties have been a force only in periods of party realignment, and none has lasted long. In Canada, by contrast, third parties have been a permanent feature in politics since the beginning of the second party system. One third party, the CCF/NDP, has played a continuing role since 1935 based on a social democratic philosophy. Others have been parties of regional protest—a reminder of how difficult it has been and still is to knit Canada's regions into a national whole.

THE AMERICAN PARTY PATTERN

As Table 12.1 indicates, the American pattern is one of long periods of relative party stability punctuated by rare shifts or upheavals. Once an American party builds a majority national coalition, it dominates politics at all levels for up to thirty years, until there is a realignment of the old coalitions. James L. Sundquist defines a realignment as "a durable shift in patterns of political behavior."[2]

Two aspects of this historical pattern need to be explained: the long periods of party stability; and the shift from one party system to another, known as party realignment.

Party stability. The stability of the party system between realignments can be explained by the long-term stability of individual and group loyalties to political parties once party coalitions are formed. A stable party system represents a stable distribution of loyalties or party identification (see Chapter 10). In the particular circumstances of each election there is always some movement of voters from one party to the other under the influence of short-term factors, particular candidates, and issues specific to that election, but such movement is usually not enough to disrupt the overall distribution of loyalties.

Over time, however, any particular alignment of loyalties tends to erode. Voters whose loyalties were created by the realigning events are joined and eventually replaced by their children, whose loyalties may not be as strong. The issues and the political leaders that created the realignment gradually fade from view, and new issues become important. In such a political climate, a realignment becomes possible.

---

2   James L. Sundquist, *Dynamics of the Party System: Alignment and Realignment of Political Parties in the United States*, Revised Edition (The Brookings Institution, 1983), 5; the original argument for the importance of critical elections in the realignment process is in Walter Dean Burnham, *Critical Elections: the Mainspring of American Politics* (Norton, 1970).

Realignment. Party systems are fairly stable over decades, but economic and social change is continuous. New issues arise and new interest groups form and these often cut across existing loyalties. The dominant party tries to deal with the new issues without disturbing its majority coalition, while the minority party tries to use the new issues to expand its own coalition.

For a realignment to take place, two conditions must be met: there must be a new issue of sufficient importance to detach large numbers of voters from their established loyalties; and the major parties must take opposing positions on the issue. It is when the major parties are attempting to deal with both old and new issues that third parties often emerge.

The Role of Third Parties

As is discussed in Chapter 13, there are strong pressures in the United States toward a two-party system. Third parties have always been confined to particular regions and have rarely lasted long. Most third parties are protest parties, formed to protest the

	Period	Majority Party	Minority Party	Significant 3rd Parties
Table 12.2 *American party systems.*	1. Founding system, 1796–1828	Jefferson Republicans	Federalists	
	2. Democratic system, 1828–60	Democrats	Whigs	Abolitionist Free Soil
	3. Civil War system, 1860–96	Republicans Prohibition	Democrats	Greenbacker Populist
	4. Industrial system, 1896–1932	Republicans	Democrats	Socialist Progressive
	5. New Deal system, 1932–68	Democrats	Republicans	Dixiecrat American Independent
	6. Divided government 1968–?	Republican dominance of presidency; democratic dominance of Congress and government, states		

Note: The boundaries between the systems are marked by presidential elections. In fact there were periods of transition between the systems.

neglect of certain interests by both major parties. The emergence of third parties has most often signaled the rise of an important new issue and a coming change in the party system. Thus the Abolitionist candidates for president in 1842 and 1844 and the Free Soil candidates in 1848 and 1852 were signs of growing anger in the North over slavery and over southern influence in Washington. These movements led to the formation of the Republican Party (1854) and the realignment of the party system (1856–60). Similarly, the appearance of western protest parties—the Grangers, the Greenbackers, and the Populists—after the 1870s reflected the economic upheaval of the times. On the heels of these protest movements, the parties were realigned in 1896.

Note that since 1968, American party politics has broken out of its historical pattern: one party (the Republicans) has dominated presidential politics while the other (the Democrats) has controlled Congress and most of the states. Possible explanations for this change in pattern are discussed at the end of the chapter.

The First Party System[3]

The first generation of American political leaders were eighteenth-century men who despised political parties as destructive of the broad consensus they believed was necessary for free government. Nevertheless, parties quickly formed in the new republic as the group of leaders who had united to create the national government found themselves bitterly divided over the direction it should take. The first party, the Republicans, formed around Thomas Jefferson in opposition to Alexander Hamilton, who as treasury secretary had set about expanding the national government's power. Jefferson favored a democratic republic of independent farmers; Hamilton and the Federalist Party saw economic development as the engine of progress.

At the time, there were property qualifications for voting, and party politics consisted mainly of maneuverings among cliques of political officeholders. Neither the Jeffersonian Republicans nor the Federalists accepted the legitimacy of an opposition party, and each expected to obliterate the other. It was not clear how far the political warfare would go as the Federalist government of President John Adams attempted to silence its opponents with the Alien and Sedition Acts of 1798. A crucial test was passed when Adams peacefully handed over power to Jefferson, the winner of the election of 1800.

Once in power, the Republicans moderated their opposition to government activism. Once out of power, the Federalist Party was unable to sustain a national

---

3   There is a substantial literature on each of the party systems. For recent summary articles, see
     L. Sandy Maisel and William G. Shade, eds., *Parties and Politics in American History: A
     Reader* (Garland Publishing, 1994).

challenge, and politics returned to something like a national consensus. The presidential nomination was decided by agreement among the members of Congress, and the succession passed from Jefferson to Madison to Monroe; all three were Virginians, and each won two terms with little opposition. The "era of good feelings" came to an end over the presidential election of 1824. General Andrew Jackson, a national hero but a political outsider, led both in popular votes and in the Electoral College but the House of Representatives passed him over to select John Quincy Adams. Furious with the political elite, Jackson turned to Martin Van Buren, who had built a powerful political organization in New York state. Van Buren secured Jackson's election in 1828.

President Jackson's policies and Van Buren's new style of machine politics polarized both the politicians and the electorate. Jackson's supporters became the Democratic Republicans and eventually the Democrats; his opponents became the National Republicans and eventually the Whigs. To help express their opposition to what they saw as the dictatorial powers of "King Andrew," the Whigs had taken the name of the eighteenth-century English opponents of the power of the king.

The Second Party System: The Founding of the Democratic Party

The second party system represented a complete break with the earlier style of politics. The spread of democratic ideas and Jackson's well-organized campaigns greatly increased public interest and participation in national politics. The new democratic politics required new forms of political organization, and it was the Democrats under Jackson and Van Buren who established those forms which would come to characterize nineteenth-century American politics: the urban "machine"; strong state-party organizations; national conventions to nominate presidential candidates and rally the national party; and the use of presidential power and federal patronage to build party organizations.

The Democratic Party claims both Thomas Jefferson and Andrew Jackson as its founders. As an organization, the party was founded under Jackson, but intellectually and in terms of its animating spirit, it can trace its descent from the old Republican Party of Thomas Jefferson. Although radically different in style, Jackson and Jefferson shared the same broad political views: both saw the independent farmer as the backbone of the republic; both saw the power of the national government as the principal threat to individual liberty and were strong supporters of state and local rights; both feared the power of financiers and big businessmen to manipulate government; and both saw themselves as supporters of "the people" against all threats to their liberties. The Democratic Party from its earliest days has seen itself as the party of the common man. Characteristically, it has been more open to outsiders and newcomers, and more pluralistic and secular than its opponents.

By the 1850s the policy differences that had shaped the second party system were becoming overshadowed by rising tensions over the future of slavery. As the number of states expanded, the southern states found themselves increasingly outnumbered; for them, it came to seem essential that slavery not be prohibited in the western territories. Many in the North perceived as a threat to their liberty even the possibility that slavery could spread outside the South. As North and South became increasingly polarized, most national institutions were torn between their northern and southern components, not least the two national parties. The Whigs, who were supported mainly by northern evangelicals (strongly opposed to slavery) and by better-off southerners (many of them slave holders), were the first party to fall apart.

Some northern Democrats made strenuous efforts to find a new compromise on the slavery issue that would hold the national Democratic coalition together. Senator Stephen Douglas's Kansas-Nebraska Act to repeal the earlier congressional ban and allow the western territories to decide the question of slavery for themselves boomeranged badly. His efforts inflamed northerners, triggered violence in the territories, and in the end failed to satisfy the South. In 1860 the southern state delegations walked out of the Democratic national convention, which nominated Douglas, and chose their own candidate. The election was fought between two northern and two southern candidates; the resulting fragmentation of the electorate allowed Abraham Lincoln, candidate of the new Republican Party, to win with 40 percent of the national vote by sweeping the northern states. For the first time, a president had been elected without any support in the South.

◄ The Founding of the Republican Party

The issue that brought about the formation of the Republican Party was opposition to slavery and to what was seen as the southern states' growing determination to impose slavery on the West. Abolitionist candidates had run in the elections of 1840 and 1844, but without making much impact. Growing dissatisfaction in the North with the equivocal positions of both major parties on the slavery issue led to the establishment of the more moderate and broadly based Free Soil Party, which contested the elections in 1848 and 1852. The growing polarization between North and South over slavery tore apart the Whig Party and in the end also split the Democrats. The new Republican Party was formed in the North out of northern Whigs and Free Soilers, most of whom were former Democrats.

The Third Party System

The sweeping victory of Abraham Lincoln and the Republicans in the northern and western states in 1860 precipitated the secession of the southern states and brought on the Civil War. As a result of the war, the Republicans became not just the anti-slavery party but the party of the Union. They proceeded to solidify their majority status outside the South.

The outbreak of the Civil War placed the Democrats on the defensive. While most northern Democrats supported the war, the party would for long be tainted by its pro-southern heritage. It was a tribute to the strength of their basic Jacksonian appeal that the Democrats survived as a national party at all. The impact of the war on Democratic Party fortunes was twofold:

First: Once the last federal troops left the southern states in 1876, the South became a solidly Democratic domain, especially after blacks were effectively excluded from politics. The total Democratic dominance of the region even spilled over into several of the border states and areas, such as southern Indiana, which had been originally settled by southerners. This Democratic hegemony lasted for a century and only started to weaken in the 1950s. The southern states thus provided the Democratic Party with a solid base of support, but for a long time its dependence on the South was a liability for the party in the rest of the country.

Second: Much of the North, and especially the midwestern and prairie states, became almost as solidly Republican as the South was Democratic. However, the Democrats retained the loyalty of groups such as the Irish, who had become an important voting block in the northern cities; and as a result they remained competitive in states like New York, New Jersey, and Connecticut.

So the Democratic Party survived during the third party system as an awkward coalition between the white South (where anti-Catholic as well as anti-black sentiment was strong) and the northern urban-party machines, which were often run by Irish Catholics.

The Republicans dominated national politics after the war, but in the 1870s their popularity began to fade. There were several reasons: middle-class revulsion at the rampant corruption in Washington and in many state governments; the emergence among Republicans of divisive moral issues, the key one being prohibition; and a sharp economic downturn that began in 1873. This latter event ended any chance the Republicans had of establishing themselves in the South; it also solidified working-class support for the Democrats in the North. Between 1874 and 1892 the two parties were in tight competition nationally, with the Democrats winning the presidency in 1884 and 1892.

The rapid growth of the American economy after the Civil War, and the accompanying development of large industrial and financial monopolies, began to polarize the United States along a new dividing line never before seen: between the industrializing states of the Northeast and Midwest and the farming and mining states of the West. Western farmers, finding themselves burdened with debt and at the mercy of the railroad and grain storage monopolies, protested that both major parties were being dictated to by business and financial interests. In general terms, the industrial states were supportive of the *laissez-faire* and sound-money policies of the national parties, while the western states wanted regulation of monopolies and a looser, more inflationary monetary policy. The latter could mean the use of silver (mined in the West) as well as gold to back the currency, or, alternatively, the use of paper currency ("greenbacks").

The western protests came in waves. Greenbacker candidates ran in several elections in the 1870s but made little impact. In the 1890s a new Populist Party was formed; in the presidential election of 1892, its candidate won several western states and close to 10 percent of the total vote. The clash of issues and values came to a head in the election of 1896. The Republicans, now convinced that industrial development and *laissez-faire* constituted the wave of the future, nominated William McKinley of Ohio. The Democratic Party was badly divided, but in the end loyalty to the heritage of Jefferson and Jackson won out and it nominated a western crusader from Nebraska, William Jennings Bryan. When the Populists also supported Bryan, the stage was set for a showdown between the old America of the independent farmer and the new, Republican vision of a business-oriented America.

In the critical election of 1896, McKinley won by sweeping all of the Northeast and Midwest, where most Americans lived. After uniting with the Populists, the Democrats picked up support in the West, while retaining the solid South; but they lost ground in the East, since Bryan, a small-town Protestant fundamentalist and supporter of prohibition, had no appeal to the urban immigrant working class.

The Fourth Party System

By identifying with the American Dream in a time of rapid economic growth, the Republican Party dominated this era to an even greater extent than the previous one. The Democratic Party, by continuing to identify with a shrinking rural America, found itself at its lowest ebb nationally.

Although the radical proposals of the Populists had been defeated, the period from 1900 to 1920 was one of substantial reform. Pressure for reform came from the Progressive movement, which was led by urban professionals whose main aim was to modernize government and clean up the political process. The Progressives never coalesced into a political party. While most of them were Republican in background, they were influential in both major parties. Republican president Teddy Roosevelt (1901–09) was a major supporter of reform, and when the Republican Party split between progressive and traditional factions in 1912, a progressive Democrat, Woodrow Wilson (1913–21), was elected.

After World War I the reform era was over. The American economy was booming, and faith in *laissez-faire* policies and traditional Republicanism had been fully restored. The Democratic Party was once again reduced to a small minority, its only stronghold the backward rural South. The attempt to rally Progressives behind the third-party candidacy of Robert LaFollette in 1924 had little impact.

The era of prosperity, *laissez-faire*, and Republicanism came to a sudden end with the stock market crash of October 1929, which ushered in the Great Depression. President Herbert Hoover accepted the dictates of classical economics that the economy would eventually return to equilibrium and was reluctant to sanction government intervention. Meanwhile, the Depression deepened, the unemployment rate soared, and rural areas found themselves doubly inflicted by widespread drought. In these circumstances, it was inevitable that the opposition Democrats would win the election of 1932. The new president, Franklin D. Roosevelt (FDR), had been a progressive member of President Wilson's Cabinet and, more recently, an activist governor of New York. He had campaigned on a fairly traditional platform, but once in office he transformed American politics.

The Fifth Party System

Politically, the contrast with the previous system was stark: the Republicans had placed their faith in market forces, and now the Democrats were resorting to active government intervention. FDR set about quickly to use the federal government's power to alleviate the Depression. The first wave of the New Deal was a massive federal intervention to regulate industry, finance, and agriculture. While most of these policies were short-lived, they indicated that the government was suddenly more than ready to tackle economic and social problems. The legacy of the New Deal would include a set of national regulatory agencies, recognition of the union movement, government management of agricultural production, and the first national welfare legislation.

Voter response to the New Deal and to FDR's charisma remade the old Democratic Party into a new majority coalition. For the first time in their history, the Republicans were reduced to a minority in most of the country. To its traditional stronghold in the South, the Democrats added most of the urban working-class groups, many of them Catholic and of non-Anglo-Saxon heritage (the "ethnic" voters). While the Irish had always been loyal Democrats, many of these other groups had never been politically mobilized before. Jewish voters, traditionally connected to the Republican Party, switched in large numbers to the Democrats. Even in the black communities in the North, which had been devoted to the Republican Party since its founding, there was movement toward the Democrats as a result of New Deal policies.

More than at any other time in American history, the division between the two parties was a class division. Working-class and labor union support went solidly to the Democrats, while the Republicans took most of the middle- and upper-class votes.

Democrats dominated urban areas in all parts of the country. Republicans generally won only in the suburbs and in rural areas outside the South. For their own historical reasons, the southern states remained one-party Democratic.

The division between the parties was also one of policy. Here, the dividing line was the New Deal. Political liberals supported the use of government to deal with economic and social problems; political conservatives opposed this and wanted to minimize both the role of government and government expenditures. The terms *liberal* and *conservative* also described the divisions within both national party coalitions. Under Roosevelt the Democratic Party outside the South became overwhelmingly liberal. The situation in the South was quite different. Since the Civil War virtually all white southerners had been Democrats. Blacks were almost completely excluded from politics, and the Republican Party scarcely existed outside a few counties in the Appalachians. While New Deal policies appealed to the poorer elements in the South, most of the southern leaders remained conservative Democrats wary of the federal government.

Paradoxically, the New Deal greatly increased the South's national influence. As part of the new majority coalition, southern Democrats came to wield great power in Congress as chairs of key committees in both Houses. Indeed, between 1938 and 1964, most attempts by liberal Democrats at further social reform were blocked in Congress by an informal conservative coalition of southern Democrats and Republicans. While they disagreed strongly with New Deal policies, southern Democrats had no incentive to give up power by leaving the party, and the rest of the party was unwilling to give the Republican Party an opening in the South by forcing the conservative southerners to leave.

Faced with a majority Democratic coalition, the minority Republican Party divided into two camps: those who advocated some accommodation with liberal policies, and those who wanted a return to traditional *laissez-faire*. Generally, the more liberal Republicans of the Northeast won out over the conservatives of the Midwest and West. After losing five presidential elections in a row between 1932 and 1948, the Republicans finally hit on a winning formula in 1952 by choosing a nonpolitician, General Dwight Eisenhower, the military commander of World War II, as their presidential candidate. But Eisenhower's two easy victories in 1952 and 1956 were largely personal triumphs and did little to change national policies or the minority status of the Republican party across the country.

In the 1960s the Democrats reasserted their dominance in national politics After John F. Kennedy's narrow victory in the presidential campaign of 1960, several factors raised the party to new heights of popularity: the appeal of a youthful, glamorous president; the wave of idealism surrounding the final stages of the civil rights movement; the surge of emotion after President Kennedy's assassination, which was ably used by his successor, Lyndon Johnson, to secure passage of the Civil Rights Act of

1964; and the capture of the Republican presidential nomination by a new set of southwestern conservatives headed by Senator Barry Goldwater.

In 1964 the Democrats won an overwhelming victory at every level. Many liberal Republicans, repelled by Goldwater's hard-line, anti-New Deal policies, had supported the Democrats. So many new liberal Democrats were elected to Congress that the conservative coalition was finally swept aside and a whole new liberal reform agenda, labeled the Great Society program, was passed into law. Many commentators believed that a new realignment had formed and predicted a new era of Democratic dominance. Yet by 1968 the Democratic Party was bitterly divided and the New Deal party system was finished. Two issues divided the Democratic Party and ended its national majority status: civil rights and the Vietnam War.

◂ The Impact of Civil Rights on the Democratic Party

In the 1960s, Democratic Party sponsorship of civil rights for black Americans placed the national party in flat opposition to white southerners, who had always been determined to maintain racial segregation. It was this direct clash that brought the century-old Democratic monopoly of southern politics to an end.

The formation of the New Deal coalition had not at first lifted the Democratic Party's traditional indifference to black interests. But during World War II rural southern blacks began migrating into the northern cities in large numbers. This increased the awareness of northern liberals about the situation in the southern states. The growing liberal concern about black rights erupted at the Democrats' national convention in 1948, when northern liberals led by Hubert Humphrey voted to place a commitment to civil rights in the party platform. The vote triggered a walkout by many southern delegates, who threw their support to an independent candidate, the "Dixiecrat" Strom Thurmond, who won four states in the Deep South in the presidential election.

In the 1950s, as the black crusade for civil rights got under way, led by Dr. Martin Luther King, both major parties found themselves caught between conflicting forces. The Democrats needed the continued support of the southern Democrats, who were using their power in Congress to block or water down civil rights legislation. Under Eisenhower the Republicans remained indifferent to civil rights issues, with Republican conservatives arguing that such matters should continue to be left to the states.

It was only in the early 1960s, after support began rising in the North for Dr. King and the black cause, and after the sight of white southern repression could no longer be avoided (because it was on television in every region), that President Kennedy fully committed the government and the Democrats to the civil rights cause. Between 1964 and 1968 a series of important civil rights measures were passed under Democratic sponsorship. When their own Democratic Party brought about the end of segregation, most white southerners abandoned the national party. In 1964 the Deep South voted for Goldwater, who supported states' rights. In 1968 the same region supported George Wallace's American Independent Party, while the rest of the South voted for Nixon. The Democrats had lost their greatest stronghold.

In the North the reaction to civil rights was twofold. First, black voters completed their shift to the Democratic Party and became that party's most reliable supporters across the country. Second, many working-class whites in the North felt threatened by the changes. As the Democrats moved to end racial discrimination in housing and employment, and as busing became widely practiced as a means to integrate the public schools in many cities, the Democrats found their support eroding among the white working class.

The Impact of the Vietnam War on the Democratic Party

The American involvement in Vietnam was a logical extension of the policy of containing communism—a policy that both major parties had supported since the start of the Cold War. This involvement had grown gradually under Eisenhower and Kennedy until President Johnson was faced with a choice: Should he increase the scale of military involvement? Or should he pull out altogether? His decision in 1965 to send American combat troops to Vietnam quickly transformed a foreign policy issue that had attracted little public attention into a burning issue of domestic politics.

The Vietnam War coincided with the entry into politics of the first of the postwar "baby boom" generation. The war clashed not only with their interests (since it was necessary to reinstitute the draft to find enough troops to send to Vietnam), but also with their idealism, which had already been aroused by the civil rights struggle. Opposition to the war flourished in the universities and developed into a loosely structured national anti-war movement that organized mass protests and marches in Washington and across the country.

Politically, the struggle was fought out within the Democratic Party. The war was being directed by President Johnson, who was strongly supported by most working-class Democrats and southerners. At the same time, however, the natural home for the anti-war movement was the Democratic Party, which since the New Deal had been the party of reform. The party that had been energized and united by its Great Society program of domestic reforms became bitterly divided over the war. In 1968 the anti-war forces devoted their energies to nominating an anti-war presidential candidate and committing the party to ending the war. Their efforts were blocked by the party leadership at the turbulent National Convention in Chicago.

Opposition to the war continued until the final American withdrawal in 1973, but after 1968 the targets were President Nixon and the Republican Party. After the Democrats were defeated in 1968, anti-war Democrats took over the national machinery of the party—a development that further alienated both white southerners, with their long military tradition, and working-class northerners, for whom support for the war was a matter of unquestioned patriotism.

⁂ The Democratic Party After 1968

The Democrats entered the 1970s badly divided. The division over the war opened up more general divisions over foreign policy. Many Democrats became critical of how their country was applying its military and economic power abroad. Many of them also supported emerging new "rights" issues: affirmative action against discrimination for minorities and for women; the rights of accused persons; opposition to the death penalty; homosexual rights; abortion rights; and so on. All of these were controversial and were instinctively opposed by socially conservative working-class and southern Democrats. The terms *liberal* and *conservative* began to be defined in terms of these and other social issues rather than economic issues.

Since the New Deal the Democratic coalition's great strength had been the party's reputation for using government to keep the economy growing. Throughout the 1950s and 1960s the postwar boom had continued to raise living standards in the United States. But in the 1970s across the Western world, confidence in the ability of governments to manage the economy began declining steadily as both inflation and unemployment rose out of control. In the United States the economic troubles peaked under President Carter. This deprived the Democrats of their traditional economic trump card in national politics, as well as their main unifying issue.

As can be seen from Table 12.2, the problems these changes caused for the Democratic Party were felt largely at the presidential level. It is at this level that divisions within a party are most difficult to conceal. On the traditional national issues—the economy, foreign policy, and some new social and cultural issues—the Democrats found themselves divided and on the defensive against a powerful new conservative attack. At the state level, Democrats found it easier to avoid these issues or to adjust their positions for local consumption.

The Democrats' national difficulties were greatly compounded by radical changes in the system for nominating presidential candidates—changes that had been brought about by the anti-war Democrats after 1968 (see Chapter 11). Once the process had been democratized and the influence of party leaders had been removed, the party activists found their influence greatly increased. Most of these activists belonged to the most liberal end of the party. As a result, the Democrats nominated several northern liberals—McGovern in 1972, Mondale in 1984, Dukakis in 1988—who had no appeal in the South or among social conservatives. They lost those elections.

The only Democrats to win the presidency since 1964 have been two southerners, Jimmy Carter and Bill Clinton. Carter, little known in the party, took skillful advantage of the new nominating system to win the nomination in 1976. The fact that Carter was a southerner and a born-again Christian broadened his appeal among conservative voters, though the most important factor in his victory was the demoralization of the Republican Party after the Watergate scandal. Clinton in 1992 won the nomination in the absence of several of the party heavyweights, and then defeat-ed the weak Republican incumbent, George Bush.

Though weak in presidential elections, the Democrats remained strong at other levels, even in the South. Although the Republican Party was picking up strength steadily in the South, the strong Democratic tradition there as well as the great increase in black voting after the Voting Rights Act of 1965 kept the Democrats viable in the southern states. The Democrats also remained strong at the state level, and this in turn helped them maintain control of Congress until 1995. In addition, congres-sional incumbents—most of them Democrats—became highly skilled at using the perquisites of office and the campaign finance laws to keep getting re-elected.

The Republican Party After 1968
Richard Nixon was elected narrowly with a minority of the total vote in 1968 and promptly set about securing his re-election. His main targets were disaffected, social-ly conservative Democrats in both the South and the North who were opposed to the civil rights revolution and changes in social and sexual mores. Nixon exploited issues such as urban crime, and attacked liberal court decisions, and automatically gained the support of those who supported the war. The Democratic Party played into his hands by nominating an anti-war candidate, Senator George McGovern, in 1972. Nixon's overwhelming victory in that year seemed to herald a realignment of the party system: a new national Republican coalition that included white southerners and northern working-class voters stolen from the Democrats.

But Nixon was so desperate to triumph that his aides resorted to a variety of ille-gal methods to help him. Such were the roots of the Watergate scandal. Nixon's attempts to cover up the Watergate scandal led to his resignation in 1974, just ahead of certain impeachment by the House of Representatives. As result of the scandal, Republicans lost heavily in that year's congressional elections; two years later, Nixon's appointed successor Gerald Ford, who had pardoned the ex-president, was defeated by Jimmy Carter.

Nixon, whose main passion was foreign policy, had pursued a pragmatic course in domestic policy. Mainly, this meant acquiescing in the Democratic Congress's initia-tives on environmental, consumer, and worker protection issues. After Nixon's down-fall the party became increasingly dominated by a new, hard-line conservatism that emphasized two things: a return to an aggressive stance against the Soviet Union (Nixon and his principal adviser Henry Kissinger had pursued detente with the Communist powers), and an aggressive anti-government stance that opposed most of what the New Deal/Great Society tradition stood for. The conservative take-over of the Republican Party was able to draw on new resources from the South, the new Christian Right, the conservative intellectual revival, and grass-roots revolts against "big government."

The South. National Democratic sponsorship of the civil rights movement in the South broke the century-old Democratic monopoly of white southern allegiance and provided an opening for the Republican Party in the southern states for the first time in its history. At the same time, the end of segregation made the South attractive to new business investment. There was an influx of northerners, and cities such as Atlanta, Dallas, and Houston grew rapidly in the 1970s. The new southern Republican party had the most success among middle-class whites in the cities and suburbs; but it also now drew on the tradition of religious conservatism across the region.

In spite of its new appeal in the generally conservative region, the Republicans did not immediately sweep the South: the Democratic tradition was too strong to be quickly displaced. Also, southern blacks voted overwhelmingly for Democrats. It was not until 1994 that Republicans constituted a majority of the southern congressional delegations, and even in 1996 they still did not control both houses of any southern state legislature.

The new Christian Right. Traditionally, conservative Christians had been wary of involvement in politics. They were, however, disturbed by many of the social changes that had transpired in American society in the 1960s and by the Supreme Court decisions banning prayer in public schools and permitting abortion. A new style of "televangelism" fed these concerns and provided linkage between various groups.[4] A group of conservative political operatives sensed that this worried religious constituency might be persuaded to mobilize itself behind the Republican Party. To coordinate the Republicans' appeal to conservative Christians, this group set up a political umbrella-group, the Moral Majority, headed by Jerry Falwell, one of the best-known TV evangelists.[5]

The conservative intellectual revival. Ever since the New Deal, liberal thinkers had held the intellectual initiative in the United States. Most conservative thinkers, of whom there were few, looked back to the *laissez-faire* era of the 1920s. By the 1970s, however, the initiative had begun to shift strongly to a new generation of conservative thinkers. Sidney Blumenthal traces the origins of this conservative revival back to 1955, when the magazine *National Review* was founded by William F. Buckley. With New Deal liberalism triumphant in the 1960s, supporters of hard anti-communist, anti–New Deal positions were greatly in the minority. Barry Goldwater's pronouncements during his 1964 presidential campaign were almost universally ridiculed by the

---

4   On the televangelism phenomenon, see Steve Bruce, *Pray TV: Televangelism in America* (Routledge, 1990).

5   See Steve Bruce, *The Rise and Fall of the New Christian Right: Conservative Protestant Politics in America, 1978–1988* (Clarendon Press, 1988).

Vice-President Gerald Ford and Mrs. Ford escort Richard Nixon and Mrs. Nixon to a helicopter on the South Lawn of the White House after Nixon's resignation.

intellectual community. But by the mid–1970s such arguments were finding a much more receptive audience.[6]

Both the turmoil over Vietnam and the extensive new programs of the Great Society had created an intellectual backlash against "liberal extremism." The downturn in the economy in the 1970s was seen as demonstrating the failure of Keynesian economics, and provided a new audience for conservative economists such as Friedrich von Hayek and Milton Friedman. The movement was joined by a number of former Democratic intellectuals, labeled "neoconservatives," who were strongly anticommunist, had supported the Vietnam War, and were disenchanted with what they saw as the excesses of liberal domestic policy in the 1960s.[7]

By the late 1970s the new conservative ideas were being developed and publicized through a network of new journals and research institutions, including think tanks such as the American Enterprise Institute and the Heritage Foundation. Conservative intellectuals had largely seized the initiative in the national political debate from the formerly dominant New Deal liberals, who were forced more and more on the defensive about their past achievements.

---

6   Sidney Blumenthal, *The Rise of the Counter-Establishment: From Conservative Ideology to Political Power* (Times Books, 1986).
7   See Gary Dorrien, *The Neo-Conservative Mind: Politics, Culture, and the War of Ideology* (Temple University Press, 1993).

Grass roots revolts against big government. The geographical roots of the new conservatism were in the southwest. Goldwater was from Arizona, Reagan from
California, and both their candidacies were heavily backed by money from wealthy
southern California entrepreneurs. The turnaround in public attitudes to government
has been dated to the "tax revolt" in California with the passage in 1978 of
Proposition 13, a voter initiative that amended the state constitution to severely limit
increases in local property taxes. Other signs were the "sagebrush rebellion" in the
western states against federal regulation of land use, and the formation of new business lobbies, such as the Business Roundtable, in reaction to increasing regulation.

All of the elements of the New Right came together behind the presidential candidacy of Ronald Reagan in 1980. Reagan, a former movie actor, had established his
political credibility as governor of California from 1967 to 1975. He had almost succeeded in winning the Republican nomination from President Ford in 1976 and won it
easily the next time. His easygoing personality and unabashed patriotism, and
his actor's ability to read convincingly from a text, made him an attractive spokesman for the conservative cause. Reagan won the presidency in 1980, with coattails
long enough to give the Republicans control of the Senate for the first time in twenty-
five years.

In office, Reagan was able to achieve the New Right's immediate objectives: to cut
income taxes substantially, increase spending on defense, and take a more aggressive
stance toward the Soviet Union. But he was faced with a Democratic House of
Representatives and luke-warm support from many moderate Republicans, so his
more sweeping plans to cut back federal programs and enact the conservative social
agenda bogged down. Reagan's personal success had surprisingly little impact on the
overall fortunes of the Republican Party. The Democrats won back the Senate in 1986,
and by the end of the decade they were almost as strongly positioned in Congress and
the states as they had been at the beginning. Clearly there had been no Republican
realignment under Reagan.

The failure of the New Right to prevent the succession of Vice President George
Bush, whose commitment to conservatism was doubtful, underscored the fact that as
a group, they lacked a new standard bearer with anything close to Ronald Reagan's
broad personal appeal. The Christian Right, seeing little progress on the social issues
most important to them, were forced to regroup. Jerry Falwell closed down his Moral
Majority organization in 1989. In 1988 the campaign of Pat Robertson, a rival
televangelist, for the Republican nomination to succeed Reagan failed badly.
Robertson, however, emerged as the Christian Right's leading figure. He was
determined to use the political process (and the Republican Party in particular)
to return America to its Christian heritage. After his political defeat, he founded
a new organization, the Christian Coalition, for which he set out a two-pronged strategy: build a national grass-roots organization, and lobby more effectively in

Washington.[8] The New Right remained in firm control of the Republican Party, but it seemed to many that by the late 1980s the conservative "revolution" might be over. A period of political and policy stalemate had set in.

THE PARTY SYSTEM IN THE NINETIES

At the start of the decade the Democrats remained firmly in control of Congress. The election of President Clinton in 1992 during an economic recession placed the policy reins back in Democratic hands. The recession had raised public anxiety about the availability and cost of health care, and Clinton set out to find a comprehensive solution to the problem, which had eluded all his Democratic predecessors since FDR. Clinton's proposal, when he finally unveiled it, was a cumbersome compromise that aroused little enthusiasm within his divided party. Different aspects of the plan were attacked by the various health care interests; the business/labor coalition the president tried to build in its support unraveled quickly; and the Republicans had no difficulty blocking action in Congress.[9] The centerpiece of the Democratic agenda had collapsed, and in the 1994 elections the Republicans took control of both houses of Congress for the first time in fifty years.

The second wave of the conservative assault on Washington came from an unexpected source: inside the House of Representatives, where the Republicans had been an impotent minority for forty years. A small group of young conservative activists who called themselves the Conservative Opportunity Society had started plotting a long-term take-over strategy in the mid–1980s. Their leader, Newt Gingrich of Georgia, had a two-part strategy: destroy the Democrats' reputation in the House, and recruit qualified conservative Republican candidates for the House.

Undermining the Democrats. Gingrich attacked the Democratic House leadership as corrupted by their long, unchallenged rule. His greatest coup came when his attacks on Speaker Jim Wright's financial dealings forced Wright to resign in 1989. The same year, the Democratic whip, Tony Coelho, also resigned over problems with his personal finances. The press picked up the corruption issue, and before long a number of scandals in the management of the House were uncovered that implicated a large number of members, most of them Democrats. In 1993 one of the most powerful Democrats, Dan Rostenkowski, chair of the Ways and Means Committee, was indicted for corruption. He eventually went to jail.

---

8   See Matthew Moen, "From Revolution to Evolution: The Changing Nature of the Christian Right," *Sociology of Religion* 55 (1994).

9   Haynes Johnson and David Broder, *The System: The American Way of Politics at the Breaking Point* (Simon & Schuster, 1996).

Table 12.3	Election		Defeat		
Turnover in membership	year	Retirement	Primary	General election	Total
of the House of					
Representatives,	1986	38	2	6	46
1986–96.	1988	23	1	6	30
	1990	27	1	15	43
	1992	65	19	24	108
	1994	48	4	34	86
	1996	50	2	20	72

Retirement figures include those seeking other offices. Figures compiled from *Congressional Quarterly, Weekly Reports.*

Gingrich's highly effective campaign against the Democratic control of Congress exploited the public's gut feeling that there was something badly wrong with how things were being done in Washington. Starting in 1992 there was a significant increase in the number of House members retiring and of incumbent members being defeated for renomination or re-election. The Democrats' advantage of incumbency was being whittled down by Gingrich's assaults.

Recruiting conservative candidates. The National Republican Congressional Committee had been involved in recruiting and training candidates for Congress for some time, but Gingrich decided a more long-range and focused campaign was needed. Using an established political action committee, GOPAC, he concentrated on finding and supporting candidates first of all for state offices. After a few years they would have the experience to run for the House. He also made an effort to motivate these candidates with a unified conservative message calling for radical change in Washington (Gingrich supplied them with tapes of his lectures).[10]

After the 1990 census, GOPAC also became actively involved in helping Republican state legislators redraw the House districts. In particular, Republicans in some southern states cooperated with black legislators in concentrating black voters in new "majority minority districts." This concentration not only increased the number of black members of Congress dramatically but also helped the Republicans by taking black, mostly Democratic, voters out of other Democratic districts.[11] The shake-up

10   On Gingrich's campaign, see Connie Bruck, "The Politics of Perception," *The New Yorker*, October 9, 1995.
11   In *Shaw v. Reno* 113 S.Ct. 2816 (1993) the Supreme Court ruled that race could not be the predominant factor in drawing district lines. As a result, in subsequent cases the majority minority districts in Georgia, Louisiana, North Carolina, Florida, Texas, Illinois, and New York had to be redrawn for the 1996 or 1998 elections.

caused by redistricting contributed to the increase in retirements and incumbent defeats in 1992.

Gingrich also initiated a much more aggressive Republican strategy in Congress. The long-established policy of the House Republican leadership had been to cooperate with the majority Democrats in return for some influence on legislation; now Gingrich and his associates adopted a confrontational approach. For example, they used the new C–Span television channel of congressional proceedings as a daily forum for attacking the Democrats and propounding conservative ideas. In 1989 Gingrich was narrowly elected to the number-two position of Republican whip; from that base, he gradually extended his control over party operations. As support for Gingrich's tactics grew, the longtime minority leader, Robert Michel, was persuaded to retire in 1994 to make way for Gingrich.

The election of President Clinton presented the Republicans with a window of opportunity in 1994, since the president's party usually loses House seats in the off-year elections. Gingrich executed an unprecedented party strategy for the elections by announcing with great fanfare a party platform to which he had persuaded most Republican members and candidates to pledge support. The "Contract with America" was a ten-point conservative program that had been carefully tested by polling and in focus groups, and from which divisive issues such as abortion, gun control, and the social agenda of the Christian Right had been excluded.

As a campaign strategy to motivate and unite the Republicans and throw the Democrats on the defensive, the contract succeeded brilliantly. Against all expectations, the Republicans gained a net fifty-three seats—the largest pickup in many years and enough for them to take control of the House for the first time since 1954.[12] The Republicans also won back control of the Senate and had a near-record performance in state gubernatorial and legislative elections.

As the new Speaker of the House of Representatives, Gingrich was in an unusually powerful position as Republican party spokesman. He had been the winning strategist and he had mapped out a coherent legislative program. Also, many of the new Republican members in both the House and Senate were conservative "true believers" who had been recruited by him over the previous ten years. Sure of his mandate, Gingrich immediately led his narrow Republican majority in the House in an all-out assault on many of the programs the Democrats had established during the Great Society era.

The vehicle to bring about the "Republican revolution" was the 1996 budget. The appropriations bills and budget resolutions not only slashed expenditures for Democratic social programs but proposed the elimination of a host of regulations

---

12 So unexpected was the Republican majority that a book on the House Republicans published earlier the same year was entitled *Congress' Permanent Minority? Republicans in the U.S. House*, William F. Connelly Jr. and John J. Pitney Jr. (Littlefield Adams, 1994).

that had been passed by both Democratic and Republican administrations. For the longer run, the House Republicans proposed radical alterations in Medicare, Medicaid, and various welfare programs. By the end of 1995, however, the radical agenda had run into the realities of the separation of powers in Washington.

First, all of the measures passed by the House had to be watered down to win the support of the moderate Republicans who held the balance of power in the Senate. Second, the radicalism of the House Republicans had the effect of unifying the Democrats in Congress and encouraging President Clinton to veto most of the Republican appropriations bills. When the congressional Republicans tried to force the president's hand by allowing large parts of the federal government to run out of funds and shut down for three weeks, their popularity fell sharply. Speaker Gingrich found himself the most unpopular politician in America. The revolution ground to a halt.[13] The 104th Congress ended in a flurry of moderate compromises between the Republicans and the president as each side realized it needed a legislative record to show the voters.

President Clinton's first term thus saw the failure of the traditional Democratic policy approach in the first two years and the failure of a radical conservative Republican agenda in the second two. The radicalism of the House Republicans enabled Clinton to position himself in 1996 as the defender of popular programs, such as Medicare and environmental regulation, and as a political and social moderate. Clinton was easily re-elected; the Republicans held on to the Congress, but with only a narrow majority in the House.

At the end of the 1990s the Democrats are still strongly placed in Washington. But while they control the government and have substantial minorities in Congress, they remain politically and intellectually on the defensive. Ever since the New Deal the party's main reason for existence has been its programs for solving economic and social problems, but the public is skeptical of big new government programs and the general preoccupation with the deficit prevents major increases in spending. As a result, the party is sharply divided between the New Deal liberals, who are strongly entrenched in the congressional leadership, especially in the House, and the moderates who accept, as President Clinton proclaimed in his 1996 State of the Union message, that "the era of big government is over." The president's second term will be a severe test of his ability to keep his party united while fending off further Republican advances.

Both politically and intellectually, the initiative still seems to lie with the Republicans, though the experience of 1995–96 has indicated that an indiscriminate assault on governmental programs is not what the American public wants. The Republican Party in Congress has become increasingly conservative, with the leader-

---

13   See David Maraniss and Michael Weisskopf, *"Tell Newt to Shut Up!"* (Touchstone, 1996).

ship in both houses now largely in
the hands of southerners. The principal division in the Republican Party
is no longer between conservatives
and moderates (though with narrow
majorities in Congress, the small
group of northern moderates can
play a pivotal role), but between the
political and economic conservatives
who dominate Congress, and the
social and religious conservatives
who control many of the state parties.

President Bush and Pat Robertson share a light moment during the President's address to the Christian Coalition dinner in Norfolk, Virginia.

By mobilizing conservative churches, Pat Robertson's Christian Coalition has built
a strong grass-roots organization. Coalition members have been encouraged to
become active in the local Republican Party: by one estimate, in 1994 Christian
activists controlled the party apparatus in eighteen states and wielded influence in
many more.[14] This grass-roots activity was accompanied by a much more politically
sophisticated lobbying operation in Washington led by Ralph Reed, executive director
of the Christian Coalition until 1997. The coalition's influence among Republicans in
Congress rests on the strength of its local organization and its connections to conservative church networks.[15]

While it is fully supportive of the other conservative issues, the Christian Coalition
sees the Republican Party essentially as a vehicle for its conservative social agenda.
The dilemma for Republican leaders is that while white evangelicals have become an
essential part of the Republican coalition, their social agenda is divisive and does not
command the support of even a majority of Republicans. The Christian Coalition
saw its social agenda sidelined once during the Reagan Administration and again in
1995–96. In 1996, because of their organizational strength among the national convention delegates, social conservatives were able to write much of their agenda into
the party platform; but later they saw that platform openly dismissed by most of the
leadership (Bob Dole claimed he had not read it), and the issues it addressed ignored
during the presidential campaign. The day after the election, Pat Robertson promised
an early organizational effort among social conservatives to back a candidate and set
the issues for the 2000 election well in advance of the nomination process.[16] For

---

14   John F. Persinos, "Has the Christian Right Taken Over the Republican Party?" *Campaigns and
      Elections,* September, 1994, 21–24.
15   On the Christian Right's role within the Republican Party in the 1990s, see Clyde Wilcox,
      "Premillenialists at the Millenium: Some Reflections on the Christian Right in the Twenty-first
      Century" *Sociology of Religion* 55 (1994), 243–261.
16   *New York Times,* November 7, 1996, B10.

Republican leaders, keeping Christian conservatives on side without becoming too heavily identified with their divisive social agenda will be an increasingly difficult challenge.

The Sixth Party System and the Question of Realignment

The New Deal party system came to an end in 1968 when, for reasons explained earlier, important elements in the national Democratic coalition broke loose from their traditional loyalties. Instead of a stable new alignment forming out of elements of the previous alignment, which Table 12.1 indicates is the historical pattern, the period since 1968 has been one of divided government. For twenty-four of the thirty years between the 1968 and 1998 elections, control in Washington has been divided between the parties. During President Carter's term, 1977–81, and in the first half of President Clinton's first term, 1993–95, the Democrats controlled both branches—something the Republicans have not achieved since 1929.

At the presidential level it seems as if a realignment has taken place. The Republican Party, after a very narrow win in 1968, easily won the elections of 1972, 1980, 1984, and 1988. The Democrats, like a typical minority party, could only win narrowly in 1976, when the Republicans were temporarily damaged by the Watergate scandal, and in 1992, when a conservative independent candidate, Ross Perot, ran strongly. Clinton's re-election in 1996 provides an example of the advantages of incumbency in a time of economic prosperity.

At the level of congressional and state elections, however, the Democrats continued their pre-1968 dominance right through to 1994. The only major success for the Republicans in that period was to control the Senate from 1981 to 1987. In every previous party system a realignment at the presidential level was accompanied by a realignment in Congress and followed by a process of realignment in most of the states.[17] This did not happen after 1968.

Starting with Nixon, the Republicans worked hard to create a new majority party through a "southern strategy" by appealing to dissident Democrats in the South and among the urban working class. This Republican effort was badly set back by the Watergate scandal of 1973–74. Everett Carl Ladd referred to Republicans after Watergate as "an exceptionally weak second party nationwide."[18] This proved the take-off point for the conservative Republican resurgence led by Reagan, which

---

17   On the working out of the realignment process at the state level, see Sundquist, *Dynamics of the Party System*.

18   Everett Carl Ladd Jr., *Where Have All the Voters Gone? The Fracturing of America's Political Parties* (Norton, 1978), 5.

	1976			1988			
	Rep	Dem	Other	Rep	Dem	Other	
Presidential vote %	48	50		54	46		
Party identification	33	52	15	41	48	11	
Members of Congress	181	354		220	315		
House	143	292		175	260		
Senate	38	62		45	55		
Governors	12	37	1	22	28	0	
State legislative seats	2370	5128	55*	2927	4469	48*	
	31%	68%		40%	60%		
State houses controlled	18	80	1	30	67	2	
Full state control (governor; both houses)	1	29		5	14		

Table 12.4

Indicators of party success at national and state levels, 1976 and 1988.

*Nebraska has only one legislative house, which is officially nonpartisan.

This is an adaptation and expansion of a table in E.C. Ladd, *Where Have All the Voters Gone?* (Norton, 1978). Reprinted with permission. Figures for 1988 from *Congressional Quarterly*. All party identification figures from *American National Elections Studies*, University of Michigan Center for Political Studies, reprinted by U.S. Bureau of the Census, *Statistical Abstract of the United States*, 1991.

triumphed in 1980 and dominated Washington through the 1980s. Reagan held a strong attraction for many working-class voters (the "Reagan Democrats") and for white evangelicals, but only the latter group permanently realigned themselves with the Republicans (see Chapter 10).

Table 12.4 compares the fortunes of the two parties at the national and state levels in 1976 and 1988. Clearly, the Republicans recovered substantially from their low point in 1976, but at the end of the Reagan years the Democrats still led by a comfortable margin both in Congress and in the states.

How is the persistence of this new split pattern to be explained? Walter Dean Burnham contends that while there has been no party realignment since 1968 as in other periods, there *has* been a radical change or realignment in voting behavior that has created a system of divided government.[19] Analysts differ as to whether a future party realignment is likely or not, but the factors that explain the change in voting behavior can also be used to explain why a party realignment has not taken place, or not taken place yet.

Just as partisan realignments in the past were created by voters who mostly voted a straight ticket (that is, voting for the same party's candidates for all offices), so the pattern of divided government has been created by massive ticket-splitting (that is, voting for the candidates of different parties for different offices). There were two key factors that opened the way for the rise of ticket splitting: the dealignment of party identification, and the decline of party organization.

Party identification. As was discussed in Chapter 10, since the early 1970s rather than a realignment of party loyalties there has been an across-the-board *dealignment* of party identification, a general decline in the strength of party loyalty, and a corresponding rise in the number of voters with only a weak identification or no identification with the parties. Thus, the decline in identification with the Democrats has not directly benefited the Republicans. Apparently there has been no realigning event or personality with sufficient impact to regalvanize party loyalties in a new, long-term pattern.

Party organization. As James L. Sundquist has documented in *Dynamics of the Party System*, while realignments took place around national issues, the process of realignment was completed down to the local level by the state party organizations. Since the 1960s the focus of political campaigning has shifted from the parties to the individual candidates, and the skills required have shifted from grass roots organizing to television advertising and fund raising. As a result, the traditional party organizations have been greatly weakened to the point where they no longer have the capacity to mobilize large numbers of voters and hold their loyalty. Realignment may no longer be possible in the traditional sense.

The shift to candidate-centered rather than party-centered campaigning has had another effect that has impeded party realignment: it has entrenched incumbents. With the collapse of party organizational strength, members must now secure their own re-election, and they have become increasingly skilled at doing so by using the advantages incumbency provides (see Chapter 6). In particular, incumbents have a huge advantage in raising campaign money from the PACs of interest groups that do business with their committees. The increasing difficulty of defeating incumbents

---

19   Walter Dean Burnham, "Critical Realignment: Dead or Alive?" in Byron E. Shafer, ed., *The End of Realignment? Interpreting American Electoral Eras* (University of Wisconsin Press, 1991).

benefited the majority Democrats throughout the 1980s. It took Gingrich's relentless assaults on the House Democrats after 1990 to weaken the advantage of incumbency and to open the door for a Republican take-over (see Table 12.3).

Alan Ehrenhalt points out that the days when prominent citizens were drafted by their party to serve for a time in political office are almost completely gone. This change in the nature of political careers is one reason why Democrats have continued to dominate politics at the congressional, state, and local levels in spite of the Republican realignment at the presidential level since 1968. Races for political office, he argues, have become almost entirely dominated by careerists driven by passion and individual ambition.[20]

The more natural home for the new breed of professional politicians is the Democratic Party, which believes in positive, problem-solving government. The Republican Party, in contrast, has increasingly cast itself as the anti-government party. It may well be that Democrats continue to dominate state and local politics because the Republican Party is unable to recruit enough candidates who can match the Democrats in motivation and persistence. Newt Gingrich's recruitment of candidates for the House who were motivated to dismantle much of the governmental structure would seem to have countered this trend. However, many of the new conservative members continue to display a distrust of government and a disdain for life in Washington. It remains to be seen how long the enthusiasm of such new conservative politicians will last.

All of the factors listed above—partisan dealignment, weak party organization, entrenched congressional incumbents, and changing patterns of candidate recruitment—are plausible when it comes to explaining why the historic process of partisan realignment has recently failed. Some political scientists have suggested other reasons why voter behavior has changed. Morris Fiorina argues that the easiest way for voters to protest against an entrenched Democratic Congress has been to support Republican presidential candidates. It may even be that many voters are deliberately seeking to balance control of the presidency and Congress between the parties.[21]

Gary Jacobson, on the other hand, has argued that more and more voters now perceive the presidency and Congress as performing different functions, and have voted for the party most likely to deliver for them in each case. Thus, voters look to Republican presidents to manage the economy and America's relations with the world, and at the same time expect the Democrats in Congress to keep delivering basic services to their constituents.[22]

---

20   Alan Ehrenhalt, *The United States of Ambition: Politicians, Power and the Pursuit of Office* (Random House/Times Books, 1991).
21   Morris Fiorina, *Divided Government* (Macmillan, 1992), Chapter 5.
22   Gary C. Jacobson, *The Electoral Origins of Divided Government: Competition in U.S. House Elections, 1946–1988* (Westview Press, 1990), Chapters 5 and 6.

The unexpected capture of both houses of Congress in 1994 by the Republicans raised new questions about the party system. Burnham argues that while the period from 1968 to 1990 marked a stable pattern of divided government, there are indications that a further shift in voter behavior began around 1990.[23] He points to the rising voter disillusionment with "politics as usual," which has led to increasing pressure on congressional incumbents and to a large increase in retirements (see Table 12.3). This same disillusionment helped independent candidate Ross Perot do well (19 percent of the vote) in the 1992 presidential election.

The fact that from 1995 through to at least 1999 the pattern of divided government was resumed, but with the parties' roles reversed, tends to confirm Fiorina's notion that some voters now prefer party balance in Washington. In 1996 President Clinton presented himself as the defender of popular programs against the excesses of the congressional Republicans; in the last week of the campaign, with Clinton's victory assured, the Republican Party ran ads in marginal House seats arguing that a Republican Congress was needed to prevent Democratic excesses.

Still, as Burnham points out, the Republican capture of Congress and many of the states in 1994 "bears many characteristics of an old-style partisan critical realignment."[24] The fact that the Republicans did not go on to win the presidency in 1996 does not necessarily contradict that analysis. Republicans did keep control of the Congress (the first time the party had won two consecutive terms in Congress since 1928), and Clinton's re-election can be attributed to the advantages of incumbency and the early mistakes of the congressional Republicans.

Thus, the further changes in political behavior that Burnham notes may indicate either a perpetuation of the kind of post-1968 fluid politics in which divided government is the most likely outcome; or it may be that the long-expected Republican realignment that started at the presidential level in 1972 is only now having its impact on Congress and the states. Perhaps the weakening of the party system has only slowed down the realignment mechanism.

---

23   Walter Dean Burnham, "Realignment Lives: The 1994 Earthquake and Its Implications," in Colin Campbell and Bert Rockman, eds., *The Clinton Presidency: First Appraisals* (Chatham House, 1996).

24   Burnham "Realignment Lives," 363.

CHAPTER 13

POLITICAL PARTIES IN THE
UNITED STATES

Political parties are the most important intermediary institutions in democratic political systems. By nominating candidates for public office and organizing to win elections, parties provide a link between officeholders that makes it easier for them to cooperate with one another and also makes it easier for the public to hold them accountable for their actions. Parties provide a means of aggregating conflict over policies and interests and directing it into democratic political channels.

Parties also help clarify and simplify the choices voters must make at election time. A candidate's party "label" usually tells the voter something important about the kinds of policies he or she is likely to support if elected. It is much easier for the average voter to find out something about the parties than it is to collect information on the individual candidates, especially since parties have usually compiled a "track record" over time.

The general term "political party" covers a wide variety of organization types. Because parties are intermediary institutions, they tend to reflect the political culture and constitutional framework within which they operate. This is why American and Canadian parties are substantially different in both organization and style.

Parties vary greatly in organizational strength. Strong parties can control the nomination process and act as a cohesive and disciplined force in politics. Weak parties may be little more than formal structures with no organizational strength—simply arenas where candidates contend for the right to use the party's name in an election.

The Influence of American Political Culture on Political Parties

American parties operate within a pervasive liberal culture. The only parties that can be successful are those advocating liberal ideas. The fact that the two major American parties share the same basic liberal principles means that the arguments between them are not about fundamentals. The parties often present sharply differing visions of American society, as in the continuing contest between the *laissez-faire* and New Deal versions of liberalism, but their joint acceptance of the American Creed limits the extent of the disagreements between them and gives the parties considerable flexibility in building broad coalitions of support. There are no ideological tests for belonging to a party; rather, the parties are open-ended, with no well-defined membership. Anyone who chooses to run for a party or public office as a Democrat or a Republican may do so.

America has always been a hostile environment for political parties. The absence of any mention of parties in the Constitution was deliberate. The framers without exception shared the conventional eighteenth-century belief that parties or factions were destructive of national unity and civic virtue, and were simply vehicles for the pursuit of narrow interests.[1] When the Federalist and Republican parties formed in the 1790s, each saw itself as a temporary necessity for combating the threat to the republic from the other. The peaceful transition of power from the Federalists to the Republicans after the election of 1800 marked a crucial transition toward democratic politics, but each party still assumed that the other would disappear and that the nation would return to a system based on nonpartisan consensus. The new breed of political operatives who emerged around Martin Van Buren in the 1820s were the first to argue that parties were inevitable in a free society and that structured competition between parties was essential to the working of the American system of democracy.[2]

Although parties became firmly established in the nineteenth century, the case against parties has always resonated with the American public. Party loyalty depends on individual members subordinating their own beliefs to those of the party—a concept that has never sat well with the strongly individualistic American spirit. In the public mind, parties have always been tainted with illegitimacy. Indeed, as will be discussed later, some of the most important political reforms of the twentieth century were specifically designed to weaken party organization in the name of increased democracy.

---

1   Richard Hofstadter, *The Idea of a Party System: The Rise of Legitimate Opposition in the United States, 1780–1840* (University of California Press, 1970).

2   Hofstadter, Chapter 6. Edmund Burke was the first to make the positive case for political parties in England, in 1770.

One of the most distinctive features of American politics, the primary election, was one of these anti-party reforms. In a primary election the party's nominee for office is decided by a vote of those registered as party supporters, rather than by the party organization. Another distinctive feature of politics in the western states, the direct initiative, which allows voters to place an issue on the ballot by petition, has similar anti-party origins. Primaries and direct democracy mechanisms are discussed later in the chapter.

The Influence of the Constitutional Structure on Political Parties

The federal system and the design of national institutions has shaped the structure of parties in the United States. Parties organize at each level at which elections are held. The vast majority of elections, including those for city and county offices, the state legislatures, and the House of Representatives, are held at the local level. Party organization has always been strongest at the local level. One of the most popular aphorisms in American politics is that "all politics is local."

The principal statewide elections are for governor and U.S. senator. (Some states also elect a few other state officials and hold statewide referenda.) In the second half of the nineteenth century, strong state parties were built in many of the states, but state party organizations were undermined by the reforms of the Progressive period and have rarely had much organizational strength in the twentieth century.

The election of the president every four years is the only national election, but because of the Electoral College, even that election is organized at the state level. The only national organization for either party has been the national convention, which meets for a week every four years to formally nominate the presidential candidate. Also, each party has an ongoing national committee, composed of delegates from the state parties, whose principal job is to organize and set the rules for the national convention. At the national level, therefore, American parties have always been extremely weak, little more than loose coalitions of independent state parties.

The parties were weakened by the constitutional separation of institutions at the national level. In a parliamentary system, to control the government a party has to win a majority of seats in the legislature, and this requires a strong national party organization. This is not the case in the United States, where the president is elected separately from the Congress. Although the president is the national leader of his party, he has very few powers that can strengthen his party. Presidents have sometimes tried to intervene in congressional elections or to discipline state parties, but these efforts have always failed because of a built-in local resistance to central control. Another consequence of the separation of powers is that the party not occupying the White House has no national leader until the next presidential campaign.

Party discipline is very weak in the United States compared to other countries because the party leaders have neither the incentive nor the means to enforce greater discipline. Given the fragmented political structure at every level, politics in the United States is always about building majority support, by persuasion, compromise, or deal making; and the parties by necessity operate in this way. Thus, party leaders have always been reluctant to lose support by disciplining members. There is in any case no formal party membership. Because primary elections are used for deciding nominations, party organizations do not even control the nomination process, so they lack the most forceful methods for enforcing discipline—denying rebels the party's endorsement and screening out unsuitable candidates.

The characteristics of the major American parties can be summarized as follows: non-ideological; open-ended/inclusive; organizationally weak; decentralized; and undisciplined.

Comparison with Canadian Parties

In complete contrast to the United States, political parties played a foundational role in Canada. David Smith points out that it was political parties that pressured Britain to grant responsible government to the Canadian colonies in the mid-nineteenth century. He points out that until World War I the "governing parties," John A. Macdonald's Conservatives (to 1891) and Wilfrid Laurier's Liberals (after 1896), played the key integrating role in establishing Canada as a nation and presiding over its westward expansion.[3]

In the Canadian parliamentary system, government and party have always been tightly linked. In order to control the government through the House of Commons, the party leader must maintain tight control over the party outside the Commons. Thus, Canadian parties have always been highly centralized and dominated by the party leader. For most of their history the two major parties were even highly integrated between the federal and provincial levels.[4] Since the 1960s, however, intergovernmental tensions have taken center stage in Canadian politics and the integrative role of the parties has weakened; as a result, formal ties between the two levels of the parties have mostly been severed.

So, Canadian parties are much more centralized and much more disciplined than American parties. The difference can be illustrated by the case of David Duke's recent candidacies for the Republican Party in Louisiana. Duke is a former leader of the Ku

---

3   David E. Smith, "Party Government in Canada," in R.K. Carty, ed., *Canadian Political Party Systems: A Reader* (Broadview Press, 1992), 533–558.

4   R.K. Carty, "Three Canadian Party Systems," in Carty, ed., *Canadian Political Party Systems*, 566.

Klux Klan and a neo-Nazi sympathizer. When he decided to run for the state legislature as a Republican in 1989, there was no party mechanism to stop him from doing so. In an effort to disassociate the party from his views, the Republican National Committee supported his opponent in the primary election for the party nomination; but it failed to defeat him, and he won the seat. Likewise, the party had no way of stopping Duke from running as a Republican for the U.S. Senate in 1990, and for governor in 1991 (he ran strongly but lost on both occasions), and once again for senator in 1996.

In contrast, Canadian parties leave the candidate selections largely to the membership in the local party associations but give the party leader the right to approve all party candidates. Party leaders sometimes reject candidates chosen at the local level. In 1988, for example, the Progressive Conservative leader vetoed the candidacy of Sinclair Stevens, a former Cabinet member who had been involved in an ethics scandal. In the Liberal Party the leader has the right to name candidates for several ridings—a power Jean Chrétien exercised in the 1993 and 1997 elections. Chrétien has also kept some MPs in line by threatening to withdraw approval of their candidacy in the next election. In 1996, MP John Nunziata was booted from the Liberal caucus for voting against the government's budget, and the Liberal association in his riding was later disbanded by party authorities. (Nunziata won his seat in 1997 as an independent candidate, defeating the Liberal candidate chosen by Jean Chrétien.)

Canadian political parties are thus much stronger organizationally than American parties; in particular, each has a centrally directed national organization. Each also has a clearly defined membership and is highly disciplined.

The Two-party System

An important characteristic of the American political scene is that it is totally dominated by two political parties, the Democrats and the Republicans. Virtually all officeholders at the national and state levels were elected as candidates of one of these two parties. There has been a two-party system throughout American history. Third parties have sometimes arisen, but they have rarely lasted long or had a national impact.

The United States is virtually alone in having such a pure two-party system. Multiparty systems are common in many countries. Even in countries where two parties predominate, such as Britain and Germany, third parties often play a significant continuing role. Canada since 1921 has had a "two party plus" system. While only the Liberals and the Progressive Conservatives have formed governments federally, the CCF/NDP has played a significant role nationally since the 1940s. It has also formed governments in several provinces, as have other provincially based parties. Currently the Reform Party is attempting to establish itself as a national party from its base in the western provinces.

There are no definitive explanations why the United States has always functioned with only two parties.[5] The absence of a viable socialist party is certainly one factor. Also, the American parties are by nature broad, inclusive, non-ideological and loosely structured coalitions, and this has tended to undercut the need for third parties. The pressure to build and maintain the broadest possible national coalition arises from the nature of the executive power in the American system. The party that elects the president controls the federal government. The first national parties were formed to elect a presidential candidate, and this has continued to be every party's main reason for existence. Small wonder, then, that every party tries to form the broadest possible national coalition, and why interest groups only deal with parties that have winning prospects. Conversely, a party that is perceived as having no possibility of winning the presidency will have difficulty holding on to its support.

Other factors have helped entrench the two-party system. The use of the single-member plurality system for legislative elections—rather than, say, some form of proportional representation—disadvantages third parties in most situations, though it has not stopped them from persisting in Canada. In addition, the two-party system has become in itself an American tradition; as a result, the laws in many states make it difficult for third-party candidates even to get on the ballot. For example, it took a great deal of money and organizational effort for billionaire Ross Perot to get his name on the presidential ballot in all states in 1992, and to get his new Reform Party on the ballot in all states in 1996.

PARTY ORGANIZATION

There have been three important periods in the development of American political parties: the Jacksonian era, when the characteristic forms of American party organization were invented; the Progressive era, when sweeping reforms to party organization were passed; and the 1960s and 1970s, during which traditional forms of party organization were largely replaced by candidate-centered organizations.

The Jacksonian Era

The characteristic forms of American party organization were created during the second party system with the advent of mass democratic politics in the 1820s and

---

5   See, for example, the classic text by V.O. Key Jr., *Politics, Parties, and Pressure Groups*, 5th Edition (Thomas Y. Crowell, 1964), 205–210.

1830s. Before then national politics had been centered on the political elite in Washington. The national electorate was limited by property qualifications for voting, and voter turnout in national elections was low. Political organization was rudimentary; for example, until 1824 the presidential nomination of the dominant Republican Party was decided by negotiations within the congressional caucus.

The spread of democratic ideas and Andrew Jackson's drive for the presidency in 1828 expanded the national electorate considerably; this expansion led to the development and spread of new forms of organization capable of mobilizing a mass electorate. The new forms were pioneered by Jackson's emerging Democratic Party. Jackson's chief organizer (and successor) was Martin Van Buren, who created the first strong, statewide party organization, the "Albany Regency" in New York state, and who was the first of a new breed of professional political organizers. Jackson's Whig opponents were appalled at this crass new form of politics, but the Democrats' success forced them to adopt the same methods.

The effect of the expansion of the electorate was to shift the focus of political organization from Washington to the grass roots, which is where voters now had to be organized if elections were to be won. Parties organized themselves at the local level, in the cities and counties. The new political techniques allowed strong party organizations to be built in many states. Nationally, however, party organization remained weak. The national convention was invented in the 1830s as a forum for nominating presidential candidates every four years and for rallying the party behind them, but, as was discussed in Chapter 10, the national convention never developed any power independent of the state parties.

The Local Political Machine

The new style of mass politics required hierarchical, military-style organizations to turn out the voters on election day. The foot soldiers in any organization were the poll captains, who were responsible for getting out the vote for their candidates in the local precincts. The poll captains were responsible to the ward leaders, who were responsible on up the chain of command to the party boss. The boss and his associates controlled the nominations and commanded the organization to get them elected.

The two problems that must be solved by any party organization are these: how to motivate the party workers so as to maintain the organization, and how to retain the loyalty of the voters. The American political machinery solved these problems through patronage, and by providing basic services to the voter.

The Patronage System

In the nineteenth century, government employees were appointed by the chief executive at each level of government. Thus, at the local level all policemen, firemen, garbage collectors, clerks, and so on were appointed by the mayor or county executive. When the party's candidate was elected mayor, city jobs were distributed by the party to its workers. In return for their jobs, the party workers were required to give back a small portion of their pay (which went into party funds) and to work for the party as required, especially on election day. City workers had every incentive to work hard for the party, since if the party lost the election they would lose their jobs.

The Party Machine and the Voter

The machine also needed to retain the loyalty of the voters. It did this by using its organization to provide services that were not provided elsewhere at that time. Part of the poll captain's job was to monitor life in his precinct. Those who were unemployed or going hungry, or were in trouble with officials or the law, could go to the party organization for help. The party held picnics for the children in summer and distributed turkeys at Thanksgiving. All the party wanted in return was their vote on election day, which most voters were only too happy to provide.

Machine politics worked best where there was a large poor or working-class population, such as recent immigrants in the cities, and the rural poor. This system flourished in an era when government services at every level were minimal. In these situations politics was a question of bread and butter, a matter of material incentives rather than national issues. The middle class generally scorned machine politics and were the main supporters of the reform candidates who from time to time tried to defeat the machines. Political machines could belong to either national party. Most of the best-known ones, such as Tammany Hall in New York City and the Cook County (Chicago) machine, were Democratic and run by Irish Americans; but some machines, such as those in Philadelphia and Pittsburgh, were Republican.[6]

State Party Organization

Machine politics worked best at the local level, where an efficient organization could monopolize electoral office for long periods of time. The larger and more diverse the area, the more difficult it was to organize. Nevertheless, in the second half of the nineteenth century several powerful statewide party organizations were built, using state patronage to reward local machines for throwing the blocks of votes they controlled behind the party candidates for state office. State party bosses were also able to obtain funds and additional patronage jobs from business in return for state contracts or favorable legislation.

As was discussed in Chapter 11, the party bosses of the big states played a key role at national conventions in picking the parties' presidential candidates. The main concern of the state leaders was whether the candidate for president "at the top of the ticket" would help or hurt their chances of winning the state and local offices that

---

6   For the history of machine politics in a major city, see Harold F. Gosnell, *Machine Politics, Chicago Model*, 2nd edition, (University of Chicago Press, 1968).

controlled the flow of patronage. If the candidate they backed became president, they could expect a share of federal patronage and possibly a Cabinet post for themselves.

The machine was the dominant form of party organization in the second half of the nineteenth century, but machine politics did not flourish in all parts of the United States. In his survey of party organizations, David Mayhew could identify only thirteen states that had a long tradition of strong local and state party organizations. These states formed a band extending from Rhode Island and Connecticut in the Northeast through to Illinois in the Midwest, with Delaware, West Virginia, Kentucky, and Missouri forming a southern border. This group included all of the largest states at the time and most of the American population.[7]

Outside of these states, in northern New England, the South, the prairies, and the West, there were isolated examples of machines operating for a time—in Boston, New Orleans, and San Francisco—but state party organizations never were able to build much strength over long periods. In these areas the parties functioned simply as arenas where various interests, regions, or individuals engaged in a continuous struggle to control nominations and elections.

◆ Machine Politics: Pro and Con

Machine politics, which lasted well into the twentieth century in some places, was an easy style of politics to criticize. From a contemporary perspective, politics should be about issues and principles, not jobs and turkeys. Government jobs and contracts should be awarded on merit rather than through political connections. Where a machine had so much control over local politics, it inevitably abused its power. Because winning elections was so crucial to maintaining the organization, corrupt practices flourished, such as ballot stuffing, voter impersonation (as in "vote early and often"), voting the graveyard, and rigging voting machines.

But some analysts have pointed out the benefits that flowed from this style of politics. Because every citizen had a vote, the machines did not discriminate and were willing to deal with everyone. At a time when government provided few services, the machines delivered benefits such as jobs widely to poor people. They were also an important means of pulling immigrants into the political system. For example, the Cook County machine was started by the Irish, but successively accommodated the Italians, Poles, and southern blacks as they arrived in Chicago in large numbers.

Not all machine candidates were corrupt. The machines recognized that in order to maximize support for the ticket or to undercut reformers, they had to nominate "clean" candidates. Some distinguished national politicians got their start with the

---

7   David R. Mayhew, *Placing Parties in American Politics: Organization, Electoral Settings, and Government Activity in the Twentieth Century* (Princeton University Press, 1986), Chapter 8.

support of local machines, including President Harry Truman (in Kansas City) and Adlai Stevenson, Democratic presidential candidate in 1952 and 1956 (in Chicago).

Furthermore, states that had no strong party organizations were often more corrupt than the ones that did. Where there was no party organization to contend with, powerful business interests, such as the Boston and Maine Railroad in New Hampshire and the Southern Pacific Railroad in California, got their way by bribing individual legislators. A strong party was more likely to exercise some control over these interests and to extract benefits from them.

The Progressive Era

The long-standing middle-class campaign to reform the political system came to a head at the beginning of the twentieth century. Between 1900 and 1920 many reforms were pushed through at the state and federal levels. The reform campaign was carried forward in the name of modernizing and democratizing the American system. A key element in the campaign was an attack on political parties as corrupt, inefficient, and a relic of more primitive political times. The explicit aim of reform was to weaken the role of the parties in the political process.[8] It was generally thought that increased democracy would cure the ills of party control of politics.

Two of the four constitutional amendments passed during this period dealt with political reform. The 17th Amendment, ratified in 1913, made the Senate directly elected. Election by state legislatures had made the Senate the stronghold of party bosses and had enabled business to "buy" seats in some states. It was contended that greatly expanding the electorate for the Senate would eliminate these forms of corruption. The 19th Amendment, ratified in 1920, gave women the vote. Female suffrage finally came about partly because many believed that women voters would help clean up the political system.

There was a great deal of legislation attacking political corruption. The Tillman Act (1907) prohibited the use of corporate funds in political campaigns. Many states passed voter registration laws to prevent party manipulation of voting. In the 1890s the "Australian" (that is, secret) ballot had largely replaced party-supplied tickets. Many cities switched to nonpartisan elections for municipal offices. Since state and local machines often controlled judicial appointments, many states began choosing their state judges through direct popular election.

Many states, particularly in the West, adopted some "direct democracy" mechanisms: the referendum, initiative, or recall. The use of direct democracy is discussed

---

8   The debate in this period over whether parties were the instrument or the enemy of democracy is recounted in Austin Ranney, *The Doctrine of Responsible Party Government* (University of Illinois Press, 1962).

at the end of the chapter. But the reforms that had the greatest impact on the party system were civil service reform and direct primaries. The former attacked the parties' most important resources; the latter attacked the parties' control of the nomination process.

◂ Civil Service Reform

The campaign to create a politically neutral career civil service at every level of government attacked the principal means by which party organizations maintained themselves: political patronage. Reformers not only attacked the patronage system as corrupt but argued that modern governments needed to be staffed by highly qualified professionals whose careers did not depend on their political contacts. The goal was a professional public service whose members were hired and promoted on merit. In exchange for guaranteed employment, these people would be required to avoid partisan political activity.

The federal Civil Service Commission was established in 1883 to oversee the hiring and training of public servants. Over the next forty years the bulk of federal government jobs were brought under civil service rules.[9] Today the president has only the power to nominate the top 3,000 policy-makers in the federal departments and boards, who form his administration. For many years the post office was the last outpost of large-scale patronage. This era ended when it was made into a separate public corporation in 1970.

◂ Primary Elections

The primary election was the most important innovation of the Progressive era, the one that had the greatest and most lasting impact on how political parties operated. A primary is an election within a party to choose that party's nominee for an office. Primaries were first used around the beginning of the century in the one-party southern states, where securing the Democratic nomination was the key to election, since there was usually no Republican candidate. Reformers in the North quickly seized upon the new invention as a means to democratize the nomination process and remove it from the hands of the party bosses. Soon after, primaries became the standard method, mandated by state laws, for determining party nominations at every level. Until the 1970s, primaries had only limited use in presidential nominations, as discussed in Chapter 11.

Most election law is state law, so primaries work in different ways in different states. Currently, twenty-eight states require voters to register by party (that almost always means as Democrat, or Republican, or independent). In these states a primary

---

9   On the struggle over civil service reform, see Stephen Skowronek, *Building a New American State: The Expansion of National Administrative Capacities, 1877–1920* (Cambridge University Press, 1982), Chapter 6.

may be *closed*, so that only voters registered with the party may vote in its primary elections; or *partially open*, so that voters registered as independent may choose which party's primary to participate in. In the twenty-two states that do not have voter registration by party, primaries are *open*, meaning that voters choose at the polling station which party's primary to participate in.

In most states the candidate with the most votes in the primary becomes the party nominee; but in some southern states a run-off primary is required between the top two candidates if no candidate receives 50 percent of the primary vote. Louisiana has a "blanket" primary in which candidates of all parties compete together; the top two candidates, regardless of party, contest the general election unless one candidate received 50 percent of the vote in the primary.

Since the power to choose party candidates is the key to maintaining a strong party organization, the introduction of primaries was most strongly resisted in those states where the parties were most powerful. In some states the impact of primaries was weakened by the requirement for candidates to obtain a certain level of support at the party convention before they could participate in the primary.

The Impact of the Progressive Reforms on the Political Parties

The Progressive reforms were intended to weaken the parties, and there is no doubt they did so. Civil service reform arose as much from the needs of modern government as from anti-party feeling, and was also happening in other countries at the same time. (In Canada, civil service reform was one of the factors that brought the first party system, which was based on the central distribution of patronage, to an end.[10]) The Tillman Act, like most American attempts to control the influence of money, was only half-heartedly enforced. The direct-democracy reforms, while they added a distinctive dimension to politics in a number of states, most notably California, were too limited to have much impact on the overall functioning of the political system. The voter registration laws, which placed the responsibility for registering on the individual voter, were an important reason why American political participation declined during the twentieth century.

The most damaging reform, from the point of view of the parties, was the introduction of primary elections. The innovation was motivated by the Americans' naive belief that more democracy was always better and that parties were by their very nature not to be trusted. It is no accident that the primary system has not been adopted outside the United States: in other countries the fact that political parties perform a necessary political function has been much more generally recognized.

---

10   Carty, "Three Canadian Party Systems," 570.

The main impact of the reforms was to weaken the parties at the state level. The era of strong state-party organizations and state-party bosses came to an end, although in a few states, such as Connecticut, strong state organizations persisted until the 1960s. The impact of the reforms was less serious on the local machines. An efficient machine had little difficulty winning a primary election and thus keeping control of nominations in its area. Civil service reform was less uniform at the local level, and many party organizations continued to control large numbers of government jobs. The New Deal period gave a boost to local Democratic machines, since President Roosevelt was willing to work with them and give them federal patronage, provided the members of Congress from machine-controlled districts supported his programs.

Machine politics declined rapidly after World War II. Machines had always done best where there was a large dependent population that needed a machine's services and was willing to accept its political leadership. With the expansion of government services during the New Deal, rising levels of education, and the general prosperity of the 1950s, the fertile ground for the old-style politics contracted steadily.

The Daley Machine in Chicago

The longest-lasting of the local political machines was the Cook County (Chicago) Democratic machine, which continued to function in the traditional manner until the end of the 1970s. The Chicago machine was led from 1955 until his death in 1976 by Richard J. Daley, who was both chairman of the Democratic Party county executive (that is, party boss) and mayor of Chicago. Daley controlled the city government and the politics of the county, including its six congressional districts, with great skill.[11]

Because he controlled the massive Chicago vote, Daley was the most powerful figure in the state Democratic Party and was able to play a key role in nominating Democratic presidential candidates at the national conventions. It was considered obligatory for candidates for the Democratic presidential nomination to make the trip to Chicago to ask for Daley's support.

In the 1960s, as the last of the old-time party bosses, Daley's role in the Democratic Party became increasingly controversial. Indeed, it was the disastrous 1968 national convention in Chicago that triggered the sweeping reform of the delegate selection process, as a result of which the power of the state leaders was taken away. Daley was the most vociferous opponent of the anti-war forces at the convention. As mayor, he was blamed when the Chicago police beat many protesters outside the convention. At the 1972 convention the anti-war forces got their own back when Daley and his hand-picked Illinois delegation were ejected from the convention for violating the new delegate selection rules.

---

11   See Melvin A. Kahn and Frances J. Majors, *The Winning Ticket: Daley, the Chicago Machine, and Illinois Politics* (Praeger, 1984).

The Cook County Democratic machine finally fell apart in the early 1980s after Daley's death. The machine had become increasingly dependent on the votes of Chicago's blacks, who by then were nearly 50 percent of the city's population. When the black community decided that the time had come for a black mayor, the machine began to fragment, with many of its leaders refusing to support a black candidate. When the first black mayor of Chicago, Walter Washington, was elected in 1983 in the face of machine opposition, the old-style political machine that had ruled the city for decades was effectively dead.[12] Yet the name Daley still has power: Richard Daley's son, Richard M. Daley, was elected mayor of Chicago in 1989.

The Decline of Party Organization Since the 1960s

In the 1960s the party organizations lost their last vestiges of the power to control nominations and deliver votes for a candidate. By then, rising educational standards had made voters less dependent on the party for political information. But the final blow was delivered by television: once candidates started using TV commercials to speak directly to the voters, the political parties lost one of their traditional functions, and candidates found it much easier to win without a party's organizational support. The use of television by parties and candidates has been tightly regulated in Canada and other countries; in the United States the only limit on its use is the availability of money.

The advent of television and the disappearance of traditional methods of party organization had a profound impact on political campaigning in the United States, in three areas: organization, campaign practices, and fund raising.

Candidate-centered organization. After the strong party organizations disappeared, candidates were forced to build their own organizations to run their campaigns. Most political organizations are now "candidate-centered." Each candidate develops a private network of contacts, interest groups, and sources of funding. Traditionally, the party organizations had made their resources available to all the party candidates; today's candidate organizations have a much narrower focus.

The rising importance of candidate-centered organizations is illustrated by the Republican strategy in Georgia in the 1990 elections. There were two statewide races that November: for senator and for governor. Realizing that incumbent Democratic senator Sam Nunn would be almost impossible to defeat, the Republicans took the drastic step of not running a candidate against him in order to increase their chances

---

12   See Samuel K. Gove and Louis H. Masotti, eds., *After Daley: Chicago Politics in Transition* (University of Illinois Press, 1982).

of winning the governorship: "Republicans decided to give Nunn a free ride to discourage him from setting in motion *his* powerful field and financial operation, a mobilization that could help the Democratic nominee for the open governorship."[13] (emphasis added)

In other words, the best political organization in Georgia belonged not to the Democratic Party but to Senator Nunn, and he would be less likely to put it into operation if he was not fighting for his own re-election.

TV-centered campaigning. Since the 1960s television has become more and more important in political campaigns. It is often less central at the local level, such as in many urban seats in the House of Representatives, since television markets are often larger than individual districts. But no candidate can expect to run well for a statewide office without a large television budget. In extreme cases, campaigns are mounted almost entirely on television. In 1994, Michael Huffington, the Republican candidate for the Senate from California, campaigned almost exclusively through television commercials, avoiding most interviews and personal appearances.[14]

Because of this dependence on television, a number of new skills are now an indispensable part of political campaigning: making television commercials, plotting schedules for TV advertising, "image" consulting, various forms of opinion polling, and so on. In earlier days, advertising companies were called in simply to make political commercials during a campaign; nowadays, most national and statewide campaigns are run by political consulting firms that provide the whole package of necessary skills for their political clients in return for substantial control over the campaign—and large fees. Political consultants have replaced traditional forms of political organization. In many political campaigns, the new, highly specialized skills have entirely replaced the traditional tasks of door-knocking and envelope-stuffing.

Fund raising. Television advertising and opinion polling have greatly increased the cost of political campaigns. Since 1976 there has been a ceiling on expenditures in presidential elections, but there are no limits in congressional or other elections. By 1994 the average cost of a campaign for the House of Representatives was over $300,000. Expenditures were, of course, higher in closely contested seats. No fewer than forty-eight House candidates spent over $1 million.[15]

For Senate elections costs are, of course, much higher in most states. In 1994 successful candidates spent around $4 million on average. The all-time record was set that year in California, where the unsuccessful Republican challenger, Michael Huffington,

---

13   *Congressional Quarterly, Weekly Report,* June 16, 1990.
14   See Sidney Blumenthal, "The Candidate," *The New Yorker,* October 10, 1994.
15   *Congressional Quarterly, Weekly Report,* June 3, 1995.

spent nearly $30 million—most of it his own money, and excluding spending on the primary. The Democratic incumbent, Diane Feinstein, spent over $14 million. The previous spending record for a Senate contest was set in 1984 in North Carolina, when the two candidates spent $25 million between them in a close and bitter race.

As Huffington discovered, the candidate who spends the most money does not always win. There is, however, strong pressure on candidates to match their opponent's spending, and most analysts agree that to be competitive a candidate must be able to spend "enough" to run a serious television campaign. In the 1980s the practice of using television commercials not just to "sell" the candidate but to attack an opponent became common. It is now assumed that a candidate must have money available to respond quickly to attack ads.

◄ The Impact of the Decline of Party Organization

The weakening of party organizations and the advent of candidate-centered organizations has affected American politics in a variety of ways. Mainly, it has fragmented the parties internally and reduced them to little more than arenas in which individuals and groups contend for office and influence, but over which party officials have little control. Parties can no longer generate loyalty or mobilize dependable bodies of supporters. Most campaigning is aimed at gaining support for a particular candidate or position. This may be why parties may no longer have the capacity to create a broad realignment of political loyalties.

The weakness of the parties has increased the impact of single-issue pressure groups. Many groups have organized themselves to push one particular issue, and support or attack candidates solely on the basis of how they stand on that issue. In earlier times party organizations mediated between these groups and the candidates. Now that parties are weaker, these groups work directly on the candidates. For example, in 1996 the Dole campaign tried frantically to moderate the demands of the pro-life and gun lobbies without losing their support.

The state and local party organizations are declining, but at the same time, the *national* committees of the parties are starting to play a larger role in coordinating campaigns across the country. In the 1980s the Republican National Committee began recruiting and training candidates for congressional and even state offices. Its Democratic counterpart eventually followed suit. Each party's national committee and House and Senate campaign committees are also doing more to fund candidates, but the law restricts them to giving a total of $10,000 for each House candidate and slightly more for the Senate, and the party's role remains marginal to the candidate's own fund raising.[16]

---

16   On the increasing importance of the party national committees, see Xandra Kayden and Eddie
        Mahe Jr., *The Party Goes On: The Persistence of the Two-Party System in the United States*
        (Basic Books, 1985).

The Problem of Campaign Financing

Concern about the growing influence of money in American political life has been building for some time.[17] The public perception is that politicians in Washington are beholden to special interest groups, from whom most campaign funds are raised. This was one of the issues on which Ross Perot campaigned effectively in 1992 and 1996. Most politicians are tired of having to spend so much of their time raising campaign funds and agree that money is a problem. The question is how to solve the problem. Since the regulation of campaign financing is one area where Canadian and American practice is strikingly different, it is worth laying out the differences.[18]

Comparison of American and Canadian Regulation of Election Expenditures

Political donations.

United States: For each campaign, political donations to a candidate are restricted to $1,000 (for individuals) and $5,000 (for PACs). All donations must be reported. Primaries are treated as separate campaigns. Larger donations are permitted to political parties, and there is a ceiling for total donations from individuals. A limit on total personal and family contributions by a candidate to his or her own campaign was struck down by the Supreme Court.

Canada: There are no restrictions on individual or corporate political donations, but all donations of $100 or over must be reported. Individuals receive tax credits on a sliding scale for donations up to $1,150.

Limits on campaign spending.

United States: A 1974 law placed restrictions on two types of campaign spending: total campaign spending by candidates, and "independent expenditures" by other groups or individuals in support of a candidate. However, these restrictions were struck down by the Supreme Court. There are therefore no limits on campaign spending, except in presidential elections.

Canada: There are strict and low limits on how much individual candidates can spend during an election campaign. There are also limits on spending by the national parties during the campaign, but no limits on expenditures before that period. Legislation from 1983 that restricted expenditures by organizations other than parties during an election campaign has been struck down by the courts.

17   For an overview of the issue, see Frank J. Sorauf, *Money in American Elections* (Scott, Foresman and Company, 1988). A critique of the current system is Elizabeth Drew, *Politics and Money: The New Road to Corruption* (Macmillan, 1983).

18   On Canadian regulation and its effects, see W.T. Stanbury, *Money in Politics: Financing Federal Parties and Candidates in Canada* (Royal Commission on Electoral Reform and Party Financing, 1991).

Public funding of campaigns.

United States: There is some public funding of presidential campaigns (see Chapter 10), but no public funding of any other campaigns.

Canada: Parties are reimbursed from public funds for 22.5 percent of their total election expenses. Candidates are reimbursed for 50 percent of their election and personal expenses, provided they receive at least 15 percent of the vote.

Political advertising on television.

United States: There are no restrictions on the purchase of television advertising by parties or candidates. Political advertisers typically pay full commercial rates.

Canada: Broadcasting outlets are required to make available a certain amount of free prime time; a further amount must be made available for political parties to purchase. The broadcast time is shared out between the parties according to an elaborate formula worked out for each election. Parties and candidates are forbidden from purchasing further time.

These strikingly different approaches to regulation make it clear how different a role political parties play in the two countries. In Canada, campaigning is almost entirely party-centered; in the United States, it is now almost entirely candidate-centered. In the United States, individual candidates now have to spend vast sums to stand any chance of election; in Canada, such high-spending campaigns are prohibited by law. Public funding, in the form of direct subsidies and tax credits, is very important in Canada, where it is generally recognized that parties play an essential public role. In the United States, the notion that parties matter receives only the most minimal and grudging recognition.

In Canada, fund raising is almost entirely a party matter; in the United States, candidates must raise most of their own funds. The approaches to regulating fund-raising are quite different in the two countries. American law severely limits donations from individuals. Since campaign costs have continued to spiral, this has forced candidates into the arms of the PACs, which can give larger amounts and have greater incentive to do so. In Canada there are no limits on either individual or corporate donations, though donations must be disclosed. The provision of tax credits to encourage small donations from individuals has been enormously beneficial. The main effect has been to level the playing field by enabling smaller parties, such as the NDP, to raise enough money to maintain the party organization and run effective national campaigns.

Both countries have tried to limit total campaign spending. In Canada there are low limits for candidates; there are also limits for the parties, though only during the short campaign period itself. In the United States, an attempt to limit spending was struck down by the Supreme Court in *Buckley v. Valeo* (1976), which defined campaign spending as protected "speech" under the First Amendment. Limits are only constitutionally acceptable when they are voluntary and part of a quid pro quo, as in the public funding provision for presidential campaigns. In Canada, the limit on campaign expenditures by other organizations was struck down by the courts as a violation of the Charter guarantee of free expression. This became an issue in the 1988 campaign, when several business groups spent heavily in support of the Free Trade Agreement, thus indirectly supporting the Conservative government.[19]

In the United States the main reason for ballooning campaign costs is the cost of buying television time. Canada has dramatically reduced the cost of campaigns for all the parties by severely restricting the use of television. Such regulations are also standard in Europe; in the United States they would be unthinkable, not to mention unconstitutional. In the United States some have proposed that television stations, which are publicly licensed, be required to provide candidates with some time free or at reduced rates; but without a restriction on buying additional time, the impact on campaign costs would be quite limited.

There is considerable public pressure for further campaign finance reform. This has been fanned by media reports of the close links between politicians and interest groups. Since 1989, however, the issue has become hopelessly bogged down in fighting between the parties. Neither party will support a change in the law that it believes will disadvantage it vis-à-vis the other party. In general terms, Democrats tend to support limits on campaign spending and increased public financing of campaigns. Republicans oppose both and lean toward removing most restrictions on fund raising, provided that all donations are reported. Both parties are nervous about changing the law concerning PACs, which have a proven track record of supporting those in power regardless of party. A consensus may now be emerging that the limits on individual donations must be raised in order for a better balance to be achieved with PACs. But in spite of public pressure, there is only a remote possibility that enough interparty agreement will develop that campaign financing practices will be comprehensively reformed.

DIRECT DEMOCRACY

For the framers of the Constitution the fact that popular sovereignty would take the form of representative government was both inevitable, given the size of the new republic, and highly desirable. James Madison believed that government by wise representatives was superior to direct rule by the people.[20] Nevertheless, for many

---

19   See Jane Hiebert, "Fair Elections and Freedom of Expression Under the Charter," *Journal of Canadian Studies* 24 (1989–90).

20   *The Federalist Papers*, Number 10.

Americans direct democracy, in the form of the New England town meetings at which local decisions are made by all the citizens, has remained an ideal. For many, direct democracy seems more democratic that representative democracy.

The idea that voters should be able to bypass the legislative process and vote for policies directly was taken up by western Populists and then by the Progressives around the turn of the century. These reformers argued that the representative system had been corrupted by the parties and special interests so that state legislatures were unresponsive to popular pressure for economic regulation and political reform. In this period direct democracy mechanisms were adopted by a number of states, especially in the West.

The principal direct democracy devices are the *initiative* whereby the collection of a certain number of signatures puts a proposed law or amendment to the state constitution to a popular vote; the *referendum* whereby certain kinds of laws can, or sometimes must, be submitted to a popular vote before they go into effect; and the *recall* whereby the collection of a certain number of signatures can remove an elected official from office or force him to face a new election before the end of his term. The specific requirements for each device vary from state to state.

The referendum is the most widely used direct democracy device around the world. In Switzerland the regular use of the referendum is built into the Constitution. Most parliamentary democracies have used the referendum on occasion to supplement the normal representative processes in dealing with particularly difficult issues. There have been two national referendums in Canada, on conscription in 1942 and on the Charlottetown constitutional agreement in 1992. The United States is in fact one of the few democracies that has never held a national referendum. There was no provision for direct democracy in the carefully balanced design of the Constitution. While proposals for a national referendum have periodically been discussed in Congress, the idea has never come close to passing. [21]

At the state level, every state except Delaware requires amendments to the state constitution to be submitted to a referendum. Roughly half the states allow a referendum to be called on a law passed by the legislature if sufficient signatures are collected, but this procedure is rarely used. Use of the recall is also fairly rare. Fifteen states allow the recall of elected state officials, but only one governor and a handful of legislators have ever been recalled. The most recent case was in Arizona in 1987, when enough signatures were collected to require Governor Mecham to face a recall election. The new election was preempted when he was impeached and convicted by the state legislature. The recall procedure is used more often at the local government level.[22]

The most commonly used direct democracy device in the American states is the initiative. The most common form is the direct initiative, which puts a proposed law or

---

21   Cronin, *Direct Democracy*, Chapter 7.
22   Cronin, *Direct Democracy*, 127–128.

state constitutional amendment directly to a popular vote, bypassing the legislative process altogether. In most cases the proposal is cast as a constitutional amendment, since an amendment can only be overturned by another amendment or the courts, whereas the legislature can amend or revoke an ordinary law. A total of twenty-four states and the District of Columbia allow the direct initiative. The number of signatures required to get a proposal on the state ballot varies in different states between 3 and 15 percent of registered voters. Some states require a balance of signatures from across the state. In most cases the device was adopted in the Progressive era. While there has been renewed interest in direct democracy in the past twenty years, only five states and the District of Columbia have adopted the initiative since 1959, with Mississippi being the latest in 1992.

In the near-century from 1898 to 1992 there were a total of 1,732 initiatives submitted to voters in the states, with well over half being submitted in the five states that have used the device most often: Oregon, California, North Dakota, Colorado, and Arizona. Resort to the initiative has varied over the years. After fairly heavy use in the early part of the century, the number of initiatives fell, reaching a low point in the 1960s. Since then, interest has increased steadily, and it is projected that the 1990s will see the greatest use of the initiative device. The success rate also seems to be increasing. Whereas only 38 percent of the 1,732 initiatives passed, the success rate since 1990 has been around 50 percent.[23]

There are a number of reasons for the increasing use of the constitutional or legislative initiative in those states which permit the procedure. One is undoubtedly the cynicism about "politics as usual" that has been a notable feature of American politics in the 1990s. Another is the disappearance of party organization and the rise of single-issue groups. Most proposed initiatives are pushed by interest groups or by groups formed around a single issue. The issues addressed by most initiatives are commonly those that political parties shy away from. Parties do not usually get involved in initiative politics.

The great majority of ballot initiatives deal with state or local issues. For example, in 1994 voters in Washington state approved a proposal to end dentists' monopoly of making and selling false teeth, while in Alaska voters defeated a proposal to move the state capital from Juneau to Wasilla. However, the initiative has also been used by groups attempting to influence the national agenda by demonstrating popular support for an issue that has been blocked in the legislative process. For example, referendum victories in key states played an important role early in the twentieth century in pressuring federal politicians to pass a constitutional amendment on woman suffrage.

---

23   David B. Magelby, "Direct Legislation in the United States," in David Butler and Austin Ranney, eds., *Referendums Around the World: The Growing Use of Direct Democracy* (Macmillan, 1994).

The best recent example has been the campaign for term limits for members of Congress. Starting with the passage of an initiative in Colorado in 1990, a national campaign coordinated by the single-issue group U.S. Term Limits saw twenty-two states approve congressional term limits, either by initiative or by legislation, as of the end of 1994. In 1995 in *U.S. Term Limits v. Thornton* the Supreme Court ruled that congressional terms could only be limited by amending the Constitution. When Congress failed to pass such an amendment, term limit supporters resorted to the initiative once more. In 1996 nine states passed (and five rejected) proposals requiring their members of Congress to vote for a term limit amendment on pain of their failure being noted on the next ballot. The constitutionality of this use of the initiative to mandate members of Congress is uncertain, and in any case seemed to have little impact, since the House again failed to pass a term limits amendment in 1997.[24]

The state of California has become the main battleground for interest groups either hoping for or fearful of a knock-on effect from the passage of a ballot initiative. The modern phase of these initiative wars started with Proposition 13 in 1978, which severely limited property taxes. While it was locally initiated, Proposition 13 became the inspiration for a national tax revolt that led to President Reagan's massive 1981 income tax cuts. In 1996 national civil rights organizations fought in vain against Proposition 209 forbidding affirmative action by state agencies. Both sides saw the California battle as potentially the start of a national movement against affirmative action. The Christian Right has also used the initiative as part of its national campaign on moral issues. Constitutional amendments to forbid local anti-gay discrimination ordinances passed in Colorado in 1992, but failed in Oregon and Idaho in 1994. An amendment to guarantee "parents' rights" failed in Colorado in 1996. An unexpected development was the passage in California and Arizona in 1996 of amendments allowing the use of marijuana for medical purposes.

Because the stakes are high for the groups involved in many of the initiative campaigns, the direct democracy process has been subjected to the same pressures as other elections. Especially in California, an initiative "industry" has grown up involving specialists in every part of the process. Many more initiatives are proposed than ever collect enough signatures to get on the ballot. The process of signature collection is handled nowadays by specialized firms. Most initiative campaigns are now run by campaign consulting firms. Spending is high in many of the initiative campaigns, but in 1978 the Supreme Court ruled unconstitutional state laws limiting expenditures.[25]

---

24   Dan Carney, "House Votes Down Amendment As Effort Loses Momentum," *Congressional Quarterly, Weekly Report*, February 15, 1997.

25   *First National Bank of Boston et al. v. Belotti* 435 U.S. 765 (1978).

Magelby reports that in 1990, two-thirds of the money spent on initiative campaigns in California came from business interests. Only 12 percent was contributed by individuals. The proportion of business spending is highest in the most expensive campaigns.[26]

In recent years the initiative process has also generated a great deal of litigation. Since the process of getting an initiative on the ballot is more cumbersome and less well-established than a regular election, one strategy for opponents has been to tie a proposal up in the courts before it even comes to a vote. Controversial initiatives are invariably challenged in court if they pass. Thus, the opponents of Proposition 209 on affirmative action went into federal court the day after the vote and won a stay (later lifted) on the grounds that the new amendment violated the U.S. Constitution. The legal challenge to the Colorado gay rights amendment succeeded when the Supreme Court ruled in *Romer v. Evans* (1996) that it violated the equal protection clause of the 14th Amendment.

The increasing use of the direct initiative has made it a regular part of the political process in the United States. The state initiative process has become an alternative method of putting issues on the national agenda. While initiative campaigns have become much like other election campaigns, the process does have some distinctive features. The parties and most candidates for office usually avoid taking sides in initiative campaigns. This removes the stabilizing factors of party and candidate identification from voter behavior (see Chapter 10). As a result, voters are highly susceptible to the short-term influences of the campaign. Public opinion is much more volatile on initiatives than in other elections,[27] although Cronin discounts the charge that voters behave less rationally on initiatives.[28] The importance of the campaign in determining the outcome, however, highlights once again the influence that campaign expenditures and corporate spending have on the electoral process.

---

26   Magelby, "Direct Legislation in the United States," 243.
27   Magelby, 249.
28   Cronin, *Direct Democracy*, Chapter 4.

CHAPTER 14

INTEREST GROUPS AND LOBBYING

An interest group is an organization formed to promote the interests of its members by influencing public policy. Interest groups lobby government on behalf of their members for a variety of benefits such as subsidies, contracts, and favorable legislation or regulations. Political parties are at the center of political life, nominating candidates for office and taking positions on a broad range of issues. In contrast, interest groups pursue a narrow range of issues that are of interest and benefit to their members. In most cases the interest of the members is an economic one.

There are a number of systemic reasons why interest groups play a more active role in the policy-making process in the United States than in other political systems—that is, why the American political system is particularly open to interest group activity. In the first place, interest groups are considered a legitimate, even necessary, element in the working of American democracy. James Madison, the principal architect of the Constitution, recognized the pursuit of private interests as the driving force behind most politics and structured his constitutional system both to control those interests and to take advantage of them. He argued that the diversity of factions and the competition between them would help prevent a majority faction from emerging and monopolizing power. To justify their activity, interest groups also cite the First Amendment guarantees of freedom of speech and the right "to petition the government for a redress of grievances."

A second reason is the relative weakness of American political parties (see Chapter 13). Noted political scientist V. O. Key Jr. commented in 1942 that "a striking feature of American politics is the extent to which political parties are supplemented by private associations founded to influence public policy."[1] In political systems with strong parties, the parties when in power control the policy-making process and are the dominant intermediaries between the government and the public. To attempt to influence policy, interests must deal with the parties, whose function is to aggregate and integrate the whole range of interest group pressures. In the American case, E.E. Schattschneider argued that "if the parties exercised the power to govern effectively, they would shut out the pressure groups."[2] However, American parties are much weaker organizations that do not dominate the policy process, and this leaves a great deal of room for direct involvement by interest groups.

The institutional structure of the American constitutional system also facilitates interest group activity. The separation between the executive and legislative branches, reinforced in recent years by strong decentralizing forces within each branch, makes the policy process in Washington a highly fragmented one. With the decentralization of power and the lack of effective party discipline (see Chapter 6), the American legislative process has developed "multiple cracks" or "multiple points for bringing influence." Because there are so many political actors in Washington who have the power to affect legislation, the potential targets for interest groups are "literally uncountable."[3] Individual members of Congress can have considerable influence on legislation. The members are thus well worth influencing, and given the limited role of party discipline, they are wide open to outside influences. While interests also lobby the executive branch, their main focus is almost always on the Congress, which holds the ultimate legislative and appropriation power and has considerable influence over the working of the executive branch.

Interest Groups in the Canadian Parliamentary Process

The main difference in the lobbying process between Canada and the United States relates to where the decision processes are located and, therefore, where lobbying activities are focused. In Canada the parlimentary system gives control over policy to the Cabinet, which is a fusion of party, parliamentary, and bureacratic elites. The Cabinet ministers are the leaders of the majority party and head the departments,

1   V.O. Key Jr., *Politics, Parties, and Pressure Groups*, Fifth Edition (Thomas Crowell and Company, 1964), 17.
2   E.E. Schattschneider, *Party Government* (Holt, Rinehart & Winston, 1942), 192.
3   Morton Grodzins, "American Political Parties and the American System," in Aaron Wildavsky, ed., *American Federalism in Perspective* (Little, Brown, 1967), 134.

which are staffed by professional civil servants. The Cabinet controls the legislative process through its parliamentary majority; as a result, Parliament is denied any independent influence over the bureaucracy. Policy-making thus takes place almost entirely within the executive branch. In the United States the effective policy-making arena is Congress; in Canada it is the executive branch. In Washington policies begin to take shape in congressional committees; in Canada, the starting point is in the middle levels of the bureaucracy.

Policy-making in Ottawa is highly centralized in the executive branch and takes place behind closed doors. Both the politicians and the civil servants operate according to codes of public solidarity and secrecy. Because of tight party discipline, Parliament plays a largely formal and passive role in policy. Unlike members of Congress, individual MPs are usually not worth lobbying.[4] There are therefore a much smaller number of decision-makers in the Canadian policy system and fewer "cracks" in the system through which interests can influence the process.

In Canada, interest groups have never been seen as a legitimate part of the political process. Business groups have of course always lobbied governments in Canada for favorable policies, but in the Canadian system the role of interests has been much less visible and in the past was often not taken for "lobbying" at all. Indeed, as Paul Pross points out, the leading text on Canadian government from the 1940s to the 1960s did not mention interest groups at all.[5]

Canadian governments have the same need as governments in the United States to deal with interest groups as a source of information and political support. The tradition in Canada has been policy-making by "elite accommodation," which involves ministers, bureaucrats, and interest group leaders seeking mutually satisfactory decisions. The principal interest groups are given access to government on policies that affect them. Indeed, historically government agencies often encouraged interests to organize in order to facilitate consultation. Such a system tends to produce incremental policy-making and is biased toward those interests which have established access in Ottawa.[6]

For most of Canadian history the party in power has played an important role in brokering among competing interests. While the party organization has limited direct influence over policy-making, it has long acted both as an important feedback mechanism for government and as a channel of access to ministers. Some party

---

4   Pross quotes John Bulloch of the Canadian Federation of Independent Business explaining why he seldom approaches MPs: "We do not have time to talk to people who have no influence." *Group Politics and Public Policy*, 77.

5   A. Paul Pross, *Group Politics and Public Policy*, Second Edition (Oxford University Press, 1992), 1.

6   Robert Presthus, *Elite Accommodation in Canadian Politics* (Cambridge University Press, 1973).

functionaries ("bagmen") have traditionally acted as middlemen, collecting money from business interests for the party coffers. The tradition in both major parties has been to appoint such party insiders to the Senate; this has been a standard method of providing business interests with the opportunity to lobby discreetly on policy.[7]

Since the 1960s there has been an expansion of government activity and a proliferation of groups attempting to influence government policy—a development similar to that in the United States. As a consequence there has been a "diffusion of power" within the previously highly centralized policy system in Ottawa, and separate policy communities and policy networks have developed around different issue areas. The nature of the interaction between government and interest groups varies between different policy communities.[8] The policy process has also been made more complex by the decentralization of the federal system in the same period (see Chapter 4)—a development that has brought the provincial governments into play on a wide range of issues.[9]

From the point of view of those trying to influence policy, the decision-making processes in the executive branch are complex, obscure, and highly contingent on who holds the key positions in the relevant department.[10] There are many fewer footholds in the system than in the United States. This means that there is probably an even greater need than in Washington for expert lobbyists who know how the executive branch works and have good contacts within it. In the past twenty years there has been considerable growth in the lobbying industry in Ottawa. Lobbyists have been required to register since 1990, and in 1997 there were around 3,000 lobbyists. The growth of lobbying has provided an opportunity for ministers, their political aides, and civil servants to exit through the "revolving door" to become lobbyists. Most often, it is the second-echelon ministers and political advisers who join the lobbying firms. Former prime ministers and leading ministers are valued for their Ottawa experience and contacts—that is, as "rainmakers"—on corporate boards or in prestigious law firms. After the exposure of questionable activities by some lobbyists during the Mulroney government,[11] the disclosure requirements were tightened in 1997.

Since the focus of lobbying in Canada is the executive branch, many of the techniques used in the United States (which are discussed below) have less relevance. Campaign donations to parties and candidates, while a factor in Canada, are much

7   Colin Campbell, *The Canadian Senate: A Lobby From Within* (Macmillan, 1978).

8   William D. Coleman and Grace Skogstad, eds., *Policy Communities and Public Policy in Canada: A Structural Approach* (Copp Clark Pitman, 1990).

9   See Pross, *Group Politics and Public Policy*, 68–74.

10   W.T. Stanbury, *Business-Government Relations in Canada: Grappling With Leviathan* (Methuen, 1986), 97–111.

11   Stevie Cameron, *On the Take: Crime, Corruption and Greed in the Mulroney Years* (Macfarlane Walter & Ross, 1994).

less central than in Washington. Lobbying methods change as a policy proposal moves up from the middle levels of the bureacracy toward Cabinet approval.[12] In the current, more diffuse policy-making system there is a greater tendency than before for interest groups to lobby parliamentary committees and individual legislators.[13] Interest groups may also engage in "advocacy advertising" to make their case on a particular issue, or in corporate advertising to bolster their public image. This parliamentary and public lobbying is usually to supplement an "inside" campaign of executive lobbying, and is not a substitute for it.

The diffusion of power within the Canadian policy-making system nevertheless remains very limited compared to the radically fragmented American system. Attempts to pressure the Canadian government need to have an integrated strategy that targets the bureaucracy and the Cabinet simultaneously. On attempts to influence budget policy, Alan Freeman writes: "For a lobby campaign to succeed, it's got to get everybody from the bureaucrats to the finance minister, and even the prime minister, on side."[14] The access given to interest groups in Canada thus lies primarily within the discretion of the government. In the centrally directed parliamentary system, the government, as the final arbiter of legislation, almost always has the upper hand over the interest groups if it chooses to use it.

Lobbying in Canada and the United States: The Free Trade Agreements, 1988 and 1993

The fierce battles over the ratification of the two North American free trade agreements provide a good example of how the different systems require a different focus for lobbying efforts. In both countries the business community—especially the large corporations—strongly supported the free trade agreements while the labor unions, environmental groups, and assorted nationalist groups were strongly opposed. Those opposed had little access to government while the agreements were being negotiated and had to focus their lobbying efforts on the ratification process. In Canada the focus was a general election campaign to determine whether the party that had negotiated the agreement or a party that promised to scrap it would form the next government.

---

12   See the extended discussion of lobbying strategies in Stanbury, Chapters 7 to 10.

13   Lobbying MPs can sometimes be successful. In 1996 a coalition of insurance brokers targeted Liberal backbenchers in order to defeat a proposal that would have granted banks the power to sell insurance. Although the final decision was made by the Cabinet, finance minister Paul Martin was quick to acknowledge the "overwhelming support from caucus for this particular decision and that was not an unimportant issue." Howlett, McKenna, and Partridge, "How the Banks Lost Big," *The Globe and Mail*, March 9, 1996.

14   Alan Freeman, "The Byzantine World of Budget Lobbying," *The Globe and Mail*, March 2, 1996.

In the United States the focus was a campaign to influence the votes of the 435 members of the House of Representatives.

In Canada the controversy came to a head over the Free Trade Agreement (FTA), which the Mulroney Conservative government negotiated with the Americans in the mid-1980s. The Liberals and the New Democrats decided to oppose the agreement. The Liberals went so far as to use their majority in the Senate to block ratification until a general election was called. All three parties treated the 1988 election as a referendum on the FTA.[15]

A variety of groups joined together in an independent campaign to oppose the agreement. The Pro-Canada Network represented thirty different national organizations and grass roots coalitions in all ten provinces. The nationalist Council of Canadians and many individual trade unions also joined the campaign. These groups spent an estimated $750,000 on anti–free trade advertising during the campaign.

The strength of the campaign against the FTA triggered the formation of the Canadian Alliance for Trade and Job Opportunities, headed by former politicians and representing thirty-five business organizations and companies. This group spent around $2 million in newspaper and billboard advertising in support of the FTA.

When the Conservatives won a large majority in the election, all sides recognized that the issue was settled and that there was no prospect of derailing the ratification in Parliament. The extension of the agreement several years later to include Mexico did not arouse Canadian fears. The Mulroney government ratified the extension in 1992.

In the United States the prospect of free trade with Canada was widely welcomed, and there was no difficulty in getting Congress to pass the necessary enabling legislation for the FTA in 1988. However, the subsequent extension of the agreement to include Mexico as part of the North American Free Trade Agreement (NAFTA) stimulated much the same fierce debate in the United States that Canada had gone through over the earlier agreement. The Bush Administration had negotiated NAFTA under "fast track" authority from Congress. Under this special procedure, Congress undertakes not to amend the agreement but simply to vote it up or down within ninety days of the agreement being submitted by the president.

President Clinton sent NAFTA to Congress in the fall of 1993. The Senate was always expected to approve the legislation, so the lobbying campaigns focused on the House, where the vote was likely to be very close. The issue was a difficult one for the president, since major elements in the Democratic Party—especially the trade unions—were strongly opposed to the deal. Thus although there was a Democratic

---

15   Hilary Mackenzie and Theresa Tedesco, "After the Decision," *Maclean's*, December 12, 1988; Janet Hiebert, "Fair Elections and Freedom of Expression Under the Charter," *Journal of Canadian Studies* 24 (1989–90), 79–83.

majority in the House, passage was not assured. Opposition to the agreement in the House was led by the Democratic whip, David Bonior.[16]

An umbrella group, the Citizens' Trade Campaign (CTC), was formed to coordinate a grass roots campaign to pressure Democratic members of Congress to vote against the agreement. The CTC represented forty-one different organizations, including thirteen unions, major environmental groups (including the Sierra Club, Friends of the Earth, and Greenpeace), the National Council of Senior Citizens, Ralph Nader's organization Public Citizen, Ross Perot's United We Stand, and Jesse Jackson's Rainbow Coalition. Although the vote on the agreement was not until November, by August the CTC had set up branches in most states and started its grass roots campaign.

To coordinate the campaign to pass NAFTA, President Clinton appointed William Daley, a Chicago lawyer and son of the late Richard Daley, legendary boss of the old Cook County Democratic machine. The strongest support came from big business. Its umbrella group, USA–NAFTA, representing thousands of corporations and trade organizations, spent several million dollars on pro-NAFTA advertising. The representatives of small business stayed out of the campaign since their main organization, the National Federation of Independent Business, had voted narrowly to oppose the agreement. The president spent some time trying to win small business support. To counter the grass roots campaign of the NAFTA opponents, the president urged the large corporations to bring groups of employees to Washington to lobby members.

The Republicans in Congress strongly supported free trade but were worried about the political strength of the opposition groups. Republican leaders promised the president they would deliver enough votes to pass the NAFTA bill provided that he could deliver 100 Democratic votes (out of 258). In the countdown to the vote, President Clinton engaged in intensive personal lobbying of Democratic members. It was reported, for example, that the Democrats from North Carolina agreed to support the bill when the president promised to reduce the tax on tobacco he had proposed to help pay for his health care reforms. In the end the bill passed rather more easily than expected—234 : 200, with 102 Democratic votes in favor.

THE EXTENT OF INTEREST GROUP INFLUENCE IN THE UNITED STATES

While interest groups have an unusual degree of access to the American policy system, estimates of the extent of interest group influence in Washington have varied. The

---

16   An account of the lobbying campaigns on NAFTA is in *The New York Times*, November 12, 13, 14, 1993.

postwar generation of political scientists, including Key and Schattschneider, saw what they labeled "pressure groups" as highly influential because of the weakness of the parties, which they deplored. In Key's view, "at bottom, group interests are the animating force in the political process."[17] By the 1960s a more benign view of "interest groups" generally prevailed. In a modern version of Madison's argument, pluralists like Robert Dahl[18] argued that interests were sufficiently divided and the political system sufficiently open to competition between groups that no one interest was likely to become dominant. Studies of lobbying activity in Congress suggested that interest group influence had been exaggerated and that such groups were simply one of a number of factors—including constituency pressures, parties, and ideology—influencing policy decisions.[19]

The predominant perspective in political science more recently has one of "critical pluralism." There is the recognition that, especially since the 1970s, there has been a broadening of participation in the policy process. A very wide range of groups engage in interest group activity, making the process distinctly pluralistic. At the same time, effective representation of interests requires organization and money, and only the largest or wealthiest interests are likely to be well represented. Minority interests or those of the poorer segments of society tend to be overwhelmed or shut out by the voices of already powerful interests. *Open* access of interests to government does not lead automatically to *equal* access.

Although a wide range of groups engage in interest group activity, the predominant interest pursued has always been economic, and most interest groups have always been business groups, whether individual corporations, trade associations, or "peak associations" such as the National Association of Manufacturers and the U.S. Chamber of Commerce. Perceptions of interest group influence have therefore generally been linked to attitudes toward the power of business to influence public policy. Indeed, interest group influence is commonly analyzed in terms of the relative strength of business vis-à-vis "countervailing" groups such as labor unions, public interest groups, and regulatory agencies.

The fact that business wields considerable influence on American public policy should come as no surprise. Given the dominance of liberal ideas in the United States, the public belief in the virtues of capitalism runs very deep. American success is

17   Key, *Politics, Parties, and Pressure Groups*, 17.
18   Robert A. Dahl, *Pluralist Democracy in the United States: Conflict and Consent* (Rand McNally, 1967).
19   See Lester Milbrath, *The Washington Lobbyists* (Rand McNally, 1963), and Raymond A. Bauer, Ithiel de Sola Pool, and Lewis Anthony Dexter, *American Business and Public Policy* (Atherton, 1963).

almost invariably attributed by Americans to the genius of their democracy and system of free enterprise. David Vogel, however, argues against the common perception that business has more influence in the United States than in other capitalist countries. Business has much more influence on government in Japan, he points out, and the environmental, equal opportunity, and health and safety regulations imposed on American business since the 1970s are generally much stricter than in other Western countries.[20]

Within the American liberal tradition there have always been two distinct attitudes toward business, stemming from the original debate between Alexander Hamilton and Thomas Jefferson. The argument over the role of commerce in American life reflects the argument that has run through American history as to which of the fundamental liberal principles should be given priority: liberty or equality. The degree of American business influence in public policy has depended on which liberal principle dominates the public mood at the time.

Alexander Hamilton saw the growth of industry as the key to progress in the new country. Manufacturing, he believed, was the best way to develop the talents of the people, and he advocated policies to support and encourage business growth. Hamilton's successors in the Whig and Republican parties advocated a national program of economic development. This positive attitude toward business crystalized in the rise of *laissez-faire* liberalism toward the end of the nineteenth century. In the *laissez-faire* tradition, which is the principal theme in modern political conservatism, "business is seen as having a unique relationship to the public welfare" and government interference with the operation of free enterprise is attacked as entirely wrongheaded. In this light, "businessmen do not appear simply as representatives of a special interest, ... they appear as functionaries performing functions that [are] regard[ed] as indispensible."[21] Accordingly, the wishes of the business community are treated with great deference—an attitude often summarized in these famous words, from Charles Wilson, President Eisenhower's defense secretary: "What's good for General Motors is good for America."[22]

The Republican "revolutionaries" in the House of Representatives recently exhibited the same classic *laissez-faire* view that business can do no wrong. No sooner did they take control after the 1994 elections than the Republican leaders invited business lobbyists to participate directly in the drafting of legislation to eliminate

20   David Vogel, *Fluctuating Fortunes: The Political Power of Business in America* (Basic Books, 1989), 14–15.

21   Charles Lindblom, quoted by Vogel, *Fluctuating Fortunes*, 5–6.

22   This well-known quotation is in fact a misquotation. What Wilson, who had been chairman of General Motors, actually said at his Senate confirmation hearing was: "I thought that what was good for our country was good for General Motors, and vice versa."

most of the health and safety regulations on American business—an effort that did not succeed.[23]

Thomas Jefferson, while not hostile to business, worried about its impact, and especially about the inequality it was bound to generate. He believed that a predominantly agricultural society was likely to remain more equal and was therefore preferable to a commercial society. In particular, the Jeffersonians were concerned about any kind of government support for business, which they saw as simply a way of distributing economic privileges and as a corrupting factor in political life.

Jefferson's vision of a predominantly agricultural republic had largely evaporated by the mid-nineteenth century, but the underlying concerns remained. The relationship between government and business became an issue again in the last quarter of the nineteenth century, a period of rapid, unregulated business expansion in the United States. As business power grew, it was met by the political protests of farmers who found themselves dependent on new banking and railroad monopolies, and of industrial workers who found themselves at the mercy of unregulated employers. Business countered the political pressures for government regulation with *laissez-faire* propaganda and by cultivating close relationships with politicians in both political parties. Nevertheless, *some* regulation of business was politically inevitable, and in the new industrial era two distinct approaches developed for curtailing the power of business: the antitrust and regulatory traditions.

The unregulated growth and increasingly national reach of American business generated a new form of managerial capitalism dominated by large corporations. In many industries dominant corporations extended their control through trusts and holding companies. Since monopoly control of the market violated both the common law prohibition on restraining trade and the *laissez-faire* argument for the virtues of competition, the new monopolies were vulnerable to public pressure for their regulation ("Bust the trusts!"). The passage of the Sherman Antitrust Act in 1890 marked the beginning of what has been a characteristically American approach to regulating large corporations.

Antitrust policy has long been "a fundamental political and cultural value" in the United States.[24] While public attention has focused on a few high-profile cases, such as the court-ordered breakup of the Standard Oil and American Tobacco trusts in 1911 and of the ATT Bell telephone system in the 1980s, much of the work of the enforcement agencies—the Federal Trade Commission (FTC) and the antitrust

---

23   See David Maraniss and Michael Weisskopf, *"Tell Newt to Shut Up!"* (Touchstone Books, 1996), Chapter 5.

24   Tony Freyer, *Regulating Big Business: Antitrust in Great Britain and America, 1880–1990* (Cambridge University Press, 1992), 1.

division of the Justice Department—involves policing restrictive or collusive practices at a lower level.

The antitrust approach to business regulation has always been most strongly supported by Democrats, and enforcement has usually been most assiduous in Democratic administrations. Even for Democrats, however, the policy presents a dilemma as the nature of markets changes. Thus, the Clinton appointees at the FTC did not challenge the proposed merger between the last two American aircraft makers, Boeing and McDonnell Douglas, because the market for aircraft is global and the United States needs a strong competitor.[25] Democratic ambivalence toward antitrust policy can also be seen in the approach the Clinton Administration has taken toward Microsoft, the computer software giant. The Justice Department has been investigating Microsoft since 1993, when competitors charged it with monopolistic practices. At the same time, Bill Gates, the founder and head of Microsoft, has emerged as the latest American business icon, whose support has been eagerly sought by President Clinton and Vice President Gore.

The alternative approach to corporate regulation has been to set up specialized regulatory agencies. The first of these was the Interstate Commerce Commission, created in 1887 to oversee railroad rates, which were the main focus of rural protest. Setting up an independent regulatory commission was intended not only to distance the commission's work from day-to-day political pressures but also to embody the growing middle-class belief that policy problems should be solved not by the market or by politics, but through the application of technical expertise by professionals. Each wave of public criticism of business, discussed below, brought new agencies created to regulate specific industries.

Regulatory policy is controversial. It was long opposed by free market economists; but in addition, some political scientists argue that after the initial reform impetus, such agencies are likely to be "captured" by the industry they were set up to regulate. It was not until the 1970s, under President Carter, that there was a serious reconsideration of the traditional regulatory approach. Since then, some of the most heavily regulated industries (trucking, the airlines, and telecommunications) have been substantially deregulated.[26]

In the 1970s a number of new agencies were established with broad mandates to require higher standards of corporate behavior in a number of areas. These agencies, such as the Environmental Protection Agency (EPA) and the Occupational Safety and

---

25   For a discussion of the current dilemmas of antitrust policy in relation to the Boeing–McDonnell Douglas merger, see Michael Hirst, "But Nary a Trust to Bust," *Newsweek*, June 2, 1997, and Steven Pearlstein and John Mintz, "Will This Mega-Merger Fly?" *The Washington Post National Weekly Edition*, June 9, 1997.

26   Martha Derthick and Paul J. Quirk, *The Politics of Deregulation* (The Brookings Institution, 1985).

Health Agency (OSHA), have proved to be strong countervailing forces, and attempts by business to curtail their powers have mostly failed owing to strong public support for environmental regulation.

Fluctuations in Business Influence

According to David Vogel, business influence in the twentieth century has fluctuated between periods of "privilege" in the 1920s, 1950s, and 1980s, when business influence was largely uncontested in Washington, and periods of "pluralism" in the 1900s, 1930s, and 1960s, when the public mood changed and business had to fight to maintain its influence against strengthened countervailing forces.[27] Vogel argues that the public is more willing to regulate the behavior of business when there is optimism about long-term economic prospects. Periods of prosperity thus pave the way for periods of business regulation. Conversely, the public is more willing to support business when it is doubtful about the future state of the economy. Andrew McFarland argues that there are cycles in interest group activity in the United States characterized by periods of business control followed by periods of reform triggered by the excesses of business. A period dominated by business interests ends when business is seen to violate "widely shared standards," thereby stimulating the rise of new countervailing groups.[28]

The three main periods in which the regulation of business activity was extended were all periods in which there was a change in the public mood, an upsurge of support for broad reform of the governmental system, and an extension of the power of the federal government.

In the Progressive era a range of new groups lobbied for political, governmental, and social reforms. There was also protest against business abuses, some of them exposed by the "muckrakers" of the popular press. These pressures led to a tightening and increased enforcement of the antitrust laws, to the creation of the Federal Reserve System to regulate banking, and to the creation of the Federal Trade Commission and the forerunner of the Food and Drug Administration to regulate abusive business practices. The Progressive era was followed by the unbridled capitalism of the 1920s. That decade saw rising prosperity, the Teapot Dome scandal involving influence peddling for oil exploration leases on federal land, and an unregulated, soaring stock market whose crash in 1929 heralded the Great Depression of the 1930s and the most radical period of reform in American history.

---

27   Vogel, *Fluctuating Fortunes.*
28   Andrew S. McFarland, "Interest Groups and Political Time: Cycles in America," *British Journal of Political Science* 21 (1991), 257–284.

The New Deal produced a radical shift in public attitudes toward the role of government. In relation to business, it brought to power followers of the Jeffersonian tradition, who doubted the capacity of unregulated markets to produce equality or even economic efficiency. Many saw expert regulators as likely to be superior to the blind forces of the market in managing the economy; it was this same spirit that lay behind the shift to Keynesian economics. This revolution in thinking produced a whole range of new agencies to regulate different industries: the stock exchange, banking, airlines, broadcasting, and transportation.

The New Deal also established a major new countervailing force by putting trade union organizing rights on a secure legal footing for the first time. Without a supportive socialist tradition, trade unions have always had to struggle to establish their legitimacy in the United States, and this remained the case even with the new status granted them during the New Deal.

In 1947 the conservative coalition in Congress passed the Taft-Hartley Act, which cut back the rights of unions to organize and engage in political activity. Organized labor is often on the defensive in Washington against further business-backed efforts to restrict their operations.[29] The peak labor organization, the American Federation of Labor–Congress of Industrial Organizations (AFL-CIO), and many of the larger unions have nevertheless been an important lobbying force in Washington. Labor has not been able to win many victories on its own, but it has been an important element within the Democratic Party coalition in the North and has played an important role in broader coalitions supporting much of the social legislation since the New Deal.

The political upheavals of the 1960s produced a new set of countervailing forces in the form of new middle-class social movements promoting civil rights, women's rights, consumer protection, and protection of the environment. As a result, new regulatory agencies with broad mandates to regulate business practices were established, the main ones being the EPA, the OSHA, and the Equal Employment Opportunities Commission (EEOC). The upsurge of social activism also left behind a range of new public-interest lobbying groups, many of them inspired by Ralph Nader, who became a permanent watchdog on the Washington scene. The environmental and public interest groups in particular have become influential players in Washington.[30]

The business community was forced to adapt to the more pluralistic policy environment in Washington in the 1970s and developed many of the lobbying strategies discussed in the next section. Business generally supported the rise of political conservatism and the move to deregulation. In some cases the necessary legislation got

---

29   On the declining size and influence of American labor unions since the 1950s, see Michael Goldfield, *The Decline of Organized Labor in the United States* (University of Chicago Press, 1987).

30   See "The Public-Interest Movement" in Vogel, *Fluctuating Fortunes*.

bogged down by conflicts within the business community. For example, the banking and insurance industries have been engaged in a long lobbying war in both the United States and Canada, with each trying to block the other from being allowed to expand into its own domain of operations.[31]

In the 1980s, business pressed for the elimination of many of the regulations adopted in the 1970s. President Reagan's method of undercutting the regulatory agencies was to appoint those hostile to the agency to head them. An obvious example was the appointment of James Watt, a well-known opponent of the environmental movement, to be Secretary of the Interior. A change in an agency's administration can have a strong impact on its effectiveness.[32] Attempts to amend the regulations quickly ran into difficulties in Congress, and the president had to back off in 1983 after a scandal involving high-level appointments to the EPA. Among the Republicans' first priorities when they took control of Congress in 1995 was a bill, drafted with the involvement of business lobbyists, to sweep away many of the regulations on business. The effort soon raised a public outcry, and the Republican leaders had to abandon their efforts.

Interest Group Activity in Congress

In the 1970s there were substantial changes in the policy process in Washington and in the environment in which interest groups had to operate: the expansion of government during the Great Society program generated an explosion of groups with a stake in lobbying Congress; there was a radical decentralization of power in both houses away from the committee chairs, which opened up the policy process in Congress; and money was injected into the policy process in a new way through reform of the campaign finance laws.

One of the most important developments of the period was the proliferation of new public-interest groups. Some groups, such as consumer groups, found their support and influence waning by the late 1970s; but others, mainly environmental groups, have become formidable fixtures on the Washington scene. The institutionalization of new countervailing forces to business has produced a much more pluralistic policy environment, though one in which the relative influence of business vis-à-vis its adversaries still fluctuates. After losing several battles over regulation in the early 1970s, business interests were forced to enter into the political process in a new and better-organized way and to acquire the skills that the new policy environment requires.

---

31   *Congressional Quarterly, Weekly Report*, March 2, 1996, 540–541; *The Globe and Mail*, March 9, 1996.

32   William F. Grover has documented the shift in the operations of the OSHA between the Carter and Reagan administrations in response to business pressure in *The President as Prisoner: A Structural Critique of the Carter and Reagan Years* (State University of New York Press, 1989).

In order to evaluate the role that interest groups play and their overall effect on policy, it is necessary to understand the methods by which interests attempt to influence the decision-makers in Washington. Larry J. Sabato quotes the manager of a political action committee (PAC) on what is necessary to be effective and influential in Washington: "You have to have three elements: a PAC, a lobbying division, and a strong grassroots organization. The lobbying is central, and you back it up with the other two."[33]

The central goal of lobbying is to collect information and establish access to decision-makers. Lobbying is then backed up with both a "carrot," in the form of campaign funds, which all members of Congress need, and a "stick," in the form of grass roots pressure that reminds the member of the attentive public in his or her district. Some interest groups, such as the National Rifle Association (NRA),[34] have been extremely influential in Washington by perfecting the use of all three elements.

LOBBYING

The currency of influence in Washington is not crude pressure or money but information. The ideal relationship between the interest group and the members of Congress or bureaucrats is based on a reciprocal exchange of information, with the lobbyist as the intermediary. What a lobbyist needs first of all is information: information on what decisions are going to be made, when, and by whom; and information on the views of the various decision-makers on the issues and on how they are likely to act. The bureaucratic and congressional processes are so complicated that it takes experience with the system and good contacts to be able to keep track of what is happening. The basic, everyday activity of the professional lobbyist, therefore, is collecting information, and making and keeping contact with members of Congress and their staffs and with bureaucrats in the executive agencies. Establishing contact not only provides information but also gives the lobbyist access to the decision-maker when decisions are being made that affect the interests of the lobbyist's employer or client.

In exchange for access, the lobbyist provides the member first and foremost with information. The member needs information, on how existing policies are working and on what effect new proposals would have. He needs arguments and statistics, to persuade himself, his colleagues, and his constituents, to counter criticism, and to justify his decisions. Thus, the activities of the lobbyist are designed to provide the

---

33   Larry J. Sabato, *PAC Power: Inside the World of Political Action Committees* (W.W. Norton, 1985), 124.

34   For more information on the NRA's effective lobbying techniques, see Robert J. Spitzer, *The Politics of Gun Control* (Chatham House, 1995), 99–115.

member of Congress with what he or she needs: information, campaign funds, and support in the member's district. In exchange, the lobbyist expects information, access, and consideration of the interests of the organization.

In dealing with the bureaucrats in the executive agencies, the lobbyist tries to establish the same relationship of reciprocal support. Since the bureaucrat is not elected, campaign funds and local support are not relevant. Bureaucrats do, however, need information and congressional support. In order to do their job well, they need accurate information on how policies are working. They also want a good working relationship with the interests they regulate. In order to maintain or expand the work of their agency, they need support from the relevant legislative and appropriations committees in Congress. The interest groups that have access to the members of Congress can be useful allies for the bureaucrats in their dealings with Congress. Thus, the lobbyist tries to obtain congressional support for the bureaucrats in exchange for information, access, and decisions favorable to their interests.

Lobbying Organizations

Lobbying in Washington has become a highly specialized, full-time business. Ideally, effective representation requires a Washington office staffed by full-time lobbyists. Because lobbying is expensive, however, only the largest organizations or groups of organizations can afford such an operation. Most businesses are represented through the lobbying operations of trade associations, such as the National Association of Realtors and the National Association of Milk Producers. Other groups with lobby offices are the "peak associations," which group together large numbers of firms or unions; the National Association of Manufacturers, the U.S. Chamber of Commerce, and the AFL–CIO are peak associations. Some large corporations, and a few unions, maintain their own public affairs or governmental affairs offices for lobbying.

The most common method of lobbying is to hire a Washington firm to handle the entire lobbying process on a particular issue. Washington is full of "political lawyers." Indeed, most law firms, public relations firms, and consultants in Washington are engaged in selling lobbying services and expert knowledge of how government operates to those with an interest in influencing particular government decisions. Lobbying services have become increasingly specialized, with some firms, for example, specializing in mobilizing grass roots support.

Lobbying depends upon having contacts and an inside knowledge of government, and there is a steady demand in the industry for those who have such credentials. Thus, many former members of Congress stay on in Washington as lobbyists once they have retired or have been defeated. The same is true for former congressional staff members, high-level civil servants, and political executives. The money to be made as a lobbyist is much greater than a government salary, and the incentive for these people to "cash in" on their expertise in government is strong.

There has been rising concern in recent years about the "revolving door" relationship that has developed between interest groups and government officials, in which officials involved in regulating a particular industry subsequently accept lucrative offers to work for firms in that industry. A number of high-profile cases have drawn negative attention to this practice. Michael Deaver, one of the troika of top White House officials during President Reagan's first term, left the White House in 1985, openly admitting his desire to "cash in" on his Reagan connection. He set up a public relations firm and was immediately inundated with clients (including the Canadian government, which hired him to lobby for tighter acid rain regulations). The crassness of Deaver's operations drew a congressional investigation as to whether he had violated the ban on lobbying his colleagues for a year. In 1987, Deaver was convicted of perjury for lying to Congress and a grand jury about his lobbying activities.

The case that focused attention on the congressional "revolving door" was that of former senator John Tower of Texas. After a long congressional career, including several years as chair of the Senate Armed Service Committee, Tower retired and accepted contracts to advise several American and British defense contractors, making several million dollars over a two-year period. Criticism of his lobbying activities was an important factor in the Senate's unprecedented refusal to confirm his nomination as defense secretary in 1989.

Since 1978, high-level officials have been banned from lobbying their former government office for one year after leaving. In 1990 the ban was broadened to prevent most lobbying of the executive branch for one year; also, the ban was extended for the first time to former members of Congress. Nevertheless, one of Ralph Nader's public interest organizations, Congress Watch, reported that over half of the 300 members of Congress, congressional staffers, and White House staffers who lost or left their jobs after the 1992 elections went to work for lobbing firms in Washington.[35]

The Operation of Political Action Committees (PACs)

The campaign finance laws were reformed in the 1970s after it was discovered that large sums of corporate money had flowed illegally into various political campaigns, in particular President Nixon's re-election campaign of 1972. The new law requires an interest group to set up a PAC, which administers a special political fund that is segregated from the other funds of the organization. Group members are invited to contribute to this fund, which must be registered with the Federal Election Commission,

---

35   *Newsweek*, September 20, 1993, 4.

which administers the rules governing how funds may be solicited and donated. PACs have thus become the principal means by which interest groups donate money to political candidates, and PAC donations have provided a steadily increasing share of the funds raised by incumbent members of Congress.

Members of Congress need a steady flow of campaign contributions to finance their next campaign and to warn off serious challengers (see Chapter 6). Lobbyists take advantage of this need by offering donations through their PACs. The unspoken quid pro quo is access to the member. Most members agree that while campaign contributions do not buy votes in Congress in the crude sense, they do buy access. It is difficult for members to slam the door in the face of a lobbyist who has contributed to their campaign.

A PAC can only donate up to $5,000 to a candidate for each election or primary. Under a 1976 ruling of the Supreme Court, however, a PAC may undertake unlimited "independent expenditures" on behalf of or against a candidate for office, provided that such expenditures are entirely independent of the candidate's own organization. A small number of wealthy PACs take advantage of this, producing television commercials to support friendly candidates and to attack those candidates who have positions contrary to the those of the interest group. In 1980, for example, a number of conservative "political" PACs spent heavily against certain liberal Democratic senators and claimed credit for the defeat of several of them. In 1996, labor union PACs spent an estimated $30 million attacking the Republican-controlled House in the districts of vulnerable Republican members. In 1996, environmental groups such as the Sierra Club and the League of Conservation Voters contributed heavily to congressional campaigns through their PACs.[36]

Groups such as the NRA use PAC funds to support candidates favorable to their interests. The NRA PAC, called the Political Victory Fund, dispenses substantial amounts in campaign funds to supportive congressional and presidential candidates and also undertakes independent expenditures on their behalf. Implementing such a strategy involves significant amounts of money. For example, the NRA spent just over $900,000 on the 1990 congressional elections.

The distribution of campaign funds by PACs has become important to the lobbying goals of organizations. This means, in the first place, that most PACs concentrate their money where it is likely to do the most good for their interests—namely, on the members of the committees that deal with the issues of the most concern to them. Thus, the members of the banking committees can expect to be offered funds by the PACs run by the American Banking Association and individual banks. Most committees have their own interest group constituencies, which are always willing to give the members PAC money. When important legislation is before the committee, PAC contributions soar.

---

36   John H. Cushman Jr., "Environmentalists Ante Up to Sway a Number of Races," *New York Times*, October 23, 1996.

A consequence of campaign funds being directed by lobbying goals is that most PAC money goes to incumbent members of Congress. It was estimated that in the 1990 election, more than 90 percent of PAC contributions went to incumbents.[37] Incumbents thus have no difficulty raising campaign funds. This is particularly true of committee chairs and others in powerful positions. One of the consequences of the Democrats losing control of the House of Representatives in 1994 was that there was a noticeable shift of business PAC money from the minority Democrats to the majority Republicans.[38] There are only a few members who refuse to accept PAC money and rely solely on campaign donations from individuals.

Most interest groups feel they have no choice but to join in the distribution of PAC money once their competitors have started. Indeed, PAC money has now become such a routine part of the election process that the impact of particular donations has been greatly lessened. Many members of Congress take advantage of the unwillingness of interest groups to offend, and solicit campaign funds from them. A common technique is for members to hold fund-raising cocktail parties and invite lobbyists, who hesitate to turn down such "invitations" even though the price of attendance can be as high as $1,000 a head. In this manner, members of Congress can extract campaign funds from interest groups, without making any specific commitments. For interest groups, PAC contributions have become a cost of staying in the process.

Grass Roots Organization

An obvious interest-group strategy is to mobilize support in the member's district, since members are always especially attentive to interests that are well represented in their district and are known to fear organized and intensive opposition back home. Thus, a strong network of local members or supporters is an important arm of an organization's lobbying arsenal. Part of the job of the Washington lobby office is to provide the organization's local supporters with information on the issues and to alert them to contact their members of Congress when important votes are coming up. A large volume of mail from his or her district taking a position on an issue is bound to get the member's attention. Another strategy is to bring influential local citizens—a major employer in the district, for example—to Washington to speak to the member.

The more districts in which any group is organized, the greater its potential influence. As was noted in Chapter 6, some large companies have deliberately spread out their facilities to increase their lobbying influence in Congress. Some interest groups, like the peanut or tobacco growers, are regionally concentrated, which limits the scope of their influence in Congress. On the other hand, there are many organizations that

---

37   *Congressional Quarterly, Weekly Report,* June 29, 1991.
38   Thomas B. Edsall, "What the Losers Lost and the Winners Won," *Washington Post National Weekly Edition,* July 31–August 6, 1995.

have national membership networks, some of them highly organized, with excellent communications between Washington and the local branches. Examples include the NRA, the American Medical Association (AMA), and the U.S. Chamber of Commerce.

One of the best examples of an effective grass roots lobbying campaign was in 1983, when the banks and other financial institutions forced Congress to repeal a law passed the previous year that required them to start withholding tax on an individual's income from interest and capital gains (in the same manner that employers deduct income tax from employee paychecks). The financial institutions had lobbied hard against the proposal in Washington in 1982, but in the end the arguments for the bill (reducing tax evasion and lowering the deficit) narrowly prevailed.

The law gave the banks until July 1, 1983, to get their administrative arrangements ready. Instead of doing so, however, they launched a massive grass roots campaign to repeal the law by enlisting the support of their customers—everyone with a savings account! Congress was deluged with hundreds of thousands of letters protesting the law. Despite considerable effort by the congressional leaders of both parties and President Reagan, the repeal passed by overwhelming majorities in both houses. Although most experts considered the law necessary, most members of Congress were simply unwilling to back a law in the face of such massive opposition from their districts—opposition that had been stimulated and organized by the banks.[39]

Interest groups will sometimes go beyond informing and mobilizing their attentive publics and attempt, through "advocacy" advertising, to influence public opinion. If an interest group has public opinion behind it, members of Congress are much more likely to be in a receptive mood for the lobbyist's message. Lobbying against public opinion, however, is uphill work. Since the methods used—direct mail and advertising—are expensive, such campaigns are usually only resorted to when the lobbying has failed or is in danger of failing to achieve the policy objective. In the case of the battle over the withholding of taxes in 1982–83, the financial institutions only resorted to an all-out public campaign after they had failed to block the legislation by lobbying in Washington.

Interest groups are more likely to engage in a public relations campaign to counter an episode or run of bad publicity. For example, the steady growth of public concern about the environment has placed some industries, such as the oil, chemical, and nuclear power industries, on the defensive. Once seen as the providers of millions of jobs and as engaged on the frontiers of technology, they are now increasingly criticized as polluters of the environment. To try to revive their sinking public image, these industries have spent millions of dollars for advertisements highlighting their positive aspects (their provision of scholarships for minority students, for example). Even the

---

39   *Congressional Quarterly, Weekly Report*, April 23, 1983, 770–772.

powerful NRA has undertaken advertising campaigns in an attempt to soften its extremist, gun-toting public image.

The Role of Interest Groups in the American Policy Process: An Overview

Interest-group lobbying has become a huge industry in Washington. There is no accurate count of the number of interests represented, but some estimates run as high as 70,000 (compared to 3,000 registered lobbyists in Ottawa.) The fact that at least two-thirds of such groups are business-related should not be surprising in such an enterprise culture as the United States. However, a range of other groups, such as environmental organizations, women's and civil rights organizations, and unions led by the AFL–CIO, have also demonstrated their power and lobbying skill in certain situations. The development of public-interest lobbying since the 1970s has also had a countervailing effect.

Central to the wave of cynicism about politics in Washington that has gripped much of the American electorate in the 1990s is the perception that politicians are in the pockets of special interests. This was one of Ross Perot's major themes in his presidential campaigns in 1992 and 1996, and the issue was picked up by the media. By 1996, the angry public mood and bad media publicity had finally generated enough pressure that Congress tightened the laws regulating lobbying: there is now an almost complete ban on accepting gifts from lobbyists, and much tighter law on lobbyist registration and on disclosure of lobbying activities and expenditures. Reforming the 1970s campaign finance law has proved much more difficult.

PACs were invented as a way of limiting the flow of interest group money, particularly business money, to political campaigns. Since the 1970s, however, the enormous growth in the number of PACs and the increased dependence of politicians on PAC donations has left the political system awash in interest group money. The one area where the campaign finance reforms of the 1970s worked well was in presidential campaigns, through the provision of public funding with expenditure limits. However, a series of fund-raising scandals in the aftermath of President Clinton's re-election campaign in 1996 has drawn attention to the degree to which large corporate and individual donations—some of them from dubious sources—have been flooding into presidential campaigns in the form of "soft money" ostensibly for "party building" purposes. The new scandals have increased public pressure for reform of the financing of both congresssional and presidential campaigns. Yet the parties remain deadlocked between conflicting philosophies and conflicting party interests. More generally, the problem is that those who have succeeded in mastering the existing system are the ones with the responsibility for reforming the system.

Members of Congress always say that campaign contributions do not buy their votes. President Clinton, faced with the revelations of dubious fund-raising practices, has said emphatically that contributions, no matter how large, never influenced his decisions on policy. They may be correct in their denials. There is now so much legal campaign money available to incumbents from interest groups that there is certainly no need to provide a quid pro quo for donations. In the words of Representative Al Swift: "There is so much money out there that anybody who gives anybody anything for it is an idiot."[40] The point is, however, that it is impossible to tell the situations where donations have had no influence from those where they have. Certainly when it comes to passing tax loopholes and favorable regulations, the system has all the appearance of "legalized bribery."[41]

It is clear that what campaign contributions do buy is access to the decision-maker—the opportunity for the group or the individual to make their case. Access provides the opportunity to influence. That is why most interest groups now feel they have no choice but to contribute. Members of Congress complain that they have to spend a great deal of their time soliciting or socializing with potential donors—in other words, listening to them make their case. The principal problem with the steady escalation of campaign giving is not that it buys votes or decisions but that it further skews access to the policy process. While it is true that the interest-group process in Washington is pluralistic and open to any group, effective representation in Washington costs money, in terms of organization and skill, and now increasingly in terms of the ability to buy access through campaign donations.

While access may not invariably buy influence, lack of access is very likely to translate into lack of influence on policy. In addition, the appearance of politicians being "bought" by special interests undermines public confidence in the fairness of the political process. As so often in American life, the fundamental debate over campaign finance reform is about whether the principle of liberty—in this case the right to petition the government—should be restricted in deference to the principle of equality—the desire to preserve equal access to the policy process.

40   *Congressional Quarterly, Weekly Report*, March 17, 1990.
41   Jonathan Alter, "Keeping it in the Bedroom," *Newsweek*, March 10, 1997, 32.

CHAPTER 15

POLICY-MAKING IN WASHINGTON

The policy-making system in Washington has been described by Richard Rose as "an organized anarchy." To the question 'Who's in charge here?' the correct constitutional answer is: No one."[1] Under the Constitution, policy-making requires the cooperation of the independent executive and legislative branches, with the judicial branch sometimes playing its own special role. The president, the executive branch, the House of Representatives, and the Senate all have their own complex internal decision-making processes; it follows that the interactions between these institutions will be even more complicated. Moreover, the members of these institutions do not operate in a vacuum, but instead must deal continuously with a variety of supra-constitutional actors. These include people in the media, who have developed complicated, symbiotic relationships with the political actors, as well as many interest groups that swarm over and around the policy process, complicating the linkages between the political actors. Both sets of supra-constitutional actors have a huge effect on how policy is made in Washington. The role of interest groups was discussed in Chapter 14.

---

1   Richard Rose, *The Postmodern President: The White House Meets the World* (Chatham House, 1988), 183.

THE MASS MEDIA

The news media have always played an important social and political role in the United States. Samuel Huntington argues that behind each surge of political reform in America there was the development of new forms of media and an expansion of their audience, helping to build popular support for change. Prior to the Revolutionary era there was an explosion in the circulation of political pamphlets. There was an increase in the number and circulation of newspapers before the Jacksonian era—from 242 newspapers with a circulation of 200,000 in 1800 to over 1,000 newspapers with a circulation of over 1,000,000 by 1829. The Progressive era saw the development of a mass popular press—the large-circulation dailies created by media tycoons such as William Randolph Hearst, and inexpensive magazines.[2]

The turbulent period of the 1960s and early 1970s produced two major developments in the media that continue to influence current politics. It was not until the 1960s that a truly national press began to emerge out of the previously highly localized newspaper markets. As a result of their reporting on Vietnam and Watergate, respectively, the *New York Times* and *Washington Post* gained new prestige and prominence, as did the national newsmagazines, *Time*, *Newsweek*, and *U.S. News and World Report*. The *Times*, followed by the *Wall Street Journal*, distributed national editions, an example followed later by *USA Today*, a new paper designed from scratch for a national audience.

The most important development of the 1960s was the emergence of television news as a force in politics. By bringing the brutality of southern racism and then the horror of the Vietnam War directly into every American home, television was credited with mobilizing public opinion on both issues. The impact of television has continued to grow. By the 1980s, television had displaced newspapers as the principal and most trusted source of news information for a majority of the population. From its emergence in the 1950s through the 1980s, American television news had a nationalizing effect, since it was dominated by the three national networks. In recent years, however, technological developments such as satellite transmission, the spread of cable, and the mushroom growth of the Internet have had a fragmenting effect, with the networks' share of the national audience declining. In another development, twenty-four-hour news channels and global satellite networks, both pioneered by CNN, have intensified news coverage and speeded up the public response, placing new pressures on politicians.

---

2   Samuel P. Huntington, *American Politics: The Promise of Disharmony* (Harvard University Press, 1981), 99–101.

Constitutional Protection of the Media

The role the media play in politics looms larger in the United States than in Canada and other Western democracies in part because of the extraordinary degree of freedom accorded the press under the Constitution. The First Amendment states that "Congress shall make no law ... abridging the freedom of speech, or of the press." The Supreme Court has reinforced this freedom from government restriction, most notably in the case of *New York Times v. United States* (1971), where the Court upheld the right of the *New York Times* and the *Washington Post* to print excerpts from the Pentagon Papers, a leaked top-secret study of U.S. decision-making during the Vietnam War, over the objections of President Nixon. Justice William O. Douglas made the argument for an unrestrained press: "Open debate and discussion of public issues are vital to our national health. On public questions there should be 'uninhibited, robust, and wide open' debate."[3]

While freedom of the press is not absolute, it is very well protected in the American system. Even the law of libel, which in Canada and other countries acts as a major constraint on reporting, has been given a very narrow scope by the American courts. The limited scope for libel litigation by politicians in America is primarily a result of a 1964 Supreme Court case, *New York Times v. Sullivan*, which provided the "central element in [the] constitutional scheme of protection" for freedom of the press. [4]

In *Sullivan* the Court found that the First Amendment requires "a federal rule [which] prohibits a public official from recovering damages for a defamatory falsehood ... unless he proves that the statement was made with actual malice."[5] The *Sullivan* ruling allows the press to report speculations and allegations about public figures without much fear of prosecution since, even if the statement turns out to be false, the burden of proof is on the public figure to prove that the media outlet knew the information was false at the time it reported it.

In Canada, by contrast, the common law tradition continues to balance freedom of the press with concern for protecting the reputation of public figures from false statements. In *Hill v. Church of Scientology of Toronto* (1995), Mr. Justice Cory, for a unanimous Supreme Court, explicitly rejected the invitation, supported by most Canadian media organizations, to adopt the *Sullivan* rule in Canada. In his lengthy critique of that rule, Cory noted that no other jurisdiction had adopted it. The United States stands alone therefore in the degree of importance it attaches to freedom of the press. Constitutional protection of this magnitude invites an aggressive and intrusive mass media.

---

3 403 U.S. 713 (1971).

4 Ronald Dworkin, *Freedom's Law: The Moral Reading of the Constitution* (Harvard University Press, 1996), 195.

5 376 U.S. 254 (1964). See Anthony Lewis, *Make No Law: The Sullivan Case and the First Amendment* (Random House, 1991).

The Role of the News Media in Washington

By its very nature, the Washington political community is susceptible to media cover-age that is both extensive and intrusive. What makes the federal government such an attractive target for news gatherers and pundits is not simply the importance of the issues and the prominence of the personalities, but also the way in which its business is conducted. The U.S. government is a system with "multiple cracks." The fact that a large number of independent actors are in a position to exercise influence on a deci-sion makes the process much more public and creates a need for communication between the actors. Whereas in a parliamentary system most of the communication takes place in private settings (within the department, Cabinet, or caucus), communi-cation in a separated system with so many different political actors requires open and public channels of discourse. John Kingdon describes why the media's role in facili-tating the discussion in Washington is crucial:

> Various people scattered both inside and outside of government, dealing with
> similar problems day in and day out, sometimes communicate with each
> other in surprisingly indirect ways. They are all busy people and their paths
> may not cross frequently in the normal course of events, but they do all read
> newspapers.[6]

More importantly, they all read the *same* set of newspapers. Papers such as the *New York Times*, the *Washington Post*, and the *Wall Street Journal*[7] are all read avid-ly by politicians, bureaucrats, lobbyists, and journalists. These sources, in combina-tion with others such as the weekly political television talk shows, several weekly jour-nals of opinion, and "insider" newssheets with a local Washington circulation, deter-mine the "stories" everyone talks about and help shape the collective perspective of the governmental actors and the media commentators. It is within this context of shared assumptions (the "conventional wisdom") that decision-making takes place in Washington. The same shared assumptions shape the news reporting transmitted to the public by the media. In this sense, politicians and reporters are all part of the same political community "inside the Beltway."

The perceived power of the media comes from their role as the principal means of political communication between Washington and the American public. While the leading newspapers play the dominant role within Washington, television dominates Washington's communications with the rest of the country. It is in this respect that the

---

6   John W. Kingdon, *Agendas, Alternatives, and Public Policies* (Little, Brown, 1984), 63.
7   In terms of political perspective, the *New York Times* and the *Washington Post* are more pop-
     ular among liberals, while the *Wall Street Journal* and the *Washington Times* are of more
     interest to conservatives.

fundamentally adversarial relationship between the press and the politicians is clear-est. In a system based on frequent elections where public opinion polling has become a way of life, what the media communicate about politics to the public is extremely important for the politicians. As a consequence, everyone in Washington is obsessed with how their actions will be reported. James Fallows quotes a member of President Clinton's White House staff: "There is no such thing as a substantive discussion that is not shaped or dominated by how it is going to play in the press."[8] Politicians go to great lengths to try to influence the media's presentation and interpretation of events.

Most politicians have adapted to this increasingly media-shaped environment and have learned to use the media to serve their own interests. As one scholar put it, "politicians are not supine victims of the television age; rather they seek to under-stand its constraints and opportunities and to turn them to their own advantage if they can."[9] The relationship between politicians and the media is a symbiotic one—the media get information and the politicians get publicity. The goal for the politicians is to ensure that media coverage is favorable, and this can be accomplished through a variety of techniques.

One form of media manipulation is the leaking of confidential information—an activity for which there is much more scope and rationale in Washington than in Ottawa. By leaking and publishing information, the political actors and the media are able to use each other for their own purposes. There are a host of opportunities and a variety of motives for leaking information, from acting out a personal grudge to stimulating opposition to a forthcoming decision.[10] The media are always eager to run an exclusive story and to cultivate confidential sources. As noted above, in the case of one of the most spectacular leaks—of the Pentagon Papers by Daniel Ellsberg, a for-mer Defense Department employee—the Supreme Court upheld the newspapers' right to publish.

Every president has at some point become infuriated by embarrassing leaks, and some administrations have gone to great lengths to try to stop them. The Nixon Administration engaged in extensive wiretapping of some of its members, and White House operatives broke into the office of Daniel Ellsberg's psychiatrist in a vain effort to find information to discredit Ellsberg. The Reagan Administration proposed sub-mitting even senior officials to lie detectors tests to identify leakers. Since the media will always protect their sources to preserve their access to inside information, leakers

---

8   James Fallows, *Breaking the News: How the Media Undermine American Democracy* (Pantheon, 1996), 187.

9   Austin Ranney, *Channels of Power: The Impact of Television on American Politics* (Basic Books, 1983), 89.

10   Stephen Hess, *The Government/Press Connection* (The Brookings Institution, 1984), at 77 lists six different types of leaks according to the personal or policy motivation of the leaker.

are rarely found. The truth is that every Washington institution, including the White House, leaks information when it suits its purposes. As columnist James Reston once noted, the American government "is the only known vessel that leaks from the top."[11]

A common method for politicians to attract favorable media attention is to manufacture what Daniel Boorstin has called a "pseudo-event." A pseudo-event is not a spontaneous occurrence; rather, it is an event created for the purpose of being reported. It is an interpretation of the news disguised as a news event.[12] An example of a common pseudo-event is a presidential news conference. Such conferences are always carefully prepared for in advance. During the conference, the president presents answers that "spin" an interpretation of events that is in his self-interest. Instead of reporting the issue itself, the press are invited to report the president's positive role in confronting the issue. A successful press conference interjects the politician between the issue and the media, who convey "the news" to the public.

Most presidents have manipulated their coverage by the media, but the undisputed master of the pseudo-event was President Reagan. Reagan, a former B-movie actor, excelled at reading from prepared texts. Michael Deaver, one of Reagan's troika of advisers (see Chapter 7), used this skill to its maximum potential by "directing" Reagan in preplanned events. As Donald Regan, Reagan's chief of staff, noted in his memoirs:

> Deaver was a master of his craft. He saw—designed—each Presidential action as a one-minute or two-minute spot on the evening network news ... and conceived every Presidential appearance in terms of camera angles ... Every moment of every public appearance was scheduled, every word was scripted, every place where Reagan was expected to stand was chalked with toe marks. The President was always being prepared for a performance.[13]

Some of Reagan's performances, such as his teary-eyed address on the fortieth anniversary of D-Day, have become legendary. The press did not cover Reagan's policies so much as they covered Reagan's performances. An effective media strategy such as Reagan's simultaneously diverts coverage away from substance; it gives the administration more leeway in policy development, and also provides the positive coverage necessary to build the president's popularity, which is important in dealing with the Congress.

All successful politicians develop a distinctive way of using television to complement their strengths. President Kennedy used press conferences to show off his quick

---

11   Quoted in Hess, *The Government/Press Connection*, 76.

12   Daniel Boorstin, *The Image: A Guide to Pseudo-Events in America* (Harper & Row, 1961), 11.

13   Donald T. Regan, *For the Record: From Wall Street to Washington* (Harcourt Brace Jovanovich, 1988), 248.

wit and his grasp of issues. President Clinton takes advantage of his ability to communicate and empathize with individuals by appearing on various phone-in talk shows and participating in televised "town hall" meetings. The multitude of opportunities presented by the media, and television in particular, are there to be seized by an experienced and media-sensitive politician.

Reagan's speeches were always dramatically staged; here he proposes an Economic Bill of Rights in a speech at the Jefferson Memorial.

Few presidents have had the media skills of President Reagan, and most politicians do not enjoy as many opportunities as the White House provides for stage-managing events. However, all successful Washington operatives have become skilled at cultivating the media. Among the most skilled in recent years have been Henry Kissinger, secretary of state under Nixon and Ford, and James Baker, Reagan's chief of staff and Bush's secretary of state. By providing the media with what they need—timely inside information, good stories, and photo opportunities—politicians are able to establish their preferred versions of reality. Cooperating with the media almost always guarantees positive personal coverage. By providing the story, the political actor creates the opportunity to explain and justify his or her own actions in a self-serving manner.[14]

The Impact of the News Media on the American Public

As the main source of information and politics, the media act as a filter between the politicians and the public. Since reporting and editing the news is always a matter of selection and emphasis, the media are always open to charges of bias—of coloring their reports with their own values. There is a fundamental sense in which this is true. The media, like all American institutions, operate within the fundamental liberal consensus of American society. In Samuel Huntington's view, the existence of the ideological consensus gives the American press their unique role as the "clergy of

---

14   This logic has worked for reporter Bob Woodward. Woodward, in the course of writing several "insider" books, has made it a practice to recreate events and conversations on the basis of information leaked by the participants. Because it is well known throughout Washington that those who do not leak to Woodward are negatively portrayed, the amount of cooperation he achieves is astounding. See Howard Kurtz, "Selecting Heroes," *Washington Post Weekly Edition*, July 29–August 4, 1996, 15.

American society." The media "act as custodians of its ultimate values; they expose and denounce deviations from those values; they bestow legitimacy on individuals and institutions who reflect those values."[15]

There are two famous cases in which the press filled the role of the liberal clergy. In the case of the civil rights movement in the early 1960s, the vividness of the television coverage of racist brutality in southern cities, backed up by sympathetic reporting about the civil rights struggle and Martin Luther King, played a significant role in finally mobilizing white sentiment in the North on the side of freedom for black citizens. In the case of the intensive media coverage of the Vietnam War, both the horrifying immediacy of the television images and press photographs and the increasing skepticism of the journalists bolstered opposition to the war. Indeed, when Walter Cronkite, the popular and trusted anchorman for the CBS Evening News, voiced his skepticism on air, President Johnson privately admitted that the war was finished. "It's all over," he told aides. Journalist David Halberstam commented, "It was the first time in history that a war had been declared over by an anchorman."[16] While this may be overstating media influence, it seems clear that the impact of the media coverage was not neutral. (The American military indeed have gone to great lengths to limit and control media access in all subsequent military engagements, such as the 1991 Gulf War.)

The press are often accused of partisan bias in their reporting. Liberals point to the concentration of media ownership and to the conservative biases of the owners and business advertisers;[17] conservatives complain about the liberal inclinations of most journalists. Thomas Patterson clears journalists of the charge of deliberate political partisanship. He argues that the way the press reports politics introduces a "random partisanship" into the process, meaning that politicians of both parties may be reported negatively or positively depending on their role in the "story" the press is telling. Most politicians get both good and bad press at different times. Thus, Jimmy Carter was helped by mostly favorable coverage in the election of 1976 but hurt by negative coverage in 1980. George Bush was helped by his press coverage in 1988 but hurt in 1992, and so on. What is involved is not political bias but journalistic bias, which arises from the requirements of the medium.

There are a number of characteristics of the press that structure its presentation of the news. In the first place, television in particular has a strong tendency to dramatize and personalize the news. Paul Weaver argues that television news reportage requires a theme or story to make its reports visually interesting and hold the viewers'

---

15   Huntington, *American Politics*, 102.
16   Quoted in Austin Ranney, *Channels of Power*, 5.
17   For an extended critique of the media from this perspective, see Michael Parenti, *Inventing Reality: The Politics of the News Media*, 2nd Edition (St. Martin's Press, 1992).

attention. Television is by nature more interpretive than print journalism. Thus, in the reporting of the 1968 presidential election campaign, Humphrey was cast as the "underdog" and received mainly positive coverage; Wallace was defined as "dangerous" and received mixed coverage; Nixon was cast as the fading front-runner and received negative coverage.[18] Patterson argues that "the stories that the journalists tell of the candidates are not harmless little tales that mix fact and fiction. They are narratives with real consequences, because they affect the images that voters acquire of the candidates. The press is the message."[19]

A second characteristic of the press is that it has a short attention span. "Its concern is the new, the unusual, and the sensational." It is always searching for "a riveting story."[20] "The press," said Walter Lippman, "is like the beam of a searchlight that moves restlessly about, bringing one episode and then another out of darkness into vision."[21] Press coverage magnifies some issues and downplays others, which may in fact have more long-term significance. By focusing on an issue, the press can raise public awareness of it, but it cannot shape or sustain public opinion on the issue. Patterson argues that with the weakening of parties and dealignment of party loyalty, the press has been pushed into the parties' former role of interpreting politics to the public—a role which by its nature it is not suited to play. Journalistic values and political values are two quite different things.

The characteristic of the press that most seriously affects the public's understanding of politics is the view of politics that has developed over the years in the profession of journalism. Politics is almost universally viewed by journalists as "essentially a game played by individual politicians for personal advancement, gain, or power."[22] Politicians are thus seen not as striving for the public good but as manipulating the public for their own selfish interests. This cynical view of politicians was reinforced by the events of Vietnam and Watergate, when the media caught two presidents lying to the public.

The Watergate scandal was the case that really established the media as the guardians of the American system. The work of two young beat reporters for the *Washington Post*, Bob Woodward and Carl Bernstein,[23] in establishing the connection between White House operatives and the mysterious break-in at the offices of the Democratic National Committee led to the uncovering of a range of illegal activities directed from the White House and eventually to the resignation of the president and the conviction of several of his associates.

---

18   Paul H. Weaver, "Is Television News Biased?" *The Public Interest* No. 26 (1972).
19   Thomas E. Patterson, *Out of Order* (Knopf, 1993), 125.
20   Patterson, 37, 29.
21   Quoted at Patterson, 207.
22   Weaver, 69.
23   See Woodward and Bernstein, *All the President's Men* (Simon and Schuster, 1974).

The early stages of the investigation posed serious risks for the *Post*. President Nixon was at the height of his powers and coasting to re-election. The administration was threatening the profitability of the *Post* company through its power to block the renewal of the broadcast licences of *Post*-owned television stations in Florida. On the other hand, the Sullivan and Pentagon Papers cases had recently shown the press that the courts were willing to give them broad constitutional protection. Ronald Dworkin notes that "it is doubtful whether the Watergate investigation, or similar exposes, would have been possible if the court had not adopted something like the Sullivan rule."[24]

The exposure of the Watergate scandals was a triumph of investigative journalism that vindicated the role of the press as the watchdog of the American system and legitimized an aggressive role for the media in scrutinizing the conduct of politicians. After Watergate, the Washington media increasingly moved beyond descriptive reporting to critical analysis of the political world, a change that some argue has contributed to an increased public cynicism about politics in general.[25] Patterson argues that Vietnam and Watergate have had a poisonous effect on relations between politicians and the press. Vindicated in their cynical view of politics, the press turned against the politicians. [26]

The number of media organizations with reporters in Washington has grown enormously in the past twenty years, and some commentators argue that the competition among media organizations, each eager to uncover its own "-gate" scandal, has in fact led to a deterioration in the quality of investigative reporting. Larry J. Sabato argues that media scrutiny of politicians has degenerated into "attack journalism," which has become increasingly intrusive into not just the public but also the private lives of politicians. Media competition, rather than broadening the scope of news coverage, has often led to "pack journalism" where everyone goes after the same "scandal" in a "feeding frenzy."[27] By contrast, the press often neglect more serious matters. An example is the complex "S and L scandals," involving the widespread misuse of depositors' funds by savings and loan institutions across the country in the 1980s. The media were very slow to catch on to and investigate this story, although it cost taxpayers billions of dollars to compensate the depositors.

---

24   Ronald Dworkin, *Freedom's Law*, 195–196.
25   See Thomas E. Patterson, "Bad News, Bad Governance," in *Annals of the American Academy of Poliical and Social Sciences*, July 1996, and Fallows, *Breaking the News*.
26   Patterson, *Out of Order*, 19.
27   Larry J. Sabato, *Feeding Frenzy: How Attack Journalism Has Transformed American Politics* (The Free Press, 1991). George Bain makes a similar case against the Ottawa media in *Gotcha! How the Media Distort the News* (Key Porter, 1994).

Washington Post reporters Carl Bernstein (left) and Robert Woodward (right). Their investigation of the Watergate scandal garnered the newspaper a Pulitzer Prize.

There is almost universal agreement that a free press is an important part of the democratic process in that it exposes and holds up to public scrutiny the actions of those in power. In fulfilling its function, however, the media find it difficult to strike the right balance in their dealings with the politicians. It is generally agreed that in an earlier period, the relationship between the leading journalists and politicians was much too cosy. Many journalists were wooed into close social relations with the Washington power brokers and ended up as apologists for official policies. Sabato labels the years 1941–66 the period of "lapdog" journalism. Now the charge against the media is that they trivialize public debate and report too little on the substance of policy issues. Even many journalists agree that the media have become overly cynical about politicians and too intrusive into their purely private lives. It seems likely that this new media aggressiveness has deterred some people from running for office or accepting high-level appointments.

Journalistic excess is not a new phenomenon. Samuel Huntington argues that each period of social upheaval is followed by a period of excessive "muckraking" (Theodore Roosevelt's term for this style of journalism).[28] Roosevelt himself warned of the cynicism that could result from such scandal-seeking:

> To assail the great and admitted evils of our political industrial life with such crude and sweeping generalizations as to include decent men in the general

---

28 Huntington, *American Politics*, 102–104.

condemnation means the searing of the public conscience. There results a general attitude either of cynical belief in and indifference to public corruption or else of a distrustful inability to discriminate between the good and the bad.[29]

The example of President Clinton may suggest that the public has become tired of scandal-mongering. From the early stages of his campaign for the Democratic presidential nomination in 1992 through his first four years in office, President Clinton was dogged by stories about his private life. Reporters came to admire his resilience but treated him with skepticism. The thinly disguised portrait of a likable but amoral presidential candidate in columnist Joe Klein's best-selling novel *Primary Colors*[30] is fairly typical of the media's view of Clinton at the end of his first term. Clinton became the most investigated president in American history, as his private life and particularly his financial dealings while governor of Arkansas in the 1980s were dug into by the media, by an independent counsel appointed by the Justice Department, and by the Republicans in Congress. Yet in spite of all the negative coverage, he coasted to an easy re-election victory in 1996. Renewed charges of scandal have had no effect on his public support.

The media are now such an inextricable part of the political process in Washington that it is easy to see them as a powerful force in their own right. The role of the media in American politics is, however, a paradoxical one. On the one hand, the media influence the way the political actors behave; on the other hand, they are manipulated by the political actors. They shape how the wider public views politics and yet as commercial operations they are ultimately dependent on maintaining public approval. The fundamental role of the media remains that of guardian of the American political culture. It is a culture that attaches great importance to a free press, so long as the press is seen to uphold the basic American values supported by the public.

POLICY COMMUNITIES IN WASHINGTON

Policy-making in Washington is shaped by ongoing interactions between the Congress, the executive departments and agencies (with periodic and selective presidential intervention), and various interest groups. The wider policy community is composed of many different clusters of actors whose continuing interests lie in particular areas of policy. Each of these discrete policy clusters is usually composed of

---

29   Quoted in Huntington, *American Politics*, 104.
30   *Primary Colors: A Novel of Politics* (Random House, 1996) was originally published as by "Anonymous." *Newsweek* columnist Joe Klein later admitted he was the author—something he had earlier strenuously denied.

the leading members of the congressional authorizing committee and appropriations subcommittee, the top civil servants in the executive agency, and the interest groups with a stake in that area of policy. Given this pattern of interaction between the three groups of actors, there is a persistent tendency for policy in a given area to be controlled by "iron triangles" or "subgovernments."

Subgovernments

Iron triangles are so called because each leg of the interlocking relationship is a reciprocal relationship: the civil servants want to maintain a close working relationship with the members of Congress, who have legislative and oversight power and who control the agency's budget; the members of Congress in turn rely on the civil servants for information that will enable them to do their job effectively and deliver favors to their districts; and the lobbyists wish to maintain access to both the relevant members of Congress and the civil servants, through the exchange of information and support.

Lobbyists, members of Congress, and civil servants share a "permanence" in the Washington community (that is, relative to the much more "transient" political executives). Because they deal with policy in the same area over a long period of time, the three groups have a strong tendency to work together on the basis of mutual accommodation and support. The close working relationship between the groups is often reinforced by the movement of personnel between them, through the "revolving door." It is not uncommon, for example, for lobbyists to become congressional staffers and vice versa, and for civil servants to be hired by interest groups. Groups of actors in a given policy area have been dubbed "subgovernments" because they dominate policy in that area, and because other political actors usually defer to the decisions reached within the specialized group. Subgovernments typically defend existing policy and try to extend it incrementally. It has been argued that collectively, such policy groupings form what amounts to a "permanent government" in Washington that is resistant to changes proposed by the "transient" presidents and political executives.

The subgovernment configuration was typical of how most domestic policy was dealt with in the post–New Deal period, a time when committee chairs were all-powerful in Congress and dominated policy within their jurisdictions. Theodore Lowi has pointed out that subgovernments work best when government policy is "distributive," and involves delivering benefits to a limited population in a policy area that draws little public attention. A good example was the sugar subgovernment that controlled sugar policy from 1934 to 1974. Through the subgovernment, quotas were set for domestic sugar growers and limited quotas were allocated to selected foreign countries. All of this stabilized sugar prices in the United States above the world price. The benefits to domestic growers and some foreign governments were considerable, while the effect on domestic consumers was largely invisible.[31]

Issue Networks

A series of important changes in the 1970s broadened the policy community in Washington and created a new decision-making environment in which the typical policy configuration was no longer the subgovernment (though some of these patterns persisted), but rather the "issue network." Issue networks involve a wider range of often competing committees, executive agencies, and interest groups, all engaged in a struggle to control policy and the policy debate in a given area.

Most of the changes in the Washington scene grew out of the policy and political upheavals of the 1960s:

New federal programs.   The 1960s and early 1970s saw an expansion of federal programs into new areas of public life such as education, urban development, transportation, health care, civil rights, the environment, and the arts. Each new program generated a new set of interest groups drawn to lobby in Washington. The expansion in government programs created an explosion in the volume of lobbying.

New political activism.   One of the important legacies of the political activism of the 1960s, and of the entry of the large "baby boom" generation into politics, was the creation of new, broadly based, national political "movements," most notably the environmental movement, a revived women's movement, and a "public interest" movement initiated by Ralph Nader. These movements reinvigorated some old interest groups and generated a host of new groups, most of them critical of established policies and of the system of subgovernments.

New sources of policy ideas.   The upsurge of reformism in the 1960s and early 1970s and the conservative reaction that set in by the mid-1970s stimulated new policy debates, which became institutionalized in "think tanks," which are privately funded policy research institutions. The oldest think tanks, such as the Brookings Institution, date back to the earlier Progressive reform era. A few new ones were founded in the intervening period, but by far the biggest expansion came in the 1970s.

Think tanks have emerged as an important source of new policy ideas and of analyses and critiques of existing policy. A number of conservative think tanks, most notably the Heritage Foundation and the American Enterprise Institute, were

---

31   See David E. Price, *Who Makes the Laws?* (Schenkman, 1972), 123–138.

established to combat the dominant liberal policy climate of the 1960s. The conservative think tanks were an important source of executive personnel and policy ideas for the Reagan Administration. Similarly in the 1980s, new liberal and moderate think tanks, such as the Progressive Policy Institute, were established to try to contest the new conservative dominance.

Congressional reform. Another result of the reform climate of the 1960s was the long-delayed reform of congressional procedures, discussed in Chapter 5. The reforms reduced the autocratic power of committee chairs, decentralized policy influence to the subcommittees, and provided new scope for individual policy entrepreneurs, especially in the Senate.

The various changes mentioned above opened up the "multiple cracks" in the decision-making process to a host of new and competing interests; this in turn created a policy system characterized much more by issue networks than by subgovernments. Indeed, new interest groups often challenged some long-standing subgovernments. The sugar subgovernment broke up in 1974 when Congress, under pressure from a range of consumer groups, refused to extend the sugar quota system. In another area, the rising influence of environmental groups both nationally and locally broke into the subgovernment composed of the Army Corps of Engineers, the Public Works Committees, and the construction industry, which had long been engaged in dredging rivers and building dams all across the country.

THE TRANSFORMATION OF SUBGOVERNMENTS INTO ISSUE NETWORKS

An example of how a policy framework can be transformed from a subgovernment into an issue network is the area of tobacco policy. Since the New Deal in the 1930s, tobacco growing has been supported by the federal government through price supports and a system of marketing quotas. Policies governing this system and the price support levels were for years tightly controlled by the "tobacco subgovernment" in Washington, which was composed of the following: key members of the House and Senate Agriculture and Appropriations Committees (who were mainly from the leading tobacco-growing states of North Carolina, Virginia, and Kentucky); bureaucrats in the Department of Agriculture; and representatives of the tobacco growers' associations and the cigarette manufacturers. The tobacco congressmen and the tobacco lobbies were powerful, smoking was a widespread habit among the public, and the decisions of the tobacco subgovernment were not contested by Congress or the president.

The first signs of change in the policy climate for tobacco appeared in the 1950s with the publication of medical research reports that linked cigarette smoking with lung cancer. Such findings, which soon grew in volume, began to be publicized in the annual reports of the Surgeon General of the United States, a federal official. Over time, the build-up of such information brought new interest groups into the debate over tobacco policy: the American Medical Association; the American Cancer Institute; other prestigious medical and public health organizations; new anti-smoking lobbies; and other public interest groups. At first, the pressure was not directed against tobacco subsidies but at smoking, and proposals were made to regulate tobacco advertising and to require health warnings on cigarette packages.

The rise of new interest groups and public pressures brought new political actors into the debate—the congressional committees dealing with public health, and other federal agencies such as the Federal Trade Commission, the Office of the Surgeon General, the Food and Drug Administration, and the Environmental Protection Agency. Eventually it became popular for members of Congress from outside the South to campaign against the tobacco lobby. By the 1980s the small, cohesive tobacco subgovernment had become a much larger and more diverse and acrimonious tobacco issue network. The cigarette industry and the tobacco growers, with their congressional allies from the tobacco-growing and manufacturing districts, found themselves fighting a losing battle against health warnings and advertising regulations and forced to defend the hitherto sacrosanct tobacco marketing system.

Some subgovernments have had extraordinary staying power. The most powerful may be the "Veterans triangle," which operated largely unchallenged into the 1990s. The Veterans triangle is composed of the usual three elements: the House and Senate Veterans Affairs Committees (composed almost entirely of veterans), the Department of Veterans Affairs, and the three main veterans' organizations—the American Legion, the Veterans of Foreign Wars, and the Disabled American Veterans.

The Veterans triangle has been characterized by the interchange of personnel between the committee staffs, the bureaucracy, and the veterans' organizations. This has made for an especially tightly knit subgovernment that has long resisted proposals for change from outside. President Clinton's choice for Veterans Affairs secretary was Jesse Brown, executive director of Disabled American Veterans.

Any proposal for a major policy change may expose a subgovernment to outside scrutiny. Paul C. Licht has related how this happened with Veterans Affairs. The promotion of the Veterans Administration, a sub-Cabinet agency, to full Cabinet status had long been a goal of the veterans' lobby. The proposal was suddenly placed on the legislative agenda when President Reagan unexpectedly endorsed the idea. However, the legislation to create the new agency had to go through the House and Senate Government Operations Committees, whose members were not tied to the Veterans triangle and who were willing to listen to critics of the existing system. Before it would create a new department, Congress insisted on a reorganization of the old one and on the establishment of an improved appeals system for veterans. The old triangle had strongly resisted both.[32]

The Veterans subgovernment has never really opened out into an issue network, since there are no strong opponents of veterans' benefits. Some have been critical of particular policies; and others have criticized the programs as unnecessarily wasteful; but both parties support the broad extension of benefits. The Republicans view them as a reward for patriotic service, the Democrats as a valuable social program. A measure of just how successful the Veterans subgovernment continues to be in defending its resources is the fact that in 1995, when Republican budget-cutting was at its height in the Congress, the budget for Veterans Affairs actually increased.[33] Secretary Brown has been an highly active and effective lobbyist for his department.

Agenda Setting

In government, there are always too many issues and not enough time. For a major change in policy to take place, the issue must first make it onto the legislative agenda. Once on the agenda, the policy alternatives are shaped within the particular policy community. Through the legislative process, the policy alternatives are sorted out and specific outcomes are determined.

John Kingdon describes the agenda-setting process as the coming together of three essentially separate streams—problems, proposals, and politics. The streams join when "a problem is recognized, a proposal is available that can be related to that problem, and the political conditions are right."[34] When the political opportunity presents itself, it takes a "policy entrepreneur" to seize the issue and move it to the top of the agenda. Kingdon uses his model to explain the sudden bursts of legislative activity that occur at rare intervals, examples being the New Deal and the Great Society program. The same model can be used to explain the much more common situation where bills that have been stuck in congressional committees for years are suddenly propelled through the final stages into legislation. Kingdon likens policy entrepreneurs to "surfers waiting for the big wave."[35]

Agenda setting is a political process. Kingdon draws a distinction between the political actors and the other members of the policy community: bureaucrats, interest groups, and policy specialists. Once an issue is on the policy agenda, the other actors play an important role in sifting through alternatives and shaping outcomes.

---

32   Paul C. Licht, *Forging Legislation* (W.W. Norton and Company, 1992).
33   *Congressional Quarterly, Weekly Report*, July 15, 1995.
34   John W. Kingdon, "Agendas, Ideas, and Policy Change," in Lawrence C. Dodd and Calvin Jillson, eds., *New Perspectives on American Politics* (Congressional Quarterly Press, 1994), 216.
35   Kingdon "Agendas, Ideas, and Policy Change," 221.

Only the political actors, however, are in a position to move an issue onto the agenda for active consideration. Even the vaunted power of the media cannot ensure that an issue will be acted upon. Kingdon quotes a reporter: "The media can help shape an issue and help structure it, but they can't create an issue."[36]

In a parliamentary system like Canada's the policy agenda is set by the Cabinet. Only a limited number of bills can be handled in any parliamentary session. The process whereby ministers and departments compete for a spot on the parliamentary agenda takes place within the executive branch. Once the Cabinet has sorted out its policy priorities, it sets the agenda for the House of Commons. Usually the government can count on its legislation being enacted by Parliament. Only occasionally is it possible for a backbench "entrepreneur" to push a private member's bill through to legislation.

In the American system there is no centralized control of the policy agenda; rather, Congress and the president compete for control. Some studies have attempted to allocate responsibility for major pieces of legislation between president and Congress. They show that before the New Deal, more than half of such legislation originated in the Congress, with the president responsible for initiating less than one-fifth. After that the president's legislative role increased substantially. Between 1946 and 1964 it was the president who initiated around half of all major bills, with most of the rest being jointly developed by the president and Congress.[37]

The president now has the biggest single role in setting the policy agenda. He lays out general proposals in the State of the Union message each January and follows them with more detailed proposals for legislation. Because he can always command media attention, the president can often force Congress to address his priorities. However, he has no control over the legislative branch, so there is no guarantee that the president's agenda will be enacted into legislation.

President Carter pushed a reluctant Congress to deal with his proposals on energy conservation. After a great deal of presidential effort, the end result was much less than he had hoped for.[38] President Clinton set the agenda for the 103rd Congress (1993–94) by proposing comprehensive legislation on health care reform. It was an issue for which the political conditions seemed right. Yet after many months of executive branch preparations, congressional negotiations, and public campaigns by interest groups for and against his proposals, no legislation reached the floor of either House.[39]

---

36   John Kingdon, *Agendas, Alternatives and Public Policies*, 63. Stephen Hess has also concluded that the role of the media as an independent force in Washington has been greatly exaggerated. See *Live from Capitol Hill: Studies of Congress and the Media* (The Brookings Institution, 1991).

37   William M. Goldsmith, *The Growth of Presidential Power*, Volume III (Chelsea House, 1974), 1390–1407.

38   See Barbara Kellerman, *The Political Presidency: Practice of Leadership* (Oxford University Press, 1984), Chapter 10.

39   See Haynes Johnson and David Broder, *The System: The American Way of Politics at the Breaking Point* (Little, Brown, 1996).

Cabinet secretaries and other political executives are often in a position to "elevate" an issue in Washington, but to get it scheduled for action, they usually require presidential support. When he was Secretary of Housing and Urban Development in the Bush Administration, Jack Kemp had plenty of ideas for new legislation but little success in gaining the backing of the president, who had no interest in urban policy. But in September 1996, David Kessler, commissioner of the Food and Drug Administration, was able to proceed with stringent new regulation of the tobacco industry because he had President Clinton's support (and Congress was unlikely to object shortly before an election). Michael Pertschuck, a former political executive, commented: "A regulator alone couldn't have done it. But a regulator and a president are a fairly formidable team."[40]

Congress finds it hard to compete with the president in setting the agenda. Because its power has been dispersed to the committees and subcommittees, and because its party leadership is weak, Congress has limited capacity to set its own agenda. The principal exception to that general rule was in the 104th Congress (1995–96), when the House Republicans set the agenda. In 1994 the Republicans under the leadership of Newt Gingrich had campaigned on an agenda, the "Contract with America," and won control of the Congress. Once in charge, the Republicans made a concerted effort to pass their complete agenda. Although they were confident that the political conditions were right for it, their efforts were stymied. Not only did they have to water down some of their proposals to pass the more moderate Republican Senate, but most of their key proposals were vetoed by the president.[41]

While it is difficult for Congress to set the legislative agenda, there are many examples of individual members of Congress successfully shepherding particular bills to completion. Mayhew cites two examples: Senate majority leader Lyndon Johnson's sponsorship of two civil rights bills in the 1950s, and Senator Edmund Muskie's leadership in passing several environmental bills in the 1970s.[42] The decentralization of power in Congress that started in the 1970s made it simpler for members other than committee chairs to initiate legislation, but at the same time made it more difficult for anyone to steer legislation through to passage.

The Policy Outlook

In Ottawa, once the Cabinet has decided to put an issue on the parliamentary agenda, it can be virtually certain of having the legislation passed within a few months.

---

40   Glenn Frankel, "An End to Smoke and Mirrors," *Washington Post National Weekly Edition* September 2–8, 1996, 29.

41   See Elizabeth Drew, *Showdown: The Struggle Between the Gingrich Congress and the Clinton White House* (Simon and Schuster, 1996).

42   Mayhew, *Divided We Govern: Party Control, Lawmaking, and Investigations, 1946–1990* (Yale University Press, 1991), 105–106.

The government usually puts some effort into rallying its party caucus and building public support, but in the last analysis, if it decides to go ahead with a bill, it can rely on its loyal majority to move it through all the legislative stages.

In Washington there are three independent institutions—the House, Senate, and the president—and all three must come to an agreement before legislation can pass. It is possible for legislation to pass over the president's veto, but this rarely happens. As Steven Smith puts it, Washington policy-making is "a three institution game."[43] The orientations of the three institutions determine the "general policy outlook" for legislation in general and for particular types of legislation. The policy outlook in each house changes to a greater or lesser extent with the elections every two years; the executive branch outlook shifts as the president moves through the four-year election cycle. Each two-year period therefore presents a different outlook for policy-making.

It is instructive to compare three successive congresses, covering the period from 1991 to 1997. The 102nd Congress (1991–93) had a Democratic majority in both houses and a Republican president. Little was accomplished. The Democratic strategy was to create issues for the 1992 election by passing bills, such as the Family and Medical Leave bill (discussed below), that President Bush would be forced to veto owing to conservative pressures within his own party. The president had almost no domestic agenda of his own.

The 103rd Congress (1993–95) had smaller Democratic majorities in both Houses and a Democratic president elected on a minority vote. The Family and Medical Leave Act was immediately passed, but otherwise little was accomplished. The Republican minority was well organized, and President Clinton had great difficulty getting his budget through on a narrowly partisan vote. The centerpiece of the president's agenda—a major health-care reform package—split his own party and got nowhere in spite of months of effort.

The 104th Congress (1995–97) had new Republican majorities in both Houses and a Democratic president. The House Republicans set the agenda with a series of "revolutionary" proposals, but by early 1996 deadlock had been reached as the president vetoed most of their ideas.[44] In the summer of 1996 the climate suddenly shifted: both the congressional Republicans and President Clinton realized they needed some accomplishments to run on in the November elections, and several compromise bills were passed, including a major reform of the welfare system.

These three congresses illustrate the rapid shifts in general policy outlook that can take place even within the two years of one Congress. The outlook for different kinds of legislation shifted from one Congress to the next. The Family and Medical Leave Act, a typical Democratic initiative, could only have been passed in the 103rd

---

43   Steven S. Smith, *The American Congress* (Houghton Mifflin, 1995), 24.
44   David Maraniss and Michael Weisskopf, *"Tell Newt to Shut Up!"* (Touchstone, 1996).

Congress. Welfare reform, a major Republican issue, could only have been passed in the 104th Congress. It was the most ideologically divided Congress, the 104th, that turned out to be the most productive, with a last-minute flurry of compromises.

Legislative productivity, which tends to be fairly steady in a parliamentary system, varies considerably in the American system. There have been brief periods when Washington functioned almost like a parliamentary system, producing a great deal of legislation in a short period under strong executive leadership: 1913–16, when Woodrow Wilson's Progressive reforms were enacted; 1933–36, when FDR's New Deal was passed; and 1965–67, when Lyndon Johnson's Great Society program was hurried through the Congress.

Historically, there have been two prerequisites for intensive policy activity in Washington: an activist president with a legislative agenda, and an influx of new members of the president's party into Congress who are committed to the president's agenda. Not all presidents define their role to include active legislative leadership; but without presidential leadership, Congress is usually incapable of sustained legislative activity. Also, without a shake–up in membership, it is difficult for Congress to over-come the resistance of entrenched subgovernments. Periods of concerted policy action tend to be brief. Presidents Wilson, Roosevelt, and Johnson eventually found them-selves in the same situation: frustrated by a Congress that refused to do their bidding though it was controlled by their own party.

Mayhew has pointed out that these three periods of rapid policy change were actu-ally just the peaks of longer periods of heightened legislative activity that involved both parties. Thus, the Progressive reform period started with Republican Theodore Roosevelt and culminated in Wilson; the scorned Republican President Hoover antic-ipated some of the New Deal reforms, which FDR continued in a more radical fash-ion; and the changes that started with Kennedy and Johnson continued into the Nixon Administration, which produced a great deal of domestic legislation, such as innova-tive environmental laws. Mayhew attributes such legislative surges to a "public mood" that for a time is supportive of change.[45] Once the public returns to its normal inat-tentive state, the policy process returns to the usual state of trench warfare.

The Policy-making Process

Within each of the three institutions whose agreement is needed to make policy, there exist strong centrifugal pressures that militate against concerted action. Within the executive branch there are departments and agencies with different perspectives and goals for legislation. Also, within an agency there are often tensions between the

---

45   Mayhew, *Divided We Govern*, 142–174.

career staff and the political executives. Only the president can make the executive branch speak with one voice on an issue and bring executive resources fully to bear in the struggle for legislation, but he must exert himself to do so. Executive branch unity is never automatic.

Put another way, the executive branch can speak and operate with authority only through the president. For this reason there is often fierce competition within the executive branch—and sometimes within the White House itself—to get the president's support for a particular position. One of the most publicized recent examples was the fierce debate over whether President Clinton should sign or veto the welfare reform bill passed by the Congress in July 1996. According to one account, the Secretaries of Housing and Urban Development, Labor, and Health and Human Services pressed for a veto, while the Secretaries of the Treasury and Commerce, along with the vice president, argued for signing. The senior White House staff were equally divided. The president decided to sign the bill.[46]

As was discussed in Chapter 5, the legislative process in both the House and the Senate has been highly decentralized since the 1970s. Before that, committee chairs wielded considerable power over policy in their areas and were the key players in the passage of legislation. For example, when President Johnson wanted a tax cut passed in 1964 he had to negotiate with Rep. Wilbur Mills, chair of the House Ways and Means Committee. Having struck a deal with Mills, the president could be sure that the tax cut would pass.[47] Ever since the concentrated power of the committee chairs was dispersed following the procedural reforms of the mid-1970s, a majority must be built for legislation at each stage of the legislative process in each house. In some situations the House Speaker can wield considerable influence, as Newt Gingrich demonstrated for a time in 1995, but in general terms there are no major power brokers any more.

The relative weakness of party discipline in Congress means that the necessary majority to carry legislation through its stages in either house almost always has to be a bipartisan one. One party or the other usually provides a base on which to construct a majority, but it is rarely enough simply to mobilize party members. Mayhew found that only 9 percent of major legislation was passed by a purely partisan majority in both houses. Conversely, he found that 70 percent of major legislation was passed by large bipartisan majorities in both houses.[48]

As R. Douglas Arnold emphasizes, what is needed to pass legislation is a broad coalition that reaches across party lines, across all three institutions, and into the

46   David Remnick, "Curious George," in *The New Yorker,* October 21 and 28, 1996, 176–177.
47   On the mode of operation of Mills, the most famous of the old-style committee "barons," see John F. Manley, "Wilbur D. Mills: A Study in Congressional Influence," *American Political Science Review* 63 (1969), 442–464.
48   Mayhew, *Divided We Govern,* 124.

wider policy community. The support of interest groups and their attentive publics is an essential ingredient in building support in Congress. Policy specialists play an important role in generating viable proposals to deal with the problems Congress has defined. In the process of persuading members of Congress that they are pursuing a politically safe course, it is always helpful to provide evidence of public support.

Broad policy coalitions do not fall into place by themselves, and Arnold emphasizes the crucial role that "coalition leaders" play[49]—especially in the Congress—in shepherding legislation through the many bottlenecks in the process. Even when the president is the principal backer of legislation, he needs active coalition builders inside the Congress. The president's own role is typically to build public and interest-group backing for his proposal, but he must also work actively with the Congress. The president's persuasive or deal-making powers are often crucial for steering legislation through difficult stages. Presidents differ greatly in the amount of will and skill they bring to the task of coalition building.[50]

Building coalitions in Congress takes a great deal of time, effort, and skill. This work is often invisible to the public and may not have any electoral payoff, since it inevitably requires flexibility and compromise. But Arnold emphasizes that however much they care about safeguarding their re-election prospects, many members of Congress are genuinely committed to making good public policy. Mayhew suggests that there is an underestimated "problem solving mentality" in Congress that leads many members to work away at building support for legislation.[51]

The will to legislate is not in itself enough; it requires considerable skill to steer a bill through the congressional maze. Arnold points to three types of strategy that coalition leaders commonly use to build support: strategies of persuasion, procedural strategies, and strategies of modification.[52] These strategies operate in conjunction with the "standard operating procedures" in Congress—logrolling and the maximum spreading of benefits—that were discussed in Chapter 6.

The preferred strategy is to persuade other political actors, interest groups and their attentive publics, and (so far as possible) the general public to support a proposal on its merits. Clearly, when there is broad support for legislating on an issue, it will be much easier to work out the details and steer a bill through its different stages. A common strategy of persuasion is to link the issue to a position that is already popular. Arnold cites how support for expensive space programs has been justified by linking them to national defense.[53] If a proposal can be linked to larger issues that already

---

49   R. Douglas Arnold, *The Logic of Congressional Action* (Yale University Press, 1990), 6–8.
50   See the case studies in Kellerman, *The Political Presidency*.
51   Mayhew, *Divided We Govern*, 130.
52   Arnold, *The Logic of Congressional Action*, Chapter 5.
53   Arnold, 93.

command widespread support—such as national defense, economic growth, the principle of equity/fairness, and, in recent years, "family values"—the chances of passage are greatly increased. Conversely, the key to defeating a proposal is often to link it to an unpopular issue. Thus, in recent years funding for the development of the space station has been threatened by those linking its cost to the budget deficit.

Procedural strategies are important in maximizing support in Congress. Members of Congress prefer to avoid taking positions on controversial issues and only feel comfortable casting votes that are politically safe. Legislation may be written so as to delegate to others—the president or a regulatory agency—the major unresolved or controversial issues. Also, legislation may be so drafted that it is open to different, even opposing, interpretations or has loopholes that allow for different outcomes.

In the pre-1970s Congress, the shaping of legislation in committee was mostly done in private, and it was not uncommon for members to vote one way in committee and the other way in public after the bill came to the floor. Under the reform rules, however, almost all votes are now on the record. Often the voting is set up so as to allow nervous members to vote on both sides of the issue—that is, to vote *for* the bill in one format and *against* it in another. Another increasingly common method of dodging responsibility is to include a number of issues together, the unpopular with the popular, in an "omnibus" or "take it or leave it" bill.

Modification is perhaps the most basic of the three strategies. In order to build a majority at each of the legislative stages, and ensure the president's signature, coalition builders must adjust proposals to attract new supporters. This can be enormously difficult to do without alienating present supporters. Some interests will be pragmatic and willing to accept "half a loaf"; others will stick to ideological positions that make compromise more difficult. The strategy of modification thus requires negotiating skills, which many members do not possess, as well as a degree of pragmatism that may be politically risky.

For most legislation, all three types of strategy are necessary. Legislating takes a great deal of time and effort, and there is no guarantee of quick success. Indeed, it is rare for a proposal to be passed into law in a single session of Congress. Proposals often stall in Congress until the political climate is supportive and all the right compromises have been found to build a majority coalition. For example, a major reform of telecommunications law had been caught between competing interests, and stuck in committee for several years, until quite suddenly in February 1996 it was able to move to passage by large majorities.[54]

---

54   *Congressional Quarterly, Weekly Report*, February 3, 1996, 289–294.

◄ The Family and Medical Leave Act, 1993

A good example of how the American legislative process commonly works is the Family and Medical Leave Act, which was signed into law by President Clinton in February 1993 after it had been in process in Congress for nearly ten years.[55]

Ronald D. Elving has traced the bill's origins to a small group of liberal Democrats who started work in 1984 on a proposal that would require businesses to provide paid maternity leave for their employees. They worked from the beginning with a coalition of women's and union groups. At first, the outlook was not good. The Democrats controlled the House, but Republicans controlled the Senate, Reagan was president, and the general mood in Washington was strongly conservative.

From its initial introduction in 1984 to its first passage by the House in 1990, the bill's supporters set out to build a majority coalition through strategies of persuasion and modification. The main objection from Republicans and moderate Democrats was that the bill imposed new costs on small businesses. An early decision was to mandate only unpaid leave. For the sake of lining up the necessary support of the first moderate Republicans, businesses with fewer than fifty employees were exempted. To stay clear of an extremely contentious issue, it was made clear that medical leave would not apply to abortions. In order to broaden interest-group backing, additional medical conditions were included. To get the support of the influential American Association of Retired Persons (AARP), the coverage was extended to include leave to look after elderly parents.

As the proposal gained broader support, it also stimulated a more active opposition, mainly from business groups that had the ear of the Republican Party, including the U.S. Chamber of Commerce. The sponsors found support among social conservatives, however, with the argument that the legislation would support families and would discourage abortion by guaranteeing women time off during pregnancy. The support of the U.S. Catholic Conference did much to line up the first conservative Republican support for the bill—most notably that of Rep. Henry Hyde, the leading opponent of abortion in the Congress.

The Democratic House leadership, while sympathetic to the bill, was unwilling to commit any effort to its passage until its supporters had built up a majority coalition. The Democratic take-over of the Senate in the 1986 election allowed a parallel bill, sponsored by Senator Chris Dodd, to start making progress there, but the Senate leader required Dodd to get the sixty votes needed to overcome a certain Republican filibuster before he would schedule a floor vote on the bill.

It was only after the bill first passed the House in 1990 that the media began to pick

---

55   The account of the legislative process leading to the passage of this act is based on Ronald D. Elving, *Conflict and Compromise: How Congress Makes the Law* (Simon and Schuster, 1995).

President Clinton signs the Family and Medical Leave Act, the first legislation of his presidency. With him is Vicki Yandle, who lost her job after staying home to take care of her daughter, diagnosed with cancer.

up on the issue. A higher public profile triggered serious procedural maneuvering around the issue. In the Senate, the Republican minority decided against a filibuster, which would have given the bill's supporters more publicity, and allowed the bill to pass on a voice (unrecorded) vote, since they knew that President Bush would veto it, which he duly did.

Sensing that public opinion was now behind the issue, the Democrats brought the bill forward again in the new Congress in 1991. They continued to broaden its support, even allowing a substitute, slightly modified version sponsored by a moderate Democrat and Rep. Henry Hyde to replace the original bill in order to emphasize that it was not simply a "liberal" issue. The bill passed both houses early in 1992, but the Democratic leadership delayed sending the bill to the White House until October to force President Bush to exercise his expected veto shortly before the presidential election.

Bush's veto of the now popular bill was one of the issues the Democrats used against him in the 1992 campaign. The election of President Clinton meant that the Democrats controlled all three institutions for the first time since 1980, and that passage of the bill was certain. Rather than reopen the issues in the hope of getting a stronger bill, the Democratic leaders decided to stick with the existing compromise. It was rushed through all its stages in the new Congress and passed overwhelmingly by bipartisan majorities in both houses. The Family and Medical Leave Act was the first piece of legislation signed by the new president in February 1993.

Policy-making in Washington: An Overview

It is clear from an overview of their policy-making processes that the Canadian and American systems of government are based on radically different principles. Policy-making in the parliamentary system is heavily concentrated in the Cabinet, whose members work closely with the civil servants of the Ottawa bureaucracy. The processes of agenda setting and shaping legislation take place within the executive branch, which determines which interests and policy experts will be consulted. Once a government bill is produced, the legislative process is essentially a formality, since it is controlled by the government's disciplined majority in the House of Commons. Efforts to change or block legislation once it is introduced into the House of Commons are usually fruitless unless the public and the government caucus are sufficiently aroused that the government is persuaded to back down.

In the American system, policy-making is a "three-institution game," with the House of Representatives, the Senate, and the executive branch each operating outside the control of the others. Since power in each of the institutions is highly decentralized, and since there are a large number of decision-makers, the policy process is open to influence at almost every point. The president can influence the policy agenda through his skill at publicizing issues and drawing media attention to them, but as President Clinton discovered with his health care proposals in 1993–94, the president has only marginal influence on the legislative process in Congress.

Once an issue reaches the political agenda, a struggle ensues within the relevant issue network or policy community to shape the outcome. Legislation is shaped as it goes through the congressional process. A majority must be built at every stage if legislation is to pass. As a consequence, the process is slow and most legislation has a long gestation period. It may slowly build support over several Congresses, like the Family and Medical Leave Act. It may become stuck at the committee stage for years (as happened with the telecommunications bill) until the necessary compromises are struck within the policy community and the policy outlook in all three institutions is favorable for passage.

CHAPTER 16

CONCLUSION

An examination of the American political system suggests three main distinguishing characteristics: the dominant role of liberal ideas; government by separated institutions; a political sense of national identity. These three characteristics are closely tied together: the fragmented constitutional structure stems from the liberal fear of governmental power; the American identity has a political content—a belief in individual liberty and pride in the genius of the constitutional system.

LIBERAL IDEAS

The root of American exceptionalism is the dominance of the liberal tradition (reinforced at most points by American Protestantism) and the absence of viable conservative and social democratic traditions. Liberal ideas have defined and limited the public debate,[1] and the resonance of alternative ideas has always been correspondingly weak. The range of politically viable options in the United States has always been

---

1   On the limiting effect of of liberalism on the political debate in America, see A. Mark Roelofs, *The Poverty of American Politics: A Theoretical Interpretation* (Temple University Press, 1992)

narrower than in Canada and other Western countries, where the alternatives to liberalism have played a much larger role in shaping public beliefs and expectations.

The central argument throughout American history has been within liberalism, between the competing principles of individual liberty and equality. Liberty has usually won the argument. In America, argues J. R. Pole, "equality is usually the language of the underdog."[2] The case for limiting individual rights for the common good has always been a difficult one to make in the United States. Yet American individualism has been constrained by a continuing concern for equality.

From the beginning, the Americans took pride in being an egalitarian society, free from the entrenched divisions of hereditary rank and privilege of the Old World. America saw itself as a new kind of society based on a new form of equality. The American commitment has always been to an equality of opportunity—social and political equality with the opportunity for economic advancement. Jefferson and Madison, among others, understood that a tension existed between the pursuit of individual happiness and the maintenance of an egalitarian society. So long as the United States remained a predominantly agricultural society, a rough balance was maintained between the two commitments.

The balance was upset by the advance of industrialization, which created new and much greater inequalities of wealth, which were inevitably translated into new social and political inequality. The argument in the twentieth century has therefore been between those who believe that America is still the land of opportunity for all and those concerned with restoring true equality of opportunity. Central to this debate is the question of the role of government.

One consequence of the dominance of liberalism has been an instinctive American distrust of government as a threat to individual liberty. The classical liberal ideal of minimal government remains a compelling one, as President Reagan demonstrated in the 1980s. ("Government is not the answer to our problems; government is the problem.") The "new liberal" conception of government as a positive instrument for enhancing the equality of opportunity did not receive much support until the New Deal. In the last twenty years the New Deal liberalism of the Democratic Party has been challenged again by classical liberalism in the modern form of conservative Republicanism, which is strongly individualistic and hostile to all but minimum government.

SEPARATED INSTITUTIONS

American liberalism is strongly entrenched by the constitutional structure. The framers set out to establish a new form of government based on liberal principles. To

---

2   J. R. Pole, *The Pursuit of Equality in American History* (University of California Press, 1978), ix.

prevent any threat to individual liberty by the accumulation of unfettered power they created a system of separated institutions that were required to share power. The institutional framework of the Constitution has proved to be extraordinarily durable and has worked very much as the framers intended, by fragmenting power at every level, thus making government action difficult.

For most of the nineteenth century the fragmentation of power was partially offset by strong political party organizations. In the twentieth century, however, just as the demands on the federal government were growing, the parties' organizational capacities were undermined, first by the anti-party reforms of the Progressives and later by the ability of candidates to communicate directly with the voters through the unrestricted use of television. The result in recent years has been the radical individualization of politics: candidate-centered campaigns and the devolution of power in Congress to subcommittees and individual members, making concerted action more difficult than ever.

Pride in the constitutional system and liberal Creed is deeply entrenched in the American consciousness, and there is no prospect of significant change. The American system of government (separated institutions with weak parties) can nevertheless be evaluated in comparison with those of Canada and most Western countries (parliamentary systems with strong parties) in terms of three basic criteria: effectiveness, democratic accountability, and policy output.

Effectiveness

The ability of the American system to meet the demands of modern government has worried American political scientists since Woodrow Wilson in the 1880s.[3] Most have advocated strengthening the executive branch by moving closer to a parliamentary system[4] or strengthening political parties to move closer to a system of responsible government.[5] Wilson himself concluded that the answer lay in strong presidential leadership, which he demonstrated during his two terms in office. The same conclusion was reached in the 1950s by Richard Neustadt, who drew on the example of FDR's leadership during the Great Depression and World War II.[6] By the late 1970s, however, the realization had set in that expectations of presidential leadership had become much

---

3   Woodrow Wilson, *Congressional Government: A Study in American Politics* (World Publishing Company, [1885], 1956).

4   The advocacy of a parliamentary system by Americans is reviewed in Thomas O. Sargentich "The Limits of the Parliamentary Critique of the Separation of Powers," *William and Mary Law Review* 34 (1993), 679–739.

5   Committee on Political Parties of the American Political Science Association, "Towards a Responsible Two-Party System" *American Political Science Review* 44 (1950).

6   Richard E. Neustadt, *Presidential Power: The Politics of Leadership* (John Wiley and Sons, 1960).

higher than the constitutional and political realities could normally accommodate. Richard Rose pointed to the limitations on presidential leadership in comparison to a parliamentary system: to the question of who is in charge in Washington, "the correct constitutional answer is: no one."[7] Each president must struggle as best he can to create a record of achievement for himself.

Democratic Accountability

A clear comparative weakness of the American separated system is that it diffuses responsibility for government action (or inaction) and thus blurs democratic accountability. The further weakening of party organizations since the 1960s has undercut their ability to bridge the institutional gap and has produced an era in which divided government has become the norm. Since any major action requires cooperation between the executive and legislative branches and usually between the parties, it is difficult for the public to accurately apportion credit for popular action (everybody can claim credit) or blame for inaction (each institution and party can blame the other).

An example of the confusion that can reign was the serious miscalculation of the Republican congressional leaders during the stalemated budget negotiations with the president in 1995–96. Confident that the public would blame the president, the Republicans refused to compromise and allowed parts of the government to shut down for three weeks. When they discovered that instead the public blamed the Congress, the Republican leaders were forced into a humiliating retreat. Only in the now unusual situation where one party controls both branches of government is it possible to hold that party responsible for what happens in Washington. The brilliant campaign waged by Newt Gingritch against the Democrats in the 1994 elections demonstrated how this can be done.

From a different perspective, it can be argued that the American system is highly democratic in that it is much more responsive to the voters than a parliamentary system. To represent local interests has always been imperative for members of Congress. The opinions of constituents always trump party loyalty and arguments for the national interest. Modern presidents are always in campaign mode, closely following the opinion polls. This hypersensitivity in Washington to grass roots opinion increases the difficulty of making unpopular decisions. In Canada, the Mulroney government had no difficulty passing the highly unpopular goods and services tax (GST), the kind of decision that it is almost impossible to make in Washington. Americans have frequently envied the effectiveness of the parliamentary system and its ability to make necessary but unpopular decisions, but the weakness of the checks on executive power

---

7   Richard Rose, *The Postmodern Presidency* (Chatham House, 1989), 183.

makes them uneasy. The examples of White House manipulation in the Watergate and Iran/Contra scandals have kept alive the ancient American fear of executive tyranny. In the parliamentary system there are in fact few short-run checks on a government with a disciplined majority.

Sargentich argues that the superiority of the American system over the parliamentary system lies in "the principle of dialogue underlying the Constitution's structure."[8] The American system is thus more democratic, since it requires a much broader debate and clear evidence of public support before major actions can be taken. In most cases, broad coalitions in support at the grass roots and among interest groups must be built, often over several years, before legislation can be passed. Steinmo and others have argued to the contrary: that the multiple cracks in the American system give unusual power to unrepresentative interest groups, which are often able to block action even in the face of popular support.[9]

Policy Output

Comparison between the policy outputs of the American and other Western nations has mostly focused on the growth of the welfare state in the twentieth century. While the difference between American and other social welfare systems is often overstated, it is the case that "American governments tend to spend somewhat less, and do somewhat less, to address the social and economic problems faced in all advanced industrial nations."[10] Explanations of this difference mostly focus on the American political culture: the dominance of liberal individualism in the United States and the weakness of the sense of community and commitment to the common good that is present in conservative and socialist thought. Steinmo prefers an institutional explanation, arguing that it is the division of political authority and responsibility and the veto power that the fragmented constitutional structure gives to interest groups which is responsible for the underdevelopment of the American welfare state.

In fact, the belief system and the constitutional structure reinforce each other. The case for limiting individual rights is always difficult to make in the United States because of the constant reinforcement of liberal individualism and the mistrust of government. The fragmented institutional system makes government action difficult and provides maximum opportunity for private interests to benefit at the expense of the public interest.

---

8   Sargentich, "The Limits of the Parliamentary Critique of the Separation of Powers," 732.

9   Sven H. Steinmo, "American Exceptionalism Reconsidered: Culture or Institutions?" in Lawrence C. Dodd and Calvin Jillson, eds., *The Dynamics of American Politics: Approaches and Interpretations* (Westview Press, 1994), 106–131.

10   Steinmo, "American Exceptionalism Reconsidered," 112.

NATIONAL IDENTITY

From a Canadian perspective it is the strength and intensity of the American sense of identity that stands out in comparison to the persistent divisions within Canada. The intensity surrounding American identity comes from its origins and accompanying sense of national mission. The American identity was forged in a revolutionary war fought in the name of universal political ideals. The two founding strains of thought—New England Puritanism, which sought to create a righteous society in the New Eden, and Enlightenment liberalism, which believed that man's natural goodness would flourish free from the artificial constraints of the Old World—came together to infuse the Americans with a sense of national destiny. This missionary vision sanctified the often brutal settlement of the continent and held the new nation together though the Civil War.

From a broader perspective, however, it is the political content of the American identity that has made it a particularly powerful integrating force throughout American history, in that it holds out the promise of political and religious freedom and of economic and social opportunity (the American Dream) to all who share America's values. Throughout the nineteenth century the Anglo-Protestant society gloried in the nobility of its ideals and resisted their universalistic import. But in the end the acculturation of millions of diverse immigrants enabled the United States to make the transition to a multiethnic, multireligious industrial society in the twentieth century.

The one internal division that the common vision could not overcome was the division caused by white racism. There was no shared history between black and white. On the Fourth of July of 1852, Frederick Douglass, the black abolitionist leader, addressed the Rochester Ladies' Anti-Slavery Society as follows:

> The blessings in which you, this day, rejoice, are not enjoyed in common. The rich inheritance of justice, liberty, prosperity, and independence, bequeathed by your fathers, is shared by you, not by me .... This Fourth [of] July is *yours*, not *mine*. You may rejoice, *I* must mourn.[11]

Even with the abolition of slavery the separation of the races remained. Unlike the immigrants, African Americans were denied access to the American Dream. It was not until the 1960s that Americans began to respond to the challenge of another great black orator, Martin Luther King Jr., to share their "rich inheritance" with black Americans. The black/white divide has been the most destructive division in American history and the most difficult to overcome. It is one area in which the meaning of America's historic commitment to equality of opportunity has yet to be fulfilled.

---

11   Frederick Douglass, "What to the Slave is the Fourth of July?" *The Frederick Douglass Papers*, Series 1, Volume 2 (Yale University Press, 1982), 359–387.

APPENDIX 1:
THE DECLARATION OF INDEPENDENCE

In Congress, July 4, 1776,

THE UNANIMOUS DECLARATION
OF THE THIRTEEN UNITED
STATES OF AMERICA

When, in the course of human events, it becomes necessary for one people to dissolve the political bonds which have connected them with another, and to assume, among the powers of the earth, the separate and equal station to which the laws of nature and of nature's God entitle them, a decent respect to the opinions of mankind requires that they should declare the causes which impel them to the separation.

We hold these truths to be self-evident, that all men are created equal; that they are endowed by their Creator with certain unalienable rights; that among these, are life, liberty, and the pursuit of happiness. That, to secure these rights, governments are instituted among men, deriving their just powers from the consent of the governed; that, whenever any form of government becomes destructive of these ends, it is the right of the people to alter or to abolish it, and to institute a new government, laying its foundation on such principles, and organizing its powers in such form, as to them shall seem most likely to effect their safety and happiness. Prudence, indeed, will dictate that governments long established, should not be changed for light and transient causes; and, accordingly, all experience hath shown, that mankind are more disposed to suffer, while evils are sufferable, than to right themselves by abolishing the forms to which they are accustomed. But, when a long train of abuses and usurpations, pursuing invariably the same object, evinces a design to reduce them under absolute despotism, if is their right, it is their duty, to throw off such government and to provide new guards for their future security. Such has been the patient sufferance of these colonies, and such is now the necessity which constrains them to alter their former systems of government. The history of the present King of Great Britain is a history of repeated injuries and usurpations, all having, in direct object, the establishment of an absolute tyranny over these States. To prove this, let facts be submitted to a candid world:

He has refused his assent to laws the most wholesome and necessary for the public good,

He has forbidden his governors to pass laws of immediate and pressing importance, unless suspended in their operation till his assent should be obtained; and, when so suspended, he has utterly neglected to attend to them.

He has refused to pass other laws for the accommodation of large districts of people, unless those people would relinquish the right of representation in the legislature; a right inestimable to them, and formidable to tyrants only

He has called together legislative bodies at places unusual, uncomfortable, and distant from the depository of their public records, for the sole purpose of fatiguing them into compliance with his measures.

He has dissolved representative houses repeatedly for opposing, with manly firmness, his invasions on the rights of the people.

He has refused, for a long time after such dissolutions, to cause others to be elected; whereby the legislative powers, incapable of annihilation, have returned to the people at large for their exercise; the state remaining, in the meantime, exposed to all the danger of invasion from without, and convulsions within.

He has endeavored to prevent the population of these States; for that purpose, obstructing the laws for naturalization of foreigners, refusing to pass others to encourage their migration hither, and raising the conditions of new appropriations of lands.

He has obstructed the administration of justice, by refusing his assent to laws for establishing judiciary powers.

He has made judges dependent on his will alone, for the tenure of their offices, and the amount and payment of their salaries.

He has erected a multitude of new offices, and sent hither swarms of officers to harass our people, and eat out their substance.

He has kept among us, in time of peace, standing armies, without the consent of our legislatures.

He has affected to render the military independent of, and superior to, the civil power.

He has combined, with others, to subject us to a jurisdiction foreign to our Constitution, and unacknowledged by our laws; giving his assent to their acts of pretended legislation:

For quartering large bodies of armed troops among us:

For protecting them by a mock trial, from punishment, for any murders which they should commit on the inhabitants of these States:

For cutting off our trade with all parts of the world:

For imposing taxes on us without our consent:

For depriving us, in many cases, of the benefit of trial by jury:

For transporting us beyond seas to be tried for pretended offences:

For abolishing the free system of English laws in a neighboring province, establishing therein an arbitrary government, and enlarging its boundaries, so as to render it at once an example and fit instrument for introducing the same absolute rule into these colonies:

For taking away our charters, abolishing our most valuable laws, and altering, fundamentally, the powers of our governments:

For suspending our own legislatures, and declaring themselves invested with power to legislate for us in all cases whatsoever.

He has abdicated government here, by declaring us out of his protection, and waging war against us.

He has plundered our seas, ravaged our coasts, burnt our towns, and destroyed the lives of our people.

He is, at this time, transporting large armies of foreign mercenaries to complete the works of death, desolation, and tyranny, already begun, with circumstances of cruelty and perfidy scarcely paralleled in the most barbarous ages, and totally unworthy of the head of a civilized nation.

He has constrained our fellow citizens, taken captive on the high seas, to bear arms against their country, to become the executioners of their friends, and brethren, or to fall themselves by their hands.

He has excited domestic insurrections amongst us, and has endeavored to bring on the inhabitants of our frontiers, the merciless Indian savages, whose known rule of warfare is an undistinguished destruction of all ages, sexes, and conditions.

In every stage of these oppressions, we have petitioned for redress, in the most humble terms; our repeated petitions have been answered only by repeated injury. A prince, whose character is thus marked by every act which may define a tyrant, is unfit to be the ruler of a free people.

Nor have we been wanting in attention to our British brethren. We have warned them, from time to time, of attempts made by their legislature to extend an unwarrantable jurisdiction over us. We have reminded them of the circumstances of our emigration and settlement here. We have appealed to their native justice and magnanimity, and we have conjured them, by the ties of our common kindred, to disavow these usurpations, which would inevitably interrupt our connections and correspondence. They, too, have been deaf to the voice of justice and of consanguinity. We must, therefore, acquiesce in the necessity which denounces our separation, and hold them as we hold the rest of mankind, enemies in war, in peace, friends.

We, therefore, the representatives of the United States of America, in general Congress assembled, appealing to the Supreme Judge of the world for the rectitude of our intentions, do, in the name, and by the authority of the good people of these colonies, solemnly publish and declare, that these united colonies are, and of right ought to be, free and independent states: that they are absolved from all allegiance to the British Crown, and that all political connection between them and the state of Great Britain is, and ought to be, totally dissolved; and that, as free and independent states, they have full power to levy war, conclude peace, contract alliances, establish commerce, and to do all other acts and things which independent states may of right do. And, for the support of this declaration, with a firm reliance on the protection of Divine Providence, we mutually pledge to each other our lives, our fortunes, and our sacred honor.

The foregoing Declaration was, by order of Congress, engrossed, and signed by the following members:

JOHN HANCOCK

New Hampshire
Josiah Bartlett
William Whipple
Matthew Thornton

Massachusetts Bay
Samuel Adams
John Adams
Robert Treat Paine
Elbridge Gerry

Rhode Island
Stephen Hopkins
William Ellery

Connecticut
Roger Sherman
Samuel Huntington
William Williams
Oliver Wolcott

New York
William Floyd
Philip Livingston
Francis Lewis
Lewis Morris

New Jersey
Richard Stockton
John Witherspoon
Francis Hopkinson
John Hart
Abraham Clark

Pennsylvania
Robert Morris
Benjamin Rush
Benjamin Franklin
John Morton
George Clymer
James Smith
George Taylor
James Wilson
George Ross

Delaware
Caesar Rodney
George Reed
Thomas M'Kean

Maryland
Samuel Chase
William Paca
Thomas Stone
Charles Carroll, of Carrollton

Virginia
George Wythe
Richard Henry Lee
Thomas Jefferson
Benjamin Harrison
Thomas Nelson, Jr.
Francis Lightfoot Lee
Carter Braxton

North Carolina
William Hooper
Joseph Hewes
John Penn

South Carolina
Edward Rutledge
Thomas Heyward, Jr.
Thomas Lynch, Jr.
Arthur Middleton

Georgia
Button Gwinnett
Lyman Hall
George Walton

Resolved, That copies of the Declaration be sent to the several assemblies, conventions, and committees, or councils of safety, and to the several commanding officers of the continental troops; that it be proclaimed in each of the United States, at the head of the army.

APPENDIX 2:

THE CONSTITUTION OF THE
UNITED STATES OF AMERICA

We the People of the United States, in Order to form a more perfect Union, establish justice, insure domestic Tranquility, provide for the common defence, promote the general Welfare, and secure the Blessings of Liberty to ourselves and our Posterity, do ordain and establish this CONSTITUTION for the United States of America.

Article I

Section 1
All legislative Powers herein granted shall be vested in a Congress of the United States, which shall consist of a Senate and House of Representatives.

Section 2
The House of Representatives shall be composed of Members chosen every second Year by the People of the several States, and the Electors in each State shall have the Qualifications requisite for Electors of the most numerous Branch of the State Legislature.

No Person shall be a Representative who shall not have attained to the Age of twenty-five Years, and been seven Years a Citizen of the United States, and who shall not, when elected, be an Inhabitant of that State in which he shall be chosen.

[Representatives and direct Taxes[2] shall be apportioned among the several States which may be included within this, Union, according to their respective Numbers, which shall be determined by adding to the whole Number of free Persons, including those bound to Service for a Term of Years, and excluding Indians not taxed, three fifths of all other Persons.][3] The actual Enumeration shall be made within three Years after the first Meeting of the Congress of the United States, and within every subsequent Term of ten Years, in such Manner as they shall by Law direct. The Number of Representatives shall not exceed one for every thirty Thousand, but each State shall have at Least one Representative; and until such enumeration shall be made, the State of New Hampshire shall be entitled to chuse three, Massachusetts eight, Rhode-Island and Providence Plantations one, Connecticut five, New York six, New Jersey four, Pennsylvania eight, Delaware one, Maryland six, Virginia ten, North Carolina five, South Carolina five, and Georgia three.

When vacancies happen in the Representation from any State, the Executive Authority thereof shall issue Writs of Election to fill such Vacancies.

The House of Representatives shall chuse their Speaker and other Officers; and shall have the sole Power of Impeachment.

Section 3

The Senate of the United States shall be composed of two Senators from each State, chosen by the Legislature thereof, for six Years; and each Senator shall have one Vote.

Immediately after they shall be assembled in Consequence of the first Election, they shall be divided as equally as may be into three Classes. The Seats of the Senators of the first Class shall be vacated at the Expiration of the second Year, of the second Class at the Expiration of the fourth Year, and of the third Class at the Expiration of the sixth Year, so that one-third may be chosen every second Year; and if Vacancies happen by Resignation, or otherwise, during the Recess of the Legislature of any State, the Executive thereof may make temporary Appointments until the next Meeting of the Legislature, which shall then fill such Vacancies.

No Person shall be a Senator who shall not have attained to the Age of thirty Years, and been nine Years a Citizen of the United States, and who shall not, when elected, be an Inhabitant of that State for which he shall be chosen.

The Vice President of the United States shall be President of the Senate, but shall have no vote, unless they be equally divided.

The Senate shall chuse their other Officers, and also a President pro tempore, in the absence of the Vice President, or when he shall exercise the Office of President of the United States.

The Senate shall have the sole Power to try all Impeachments. When sitting for that purpose they shall be on Oath or Affirmation. When the President of the United States is tried, the Chief justice shall preside: And no person shall be convicted without the Concurrence of two thirds of the Members present.

Judgment in Cases of Impeachment shall not extend further than to removal from Office, and disqualification to hold and enjoy any Office of honor, Trust, or Profit under the United States: but the Party convicted shall nevertheless be liable and subject to Indictment, Trial, Judgment and Punishment, according to Law.

Section 4

The Times, Place and Manner of holding Elections for Senators and Representatives, shall be prescribed in each State by the Legislature thereof; but the Congress may at any time by Law make or alter such Regulations, except as to the Places of Chusing Senators.

The Congress shall assemble at least once in every Year, and such Meeting shall be on the first Monday in December, unless they shall by Law appoint a different Day.

Section 5

Each House shall be the Judge of the Elections, Returns and Qualifications of its own Members, and a Majority of each shall constitute a Quorum to do Business; but a smaller number may adjourn from day to day, and may be authorized to compel the Attendance of absent Members, in such Manner, and under such Penalties, as each House may provide.

Each House may determine the Rules of its Proceedings, punish its Members for disorderly Behaviour, and, with the Concurrence of two thirds, expel a Member.

Each House shall keep a journal of its Proceedings, and from time to time publish the same, excepting such Parts as may in their Judgment require Secrecy; and the Yeas and Nays of the Members of either House on any question shall, at the Desire of one fifth of those Present, be entered on the Journal.

Neither House, during the Session of Congress, shall, without the Consent of the other, adjourn for more than three days, nor to any other Place than that in which the two Houses shall be sitting.

Section 6

The Senators and Representatives shall receive a Compensation for their Services, to be ascertained by Law, and paid out of the Treasury of the United States. They shall in all Cases, except Treason, Felony, and Breach of the Peace, be privileged from Arrest during their Attendance at the Session of their respective Houses, and in going to and returning from the same; and for any Speech or Debate in either House, they shall not be questioned in any other Place.

No Senator or Representative shall, during the Time for which he was elected, be appointed to any civil Office under the Authority of the United States, which shall have been created, or the Emoluments whereof shall have been increased, during such time; and no Person holding any Office under the United States shall be a Member of either House during his continuance in Office.

Section 7

All Bills for raising Revenue shall originate in the House of Representatives; but the Senate may propose or concur with Amendments as on other bills.

Every Bill which shall have passed the House of Representatives and the Senate, shall, before it becomes a Law, be presented to the President of the United States; if he approve he shall sign it, but if not he shall return it, with his Objections, to that House in which it shall have originated, who shall enter the Objections at large on their Journal, and proceed to reconsider it. If after such Reconsideration two thirds of that

House shall agree to pass the bill, it shall be sent, together with the objections, to the other House, by which it shall likewise be reconsidered, and if approved by two thirds of that House, it shall become a Law. But in all such Cases the Votes of both Houses shall be determined by Yeas and Nays, and the Names of the Persons voting for and against the Bill shall be entered on the Journal of each House respectively If any Bill shall not be returned by the President within ten Days (Sundays excepted) after it shall have been presented to him, the Same shall be a Law, in like Manner as if he had signed it, unless the Congress by their Adjournment prevent its Return, in which Case it shall not be a Law.

Every Order, Resolution, or Vote to which the Concurrence of the Senate and House of Representatives may be necessary (except on a question of Adjournment) shall be presented to the President of the United States; and before the Same shall take Effect, shall be approved by him, or being disapproved by him, shall be repassed by two thirds of the Senate and House of Representatives, according to the Rules and Limitations prescribed in the Case of a Bill.

Section 8
The Congress shall have Power To lay and collect Taxes, Duties, Imposts and Excises, to pay the Debts and provide for the common Defence and general Welfare of the United States; but all Duties, Imposts and Excises shall be uniform throughout the United States;

To borrow money on the credit of the United States;

To regulate Commerce with foreign Nations, and among the several States, and with the Indian Tribes;

To establish a uniform rule of Naturalization, and uniform Laws on the subject of Bankruptcies throughout the United States;

To coin Money, regulate the Value thereof, and of foreign Coin, and fix the Standard of Weights and Measures;

To provide for the Punishment of counterfeiting the Securities and current Coin of the United States;

To establish Post Offices and post Roads;

To promote the Progress of Science and useful Arts, by securing for limited Times to Authors and Inventors the exclusive Right to their respective Writings and Discoveries;

To constitute Tribunals inferior to the Supreme Court;

To define and punish Piracies and Felonies committed on the high Seas, and Offenses against the Law of Nations;

To declare War, grant Letters of Marque and Reprisal, and make Rules concerning Captures on Land and Water;

To raise and support Armies, but no Appropriation of Money to that Use shall be for a longer Term than two Years;

To provide and maintain a Navy;

To make Rules for the Government and Regulation of the land and naval forces;

To provide for calling forth the Militia to execute the Laws of the Union, suppress Insurrections and repel Invasions;

To provide for organizing, arming, and disciplining the Militia, and for governing such Part of them as may be employed in the Service of the United States, reserving to the States respectively, the Appointment of the Officers, and the Authority of training the Militia according to the discipline prescribed by Congress;

To exercise exclusive Legislation in all Cases whatsoever, over such District (not exceeding ten Miles square) as may, by Cession of particular States, and the acceptance of Congress, become the Seat of the Government of the United States, and to exercise like Authority over all Places purchased by the Consent of the Legislature of the State in which the Same shall be, for the Erection of Forts, Magazines, Arsenals, Dock-yards, and other needful Buildings;—And

To make all Laws which shall be necessary and proper for carrying into Execution the foregoing Powers, and all other Powers vested by this Constitution in the Government of the United States, or in any Department or Officer thereof.

Section 9

The Migration or Importation of such Persons as any of the States now existing shall think proper to admit, shall not be prohibited by the Congress prior to the Year one thousand eight hundred and eight, but a tax or duty may be imposed on such Importation, not exceeding ten dollars for each Person.

The privilege of the Writ of Habeas Corpus shall not be suspended, unless when in Cases of Rebellion or Invasion the public Safety may require it.

No bill of Attainder or ex post facto Law shall be passed.

No capitation, or other direct, Tax shall be laid unless in Proportion to the Census or Enumeration herein before directed to be taken.

No Tax or Duty shall be laid on Articles exported from any State.

No Preference shall be given by any Regulation of Commerce or Revenue to the Ports of one State over those of another: nor shall Vessels bound to, or from, one State, be obliged to enter, clear, or pay Duties in another.

No Money shall be drawn from the Treasury, but in Consequence of Appropriations made by Law; and a regular Statement and Account of the Receipts and Expenditures of all public Money shall be published from time to time.

No Title of Nobility shall be granted by the United States: And no Person holding any Office of Profit or Trust under them, shall, without the Consent of the Congress, accept of any present, Emolument, Office, or Title, of any kind whatever, from any King, Prince, or foreign State.

Section 10

No State shall enter into any Treaty, Alliance, or Confederation; grant Letters of Marque and Reprisal; coin Money; emit Bills of Credit; make any Thing but gold and silver Coin a Tender in Payment of Debts; pass any Bill of Attainder, ex post facto Law, or Law impairing the Obligation of Contracts, or grant any Title of Nobility.

No State shall, without the Consent of the Congress, lay any Imposts or Duties on Imports or Exports, except what may be absolutely necessary for executing its inspection Laws; and the net Produce of all Duties and Imposts, laid by any State on Imports or Exports, shall be for the use of the Treasury of the United States; and all such Laws shall be subject to the Revision and Control of the Congress.

No state shall, without the Consent of Congress, lay any duty of Tonnage, keep Troops, or Ships of War in time of Peace, enter into any Agreement or Compact with another State, or with a foreign Power, or engage in War, unless actually invaded, or in such imminent Danger as will not admit of delay.

Article II

Section 1

The executive Power shall be vested in a President of the United States of America. He shall hold his Office during the Term of four years, and, together with the Vice President, chosen for the same Term, be elected, as follows:

Each State shall appoint, in such Manner as the Legislature thereof may direct, a Number of Electors, equal to the whole Number of Senators and Representatives to which the State may be entitled in the Congress: but no Senator or Representative, or Person holding an Office of Trust or Profit under the United States, shall be appointed an Elector.

[The Electors shall meet in their respective States, and vote by Ballot for two persons, of whom one at least shall not be an Inhabitant of the same State with themselves. And they shall make a List of all the Persons voted for, and of the Number of Votes for each; which List they shall sign and certify, and transmit sealed to the Seat of the Government of the United States, directed to the President of the Senate. The President of the Senate shall, in the Presence of the Senate and House of Representatives, open all the Certificates, and the Votes shall then be counted. The Person having the greatest Number of Votes shall be the President, if such Number be a Majority of the whole Number of Electors appointed; and if there be more than one who have such Majority, and have an equal Number of Votes, then the House of Representatives shall immediately chuse by Ballot one of them for President; and if no Person have a Majority, then from the five highest on the List the said House shall in like Manner chuse the President. But in chusing the President, the Votes shall be taken by States, the Representation from each State having one Vote; a quorum for this Purpose shall consist of a Member or Members from two-thirds of the States, and a Majority of all the States shall be necessary to a Choice. In every Case, after the Choice of the President, the Person having the greatest Number of Votes of the Electors shall be the Vice President. But if there should remain two or more who have equal votes, the Senate shall chuse from them by Ballot the Vice President.]⁴

The Congress may determine the Time of chusing the Electors, and the Day on which they shall give their Votes; which Day shall be the same throughout the United States.

No person except a natural-born Citizen, or a Citizen of the United States, at the time of the Adoption of this Constitution, shall be eligible to the Office of President; neither shall any Person be eligible to that Office who shall not have attained to the Age of thirty-five years, and been fourteen Years a Resident within the United States.

In Case of the Removal of the President from Office, or of his Death, Resignation, or Inability to discharge the Powers and Duties of the said Office, the same shall devolve on the Vice President, and the Congress may by Law provide for the Case of Removal, Death, Resignation, or Inability, both of the President and Vice President, declaring what Officer shall then act as President, and such Officer shall act accordingly, until the disability be removed, or a President shall be elected.

The President shall, at stated Times, receive for his Services a Compensation, which shall neither be increased nor diminished during the Period for which he shall have been elected, and he shall not receive within that Period any other Emolument from the United States, or any of them.

Before he enter on the execution of his Office, he shall take the following Oath or Affirmation:—"I do solemnly swear (or affirm) that I will faithfully execute the Office of President of the United States, and will, to the best of my Ability, preserve, protect, and defend the Constitution of the United States."

Section 2

The President shall be Commander in Chief of the Army and Navy of the United States, and of the Militia of the several States, when called into the actual Service of the United States; he may require the Opinion, in writing, of the principal Officer in each of the executive Departments, upon any subject relating to the Duties of their respective Offices, and he shall have Power to Grant Reprieves and Pardons for Offenses against the United States, except in Cases of Impeachment.

He shall have Power, by and with the Advice and Consent of the Senate, to make Treaties, provided two-thirds of the Senators present concur; and he shall nominate, and by and with the Advice and Consent of the Senate, shall appoint Ambassadors, other public Ministers and Consuls, Judges of the supreme Court, and all other Officers of the United States, whose Appointments are not herein otherwise provided for, and which shall be established by Law: but the Congress may by Law vest the Appointment of such inferior Officers, as they think proper, in the President alone, in the Courts of Law, or in the Heads of Departments.

The President shall have Power to fill up all Vacancies that may happen during the Recess of the Senate, by granting Commissions which shall expire at the End of their next Session.

Section 3

He shall from time to time give to the Congress Information of the State of the Union, and recommend to their Consideration such Measures as he shall judge necessary and expedient; he may, on extraordinary occasions, convene both Houses, or either of them, and in Case of Disagreement between them, with respect to the Time of Adjournment, he may adjourn them to such Time as he shall think proper; he shall receive Ambassadors and other public Ministers; he shall take care that the Laws be faithfully executed, and shall Commission all the Officers of the United States.

Section 4

The President, Vice President and all civil Officers of the United States, shall be removed from Office on Impeachment for, and Conviction of, Treason, Bribery, or other high Crimes and Misdemeanors.

Article III

Section 1

The judicial Power of the United States, shall be vested in one supreme Court, and in such inferior Courts as the Congress may from time to time ordain and establish. The Judges, both of the supreme and inferior Courts, shall hold their Offices during good Behaviour, and shall, at stated Times, receive for their Services, a Compensation, which shall not be diminished during their Continuance in Office.

Section 2

The judicial Power shall extend to all Cases, in Law and Equity, arising under this Constitution, the Laws of the United States, and Treaties made, or which shall be made, under their Authority;—to all Cases affecting ambassadors, other public ministers and consuls;—to all cases of admiralty and maritime Jurisdiction;—to Controversies to which the United States shall be a Party;—to Controversies between two or more states;—between a State and Citizens of another State;[5]—between Citizens of different States—between Citizens of the same State claiming Lands under Grants of different States, and between a State, or the Citizens thereof, and foreign

States, Citizens, or Subjects.

In all Cases affecting Ambassadors, other public Ministers and Consuls, and those in which a State shall be Party, the supreme Court shall have original Jurisdiction. In all the other Cases before mentioned, the supreme Court shall have appellate Jurisdiction, both as to Law and Fact, with such Exceptions, and under such Regulations as the Congress shall make.

The trial of all Crimes, except in Cases of Impeachment, shall be by Jury; and such Trial shall be held in the State where the said Crimes shall have been committed; but when not committed within any State, the Trial shall be at such Place or Places as the Congress may by Law have directed.

Section 3

Treason against the United States, shall consist only in levying War against them, or in adhering to their Enemies, giving them Aid and Comfort. No Person shall be convicted of Treason unless on the Testimony of two Witnesses to the same overt Act, or on Confession in open Court.

The Congress shall have power to declare the Punishment of Treason, but no Attainder of Treason shall work Corruption of Blood, or Forfeiture except during the Life of the Person attainted.

Article IV

Section 1

Full Faith and Credit shall be given in each State to the public Acts, Records, and judicial Proceedings of every other State. And the Congress may by general Laws prescribe the Manner in which such Acts, Records and Proceedings shall be proved, and the Effect thereof.

Section 2

The Citizens of each State shall be entitled to all Privileges and Immunities of Citizens in the several States.

A Person charged in any State with Treason, Felony, or other Crime, who shall flee from justice, and be found in another State, shall on demand of the executive Authority of the State from which he fled, be delivered up, to be removed to the State having Jurisdiction of the crime.

No Person held to Service or Labour in one State, under the Laws thereof, escaping into another, shall, in Consequence of any Law or Regulation therein, be discharged from such Service or Labour, but shall be delivered up on Claim of the Party to whom such Service or Labour may be due.

Section 3

New States may be admitted by the Congress into this Union; but no new State shall be formed or erected within the jurisdiction of any other State; nor any State be formed by the junction of two or more States, or parts of States, without the Consent of the Legislatures of the States concerned as well as of the Congress.

The Congress shall have Power to dispose of and make all needful Rules and Regulations respecting the Territory or other Property belonging to the United States; and nothing in this Constitution shall be so construed as to Prejudice any Claims of the United States, or of any particular State.

Section 4

The United States shall guarantee to every State in this Union a Republican Form of Government, and shall protect each of them against Invasion; and on Application of the Legislature, or of the Executive (when the Legislature cannot be convened) against domestic Violence.

Article V

The Congress, whenever two-thirds of both Houses shall deem it necessary, shall propose Amendments to this Constitution, or, on the Application of the Legislatures of two-thirds of the several States, shall call a Convention for proposing Amendments, which, in either Case, shall be valid to all Intents and Purposes, as part of this Constitution, when ratified by the Legislatures of three-fourths of the several States, or by Conventions in three-fourths thereof, as the one or the other Mode of Ratification may be proposed by the Congress; Provided that no Amendment which may be made prior to the Year One thousand eight hundred and eight shall in any Manner affect the first and fourth Clauses in the Ninth Section of the first Article; and that no State, without its Consent, shall be deprived of its equal Suffrage in the Senate.

Article VI

All Debts contracted and Engagements entered into, before the Adoption of this Constitution, shall be as valid against the United States under this Constitution, as under the Confederation.

This Constitution, and the Laws of the United States which shall be made in Pursuance thereof; and all Treaties made, or which shall be made, under the Authority of the United States, shall be the supreme Law of the Land; and the Judges in every

State shall be bound thereby, any Thing in the Constitution or Laws of any State to the Contrary notwithstanding.

The Senators and Representatives before mentioned, and the Members of the several State Legislatures, and all executive and judicial Officers, both of the United States and of the several States, shall be bound by Oath or Affirmation to support this Constitution; but no religious Tests shall ever be required as a qualification to any Office or public Trust under the United States.

Article VII

The Ratification of the Conventions of nine States shall be sufficient for the Establishment of this Constitution between the States so ratifying the same.

Done in Convention by the Unanimous Consent of the States present the Seventeenth Day of September in the Year of our Lord one thousand seven hundred and Eighty seven, and of the Independence of the United States of America the Twelfth. In Witness whereof We have hereunto subscribed our Names.[6]

George Washington
President and deputy from
Virginia

New Hampshire
John Langdon
Nicholas Gilman

Massachusetts
Nathaniel Gorham
Rufus King

Connecticut
William Samuel Johnson
Roger Sherman

New York
Alexander Hamilton

New Jersey
William Livingston
David Brearley
William Paterson
Jonathan Dayton

Pennsylvania
Benjamin Franklin
Thomas Mifflin
Robert Morris
George Clymer
Thomas FitzSimmons
Jared Ingersoll
James Wilson
Gouverneur Morris

Delaware
George Read
Gunning Bedford, Jr.
John Dickinson
Richard Bassett
Jacob Broom

Maryland
James McHenry
Daniel of St. Thomas Jenifer
Daniel Carroll

Virginia
John Blair
James Madison, Jr.

North Carolina
William Blount
Richard Dobbs Spaight
Hugh Williamson

South Carolina
John Rutledge
Charles Cotesworth
  Pinckney
Charles Pinckney
Pierce Butler

Georgia
William Few
Abraham Baldwin

Articles in Addition to, and Amendment of, the Constitution of the United States of America, Proposed by Congress, and Ratified by the Legislatures of the Several States, Pursuant to the Fifth Article of the Original Constitution[7]

Amendment I

Congress shall make no law respecting an establishment of religion, or prohibiting the free exercise thereof; or abridging the freedom of speech, or of the press; or the right of the people peaceably to assemble, and to petition the Government for a redress of grievances.

Amendment II

A well regulated Militia, being necessary to the security of a free State, the right of the people to keep and bear Arms shall not be infringed.

Amendment III

No Soldier shall, in time of peace, be quartered in any house, without the consent of the Owner, nor in time of war, but in a manner to be prescribed by law.

Amendment IV

The right of the people to be secure in their persons, houses, papers, and effects, against unreasonable searches and seizures, shall not be violated, and no Warrants shall issue, but upon probable cause, supported by Oath or affirmation, and particularly describing the place to be searched, and the persons or things to be seized.

Amendment V

No person shall be held to answer for a capital or otherwise infamous crime, unless on a presentment or indictment of a Grand Jury, except in cases arising in the land or naval forces, or in the Militia, when in actual service in time of War or public danger; nor shall any person be subject for the same offence to be twice put in jeopardy of life or limb; nor shall be compelled in any criminal case to be a witness against himself, nor be deprived of life, liberty, or property, without due process of law; nor shall private property be taken for public use, without just compensation.

Amendment VI

In all criminal prosecutions, the accused shall enjoy the right to a speedy and public trial, by an impartial jury of the State and district wherein the crime shall have been committed, which district shall have been previously ascertained by law, and to be informed of the nature and cause of the accusation; to be confronted with the witnesses against him; to have compulsory process for obtaining witnesses in his favour, and to have the Assistance of Counsel for his defence.

Amendment VII

In suits at common law, where the value in controversy shall exceed twenty dollars, the right of trial by jury shall be preserved, and no fact tried by a jury, shall be otherwise reexamined in any Court of the United States, than according to the rules of the common law.

Amendment VIII

Excessive bail shall not be required, nor excessive fines imposed, nor cruel and unusual punishments inflicted.

Amendment IX

The enumeration of the Constitution, of certain rights, shall not be construed to deny or disparage others retained by the people.

Amendment X

The powers not delegated to the United States by the Constitution, nor prohibited by it to the States, are reserved to the States respectively, or to the people.

Amendment XI [1798]

The Judicial power of the United States shall not be construed to extend to any suit in law or equity, commenced or prosecuted against one of the United States by Citizens of another State, or by Citizens or Subjects of any Foreign State.

Amendment XII [1804]

The Electors shall meet in their respective States and vote by ballot for President and Vice-President, one of whom, at least, shall not be an inhabitant of the same State with themselves; they shall name in their ballots the person voted for as President, and in distinct ballots the person voted for as Vice-President, and they shall make distinct lists of all persons voted for as President, and of all persons voted for as Vice-President, and of the number of votes for each, which lists they shall sign and certify, and transmit sealed to the seat of the government of the United States, directed to the President of the Senate;—The President of the Senate shall, in the presence of the Senate and House of Representatives, open all the certificates and the votes shall then be counted;—The person having the greatest number of votes for President, shall be the President, if such number be a majority of the whole number of Electors appointed; and if no person have such majority, then from the persons having the highest numbers not exceeding three on the list of those voted for as President, the House of Representatives shall choose immediately, by ballot, the President. But in choosing the President, the votes shall be taken by states, the representation from each state having one vote; a quorum for this purpose shall consist of a member or members from two-thirds of the states, and a majority of all the states shall be necessary to a choice. And if the House of Representatives shall not choose a President whenever the right of choice shall devolve upon them, before the fourth day of March next following, then the Vice-President shall act as President, as in the case of the death or other constitutional disability of the President.—The person having the greatest number of votes as Vice-President, shall be the Vice-President, if such number be a majority of the whole number of Electors appointed, and if no person have a majority, then from the two highest numbers on the list, the Senate shall choose the Vice-President; a quorum for the purpose shall consist of two-thirds of the whole number of Senators, and majority of the whole number shall be necessary to a choice. But no person constitutionally ineligible to the office of President shall be eligible to that of Vice-President of the United States.

Amendment XIII [1865]

Section 1

Neither slavery nor involuntary servitude, except as a punishment for crime whereof the party shall have been duly convicted, shall exist within the United States, or any place subject to their jurisdiction.

Section 2

Congress shall have power to enforce this article by appropriate legislation.

Amendment XIV [1868]

Section 1

All persons born or naturalized in the United States, and subject to the jurisdiction thereof, are citizens of the United States and of the State wherein they reside. No State shall abridge the privileges or immunities of citizens of the United States; nor shall any State deprive any person of life, liberty, or property, without due process of law; nor deny to any person within its jurisdiction the equal protection of the laws.

Section 2

Representatives shall be apportioned among the several States according to their respective numbers, counting the whole number of persons in each State, excluding Indians not taxed. But when the right to vote at any election for the choice of electors for President and Vice-President of the United States, Representatives in Congress, the Executive and Judicial officers of a State, or the members of the Legislature thereof, is denied to any of the male inhabitants of such State, being twenty-one years of age, and citizens of the United States, or in any way abridged, except for participation in rebellion, or other crime, the basis of representation therein shall be reduced in the proportion which the number of such male citizens shall bear to the whole number of male citizens twenty-one years of age in such State.

Section 3

No person shall be a Senator or Representative in Congress, or elector of President and Vice-President, or hold any office, civil or military, under the United States, or under any State, who, having previously taken an oath, as a member of Congress, or as an officer of the United States, or as a member of any State legislature, or as an executive or judicial officer of any State, to support the Constitution of the United States, shall have engaged in insurrection or rebellion against the same, or given aid or comfort to the enemies thereof. But Congress may by a vote of two-thirds of each House, remove such disability.

Section 4
The validity of the public debt of the United States, authorized by law, including debts incurred for payment of pensions and bounties for services in suppressing insurrection or rebellion, shall not be questioned. But neither the United States nor any State shall assume or pay any debts or obligation incurred in aid of insurrection or rebellion against the United States, or any claim for the loss or emancipation of any slave; but all such debts, obligations, and claims shall be held illegal and void.

Section 5
The Congress shall have the power to enforce, by appropriate legislation, the provisions of this article.

Amendment XV [1870]

Section 1
The right of citizens of the United States to vote shall not be denied or abridged by the United States or by any State on account of race, color, or previous condition of servitude—

Section 2
The Congress shall have power to enforce this article by appropriate legislation.

Amendment XVI [1913]

The Congress shall have power to lay and collect taxes on incomes, from whatever source derived, without apportionment among the several States, and without regard to any census or enumeration.

Amendment XVII [1913]

The Senate of the United States shall be composed of two Senators from each State, elected by the people thereof, for six years; and each Senator shall have one vote. The electors in each State shall have the qualifications requisite for electors of the most numerous branch of the State legislatures.

When vacancies happen in the representation of any State in the Senate, the executive authority of such State shall issue writs of election to fill such vacancies: *Provided*, That the legislature of any State may empower the executive thereof to make temporary appointments until the people fill the vacancies by election as the legislature may direct.

This amendment shall not be so construed as to affect the election or term of any Senator chosen before it becomes valid as part of the Constitution.

Amendment XVIII [1919]

Section 1
After one year from the ratification of this article the manufacture, sale, or transportation of intoxicating liquors within, the importation thereof into, or the exportation thereof from the United States and all territory subject to the jurisdiction thereof for beverage purposes is hereby prohibited.

Section 2
The Congress and the several States shall have concurrent power to enforce this article by appropriate legislation.

Section 3
This article shall be inoperative unless it shall have been ratified as an amendment to the Constitution by the legislatures of the several States, as provided in the Constitution, within seven years from the date of the submission hereof to the States by the Congress.

Amendment XIX [1920]

The right of citizens of the United States to vote shall not be denied or abridged by the United States or by any State on account of sex.

Congress shall have power to enforce this article by appropriate legislation.

Amendment XX [1933]

Section I
The terms of the President and Vice-President shall end at noon on the 20th day of January, and the terms of Senators and Representatives at noon on the 3d day of

January, of the years in which such terms would have ended if this article had not been ratified; and the terms of their successors shall then begin.

Section 2

The Congress shall assemble at least once in every year, and such meeting shall begin at noon on the 3d day of January, unless they shall by law appoint a different day.

Section 3

If, at the time fixed for the beginning of the term of the President, the President elect shall have died, the Vice-President elect shall become President. If a President shall not have been chosen before the time fixed for the beginning of his term or if the President elect shall have failed to qualify, then the Vice-President elect shall act as President until a President shall have qualified; and the Congress may by law provide for the case wherein neither a President elect nor a Vice-President elect shall have qualified, declaring who shall then act as President, or the manner in which one who is to act shall be selected, and such person shall act accordingly until a President or Vice-President shall have qualified.

Section 4

The Congress may by law provide for the case of the death of any of the persons from whom the House of Representatives may choose a President whenever the right of choice shall have devolved upon them, and for the case of the death of any of the persons from whom the Senate may choose a Vice-President whenever the right of choice shall have devolved upon them.

Section 5

Sections 1 and 2 shall take effect on the 15th day of October following the ratification of this article.

Section 6

This article shall be inoperative unless it shall have been ratified as an amendment to the Constitution by the legislatures of three-fourths of the several States within seven years from the date of its submission.

Amendment XXI [1933]

Section 1

The eighteenth article of amendment to the Constitution of the United States is hereby repealed.

Section 2

The transportation or importation into any State, Territory, or possession of the United States for delivery or use therein of intoxicating liquors, in violation of the laws thereof, is hereby prohibited.

Section 3

This article shall be inoperative unless it shall have been ratified as an amendment to the Constitution by conventions in the several States, as provided in the Constitution, within seven years from the date of the submission hereof to the States by the Congress.

Amendment XXII [1951]

No person shall be elected to the office of the President more than twice, and no person who has held the office of President, or acted as President, for more than two years of a term to which some other person was elected President shall be elected to the office of the President more than once.

But this Article shall not apply to any person holding the office of President when this Article was proposed by the Congress, and shall not prevent any person who may be holding the office of President, or acting as President, during the term within which this Article becomes operative from holding the office of President or acting as President during the remainder of such term.

This article shall be inoperative unless it shall have been ratified as an amendment to the Constitution by the legislatures of three-fourths of the several states within seven years from the date of its submission to the states by the Congress.

Amendment XXIII [1961]

Section I

The District constituting the seat of Government of the United States shall appoint in such manner as the Congress may direct:

A number of electors of President and Vice-President equal to the whole number of Senators and Representatives in Congress to which the District would be entitled if it were a State, but in no event more than the least populous State; they shall be in addition to those appointed by the States, but they shall be considered, for the purposes of the election of President and Vice-President, to be electors appointed by a State; and they shall meet in the District and perform such duties as provided by the twelfth article of amendment.

Section 2
The Congress shall have power to enforce this article by appropriate legislation.

Amendment XXIV [1964]

Section 1
The right of citizens of the United States to vote in any primary or other election for President or Vice President, for electors for President or Vice President, or for Senator or Representative in Congress, shall not be denied or abridged by the United States or any state by reason of failure to pay any poll tax or other tax.

Section 2
The Congress shall have the power to enforce this article by appropriate legislation.

Amendment XXV [1967]

Section 1
In case of the removal of the President from office or of his death or resignation, the Vice President shall become President.

Section 2
Whenever there is a vacancy in the office of the Vice President, the President shall nominate a Vice President who shall take office upon confirmation by a majority vote of both Houses of Congress.

Section 3
Whenever the President transmits to the President Pro Tempore of the Senate and the Speaker of the House of Representatives his written declaration that he is unable to discharge the powers and duties of his office, and until he transmits to them a written declaration to the contrary, such powers and duties shall be discharged by the Vice President as Acting President.

Section 4
Whenever the Vice President and a majority of either the principal officers of the executive departments or of such other body as Congress may by law provide, transmit to the President Pro Tempore of the Senate and the Speaker of the House of Representatives their written declaration that the President is unable to discharge the

powers and duties of his office, the Vice President shall immediately assume the powers and duties of the office as Acting President.

Thereafter, when the President transmits to the President Pro Tempore of the
Senate and the Speaker of the House of Representatives his written declaration that
no inability exists, he shall resume the powers and duties of his office unless the Vice
President and a majority of either the principal officers of the executive departments
or of such other body as Congress may by law provide, transmit within four days to
the President Pro Tempore of the Senate and the Speaker of the House of
Representatives their written declaration that the President is unable to discharge the
powers and duties of his office. Thereupon Congress shall decide the issue, assem-
bling within forty-eight hours for that purpose if not in session. If the Congress, within twenty-one days after receipt of the latter written declaration, or, if Congress is not
in session, within twenty-one days after Congress is required to assemble, determines
by two-thirds vote of both Houses that the President is unable to discharge the powers and duties of his office, the Vice President shall continue to discharge the same as
Acting President; otherwise, the President shall resume the powers and duties of his
office.

Amendment XXVI [1971]

Section 1
The right of citizens of the United States, who are eighteen years of age or older, to
vote shall not be denied or abridged by the United States or by any State on account
of age.

Section 2
The Congress shall have the power to enforce this article by appropriate legislation.

Amendment XXVII [1992]

No law varying the compensation for the service of Senators and Representatives shall
take effect until an election of Representatives shall have intervened.

Notes

[1]This version, which follows the original Constitution in capitalization and spelling, was published by the United States Department of the Interior, Office of Education, in 1935.

[2]Altered by the Sixteenth Amendment.

[3]Negated by the Fourteenth Amendment.

[4]Revised by the Twelfth Amendment.

[5]Qualified by the Eleventh Amendment.

[6]These are the full names of the signers, which in some cases are not the signatures on the document.

[7]This heading appears only in the joint resolution submitting the first ten amendments, which are collectively known as the Bill of Rights. They were ratified on December 15, 1791.

Appendix 3:
Federalist Paper No. 10
James Madison

Among the numerous advantages promised by a well-constructed Union, none deserves to be more accurately developed than its tendency to break and control the violence of faction. The friend of popular governments never finds himself so much alarmed for their character and fate as when he contemplates their propensity to this dangerous vice. He will not fail, therefore, to set a due value on any plan which, without violating the principles to which he is attached, provides a proper cure for it. The instability, injustice, and confusion introduced into the public councils have, in truth, been the mortal diseases under which popular governments have everywhere perished, as they continue to be the favorite and fruitful topics from which the adversaries to liberty derive their most specious declamations. The valuable improvements made by the American constitutions on the popular models, both ancient and modern, cannot certainly be too much admired; but it would be an unwarrantable partiality to contend that they have as effectually obviated the danger on this side, as was wished and expected. Complaints are everywhere heard from our most considerate and virtuous citizens, equally the friends of public and private faith and of public and personal liberty, that our governments are too unstable, that the public good is disregarded in the conflicts of rival parties, and that measures are too often decided, not according to the rules of justice and the rights of the minor party, but by the superior force of an interested and overbearing majority. However anxiously we may wish that these complaints had no foundation, the evidence of known facts will not permit us to deny that they are in some degree true. It will be found, indeed, on a candid review of our situation, that some of the distresses under which we labor have been erroneously charged on the operation of our governments; but it will be found, at the same time, that other causes will not alone account for many of our heaviest misfortunes; and, particularly, for that prevailing and increasing distrust of public engagements and alarm for private rights which are echoed from one end of the continent to the other. There must be chiefly, if not wholly, effects of the unsteadiness and injustice with which a factious spirit has tainted our public administration.

By a faction I understand a number of citizens, whether amounting to a majority or minority of the whole, who are united and actuated by some common impulse of passion, or of interest, adverse to the rights of other citizens, or to the permanent and aggregate interests of the community.

There are two methods of curing the mischiefs of faction: the one, by removing its causes; the other, by controlling its effects.

There are again two methods of removing the causes of faction: the one, by destroying the liberty which is essential to its existence; the other, by giving to every citizen the same opinions, the same passions, and the same interests.

It could never be more truly said than of the first remedy that it was worse than the disease. Liberty is to faction what air is to fire, an ailment without which it instantly expires. But it could not be a less folly to abolish liberty, which is essential to political life, because it nourishes faction than it would be to wish the annihilation of air, which is essential to animal life, because it imparts to fire its destructive agency.

The second expedient is as impracticable as the first would be unwise. As long as the reason of man continues fallible, and he is at liberty to exercise it, different opinions will be formed. As long as the connection subsists between his reason and his self-love, his opinions and his passions will have a reciprocal influence on each other; and the former will be objects to which the latter will attach themselves. The diversity in the faculties of men, from which the rights of property originate, is not less an insuperable obstacle to a uniformity of interest. The protection of these faculties is the first object of government. From the protection of different and unequal faculties of acquiring property, the possession of different degrees and kinds of property immediately results; and from the influence of these on the sentiments and views of the respective proprietors ensues a division of the society into different interests and parties.

The latent causes of faction are thus sown in the nature of man; and we see them everywhere brought into different degrees of activity, according to the different circumstances of civil society. A zeal for different opinions concerning religion, concerning government, and many other points, as well of speculation as of practice; an attachment to different leaders ambitiously contending for pre-eminence and power; or to persons of other descriptions whose fortunes have been interesting to the human passions, have, in turn, divided mankind into parties, inflamed them with mutual animosity, and rendered them much more disposed to vex and oppress each other than to co-operate for their common good. So strong is this propensity of mankind to fall into mutual animosities that where no substantial occasion presents itself the most frivolous and fanciful distinctions have been sufficient to kindle their unfriendly passions and excite their most violent conflicts. But the most common and durable source of factions has been the various and unequal distribution of property. Those who hold and those who are without property have ever formed distinct interests in society. Those who are creditors, and those who are debtors, fall under a like discrimination. A landed interest, a manufacturing interest, a mercantile interest, a moneyed interest, with many lesser interests, grow up of necessity in civilized nations, and divide them into different classes, actuated by different sentiments and views. The regulation of these various and interfering interests forms the principal task of modern legislation and involves the spirit of party and faction in the necessary and ordinary operations of government.

No man is allowed to be a judge in his own cause, because his interest would certainly bias his judgment, and, not improbably, corrupt his integrity With equal, nay with greater reason, a body of men are unfit to be both judges and parties at the same time; yet what are many of the most important acts of legislation but so many judicial determinations, not indeed concerning the rights of single persons, but concerning the rights of large bodies of citizens? And what are the different classes of legislators but advocates and parties to the causes which they determine? Is a law proposed concerning private debts? It is a question to which the creditors are parties on one side and the debtors on the other. justice ought to hold the balance between them. Yet the parties are, and must be, themselves the judges; and the most numerous party, or in other words, the most powerful faction must be expected to prevail. Shall domestic manufacturers be encouraged, and in what degree, by restrictions on foreign manufacturers? [These] are questions which would be differently decided by the landed and the manufacturing classes, and probably by neither with a sole regard to justice and the public good. The apportionment of taxes on the various descriptions of property is an act which seems to require the most exact impartiality; yet there is, perhaps, no legislative act in which greater opportunity and temptation are given to a predominant party to trample on the rules of justice. Every shilling with which they overburden the inferior number is a shilling saved to their own pockets.

It is in vain to say that enlightened statesmen will be able to adjust these clashing interests and render them all subservient to the public good. Enlightened statesmen will not always be at the helm. Nor, in many cases, can such an adjustment be made at all without taking into view indirect and remote considerations, which will rarely prevail over the immediate interest which one party may find in disregarding the rights of another or the good of the whole.

The inference to which we are brought is that the *causes* of faction cannot be removed and that relief is only to be sought in the means of controlling its *effects*.

If a faction consists of less than a majority, relief is supplied by the republican principle, which enables the majority to defeat its sinister views by regular vote. It may clog the administration, it may convulse the society; but it will be unable to execute and mask its violence under the forms of the Constitution. When a majority is included in a faction, the form of popular government, on the other hand, enables it to sacrifice to its ruling passion or interest both the public good and the rights of other citizens. To secure the public good and private rights against the danger of such a faction, and at the same time to preserve the spirit and the form of popular government, is then the great object to which our inquiries are directed. Let me add that it is the great desideratum by which alone this form of government can be rescued from the opprobrium under which it has so long labored and be recommended to the esteem and adoption of mankind.

By what means is this object attainable? Evidently by one of two only. Either the existence of the same passion or interest in a majority at the same time must be prevented, or the majority, having such coexistent passion or interest, must be rendered, by their number and local situation, unable to concert and carry into effect schemes of oppression. If the impulse and the opportunity be suffered to coincide, we well know that neither moral nor religious motives can be relied on as an adequate control. They are not found to be such on the injustice and violence of individuals, and lose their efficacy in proportion to the number combined together, that is, in proportion as their efficacy becomes needful.

From this view of the subject it may be concluded that a pure democracy, by which I mean a society consisting of a small number of citizens, who assemble and administer the government in person, can admit of no cure for the mischiefs of faction. A common passion or interest will, in almost every case, be felt by a majority of the whole, a communication and concert results from the form of government itself; and there is nothing to check the inducements to sacrifice the weaker party or an obnoxious individual. Hence it is that such democracies have ever been spectacles of turbulence and contention; have ever been found incompatible with personal security or the rights of property; and have in general been as short in their lives as they have been violent in their deaths. Theoretic politicians, who have patronized this species of government, have erroneously supposed that by reducing mankind to a perfect equality in their political rights, they would at the same time be perfectly equalized and assimilated in their possessions, their opinions, and their passions.

A republic, by which I mean a government in which the scheme of representation takes place, opens a different prospect and promises the cure for which we are seeking. Let us examine the points in which it varies from pure democracy, and we shall comprehend both the nature of the cure and the efficacy which it must derive from the Union.

The two great points of difference between a democracy and a republic are: first, the delegation of the government, in the latter, to a small number of citizens elected by the rest; secondly, the greater number of citizens and greater sphere of country over which the latter may be extended.

The effect of the first difference is, on the one hand, to refine and enlarge the public views by passing them through the medium of a chosen body of citizens, whose wisdom may best discern the true interest of their country and whose patriotism and love of justice will be least likely to sacrifice it to temporary or partial considerations. Under such a regulation it may well happen that the public voice, pronounced by the representatives of the people, will be more consonant to the public good than if pronounced by the people themselves, convened for the purpose. On the other hand, the effect may be inverted. Men of factious tempers, of local prejudices, or of sinister designs, may, by intrigue, by corruption, or by other means, first obtain the suffrages, and then betray the interests of the people. The question resulting is, whether small or extensive republics are most favorable to the election of proper guardians of the public weal; and it is clearly decided in favor of the latter by two obvious considerations.

In the first place it is to be remarked that however small the republic may be the representatives must be raised to a certain number in order to guard against the cabals of a few; and that however large it may be they must be limited to a certain number in order to guard against the confusion of a multitude. Hence, the number of representatives in the two cases not being in proportion to that of the constituents, and being proportionally greatest in the small republic, it follows that if the proportion of fit characters be not less in the large than in the small republic, the former will present a greater option, and consequently a greater probability of a fit choice.

In the next place, as each representative will be chosen by a greater number of citizens in the large than in the small republic, it will be more difficult for unworthy candidates to practice with success the vicious arts by which elections are too often carried; and the suffrages of the people being more free, will be more likely to center on men who possess the most attractive merit and the most diffusive and established characters.

It must be confessed that in this, as in most other cases, there is a mean, on both sides of which inconveniencies will be found to lie. By enlarging too much the number of electors, you render the representative too little acquainted with all their local circumstances and lesser interests; as by reducing it too much, you render him unduly attached to these, and too little fit to comprehend and pursue great and national objects. The federal Constitution forms a happy combination in this respect; the great and aggregate interests being referred to the national, the local and particular to the State legislatures.

The other point of difference is the greater number of citizens and extent of territory which may be brought within the compass of republican than of democratic government; and it is this circumstance principally which renders factious combinations less to be dreaded in the former than in the latter. The smaller the society, the fewer probably will be the distinct parties and interests composing it; the fewer the distinct parties and interests, the more frequently will a majority be found of the same party; and the smaller the number of individuals composing a majority, and the smaller the compass within which they are placed, the more easily will they concert and execute their plans of oppression. Extend the sphere and you take in a greater variety of parties and interests; you make it less probable that a majority of the whole will have a common motive to invade the rights of other citizens; or if such a common motive exists, it will be more difficult for all who feel it to discover their own strength and to act in unison with each other. Besides other impediments, it may be remarked that, where there is a consciousness of unjust or dishonorable purposes, communication is always checked by distrust in proportion to the number whose concurrence is necessary.

Hence, it clearly appears that the same advantage which a republic has over a democracy in controlling the effects of faction is enjoyed by a large over a small republic—is enjoyed by the Union over the States composing it. Does this advantage consist in the substitution of representatives whose enlightened views and virtuous sentiments render them superior to local prejudices and to schemes of injustice? It will not be denied that the representation of the Union will be most likely to possess these requisite endowments. Does it consist in the greater security afforded by a greater variety of parties, against the event of any one party being able to outnumber and oppress the rest? In an equal degree does the increased variety of parties comprised within the Union increase this security. Does it, in fine, consist in the greater obstacles opposed to the concert and accomplishment of the secret wishes of an unjust and interested majority? Here again the extent of the Union gives it the most palpable advantage.

The influence of factious leaders may kindle a flame within their particular States but will be unable to spread a general conflagration through the other States. A religious sect may degenerate into a political faction in a part of the Confederacy; but the variety of sects dispersed over the entire face of it must secure the national councils against any danger from that source. A rage for paper money, for an abolition of debts, for an equal division of property, or for any other improper or wicked project, will be less apt to pervade the whole body of the Union than a particular member of it, in the same proportion as such as malady is more likely to taint a particular county or district than an entire State.

In the extent and proper structure of the Union, therefore, we behold a republican remedy for the diseases most incident to republican government. And according to the degree of pleasure and pride we feel in being republicans ought to be our zeal in cherishing the spirit and supporting the character of federalists.

APPENDIX 4:
FEDERALIST PAPER NO. 51
JAMES MADISON

To what expedient, then, shall we finally resort, for maintaining in practice the necessary partition of power among the several departments as laid down in the Constitution? The only answer that can be given is that as all these exterior provisions are found to be inadequate, the defect must be supplied, by so contriving the interior structure of the government as that its several constituent parts may, by their mutual relations, be the means of keeping each other in their proper places. Without presuming to undertake a full development of this important idea I will hazard few general observations which may perhaps place it in a clearer light, and enable us to form a more correct judgment of the principles and structure of the government planned by the convention.

In order to lay a due foundation for that separate and distinct exercise of the different powers of government, which to a certain extent is admitted on all hands to be essential to the preservation of liberty, it is evident that each department should have a will of its own; and consequently should be so constituted that the members of each should have as little agency as possible in the appointment of the members of the others. Were this principle rigorously adhered to, it would require that all the appointments for the supreme executive, legislative, and judiciary magistracies should be drawn from the same fountain of authority, the people, through channels having no communication whatever with one another. Perhaps such a plan of constructing the several departments would be less difficult in practice than it may be in contemplation appear. Some difficulties, however, and some additional expense would attend the execution of it. Some deviations, therefore, from the principle must be admitted. In the constitution of the judiciary department in particular, it might be inexpedient to insist rigorously on the principle: first, because peculiar qualifications being essential in the members, the primary consideration ought to be to select that mode of choice which best secures these qualifications; second, because the permanent tenure by which the appointments are held in that department must soon destroy all sense of dependence on the authority conferring them.

It is equally evident that the members of each department should be as little dependent as possible on those of the others for the emoluments annexed to their offices. Were the executive magistrate, or the judges, not independent of the legislature in this particular, their independence in every other would be merely nominal.

But the great security against a gradual concentration of the several powers in the same department consists in giving to those who administer each department the necessary constitutional means and personal motives to resist encroachments of the others. The provision for defense must in this, as in all other cases, be made commensurate to the danger of attack. Ambition must be made to counteract ambition. The interest of the man must be connected with the constitutional rights of the place. It may be a reflection on human nature that such devices should be necessary to control the abuses of government. But what is government itself but the greatest of all reflections on human nature? If men were angels no government would be necessary. If angels were to govern men, neither external nor internal controls on government would be necessary. In framing a government which is to be administered by men over men, the great difficulty lies in this: you must first enable the government to control the governed; and in the next place oblige it to control itself. A dependence on the people is, no doubt, the primary control on the government; but experience has taught mankind the necessity of auxiliary precautions.

This policy of supplying, by opposite and rival interests, the defect of better motives, might be traced through the whole system of human affairs, private as well as public. We see it particularly displayed in all the subordinate distributions of power, where the constant aim is to divide and arrange the several offices in such a manner as that each may be a check on the other—that the private interest of every individual may be a sentinel over the public rights. These inventions of prudence cannot be less requisite in the distribution of the supreme powers of the State.

But it is not possible to give to each department an equal power of self-defense. In republican government, the legislative authority necessarily predominates. The remedy for this inconveniency is to divide the legislature into different branches; and to render them, by different modes of election and different principles of action, as little connected with each other as the nature of their common functions and their common dependence on the society will admit. It may even be necessary to guard against dangerous encroachments by still further precautions. As the weight of the legislative authority requires that it should be thus divided, the weakness of the executive may require, on the other hand, that it should be fortified. An absolute negative on the legislature appears, at first view, to be the natural defense with which the executive magistrate should be armed. But perhaps it would be neither altogether safe nor alone sufficient. On ordinary occasions it might not be exerted with the requisite firmness, and on extraordinary occasions it might be perfidiously abused. May not this defect of an absolute negative be supplied by some qualified connection between this weaker department and the weaker branch of the stronger department, by which the latter may be led to support the constitutional rights of the former, without being too much detached from the rights of its own department?

If the principles on which these observations are founded be just, as I persuade myself they are, and they be applied as a criterion to the several State constitutions, and to the federal Constitution, it will be found that if the latter does not perfectly correspond with them, the former are infinitely less able to bear such a test.

There are, moreover, two considerations particularly applicable to the federal system of America, which place that system in a very interesting point of view.

First. In a single republic, all the power surrendered by the people is submitted to the administration of a single government; and the usurpations are guarded against by a division of the government into distinct and separate departments. In the compound republic of America, the power surrendered by the people is first divided between two distinct governments, and then the portion allotted to each subdivided among distinct and separate departments. Hence a double security arises to the rights of the people. The different governments will control each other, at the same time that each will be controlled by itself.

Second. It is of great importance in a republic not only to guard the society against the oppression of its rulers, but to guard one part of the society against the injustice of the other part. Different interests necessarily exist in different classes of citizens. If a majority be united by a common interest, the rights of the minority will be insecure. There are but two methods of providing against this evil: the one by creating a will in the community independent of the majority—that is, of the society itself; the other, by comprehending in the society so many separate descriptions of citizens as will render an unjust combination of a majority of the whole very improbable, if not impracticable. The first method prevails in all governments possessing an hereditary or self-appointed authority. This, at best, is but a precarious security; because a power independent of the society may as well espouse the unjust views of the major as the rightful interests of the minor party, and may possibly be turned against both parties. The second method will be exemplified in the federal republic of the United States. Whilst all authority in it will be derived from and dependent on the society, the society itself will be broken into so many parts, interests and classes of citizens, that the rights of individuals, or of the minority, will be in little danger from interested combinations of the majority. In a free government the security for civil rights must be the same as that for religious rights. It consists in the one case in the multiplicity of interests, and in the other in the multiplicity of sects. the degree of security in both cases will depend on the number of interests and sects; and this may be presumed to depend on the extent of country and number of people comprehended under the same government. This view of the subject must particularly recommend a proper federal system to all the sincere and considerate friends of republican government, since it shows that in exact proportion as the territory of the Union may be formed into more circumscribed Confederacies, or States, oppressive combinations of a majority will be facilitated; the best security, under the republican forms, for the rights of every class of citizen, will be diminished; and consequently the stability and independence of some member of the government, the only other security, must be proportionally increased. justice is the end of government. It is the end of civil society. It ever has been and ever will be pursued until it be obtained, or until liberty be lost in the pursuit. In a society under the forms of which the stronger faction can readily unite and oppress the weaker, anarchy may as truly be said to reign as in a state of nature, where the weaker individual is not secured against the violence of the stronger; and as, in the latter state, even the stronger individuals are prompted, by the uncertainty of their condition, to submit to a government which may protect the weak as well as themselves; so, in the former state, will the more powerful factions or parties be gradually induced, by a like motive, to wish for a government which will protect all parties, the weaker as well as the more powerful. It can be little doubted that if the State of Rhode Island was separated from the Confederacy and left to itself, the insecurity of rights under the popular form of government within such narrow limits would be displayed by such reiterated oppressions of factious majorities that some power altogether independent of the people would soon be called for by the voice of the very factions whose misrule had proved the necessity of it. In the extended republic of the United States, and among the great variety of interests, parties, and sects which it embraces, a coalition of a majority of the whole society could seldom take place on any other principles than those of justice and the general good; whilst there being thus less danger to a minor from the will of a major party, there must be less pretext, also, to provide for the security of the former, by introducing into the government a will not dependent on the latter, or, in other words, a will independent of the society itself. It is no less certain than it is important, notwithstanding the contrary opinions which have been entertained, that the larger the society, provided it lie within a practicable sphere, the more duly capable it will be of self-government. And happily for the *republican cause*, the practicable sphere may be carried to a very great extent by a judicious modification and mixture of the federal principle.

APPENDIX 5:
PRESIDENTS AND CONGRESSES
1789–1998

Year	President and vice president	Party of president	Congress	House Majority party	House Minority party	Senate Majority party	Senate Minority party
1789-1797	**George Washington**	None	1st	38 Admin	26 Opp	17 Admin	9 Opp
	John Adams		2d	37 Fed	33 Dem-Rep	16 Fed	13 Dem-Rep
			3d	57 Dem-Rep	48 Fed	17 Fed	13 Dem-Rep
			4th	54 Fed	52 Dem-Rep	19 Fed	13 Dem-Rep
1797-1801	**John Adams**	Federalist	5th	58 Fed	48 Dem-Rep	20 Fed	12 Dem-Rep
	Thomas Jefferson		6th	64 Fed	42 Dem-Rep	19 Fed	13 Dem-Rep
1801-1809	**Thomas Jefferson**	Dem-Rep	7th	69 Dem-Rep	36 Fed	18 Dem-Rep	13 Fed
	Aaron Burr (to 1805)		8th	102 Dem-Rep	39 Fed	25 Dem-Rep	9 Fed
	George Clinton (to 1809)		9th	116 Dem-Rep	25 Fed	27 Dem-Rep	7 Fed
			10th	118 Dem-Rep	24 Fed	28 Dem-Rep	6 Fed
1809-1817	**James Madison**	Dem-Rep	11th	94 Dem-Rep	48 Fed	28 Dem-Rep	6 Fed
	George Clinton (to 1813)		12th	108 Dem-Rep	36 Fed	30 Dem-Rep	6 Fed
	Elbridge Gerry (to 1817)		13th	112 Dem-Rep	68 Fed	27 Dem-Rep	9 Fed
			14th	117 Dem-Rep	65 Fed	25 Dem-Rep	11 Fed
1817-1825	**James Monroe**	Dem-Rep	15th	141 Dem-Rep	42 Fed	34 Dem-Rep	10 Fed
	Daniel D. Tompkins		16th	156 Dem-Rep	27 Fed	35 Dem-Rep	7 Fed
			17th	158 Dem-Rep	25 Fed	44 Dem-Rep	4 Fed
			18th	187 Dem-Rep	26 Fed	44 Dem-Rep	4 Fed
1825-1829	**John Quincy Adams**	Nat-Rep	19th	105 Admin	97 Jack	26 Admin	20 Jack
	John C. Calhoun		20th	119 Jack	94 Admin	28 Jack	20 Admin
1829-1837	**Andrew Jackson**	Democrat	21st	139 Dem	74 Nat Rep	26 Dem	22 Nat Rep
	John C. Calhoun (to 1833)		22d	141 Dem	58 Nat Rep	25 Dem	21 Nat Rep
	Martin Van Buren (to 1837)		23d	147 Dem	53 AntiMas	20 Dem	20 Nat Rep
			24th	145 Dem	98 Whig	27 Dem	25 Whig
1837-1841	**Martin Van Buren**	Democrat	25th	108 Dem	107 Whig	30 Dem	18 Whig
	Richard M. Johnson		26th	124 Dem	118 Whig	28 Dem	22 Whig
1841	**William H. Harrison**	Whig					
	John Tyler						

Year	President and vice president	Party of president	Congress	House Majority party	House Minority party	Senate Majority party	Senate Minority party
1841–1845	**John Tyler**	Whig	27th	133 Whig	102 Dem	28 Whig	22 Dem
	(VP vacant)		28th	142 Dem	79 Whig	28 Whig	25 Dem
1845–1849	**James K. Polk**	Democrat	29th	143 Dem	77 Whig	31 Dem	25 Whig
	George M. Dallas		30th	115 Whig	108 Dem	36 Dem	21 Whig
1849–1850	**Zachary Taylor˙**	Whig	31st	112 Dem	109 Whig	35 Dem	25 Whig
	Millard Fillmore						
1850–1853	**Millard Fillmore**	Whig	32d	140 Dem	88 Whig	35 Dem	24 Whig
	(VP vacant)						
1853–1857	**Franklin Pierce**	Democrat	33d	159 Dem	71 Whig	38 Dem	22 Whig
	William R. King		34th	108 Rep	83 Dem	40 Dem	15 Rep
1857–1861	**James Buchanan**	Democrat	35th	118 Dem	92 Rep	36 Dem	20 Rep
	John C. Breckinridge		36th	114 Rep	92 Dem	36 Dem	26 Rep
1861–1865	**Abraham Lincoln˙**	Republican	37th	105 Rep	43 Dem	31 Rep	10 Dem
	Hannibal Hamlin (to 1865)		38th	102 Rep	75 Dem	36 Rep	9 Dem
	Andrew Johnson (1865)						
1865–1869	**Andrew Johnson**	Republican	39th	149 Union	42 Dem	42 Union	10 Dem
	(VP vacant)		40th	143 Rep	49 Dem	42 Rep	11 Dem
1869–1877	**Ulysses S. Grant**	Republican	41st	149 Rep	63 Dem	56 Rep	11 Dem
	Schuyler Colfax (to 1873)		42d	134 Rep	104 Dem	52 Rep	17 Dem
	Henry Wilson (to 1877)		43d	194 Rep	92 Dem	49 Rep	19 Dem
			44th	169 Dem	109 Rep	45 Rep	29 Dem
1877–1881	**Rutherford B. Hayes**	Republican	45th	153 Dem	140 Rep	39 Rep	36 Dem
	William A. Wheeler		46th	149 Dem	130 Rep	42 Dem	33 Rep
1881	**James A. Garfield˙**	Republican	47th	147 Rep	135 Dem	37 Rep	37 Dem
	Chester A. Arthur						
1881–1885	**Chester A. Arthur**	Republican	48th	197 Dem	118 Rep	38 Rep	36 Dem
	(VP vacant)						
1885–1889	**Grover Cleveland**	Democrat	49th	183 Dem	140 Rep	43 Rep	34 Dem
	Thomas A. Hendricks		50th	169 Dem	152 Rep	39 Rep	37 Dem
1889–1893	**Benjamin Harrison**	Republican	51st	166 Rep	159 Dem	39 Rep	37 Dem
	Levi P. Morton		52d	235 Dem	88 Rep	47 Rep	39 Dem
1893–1897	**Grover Cleveland**	Democrat	53d	218 Dem	127 Rep	44 Dem	38 Rep
	Adlai E. Stevenson		54th	244 Rep	105 Dem	43 Rep	39 Dem
1897–1901	**William McKinley˙**	Republican	55th	204 Rep	113 Dem	47 Rep	34 Dem
	Garret A. Hobart (to 1901)		56th	185 Rep	163 Dem	53 Rep	26 Dem
	Theodore Roosevelt (1901)						

Year	President and vice president	Party of president	Congress	House Majority party	House Minority party	Senate Majority party	Senate Minority party
1901-1909	**Theodore Roosevelt**	Republican	57th	191 Rep	151 Dem	55 Rep	31 Dem
	(VP vacant, 1901-1905)		58th	208 Rep	178 Dem	57 Rep	33 Dem
	Charles W. Fairbanks		59th	250 Rep	136 Dem	57 Rep	33 Dem
	(1905-1909)		60th	222 Rep	164 Dem	61 Rep	31 Dem
1909-1913	**William Howard Taft**	Republican	61st	219 Rep	172 Dem	61 Rep	32 Dem
	James S. Sherman		62d	228 Dem	161 Rep	51 Rep	41 Dem
1913-1921	**Woodrow Wilson**	Democrat	63d	291 Dem	127 Rep	51 Dem	44 Rep
	Thomas R. Marshall		64th	230 Dem	196 Rep	56 Dem	40 Rep
			65th	216 Dem	210 Rep	53 Dem	42 Rep
			66th	240 Rep	190 Dem	49 Rep	47 Dem
1921-1923	**Warren G. Harding**˙	Republican	67th	301 Rep	131 Dem	59 Rep	37 Dem
	Calvin Coolidge						
1923-1929	**Calvin Coolidge**	Republican	68th	225 Rep	205 Dem	51 Rep	43 Dem
	(VP vacant,	1923-1925)	69th	247 Rep	183 Dem	56 Rep	39 Dem
	Charles G. Dawes		70th	237 Rep	195 Dem	49 Rep	46 Dem
	(1925-1929)						
1929-1933	**Herbert Hoover**	Republican	71st	267 Rep	167 Dem	56 Rep	39 Dem
	Charles Curtis		72d	220 Dem	214 Rep	48 Rep	47 Dem
1933-1945	**Franklin D. Roosevelt**˙	Democrat	73d	310 Dem	117 Rep	60 Dem	35 Rep
	John N. Garner		74th	319 Dem	103 Rep	69 Dem	25 Rep
	(1933-1941)		75th	331 Dem	89 Rep	76 Dem	16 Rep
	Henry A. Wallace		76th	261 Dem	164 Rep	69 Dem	23 Rep
	(1941-1945)		77th	268 Dem	162 Rep	66 Dem	28 Rep
	Harry S Truman (1945)		78th	218 Dem	208 Rep	58 Dem	37 Rep
1945-1953	**Harry S Truman**	Democrat	79th	242 Dem	190 Rep	56 Dem	38 Rep
	(VP vacant, 1945-1949)		80th	245 Rep	188 Dem	51 Rep	45 Dem
	Alben W. Barkley		81st	263 Dem	171 Rep	54 Dem	42 Rep
	(1949-1953)		82d	234 Dem	199 Rep	49 Dem	47 Rep
1953-1961	**Dwight D. Eisenhower**	Republican	83d	221 Rep	211 Dem	48 Rep	47 Dem
	Richard M. Nixon		84th	232 Dem	203 Rep	48 Dem	47 Rep
			85th	233 Dem	200 Rep	49 Dem	47 Rep
			86th	283 Dem	153 Rep	64 Dem	34 Rep
1961-1963	**John F. Kennedy**˙	Democrat	87th	263 Dem	174 Rep	65 Dem	35 Rep
	Lyndon B. Johnson						

Year	President and vice president	Party of president	Congress	House Majority party	House Minority party	Senate Majority party	Senate Minority party
1963-1969	**Lyndon B. Johnson**	Democrat	88th	258 Dem	177 Rep	67 Dem	33 Rep
	(VP vacant, 1963-1965)		89th	295 Dem	140 Rep	68 Dem	32 Rep
	Hubert H. Humphrey		90th	247 Dem	187 Rep	64 Dem	36 Rep
	(1965-1969)						
1969-1974	**Richard M. Nixon****	Republican	91st	243 Dem	192 Rep	57 Dem	43 Rep
	Spiro T. Agnew***		92d	254 Dem	180 Rep	54 Dem	44 Rep
	Gerald R. Ford****						
1974-1977	**Gerald R. Ford**	Republican	93d	239 Dem	192 Rep	56 Dem	42 Rep
	Nelson A. Rockefeller****		94th	291 Dem	144 Rep	60 Dem	37 Rep
1977-1981	**Jimmy Carter**	Democrat	95th	292 Dem	143 Rep	61 Dem	38 Rep
	Walter Mondale		96th	276 Dem	157 Rep	58 Dem	41 Rep
1981-1989	**Ronald Reagan**	Republican	97th	243 Dem	192 Rep	53 Rep	46 Dem
	George Bush		98th	269 Dem	165 Rep	54 Rep	46 Dem
			99th	253 Dem	182 Rep	53 Rep	47 Dem
			100th	257 Dem	178 Rep	54 Dem	46 Rep
1989-1993	**George Bush**	Republican	101st	262 Dem	173 Rep	55 Dem	45 Rep
	Dan Quayle		102d[1]	267 Dem	167 Rep	56 Dem	44 Rep
1993-	**Bill Clinton**	Democrat	103d	258 Dem	176 Rep	57 Dem	43 Rep
	Albert Gore, Jr.		104th	230 Rep	204 Dem	52 Rep	48 Dem
			105th	227 Rep	207 Dem	55 Rep	45 Dem

ABBREVIATIONS: **Admin** = Administration supporters; **AntiMas** = Anti-Masonic; **Dem** = Democratic; **Dem-Rep** = Democratic-Republican; **Fed** = Federalist; **Jack** = Jacksonian Democrats; **Nat Rep** = National Republican; **Opp** = Opponents of administration; **Rep** = Republican; **Union** = Unionist; **Whig** = Whig.

*Died in office. **Resigned from the presidency. ***Resigned from the vice presidency. ****Appointed vice president.

[1] From the 102d Congress, the House has had one Independent-Socialist member.

GLOSSARY

Alien and Sedition Acts: A series of laws passed by Adams administration in 1798 authorizing the deportation of undesirable aliens and making it a crime to criticize the government. They were aimed at silencing the pro-French sentiment of the Jeffersonian Republicans. The laws were repealed once Jefferson became president in 1801.

American Creed: The core set of liberal beliefs held by most Americans since the founding of the republic. The principle concepts are individual liberty and equality. See Chapter 2.

American Dream: The belief widely inculcated since the late nineteenth century that America is the land of opportunity in which all citizens can rise to the highest levels.

American Federation of Labor–Congress of Industrial Organization (AFL-CIO): The labor peak organization, created by the 1955 merger of the AFL, established in 1881, and the CIO, established in the 1930s.

American Protestantism: The dominant form of religion in America from the beginning. American Protestantism is often divided by scholars into its mainline and evangelical wings. Protestantism in America has been marked by the development of a multiplicity of new churches and sects.

American Revolution: Also referred to as the War of Independence, established American sovereignty through the rejection of British colonial rule. Waged between the years 1775 and 1777, the American Revolution ended with the Treaty of Versailles (1783), in which Britain officially recognized the independence of the American colonies.

Appropriations: The congressional process that approves the spending of government funds for particular purposes.

Articles of Confederation: The agreement between the newly independent American states in 1781 forming the first government for the United States. A weak form of federation, the Articles were replaced by the U.S. Constitution in 1789.

Bill of Rights: The first ten amendments to the U.S. Constitution. Created as a response to fears about the new national government. Modeled on the English Bill of Rights of 1688, the American Bill of Rights was the inspiration for many later declarations of rights including the Canadian Charter of Rights and Freedoms. See Chapter 3.

Caucus: 1. A meeting of members of the same party. **2.** In both houses of Congress, a closed meeting of all representatives of the same party. There are also caucuses of members with particular interests that may cross party lines, for example, the Congressional Black Caucus. **3.** A meeting of local party activists to select delegates to the party's national convention. See Chapter 11.

Christian Coalition: A grass roots organization, linked to conservative church networks, formed by Rev. Pat Robertson in 1989 to lobby on conservative social issues.

Christian Right: Mobilization of conservative Christians for political action on social issues. An important part of the Republican Party coalition since the 1970s. See Chapter 12.

Civil Rights Acts: Federal laws prohibiting racial discrimination. The first set of these laws was passed by Congress in the years following the Civil War (1866–1875). The second set of laws was passed between 1957 and 1968 as a result of pressure from the civil rights movement. The most significant of these laws were the Civil Rights Act of 1964, which prohibited racial segregation in public accommodation and race and sex discrimination in employment, and the Voting Rights Act of 1965, which provided federal guarantees of black voting rights.

Civil War: Waged between 1861 and 1865, the war was triggered by the secession of eleven southern states after election of President Lincoln. The remaining states rallied behind the federal government to preserve the Union.

Confirmation: The process by which the Senate approves the appointment of high-level executive or judicial appointments nominated by the president.

Constitutional Convention: The Constitutional Convention, a meeting of representatives of 12 of the 13 original states, met in Philadelphia from May 25 to September 18, 1787. It was at this convention that the U.S. Constitution was written.

Continental Congress: A meeting of representatives of the American colonies to coordinate action against British colonial rule. The first session met in September 1774.

The second session, which began in September 1775, approved the Declaration of Independence and later ratified the Articles of Confederation.

Dealignment: The weakening of party identification among voters, particularly since 1968. An important consequence of dealignment has been a great increase in split-ticket voting, leading to an era of divided government in Washington. See Chapter 10.

Declaration of Independence: The document, written mainly by Thomas Jefferson, was approved by the second Continental Congress on the Fourth of July, 1776. It was a declaration of liberal principles that justified the colonies' rejection of British colonial rule.

Direct Democracy: A mechanism used in many of the states whereby citizens can bypass the legislative process and vote directly on issues. See Chapter 13.

Electoral College: The method of indirectly electing the president established by Article II, Section 1, and the 12th Amendment to the Constitution. See Chapter 3.

Emancipation Proclamation: Issued by President Lincoln on January 1, 1863, under his emergency war powers, declaring the freedom of the slaves in the states of the Confederacy.

Enlightenment: The rise of liberal rationalism in the second half of the eighteenth century. An important influence on the thinking of many of the American founders, notably Thomas Jefferson.

Federalist Papers: A series of articles written by James Madison, Alexander Hamilton, and John Jay between 1787 and 1788. This collection was intended to persuade the states to ratify the new U.S. Constitution; it is now considered to be the most important commentary on the meaning of the Constitution. Of particular importance are Numbers 10 and 51, in which Madison explained his theory of political "factions" and how the separation of powers can counter the tyranny of the majority.

Federalist Party: The first American political party, formed in the 1790s by the supporters of John Adams and Alexander Hamilton in opposition to Thomas Jefferson's Republican Party. It faded as a national party after 1808.

Filibuster: Tactic used in the Senate to prevent a vote by prolonging debate on an issue. A filibuster can only be ended by a vote to close debate by sixty senators. The tactic is used as a blocking and negotiating tool.

Gettysburg Address: Short speech by President Lincoln in 1863 at the dedication of the Union cemetery at the site of the Battle of Gettysburg. It has become famous as a statement of America's fundamental commitment to democratic government. See Chapter 2.

GOP (Grand Old Party): Common term for the Republican Party, dating from the period immediately after the Civil War.

Great Society: Name given to President Johnson's ambitious program of liberal legislation from 1965 to 1968. Seen as an expansion of New Deal policies, it notably included the Medicare and Medicaid programs.

Hamilton, Alexander (1755–1804): The influential first Secretary of the Treasury. His policies favoring a strong national government and support for business were strongly opposed by Thomas Jefferson.

Initiative: The principal means of direct democracy used in many of the states whereby a proposed law or constitutional amendment can be taken directly to the voters on the collection of a certain number of signatures.

Iran/Contra: Reagan Administration scandal, uncovered in 1986, in which arms were secretly sold to Iran and the proceeds used to fund the anti-Communist Contra rebels in Nicaragua in violation of the law.

Jackson, Andrew (1767–1845): President from 1829 to 1837 and founder of the Democratic Party. Jackson presided over the rise of mass democracy in America and the invention of the new forms of party organization.

Jefferson, Thomas (1743–1826): Author of the Declaration of Independence and president from 1801 to 1809. The major intellectual influence on the development of American liberal ideas.

Keynes, John Maynard (1883–1946): British economic theorist whose ideas were summarized in the *General Theory of Employment, Interest and Money* (1936). He had a major impact on economic policy and reinforced New Deal liberalism in the United States. Keynes argued that government was responsible for regulating the overall level of economic activity.

***Laissez-faire*:** Economic theory propagated in the mid-nineteenth century that argued against government intervention in the natural laws of economics. Also known as free enterprise or free market economics.

Lincoln, Abraham (1809–1865): President from 1861 to 1865. The first Republican president, his election triggered the secession of the southern states. His leadership during the Civil War, culminating in his assassination, and his eloquent restatement of America's commitment to equality and democracy have made him an American icon.

Locke, John (1632–1704): English liberal political theorist whose ideas had a profound impact on the American founders. Locke's views on toleration and religious freedom were adopted by Madison and Jefferson.

Machine Politics: System of party organization based on patronage and the provision of basic services to voters that enabled the party bosses to maintain political control of many American cities in the nineteenth century. Last of this style of political machine was the Democratic Cook County (Chicago) organization, led by Mayor Richard J. Daley until his death in 1976.

Madison, James (1751–1836): Principal theorist of the Constitution; worked closely with Jefferson on the Virginia Statute of Religious Liberty and the Virginia and Kentucky Resolutions; president from 1809 to 1817.

Marshall, John (1755–1835): The most influential of the early chief justices of the Supreme Court (1801–1835). His precedents established the Constitution as the supreme law of the land, including the right of the Court to declare acts of Congress and the states unconstitutional.

McCarthyism: An extreme form of anti-Communist paranoia that gripped Washington in the late 1940s and early 1950s. Named after Republican senator Joseph McCarthy of Wisconsin, the most flamboyant anti-Communist crusader of that period.

Medicare/Medicaid: Great Society entitlement programs passed in 1965 that provide health insurance for those over age 65 (Medicare) and those on welfare (Medicaid).

National Association for the Advancement of Colored People (NAACP): An organization, founded in 1909, dedicated to promoting the interests of black Americans. Through use of judicial test cases, the group's legal staff prompted *Brown v. the Board of Education* (1954) and other decisions declaring racial discrimination unconstitutional. See Chapter 9.

National Committees: Committees of the Democratic and Republican parties that govern the parties between national conventions.

National Rifle Association: A powerful interest group that advocates the right of Americans to keep arms and that resists any government regulation of firearms.

New Deal: The programs initiated by President Roosevelt and the Democratic Party between 1933 and 1936 in response to the economic and social crisis of the Great Depression. New Deal liberalism advocated a positive role for government in tackling economic and social problems.

North American Free Trade Agreement (NAFTA): A 1992 agreement leading to the eventual elimination of tariffs on trade between Canada, the United States, and Mexico.

Off-year Elections: Elections for the House of Representatives and one-third of the Senate that do not coincide with a presidential election (e.g., 1990, 1994, and 1998).

Office of Management and Budget (OMB): Instituted in 1970, replacing the Bureau of the Budget in the Executive Office of the President, it is the central agency responsible for preparing the president's budget. It reviews the spending plans and regulations of all other departments.

Pentagon Papers: A highly detailed and top secret defense department report detailing American involvement with Vietnam that was leaked to the *New York Times* and *Washington Post* by Daniel Ellsberg, a former department official, in 1971.

Perot, Henry Ross (1930–): Texas billionaire who was an independent candidate for president in 1992 (19 percent of the vote) and the presidential nominee for the Reform Party in 1996 (9 percent). His main issue was the need to balance the budget.

Pledge of Allegiance: A short patriotic statement affirmed in American schools each day. See Chapter 1.

Political Action Committee (PAC): Since 1974, the vehicle through which interest groups may legally contribute to political campaigns. The group must establish a "separate segregated fund" contributed for political purposes, which must be kept apart from the group's regular funds. PAC donations to a campaign are limited to $5,000.

Political Appointees (Executive): Those appointed by the president to the top levels of the executive departments and regulatory agencies, who collectively form the administration.

Populist Party: Agrarian party with strong support in the Midwest and southern states in the 1890s protesting against the control of government policy by business and financial monopolies.

Primary Elections: In the twentieth century, the standard method of nominating party candidates for elective office by a vote of party members. In the case of a presidential primary, delegates are selected to the party's national convention to nominate the party's candidate for president. See Chapter 11.

Progressivism: A political reform movement, influential in both the Democratic and Republican parties from around 1900 to 1920, that sought to modernize the American political system for the industrial age. Among the reforms promoted were civil service reform, primary elections, women's suffrage, and early forms of social welfare legislation.

Puritans: Dissenting Protestants who were critical of the established churches and sought to build a society on scriptural principles. They formed many of the original settlements in New England and their influence was widespread across the American colonies. Stemming from the Puritan tradition, pressure for moral reform has been a recurring factor in American politics, most recently among the Christian Right. See Chapter 2.

Realignment: A durable change in patterns of political behavior establishing the long-term dominance of one of the major political parties. Realignment is triggered by the emergence of a major new issue that disrupts traditional patterns of political behavior. Thus, the response to the New Deal established the dominance of the Democratic Party from the 1930s through to the 1960s. See Chapter 12.

Republican Party: 1. The party formed by Thomas Jefferson and his supporters in 1790s in opposition to the Federalist Party. In 1828 the party began to split into the Democratic and Whig Parties. **2.** The party formed by the 1854 coalition of anti-slavery Whigs and Democrats that elected President Lincoln in 1860. The modern-day Republican Party stems from this coalition.

Regulatory Agencies: Government agencies charged with regulating specific industries or activities. They are set up outside the regular departmental structure of the executive in order to insulate them from immediate political pressures. Members of the agency boards are nominated and confirmed for set terms.

Roosevelt, Franklin D. (FDR) (1882–1945): Democratic president from 1933 till his death in 1945. Roosevelt served an unprecedented four terms, through the crises of the

Great Depression and World War II. His New Deal liberalism and international leadership set the framework for American policy for the following fifty years.

Soft Money: Since 1979, the campaign finance law has allowed the national parties to raise money for "party-building activities" free from the limits imposed on other donations. Particularly since the presidential election of 1992, this legal loophole has been abused on a massive scale to evade the limits on campaign fund-raising and spending.

State of the Union: An annual message delivered by the president to congress in January outlining his plans and goals for the legislative session. Such a report is constitutionally required by Article II, Section 3.

de Tocqueville, Alexis (1805–1859): A young French aristocrat and political theorist who toured America in 1831 and 1832 to study the workings of a democracy. His astute reflections on American life and institutions in his two-volume *Democracy in America* (1835/1840) are still widely quoted.

Vietnam War: As part of the American Cold War effort to contain the spread of communism in Asia, large numbers of American ground troops fought in Vietnam from 1965 until their withdrawal in 1973. The war provoked bitter domestic opposition, in particular, it divided the Democratic Party. As the first war America lost, it had a lasting impact on subsequent American foreign policy.

Wallace, George (1919–): Democratic governor of Alabama who was a candidate for president in each election from 1964 to 1976. He was the voice of white southern racism and northern anxiety about the impact of the civil rights revolution.

War of 1812: Triggered by British interference with American shipping during the war with Napoleon. The Americans felt it necessary to reassert their independence by attacking the British colony of Upper Canada. Generally rated a draw.

Watergate: Scandal that led to the resignation of President Nixon in 1974 involving the widespread abuse of executive powers. See Chapter 8.

Whig Party: Party formed in 1830s in opposition to Andrew Jackson's Democratic Party. The Whig Party fell apart over the issue of slavery in the mid-1850s.

Wilson, Woodrow (1856–1924): Political scientist and Democratic president from 1913 to 1921. Wilson was an exponent of strong presidential leadership who led the Congress to pass a series of progressive reforms.

PHOTOGRAPH CREDITS

INDEX